Creating French Culture

Creating French Culture

Treasures from the Bibliothèque nationale de France

Introduction by *Emmanuel Le Roy Ladurie*

Edited by *Marie-Hélène Tesnière*, Bibliothèque nationale de France
and *Prosser Gifford*, Library of Congress

Yale University Press, New Haven and London
in association with the Library of Congress, Washington
and the Bibliothèque nationale de France, Paris

Copyright © 1995 by The Library of Congress and the Bibliothèque nationale de France.

Designed by Michael Rock . Susan Sellers Partners, New York City, and John Gambell Graphic Design, New Haven, Connecticut.
Set in Linotype Didot by Highwood Typographic Services, Hamden, Connecticut.
Printed in Japan by Toppan.

Library of Congress Cataloging-in-Publication Data

Creating French culture : treasures from the Bibliothèque nationale de France / edited by Marie-Hélène Tesnière and Prosser Gifford.

p.   cm.

ISBN 0-300-06283-4 (alk. paper)

1. Bibliothèque nationale (France)—Exhibitions.   2. Bibliographical exhibitions

—Washington (D.C.)   3. France—Civilization—Exhibitions.   4. Rare books—France—Pairs—Exhibitions.   5. Manuscripts—France—Paris—Exhibitions.

I. Tesnière, Marie-Hélène.   II. Gifford, Prosser.

Z798.P22C74   1995

016.944'074'753—dc20   95-6886

CIP

A catalogue record for this book is available from the British Library.

The paper in this book meets the guidelines for permanence and durability of the Committee on Production Guidelines for Book Longevity of the Council on Library Resources.

10 9 8 7 6 5 4 3 2 1

The publication of this catalogue and
the mounting of the exhibition it describes
are made possible through the generous gifts
of the following donors:

The Florence Gould Foundation

Worms et Cie.

Cogema, Inc.

Schlumberger Foundation, Inc.

Mr. and Mrs. Michel David-Weill

Mr. Raja N. Sidawi

Mr. Daniel Rose

Mr. Leonard L. Silverstein

M. Arnaud de Vitry

Mr. Edward H. Tuck

Mr. and Mrs. Ezra N. Zilka

Contents

Maps on pages xx, 34, 168, 276, and 388

Foreword

The exhibition described in this catalogue is the second in a series sponsored by the Library of Congress, designed to bring to the American public some of the highly valued – and often unique – treasures of the world's great libraries. The first in the series, held in the galleries of the Jefferson Building at the Library of Congress in early 1993, was entitled *Rome Reborn: The Vatican Library and Renaissance Culture*. It focused upon the collections of the Vatican Library gathered during the Renaissance. The works revealed extraordinary achievements in many fields of intellectual endeavor, beginning with the recovery of classical knowledge (in science, mathematics, and geography), treating the creation of Renaissance Latin literature, Renaissance music, and the study of anatomy and practical medicine, and finally following the explosion of exploration and the consequent knowledge of distant cultures and languages, with all their implications for philosophy, political theory, and theology.

The current exhibit differs both in scope and in theme from the first. This historical canvas covers twelve centuries, from the time of Charlemagne to modern France. And the theme reveals the relationship between culture and power in France, developing the conception of culture as simultaneously an instrumentality and one of the indicia of central authority, whether religious or secular. Very early in the gathering of France into a unified entity, the significance of language, of script, of print becomes both a source and a mark of power, of royal authority, and ultimately of the state.

The marriage of culture and power is difficult for Americans to understand, born as we are under written documents that set free, that set bounds upon central authority, that are sceptical and separatist with respect to power, that use a language – English – voracious in its inclusion and adaptation of other modes of speech. It is difficult to imagine an English monarch saying "L'Etat, c'est moi," or an English Academy (much less an American) trying to purify the language. To follow the essays and study the objects in this catalogue is to realize that the French tradi-

ix

tion is different. Louis XIII, Richelieu, Louis XIV, Napoléon were only the most successful in the deliberate and self-conscious use of cultural artifacts and symbols to enhance and amplify state power. Even the revolutionaries of 1789–1794 turned the traditions of cultural and symbolic power to their own political purposes.

We are deeply indebted to Emmanuel Le Roy Ladurie, who when he was the administrateur général of the Bibliothèque Nationale conceived the idea for this exhibit, selected Marie-Hélène Tesnière as the French coordinator of the project, agreed on the theme, and set many of the curators to work. When on January 1, 1994, the Bibliothèque Nationale merged with the Bibliothèque de France to become the Bibliothèque nationale de France (BnF), Jean Favier as the president of the new institution undertook to support this joint project with enthusiasm. We are grateful to him and to Philippe Bélaval, the director general, for their assistance in many ways with the institutional cooperation necessary to sustain such an ambitious project.

This catalogue is itself an example of cultural interpretation. All the object descriptions are written by specialists and curators at the BnF, as are the four French essays discussing the growth of the collections of the Bibliothèque nationale de France and its precursors. The four American essayists, on the other hand, stand back from the collections to inquire how some of these objects reveal the relationships between culture and power in France across the twelve centuries represented in the exhibition. We believe that this exhibition and its accompanying catalogue will support a variety of inquiries, from initial acquaintance with the glories of the French manuscripts to scholarly study of the politics of belief, from the beautiful physical intricacies of bindings and medals to the remarkably layered reworkings of Proust. We are most grateful that these French national treasures, products often of crucial political and intellectual moments in French history, can be shared with the American public in a way that makes their beauty and their significance palpable.

James H. Billington
The Librarian of Congress

Foreword

To say that a national library derives from national power is self-evident to the French. An ancient tradition which makes the state responsible for all sectors of national activity leads to this contemporary political reality: that the state is responsible for the support of culture, if not for culture itself. Whoever denies this premise by asserting the independence of cultural creativity would soon revert to it by insisting that the state was neglecting its duties by not providing support. Other arrangements are conceivable, but they would upset the historical relationship between French society and the state. A millennium of custom and thought is not readily changed.

The Bibliothèque Nationale, historically, was at the outset the "librairie" – our English-speaking friends still say "library" – created by the kings following in the footsteps of Charles V. He was a wise king who in the fourteenth century surrounded himself with jurists and philosophers in order to give the monarchy an ideological framework and to uphold its position in the spiritual realm that was part of the City of God. Meanwhile, in Avignon the pope was forming a library through which he sought to demonstrate his temporal prestige and intellectual influence. The books of Avignon were dispersed, and the library of the Louvre barely outlived Charles V, but the princes took over the task. Charles V's brothers, the dukes of Burgundy, Berry, and Anjou, were the first collectors of valuable manuscripts in their day. Men with great power under an ailing king, they appropriated to themselves certain attributes of royal power, which included artistic and intellectual patronage and the definition of taste. The dukes of Orléans of the Valois line made their library at Blois one of the gems of their court. The last of that line, on becoming Louis XII, brought this treasured library to the monarchy.

It was still a library of manuscripts. The work of the printer, considered then a poor substitute for the handwork of calligraphers, appeared belatedly among the treasures. But the "bibliothèque" – during the Renaissance in France, the Greek term came to be preferred over that derived from Latin—went on to diversify its collections and to transform itself from what had been merely a collection of curiosities much like a painting gallery into a center for literary and artistic endeavors. Coins and medals were added from the great collection of Gaston d'Orléans, the uncle of Louis XIV. Thanks to far-seeing collectors, maps and prints augment the book collection starting in the seventeenth century. The modern era would add the tools to bolster all aspects of creativity, as well as different means for diffusing knowledge. Audiovisual and other electronic technologies are only the most recent of these advances.

Because it was "national," what had been the library of the kings became a participant in defining the role of public authorities in the democratization of learning. The "librairie" of the Middle Ages had contributed to connoisseurs' pleasure with both texts and illuminations. The "bibliothèque" of the Renaissance had been the laboratory of the humanists. The library of today is both a lode to be mined by scholars, whether teachers or students, and a fabulous cultural resource from which we all benefit in one way or another.

This dual role is nothing new; a seventeenth-century library regulation already provided access for laymen one day a week. What is new is the firm commitment by the authorities to address these two different but complementary needs. Since books—and whatever today enhances without supplanting them—have been and will continue to be the product of liberating creativity, it becomes a public responsibility to make them available to all citizens. This becomes evident when one notices that, parallel to the central government, many other smaller governmental entities, cities, and counties are determined to provide their citizens with access to culture by opening libraries and enhancing them with the new information technology.

Construction of a building like the one now going up on the site known as Tolbiac —that is to say, on the left bank of the Seine, just upriver from the Austerlitz train station—was discussed as early as the 1970s, when debate focused on whether to create a "BN II" or simply to continue to expand the original BN on rue de Richelieu. The debate raged for a long time, even as the acquisition of space near the library gave the BN some breathing room. Although saturation was postponed for a few years, and an auditorium was added, the future was in no way assured. The key problems remained unsolved: where to put the hundreds of readers turned away for lack of space, where to store the thousands of books to be acquired in the century to come, and how to accommodate the installation of new technologies for storing and transmitting knowledge.

It was in 1988 that the idea of a totally new building was first publicly proposed by President François Mitterrand. The plan became official in 1989, and architect Dominique Perrault won the design competition the following year. A Public Corporation for the Bibliothèque de France (Etablissement Public de la Bibliothèque de France) was established to oversee the planning, scheduling, and basic groundwork, headed by journalist Dominique Jamet. Meanwhile, the Bibliothèque Nationale, under the leadership of historian Emmanuel Le Roy Ladurie, was responsible not only for maintaining the library on rue de Richelieu in good working order but also for planning the "bibliotheconomics" of the future institution.

The initial design sparked numerous controversies. Because much of the criticism stemmed from the fact that technical details had not yet been worked out, it resulted in useful modifications to the plan. There was also much deliberation about creating a "divide" between material to remain at rue de Richelieu and material to go to Tolbiac; some plans envisaged transferring everything, others divided the collection chronologically by establishing a cutoff date. It was finally decided that Tolbiac would house all printed material—books and periodicals—as well as the entire range of audiovisual and technological equipment, while Richelieu would retain manuscripts, engravings, photographs, maps, coins, medals, antiques, and music, as well as the "performing arts" collection to be transferred from the Arsenal library.

The design of the new building calls for four glass towers at the corners of a vast, two-story base enclosing a large garden. The ground floor, or "lower garden," will house a library for specialists, containing the post-Gutenberg part of the nation's historic collection, to be complemented by future copyright deposits and new acquisitions. Basically, it will function like today's Bibliothèque Nationale, though endowed with twenty-one hundred readers' desks, a unified catalogue system, and the possibility of computerized access to texts. The second floor, or "upper garden," will provide a library for the general public, with fifteen hundred readers' desks as well as lecture and exhibition facilities. The upper-garden library will ultimately contain four hundred thousand volumes, now being acquired. In other words, none of the treasures from the age-old Royal Library will be threatened by overintensive use resulting from wide-open stacks; the nation's historic collection will still be reserved for scholars.

Two types of storerooms are being built to accommodate a total of 250 miles of shelving—twice as much as is currently needed for the twelve million books and three hundred thousand sets of periodicals accumulated over the past five hundred years. Storerooms in the base of the building behind the lower-garden reading rooms will house two-thirds of the current collection right from opening day. The rest will go to the top floors of the towers, above the offices, in storerooms protected by a double facade of glass, two pockets of air, and double-faced wooden shutters. Air-conditioning will complete the conservation environment; in contrast, at rue de Richelieu air-conditioned storage is the exception even today. The books at Tolbiac will therefore be better conserved than ever before.

Books will be carried by an automatic system that maintains the volume in an upright position wherever it goes. It will be offloaded only when it is actually handed to the reader.

It is worth pointing out that no storage or reading room is located underground. The vast garden in the center is at the normal ground level for that part of Paris, and the rooms surrounding it are no lower than the restaurants and shops around the garden of the Palais-Royal, of comparable size. Even if the Seine were to rise above the high-water mark of 1910 (when the flow of the river was completely unregulated, producing the greatest catastrophe Paris had seen in two thousand years), the basements on rue de Richelieu would be flooded long before the Tolbiac storerooms.

The Bibliothèque nationale de France (BnF) will therefore exist on two main sites, both in the center of town and easily reachable by public transportation (including "Meteor," the new express subway line due to open in 1998). The periodical conservation center in Versailles will become a thing of the past, and only the technical restoration workshops in Provins and Sablé will remain outside of Paris, joined by the new Centre Technique du Livre that has just been built in the suburb of Marne-la-Vallée.

The Tolbiac building was completed on schedule, March 23, 1995, when Dominique Perrault officially handed me the key–that is to say, the magnetic card. A week later, President Mitterrand officially inaugurated the site in the company of Mayor Jacques Chirac and several government ministers.

But the library still has to be assembled. For that, scholarly scaffolding has been and remains as significant as the construction work. A general inventory (*récolement général*, or shelf-reading) was conducted–the first in forty years–to verify the state of collections accumulated throughout the centuries. A retrospective conversion of the old catalogues is under way, in order to transform thirty-nine different catalogues –the oldest dating from the sixteenth century, the youngest being a BN-Opale computer application–into a single computerized one. The operation is already complete as far as the general catalogues go and should include the special catalogues before Tolbiac opens. A CD-ROM is also being planned. Connection with the Internet will ensure efficient access to bibliographic resources abroad.

Microfilming has been under way for half a century and will be enhanced by digital technology–some hundred thousand books should be digitized by opening day. This will not only allow access to works too damaged or fragile to handle but will also permit on-line loans to other libraries (under conditions currently subject to legal negotiations with publishers).

Thus networks are proliferating. One network involves sharing acquisitions (foreign books, subscriptions to foreign periodicals, and so on) with a few dozen specialized libraries, generally belonging to university research centers, which will thereby become "affiliated hubs" (*pôles associés*). Another network is designed to produce a union catalogue of French libraries which, as a result of their history, are often full of treasures completely hidden from those without direct access. Indeed, many municipal and university libraries now house collections that originally belonged to abbeys and monasteries or were donated by scholars and bibliophiles. Many have focused their acquisition policy on a field specific to that city or university. Pooling all this information, then linking it to the BnF's comprehensive catalogue, will mean finally offering scholars the possibility of pinpointing required documents.

Two crucial systems are still under construction: one for information processing and the other for audiovisual access. After an open competition, contracts were awarded to specialized firms that are now mobilizing highly competent teams. The life of the Bibliothèque nationale de France will ultimately depend on the effectiveness of an information processing system that must simultaneously manage personnel, funds, purchases, acquisitions, and cataloguing, as well as the daily flow of readers and queries (with the possibility of reserving books from home via France's

"Minitel" telex system); in short, it must offer everyone a bibliographic research tool that matches the wealth and diversity of sources in question. The first stage of this system should be launched in the fall of 1995; its effectiveness will determine how swiftly the second stage will be implemented.

Finally, there's the move. Some fifty thousand books and magazines will leave for Tolbiac every day for a whole year. They will find a safe home on arrival. Meanwhile, the Richelieu reading rooms will remain in operation until a month before Tolbiac opens. That final month–only twice the annual closing period–will be devoted to moving the most commonly requested materials, which would otherwise have been unavailable during the transfer.

Obviously, such a vast undertaking would have utterly failed without the competence and devotion of the many teams in charge of the various "work sites." At all levels, staff of the old Bibliothèque Nationale and Public Corporation for the Bibliothèque de France have displayed an exceptional spirit of cooperation. Thanks to General Director Philippe Bélaval and the ten executive directors, I have been able to count on everyone pulling together, working toward the common goal of making the Bibliothèque nationale de France a worthy member of the elite club of the world's great libraries.

Once Tolbiac has opened its doors to thousands of readers–specialists and general public alike–another enterprise will begin. Richelieu will be remodeled to enable the specialized departments to take advantage of the space and working conditions conducive to enhanced development and prestige.

What we are presenting to the American public today is a selection of the treasures of the Bibliothèque nationale de France. Organized around a theme developed in the days of my friend and predecessor Emmanuel Le Roy Ladurie, this selection does not include all the finest pieces from the library's collection but rather fine items that contribute to a consideration of the historical relationship between books and the power of government. I hope that it conveys to Americans not only France's rich heritage but also our faith in the future of a civilization that, I am convinced, will continue to encourage thousands of men and women to pour into libraries in search of the wider world.

Jean Favier
Membre de l'Institut
Président de la Bibliothèque
nationale de France

Acknowledgments

A catalogue of this size and complexity can be completed only with the assistance of a great many dedicated people, in this instance working in two languages on both sides of the Atlantic Ocean.

There would be no catalogue at all without the timely and generous support of the Florence Gould Foundation, which gave an early grant enabling us to proceed with the two years' labor necessary to complete the catalogue.

As the volume itself testifies, many people at the Bibliothèque nationale de France became involved with the project, including some, such as those assuring photographic quality, who are unknown to me, or others behind the scenes, such as Catherine Goérès, who handled all the invoices and payments for photographic orders. Marie-Hélène Tesnière undertook the strenuous, lengthy, and difficult task of coordinating the object descriptions supplied by her colleagues at the BnF. Their names and titles are listed elsewhere in the book, so I will not repeat them here. It should be noted, however, that many of them wrote descriptions of a number of items, and in addition Florence Callu, Antoine Coron, and Marie-Hélène Tesnière herself wrote introductory essays to parts of the catalogue. Thus, the curatorial work for this catalogue has been performed wholly in Paris, making both the catalogue and the exhibition a genuinely joint venture of two great national libraries.

The gestation of this project spanned several years. Work on the catalogue began under the leadership of Emmanuel Le Roy Ladurie, who was then administrateur général of the Bibliothèque Nationale. He initiated the project in conversations with James H. Billington, the Librarian of Congress, and he has written the introduction to the volume as well as the short essay introducing the seventeenth- and eighteenth-century materials. Jean-Pierre Guéno gave much of his energy and encouragement to the project in the early stages, and Philippe Zoummeroff, a generous friend of the Bibliothèque, made possible several trips of key BN staff to Washington during the early stages of the project. On January 3, 1994, a new organization came

xvii

into being combining the Bibliothèque Nationale with the Bibliothèque de France (Tolbiac) into the Bibliothèque nationale de France. Jean Favier became the president of the BnF and Philippe Bélaval the director general. They have both been most supportive of the project, as has Roland Schaer, director of cultural development, and, assisting him, Thierry Grillet.

The American authors who wrote essays for this volume were recruited early and were helpful in many ways—with advice on translations, explications of the significance of certain objects, and general guidance on aspects of French history. John J. Contreni, Elizabeth A. R. Brown, Orest Ranum, and Peter Gay each contributed much more to the catalogue than the signed essay in the volume, and I am personally grateful for their continuing interest and enthusiasm.

The writing done at the BnF in Paris was of course all in French, which means that translation of most of the catalogue copy into English became an essential and time-consuming aspect of the whole process. Three translators worked on the volume—Philip A. Knachel, formerly with the Folger Library; Steven R. Sachs, of Annapolis, Maryland; and Deke Dusinberre, an American who has done distinguished work in Paris for ten years as a free-lance translator. Their task was not easy, because the French curators and authors wrote in a number of styles and in some instances used technical terms for which English equivalents are not always readily available. We are much indebted to all three translators for their exacting efforts. Vincent Giroud of the Beinecke Rare Book and Manuscript Library at Yale University was helpful in the early stages of this project.

Many people at the Library of Congress also participated in the preparation of the catalogue. Above all, Evelyn Sinclair of the library's Publishing Office went over every aspect of the manuscript with an experienced editor's eye, querying and improving as she went. Dana J. Pratt, as director of publishing before he retired, showed great enthusiasm for this project. John Y. Cole, who became acting director of the Publishing Office in addition to his other duties, has been helpful at every stage, starting with the original discussions with potential publishers. Margaret Wagner of the Publishing Office has assisted us with the countless issues that a complicated book entails. Anita Herrick, who joined me part-time to assist with fundraising, has been invaluable in her ability to speak and write fluent French and to attend to the many details of fundraising and other correspondence. Essential secretarial help was given at crucial points by Cora Dubitsky in my office. Carol Armbruster, the French and Italian specialist in the library's European Division, has contributed her extensive knowledge of the library's own French collections as well as her long familiarity with the resources of the Bibliothèque Nationale. Norma Baker and her colleagues in the library's Development Office worked assiduously to augment the funds needed to carry out the project. The full list of donors, French and American, who made the catalogue, exhibition, and related events possible, is printed at the beginning of the volume. We hope that the results of their generosity convey part of our gratitude for their support. Finally, the Librarian of Congress, James H. Billington, has always kept faith with the project, sure of the significance of cooperation between two great national libraries, both concerned to preserve the great treasures of the past while developing rapidly the digital resources for the future.

We have tried the patience of more than a few people at Yale University Press, I am sure, with delays, troubles with translation, and other problems. Judy Metro and Harry Haskell, in particular, have been most effective—although sometimes exasperated—as editor and copy editor, insisting on what has to be done to produce a book of the quality and coherence finally displayed. They have our heart-felt thanks, although there must have been times when they doubted whether there would ever *be* a catalogue. Our original judgment about the excellence of Yale University Press has been amply justified.

Prosser Gifford
Director of Scholarly Programs
The Library of Congress

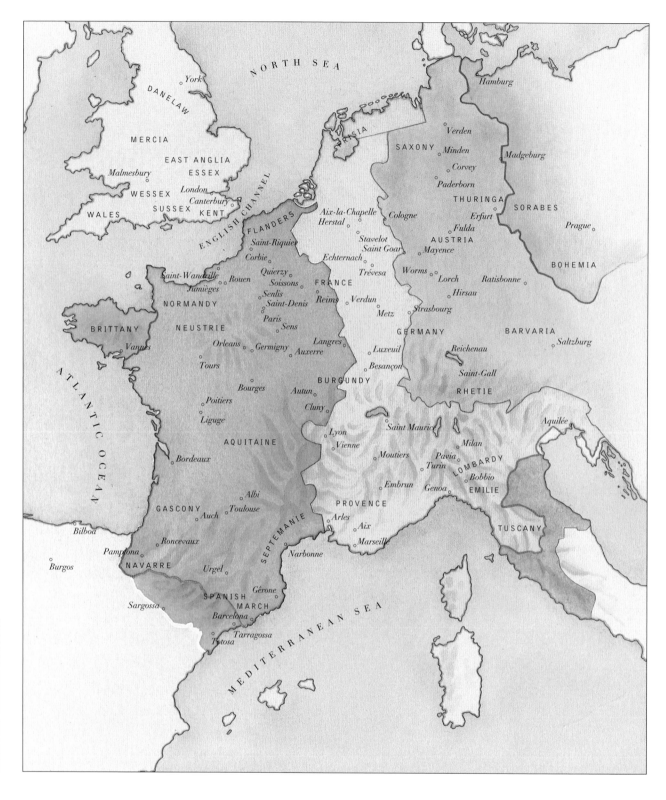

NORTH SEA

York

DANELAW

MERCIA

EAST ANGLIA
ESSEX

Malmesbury

WESSEX *London*
Canterbury
WALES SUSSEX KENT

Hamburg

SAXONY *Verden*
Minden
Corvey *Madgeburg*
Paderborn
THURINGA
SORABES
Erfurt
Prague
Fulda
BOHEMIA

ENGLISH CHANNEL

FLANDERS

Aix-la-Chapelle
Herstal

Cologne

AUSTRIA
Mayence

Saint-Riquier
Corbie

Stavelot
Saint Goar

Echternach

Worms
Lorch
Ratisbonne

Saint-Wandrille
Jumièges
Rouen
Quierzy
Soissons
Senlis

Trévesa

FRANCE

Hirsau

NORMANDY

Reims
Verdun
Metz
Strasbourg
GERMANY

BARVARIA
Saltzburg

BRITTANY

NEUSTRIE
Saint-Denis
Paris
Sens

Langres
Auxerre
Luxeuil
Besançon

Reichenau

RHETIE

Vannes

Orleans
Germigny

Saint-Gall

Tours

BURGUNDY

Aquilée

ATLANTIC OCEAN

Bourges
Autun
Cluny

Lyon
Vienne
Saint Maurice
Milan
Moutiers
Pavia
Turin
LOMBARDY
Bobbio
Genoa
EMILIE

Poitiers
Liguge

AQUITAINE

Bordeaux

Embrun

Albi
Toulouse

PROVENCE

Arles
Aix
Marseille

TUSCANY

Bilboa

GASCONY
Auch

SEPTEMANIE

Roncevaux
Pamplona
NAVARRE
Urgel

Narbonne

MEDITERRANEAN SEA

Burgos

Gérone
SPANISH
MARCH
Sargossa
Barcelona
Tarragossa
Tortosa

THE CAROLINGIAN WORLD

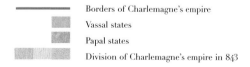

Borders of Charlemagne's empire

Vassal states

Papal states

Division of Charlemagne's empire in 843

Chronology of the History of France

POLITICAL EVENTS		CULTURAL EVENTS	
MEROVINGIANS			
481–511	Reign of Clovis		
496	Baptism of Clovis		
		594	Death of Gregory of Tours
629–639	Reign of Dagobert		
		657	Bathildis founds the abbey of Corbie
732	Charles Martel defeats the Arabs at Poitiers		
CAROLINGIANS			
751–768	Reign of Pepin		
768–814	Reign of Charlemagne		
		772	Maurdramme becomes abbot at Corbie; beginning of Carolingian minuscule
		776	Construction of the first abbey of Saint-Denis
		781–785	*Evangéliaire de Godescalc*
		785	Construction of the palace at Aix-la-Chapelle
		789	The *Admonitio generalis*, promulgated by Charlemagne, devotes a chapter to schools and the copying of manuscripts
800	Imperial coronation of Charlemagne on Christmas Day at Rome		
		810	*Evangiles du couronnement*
814–840	Reign of Louis the Pious		

xxi

CREATING FRENCH CULTURE

POLITICAL EVENTS	CULTURAL EVENTS
	827 Louis the Pious offers the abbey of Saint-Denis a Greek manuscript of the works of Pseudo-Dionysius the Areopagite
840–877 Reign of Charles the Bald	
842 The "Serments de Strasbourg": the oldest document in French	
843 Treaty of Verdun, dividing the Carolingian empire	
845–857 Norman invasions	
	877 Assemblée at Quierzy: Charles the Bald leaves his books to his son Louis and the abbeys of Saint-Denis and Notre-Dame de Compiègne
885–886 Siege of Paris by the Normans	
	910 Establishment of the first Cluniac monastery by Guillaume d'Aquitaine
911 Treaty of Saint-Clair-sur-Epte: territory around Rouen and the mouth of the Seine River ceded to Rollo; this region eventually became known as Normandy	

CAPETIANS

POLITICAL EVENTS	CULTURAL EVENTS
987–996 Reign of Hugh Capet: Proclaimed king by the Assemblée of Noyon, Hugh Capet is crowned at Reims by Archbishop Adalbéron	
	1037–1067 Founding of the abbey of Jumièges
	1062–1080 Founding of the abbeys of Caen, La Trinité, and Saint-Étienne
1066 Battle of Hastings: William of Normandy conquers England	1066–1077 Bayeux Tapestry
1095 Council of Clermont: Pope Urban II preaches the First Crusade	
	1098 Establishment of Cîteaux by Robert de Molesme
1099 Capture of Jerusalem by the Crusaders	
	ca. 1090s *Chanson de Roland*
	1100 Completion of the cloister of the abbey of Moissac
1108–1137 Reign of Louis the Fat	
	1113 Foundation of Saint-Victor in Paris by Guillaume de Champeaux
	1115 Foundation of Clairvaux by the future Saint Bernard
1137–1180 Reign of Louis VII	
	1142 Death of Abélard
	1146 Saint Bernard preaches the Second Crusade at Vézelay
1151 Death of Suger, abbot of Saint-Denis	

VALOIS

xxiii

1329	At Amiens, Edward III gives homage to the king of France for the Guyenne

1334–1342 Construction of the Palace of the Popes at Avignon

1337 Confiscation of the Guyenne by Philip VI because of failure of feudal obligations; Edward III annuls his homage to the king of France and asserts the Capetian heritage: Beginning of the Hundred Years War

1348 Outbreak of the Black Death

1350–1364 Reign of John the Good

1356 Battle of Poitiers: capture of John the Good by the English

ca. 1350 Portrait of John the Good

1368 The Royal Library is transferred to the Louvre in the Falconry Tower

after 1375 Development of International Gothic

1376 Tapestries of the Apocalypse at Angers

1380–1422 Reign of Charles VI: France is governed by the king's uncles during his minority, 1380–1388, and his intermittent bouts of madness, 1392–1422

1395 Jean Gerson becomes the chancellor of the University of Paris

1407 Assassination of the duke of Orléans on the orders of John the Fearless; France splits into two camps, the Armagnacs and the Burgundians

1410–1416 The *Très Riches Heures* by Limbourg brothers for Jean, duke of Berry

1415 Resumption of the Franco-English wars: The English king, Henry V, crushes the French troops at Agincourt; the prince-poet Charles d'Orléans is taken prisoner

1418 Massacre in Paris of the Armagnacs by the Burgundians; the dauphin flees Paris

1420 Treaty of Troyes between France and England

1422–1461 Reign of Charles VII: The dauphin proclaims himself king at Mehun-sur-Yèvre in defiance of the Treaty of Troyes, which had deprived him of his right to the crown

1428 Joan of Arc, leading the army of Charles VII, liberates Orléans from the English and conducts the king to Reims to be crowned

1431 Joan of Arc is burned at Rouen as a heretic

1436 The Ile de France is reconquered by Charles VII

1437 Entry of Charles VII into Paris

1438 Pragmatic Sanction of Bourges

1444 Fouquet paints the portrait of Charles VII

1450 The library of the abbey of Saint-Denis possesses 1,600 volumes

1454 Ordonnances on the reformation of justice

1461–1483 Reign of Louis XI

1470 The first Parisian printing press set up in the library of the Sorbonne by masters Guillaume Fichet and Johannes Heynlin; *Barzizza* is the first book printed in Paris

1477 Defeat and death of Charles the Bold, duke of Burgundy; the king of France officially takes possession of Burgundy

1480 Death of René of Anjou; after the death of his heir, Charles of Maine, in 1481, Maine, Anjou, and Provence enter the royal domain

1483–1498 Reign of Charles VIII

1489 First edition of Villon

1491 Anne of Beaujeu arranges the marriage of her brother, Charles VIII, to Anne of Brittany, heiress of the duchy

1492 Discovery of America by Christopher Columbus

1494 Beginning of the war with Italy sparked by the claim of Charles VIII to the kingdom of Naples

1495 Charles VIII enters Naples

1498–1515 Charles VIII dies without heir and the crown passes to Louis of Orléans, the great-grandson of Charles V; after having repudiated his wife, Jeanne, daughter of Louis XII, the king marries Anne of Brittany

1499 Louis XII continues the Italian campaigns; conquest of Milan and Genoa

XXV

1503 Leonardo da Vinci's *Mona Lisa*

1503–1508 Bourdichon's *Grandes Heures d'Anne de Bretagne*

1504 Surrender of French troops at Gaëta	
1515–1547 Reign of Francis I: Louis XII dies without heir and the crown passes to Francis of Angoulême, great-grandson of Charles V; Francis I immediately proclaims his rights over Milan	
1515 Victory of Marignan over the Swiss allies of the duke of Milan	1515 Leonardo da Vinci in France
	1529 Guillaume Budé's *Commentarii linguae graecae*
	1530 Founding of the Collège de France
1532 Brittany united with France	
1534 Affaire des Placards; exploration of Canada by Jacques Cartier	1534 Foundation at Paris of the Society of Jesus by Ignatius of Loyola; Rabelais's *Gargantua*
	1536 Calvin's *Institution de la religion chrétienne*
	1537 With the Edict of Montpellier, Francis I institutes the "legal deposit"
	1539 Ordonnances of Villers-Cotterets substituting French for Latin in judiciary proceedings
	1540 Death of Budé
	1544 The royal libraries of Blois and Fontainebleau
1545–1563 Council of Trent	
1547–1559 Reign of Henry II	
	1553 Execution of Michel Servet; death of Rabelais
1560 Beginning of the Wars of Religion	
1572 Saint Bartholomew's Day Massacre	
	1576 Jean Bodin's *Six livres de la République*
	1580 Montaigne's *Essais*

BOURBONS

1589–1610 Reign of Henry IV: In 1589 the last Valois king, Henry III, dies without heir and the crown returns to the Bourbon line through Henry of Navarre, a descendant of Saint Louis	
1594 Coronation of Henry IV at Chartres and entry into Paris	
1598 Edict of Nantes: the king grants Protestants liberty of conscience and authority to practice their religion in various "cities of safety"	
	1604 Completion of the Pont Neuf
1607 Béarn united with France	
1608 Founding of the city of Québec by Champlain	

1610	Assassination of Henry IV by Ravaillac		
1610–1663	Reign of Louis XIII, with regency of Marie de Médicis, 1600–1614		
		1612	Completion of the Place Royale and the Place des Vosges in Paris
1614	The coming of age of Louis XIII		
		1621	Posthumous publication of the *Journal* of L'Estoile
1624	Beginning of the Richelieu ministry		
1627–1628	Siege and surrender of La Rochelle		
		1631	Founding of *La Gazette* by Théophraste Renaudot
		1635	Founding of the Académie Française
		1636	Corneille's *Cid*
		1637	René Descartes's *Discours de la méthode*
		1640	Establishment of the Royal Printing Office
1642	Death of Richelieu; Mazarin is appointed counsel by the king	1642	Completion of the chapel of the Sorbonne in Paris
1643–1715	Reign of Louis XIV, with regency of Anne of Austria, 1643–1651		
		1645	Mansart begins the Val de Grâce
1648	The parliamentary Frond party	1648	Foundation of the Académie Royale de Peinture et de Sculpture
1650–1653	The Frond party of princes		
		1656	Mlle de Scudéry publishes *Clélie*
		1658	Foundation of the Académie des Sciences; construction and decoration of Fouquet's palace at Vaux-le-Vicomte; Lully is named superintendent of the king's music
1661	Death of Mazarin; personal government by Louis XIV; arrest of Fouquet		
		1663	Foundation of the Académie des Inscriptions et Belles-Lettres; Le Vau lays out the gardens at Versailles
		1664	Festival of the Enchanted Isle at Versailles
		1665	Molière's *Don Juan*; foundation of *Journal des savants*
1667	Turenne's campaign in Flanders		
1668	Conquest of Franche-Comté	1668	La Fontaine's *Fables*
		1670	Publication of Pascal's *Pensées*
1672–1678	War with Holland		
1673	Discovery of the Mississippi River by Joliette and Father Marquette	1673	Death of Molière
1678	Vauban is named "Commissaire Général des Fortifications de France"		

xxvii

		1680	Founding of the Comédie Française
1682	The king at Versailles; Sieur de La Salle takes possession in the name of the king of France of the Mississippi and Ohio territories		
1683	Death of Colbert		
1684	Probable date of the secret marriage of Louis XIV and Mme de Maintenon		
1685	Revocation of the Edict of Nantes, a measure which provokes the mass exodus of Protestants toward England, Germany, and Holland		
		1686	Construction of the Place des Victoires in Paris
1695	Completion of the Palace of Versailles		
		1697	Charles Perrault's *Contes*
		1699	Fénelon's *Télémaque*
		1706	Mansart completes the dome of Les Invalides
1711	Death of the Grand Dauphin, son of Louis XIV		
1715–1774	Reign of Louis XV, with regency of Philippe d'Orléans, 1715–1723		
		1721	Montesquieu's *Lettres persanes*
1723	Louis XV comes of age		
		1726	Publication of Mme de Sévigné's *Lettres*
		1739	Buffon becomes manager of the Jardin des Plantes
		1748	Montesquieu's *Esprit des lois*
		1751	Diderot and D'Alembert begin the publication of the *Encyclopédie*
		1752	First condemnation of the *Encyclopédie*
		1759	Second condemnation of the *Encyclopédie*; Voltaire's *Candide*
		1762	Rousseau's *Contrat social*
1766	Lorraine united with France		
		1767	Expulsion of Jesuits from France
1774–1792	Reign of Louis XVI		
1777	Lafayette arrives in America with other young aristocrats to help in the revolt against the English state		
1781	Surrender of the English to Franco-American forces at Yorktown		
		1782	Cholderlos de Laclos's *Liaisons dangereuses*
		1783	Beaumarchais's *Mariage de Figaro*; Montgolfier invents the hot air balloon

REVOLUTION

1789	Opening of the Estates General at Versailles		
1789	June 20: Tennis Court Oath		
1789	July 14: Taking of the Bastille		
	August 4: The Assemblée enacts the abolition of privileges		
	August 26: Vote of the Assemblée on the "Déclaration des droits de l'homme et du citoyen"		
	November 2–4: The property of the church is placed at the disposition of the nation		
1790	Suppression of monastic orders	1790	Founding of the Archives Nationales

REPUBLIC

1792	Proclamation of the Republic	1792	The Royal Library becomes the Bibliothèque Nationale; Rouget de Lisle's "Chant de guerre pour l'armée du Rhin," or "La Marseillaise," later adopted as the national anthem
1793	January 21: Beheading of Louis XVI		
		1795	Adoption of the metric system
		1796	Manuscripts of the Sorbonne and of Saint-Germain-des-Prés enter the Bibliothèque Nationale
1797	The French occupy Venice		
1798–1799	Napoléon's expedition in Egypt		
1799	Napoléon's coup d'état		
1800–1804	Consulate: Napoléon receives the plan for the Code Civil; signing of the Concordat		
1802	Founding of the Légion d'Honneur	1802	François-René Chateaubriand's *Génie du Christianisme* and *René*
1803	Sale of Louisiana to the United States		

FIRST EMPIRE

1804	May 18: Proclamation of the Empire		
	December 2: Napoléon is crowned emperor at Notre-Dame		
1805	December 2: Victory at Austerlitz		
		1809–1826	*La Description de l'Egypte*
		1810	Mme de Staël's *De l'Allemagne*
1811	May: The French at Moscow; November: Crossing of the Berezina		
1814	April 6: Abdication of Napoléon		

	POLITICAL EVENTS		CULTURAL EVENTS
1814–1815	First Restoration (Louis XVIII)		
1814	Constitutional charter conceded by the king		
1815	February–June: The Hundred Days		
1815	June 18: Battle of Waterloo		
1815–1830	Second Restoration		
1821	May 5: Death of Napoléon on Saint-Helena	1821	Alphonse de Lamartine's *Méditations poétiques*
		1822	Champollion deciphers the Rosetta Stone
1824	Deaths of Louis XVIII and Charles X		
		1826	Niépce invents photography
		1828	Founding by Jomard of the Geographic Deposit, which would become the Department of Maps and Plans
1830	July 27–29: Three Glorious Days of the Revolution of 1830		

JULY MONARCHY

	POLITICAL EVENTS		CULTURAL EVENTS
1830–1848	The July Monarchy: The duke of Orléans becomes "king of the French" under the name Louis-Philippe	1830–1842	Auguste Comte's *Cours de philosophie positive*
		1831	Stendhal's *Rouge et le noir*
		1833	Opening of a public reading room at the Bibliothèque Nationale; first volume of Michelet's *Histoire de France*
		1834	Prosper Mérimée appointed inspector of historical monuments
		1835–1840	Alexis de Tocqueville's *De la Démocratie en Amérique*
		1842–1848	Honoré de Balzac's *Comédie humaine*
		1843–1864	Restoration of Notre-Dame de Paris by Viollet-le-Duc
		1844	Alexandre Dumas's *Trois mousquetaires*
		1846	Mérimée's *Carmen*
1848	February 22–24: Fall of the July Monarchy; the Second Republic		
		1849–1850	Chateaubriand's *Mémoires d'outre-tombe*

SECOND EMPIRE

	POLITICAL EVENTS		CULTURAL EVENTS
1852	December 2: Louis Napoléon becomes emperor		
1853	Haussmann begins reconstruction of the Parisian infrastructure—avenues, parks, monuments, water distribution—giving the city its present aspect		
		1857	Charles Baudelaire's *Fleurs du mal;* Gustave Flaubert's *Madame Bovary*
1860	Piedmont cedes Savoy and Nice to France		

CREATING FRENCH CULTURE

		1862	Victor Hugo's *Misérables*
		1863	Salon des Refusés
		1863–1877	Emile Littré's *Dictionnaire de la langue française*
		1867	Pierre Larousse's *Grand Dictionnaire universel*
		1868	Inauguration of Labrouste's main reading room on the location of Mazarin's stables; it receives 46,000 readers

THIRD REPUBLIC

1870	The Third Republic		
1871	March–June: The Paris Commune	1871–1893	Emile Zola's *Rougon-Macquart*
		1872	Monet's *Impression Soleil levant*
		1874–1905	Léopold Delisle serves as director of the Bibliothèque Nationale
		1876–1910	Sacré Coeur in Paris
1881	Law requiring free primary education	1881	Victor Hugo wills his manuscripts to the Bibliothèque Nationale, inaugurating the tradition of important modern literary bequests
		1885	Death of Hugo
		1886	Arthur Rimbaud's *Illuminations;* Bartholdi's Statue of Liberty
		1888	Creation of the Institut Pasteur
		1889	Universal Exposition in Paris; construction of the Eiffel Tower
1893	Entry of the French into Timbuktu		
1894	Trial of Capt. Alfred Dreyfus		
1898	Emile Zola's *J'accuse*		
		1902	André Gide's *Immoraliste;* Claude Debussy's *Pelléas et Mélisande*
		1903	First Tour de France; Marie Curie's *Recherches sur les substances radioactives*
1905	Legal separation of church and state		
		1907	Picasso's *Demoiselles d'Avignon*
		1910	Charles Peguy's *Mystère de la charité de Jeanne d'Arc*
		1913	Blaise Cendrars's *Prose du Transsibérien*
		1913–1927	Marcel Proust's *A la Recherche du temps perdu*
		1920	Tristan Tzara's *Manifeste Dada*
		1922	Death of Proust
		1924	Installation of electric lighting at the Bibliothèque Nationale
		1929	Paul Claudel's *Soulier de satin;* Marc Bloch and Lucien Febvre found *Les Annales*

			1930–1940	Julien Cain serves as director of the Bibliothèque Nationale
			1933	André Malraux's *Condition humaine*
			1938	Jean-Paul Sartre's *Nausée*
1939	Great Britain and France declare war on Germany			
1940	Marshal Pétain forms the Vichy government; June 18: General de Gaulle appeals from London for the French to continue the war			
1944	June 6: Landing of Allies in Normandy			
1945	May 8: Germany surrenders		1945–1964	Julien Cain serves again as director of the Bibliothèque Nationale

FOURTH REPUBLIC

1946	The Fourth Republic			
			1947	Albert Camus's *Peste*

FIFTH REPUBLIC

1958–1969	Charles de Gaulle, president of the Republic			
1958	Creation of the Ministry of Cultural Affairs			
1969–1974	Georges Pompidou, president of the Republic			
1974–1981	Valéry Giscard d'Estaing, president of the Republic			
			1980	Death of Sartre; Marguerite Yourcenar is the first woman named to the Académie Française
1981–1995	François Mitterrand, president of the Republic			
			1988	July 14: The president announces the plan for the Bibliothèque nationale de France
			1989	Dominique Perrault chosen to be the architect of the new library
			1994	January: Founding of the Bibliothèque nationale de France, combining the Bibliothèque Nationale with the Bibliothèque de France

Introduction

What is the Bibliothèque nationale de France (BnF), until recently known simply as the Bibliothèque Nationale (BN)?[1] What relationships has the library had not only with culture but, almost as important, with power? At the outset there was the Bibliothèque Royale (Royal Library), alias the Librairie, or Bibliothèque, du Roi (King's Library). This institution, which was always eminently political (though not *just* political), can be said to have begun under Charles V in the late fourteenth century (1364–1380).

The Beginnings

Charles was a very literate monarch. In 1368 he brought together more than a thousand manuscripts in the Falconry Tower of the Louvre. Unfortunately, upon the death of King Charles VI (the Mad) in 1422, they were dispersed by the duke of Bedford, who oversaw the English occupation in Paris during that period. Some of the manuscripts were sold and/or sent to England; many were lost forever. Nonetheless, the BnF still possesses some sixty of Charles V's volumes, one of which (Département des Manuscrits NAF 18867) was repurchased in Great Britain during my term of office. Some years ago it was suggested that a stone taken from the tower of the Louvre be placed in the foundations of the BnF's new buildings at Tolbiac. The idea underscored the relationships between culture, as embodied by the royal or republican library, and power, symbolized in times past by the massive tower of the Louvre. In fact, as we shall see, a history of the Bibliothèque Nationale has to be based on, among other things, the chronology of the monarchy.

Charles VII (1422–1461), although a person of some cultivation, had too much to do fighting the English–part of the time alongside Joan of Arc–to devote attention to his *librairie*. It was Louis XI's accession to the throne in 1461 that marked an unquestionable revival of royal interest. Louis was a stern king of exceptional political capacities. Furthermore, his behavior was that of an educated man, an admirer of Italian culture–before the death of his father, he governed the province of Dauphiné, immediately adjacent to Piedmont. He purchased many beautiful manuscripts, as well as confiscating some fine private libraries by questionable means (which were contested during his lifetime).[2] In his reign the Royal Library continued to grow, though it still contained no printed books, despite the fact that printing had been perfected in the era of Gutenberg, beginning in 1452. It seems that Louis XI saw no good reason to add incunabula to his collection of manuscripts.

Louis's son, Charles VIII (1483–1498), was also powerfully drawn to beautiful manuscripts. As the principal actor in a war that would take him down as far as Naples, he became especially interested in the superb manuscripts of southern Italy. Indeed, his presence there in 1495 signaled a veritable turning point in the biological and cultural evolution of France: biological, in that it resulted in the introduction of syphilis to the country; cultural, because it marked an important break with late Gothic style in illuminated manuscripts, when everything had been touched by ancient and Italian influences. This break is reflected by the illuminations in the Italian manuscripts that Charles VIII seized and brought back to France, as well as in the French manuscripts produced subsequent to those Italian incursions. Moreover, Charles VIII was the first king to ensure that *printed* works found their way into the Royal Library–a library which, come what may, would never be dispersed and whose collections each sovereign from then on would strive to enlarge.

Louis XII (1498–1515), the uncle and successor of Charles VIII, was a notable collector. Moving the library to Blois, he first arranged for the preservation of the magnificent collections of his father, Charles d'Orléans. Charles was a remarkable man of learning, a collector of the first rank, a talented poet, and heir to the fine library which had belonged to his own father, Duke Louis d'Orléans, grandfather of Louis XII and an enlightened amateur. Furthermore, when new wars in Italy drew Louis XII to Milan, the monarch carried a substantial number of works home from Lombardy. To the existing collections in France, he also added manuscripts of northern and Burgundian provenance, collected previously by the great Flemish librarian Louis de La Gruthuyse. Louis XII's love for books and manuscripts was reinforced by his wife, Anne de Bretagne. Even before her marriage, the queen had taken an interest in the production of extremely valuable calligraphed and illuminated works. She cast a personal aura of splendor over the intellectual and cultural life of the French court. Through her the Royal Library acquired some extraordinary manuscripts, in particular *Les Grandes Heures d'Anne de Bretagne* (The book of hours of Anne de Bretagne), in which page after page of delicate and meticulous illuminated drawings of hundreds of flowers and insects unfold to view.

The library received a new burst of vitality from Louis XII's successor, Francis I (1515–1547). Francis was a humanist, but his culture did not exceed the bounds considered suitable for a gentleman who wanted to avoid the pedantry of the professional scholar. He was, however, unquestionably fond of literature to the extent of forcing his ambassadors to learn Greek so that they could acquire manuscripts for him in Italy and the Orient. Francis appointed men like Guillaume Budé, a great Hellenist, and Lefèvre d'Etaples, a famous humanist, to head his library, which beginning in 1544 was located at Fontainebleau. The combined influence of these two men proved of substantial importance to the long-term growth of the Royal Library.

Francis I was responsible for a decision that was as crucial in the history of the Bibliothèque nationale de France as it would be in the history of other national libraries throughout the world. For it was he who in 1537 established the *dépôt légal* (similar to the book deposit requirement under United States copyright law), obliging printers and publishers to submit to the royal authorities ("in our castle at Blois") a copy of each book published in France. This decision reflected a determination to crack down on the Protestants, who were publishing and reading a quantity of heterodox books in that period, but it also revealed Francis's genuine passion to preserve books. Nonetheless, the 1537 decree concerning "legal deposit" would not be applied systematically in France until abbé Bignon became master of the Royal Library in the eighteenth century. He was substantially responsible for the wealth of early books now in our collections. It should be noted, too, that a legal deposit is inseparable from the notion of a national library, and that most national libraries throughout the world benefit from such a requirement. It has been said, with tongue in cheek, that the way to recognize a nation is by the fact that it has a national library, and that a national library exists by virtue of legal deposit. In principle, it matters little whether the legal deposit involves only a few volumes each year in a small state or some forty thousand books a year in a country like France.

Henry II (1547–1559) made a mark for himself by ordering fine bindings from French artists. Indeed, French bookbinding achieved its golden age in the mid-sixteenth century and not, as is sometimes believed, in the seventeenth and eighteenth centuries, brilliant though the later period may have been in terms of the *habillage*, or presentation, of books. While carrying on Francis I's policy and undergoing, besides, the beneficial influence of his mother, Catherine de Médicis, Charles IX (1550–1574) took care to name a gifted Hellenist, Jacques Amyot, to direct his library. Its expansion nevertheless slowed between 1562 and 1595 because of the regrettable course of the Wars of Religion. Actually, the Royal Library was still small, having grown from 2,700 works in about 1544 to 3,650 around 1567. After its move to Paris, perhaps in 1568, it was shunted from one building to another for decades until Colbert finally found a home for it at its present site in the rue de Richelieu in the late 1600s.

In the reign of Henry IV (1589–1610), library expansion resumed, especially after the conclusion of the Wars of Religion in 1595. This new beginning was owing in particular to the hundreds of Greek manuscripts from the Ridolfi library that the king acquired from the late Catherine de Médicis. When the monks of Saint-Denis, ruined by war and pillage, wanted to sell a fine Carolingian Bible, Parlement decreed that it be deposited in the library. This is Charles the Bald's second Bible, which the BnF still possesses. Henry IV reportedly wanted to move his library to the Left Bank of Paris and thought of placing it at a site now occupied by the Collège de France, but nothing of this sort happened.

The decades which followed, distinguished by the ministries of cardinals Richelieu and Mazarin, saw a certain stagnation in the library. The two prelates incarnated absolutism to a greater degree than Louis XIII (1610–1643) or the young

Louis XIV in the years prior to his personal reign (1643–1661). Both cardinals concentrated their attention on their own collections: Richelieu assembled his at the Sorbonne (the Bibliothèque Nationale recovered part of it during the French Revolution), while Mazarin brought his books to the Collège des Quatre Nations, now the Institut de France, where some of them are still kept. As a result, the Royal Library still had "only" 6,000 manuscripts and 10,700 printed books when Mazarin died in 1661.

The Extraordinary Years

Everything would change between 1661 and 1799—a period that I describe in an essay elsewhere in this catalogue. It will suffice here to observe that in this extraordinary century and a half the Bibliothèque Nationale was aided greatly by personalities (one might say politicians) of major importance: Colbert, Louis XIV himself, the Louvois-Letellier family, and abbé Bignon, that commendable administrator in the Age of Enlightenment (although his notorious womanizing prevented him from becoming a bishop). Then came the prodigious revolutionary years, when two directors of the library were guillotined by the "Power" (Jacobin power, of course) and a third committed suicide. But happy events balanced the many painful ones. After all, wouldn't it be worth going to the guillotine even today if one could (in a manner of speaking) get in exchange hundreds of thousands of rare books, manuscripts (many of them truly marvelous), prints, medals, ancient and famous maps—though unfortunately at the clergy's expense, to be sure, between 1790 and 1800..., but in the most legal way in the world.

This incredible expansion of our collections, which created a kind of traffic jam in the stacks, was followed by a less exhilarating, and even somewhat disillusioning, period extending into the early nineteenth century. Money and qualified personnel were in short supply, and inadequate leadership and internal quarrels compounded the difficulty. Once the Great Terror of 1793–1794 had run its course, the position of director general was eliminated and the library was administered collectively by the department heads, or *gardes* (keepers). To be more exact, the keepers (who were selected by cooptation) elected a director whose powers expired at the end of each year. When Napoléon Bonaparte became consul and de facto dictator some years later, he put an end to this ineffective management system by creating the position of *administrateur* (not long ago one still spoke of the *administrateur général*). This is the position I occupied from the autumn of 1987 to the beginning of 1994—which in effect makes me a legacy from the Bonapartist era!

Furthermore, everyone felt somewhat cramped in buildings that had become inadequate and outmoded, particularly after 1800, when the library became accessible to an ever larger and more demanding public. (As a bad joke would have it, a library would be a fine place if it weren't for the readers.) The overcrowding was aggravated by the very limited schedule of hours when the library was open. Since candles were forbidden, the public was admitted only during daylight hours—from 10 a.m. to 2 p.m. Today the library operates from 9 a.m. to 8 p.m., and at the Tolbiac location it is expected to be open from 9 a.m. to 9 p.m. Tight budgets will perhaps continue to make these conveniences difficult to implement; overtime costs in France are high. But let us pray. . . .

For certain periods in the nineteenth century, the Ministry of the Interior had administrative oversight of the Bibliothèque Nationale. Later the library was administered by the Ministry of National Education, and today it is part of the Ministry of Culture, which is housed close by in the Palais Royal. Perhaps, in fact, it is better to be a large institution like the Bibliothèque Nationale in a medium-sized ministry like that of culture than to be a medium-sized entity in an enormous ministry like that of national education (which is sometimes said to control more people than the Red Army did in its glory days). That said, there was a time when an administrateur général was hard pressed to get a minister's attention for more than two full minutes. As a former administrateur once told me, "You were sure that the sound of your voice carried to the minister's ear, but you were not absolutely certain that the meaning of your words reached his little grey cells." Happily, those days are over. The Ministry of the Interior, which supervises the French national police, still plays a not insignificant role in the library's affairs, since by law it too receives a copy of each work published in France. This is a distant echo of the era when my country still had censorship. Many years ago, under De Gaulle, I remarked to one of our ministers of the interior that he could have built his own national library. The minister apparently misunderstood and answered that he would rather give the books to the policemen's children and to visiting statesmen. . . . Well, why not?

In the early nineteenth century, the Bibliothèque Nationale was not only a library but also a center for teaching and research. In 1795 Lakanal, one of the great specialists in pedagogy, decided that the French School of Oriental Languages should become an active part of the Bibliothèque Nationale. "Difficult" languages, as they were referred to at the time, including Turkish, Arabic, and even Malay, were taught in the rue de Richelieu building because of the ready availability of Oriental and other manuscripts. Several generations later, the School of Oriental Languages was separated from the library, and today it is wholly independent.

During the early 1800s, as well, plans were laid to move the Bibliothèque Nationale. It was feared that the Opéra, then located just across the street on the site of the present Place Louvois, was a potential fire hazard. Even after the old Opéra was demolished—not by fire!—the plans continued to be aired. Under Napoléon I a move to the Louvre was considered. Thereafter discussion turned successively to the church of the Madeleine, the Institut de France on the Left Bank, the Mint, the Quai d'Orsay (the present Ministry of Foreign Affairs), the Place Dauphine, the church of Saint-Sulpice, and an old livestock market. There was also talk of moving the library to the rue Saint-Jacques, the old axis of Paris formerly traveled by pilgrims en route to Saint James of Compostello in Spain. Other locations put forward were the Palais Bourbon (which now houses the Chambre des Députés), the Hôtel de Ville (City Hall), and the boulevard des Champs-Elysées. It was even suggested that the library be laid out out in the form of a circular *panoptique*, similar to Michel Foucault's design for a prison at the turn of the nineteenth century. At the center of this cartwheel-like structure, a single guard—seated, I suppose, in a swivel chair—would have scanned the corridors on the lookout for book thieves. The answer to a curator's nightmare?

The Second Empire (1852–1870) was a remarkable period for the Bibliothèque Nationale. Napoléon III had an altogether positive influence in some ways (perhaps aided by the favorable trend of the general economy), while pointing the country in the direction of disastrous wars, including the one in Mexico and especially the war against Prussia in 1870. He strengthened the power of the administrateur général, in keeping with the authoritarian coloring of his regime, and raised the salaries of the staff. During his reign a second reading room was put in service for readers who were neither scholars nor specialists. And, wonder of wonders, it was even open on Sundays! (This may seem unsurprising in the United States, but it is not necessarily so in France, if only because of the extra salary costs. Sunday opening is sure to be introduced at Tolbiac in the years to come.) Another innovation of the Second Empire was the introduction of central heating, which previously had been out of the question because of the fire hazard. The heated building did, however, attract the homeless, who in our own century have been turned away, if for no other reason than the small annual fee required for a reader's card.

In 1857 was formed the Mérimée Commission, named after the French author who imagined Carmen, one of Spain's most remarkable mythological figures. Prosper Mérimée was also in charge of historical monuments throughout the country, and deserves as much credit as Viollet-le-Duc for the Gothic Revival and the rescue of many medieval churches. Charged with the inquiry into the Bibliothèque Nationale, Mérimée minced no words in the commission's final report. He criticized the impotent administration, especially the administrateur, who was short-circuited by the collective council of heads of departments (of printed books, engravings, medals, and so on). He advocated the need for a sole head. (As one was apt to say in Paris some years ago, with an eye to the example of collective management in Yugoslavia, which was then very popular in France, "Collective management is good, but you need somebody in charge.") Furthermore, Mérimée called attention to the lack of zeal, if not the downright rudeness, of certain staff members (fortunately, only a few), and he objected to the presence at the BN of the Department of Engravings, which he felt belonged at the Louvre. (Where to put engravings, coins, and medals at the BN has been the source of recurring controversy over the years.) Mérimée was not the first to complain about the lack of funds for book acquisition and binding. He noted the excessive cataloguing delays and the faulty operation of the dépôt légal. What is more, many readers, he reported, came to get obscene books, even when "Hell" was beginning its career. (I should explain that Hell, today, is a special stack area reserved for erotic or pornographic books. It continues to generate immense curiosity on the part of the public. Although it remains an excellent place to preserve the literature consigned to it, Hell is no match for what appears today on many of our film and television screens.)

From Labrouste to the BnF

Henri Labrouste (1801–1875) was the great architect of French libraries in the nineteenth century. From 1843 to 1850 he built Sainte-Geneviève, which not long ago attracted the interest of the builders of the new municipal library in San Francisco. In 1859 he presented the authorities with his plan for the Bibliothèque Nationale. It was the age when Haussmann was rebuilding Paris and when cast-iron architecture was the vogue both in France and in England. Labrouste's plans (which called for remodeling the library without rebuilding it from scratch) were implemented fully.

The only important change was made for reasons of security: the arcade that Labrouste intended to face the rue de Richelieu was replaced by a solid wall. Among the features that were retained was the multidomed reading room inspired by the church (now mosque) of Saint Sophia in Constantinople. The vaulting has a magical effect on our readers, many of whom despair at having to leave for Tolbiac, however necessary, even indispensable, the move may be.

In the reading room for printed materials, now known as the Labrouste Room, the architect centralized the bookstacks in logical fashion behind the space allotted to the readers, so that materials could be easily and rapidly paged. The five stack floors and ceilings allowed natural light to penetrate the storage area from top to bottom. The clever arrangement of gratings and transparent floors was much admired when the new storage area was opened, so much so that German librarians often adopted it. Unfortunately for them, during the bombing raids in World War II, fire spread rapidly from one floor to the other through the openwork framing.

The stacks held a million books when Labrouste's work was completed in 1873; now the central stack area alone contains nine million. The growth of the collections presented perplexing problems, which until recently were resolved by the creation of new floors above and below the Labroustian structure and by the insertion of new stacks, so that the five original floors are now ten. Much of the work accomplished goes back to my distinguished predecessor, Julien Cain, who held the post of administrateur général from 1930 to 1964 (with the exception of the years 1940–1945). Although I am full of admiration for Cain and his work, he may perhaps be faulted for failing to keep abreast of the technological efficiencies that benefited American libraries beginning in the 1950s.

On the strength of Labrouste's work in particular, the Bibliothèque Nationale was a leader among world libraries in the years 1860–1870. After 1900, however, England and, still more, the United States achieved unquestioned preeminence, for a variety of reasons. To me, the principal one seems to be the emergence of English as the international scientific language of choice. This Anglo-Saxon superiority led to a corresponding shift in writing in the French language, which thereafter limited French books present in the library largely to those dealing with literature, history, and other fields of the humanities. Second, American libraries–like American museums–have benefited from the remarkable patronage of individuals like Andrew Carnegie. This situation has no parallel in France, where for so long all support came from public funds meagerly allocated, especially after 1900. (It is true that in France the education of an *honnête homme* was considered dependent on Latin and Greek classics and not on huge libraries.)

As early as the seventeenth century, and especially in the eighteenth century with abbé Bignon, attempts were made to catalogue the library's holdings, but much remained to be done. The field of library science stagnated in France for a long time, despite the enormous growth in the collections during the revolutionary period. Some improvement began in the mid-nineteenth century with an administrateur named Jules Taschereau, who, as a curator and then as administrateur général, had earned a reputation for his emphasis on cataloguing, particularly in French history and the medical sciences. Those efforts became well focused under another administrateur, Léopold Delisle, who was one of the great officials of our library in the late nineteenth century. It was he who began the staggering task of preparing a printed catalogue, based on cards that had long existed. He started the job when he was in his sixties and did not leave the rue de Richelieu until he was obliged to step down at the age of nearly eighty. (Today the mandatory retirement age for French government employees in such positions is sixty-five, contrary to the situation in the United States, where no age limit exists for federal employees.) Putting together the printed catalogue of the Bibliothèque Nationale, which comprises 231 volumes (or 232 *tomes* – Voltaire alone occupies two tomes), took nearly a century: it was finally completed in the 1980s. The project did not lack for scoffers, who criticized our alleged slowness on account of the care lavished on the catalogue. In fact, the quality of the finished work was remarkable. Today, thanks to it, we can move quite easily into the computerization of the titles and call numbers of our printed collection.

As I explained earlier, the position of administrateur général is not without danger. After the fall of France in 1940, Julien Cain was dismissed by the Vichy government. Later he was arrested by the Germans and prevented from resuming his duties as administrateur général until 1945. He remained at the post until 1964, when he reached the mandatory retirement age. Beginning with Cain, who was for this long period one of the best directors of the Bibliothèque, "homogeneity" in the particular destiny of the institution was guaranteed. The final series of administrateurs généraux – followed, in the end, by a président – was characterized, in fact, by a remarkable mutual solidarity. Georges Le Rider, Alain Gourdon, André Miquel, and myself, administrateurs généraux from 1974 through 1993, and Jean Favier, the current président, all belong more or less to the same generation – the generation of top functionaries shaped by graduate study at universities in the period immediately following World War II, who acceded to high-level professorial or public service positions during the first ten or fifteen years of the Fifth Republic. Because of this, continuing innovation is assured, not to be interrupted by the variety of individuals who take the leadership role.

Emmanuel Le Roy Ladurie
Membre de l'Institut
Professeur au Collège de France

1 On the history of the Bibliothèque Nationale, see Simone Balayé, *La Bibliothèque Nationale des origines à 1800* (Paris, 1988).

2 The collection of Cardinal la Balue was one of those confiscated.

I

Monarchs and Monasteries: The Early Years

QVOD VATES BELLVM CREVIT NON ESSE DVELLVM
EDIDIT & MVLTIS · VOBIS QVI CERNERE VVLTIS
EST IOSEPHVS DICTVS FERT LIBRVM CORPORE PICTVS

QVOD VATES BELLVM CREVIT NON ESSE DVELLVM
EDIDIT & MVLTIS · VOBIS QVI CERNERE VVLTIS
EST IOSEPHVS DICTVS FERT LIBRVM CORPORE PICTVS

1 Images of Power and Culture in the Carolingian and Monastic Periods

From the Eighth to the Twelfth Century

John J. Contreni

Power and culture are words particularly rich in meaning. Power suggests force and work, getting something done. There is a suggestion of intentionality in power, often in the context of political power. But power can be more subtle, as in the power of centuries-old tradition or art or words to move and to inspire. Power can also produce consequences unintended by those who wield it. Culture, a word originally associated with farming, also evokes several meanings. "High" culture suggests the life of the mind, or art and literature. But culture serves also to describe values and social traits, as in political culture and peasant culture.

When we link power and culture and set out to explore the relationship between such fissiparous concepts, we enter an exciting landscape, one strewn with high intentions, reversals of fortune, and unexpected outcomes. Who in the middle of the eighth century would have thought that three centuries later monks would be shaping European values? Or that all during those centuries warrior-kings would encourage and support culture? Or that the culture they encouraged would empower religious leaders to correct and challenge kings? The experience of power and culture in France between the times of Charlemagne (768–814) and Saint Louis (1226–1270) was punctuated at key moments by the creation of magnificent treasures. Who views these objects today glimpses something of the many manifestations of power and culture in earliest France.

Carolingian Kingship

Early in 849 Charles and Lothar, the warring sons of Louis the Pious (814–840), agreed to patch up their differences. In the thirty-five years since their grandfather, Charlemagne, had died, the kingdom of the Franks had been racked by dissension among the fractious members of the Carolingian family. The stakes in the internecine struggle were high—the right to claim authority and power in the wealthiest and most sophisticated political state yet created in the Middle Ages.

3

Power in the Carolingian world rested on the control of wealth and the command of troops. But that was not all. What made the Carolingian moment a special one in the history of medieval Europe was the readiness of Carolingian leaders to draw on cultural resources to legitimate and embellish their power.

When Lothar commissioned the monks of Saint-Martin of Tours to produce a deluxe manuscript of the Gospels, his stated intention was to bind himself and his family to the power of the prayer community at the abbey (see cat. 4). His gift also commemorated the new era of concord between Lothar (840–855) and Charles (840–877), since the abbey of Saint-Martin was located in Charles's kingdom. That a book could be freighted with so many functions—in addition to its primary one of carrying a text—testifies to the nexus of religion, politics, and culture achieved under the Carolingians.

This nexus derived from powerful historical traditions which the Carolingians inherited and crystallized in their literature and in much of their art. One ingredient in the tradition of leadership, of course, was kingship. Whatever kingship meant to the various Germanic tribes before they came into the Roman Empire, by the time they settled in the West it had become a complex and changing institution in which old and new ingredients combined. Kingship was rooted in a family, a dynasty, and its essential elements were personal. The king was a war-leader. His ability to command the respect and loyalty of the leading warrior elements of his society directly affected his ability to wield power. By the mid-eighth century, when the Carolingian family deposed the Merovingian dynasty to become kings in Francia, the king had become a religious figure as well. Whether he was (in modern terms) a quasi-religious figure, a sacred king, or a sacral king is debatable. It is not clear that such distinctions troubled early medieval kings and their entourages. Indeed, the ambiguity of their roles gave them more room for creative action.

Several strands of thought combined to surround kings with the aura of sanctity and, thus, to aggrandize their power. Roman emperors, both pagan and Christian, freely operated in the religious sphere, and Byzantine emperors continued to do so after the fall of the empire. In the West, Germanic kings, even newly minted Christians such as Clovis, were celebrated for their priestlike qualities. But these kings did not take their cues from emperors. The special features of early medieval kingship are rooted in the Bible or, rather, in the application of the biblical worldview to the newly emerging European culture.

The Bible provided two important elements to the new definition of royal power. The Scriptures defined the divine origins of power in both general and specific terms. Thus John 4.27: "No one can receive anything except what is given him from heaven." It was Paul, however, who coined the phrase that kings would append to their names for centuries (1 Cor. 15.10): "But *by the grace of God* I am what I am." It was also Paul who provided the bluntest justification for royal authority (Rom. 13.1–2, 6): "Let every person be subject to the governing authorities. For there is no authority except from God, and those that exist have been instituted by God. . . . The authorities are the ministers of God." In the early Middle Ages, clergy eager to sacralize power no doubt interpreted texts such as these to kings who were equally eager for the legitimation conferred by divine warrant. Christ in early medieval art was depicted as a king and lawgiver. Kings were blessed and anointed at their inaugurations; religious ceremonies also celebrated their victories.

The Scriptures, especially the Old Testament, also provided rulers with models of kingship. Among the artists, poets, and scholars who frequented his court, Charlemagne was known as David, as much for his leadership of the new chosen people as for his patronage of the arts. But it was King Josiah who inspired Carolingian leaders to make cultural matters matters of state.

Josiah (2 Kings 22.11) began to rule the Israelites when he was eight years old, according to the biblical account. For the first eighteen years of his reign he ruled, as had his predecessors, in ignorance of the law of God. Then one of his priests found a book containing the law of God and had it read to the king. "And when the king heard the words of the book of the law, he rent his clothes... for great is the wrath of the Lord that is kindled against us, because our fathers have not obeyed the words of this book, to do according to all that is written concerning us." After consulting his advisers, Josiah gathered all his people, "both small and great," and "made a covenant before the Lord, to walk after the Lord and to keep his commandments and his testimonies and his statutes, with all his heart and all his soul, to perform the words of this covenant, that were written in this book."

The Social Function of Culture

The implications of Josiah's kingship for book learning and for the power of words are striking. What struck the Carolingians was the key role the king played in the reform of society. It was the king who made the covenant with the Lord, who assured that his people "great and small" would walk in the ways of the Lord. This powerful message took root among Carolingian leaders, who over and over again returned to biblical models of sacred kingship to describe their own positions in medieval society.

The example of Josiah is evoked, for example, in the General Admonition (*Admonitio generalis*), one of the great reforming documents of the Carolingian period, addressed to all the ranks of the clergy and to secular leaders alike. The description of Josiah in the document as a king who corrected his wayward people and restored them to the "words of the book of the law" occurs just before the presentation of eighty-two articles intended "to correct what is erroneous, to cut away what is inadmissible, to strengthen what is right."[1] Amid the canons addressing clerical discipline, encouraging the observance of the Sabbath, inveighing against sin and abuses of all kinds, one specifically obliged monks and priests to conduct themselves in a praiseworthy manner and to establish schools

> that many may be drawn to God's service by their upright way of life and they may gather and associate to themselves not only children of servile condition but also the sons of freemen. And let schools for teaching boys the psalms, the *nota*, singing, computation and grammar be created in every monastery and episcopal residence. And correct catholic books properly, for often, while people want to pray to God in the proper fashion, they yet pray improperly because of uncorrected books. And do not allow your boys to corrupt them, either in reading or in copying; and if there is need to copy the gospel, Psalter or missal, let men of full age do the writing, with all diligence.[2]

5

This passage, which without too much exaggeration might be called the manifesto of the Carolingian cultural program, prompts several observations. It focused almost exclusively on the clergy or those intended for the clerical state. Of this group, only boys and men are mentioned. One might also observe the rudimentary and practical nature of the recommendations, which emphasized the proper understanding and use of language, mastery of Tironian notes (a system of shorthand notation), of chant, of computus (calculation), and, of course, proper copying of books.

Europe's First Book Culture

The story about Josiah highlights another important ideal of Carolingian culture—the notion that wisdom and the keys for a good society could be found in words and in books. This is all the more remarkable since the great majority of people in the Carolingian realms could not read. But priests and monks were supposed to know how to read so that they could act as informed guides on the path of spiritual salvation. It must have seemed at first a daunting task to build a culture that depended on knowledge of the written word in a society that was largely unschooled and illiterate.

The directions Carolingian leaders gave to improve this situation were simple. In addition to requiring that books be copied carefully, they fashioned a program of reading and study that would enable priests and monks to unpack all the meanings of the Word. What was essentially a one-book culture became a many-book culture. The Bible was written in an alien language—Latin—and so grammar had be studied in order to comprehend and appreciate its words. The Bible was the product of a Jewish society that was geographically, chronologically, and culturally distant from that of the Frankish world of the eighth and ninth centuries. Finally, the words of the Bible were charged with meanings whose comprehension required skill in music, dialectic, geometry, rhetoric, and the other arts. Cultivation of the arts as keys to sacred knowledge helped to justify the wisdom of the ancients, particularly the Roman pagans, in a Christian society.

The value of books in Carolingian culture went beyond the intellectual. Books counted as treasure and were fitted with sumptuous covers worthy of the riches they held within. Books of great material value also formed an important part of the venerable gift-giving tradition among the Franks, as Lothar's gift to the monastic community of Saint-Martin indicates. It is important to remember that the book culture of the Carolingians served utilitarian ends and was not some ivory-tower enterprise or societal ornament. Lothar was, after all, inspired by a political treaty when he commissioned his book (cat. 4). Books and the study of the texts and words in books prepared the "soldiers of Christ" to lead their people to paradise. Even though few could read, reading and books achieved enormous status among Carolingians.

The valorization of the written word and the creation of a program of studies centered around the explication and comprehension of texts in the eighth and ninth centuries would hardly have been possible without the simultaneous investment by Carolingian political and religious leaders in schools and the scholars who taught in them. The concentrated support of kings, bishops, and abbots left its mark in the activities of some 150 known cultural and intellectual centers scattered throughout eighth- to eleventh-century Europe. These centers, it has been estimated, produced some fifty thousand manuscripts in the ninth century alone.[3] The material resources required to produce this cultural wealth suggest that the application of political and religious power to programs of intellectual and cultural renewal bore fruit.

Certain centers blessed with royal favor and patronage played leading cultural roles in the Carolingian kingdoms. The courts of the Carolingian monarchs themselves served as important centers for book collection, book production, and dissemination (see cat 2).[4] Scores of surviving manuscripts have been traced to the courts of Carolingian rulers and their queens and to those of their relatives. Many deluxe books, like Rorico's Bible and Lothar's Gospels (cats. 3 and 4), were intended as gifts. Royal books also served another function when they were used to establish standard, authoritative texts of Bibles, law codes, and liturgical books such as sacramentaries and antiphonaries. From Pippin III (741–768) to Charles the Bald (840–877), Carolingian rulers and their families were active participants in cultural life. They commissioned texts for their own use and, as the controversies over images and predestination demonstrate, they took keen interest in questions of theological orthodoxy.

If the Carolingians had succeeded only in animating cultural life at their courts, their achievement would have evaporated even as the power of their dynasty began to weaken after the death of Charles the Bald. The stimulus royal power gave to culture, however, was broadly based and outlived the dynasty in centers all over the Frankish kingdom.

Saint-Denis

The monastery of Saint-Denis, six miles north of the heart of Paris, was one of the most important Carolingian cultural centers. Saint-Denis was first a cultic center in the restricted meaning of the word—the site held the bones of Saint Dionysius (Saint Denis in French), the first bishop of Paris, who reportedly died a martyr's death on Montmartre in the mid-third century and carried his severed head to the future site of the abbey named after him. Saint-Denis enjoyed royal favor early on. Dagobert I (d. 639), one of the most powerful Merovingian kings, was especially fond of the abbey and added to its material resources. When he died, he ordered that his body be buried at the monastery. Saint-Denis's stature as a royal monastery continued to grow in the Carolingian period. Charles Martel entrusted his son, the future Pippin III, to the monks of Saint-Denis for his early education. When Pippin moved to replace the last Merovingian king, Saint-Denis's abbot played a key role in the drama. In 754 Pope Stephen II journeyed from Rome to Saint-Denis to consecrate Pippin as the new king of the Franks.

Saint-Denis's fortunes soared along with those of the new royal family. The monastery provided the Carolingians with skilled administrators and also with propaganda glorifying the Franks and, especially, the Carolingians. Its wealth and connections with Italy made its *scriptorium* an important source of manuscripts and one of the wellsprings of the Carolingian renaissance. Its metalworking shops may have

7

produced the "Throne of Dagobert" which a later abbot, Suger (1081–1151), found in the monastery and in a burst of wishful thinking attributed to the seventh-century ruler whose patronage of the monastery he particularly valued and emphasized (see cat. 5).[5]

Excessive zeal of this sort, coupled with a muddled sense of history, enabled Saint-Denis in the ninth century to play a part in the cultural definition of power politics. Somehow, the patron of the monastery, Dionysius, became conflated with the Athenian whom Paul converted, Dionysius the Areopagite (Acts 17.34). This Dionysius, in turn, was credited with a series of sixth-century writings which combined mystical theology and Neoplatonic philosophy. In 827, the Byzantine emperor Michael II presented Louis the Pious with a copy of what is now known as the Pseudo-Dionysian corpus. The manuscript, written entirely in Greek, was translated twice, first by Abbot Hilduin of Saint-Denis and then for Louis's son, Charles the Bald, by the renowned Irish scholar John Scottus (ca. 810–ca. 870; cat. 8).

The imperial gift and the royal interest in its translation into Latin helped to establish a new, Neoplatonic current in European intellectual life and political ideology. The current grew wider when John Scottus translated other Greek authors such as Maximus the Confessor, and when Greek prayers and Greek studies flourished in Charles the Bald's kingdom. Charles's own adoption of Byzantine dress to underscore his imperial dignity no doubt was inspired by the palpable Grecizing atmosphere of his court—even if his dress struck some as arrogant.[6] Charles served as the lay abbot of Saint-Denis and tried to protect it against Viking raids. According to the terms of his will, part of his personal collection of books went to Saint-Denis (see cat. 7).

Corbie

Saint-Denis was not alone in the royal favor it received and the cultural impact it had on Carolingian society. The monastery of Corbie, another royal foundation with intimate links to the Carolingians, was founded on the Somme near Amiens by the Merovingian Balthildis and her son, Chlothar III, sometime between 657 and 661. A thousand years later, the great French Benedictine scholar Jean Mabillon, reflecting on the history of the important French monastic establishments, would conclude that "Corbie in Picardy seems to have surpassed them all."[7]

What factors contributed to Corbie's renown? First, wealth and connections. Corbie's benefactors in the seventh and eighth centuries endowed the community with thousands of acres of fertile land. Royal grants exempted Corbie from tolls, rents, and the sometimes onerous visits of royal agents who expected their hosts to maintain them and their retinues when they came calling. Corbie was even exempted from supervision by the local bishop. Corbie supported the coup which brought the Carolingians to power in the mid-eighth century and retained its privileges as well as its privileged place in the constellation of royal monasteries. Charlemagne's cousin, Adalhard, served as abbot of Corbie. The statutes Adalhard wrote for the monastery in 822 give some indication of the size of the community, since Adalhard was concerned to provide for over 500 brethren, 350 of whom were monks. For the ninth century, this was a gigantic number—larger than the communities at both Saint-Denis and Saint-Martin-de-Tours.[8]

But wealth and size were not Corbie's only claims to renown. Corbie, after all, was a monastery. Its most enduring contributions to the new Europe the Carolingians were fashioning were intellectual and cultural. Corbie monks collected books, copied books, and wrote their own books. Hadoard, Ratramnus, and Radbertus especially used the outstanding collection in Corbie's library to make original contributions to the literature of theology, biography, and polemic.

Corbie was one of the centers in the eighth century whose scribes began to perfect the clear and legible script type for which the Carolingian period is justly famous, the Carolingian minuscule. The Bible that Abbot Maurdramnus (ca. 771–783) had copied at Corbie (today conserved at the Bibliothèque Municipale in Amiens, MSS 6–9, 11, 12) is one of the earliest calligraphic examples of the new script type. With only a few changes in letter forms, Carolingian minuscule has been in use in the Western world and beyond since the advent of the printing press. The new script was not invented at Charlemagne's court in response to his command in the General Admonition that greater attention be paid to the copying of manuscripts so that errors would not creep into the sacred books. Implicitly, however, royal interest in how words were put on a page favored the development of a nascent script that promised to yield the results the king desired.

Like the rapid cursive script, the new minuscule script used lowercase letters, but unlike cursive, which ran words together, the new script tended to separate letters within words, and words from each other, for easier comprehension. If script became less dynamic, it also became simpler and more legible. Scribes at the end of the eighth century had begun to print when they copied their texts. It would be a mistake, however, to regard Carolingian scribes as mere technicians of writing. The program of religious reform initiated by royal courts created a culture of words, since it was in the sacred texts that the inspiration for and standards of a religious society were to be found. It is no coincidence that the earliest codices copied in the new script, like Maurdramnus's Bible, are predominantly liturgical books.[9] It was, after all, "the gospels, Psalters, or missals" that most concerned Charlemagne in the General Admonition. Scribes were acutely aware of the deeper significance of their task. In the words of David Ganz, "The book is both prayer and tribute, and as tribute it embodies individual toil, a toil subordinate to the goal."[10] When they reflected on their toil, scribes often called to mind another kind of culture when they compared their pens to the farmer's plow. As their pens moved across the page, they too were planting seeds, the seeds of eternal glory. Dagulf, a scribe in Charlemagne's court in the mid-790s, when he finished copying a Psalter (now Vienna, Österreichische Nationalbibliothek, MS 1861) in a verse colophon at the end of the manuscript, celebrated not his achievement but the words he had copied: "Behold the golden letters paint David's psalms. Songs like these should be ornamented so well. They promise golden kingdoms and a lasting good without end."[11]

It was the scriptoria of medieval Europe that fashioned the tools of the new culture. The study of script teaches an important lesson about that culture. Despite the drive for uniformity, cultural life exhibited the same kind of diversity as political life. Lofty statements, even when issued by potent political powers, could not guarantee uniformity of belief or practice, even in such a fundamental, seemingly mechanical activity as handwriting. Carolingian scribes, for example, invented the symbol for

9

the question mark by adapting the musical symbol for a quavering and rising tone. But the new symbol took on different shapes at the palace school of Charlemagne, Saint-Denis, Corbie, Monte Cassino, the palace school of Charles the Bald, and elsewhere.[12] Such idiosyncrasies enable palaeographers to localize manuscripts. One of the most puzzling and intriguing of such scribal peculiarities concerns Corbie.

Alongside the developing Carolingian script typical of the time of Abbot Maurdramnus and later, a second Corbie script with somewhat archaic features was also produced. This second Corbie script, known as the "Corbie *a-b* script" from its most characteristic letter forms, survives in thirty-five manuscripts and manuscript fragments, including Corbie's copy of Jerome's commentary on Isaiah now in the Bibliothèque nationale de France (MS Lat. 11627; cat. 1). This manuscript perfectly illustrates the close relationship that existed between the two script types at Corbie, for a scribe using the Maurdramnus script wrote folio 136v, and corrections in Maurdramnus script appear on folios 214–15.[13] But why would one copying center support two script types? Close study of the *a-b* manuscripts has yielded important results not only for the history of script but also for the history of Carolingian culture. The Corbie *a-b* script, it now appears, was written not by Corbie monks but by nuns, who used their skills to copy manuscripts for Corbie (especially during the abbacy of Adalhard) and other centers, and doubtless for their own use as well.[14]

The role of women (such as the *a-b* scribes) in Carolingian culture illustrates the disjuncture that often characterized the interplay of power and culture. On a prescriptive level, Carolingian legislation imposed new regulations on the lives of religious women with the intention of cloistering their activities. The General Admonition clearly envisioned a reform program propelled by "boys" and "men," since women could never become priests, the "soldiers of the church." Nevertheless, religious women had the same obligations as their male counterparts. As religious "professionals," they had to know how to pray, read, and sing in Latin to participate in their faith. And since a decree of 802 prohibited men from entering female monasteries (except for the priest, who had to leave right after saying Mass), women had to become teachers in their own communities. Those communities could also include young boys such as Paschasius Radbertus, an orphan who was raised by the community of nuns at Soissons. Paschasius became a monk at Corbie, where he began a brilliant career as a theologian and became abbot in 843. He never forgot the women who raised him and dedicated three of his works to them—not out of gratitude but in response to the searching theological questions they posed.

The examples of the Corbie *a-b* script and of other female writing centers and of the Soissons community and other female communities document female participation in the book culture of the Carolingian world, despite official restrictions. Women also contributed to that culture by keeping annals and writing saints' lives and histories. Dhuoda, the most visible female author of the Carolingian period, is made even more remarkable by her lay status. She wrote her *Guidebook* in the early 840s to instruct her son, William, in a way of life that blended Christian principles with the aristocratic virtues of family loyalty and respect for paternal authority. That she expected her sixteen-year-old son to read her book and went on to urge him to read many of the books of leading scholars to learn more about God suggests that

William was himself well educated and that Carolingian book culture had penetrated from the monasteries and cathedrals at least into the upper echelons of aristocratic lay society. Judith, the second wife of Louis the Pious, impressed contemporaries with her intellect. Count Eberhard of Friuli collected a remarkable set of books that he willed to his sons and daughters—one of the women inherited her father's copy of the Lombard laws. Other Carolingian laymen such as Einhard, the biographer of Charlemagne, and Nithard, the historian of Charles the Bald's reign, felt the cultural effects of the Carolingian program of religious reform.

Reims

Among the exemplars of Carolingian power and culture, Reims occupied a special place. It was at Reims that religious culture and political power in France began their historical journey when Bishop Remigius baptized Clovis in 496, thereby bringing the king and his Franks into the Christian religion. The reputation of the cathedral town of Reims, initially eclipsed in the early Carolingian period by royal monasteries such as Saint-Denis, rebounded in the ninth century. Astute, hardheaded bishops such as Ebbo (816–835) and Hincmar (845–882) maneuvered Reims into the mainstream of Carolingian politics and culture, a stream, as it turned out, that moved swiftly and was filled with dangerous shoals. While the contributions of both bishops to the cultural life of Reims and the Carolingian world was spectacular, their episcopacies demonstrate dramatically just how unsettled the relationship between political and religious culture was in the early Middle Ages.

Ebbo was the son of young Louis the Pious's wetnurse and a childhood playmate of the future emperor. Louis freed Ebbo from his status as a serf and in 816 named his intelligent and engaging companion to the archbishopric of Reims. Ebbo's enemies later in life, all noble ecclesiastics, would blame Ebbo's social origins for his political problems. But that was in the future. Ebbo used the resources of his new position to launch a remarkable program of manuscript copying and illumination.[15] The special qualities of the artwork produced in his diocese under his patronage, especially at the monastery of Hautvillers, have been attributed to several sources—late Roman models, Greek illuminators from the entourage of Louis the Pious, and the artistic and technical genius of local artists inspired not by models but by texts. Whatever the source of their inspiration, the artists who worked for Ebbo produced images of unusual power and liveliness (cat. 6).

Ebbo, of course, was first of all a bishop. And as spiritual leader of what the bishops of Reims liked to think was the first church in the kingdom of the Franks and as a close intimate of the court, Ebbo inevitably became involved in the power struggles of Louis the Pious's reign. Bishops such as Ebbo were among the first generation of church leaders to feel the impact of the Carolingian reform movement in their own intellectual and spiritual formations. They were interested and knowledgeable about theories of governance not in the abstract but as such learning applied to the issues of their day. Ironically, Louis the Pious's continued sponsorship of "right religion" and of reform in his realm encouraged a more active and independent episcopate. When Louis's plans for the disposition of his realm after his death antagonized his sons (around whom various parties coalesced), religious leaders entered the fray. The justification for ecclesiastical involvement in political life was exactly the same as that for royal power: biblical precedent. Whereas kings began to think of themselves as Old Testament monarchs, bishops argued that they fulfilled the role of Old Testament prophets. At a synod convened in Paris in 829, the assembled bishops instructed the Emperor Louis on his duties and warned him that if his neglect threatened the peace and concord of the realm, they would intervene.

Four years later a group of bishops, Ebbo included, did exactly that when they supported the rebellion of Louis's eldest son, Lothar, against his father, all in the name of unity and peace. Louis was forced to admit his sinfulness and to renounce his power. "Samuel had once again deposed Saul, or so it seemed."[16] By 835 Louis, benefiting from widespread revulsion provoked by his sons' rebellion, regained his throne; Ebbo lost his and was deposed from Reims. He eventually landed in Lothar's kingdom, where he became bishop of Hildesheim.

For ten years the see at Reims remained vacant, until Hincmar was appointed in 845. He would serve as archbishop of Reims and staunch advocate of episcopal power for almost forty years, until his death in 882. Reims remained a vibrant cultural center under its new leader (see cat. 9). The Reims scriptorium turned its energies to producing books for learning, especially books that mirrored the interests of Archbishop Hincmar, an exemplar of the active, learned prelate of Carolingian times. His interests included the church fathers and law. He wrote history and hagiography, especially a life of his sixth-century predecessor, Remigius, which boosted the claims of Reims. He wrote several treatises intended to instruct princes in the conduct of their power. Hincmar's pastoral concern focused on the local level and the administration of parishes as well as on the larger scale when he tried to keep suffragan bishops subordinated to him. He was a master at polemic, as recalcitrant bishops and kings learned.

Hincmar also raised his voice against one of the most celebrated achievements of the Carolingian cultural program—the integration of the Roman classics into Christian culture. The classical element in Carolingian culture has long attracted notice, if only to give the patrons, scribes, and collectors of the Carolingian world credit for preserving the works of classical antiquity. Carolingian interest in the classics, however, was not simply a rescue mission. The integration of the works of pagan antiquity into the new European culture in the eighth and ninth centuries came only at the end of a long and tortuous debate among Christian scholars about the relationship of pagan learning to Christian. Jerome's dream in the fourth century that he was barred from heaven because he was judged a Ciceronian, not a Christian, is only one early and eloquent testimony to the cultural conflict that troubled scholars.

By Hincmar's time in the ninth century, the pagan classics had been "Christianized" and formed an important component of Carolingian learning, where they served as stepping-stones to Christian wisdom. Schoolchildren learning Latin studied Virgil and the guides that helped to explain Virgil's vocabulary and allusions. They also studied histories, geographies, mythology, and poetry from the pagan past as their studies advanced. A comfortable familiarity with pagan literature inculcated from school days developed among the cultural leaders of the Frankish kingdoms.

In some cases familiarity bred enthusiasm. Frankish origins were traced back to Troy. Monks and nuns sprinkled their letters to each other with allusions to Pluto or Erebus, the Roman underworld, and without any apparent sense of contradiction described Christ as the "lord of Olympus." In other cases familiarity with the classics bred distrust and revulsion. Hincmar of Reims, whose own scriptorium copied classical works, thought that the mania for things Roman had gone too far, especially in the political realm. The Old Testament continued to serve kings, but when they also began to adopt imperial titles that conjured images of pagan Rome, he became uneasy. The archbishop could not influence the imperial ideologies of Charlemagne or of his son Louis the Pious. But as a supporter of Charles the Bald, Hincmar was ideally placed to try to curb what he saw as a dangerous trend in Frankish politics. When it became apparent that Charles would travel to Rome in 875 for his imperial coronation, Hincmar opposed Charles's plan. Taking his cue from Augustine of Hippo, a great critic of Rome, Hincmar knew that Roman concepts of power were based on pride, arrogance, brutality, and the pursuit of self-glory. Charles and his subjects did not need this kind of leadership. Christian kingship, with its emphasis on Christian principles, the pursuit of virtue, and the correction of society, was what was required. Most of all, Hincmar pointed out, in the face of the imminent threats the kingdom faced, Charles's people needed him home, not chasing titles in Italy. Charles did not follow Hincmar's advice and was crowned emperor in 875, but he died within two years. Hincmar shortly after recorded the report of a visionary who saw the king in the afterlife and was asked by Charles to tell Hincmar how much he was suffering for failing to follow the bishop's good advice.[17]

The Culture of Monasticism

In the generation after Charles, the Frankish kingdom continued to refract. The temporary unity of the realm fell victim to the emergence of regional kingships all across the map of Carolingian Europe. In the eastern, German-speaking portion of the old Carolingian Empire, a new dynasty founded by Duke Henry of Saxony replaced the Carolingians in 918. To the west, the last Carolingian was replaced (ironically with the help of the archbishop of Reims, Adalbero) by Hugh Capet, first king in the new line of Capetians. Numerous members of the Carolingian family still held powerful positions in both new realms and in the other regional principalities that split off from the ninth-century empire. Both the Ottonians in the east and the Capetians in the west contracted marriage alliances with Carolingians and continued to promote Carolingian political and cultural programs. The Capetians made Saint-Denis into a royal necropolis and chroniclers such as Adhémar de Chabannes (989–1034) reported their rise to power much as the *Liber historiae Francorum* and Einhard had for the Carolingians (cat. 12).

Cultural changes mirrored political fluctuations. Some of the older centers of cultural leadership, such as Saint-Martin in Tours, played less significant roles in the tenth, eleventh, and twelfth centuries. Viking raids, local warfare, and the more pro-

13

saic ebb and flow of talents and resources took their toll. As new political configurations began to assemble their constituent parts out of the elements of the old order, so too new impulses grounded in tradition began to animate cultural life in France. The new impulses came from an unlikely source: reform movements emanating from France's monasteries.

Benedict of Aniane (ca. 750–821), true to the Carolingian reform program, attempted to organize monastic life in Frankish lands around strict adherence to the Rule of Benedict. The political support of Louis the Pious lent authority and an element of compulsion to Benedict's reforms, which were not greeted with universal enthusiasm in the monastic establishment. The political turmoil of the Carolingian world, in which the wealth and political power of monasteries played an integral part, and continued lay control of monasteries also conspired to compromise Benedict of Aniane's vision of an authentic monastic life. Benedict, however, had fashioned the model reformers of a later age would emulate.

The monastic reform movement that began in the tenth century was a grass-roots effort led by hermits and pious laymen who feared for their souls. In 909 one of these laymen, Duke William III of Aquitaine (886–918), endowed the monastery of Cluny on his lands near Mâcon in Burgundy. His intentions were local and personal—he could hardly have imagined that twentieth-century historians would describe the fruits of his efforts as the "Cluniac empire." His thoughts were only for the salvation of his soul. Although he could not "despise all things," as Christ had commanded the rich man who wanted to follow him, at least William could have a congregation of holy men who *did* despise all things to intercede for him. William knew that the key to monastic purity (and thus the efficacy of monastic prayers) lay in monastic control of Cluny, free from local secular and episcopal meddling. He promised that neither he nor his family would interfere in monastic affairs—especially in the crucial selection of the abbot. William made the saints, Peter and Paul, the proprietors of the monastery and handed over supervision of Cluny to the pope. This grand gesture had little effect in the tenth century, when the papal horizon was limited essentially to Rome and central Italy, but when the number of monasteries that followed the model of Cluny grew and spread all across Europe, the papal connection helped Cluniac monasteries to remain independent, especially from local supervision by bishops.

The independence of Cluniac monasteries went hand in hand with their dependence on Cluny itself. As Cluny's abbots, especially the long-lived Odilo (994–1048) and Hugh (1049–1109), traveled all over Europe, often at the invitation of local nobles and religious reformers, the network of monasteries attached to the hub at Cluny grew more complex. If the Cluniac spiritual empire was "ramshackle,"[18] it still was a potent force shaping European cultural life. Cluny has received much of the credit for the eleventh-century papacy's attack on lay control of spiritual institutions and other abuses of political power, especially in the Holy Roman Empire. But Cluny was never inimical to laymen and laywomen and, indeed, thrived because of their active support of Cluniac spiritual life.

What was it that gave this monastic movement such broad cultural appeal? One answer is found in William's foundation charter, an answer that was repeated in other charters by which lay landowners endowed reformed monasteries. These donors were haunted by their perceptions of the sinfulness of the world and of their own lives. By the tenth and eleventh centuries the monastic view of the world and of humanity pervaded medieval society. So, too, did the remedy for sinfulness— prayer. Monks prayed ceaselessly for their communities, including nonmonks such as Duke William who lived outside the walls of the monasteries. By their gifts and donations, the patrons of Cluny and other reformed monasteries could attach them-selves to spiritual life of the community. They could become "the neighbor of Saint Peter."[19]

The real power of Cluny, then, was rooted in prayer (see cat. 14). The routine of monastic life in Cluniac houses, inspired by Benedict of Aniane's vision, devoted increasing amounts of time and energy to elaborate prayer services and rituals. It is in these services, in the liturgy, that the gulf between the divine and the human seemed to close and that Christ and the saints joined earthly communities. One can only imagine how chanting, processions, candles, the fragrance of incense, the dis-play of relics, and the powerful words of prayer and song impressed medieval wor-shippers who gathered in highly decorated Cluniac churches. This visible, external-ized religious culture drew the scorn of Bernard of Clairvaux (1091–1153), but the "Romanesque renaissance" attests to the attraction of the new spirituality. All over France, major new monastic complexes were erected in the eleventh and twelfth centuries. Sometimes, as in the case of Saint-Denis during the time of Abbot Suger (1081–1151), new, grander buildings replaced or were added to earlier ones. William's foundation at Cluny was repeatedly enlarged by its abbots, until in 1130 Abbot Hugh completed the greatest basilica in Europe at the time, a huge building more than five hundred feet long with four transepts, fifteen towers, and five chapels. Little remains of Hugh's basilica, which was almost totally destroyed in the French Revolution. The critical, though eloquent, words of Bernard of Clairvaux capture something of the gaudy liveliness of Cluny's interior decorations, which had pene-trated even into the monastic cloister:

> What profit is there in those ridiculous monsters, in that marvellous and deformed come-
> liness, that comely deformity? To what purpose are those unclean apes, those fierce lions,
> those monstrous centaurs, those half-men, those striped tigers, those fighting knights,
> those hunters winding their horns? Many bodies are there seen under one head, or again,
> many heads to a single body. Here is a four-footed beast with a serpent's tail; there a fish
> with a beast's head. Here again the forepart of a horse trails half a goat behind it, or a
> horned beast bears the hinder quarters of a horse. In short, so many and so marvellous are
> the varieties of divers shapes on every hand, that we are more tempted to read in the mar-
> ble than in our books.[20]

Despite Bernard's fears, monks in France's Romanesque monasteries did read their books. What monastic architects wrought in stone, scribes emulated on parchment, especially in the liturgical manuscripts whose vivid colors and twisting shapes remind the viewer of the power of art and of words (see cats. 10, 11, and 13).

Those varied hues and sinuous shapes can serve also to limn France's first great experience of power and culture from the time of Charlemagne to the age of Saint Louis. The power of politics, of religion, of words, and of art combined and recombined in different historical contexts to produce not one culture but several. In the end, the culture of the Carolingian Renaissance and the Romanesque abbeys bequeathed a rich and multivalent heritage to the future – one that would remain accessible through the treasures one age passed to another.

1 *Charlemagne: Translated Sources,* trans. P. D. King (Kendal, 1987), 209.

2 Ibid., 217.

3 Rosamond McKitterick, *The Carolingians and the Written Word* (Cambridge, 1989), 163.

4 See Bernhard Bischoff, *Manuscripts and Libraries in the Age of Charlemagne,* trans. Michael M. Gorman (Cambridge, 1994); and Rosamond McKitterick, "Royal Patronage of Culture in the Frankish Kingdoms under the Carolingians: Motives and Consequences," in *Committenti e produzione artistico-letteraria nell'alto medioevo occidentale,* vol. 39 of Settimane di studio del Centro Italiano di Studi sull'Alto Medioevo (Spoleto, 1992), 93–135.

5 See Jean Hubert, "Le Fauteuil de Dagobert," *Demareteion* 1 (1935): 17–27; and Blaise de Montesquiou-Fezensac and Danielle Gaborit-Chopin, *Le trésor de Saint-Denis: Inventaire de 1634,* 3 vols. (Paris, 1973–1977), 3:116–18.

6 See the hostile account in *The Annals of Fulda,* trans. Timothy Reuter, Ninth-Century Histories 2 (Manchester, 1992), 79 (A.D. 876), and the more matter-of-fact report in *The Annals of St-Bertin,* trans. Janet L. Nelson, Ninth-Century Histories 1 (Manchester, 1991), 194 (A.D. 876).

7 *Traité des études monastiques* (Paris, 1691), 131.

8 See David Ganz, *Corbie in the Carolingian Renaissance* (Sigmaringen, 1990), 26.

9 See David Ganz, "The Preconditions for Carolingian Minuscule," *Viator* 18 (1987): 28.

10 Ibid., 32.

11 Trans. David Ganz, ibid., 30.

12 For examples, see Bernhard Bischoff, *Latin Palaeography: Antiquity and the Middle Ages,* trans. Dáibhí O Crónín and David Ganz (Cambridge, 1990), 169–70.

13 See Ganz, *Corbie in the Carolingian Renaissance,* 142, and also 48–56 ("Problem of the AB Scriptorium").

14 See T. A. M. Bishop, "The Scribes of the Corbie *a-b,*" in Peter Godman and Roger Collins, eds., *Charlemagne's Heir: New Perspectives on the Reign of Louis the Pious (814–840)* (Oxford, 1990), 523–36.

15 See Jean Porcher, "Les manuscrits à peinture," in J. Hubert, J. Porcher, and W. F. Volbach, eds., *L'empire carolingien* (Paris, 1968), 92–123.

16 Pierre Riché, *The Carolingians: A Family Who Forged Europe,* trans. Michael Idomir Allen (Philadelphia, 1993), 156.

17 See Lawrence Nees, *A Tainted Mantle: Hercules and the Classical Tradition at the Carolingian Court* (Philadelphia, 1991), 235–57.

18 C. H. Lawrence, *Medieval Monasticism: Forms of Religious Life in Western Europe in the Middle Ages* (London, 1984), 85.

19 See Barbara H. Rosenwein, *To Be the Neighbor of Saint Peter: The Social Meaning of Cluny's Property, 909–1049* (Ithaca, 1989) and *Rhinoceros Bound: Cluny in the Tenth Century* (Ithaca, 1982).

20 "Apologia to William, Abbot of St.-Thierry," in Elizabeth Gilmore Holt, ed., *A Documentary History of Art,* vol. 1 (Garden City, N.Y., 1957), 21.

FLAVII IOSEPHI IN LIBRO HISTORI-
ARVM IVDAICI BELLI INCIPIT PRE-
PHATIO OBIECTIONIS IN EOS QVI HOC
IDEM OPERIS CONATI SVNT ADGREDI

VONIAM bellum quod cum p̄ oculo
romano gessere iudei omniu maximu quae
nr̄a etas uidit queq̄ auditu p̄cepimus. ciui
tates cu ciuitatib; gentesue comisse cu gen
tib; quidam non quod reb; interfuerint. sed
uana & incongrua narrancium sermones
aurib; colligentes oratoru more p̄scribunt.
Qui ū p̄sto fuer̄ aud romanoru obsequio
aud odio iudeoru contra fidem rerum falsa
confirmant. Scriptis aut eoru partim
accusatio partim laudatio continetur.
usqua ū ex acta fides reppitur historie. Id circo statui que iacio bar
baris antea miss patria lingua digesta & greca. nunc his q romano im
perio regunt exponere. Iosephus matathie fili ebreus genere sacerdos
ex iherosolimis qui & inicio cu romanis bello conflixi postea gestis quia
necessitas exegit interfui. Ham cu hic ut dixi motus grauissim̄ exort̄ e
romanu q̄de p̄ptim domestic moib; abebat. Iudoru aut q etate ualidi
& ingenio turbulenti erant. manu simul ac pecunia iugentes adeo t̄pub;
insolent abusi s̄ ut p̄ tumultus magnitudin̄. hos possidendaru spes
illos amittendaru parciu ouentis maceris inuadere. Q̄m iudei cunctos
etiam qui trans euphraten eent gentiles suos secu rebellaturos ee credi
derant. romanos aut chinitimi galacie irritabant. nec man̄ scelestia quies
cebat. dissessionu que plena erant oīa post neronē. Et multos quidem
reges temp̄ adortabat lucri aut cupidine pars aut militaris mutationē
p̄senciu desidrabat. Itaq̄ indignu ee duxi errante intantis reb; dissimu
lare ueritate. & parthos quidem ac babilonios arabumq̄ remotissimos
& ultra euphraten gentis nr̄e incolas. Itq̄ adiabenos mea diligentia
uera cognoscere. unde cepisse bellu quantisq̄ cladib; constiti nr̄a quoue
modo desisse. Attor ū romanoru q̄s dā qui militia secuti non essent.

Je cõmence le plogue
sur la translacion
dun liure apelle
polictatiq. comple
de tres excellent doc
teur. a saincte Jehan
de salusbery. le quel fist translater de
latin en francois. tresexcellent et puis
sant / tres crestien et misericort prince
le tres noble roy de france. Charles
quint de ce nom. lan de grace. ay. cc.
lxxv. et de son regne le vi. Et afin q̃
ceulz qui le dit liure translate lirõt
aient plus grãt desir de le lire et de le bie
mettre en leur memoire / celu qui le
translata mist au commencement

Eat vn plogue a
lp q̃ la mendaa
iue on du liure
nit et du tres no
sapi ble roy qui le
eua fist trãslater
au et qui afflue prudenca. pu
z. caplo C Ceste parole dit q̃
lõme est benoit qui treuue sapiece
et qui afflue largement de prude
ce. C Le tres glorieus docteur mõ
seigñeur saint aubroise en con
siderãt diuerses opinions de bea
titude et beaute que plusieurs genz
ont par le monde. et par especial
de tele cõme on la puet auoir en

2 Medieval Collections of the Bibliothèque nationale de France

From the Eighth to the Fifteenth Century

Marie-Hélène Tesnière

The medieval collection of the Bibliothèque nationale de France consists of three large groupings of material: monastic and university collections, royal collections, and seigneurial or lay collections.[1] When Louis XII ascended to the throne in 1498—the date usually associated with the official establishment of the Bibliothèque du Roi, or Royal Library—its holdings consisted of more than fifteen hundred manuscripts and printed works. By 1995 the medieval collection of the BnF amounted to more than thirty thousand manuscripts and about eight thousand incunabula (books printed prior to 1500). More than any other European library, the BnF has benefited in a variety of ways from centralized government. Its vaults hold the manuscripts of the abbey of Corbie (Somme) (cat. 1), as well as those of Moissac (Tarn-et-Garonne) (cat. 11), Saint-Martial de Limoges (cat. 12), Saint-Denis (cats. 7–9), and Saint-Germain-des-Prés (Paris) (cat. 13), to mention only the large monastery collections.

Monastic Collections

Prayer and reading were the basis of the Benedictine Rule, thereby conditioning literary culture in the first centuries of the Middle Ages (eighth–twelfth centuries). At the heart of the monastery was its collection of books, the original meaning of the Greek word for library, *bibliotheca*. The library bore no resemblance, however, to a modern library which brings together many books in a common room intended for silent reading. Often the monastic library was but a modest collection of books scattered about in various places according to the monks' needs. The most precious liturgical books were kept in the chapel as part of the monastery's collection of valuable liturgical ornaments and furnishings (copes, ciboria, patens, and so on). The book which loomed above all others in its sanctity, the Bible, was kept closest to the tomb of the monastery's patron saint (cat. 3). The other books were dispersed among the abbot's living quarters, the refectory, the infirmary (cat. 33), the dormitory, and the cloisters, laid flat in a chest, a cabinet, or a wall recess. This dispersal of texts can be explained not only by the requirements of monastic life but also by the fact that, until the fourteenth century, reading was done not in silence but aloud, with the words spoken in a low voice.

"Claustrum sine armario, castrum sine armamentario" (a cloister without a book-case [is like a] castle without a weapons case).[2] The need to have at hand liturgical works for the celebration of religious Offices, plus Bibles and patristic commentaries for the spiritual edification of the monks, and grammatical or encyclopedic texts for the training of novices, led each monastery of any importance to establish a *scriptorium* where the monks produced the required books. For that reason abbeys were the main centers of manuscript production until the twelfth century.

Thus the monastic library and scriptorium were inextricably linked in the early Middle Ages, thereby governing for centuries the way in which culture was disseminated. Indeed, the first French printing press would be set up in 1470 on the premises of the library of the Collège de Sorbonne (cat. 45) at a time when the university still operated as a religious institution. The library and scriptorium were supervised by the *armarius*, or librarian, a personage of highest importance. The position called for a person of education and authority; often the prior himself assumed simultaneously the responsibilities of keeper of the liturgical treasures and head of the scriptorium.

All stages of book making took place within the monastery. These included preparation of parchment starting from the sheepskin,[3] the assembly of gatherings of folded leaves of parchment, the drypoint ruling of lines and borders to guide the writing, the fabrication of ink from oak gall and vitriol, and, finally and above all, the long and painstaking labor of transcribing the text.[4] One copyist remarked of this exhausting task that it "dims the sight, bows the spine, cracks the ribs and breaks the aching back."[5] Copywork, no matter how carefully corrected, rendered each manuscript copy unique and at the same time made it extremely expensive. Next the work was proofed, illuminated, and then bound.

Since liturgical books as the bearers of God's word played a central part in religious observances, they were expected to be worthy of their purpose, and therefore had to be sumptuous.[6] The most important of these was the Sacramentary, the celebrant's book, containing the sacred prayers which the priest read at the altar during the Eucharist. The opening words of the Preface and Canon (*Vere dignum* and *Te igitur*) were frequently decorated with an interlaced design in purple and gold, while the prayers themselves were copied in gold uncials (cat. 7).

Evangelistaries were even more lavishly decorated. Because it contained the word of God, an Evangelistary would be carried in solemn procession through the church to the altar and then to the *ambo* (or raised platform), where the deacon read the Gospel at the appropriate time. In the early Middle Ages an Evangelistary often comprised the Gospels plus the list of pericopes, the selected passages to be read. Sometimes the Evangelistary went under the name *comes*, from the Latin *comma*, meaning section of pericopes. Its interior and exterior decoration resemble the work of a goldsmith (cat. 2) with intricately adorned initials and gold-and-silver script illuminating the purple-colored parchment, not to mention its magnificent binding covered with precious stones and ivory sheets. A portrait of the Evangelist (cat. 6) illustrated the beginning of each Gospel in the same author-portrait fashion the ancients had employed (cat. 9). The Canon tables were often enlivened by an arcade pattern featuring early Christian motifs, sometimes including the Fountain of Life (also found in certain Ethiopian manuscripts; cat. 97).

Then came the Gradual (cat. 10) used by the cantor stationed on the lower steps of the ambo–the volume gets its name from the Latin *gradus*, or step. The Gradual could be held in the hand, enabling the cantor to read out the appropriate chants of the mass (those subject to daily change) as he conducted the *schola cantorum*, or choir.

The intrinsic value of these lavish manuscripts meant that the first monastic libraries were veritable treasure houses.

The book whose importance overshadowed all others was the Bible. Reading and studying it provided the monk with one of his principal activities. Saint Benedict himself exclaimed, when drawing up the Benedictine Rule, "Quam enim pagina, aut quis sermo divinae auctoritatis veteris ac novi Testamenti non est rectissima norma vitae humanae?" (What page or what word of divine authority from the Old or New Testament is not a most righteous rule for human life?).[7]

Monasteries had therefore to possess at least several copies of the Bible. And for that reason Bibles were always listed first in inventories and catalogues–this practice persisted into the nineteenth century in the systematic classification of the Latin manuscripts confiscated from the large Parisian monasteries during the French Revolution. One should not be misled, however. Single volumes containing the complete Bible–those that Cassiodorus advocated in his *Institutiones*–still remained fairly rare in the early Middle Ages because of their great cost.

Single-volume Bibles were the glory of the scriptorium of Saint-Martin-de-Tours in the ninth century. During the abbacy of Fridugisus (804–834), the successor to the famous Anglo-Saxon theologian Alcuin of York, the scriptorium functioned like a veritable publishing house, producing multiple anthologies of texts on Saint Martin plus magnificent calligraphic and decorated Gospels, and complete Bibles (*pandects*) in large format, which by recent count are extant in forty-five copies (cat. 3). They are works of remarkable finesse whose expert arrangement of scripts and relative scale enhance the regularity and readability of Carolingian minuscule.

Certain abbeys were important centers of artistic production. The example of Saint-Amand-en-Pévèle near Valenciennes (Nord) comes to mind–a monastery which in the early Middle Ages produced numerous sacramentaries decorated in Franco-Saxon style (cat. 7) for other monasteries. Likewise, in the eleventh and twelfth centuries the abbey of Moissac (Tarn-et-Garonne) was a brilliant center of Aquitaine decoration (cat. 10).

Other abbeys became special centers of study and learning. Of these Saint-Denis stood in the forefront.[8] Its renowned school was where Hincmar (806–882), the future archbishop of Reims, received his training. Study of Greek became a specialty at Saint-Denis (cat. 8) in an effort to broaden knowledge of the works of Dionysius the Areopagite (also called Pseudo-Dionysius), whom the monks (mistakenly) identified with their patron saint. No doubt because of that identification, the abbey introduced Greek prayers and readings in its liturgy. And ever since the abbacy of Suger (1122–1151), the monastery harbored an outstanding school of history. It produced the *Grandes Chroniques de France*, which may in some ways be considered the "first" official history of France (cat. 27).

Exchanges between abbeys led to the circulation of manuscripts. Thanks to them it is possible to trace the links between centers like Saint-Denis (cat. 8), Reims, Saint-Amand (cat. 7), or Reichenau in the Carolingian period. Similarly, the mother houses of some orders supplied their daughter houses with a collection of books so that the liturgy, traditions, and culture appropriate to that community could be handed on. A manuscript from the powerful abbey of Cluny, made for the priory of Saint-Martin des Champs, for example, not only illustrates prayers to the Virgin but also the feast of the Transfiguration—a feast which Cluny had newly instituted (cat. 14).

Knowledge varies considerably regarding the number of books that monasteries possessed because the fragmented and partial inventories do not adequately dovetail with what may be deduced from the study of the manuscripts themselves. Although a rather large number (sixty-five) of manuscripts originating from Saint-Denis have been identified thanks to their late thirteenth-century shelfmarks consisting of two letters followed by a "cross potent" (with crossbars at the end of each arm: cat. 9), no inventory from this period has survived. So other external evidence is used to estimate the size of the library in the second half of the fifteenth century at approximately fifteen hundred volumes—an enormous number for that date.

The Royal Collections

The purple and gold of the Gospels of Godescalc,[9] the Gospels of Lothar (cat. 4),[10] and the first and second Bibles of Charles the Bald[11] provide dazzling testimony to the opulence of the libraries assembled by Carolingian monarchs.

According to Einhard, Charlemagne's biographer, the emperor did not know how to write and so hid a wax tablet and a sheet of parchment under his pillow so that in leisure moments he could practice tracing letters.[12] Such studied application *(studium discendi)* was a hallmark of the emperor's cultural policy; religious and educational uniformity thus became key aspects of the Carolingian Renaissance. The emperor knew Latin and understood Greek. At mealtimes he arranged to have someone read Saint Augustine's *De civitate Dei* (City of God) to him. In his palace at Aachen he established one of the most magnificent libraries in Europe, which, according to Einhard, was to be sold off at his death to benefit the poor—proof of Charlemagne's generosity. Only the liturgical books in the *capella regis* (royal chapel), which he had had made on his order, plus books he had acquired or inherited from his father, were to be kept together, intact.[13] But Einhard's assertions must be taken with caution. Bernhard Bischoff has demonstrated in fact that in addition to the manuscripts of the capella regis, Louis the Pious inherited a part of his father's library.[14]

> Quis saltem poterit seriem enumerare librorum,
> quos tua de multis copulat sententia terris,
> Sanctorum renovans patrum conscripta priorum.[15]

(Who could list the many books you have collected from so many places, revealing the writings of the first holy Fathers?)

The sovereign's library was richly supplied with ancient copies collected from virtually everywhere. The many foreign scholars Charlemagne attracted to his court made the palace academy and school a leading intellectual center. From Italy he recruited the deacon Peter of Pisa, who taught him Latin, the Lombards Paulin (future bishop of Aquileia) and Paul the Deacon, and Alcuin of York, whom he had met in Parma and who at Aachen and then at Tours was the veritable promoter of the Carolingian Renaissance. Charlemagne's library was thereby endowed with the ancient manuscripts these scholars brought with them from York or Ravenna, as well as with their own works dedicated to the king.

Indeed, the library, for which only a partial catalogue listing some twenty titles of classical authors has survived,[16] was in a sense conceived as a reference library. A good example from the liturgical sphere was Charlemagne's instructions to Abbot Théodemar in 787 to send the autograph copy of Saint Benedict's Rule from the monastery at Monte Cassino. Deposited in the palace library, the manuscript was used as an early type of *exemplar* (model) for the copies required by each diocese.

What was true for liturgy and patristics also applied to ancient culture. The library thereby became an essential center for the preservation and transmission of classical heritage. Many texts of ancient authors that can be traced back to the Carolingian era are thought to derive from textual models held in the palace library. Such was the case of a fifth-century manuscript of the Third Decade of Livy's *History of Rome*,[17] which most likely belonged to Charlemagne's library and which was copied later in Tours about 800.[18] This same fifth-century manuscript was later housed at the great abbey of Corbie, which evidently functioned as an important relay in transmitting to the present day the classical heritage preserved by the palace library.

Similarly, three manuscripts of Bede's *Historia ecclesiastica gentis Anglorum* held by the Bibliothèque Nationale,[19] which had been copied in the course of the ninth century in various places in France, go back to an Anglo-Saxon manuscript[20] that was augmented with additions in the Carolingian period – probably in the emperor's library.

The transmission of texts was made easier because of the ties which the emperor's former entourage retained at court and at the Palace School. After becoming bishops or abbots, they naturally had recourse to the emperor's library to found libraries which would satisfy their own needs. Such, for example, was the case of Angilbert, abbot of Saint-Riquier (789–814) and Charlemagne's son-in-law. Although we can identify only some ten volumes with certainty as having formed a part of Charlemagne's collection, it is clear that his library was a crucial link in the transmission of ancient culture.

The illustrious emperor's successors were even more partial to books. Under Louis the Pious (814–840), the library continued to be a rich resource (cat. 8), well supplied to satisfy the copyists' needs. The School of Reims, consisting of a group of scribes and painters from the abbey of Hautvillers directed by Ebbo (816–835/845), archbishop of Reims, foster brother of the king and his former librarian, seems to have drawn on the sovereign's library for its models. This is suggested by a copy of the Coronation Gospels made at Reims in the second quarter of the ninth century, which communicated to the Carolingian world the illusionist painting of antiquity (cat. 6), as well as by a copy of an ancient Terence (cat. 9).

Charles the Bald, who reigned from 840 to 877 and who was educated by Walafrid Strabo, had more eclectic tastes. Certainly he was the most cultivated of the Carolingian rulers. According to Rosamond McKitterick,[21] his library must have amounted to some fifty volumes. He was a more active patron than his predecessors, supporting the work of scholars like Hincmar of Reims and John Scottus Eriugena, and showing interest in theological controversies.[22] Charles also had his cousin Nithard edit a history (*De dissentionibus filiorum Hludovici Pii*) which contains the famous Strasbourg oaths, the oldest text in French and in Germanic.[23]

Whether a scriptorium and palace school survived from Charlemagne's day is uncertain. Rather, it seems that Charles commissioned manuscripts from the scriptoria of large abbeys such as Saint-Amand near Valenciennes (cat. 7), which produced numerous sacramentaries in addition to the second Bible of Charles the Bald (BnF Lat. 2). The Bible was presented to the king between 870 and 875—a magnificent manuscript all in gold—to mark the ruler's reconciliation with his son Carloman, abbot of Saint-Amand, the murderer of his brother Charles of Aquitaine. The Bible later went to Saint-Denis. Indeed, upon Charles the Bald's death his library was divided in accordance with his wishes among the royal abbeys of Saint-Denis and Notre-Dame of Compiègne and his son. But with the exception of this superb volume, it has not yet been possible to determine definitely which manuscripts from Saint-Denis came from Charles the Bald's library.

Leaping forward several centuries, let us picture the Sainte-Chapelle, newly constructed and consecrated on April 26, 1248, with its upper chapel directly connected to the royal apartments. A gallery in the apse housed the churchlike reliquary that presented the Great Relics for veneration by the sainted king Louis IX (1226–1270) and by the faithful: the Crown of Thorns, a piece of the True Cross, and the point of the Holy Lance.[24] With its pinnacles, lacy gables, iridescent rose windows, and luminous stained glass medallions depicting scenes from the Old and New Testaments side by side, the Sainte-Chapelle was (and is) one of the most beautiful achievements of Gothic art. More than that, it was a veritable symbol whose delicate architecture subsequently featured the admirable paintings in the Psalter that once belonged to the king.[25] Furthermore, the special light from its lead-lined stained glass windows was faithfully reproduced in the medallions in the beautiful illustrations of the so-called *Bibles moralisées* produced during Saint Louis's reign.[26]

Indeed, a small structure—almost a scale model of the chapel[27]—once stood against the north side of the Sainte-Chapelle. Whereas the ground floor of this structure served as the sacristy of the lower chapel and the second floor (or *revestiaire*) served simultaneously as sacristy for the upper chapel and treasure house for valuable relics (probably including liturgical manuscripts such as the Gospels of the Sainte-Chapelle[28]), the third floor—reserved for the king's use and accessible via an exterior stairway—housed yet another "treasure." For that is where the royal archives and the library were kept.

In this suitable and safe (*aptum et fortem*) place–singularly inviolable[29]–the king assembled on his return from a crusade in 1254 (cat. 17) a great many complete texts (*originalia*) of the works of Saint Augustine, Saint Ambrose, Saint Jerome, Saint Gregory, and other doctors of the church, which he had had copied in the monastery libraries of the kingdom.[30] The king was in fact very concerned to ensure that reliable versions (*utiles et authentici*) of the holy texts were circulated in conformance with a spirit of orthodoxy and universalism. Although he used the library personally, reading and translating to his entourage, Louis also seems to have been generous in opening it to the learned (*litterati et religiosi familiares nostri*). Prominent among them, of course, was the Dominican Vincent de Beauvais (d. 1264), *lecteur* in the Cistercian abbey of Royaumont in 1246–1247. His impressive *Mirror of the World* (*Speculum majus*), also entitled *Bibliotheca mundi,* is a monumental compilation of what was known at the time in every field of knowledge (nature, science, history). It has been suggested that the list of sources used by Vincent de Beauvais constitutes a virtual inventory of the king's library.

The few extant manuscripts identified as belonging to Saint Louis's patristic library correspond perfectly to his monastic ideals.[31] The copies are sober, meticulously prepared but without illustration. Upon the king's death his manuscripts were divided up among the mendicant orders: the Dominicans and Franciscans of Paris, monks of Royaumont, and Dominicans of Compiègne.

Another set of books passed to his son, the future Philip III the Bold. These richly decorated books were part of the capella regis and accompanied the king in his travels (where they were kept when he was in Paris remains unclear). Six copies from the series are extant, including a Psalter (Lat. 10525) and a small portable Bible that belonged to the king (Lat. 10426), and also the Psalter of his mother, Blanche of Castile (Bibliothèque de l'Arsenal 1186). Mention should also be made of the manuscripts that were stored in the chapels attached to the royal residences, notably a Psalter whose edges are decorated with the arms of France and of Castille and which may have belonged to the chapel at Saint-Germain-en-Laye (cat. 16).

A century later the scene changed to the Louvre, more specifically the Tour de la Fauconnerie (Falconry Tower), on the present site of the Pavillon de l'Horloge (Clock Tower).[32] The foundations of the original tower were brought to light by work on the Grand Louvre, where they are now on display. It was some time around 1368 that King Charles V (1364–1380) moved the library from Sainte-Chapelle onto two, later three floors in the tower. The books were laid flat on stands running along the walls. The finest manuscripts–"bien escript et bien historyé" (well written and well decorated), covered in red leather or velvet–were stored on the second floor, protected from insects by wall and vault paneling in cypress and wood from Ireland.[33] To be sure, beautiful Bibles and a number of copies of Vincent de Beauvais's *Miroir historial* were present, but more recent works were especially in evidence as a result of royal commissions (Nicole Oresme, Raoul de Presles, Denis Foulechat). The third floor seems to have been reserved for courtly romances, adventure stories, and allegorical fiction (*Roman de la rose*). On the fourth floor, space was given to arithmetic, astronomy, medicine, natural science, and astrology–for which the king nurtured a passionate interest. The total collection amounted to 910 volumes–and to these must be added another 250 divided among the royal residences at Melun, Beauté-sur-Marne, Saint-Germain-en-Laye, and Vincennes.

To look after his books, Charles V created the office of keeper of the library the following year. The appointment went to one of his *valets de chambre*, Gilles Malet, a very well regarded individual who above all was reputed to read well.[34] The inventory he prepared in 1373 gives insight into the library's composition and provides the earliest known documentation on the administration of a royal library. The original inventory no longer exists, but it was copied in 1380[35] and then revised in 1411 to include the *incipits* (opening words) of the second and last folios of each volume. For the first time, this system allows for the positive identification of the exact manuscripts of a French king's library.[36] Of the more than one thousand volumes which composed it, about one hundred have survived. Some sixty are now in the BnF. The last one to be discovered was acquired by the library in 1988.[37]

Charles V's tastes in books followed that of his ancestors, who, especially from the fourteenth century on, had striven to collect beautiful manuscript copies.[38] Among them, women like Jeanne d'Evreux and Bonne de Luxembourg (cat. 24), Charles V's own mother, were major collectors. Albeit for traditional cultural reasons, King John the Good (1350–1364), Charles V's father, inaugurated the trend in translation that characterized the late fourteenth century by entrusting the translation of the Bible to Jean de Sy and the translation of Livy's *History of Rome* to Pierre Bersuire (cat. 42).

Charles V's library included volumes inherited from his ancestors. The most beautiful liturgical books such as the Breviary of Philip the Fair (cat. 19) were stored in the keep of the château of Vincennes. Other precious volumes were housed on the second floor of the Falconry Tower, like the manuscript of Guillaume de Saint-Pathus's *Vie et miracles de Saint Louis*, complete with ninety miniatures (cat. 23). Also kept there were manuscripts of works the king had commissioned from his accredited copyists, Raoulet d'Orléans and Henri du Trévou (cat. 25) or his illuminators (cats. 25, 26, 27), notably translations of Saint Augustine's *City of God* by Raoul de Presles, Valerius Maximus's *Memorable Deeds and Sayings* by Simon de Hesdin and Nicolas de Gonesse, and Aristotle's *Politics, Economics, and Ethics* by Nicole Oresme (cat. 26). This library of works in French was designed to satisfy the need of the king and his councilors for guidance in political administration, as exemplified by the Aristotle translations, which the monarch categorized as "very necessary." The library also helped to underscore the king's political authority as much by the magnificence of his manuscripts as by the political thrust of the texts and their illumination. Thus Raoul de Presles, in his prologue to the translation of Saint Augustine's *City of God*, made reference to the legend of the fleurs-de-lis, and the new illustration of the *Grandes Chroniques de France* stressed the dynastic continuity of the kings of France (under serious challenge during the Hundred Years War).

In all the dedicatory scenes[39] the ruler is pictured as a "wise king," sometimes seated before his "book wheel" (cat. 25) or garbed like a university master, delighting in the books presented to him. Thanks to the many books "put into French" that he commissioned and circulated, he seems to have defined a genuine cultural policy. The copies, produced for his manuscript-loving brothers, the dukes of Berry, Burgundy, and Bourbon, ensured the propagation throughout the high lay aristocracy of the cultural model which emanated from the king and the royal entourage. Thus gradually, over the course of a century or more, the old feudal nobility acquired a shared historic and national consciousness. This part of Charles V's library more or less served as a model for the numerous small aristocratic libraries of the fifteenth century, which themselves soon influenced the appearance of the first incunabula.

On the king's death, his son Charles VI (1380–1422) inherited the library in the Louvre and maintained Gilles Malet in office. But Charles VI suffered from bouts of madness (cat. 28) and his uncles, keen book lovers that they were, borrowed manuscripts from here and there, some of which never reentered the royal collection (cat. 25). Worse yet, in 1424 the duke of Bedford, regent of the kingdom, purchased for the sum of 1,200 *livres* the 843 manuscripts remaining in the Louvre which Garnier de Saint-Yon had inventoried. Transported to England in 1429, they were dispersed after the duke's death in 1435. Thus the vagaries of the Hundred Years War led to the dispersal of Charles V's library. That collection, apparently the first in France to have been administered in a rational manner in terms of management, acquisition, and preservation, and which was designed to be an inalienable endowment of the crown may be considered the "first" French royal library.

Although Charles VII and Louis XI (1461–1483) were monarchs of considerable refinement–the first enamored of history, the second of Italian culture (cat. 48)– almost nothing is known about the libraries they established in their residences on the banks of the Loire, especially Montils-lès-Tours and Plessis-lès-Tours. At best, a few individual volumes belonging to them have been identified, like the *Statuts de l'Ordre de Saint-Michel* (Statutes of the Order of Saint Michael) illuminated by Fouquet (cat. 44). A little more is known about the manuscripts that Charlotte of Savoy, Louis XI's wife, kept at her castle at Amboise (Loire Valley). Among the approximately one hundred manuscripts in her possession were some thirty that had formerly belonged to Louis XI (liturgical books, *The Treasure of Wisdom*, Froissart's *Chronicles*, books of remedies, trials of the princes of the blood), which Charlotte handed down to her son.

The advent of Charles VIII (1483–1498) inaugurated a new era for the Royal Library, as a direct result of new printing technologies and of French military incursions into Italy. In 1488 the king founded the office of royal printer and appointed Pierre le Rouge to the post. The *Mer des histoires* (a kind of universal chronicle interspersed with excerpts from the *Grandes Chroniques de France*), which Pierre le Rouge printed on very fine vellum and carefully illuminated, was the first and most splendid French printed book to become part of the royal collection (cat. 49). Antoine Vérard, another Parisian publisher and adapter of texts, presented the king and his cousin Charles of Angoulême with some very lovely printed imitations of manuscripts, such as the *Lancelot* illustrated by Master Jacques of Besançon (cat. 53), the reading of which is said to have encouraged the king's "Italian dream." But the Royal Library remained primarily a collection of manuscripts into the seventeenth century at least.

From Naples–where he had gone to secure recognition of his right to succeed René of Anjou (d. 1481)–Charles VIII brought back to Amboise a large part of the collections which the House of Aragon had accumulated in Naples since the time of

27

Alphonse V (d. 1458). The roughly 450 manuscripts and 200 printed books carried off by Charles became the substantial core of the Italian holdings of the Manuscript Department of the Bibliothèque nationale de France. These materials were later augmented by the Visconti and Sforza manuscripts which Louis XII brought back from his campaigns in the duchy of Milan. It was also under Louis XII that a major part of aristocratic lay collections were acquired for the Royal Library.

Aristocratic and Private Collections

With urbanization and the advancement of teaching in universities and schools, books and learning escaped from the monasteries and the world of clerics. Lay printshops were set up near the universities (rues Saint-Jacques and Saint-Séverin in Paris). The infatuation of the aristocracy and the bourgeoisie with vernacular literature spurred the rise of private libraries in the fourteenth and fifteenth centuries.[40] Of course, many people still owned only a Psalter or a book of hours which, though a book of worship, also served as a primer and a place to record family births and deaths. Manuscripts, after all, continued to be very expensive. In Hainaut in 1337 according to the Sire de Naast's inventory, a book of hours was valued at the price of a sow and six piglets and a Bible at two cows (four livres); a Psalter was worth a mare or two pigs.[41] Discussion here will focus on the most active groups of collections, those which frequented and stimulated the world of books and writing.

First and foremost came the milieu of the chancellory, namely, the chancellors, notaries, and royal secretaries whose number and influence grew during the reigns of Saint Louis and Philip the Fair as the royal bureaucracy developed and broadened. Men like Guillaume Flote (chancellor of France between 1338 and 1348), Arnaud de Corbie (chancellor of France several times between 1388 and 1412),[42] and Guillaume Jouvenel des Ursins (Charles VII's chancellor from 1445), owned manuscripts worthy of kings and princes. Their close relationship to royalty, for that matter, suggests the likelihood of exchanges and loans. Thus the superb manuscript of Gossouin de Metz's *Image du Monde* made for Guillaume Flote (cat. 20), which later in the fifteenth century came into the duke of Berry's possession, may have been used as a model for the volume King John the Good commissioned about 1340–1350 and which later turned up in the library of Charles V.[43] Working alongside the chancellor were the notaries and royal secretaries who dispatched writs in the king's name, themselves assisted by a swarm of clerics who formed a breeding ground for new ideas.[44] Highly intelligent and skilled in the use of Latin rhetoric, these ranks produced the first satirists like Gervais du Bus,[45] early humanists like Jean de Montreuil, Nicolas de Clamanges, Jean Lebègue, and Laurent de Premierfait (cat. 32), and even political writers lamenting France's misfortunes like Alain Chartier (cat. 34) and Pierre le Fruitier, a somewhat "shady" character known as Salmon (cat. 28). Though educated as clerics, they nonetheless kept open minds regarding ancient literature and vernacular texts as reflected in their libraries.[46] Newly ennobled, they comprised a wealthy, intellectual, and cultivated bourgeoisie in the second half of the fifteenth century, ready to commission manuscripts from great artists–Etienne Chevalier, to cite one example, ordered a marvelous book of hours from the great Fouquet.[47]

Next came the princely patrons, the dukes Jean of Berry (1340–1416), Louis of Bourbon (1337–1410), John the Fearless, and Philip the Bold (1342–1404) of Burgundy, who made Paris the capital of manuscript illumination in the late fourteenth and early fifteenth centuries.[48] They provided work to artists like the Limbourgs, Jacquemart de Hesdin, and André Beauneveu (cat. 29). They granted stipends to writers who dedicated works sometimes to one patron, sometimes to another. The famous preacher Jacques Legrand, for instance, dedicated his *Archiloge Sophie* to Louis of Orléans but his *Livre des bonnes moeurs* (Book of good morals) (cat. 33) to Duke Jean of Berry. The dukes placed orders with friends who were part-time bookdealers doubling as financial and artistic advisors—for example, one Jacques Raponde, a merchant from Lucca established in Paris, from whom Philip the Bold bought three manuscripts of Hayton's *Fleur des histoires de la Terre d'Orient*, keeping one for himself (cat. 31) and offering the others to his brother, Jean of Berry, and his nephew, Louis of Orléans. In short, these princes were the driving force behind the production of luxurious manuscripts.

Furthermore, they spurred a new approach to reading insofar as they encouraged a new type of legibility in the texts they commissioned (or were given), by making the pictorial image paramount. Extensive visual cycles of one hundred to two hundred miniatures supported and guided the reader, chapter by chapter. Such illustrations were increasingly planned by the author, as with Laurent de Premierfait and his translation of Boccaccio's *De casibus virorum illustrium* (cat. 32).

The inventories of books owned by the duke of Berry and the duke of Burgundy afford only a pale reflection of the brilliant cultural life they stimulated. Only some 80 manuscripts, now widely dispersed, have survived from the 335 that the duke of Berry kept in his residences in Paris and Bourges, as well as in his delightful castle of Mehun-sur-Yèvre near Bourges. Often it is still possible to make out the duke's own signature or his ex libris, written in lovely Gothic script by his secretary, Jean Flamel. More than 40 percent of the duke of Berry's collection consisted of lavishly decorated liturgical books and Bibles. Much of the remainder was devoted to Latin and French classics, differing in that respect from the collections of the dukes of Burgundy, in which vernacular romances and chivalric literature were much better represented (cat. 38).[49]

A little later the courts of Blois and Angers, presided over by prince-poets such as Charles of Orléans (1364–1465) and René of Anjou (1409–1480), attracted poets like Villon (cat. 50) and stimulated book production in the Loire valley and western France (cats. 35, 36, 37). But though both princes were writers and poets (cat. 36), endowing literature with its letters of nobility, their collections hardly resembled one another. For Charles of Orléans and his wife, Marie of Clèves (cat. 37), the library was not for show but for reading and study (240 volumes); René of Anjou's collection of 130 volumes, on the other hand, was more suited to a creative and educated cleric than to a layman.

Mention should be made of other significant collections held by the great fifteenth-century feudal lords, such as Prigent de Coëtivy, Jacques d'Armagnac, and Louis of Bruges, lord of Gruthuyse. They loved books and gave them careful attention. Jacques d'Armagnac, count of la Marche and of Castres, duke of Nemours and peer of France (1433–1477), inscribed above his signature at the end of his volumes

29

the number of folios and *histoires* (miniatures) that the volume contained and the residence to which the manuscript was assigned–normally his castle at Carlat (Cantal) in La Marche (cat. 21). He had inherited some books from his great-great-grandfather, the duke of Berry. But, as an unrepentant conspirator, he was arrested in 1477 and then executed. His library was divided between Pierre de Beaujeu and Tanguy II Du Châtel, and about 120 of those volumes survive today.

Also extant are 140 manuscripts from the very fine library of Louis of Bruges, lord of Gruthuyse (1422–1492), a magnificent patron and advisor to the dukes of Burgundy. These volumes later joined the royal collection under Louis XII and the arms of their former owner can now only be read in palimpsest on the verso of the first folio. The texts were often written in the beautifully dark and heavy bastard script of Burgundy. Louis was one of those collectors who bridged the two worlds of manuscripts and printed books. Apparently some manuscripts in his collection were used as models by the Bruges printer Colard Mansion. But for a long time to come during the sixteenth century, book lovers' libraries continued to be collections of manuscripts. It is not uncommon, in fact, to find manuscripts modeled on a printed book, as happened in the late fifteenth century with a manuscript copy of the *Danse Macabre* based on Guy Marchant's printed edition of 1486–1487.

Some of these ecclesiastical, royal, and private collections have been reconstituted thanks to the comparison of ex libris (cat. 9), colophons (cat. 40), anagrams, and emblems (cat. 37) and heraldic signs (cat. 35), along with paleographical (cat. 1), physical, and of course artistic (cat. 44) evidence. Acquired by today's Bibliothèque nationale de France over the centuries by gift, purchase, bequest, and confiscation, these collections now constitute a priceless treasure. This living museum, revitalized and enriched day after day by discoveries from many researchers, provides fabulous testimony on medieval culture.

1 The principal work on the history of the medieval collections of the BNF remains that of Léopold Delisle, *Le Cabinet des Manuscrits de la Bibliothèque Impériale*, 3 vols. and 1 album (Paris, 1868–1881); supplement by E. Poulle (Paris, 1977). See also *Histoire des bibliothèques françaises*, vol. 1, *Les bibliothèques médiévales: Du VIe siècle à 1530*, ed. André Vernet (Paris, 1989); and the introduction by François Avril in Colette Beaune, *Le miroir du pouvoir* (Paris, 1989), 10–29. We should also thank François Avril for his advice and suggestions.

2 Cited by Pascale Bourgain, "L'édition des manuscrits," in *Histoire de l'édition française*, vol. 1, *Le livre conquérant: Du Moyen Age au milieu du XVIIe siècle* (Paris, 1982), 67.

3 "The basic steps in making parchment consisted of soaking the skins in quicklime for several days; next they were stretched on a frame and the hair and any irregularities removed before drying. Prior to writing on them, the copyist cleaned the parchment with a scraper and then with a pumice-stone removed the last traces of hair and ligaments." Jean Vezin, "La réalisation matérielle des manuscrits latins pendant le haut Moyen Age," in *Codicologica 2: Eléments pour une*

codicologie comparée (Leiden, 1978), 19. For a more general description, see *Le livre au Moyen Age*, ed. Jean Glénisson (Paris, 1989).

4 The copyists usually copied three or four pages a day.

5 Cited by Jean Vezin, "La fabrication du manuscrit," in *Le livre conquérant*, 32.

6 Eric Palazzo, *Histoire des livres liturgiques: Le Moyen Age: Des origines au XIIIe siècle* (Paris, 1993).

7 Chap. 73 of the Benedictine Rule. See Dom Jacques Dubois, "Comment les moines chantaient et goûtaient les Saintes Ecritures," in *Le Moyen Age et la Bible*, ed. Pierre Riché and Guy Lobrichon (Paris, 1984), 261.

8 Donatella Nebbiai-Dalla Guarda, *La bibliothèque de l'abbaye de Saint-Denis en France, du IXe siècle au XVIIIe siècle* (Paris, 1985).

9 BNF NAL 1023. See Joachim E. Gaehde, *Carolingian Painting* (New York, 1976), 32–35 and pls. 1–3 (orig. published as *Peinture carolingienne*).

10 Ibid., 82–87 and pls. 24–26.

11 Ibid., 125–28 and pl. 48.

12 But, having begun too late, Charlemagne achieved rather poor results: "Temptabat scribere tabulasque et codicellos ad hoc in lecto sub cervicalibus circumferre solebat, ut vacuum tempus esset manum litteris effigiendis adsuesceret; sed parum successit labor: praeposterus ac sero inchoatus." Einhard, *Vie de Charlemagne*, ed. and trans. Louis Halphen, 5th ed. (Paris, 1981), 76–77.

13 Ibid., 98: "Cappellam, id est ecclesiasticum ministerium, tam id quod ipse fecit atque congregavit, quam quod ad eum ex paterna hereditate pervenit, ut integrum esset neque ulla divisione scinderetur ordinavit. Si qua autem invenirentur aut vasa aut libri aut alia ornamenta quae liquido constaret eidem cappellae ab eo conlata non fuisse, haec qui habere vellet dato justae aestimationis pretio emeret et haberet. Similiter et de libris, quorum magnam in bibliotheca sua copiam congregavit, statuit ut ab his qui eos habere vellent justo pretio fuissent redempti pretiumque in pauperes erogatum."

14 Bernhard Bischoff, "Die Hofbibliothek Karls des Grossen," in *Mittelalterliche Studien: Ausgewählte Aufsätze zur Schriftkunde und Literaturgeschichte,* vol. 3 (Stuttgart, 1981), 148–69 and tables V–X (previously published in *Karl der Grosse: Lebenswerk und Nachleben,* vol. 2, *Das geistige Leben* [Düsseldorf, 1964], 42–62) translated into English by Michael Gorman (Cambridge, 1994), 68–74; and also *Die Hofbibliothek unter Ludwig dem Frommen,* ibid., 170–86 and tables XI and XII (previously published in *Medieval Learning and Literature: Essays Presented to Richard William Hunt,* ed. J. J. G. Alexander and M. T. Gibson (Oxford, 1976), 3–22.

15 Wicbodis poem in honor of Charlemagne in *Poetae latini aevi Carolini (MGH),* ed. Ernestus Duemmler, vol. 1, pt. 1 (Berlin, 1880), 96; cited by Bischoff, who believes that these verses may refer to a circular letter sent through the empire about 780 ("Hofbibliothek Karls des Grossen," 154–55).

16 Lucan, Statius, Tibullus, Horace, Martial, Cicero, Sallust; see B. Bischoff, in *Mittelalterichen Studien,* 3:166 and table X (Berlin, Staatsbibliothek Preussischer Kulturbesitz, ms Diez B.66, pp. 218–19).

17 BNF Lat. 5730 (*CLA* V, 562).

18 Vatican Library, Regin. Lat. 762 (*CLA* I, 109); see Bischoff, "Hofbibliothek Karls des Grossen," 168–69.

19 Lat. 5226 (Loire, 3rd or 4th quarter of the 9th century); Lat. 5227 (France, 9th century); and Lat. 5227A (Tours, 3rd quarter of the 9th century).

20 Cambridge (England) University Library, ms Kk. V. 16 (*CLA* II, 139), cited by Bischoff, "Hofbibliothek Karls des Grossen," 160–61; English trans., 67–68.

21 Rosamond McKitterick, "Charles the Bald and His Library," *English Historical Review* 95 (1980): 29–47.

22 The manuscript BNF Lat. 2855, fols. 1–62, is probably the dedication copy to the sovereign of Paschase Radbert's *De eucharistia.*

23 A unique copy has survived (BNF Lat. 9768), which dates from the late 9th century and seems to have been made in the abbey Saint-Médard de Soissons.

24 See fol. 67 of BNF Fr. 5716, the *Life and Miracles of Saint Louis,* by Guillaume de Saint-Pathus.

25 BNF Lat. 10525. Facsimile: *Le Psautier de saint Louis,* ed. Marcel Thomas (Graz, 1972).

26 Especially BNF Lat. 11560.

27 It was destroyed in 1781, but a drawing of it by C. de Froideau has survived (BNF, Cabinet des Estampes), reproduced in Jean-Pierre Babelon, *Le Palais de Justice, la Conciergerie, la Sainte-Chapelle de Paris* (Paris, 1973), 78. See also J. Guéroult, in *Mémoires de la Fédération des Sociétés Historiques et Archéologiques de Paris et de l'Ile-de-France* 1 (1949): 157–67.

28 BNF Lat. 8892 and 17326.

29 Inviolable because it was located above the sacristy.

30 Geoffroy de Beaulieu, his almoner, tells us that in imitation of the sultan of Egypt who had collected in his library all references of Arab philosophy, the saintly king decided to do the same for texts of the Holy Scriptures.

31 BNF Lat. 16357 and 17437, and Boston, Museum of Fine Arts 06.138; cited by Robert Branner, "Saint Louis et l'enluminure parisienne au XIIIe siècle," in *Septième centenaire de la mort de saint Louis: Actes du Colloque de Royaumont et Paris (21–27 mai 1970)* (Paris, 1976), 69–84, esp. 71; and also Branner, *Manuscript Painting in Paris During the Reign of Saint Louis* (Berkeley, 1977).

32 *La librairie de Charles V* (notes by François Avril), exhibition at the Bibliothèque Nationale (Paris, 1968).

33 It is not certain that wood from Ireland was rare and precious. According to Cyrien Monget (*La Chartreuse de Champmol* [Montreuil-sur-Mer, 1898], 59–60), the wood involved came from Holland and was oak hewn along a specific line.

34 "Le roy Charles avoit un sien varlet de chambre, lequel pour cause que en lui savoit plusieurs vertus, moult amoit; celluy par especial, sur tous autres souverainement bien lisoit et bien ponctoit, et tel entendens homs estoit, comme il pert" (Christine de Pisan). Cited by Léopold Delisle, *Recherches sur la librairie de Charles V,* vol. 1 (Paris, 1907), 10.

35 BNF Fr. 2700, fols. 2–37, and Collection Baluze 397.

36 BNF Fr. 2700, fols. 40–49 and 53–133.

37 BNF NAF 18867: book of astrology in French offered to the dauphin shortly after 1359.

31

38 François Avril, *Manuscript Painting at the Court of France, 1310–1380* (New York, 1978); orig. published as *L'enluminure à la cour de France* (Paris, 1978).

39 See R. Sherman, *Portraits of Charles V of France (1338–1380)* (New York, 1969) and "Representations of Charles V of France (1338–1380) as a Wise Ruler," *Medievalia et Humanistica* 2 (1971): 83–96.

40 Geneviève Hasenohr, "L'essor des bibliothèques privées aux XIVe et XVe siècles," in *Histoire des bibliothèques françaises*, vol. 1, *Les bibliothèques médiévales: Du VIe siècle à 1530*, ed. André Vernet (Paris, 1989), 214–63.

41 Cited by Hasenohr, ibid., 231.

42 M.-H. Tesnière, "Les manuscrits copiés par Raoul Tainguy: Un aspect de la culture des grands officiers royaux au début du XVe siècle," *Romania* 107 (1986): 282–386.

43 BNF Fr. 25344. See *La librairie de Charles V* (notes by François Avril), p. 83, no. 155.

44 Robert-Henri Bautier, "Les notaires et secrétaires du roi des origines au milieu du XVIe siècle," in André Lapeyre and Rémy Scheurer, *Les notaires et secrétaires du roi sous les règnes de Louis XI, de Charles VIII et de Louis XII (1461–1515)* (Paris, 1978), xiii–xix.

45 Notary from 1313 and author whose best-known manuscript of the *Roman de Fauvel* is the revised version held by the BNF (Fr. 146); facsimile with introduction by E. Roesner, F. Avril, and N. Regalado (New York, 1990).

46 Hasenohr, "Essor des bibliothèques privées," 239–240.

47 Book of hours whose leaves unfortunately are now scattered among libraries in Paris (BNF NAL 1416 and Museum of the Louvre), Chantilly, and London (British Library). See F. Avril and N. Reynaud, *Les manuscrits à peintures en France, 1440–1520* (Paris, 1993), 133–36, no. 68.

48 *Les fastes du Gothique: Le siècle de Charles V* (Paris, 1981).

49 Hasenohr, "Essor des bibliothèques privées," 248–57.

boudre et ostoit son:
chapeon et la coife.
Et lors puis que il es
toit entre ou cuer de
leglise il naloit pas
sus les piez iusques
a lautel. Aincois i a
loit a genoulz. et quãt
il estoit deuant lautel
il disoit premieremēt
son confiteor par soy

meismes a mains
iointes amoult de
souspirs et de gemis
semens et doncques
il receuoit en ceste ma
niere le urai cors ihe
sucrist de leuesque
ou du prestre
de sa tres grant deuo
cion a la sainte croiz
aouurer ihc

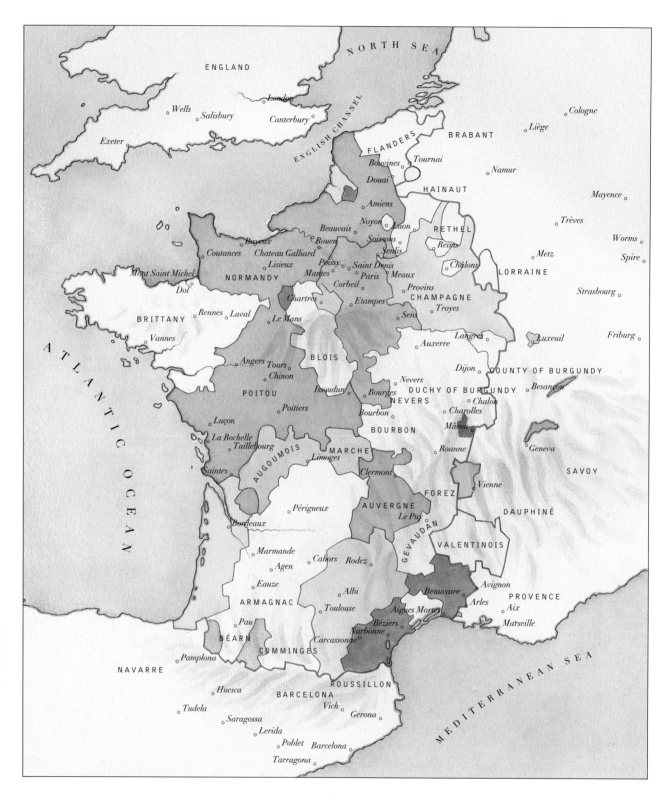

NORTH SEA

ENGLAND

Wells
Salisbury
London
Canterbury
Exeter

ENGLISH CHANNEL

FLANDERS
Bouvines
Douai
Tournai

BRABANT

Cologne
Liège

Namur

Mayence

HAINAUT

Trèves

Amiens
Noyon
Beauvais
Laon
Soissons
Reims
RETHEL

Worms

Bayeux
Rouen
Senlis
Châlons
LORRAINE

Spire

Coutances
Chateau Galliard
Poissy
Saint Denis
Meaux
Metz

Mont Saint Michel
Lisieux
Mantes
Paris
Strasbourg

Dol
NORMANDY
Corbeil
Provins
CHAMPAGNE

Chartres
Etampes
Troyes
Friburg

BRITTANY
Rennes
Laval
Le Mans
Sens
Langres
Luxeuil

Vannes
Auxerre
Dijon
COUNTY OF BURGUNDY

Angers
Tours
BLOIS
Nevers
Besançon

Chinon
Bourges
DUCHY OF BURGUNDY

POITOU
Issudun
NEVERS
Chalon

Poitiers
Bourbon
Charolles
Mâcon

Luçon
BOURBON
Roanne
Geneva

La Rochelle
Taillebourg
MARCHE
SAVOY

Saintes
AUGOUMOIS
Limoges
Clermont
Vienne
FOREZ

Périgueux
AUVERGNE
Le Puy
DAUPHINÉ

Bordeaux
GEVAUDAN
VALENTINOIS

Marmande
Cahors
Rodez
Avignon
PROVENCE

Agen
Beaucaire
Arles
Aix

Eauze
Albi
Aigues Mortes
Marseille

ARMAGNAC
Toulouse

Pau
Béziers
Narbonne

BÉARN
Carcassonne

COMMINGES
Pamplona

NAVARRE
ROUSSILLON

Huesca
BARCELONA
MEDITERRANEAN SEA

Tudela
Vich
Gerona

Saragossa

Lerida

Poblet
Barcelona

Tarragona

ATLANTIC OCEAN

FRANCE IN THE 13TH AND 14TH CENTURIES

Borders of the kingdom in 1180

Borders of the kingdom in 1328

Royal domain in 1180

Growth of royal domain by 1223

Growth of royal domain by 1270

Growth of royal domain by 1328

Counties held by the English in 1223 but no longer in 1328

English possessions in 1328, at the beginning of the

Hundred Years War

Catalogue Numbers 1–54

I

SAINT JEROME

Commentarium in Esaiam
(Commentary on Isaiah)

Département des Manuscrits, Lat. 11627,
fols. IV–2

*Parchment; III + 340 + III fols.; 385 × 240 mm;
modern binding. Written at the end of the 8th century in a script known as Corbie a-b. Described
from the 11th century in all the monastery inventories. On fol. 340v, a 13th-century ex libris of the
monastery of Corbie: "Liber sancti Petri Corbeie
quem furatus fuerit quis anathema sit, amen fiat."
Acquired by the monastic library of Saint-Germain-
des-Prés in Paris in 1638 and became part of the
national collections in 1795–1796, following the
confiscation of church property.*

In the Carolingian period (8th–9th centuries), the royal monastery of Corbie
(Somme) was one of the most brilliant centers of intellectual and religious culture in
the Western world. Day and night, 350
monks celebrated nonstop religious services,
the *laus perennis* (perpetual praise). The
abbey's famous school produced such

renowned exegetes as Paschasius Radbertus and Ratramnus of Corbie. Its scriptorium was one of the most productive of this period. Founded in the mid-7th century by monks from the house of Saint Columba at Luxeuil under the patronage of Queen Bathildis, the monastery maintained close ties with the royal court. Its relations with the other Columbanian monasteries, stretching from the British Isles to Italy (Bobbio), placed it at the crossroads of Mediterranean and Anglo-Saxon influences.

The monastery's fame dates from the abbacy of Adalhard (751–826), a significant political and religious figure who was a first cousin of Charlemagne and a close friend of Alcuin. Corbie's library at the time was considered the finest in the West during its heyday. More than eighty surviving 8th- and 9th-century manuscripts are traditionally attributed to Corbie—an exceptionally large number for this period—and are today preserved in the BNF and in libraries in Amiens and St. Petersburg. The monastery's collections naturally included a considerable number of biblical commentaries such as this commentary by Saint Jerome on the Book of Isaiah, dating from the end of the 8th century.

The manuscript's frontispiece is a fine example of a decorative style, still Merovingian in spirit, with the letters defined in delicate tones of green, orange, and brown, which seems to derive from the carpet pages found in Anglo-Saxon illumination. The title of Jerome's commentary (*In Christi nomine incipit explanatio in Esaia prophete libri decimi sancti Hieronimi presbyteri. Incipit prologus*) is inscribed in capital letters framed within a double arcade, a Lombard motif transmitted through the monastery of Luxeuil; the interlacing design of the pillars is reminiscent of Anglo-Saxon manuscripts. Two birds bear small human riders.

The elegance of the script is remarkable. The exceptional Corbie *a-b* calligraphy distinguished by the particular profile of the letters *a* and *b* is the last of the pre-Carolingian scripts. The way in which the letters are traced, their *ductus,* derives from the tight diplomatic script of Merovingian royal charters, and at the same time it antici-

pates the Carolingian minuscule by its measured flow and studied form. It belongs to the drive for clarity and simplicity inherent in 8th-century expression and is an example of the patient effort involved in search for a new script which ultimately resulted in the birth of Carolingian minuscule.

David Ganz recently questioned the attribution of this *a-b* script to the Corbie scriptorium. There is no doubt, however, that this manuscript and its twin, manuscript BNF Lat. 12155 (Jerome's commentary on the Book of Ezekiel), originated from the same period and workshop; both belonged to the abbey library in the 11th century and were among the most precious manuscripts in the collection. Regularly figuring in the abbey inventories, this manuscript was acquired in 1638 by the monastery of Saint-Germain-des-Prés, one of some four hundred of the finest items from the monastic library of Corbie which thus found their way to Paris.

Marie-Hélène Tesnière

Léopold Delisle, *Le Cabinet des Manuscrits de la Bibliothèque Impériale,* vol. 2 (Paris, 1874), 104–41, 427–40. *Corbie, abbaye royale, Colloque du centenaire* (Lille, 1963). Françoise Gasparri, "Le scriptorium de Corbie à la fin du VIIIe siècle et le problème de l'écriture a-b de Corbie," *Scriptorium* 20 (1966): 265–72. Jean Porcher, "Les manuscrits à peinture," in J. Hubert, J. Porcher, and W. F. Volbach, *L'Europe des invasions* (Paris, 1967), esp. 165–205. Ursula Winter, "Die Mittelalterlichen Bibliothekskataloge aus Corbie…" (diss., University of Berlin, 1972). Christian de Mérindol, *La production des livres peints à l'abbaye de Corbie au XIIe siècle* (Lille, 1976), 840–42. Hartmut Atsma, ed., *La Neustrie: Les pays au nord de la Loire de 650 à 850* (Sigmarinen, 1989) with articles by Pierre Riché, Jean Vezin, Florentine Mütherich, and David Ganz. D. Ganz, *Corbie in the Carolingian Renaissance* (Sigmarinen, 1990).

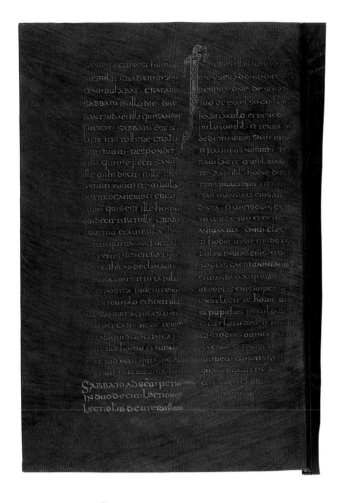

2

Lectionary on Purple Vellum

Département des Manuscrits, Lat. 9451,
fol. 31v

*Parchment; IV + II + 198 + II + IV fols.; 332 × 224
mm. Binding from the Restoration period, in red
morocco guilloché, gilt-tooled aux petits fers,
signed Bozérian the Younger, gilt edges. Northern
Italy (Monza?), ca. 800, made for Pipin, king of
Italy (?). Written in minuscule (fols. 1–12v) and in
uncial (fols. 12v–198). Formerly in the library of
Charles, duke of Rohan, prince of Soubise; purchased by the Bibliothèque Nationale at the sale of
this collection in 1789.*

Gospels and lectionaries figure among the
richest manuscripts of the early Middle
Ages–despite the admonitions of Saint
Jerome, who inveighed against having the
Gospels written so sumptuously in gilded
uncial on purple parchment. The privileged
place of biblical readings in the liturgy of the
Mass explains the lavishness of liturgical
manuscripts such as this one. Considered the
image of the divine Word, these manuscripts
were carried in church processions to the
altar and then to the ambo, or pulpit, where

the deacon conducted the reading. Gold, silver, and purple, as used here, symbolized the
celestial kingdom, the reward of eternal life,
and the radiating splendor of God's Word.

This magnificent full lectionary (*liber
comitis*) contains in extenso the biblical readings (Old Testament, Epistles, and Gospels)
of the religious service for the complete
liturgical cycle (from Christmas to Christmas)
and for the independent celebrations of the
cycle. It is written in silver letters on a very
supple, dark-purple parchment probably
imported from Byzantium. The title headings
for the readings are painted in gold and decorated with initials in finely ornamented
filigree. A veritable goldsmith's work, the letters are formed of tracery ribbons, with con-
tours emphasized by fine dotted lines in
gold. The regular and majestic script is a
beautiful uncial calligraphy, a type of majuscule derived from Roman cursive. The uncial
script was a sober script suitable for the
books of the Bible. An uncial *M* written with
a double circular arc and completed by two
heads of birds begins (fol. 32) the fourth
reading for the Saturday of the Quadre-
gesima of spring: "Item ubi supra, Lectio
Libri Sapientie: Miserere nostri, Deus omni-
um" (Likewise, as above, the Reading of the
Book of Wisdom: Pity us, God of all things)
(*Liber Jesu filii Sirach* 36.1–10).

The script and ornamentation date the
manuscript to the period of Charlemagne
and place its origin in northern Italy, probably in the region around Monza, a city ten
kilometers from Milan where all the
Lombard kings were crowned–including
Desiderius, the last one, defeated by
Charlemagne in 774. Paleographic and decorative criteria situate this document among
seven Carolingian manuscripts that can be
attributed to this region (the others being
BNF Lat. 653; Karlsruhe Aug. CCLXI; Vienna

3
Bible of Count Rorico
Département des Manuscrits, Lat. 3, fol. 183v

*Parchment; I + A + 409 + 1 fols.; 485 × 375 mm.
17th-century binding in red morocco* à la fanfare,
*restored. Written at the scriptorium of Saint-
Martin-de-Tours, ca. 835, for Count Rorico, duke of
Maine (d. 841), and entrusted by him to the abbey of
Saint-Maur-de-Glanfeuil. Transferred to Saint-
Maur-des-Fossés about 868 with the threat of
Viking invasion, entering the collection of Philippe
Hurault, bishop of Chartres, at the turn of the 17th
century and reaching the Bibliothèque Royale in
1622.*

In the first half of the 9th century the abbey
of Saint-Martin-de-Tours was a major center
of literary production and manuscript copying. No fewer than forty-five Bibles (some
now extant only in fragments) have been
identified as having originated from the famous scriptorium before it was overrun by
the Vikings in 853. Most are enormous, with
more than 400 folios, and of monumental format (55 × 40 cm), written in two columns fifty
lines in length, and containing the complete
biblical text *(pandecta)* with prologues and
Canon tables. The clear and spacious layout
of the page is enhanced by a typographic approach that increases its elegance and legibility. The title of each book of the Bible is inscribed in large capital letters on alternately
red and brown lines. Because of the sacred
nature of the book, the title (fol. 183v: Book of
Hosea) is inscribed in silver letters, now unfortunately oxidized, laid on the purple cartouche. The prologue of each book of the
Bible is written in majestic uncial for the incipit, followed by semi-uncial for the rest of
the text. The beginning of the book itself likewise has an incipit in majestic uncial, followed by semi-uncial shaped by the form of
the opening ornamental initial. Here, however, the body of the text continues directly
after the initial in a fine Carolingian minuscule specific to the Tours scriptorium. The
harmony and clarity of this new script are
one of the most evident signs of the Carolingian Renaissance.

In all likelihood it was Alcuin who started
Tours on the road to this editorial prosperity.
Before assuming the direction of the abbey
in 796 (he remained there until his death in

1616; Wolfenbüttel Helmst. 513; and Saint
Gall 108 and 227). The grandeur of its decoration suggests a royal origin similar to that of
BNF Lat. 653, which bears a dedication to a
prince of the Carolingian family. This indi
cates that it may have been made for the
royal chapel of Charlemagne's second son,
Pipin, who was king of Italy from 780 to 810
and who seems to have had contact with the
Monza scriptorium.

According to an 18th-century description
written when the manuscript belonged to
Charles, duke of Rohan, prince of Soubise
(d. 1787), the lectionary formerly had a luxurious metal binding *en ronde bosse.* In 1789,
when that bibliophile's collection was sold,
the Bibliothèque Nationale purchased it for
the sum of 2,000 livres. The binding had
already been missing for a century when the
lectionary was rebound by Bozérian the
younger in red morocco *guilloché* and gilded
aux petits fers.

Marie-Hélène Tesnière

Léopold Delisle, *Le Cabinet des Manuscrits de la Bibliothèque
Impériale*, vol. 3 (Paris, 1881), 213 and pl. IX. E. A. Lowe,
Codices Latini Antiquiores, pt. 5, *France* (Oxford and Paris,
1950), no. 580. Robert Amiet, "Un 'comes' carolingien inédit
de Haute-Italie," *Ephemerides liturgicae* 83 (1959): 335–67. Kurt
Holter, "Der Buchschmuck in Süddeutschland und
Oberitalien," in *Karl der Grosse*, vol. 3, *Karolingische Kunst*, ed.
Wolfgang Braunfels and Hermann Schnitzler (Düsseldorf,
1965), 93–94. Bernhard Bischoff, "Panorama der Hand-
schriftenüberlieferung aus der Zeit Karls des Grossen," in
Karl der Grosse, vol. 2, *Das geistige Leben*, ed. Bernhard
Bischoff (Düsseldorf, 1965), 250. Klaus Gamber, *Codices
Liturgici Latini Antiquiores*, rev. ed. (Freiburg, Switzerland,
1968), 2:472–73, no. 1210. François Avril and Yolanta Zaluska,
*Manuscrits enluminés d'origine italienne à la Bibliothèque
Nationale*, vol. 1, *VI–XIIe siècles* (Paris, 1980), 9, no. 17 and pl.
IV. *Dix siècles d'enluminure italienne (VI–XVIe siècles)*, exhibition
at the Bibliothèque Nationale (Paris, 1984), 17, no. 3. Eric
Palazzo, *Histoire des livres liturgiques: Le Moyen Age, des origines
au XIIIe siècle* (Paris, 1993), 103–23.

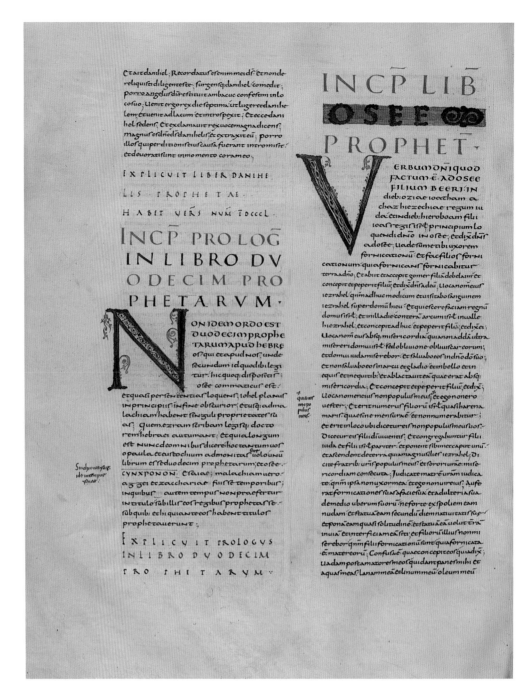

804), he had headed the Scola Palatina at
Aix-la-Chapelle (Aachen) and was one of the
moving spirits behind Charlemagne's
reforming zeal. During his sojourn at Tours
he revised at Charlemagne's request the text
of the Bible. Contrary to traditional belief, he
did not edit an official text of the Bible. In
fact, however, the popularity and influence
–albeit posthumous–of Alcuin's revision of
the Vulgate assured the triumph of Jerome's
Vulgate over the Vetus Latina.

Contemporaries greatly admired these
splendid Bibles. The scriptorium of Tours
produced at least two a year, an impressive
number given their size. They were intended

for the emperor, for the great princes or bishops of the Carolingian family, or for other monasteries. A note inscribed at the end of this copy (fol. 409), asking readers to pray for the patron who sponsored its production, informs us that it was copied for one of Charlemagne's sons-in-law, Count Rorico, duke of Maine. The count offered it to the abbey of Saint-Maur-de-Glanfeuil near Angers—a monastery which he helped restore—around 838–839. In 868 the monks of Saint-Maur-de-Glanfeuil, fleeing the invading Vikings, took it along with the relics of their patron saint to a place not far from Paris on the banks of the Marne, which would later be called Saint-Maur-des-Fossés. The life of Saint Maur was then copied onto the last pages (fols. 393–407), as were some chapters of the polyptyque of the abbey (preliminary folio and fols. 407v–408). The Bible was thereafter kept beside the saint's tomb. It is not known under what circumstances it came into the hands of Philippe Hurault, bishop of Chartres (1598–1621), before entering the collection of the Bibliothèque Royale in 1622.

Marie-Hélène Tesnière

Léopold Delisle, *Le Cabinet des Manuscrits de la Bibliothèque Impériale,* vol. 3 (Paris, 1881), 250–52. Samuel Berger, *Histoire de la Vulgate pendant les premiers siècles du Moyen Age* (Paris, 1893). Emile Lesne, *Histoire de la propriété ecclésiastique en France,* vol. 4, *Les livres, "scriptoria" et bibliothèques du commencement du VIIIe siècle à la fin du XIe siècle* (Lille, 1938), 140–90. Bonifatius Fischer, "Bibeltext und Bibelreform unter Karl dem Grossen," in *Karl der Grosse,* vol. 2, *Das geistige Leben,* ed. Bernhard Bischoff (Düsseldorf, 1965), 156–216. Bonifatius Fischer, "Die Alkuinbibel," in *Die Bibel von Moutier-Grandval* (Bern, 1971), 49–96. *La Neustrie: Les pays au nord de la Loire de Dagobert à Charles le Chauve (VIIe–IXe siècles),* ed. Patrick Périn and Laure-Charlotte Feffer, exhibition at Rouen, 1985, no. 84 (Marie-Thérèse Gousset). Pierre Petitmengin, "La Bible de Rorigon," in *Mise en page et mise en texte du livre manuscrit,* ed. Henri-Jean Martin and Jean Vezin (Paris, 1990), 78–83.

4

Gospels of Lothar

Département des Manuscrits, Lat. 266, fols. IV–2

Parchment; IV + 221 + III fols.; 320 × 245 mm. Binding from 17th–18th century, red morocco with royal arms. Ordered in Tours by Emperor Lothar between 849 and 851; in the collections of the abbey of Pontiffroy, in Metz, 1367; Chambre de Comptes in Blois; Bibliothèque Royale in Blois.

Throughout the medieval period the text of the Gospels was the subject of a great many finely, indeed lavishly, produced copies. The decoration of these manuscripts attained a level of magnificence unequaled in the Carolingian period. The Gospels of Lothar is a particularly splendid example of this deluxe production, whose blossoming in the 9th century was stimulated by the patronage of the imperial court.

A long Latin poem inscribed at the beginning of the volume informs us that it was produced in and for the monastery dedicated to Saint Martin (probably Saint-Martin-de-Tours) at Emperor Lothar's request through the intermediary of a certain Sigilaus. Since Tours was located within the territory of Charles the Bald, with whom Lothar, his half-brother, quarreled until 849, the manuscript must have been produced after that date and before Ermingarde, wife of Lothar, whose name is also mentioned in the poem, died in 851.

Nothing was spared to show off the exceptional nature of the sacred text and the eminence of the individual who had ordered its

41

production. Copied in that wonderfully clear Carolingian minuscule script (named after Charlemagne, its promoter), the manuscript contains nine pages of incipits with borders, twelve Canon tables containing the Gospel concordances drawn up by Eusebius of Caesarea, five large decorated letters, and six illustrations, depicting not only the customary series representing the Evangelists (fols. 22v, 75v, 112v, and 171v) but Christ in majesty (fol. 2v) and Lothar I in person (fol. iv). The emperor is shown seated on his throne surrounded by two bodyguards, pointing his finger toward the dedicatory poem transcribed in plain gilt capital letters on the facing leaf. This portrait is one of the oldest existing medieval representations of a contemporary individual.

The painter was an artist whose work is evident in another masterpiece of Carolingian illumination. He is the third painter identified by W. Koehler in Charles the Bald's first Bible (BNF Lat. 1), the key work produced by the School of Tours. In comparison with Charles the Bald's Bible, the Master of the Gospels of Lothar demonstrates greater expressiveness, a development which may be attributable to the influence of manuscripts produced by the School of Reims. The decoration of the initials and the architectural arcades of the canon tables display another tendency of the School of Tours. Drawn with gold and silver leaf, the metallic and flat decorative silhouette stands out on the parchment background, following a technique already used in Tours as early as the second quarter of the 9th century in the Gospels of Saint Gauzelin in the treasury of the cathedral in Nancy.

François Avril

E. K. Rand, *Studies in the Script of Tours,* vol. 1, *A Survey of the Manuscripts of Tours* (Cambridge, Mass., 1929), 157–58, pls. CXXXIV–CXXXVIII. W. Koehler, *Die karolingischen Miniaturen,* vol. 1, *Die Schule von Tours* (Berlin, 1930–33), 1:241, 403–05; 2:334–36, pls. 98–105. J. Hubert, J. Porcher, and W. F. Volbach, *L'empire carolingien* (Paris, 1968), 144–46, figs. 132–33. F. Mütherich and J. E. Gaehde, *Carolingian Painting* (New York, 1976), 14, 26, pls. 24–26. H. L. Kessler, *The Illustrated Bibles from Tours* (Princeton, 1977), esp. figs. 61, 79–81, 198.

5

Dagobert's Throne

Cabinet des Médailles, no. 651 (Inventaire des Monuments du Moyen Age). Replica cast directly from original.

Original armchair in bronze, partly gilded, 135 cm (height) × 78 cm (width). France, late 8th–9th century(?). Until 1791, part of the collection of relics and ornaments of the abbey of Saint-Denis.

Four panther's heads adorn the legs of this bronze chair, finished with braces and crosspieces. The armrests, surmounted in front by small globes and at the back by bearded heads, are composed of two openwork plaques, the lower one featuring a rosette motif and the upper one employing foliate decoration. The triangular back is decorated with three rings and foliate scrolls; it is generally assumed that a cross was originally set in the central ring. In the 12th century, as Abbot Suger explained in his *De administratione,* the throne was repaired: the crossbraces were secured by rivets and the right rear leg replaced, making the chair, which had been foldable until that date, rigid. A cruder restoration was undertaken in 1802, when Napoléon wanted to use the famous chair during the ceremonies for the founding of the Légion d'Honneur.

"Dagobert's throne" is a complex vestige that poses numerous unanswered questions regarding its initial purpose and the dates when its various parts were crafted. Several stages of execution can be detected in the seat, on one hand, and in the back and armrests, on the other. The seat is now no longer thought to date from antiquity or to be a Carolingian imitation of antiquity, but rather is believed to be Merovingian. The back and armrests, however, are attributed to the Carolingian period.

Suger's 12th-century reference to the bronze armchair indicates that it belonged to the abbey of Saint-Denis at a very early date. In the Middle Ages, religious institutions maintained rich and magnificent collections of relics, liturgical vessels, vestments, furs, scientific instruments, games, jewels, books, and so on, each object providing a concrete expression not only of the church's power but also of the legitimacy of royal authority as perceived by the king's subjects and by other monarchs. The treasure hoard of the basilica of Saint-Denis is mentioned in documents as early as the 8th and 9th centuries, and its first detailed inventory dates from the 10th century.

Following classical and early Christian practices, such treasures throughout the Middle Ages and up to the 18th century served as reserve capital, convertible into cash whenever the need arose. In the event of war or a major expense, the abbot or the king could have a particular precious object melted down or pawned, to be restored to the hoard when conditions permitted. The history of the treasury of Saint-Denis offers an excellent illustration of this custom, since the monks and the princes drew on it numerous times. Louis XVI was only following custom, then, when in the torment of the French Revolution he took the first steps to have the silver objects of the churches melted down in 1790 on a motion of the Assemblée Nationale. As early as January 18, 1791, however, the Commission des Monuments drafted a series of directives intended to protect works whose artistic or historic value exceeded their monetary value.

Thus it was on September 30, 1791, that a first group of fourteen items deemed to be of artistic and scientific value was moved from Saint-Denis to the Bibliothèque Nationale. Special precautions were taken for the transport of Dagobert's throne, testifying to the prestige that surrounded the fragile chair. In the years that followed, still other precious pieces from the abbey's treasury came to enrich the collection of the Cabinet des Médailles, which retains to this day the most valuable of the surviving objects.

Irène Aghion

B. de Montesquiou-Fezensac and D. Gaborit-Chopin, *Le trésor de Saint Denis*, vols. 1–3 (1971–77), 116–18, pls. CI, CII. *Ingelheim am Rhein, 774–1974*, exhibition at Ingelheim (Ingelheim, 1974), 399–401. *La Neustrie*, exhibition (Rouen, 1985), 47, 289. *1789: Le Patrimoine libéré*, exhibition at the Bibliothèque Nationale (Paris, 1989), 137–38, no. 79. *Le trésor de Saint-Denis*, exhibition at the Musée du Louvre (Paris, 1991), 63–68, no. 5.

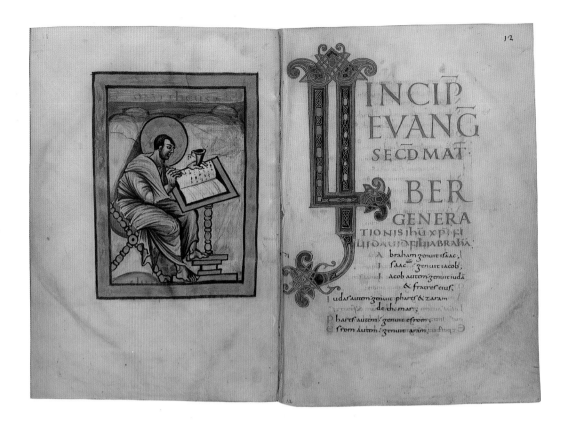

6

Gospels of the School of Reims

Département des Manuscrits, Lat. 265,
fols. 11v–12

Canones Evangeliorum (fols. 4–9v); *Quattuor
Evangelia* (fols. 10–216); *Capitulare
Evangeliorum* (fols. 217–233v)

*Parchment; II + 234 + II fols.; 285 × 200 mm.
Bound in red-grained leather with the arms of
Louis-Philippe on the spine; gilt edges. School of
Reims, second quarter of the 9th century; copy of
the Coronation Gospels of Vienna. Manuscript erro-
neously thought to have been in the library at Blois;
entered the Bibliothèque Royale in 1622 with the
collection of Philippe Hurault, bishop of Chartres
(1598–1621).*

Although the Carolingian minuscule emanating from the palace school enjoyed wide
usage, acting as a catalyst for cultural
unification of the empire, the artistic style of
imperial manuscript decoration, as in the
famous Evangelary of Godescalc (ca. 781–783)
(BNF NAL 1023), was not so widely appreciated
and copied. Rather, a style quite different
from that of the palace school, developed at
the same period in the same location, provoked fruitful imitations and adaptations

from 820 to the mid-9th century, first at Reims and then at Tours and Metz. Each center assimilated these imitations and adaptations within its own stylistic development.

The leading example of this style is found in the superb Gospels on purple vellum called the Coronation Gospels, now preserved in the Schatzkammer of the Hofburg in Vienna. They were probably produced around 790–800 for Charlemagne's young son Louis, later Louis the Pious. Greek artists from northern Italy may have been responsible for these Gospels. This style revives the artistic tradition of Hellenistic antiquity of four centuries earlier in its illusionistic motifs: for example, the noble bearing of the individuals and a sense of volume and at the same time of spatial liberty. According to legend, Emperor Otto III found the Coronation Gospels on Charlemagne's knees when he opened his tomb at Aachen in 1000. In any case, this manuscript, or at least a close copy, must have been at Reims during the archiepiscopate of Ebbo (816–835/845), because our Gospels contains a precise copy of the portraits of the Evangelists found in the Coronation Gospels and in fact belongs to the School of Reims. The relationship between these two manuscripts in Reims is reinforced by the close familial and political ties between Louis the Pious and Ebbo, the mercurial archbishop. Son of Louis the Pious's nurse, Ebbo was raised with Louis and later became his librarian.

The manuscript, copied with elegant refinement on the finest quality parchment, was produced at Reims in the second quarter of the 9th century. As was traditional, it contained the complete text of the four Gospels (fols. 10–216), preceded by tables of Gospel concordances and the ten Canons of Eusebius of Caesarea (fols. 4–9v) and followed by the *Capitulare Evangeliorum* (fols. 217–233v), a list of readings of the religious Offices appropriate to the cycle of the liturgical year. As was customary in Carolingian illumination, only the Canon tables and the beginning of the Gospels are illustrated. Antique-style arcades crowned alternately with pediments and arches frame the Canon tables. On the arch of the last Canon, that of

the Gospel of Saint John (fol. 9v), two peacocks flank a tree of life–a common motif in paleo-Christian frescoes and mosaics. They turn to the exterior to announce to the faithful the "Good News of the Resurrection," symbolized here by the gilded scroll they hold in their beaks. Each book of the Gospel is introduced by the portrait of its Evangelist in imitation of the author portraits that introduced the texts of the papyrus scrolls of classical antiquity. (In this one, the portrait of Luke is missing.) These portraits are in fact precise reproductions of those of the Coronation Gospels, with their oversized nimbuses and their omission of the usual Evangelist symbol inspiring each author. On fol. 11v, in a space devoid of decoration and on a bluish background highlighted with rose-colored cloud forms, Matthew, majestically draped in a white toga with stiffly drawn folds, writes his *Liber generationis*. The beginning of the Gospel text appears on the facing page. The title is written in gilt letters. The two initials (*LI*) of the *Liber generationis* are decorated in the Reims style.

Marie-Hélène Tesnière

Wilhelm Koehler, *Die karolingischen Miniaturen: Die Gruppe der Wiener Krönungs-Evangeliars* (Berlin, 1960). *Charlemagne: Oeuvre, rayonnement et survivances,* exhibition at Aix-la-Chapelle, 1965 (Düsseldorf, 1965), esp. 296, no. 483. Florentine Mütherich, "Die Buchmalerei am Hofe Karls des Grossen," in *Karl der Grosse: Lebenswerk und Nachleben,* vol. 3, *Karolingische Kunst,* ed. W. Braunfels and H. Schnitzler (Düsseldorf, 1965), 10–53, esp. 51. Jean Porcher, "Les manuscrits à peinture," in J. Hubert, J. Porcher, and W. F. Volbach, *L'empire carolingien* (Paris, 1968), 92–123.

45

7

Sacramentary–Use of Saint-Denis
Département des Manuscrits, Lat. 2290,
fols. 18v–19

*Parchment; II + 182 + II fols.; 280 × 215 mm. Bound
in red shagreen with the arms of Napoléon III.
Probably written and illustrated in the scriptorium
of the abbey of Saint-Amand-en-Pévèle, third or
fourth quarter of the 9th century. Franco-Saxon
school; made for the abbey of Saint-Denis; probably left the abbey in 1567 and successively owned by
Nicolas Lefèvre (1544–1612), Jacques-Auguste De
Thou (1553–1617), and Jean-Baptiste Colbert
(1619–1683), before entering the Bibliothèque Royale
in 1732 with Colbert's collection.*

The real flowering of the royal abbey of
Saint-Denis began in the reign of Charles
the Bald who, as lay abbot from 867 to 877,
was one of its principal benefactors. Apart
from the donation of numerous objets d'art
from the treasury of Saint-Denis that can be
ascribed to him (for instance, the Ptolemy
chalice and the so-called Charlemagne jewel-
case), Charles the Bald in 877 willed part of
his library to the abbey. The remainder of the
library was to be divided between the abbey
of Notre-Dame at Compiègne, which Charles
had founded in 875, and his son, the future
Louis the Stammerer. But apart from the

very beautiful Bible known as the Second Bible of Charles the Bald (BNF Lat. 2), it is uncertain which of Saint-Denis's manuscripts really belonged to this sovereign.

The Saint-Denis sacramentary is part of a group of eight sacramentaries copied and illustrated for the use of specific abbeys at the monastery of Saint-Amand-en-Pévèle near Valenciennes in the second half of the 9th century. They are recognizable by a square and spacious Caroline minuscule (compare Lat. 2291), and by their full-page Franco-Saxon illuminations (Reims, Bibliothèque Municipale 213). The monastery of Saint-Amand, during the abbacy of Charles the Bald's son Carloman (867–870) and later that of his archchancellor Gozlin (878–886), enjoyed a flourishing scriptorium. The rich ornamentation of this manuscript suggests that it was prepared at Charles the Bald's request for his favorite abbey, Saint-Denis; or perhaps Gozlin, also abbot of Saint-Germain-des-Prés and Saint-Denis, ordered it himself.

Before the birth of the missal, the sacramentary was in a real sense the celebrant's liturgical book. There is no doubt that this sacramentary was written for use at Saint-Denis. From the calendar the following celebrations may be noted: dedication of the church of Saint-Denis (Feb. 24), the *invention* or finding of the relics of Saint Denis the martyr and his companions Rusticus and Eleutherius (April 22), consecration of the altar of Peter and Paul (July 28), Passion of the Martyrs (Oct. 9), and their vigil. The canon of the Mass refers to Saint Denis and his companions in the prayers of the Libera nos, and special Masses are dedicated to them, as well as to other martyrs whose relics the abbey preserved (Saint Cucuphat and Saint Hippolyte, for example). Not to mention the *Missa greca* directly after the calendar (fols. 7v–8), in which the Greek is transcribed in Latin characters, recalling the abbey's reputation as a center of Greek study.

As was customary for Carolingian sacramentaries, only the preface (fol. 19) and the canon of the Mass (fol. 20) are illustrated, in this case in the very beautiful, purely ornamental Franco-Saxon style – a style that

marked the end of Carolingian illumination. The two pages (fols. 18v–19) are defined by a frame crafted in gilded blocks reminiscent of the goldsmith's art, white interlacing worked in with brilliantly hued geometrical motifs. The effect is reinforced by the fine red dotted lines. On the left-hand page the beginning of the prayer "Per omnia saecula" appears in gold letters, and on the right-hand page a very beautiful decoration of the *Vere* that begins the responses "Vere dignum et justum...." Here all is harmony and elegance in a successful combination of forms, colors, and script.

The manuscripts of Saint-Denis were dispersed when the Huguenots sacked the abbey in 1567. It is probably about this date that the the Saint-Denis sacramentary found its way, with twenty-five others of the same origin, into the collection of the bibliophile Nicolas Lefèvre, who may have been Louis XIII's preceptor. It then came into the possession of Jacques-Auguste de Thou (1553–1617), president of the Parlement of Paris, whose collection of manuscripts from Saint-Denis included fifty volumes. It then entered the collection of Jean-Baptiste Colbert (1619–1683), reaching the Bibliothèque Royale in 1732.

Marie-Hélène Tesnière

Abbé Victor Leroquais, *Les sacramentaires et les missels manuscrits des bibliothèques publiques de France*, vol. 1 (Paris, 1924), 19–21, no. 7, introduction, pl. X. André Boutemy, "Quel fut le foyer du style franco-saxon?" in *Annales du Congrès Archéologique et Historique de Tournai* 1949: 1–25. Michel Huglo, "Les Chants de la 'Missa greca' de Saint-Denis," in *Essays Presented to Egon Wellesz*, ed. Jack Westrup (Oxford, 1966), 74–83. Rosamond McKitterick, "Charles the Bald (823–877) and His Library: The Patronage of the Learning," *English Historical Review* 95 (1980): 29–47. Donatella Nebbiai-Dalla Guarda, *La bibliothèque de l'abbaye de Saint-Denis en France, du IXe au XVIIIe siècle* (Paris, 1985). Pierre-Marie Gy, "La Mise en page du Canon de la messe," in *Mise en page et mise en texte du livre manuscrit*, ed. Henri-Jean Martin and Jean Vezin (Paris, 1990), 112–16.

8

PSEUDO-DIONYSIUS
THE AREOPAGITE
Opera (Works)

Département des Manuscrits, Grec 437,
fols. 123v–124

*Parchment; 216 fols.; 250 × 175 mm. Bound in mar-
bled calf, spine in red leather with the monogram of
Louis-Philippe. Constantinople, before 827. Offered
by Michael II the Stammerer to Louis the Pious in
827, who gave it to the abbey of Saint-Denis;
belonged to the De Mesmes collection; acquired by
the Bibliothèque Royale in 1706.*

More than just a book, this item is a relic.
Despite the austere appearance its solid
majuscule script and lack of decoration give
it, it enjoys more than one claim to fame.
A Byzantine manuscript of the works of
Pseudo-Dionysius the Areopagite, copied in
Constantinople in the early 9th century
when iconoclasm was at its height, the *Opera*
was carried by the ambassadors of the
Byzantine emperor Michael II the Stammerer
to Compiègne in 827 for solemn presentation
to Louis the Pious.

The choice of such a gift can be explained
by the confusion that then existed between
Dionysius (Saint Denis), proselytizer among
the Gauls, bishop of Paris, and martyr in
whose honor the abbey that bears his name
was founded, and Dionysius the Areopagite,
Saint Paul's Athenian disciple whose conversion in the first century is described in
the Acts of the Apostles. The Areopagite was
credited with a theological and mystical
summa which was particularly revered

(*The Divine Names, Mystical Theology, The
Celestial Hierarchy, The Ecclesiastical
Hierarchy*), although in reality these works
were written by a Neoplatonic Christian of
the late 5th century, who chose to express his
faith in the language of Plotinus and Proclus.

The legend was so beautiful that Louis
found it perfectly natural to deposit the precious manuscript in the abbey of Saint-
Denis. He did so on the eve of Oct. 8, 827,
the saint's feast day. That night nineteen
miraculous cures were reported. Whether or
not there were such miracles, a cultural miracle did occur. Thanks to the initiative of
Abbot Hilduin, an ardent hagiographer of
the abbey's founding saint, the abbey would
become one of the rare intellectual centers
in the Carolingian world to take an interest
in Hellenism. The Pseudo-Dionysian corpus
was soon translated into Latin, probably by
Greek monks who had come from a Roman
monastery. Then an Irishman, John Scottus
Eruigena (ca. 810–ca. 870), proposed a new
translation, and the medieval West discovered a metaphysical thought whose influence
on its own contemplative development was
substantial.

Three centuries later, Peter Abelard
(1079–1142) took holy orders and retired to
the abbey of Saint-Denis. There, he endeavored to prove by a study of the documents
that the identification of Dionysius the
Areopagite with the patron of the abbey
derived more from fantasy than from reality.
He probably examined this very manuscript.
History sometimes assumes the appearance
of legend.

Marie-Odile Germain

Henri Omont, "Manuscrit des oeuvres de saint Denis
l'Aréopagite envoyé de Constantinople à Louis le
Débonnaire en 827," *Revue des études grecques* 17 (1904):
130–36.Gabriel Théry, *Etudes dionysiennes*, 2 vols. (Paris,
1932–37).Raymond J. Loenertz, "La légende parisienne de
saint Denys l'Aréopagite: Sa genèse et son premier témoin,"
Analecta bollandiana 69 (1951): 217–37.Paul Lemerle, *Le
premier humanisme byzantin* (Paris, 1971), 13–16. Donatella
Nebbiai-Dalla Guarda, *La bibliothèque de l'abbaye de Saint-
Denis en France, du IXe au XVIIIe siècle* (Paris, 1985), 29–35, 74,
201.

9

TERENCE

Comoediae (Comedies)

Département des Manuscrits, Lat. 7899, fols. 2v–3

Parchment; 176 fols.; 260 × 220 mm. Bound in fawn-colored calf with the royal arms and monogram of Charles IX. School of Reims, 9th century. Belonged to the abbey of Saint-Denis from the 9th century until 1595, when it was acquired by the Bibliothèque Royale.

The Latin comic poet Terence (ca. 185–159 B.C.), imitator of Menander, his Greek predecessor, enjoyed great success—not so much in his own brief lifetime as in the late Roman Empire, when his fame exceeded that of Plautus. Studies of libraries in late antiquity reveal that Terence's *Comedies* occupied a prominent place. Each of his plays poses a psychological or moral problem, such as the role of education in *The Adelphi*, from which Molière drew his inspiration for *L'Ecole des maris* (School for husbands) in the 17th century.

The moralizing tendency of Terence's work found an approving echo in literature of the Christian era. Commentaries insisting on the moral meaning of Terence proliferated and are known from later citations, though it is difficult to identify the authors. The famous 4th-century grammarian Donatus was perhaps one of them, along with Eugraphius in the following century. It is not surprising, then, that Terence's *Comedies* was one of the basic texts for whose transmission the Carolingians were responsible. His works were henceforth regarded as classics and considered an educational must, even for monks. In the manuscript exhibited here, the 13th-century call number "OB +" (fol. 3) and the 15th-century ex libris (fol. 41) of Saint-Denis (where it may have been acquired as early as the 9th century) suggest this use.

Lat. 7899 is one of the four oldest manuscripts of Terence outside of those copies executed in late antiquity. Its 149 illustrations were done by two artists from Reims, exhibiting the extraordinary aptitude of the School of Reims to assimilate the style of Roman painting and even surpass it in tension of design and spontaneity of line. The artists' pen-and-ink drawing technique gives expression to gestures and infuses even minor scenes with a dramatic tension that has no equivalent in Carolingian art. The volume begins with an antique-style portrait of the author, shown between two actors (fol. 2).

Each comedy—for instance, *Andria* (fol. 2v)—
is preceded by the representation of a
wardrobe where the appropriate masks for
each role are stored, sometimes accompanied
by abbreviations of the Latin names of the
characters ("Si" for "Simo," "So" for "Sosia,"
"Pam" for "Pamphilus," and so on). Facing
this wardrobe, the servant of Chrémès recites
the prologue (fol. 3).

This manuscript represents one of the
most important productions of the Carolingian Renaissance, given its role in transmitting the cultural heritage of antiquity.

Marie-Thérèse Gousset

H. Omont, *Comédies de Térence: Reproduction des 151 dessins du
manuscrit latin 7899 de la Bibliothèque Nationale* (Paris, 1904). L.
W. Jones and C. R. Morey, *The Miniatures of the Manuscripts of
Terence Prior to the Thirteenth Century* (Princeton, 1931), 53–67
and plates. J. Porcher, in J. Hubert, J. Porcher, and W. F.
Volbach, *L'empire carolingien* (Paris, 1968), 187–88, 352, figs.
172–73. A. Vernet, "La transmission des textes en France," in
La cultura latina nell'occidente latino dal VII all'XI secolo, vol. 22
of Settimana di studi sull'alto medioevo (Spoleto, 1975),
106–07. J. E. Gaehde and F. Mütherich, *Carolingian Painting*
(London, 1977), 20–21, 29, ills. III and IV. M. D. Reeve,
"Terence," *Texts and Transmissions: A Survey of Latin Classics*,
ed. L. D. Reynolds (Oxford, 1983). D. Nebbiai-Dalla Guarda,
*La bibliothèque de l'abbaye de Saint-Denis en France, du IXe au
XVIIIe siècle* (Paris, 1985), 74, 218–19. J. N. Grant, *Studies in the
Textual Tradition of Terence* (Toronto, 1986), esp. 22, 190.

10

Gradual–Use of Saint-Michel de Gaillac
Département des Manuscrits, Lat. 776, fol. 5

*Gradual with proses and sequences, followed by a
tonary. Parchment; III + 155 + III fols.; 406 × 270
mm. Bound in red morocco with the arms and
monogram of Jean-Baptiste Colbert. Made for the
abbey of Saint-Michel-de-Gaillac, near Albi,
toward the mid-11th century, certainly before 1079,
when the abbey became attached to La Chaise-
Dieu. Decoration and "neumes aquitains." Entered
Colbert's collection after 1672 (note the binding) and
was acquired for the royal collection in 1732.*

The Gradual was a basic book of the liturgy
that originally contained the chants of the
Proper of the Mass (Introit, Gradual, Alleluia,
Offertory, Communion), arranged according
to the various feasts throughout the liturgical
year. Its name was derived from the first
steps (*gradus*) of the ambo or pulpit where
the cantor stood to deliver the responses.
The gradual might vary from region to
region by the addition of proses and
sequences.

Completed in the mid-11th century for the
monastery of Saint-Michel-de-Gaillac near
Albi, this splendid Gradual testifies to the
astonishing cultural wealth of monasteries in
the Aquitaine region of the south of France
in the 11th-century. The large ornamental initial *A* (fol. 5) that begins the Introit of the
first Sunday of Advent ("Ad te levavi animam
meam...": Ps. 24.1, in imbricated lettering) is
one of the finest known examples of the
early Aquitanian style. Remarkably decorative, embellished with marvelously colored
geometric designs and interlacing, the manuscript exhibits a style that prevailed between
1050 and 1150 in France, from Limoges to the
Pyrénées and into Spain. Knots of intricate
interlaced design ending in spear- or fan-
shaped palm-leaf ornaments stand out
against vivid and contrasting colors typical
of the south of France—yellow, red, and
apple-green—the whole delicately set against

ELENAVIANIMMEM

a purple-colored background. In the center of the *A*, the little haloed figure is difficult to interpret. Is it God, to whom the text invites Christians to raise their souls? Or is it David, the author of the psalm?

This Gradual is equally crucial to the history of music. Far from imperial centers of power, Aquitaine continued to use the Gallican chant longer than anywhere else. The Gallican chant was used in Gaul before the introduction of the Gregorian chant by the Carolingians, and the Gregorian reform of the 11th century led to its disappearance. No complete collection of this chant has survived, hence the interest of the Gallican elements in this Gradual. Especially important are the mass of Saint Michael, patron saint of the monastery (fol. 116), the liturgy for Rogations, and the Offices of the Dead, observances to which the people were particularly devoted. The perfection of the script makes this Gradual a splendid example of Aquitaine musical notation in neumes distinguished by the use of separate dots.

The provenance of this manuscript before Colbert acquired it, perhaps in 1682, is uncertain. Colbert had it bound, as was his custom, in red morocco with his coat of arms "d'or à la couleuvre (*coluber*) ondoyante en pal d'azur" (or with an undulating snake on azure pale). Above his arms are a marquis's crown and the decorative chains of the royal orders, whose "Grand Trésorier" (chief treasurer) he became in 1685. His monogram formed from the interlaced initials *JBC* accompanied by a snake framed by filigree appears on the spine of the manuscript. The use of this monogram dates from 1672. The manuscript also bears on its spine the gold letters *Antiphonarium albiense*, the title by which the Gradual was generally known. The magnificent manuscript collection which Colbert (d. 1683) had assembled entered the royal collection in 1732 when one of Colbert's descendants, the count de Seignelay, sold it to the king.

Marie-Hélène Tesnière

J. Porcher, *L'art roman à Saint-Martial-de-Limoges*, exhibition catalogue (Limoges, 1950). Michel Huglo, "Les 'preces' des graduels aquitains empruntés à la liturgie hispanique," *Hispania sacra* 8 (1955): 361–83. *Le graduel romain: Édition critique par les moines de Solesmes*, vol. 2, *Les sources*, ed. M. Huglo (Abbaye Saint-Pierre de Solesmes, 1957), 93–94. M. Huglo, *Les tonaires: Inventaire, analyse, comparaison* (Paris, 1971), 140–44. M. Huglo, "La tradition musicale aquitaine: Répertoire et notations," in *Liturgie et musique (IXe–XIVe s.)*, Cahiers de Fanjeaux 17 (Toulouse, 1982), 253–68. Denise Bloch, "La bibliothèque de Colbert," in *Histoire des bibliothèques françaises*, vol. 2, *Les bibliothèques sous l'Ancien Régime, 1530–1789* (Paris, 1988), 159–79. *De Toulouse à Tripoli: La puissance toulousaine au XIIe siècle (1080–1208)*, exhibition at the Musée des Augustins, Toulouse, Jan. 6–March 20, 1989, pp. 59–60 (F. Avril), pp. 61–65 (O. Cullin), and pp. 223–24, no. 325 (Y. Zaluska and O. Cullin).

II

FLAVIUS JOSEPHUS

De bello judaico (About the Judaic war), translated into Latin by Rufinus

Département des Manuscrits, Lat. 5058, fols. 2v–3

Parchment; IV + 169 + IV fols.; 367 × 246 mm. Bound with the monogram of Louis XV on the spine. Abbey of Moissac (Tarn-et-Garonne), ca. 1100. In the monastery's collection until 1678, when the Moissac manuscripts entered Jean-Baptiste Colbert's collection, before becoming a part of the Bibliothèque Royale in 1732.

When Cassiodorus devised a course of reading and study for the monks of Vivarium in the middle of the 6th century, he ranked Flavius Josephus as a leading Christian historian indispensable to their education, notably emphasizing two books, *Antiquitates Judaicorum* (Jewish antiquities) and *De bello judaico*, which had recently been translated from Greek into Latin on Cassiodorus's initiative. The course of study that Cassiodorus conceived in his *Institutiones* survived for more than a thousand years. Thus Flavius Josephus, along with Eusebius of Caesarea, Orosius, Bede, and Isidore of Seville, was one of the essential components of Christian historical education during the entire Middle Ages. Because his writings supplied a wealth of information about the historic milieu in which Christianity was born, his two books were widely used by all biblical commentators. They were read in monasteries, and especially at Cluny, when the monks were assembled in the refectory or in private during Lent.

This splendid manuscript containing the *De bello judaico* was copied about 1100 at the Cluniac abbey of Moissac (Tarn-et-Garonne). Located in the Quercy region and known for its impressive Romanesque sculpture and its importance as a center of transmission of Cluniac culture to Spain, Moissac was then at the height of its power and influence. The Cluniac monks who had reformed the abbey and restored its liturgy had brought manuscripts with them. The copying of these and other manuscripts spawned the Moissac scriptorium, which was especially productive at the end of the 11th and the beginning of the 12th centuries.

On the facing pages that open the manuscript (fols. 2v–3), Flavius Josephus is shown offering his work as homage to the emperors Titus and Vespasian, one of whom holds a

53

scepter, the other a globe. The crowd presses in behind the author to listen to the reading. This majestic and dynamic drawing is faintly highlighted with subdued colors (ultramarine, bronze-green, red ocher). According to François Avril, this drawing reflects a Moissac artist's interpretation of models made fashionable by artists of the Loire valley, an artistic center of the highest order in the mid-11th century. On folio 7, a beautifully embellished letter in the Aquitanian style with winged lions among foliate scrolls bears comparison, in its execution, with the sculpted decoration of the capitals of the abbey's cloister.

Moissac, for all its brilliance in the Middle Ages, sank into oblivion in the 16th century. On Colbert's instructions, Nicolas-Joseph Foucault, intendant for the "généralité" of Montauban, visited the monasteries in his district in search of intellectual treasures and so discovered the library of Moissac and its 141 manuscripts, covered with dust and left to the rats. When informed of the find, Baluze, Colbert's librarian, immediately recognized the collection's importance. Foucault acquired the manuscripts and dispatched them in 1678 to Paris for Colbert's library. The canons received in exchange, and rather tardily at that, a modest sum of money. Colbert's fine collection joined the royal collections in 1732, when the count de Seignelay, one of his descendants, sold it to the king.

Marie-Hélène Tesnière

Léopold Delisle, *Le Cabinet des Manuscrits de la Bibliothèque Impériale*, vol. 1 (Paris, 1868), 457–59, 518–24. Chanoine Etienne Delaruelle, "Une miniature de Moissac et la 'Majestas Domini,'" *Annales du Midi* 68 (1956): 153–63. Jean Porcher, "L'enluminure romane en Quercy," in *Quercy roman* (Paris, 1959), 136–40 and esp. pls. 17 and 18. J. Porcher, *L'enluminure française* (Paris, 1959), 25–28. Jean Dufour, *La bibliothèque et le scriptorium de Moissac* (Geneva and Paris, 1972), esp. 140–41. J. Dufour, "La composition de la Bibliothèque de Moissac à la lumière d'un inventaire du XVIIe siècle nouvellement découvert," *Scriptorium* 35 (1985): 175–226. François Avril, "Les arts de la couleur," in *Les royaumes d'Occident* (Paris, 1983), 185–88. Denise Bloch, "La bibliothèque de Colbert," in *Histoire des bibliothèques françaises*, vol. 2, *Les bibliothèques sous l'Ancien Régime, 1530–1789* (Paris, 1988), 158–79 and esp. 161–62. Hélène Toubert, "La double page illustrée," in *Mise en page et mise en texte du livre manuscrit*, ed. Henri-Jean Martin and Jean Vezin (Paris, 1990), 373

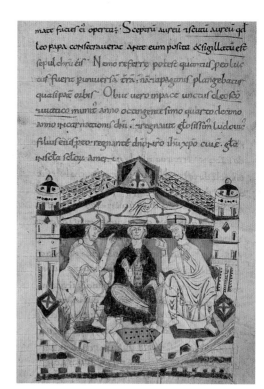

12

ADHÉMAR DE CHABANNES
Historia (Chronicle)
Département des Manuscrits, Lat. 5927, p. 157

Adhémar de Chabannes, Historia *(pp. 1–262); Conventum inter comitem et Hugonem [Guillaume V, duke of Aquitaine, and Hugues IV of Lusignan] (pp. 265–80); Einhard,* Vita Caroli Magni *(pp. 280–300).*

Parchment; VIII + 301 + VIII pp.; 330 × 230 mm. Angoulême, mid-11th century; completed at Saint-Martial de Limoges, early 12th century. Belonged to Pierre Pithou, Jacques-Auguste de Thou, and then J.-B. Colbert; acquired by the Bibliothèque Royale in 1732 with Colbert's collection.

The breakup of centralized political power in France in the 10th and 11th centuries was accompanied by a regionalization of culture, especially of historical knowledge, which was thereafter confined to local territories. This was true of the historigraphical school in Aquitaine of which Adhémar de Chabannes (ca. 988–1034) was a brilliant representative. A monk first at Saint-Cybard in Angoulême and then at Saint-Martial in Limoges, Adhémar wrote a chronicle, or *Historia*, that traced the history of the Franks from their Trojan origins until 1028. His first two books were compilations, with some annotations, of Carolingian histories and annals. But Adhémar's personal account begins in the third book, from the date 83o. It constitutes the principal source for the history of west central France in the 10th and 11th centuries.

Located in the center of France, at the northern limit of the *langue-d'oc*-speaking regions, the abbey of Saint-Martial de Limoges was an important stopping point on the pilgrimage route leading to Santiago de Compostela. After the Council of Limoges declared in 1029 that Saint Martial had been one of Christ's apostles, numerous pilgrims and leading figures of the day came to venerate his tomb, bringing with them news and information. About 1030, Adhémar offered the abbey his collection of eleven manuscripts and set off for a pilgrimage to the Holy Land, where he died in 1034. Fifteen manuscripts of Adhémar's *Historia* survive, some of them autographs.

This manuscript was probably copied in the mid-11th century at Saint-Cybard in Angoulême. A painting at the beginning of book 3 (p. 157) depicts Louis the Pious, Charlemagne's successor, as *basileus* ("king"), enthroned beneath the hand of God and flanked by the envoys of Leo V, the emperor of the Orient. The Aquitanians cherished Louis the Pious because he had been consecrated king of Aquitaine in 781 before acceding to the emperorship.

The text of Adhémar's *Historia* was originally preceded in the manuscript by the *Revelationes* of the Pseudo-Methodius and by a sermon of Saint Leo, both of which are now preserved in Lat. 3796 (fols. 8–27). The manuscript also contains a fascinating document (*Conventum*) that sheds light on feudal relationships in the Poitou region in the 11th century and has the additional interest of being written in a Latin transcribed directly from the vernacular language spoken in Poitou about 1030.

The manuscript was apparently completed at Saint-Martial de Limoges in the early 12th century, when a fragment of Einhard's Life of Charlemagne was added to it.

When the canons of Limoges sold their collection to the king of France in 1730, this volume had already left the monastery. It was in 1732 that it reached the royal collection with Colbert's manuscripts, after having passed through the hands of such great bibliophiles as Pierre Pithou (1549–1596) and Jacques-Auguste de Thou (1553–1617).

Marie-Hélène Tesnière

Adhémar de Chabannes, *Chronique*, published after the manuscripts, by Jules Chavanon (Paris, 1897). Jean Porcher, *L'art roman à Saint-Martial de Limoges: Les manuscrits à peintures, historique de l'abbaye, la basilique*, (Limoges, 1950), esp. no. 24. W. M. Hackett, "Aspects de la langue vulgaire du Poitou d'après un document latin du onzième siècle," in *Mélanges offerts à Rita Lejeune*, vol. 1 (Gembloux, 1969), 13–22. Danielle Gaborit-Chopin, *La décoration des manuscrits à Saint-Martial de Limoges et en Limousin du IXe au XIe siècle* (Paris, 1969), 32n26, 92n34, 104, 209, and figs. 116, 132. François Avril, book review of the preceding work in *Bulletin monumental* 1970: 259–61. Richard Allen Landes, *The Making of a Medieval Historian: Ademar of Chabannes and the Aquitaine at the Turn of the Millennium* (Princeton, 1985).

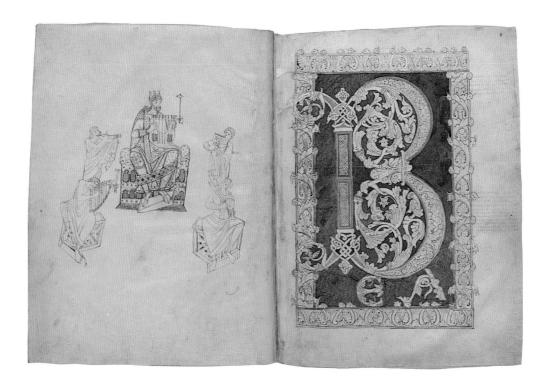

13
Psalter-Hymnal of Saint-Germain-des-Prés
Département des Manuscrits, Lat. 11550, fols. 7v–8

Parchment; 329 fols.; 435 × 315 mm. Made in the scriptorium of the abbey of Saint-Germain-des-Prés about the mid-11th century (after 1029). Illustrated by a certain Ingelardus, whose name appears in Lat. 11751 (fol. 145v) in colophon form using colored text and "enclosed letters." Acquired by the Bibliothèque Nationale in 1795–1796.

Throughout the Middle Ages, the Parisian abbey of Saint-Germain-des-Prés was a well-known and influential intellectual center from its royal beginnings to the 18th century. Its distinction, especially in the 17th and 18th centuries, stemmed from the brilliant work of its monks, at whose forefront figured Dom Jean Mabillon (1632–1707), the founder of modern historical criticism.

When Childebert, the son of Clovis, returned from Spain about 531, legend says that he founded—apparently on the advice of his chaplain (who became Saint Germain)—a basilica designed to receive the relics of Saint Vincent of Saragossa and the True Cross that he had wrested by conquest from the Visigoths of Spain. Rapidly, monks gathered around this church, located in the meadows on the left bank of the Seine River. The prosperity of the abbey dates from the 11th century. During the abbacy of Adélard (1031–1063), successor of the famous William of Volpiano, the monastery maintained a flourishing scriptorium. Only ten manuscripts survive from the exceptional production identified by the homogeneity of its decoration as emanating from the workshop of Ingelardus, who signed Lat. 11751 as *scriptor* (fol. 145v).

This great Psalter-hymnal, a masterpiece of Ingelardus's workshop, is one of the rare and magnificent surviving examples of Romanesque art from the Ile-de-France region. It is distinguished in its decoration by a drawing style firm and sober yet full of grace and harmony, reinforced with striking green, vermillion, and purple backgrounds that emphasize an alphabet of letters characterized by somewhat complex tracery and foliate ornamentation. The Psalter proper is introduced by a traditional representation of David and his musicians (fol. 7v). Sumptuously dressed, David is seated in the center on a throne decorated with ornamental arches. He is playing the lyre. Four musicians are grouped around him and, in a most realistic pose, are turned toward him as if tuning their instruments; the player of the reed horn raises his finger, the harpist with harp braced against his shoulder listens; the player of the rebec plucks a string while holding his bow; the flutist blows his reed pipe. On the facing folio (fol. 8), a magnificent *B*–the first letter of "Beatus vir qui non abiit in consilio impiorum" (Happy is the man who does not follow the advice of the wicked)–with tracery and foliage begins the Psalter. It is framed by palmettes ending in floral or animal forms that enclose the letter and lend it depth and space. The text of the psalm continues over two folios with a

succession of leafwork letters characteristic of the scriptorium.

The hymnal contains hymns in honor of Saint Vincent of Saragossa (fols. 256–257) and hymns (fol. 270) and litanies (fol. 307) in honor of Saint Germain, confirming the manuscript's attribution to the abbey of Saint-Germain-des-Prés. A litany in honor of Saint Martial, the apostle (fol. 303), furnishes the terminus a quo for determination of the date, since the Council of Limoges affirmed the apostolicity of the saint in 1029.

In 1790 the abbey of Saint-Germain-des-Prés was abolished. Most of its very beautiful manuscript collection (more than 9,000 volumes) was acquired by the Bibliothèque Nationale in 1795–1796.

Marie-Hélène Tesnière

Léopold Delisle, *Le Cabinet des Manuscrits de la Bibliothèque Impériale*, 3 vols. (Paris, 1868–1881), 2:40–58. Chanoine Victor Leroquais, *Les psautiers manuscrits latins des bibliothèques publiques de France*, vol. 2 (Mâcon, 1940–1941), 105–10, no. 334. *Les manuscrits à peintures en France du VIIe au XIIe siècle*, exhibition at the Bibliothèque Nationale (Paris, 1954), 88, no. 246. Yvonne Deslandres, "Les manuscrits décorés au XIe siècle à Saint-Germain-des-Prés par Ingelard," *Scriptorium* 9 (1955): 1–16 and plates. Maurice Coens, "Litanies de Saint-Germain-des-Prés," in *Recueil d'études bollandiennes* (Brussels, 1963), 300–307. Tilman Seebass, *Musikdarstellung und Psalter-illustration im frühen Mittelalter: Studien ausgehend von einer Ikonologie der Handschrift Paris Bibliothèque Nationale Fonds Latin 1118* (Berlin, 1973), 184 and pl. on p. 108. Charles Samaran and Robert Marichal, *Catalogue des manuscrits en écriture latine portant des indications de date, de lieu ou de copiste...*, vol. 3 (Paris, 1974), 241 and pl. XVI. *1789: Le patrimoine libéré: 200 trésors entrés à la Bibliothèque Nationale de 1789 à 1799*, exhibition at the Bibliothèque Nationale (Paris, 1989), 170, no. 99.

14

*Liturgical and Historical Miscellany
Concerning Cluny, Attributed to Peter
the Venerable*

Département des Manuscrits, Lat. 17716,
fol. 23

*Complete Office for the celebration of the
Transfiguration (fols. 7v–13, 15–22); proses and
responses in honor of the Virgin (fols. 23–24v);
interpolated version of the* De miraculis *of Peter
the Venerable entitled* De cluniacensi cenobio et
de religione et honestate fratrum ibidem Deo
serventium et de his qui illic divinitus con-
tigerunt ex relatione Domini venerabilis
Cluniacensis abbatis *(fols. 25–70v); various letters
from the abbots of Cluny and charters establishing
its rights, all dated before 1189 (fols. 70v-100v).*

*Parchment; III + 101 + III fols.; 362 × 258 mm.
Produced at Cluny at the end of the 12th century,
after 1189. Given to Saint-Martin-des-Champs at an
unknown date; acquired by the Bibliothèque
Nationale with 141 other manuscripts from Saint-
Martin in 1797.*

The powerful Cluniac order, centered around
and more or less feudally dependent on the
monastery of Cluny and its prestigious
abbot, answered directly to the pope, rather
than (as was customary) to local ecclesiastical
authority. At the beginning of the 12th century, the order numbered some twelve hundred
houses in Europe, divided among abbeys,
"daughter houses," and priories. Cluniac
monks–so-called black monks–were choir
monks. Little involved with theological
abstractions and freed from manual labor,
their chief occupation was celebrating the
Divine Office, chanting the Psalms, and reading spiritual literature, all for the greater
glory of God.

This liturgical and historical miscellany,
attributed to Peter the Venerable, was copied
and illustrated at the scriptorium of Cluny at

the end of the 12th century for the priory of Saint-Martin-des-Champs in Paris. The magnificent illustrated manuscript thereby transmitted to a major daughter house, Saint-Martin, the liturgical, doctrinal, and monastic ideals propounded by the engaging, open-minded, and cultivated Peter the Venerable, the last great abbot of Cluny (1122–1156).

The manuscript is as important for its contribution to textual tradition as it is to the history of Cluniac illumination. It contains a slightly interpolated version of Peter the Venerable's *De miraculis,* a collection of *exempla* with a doctrinal slant. The text notably recounts the life of the great Cluniac, Matthew of Abano (d. 1135), former prior of Saint-Martin-des-Champs, who at the beginning of Peter's abbacy helped him to reform the abbey. This manuscript in fact provides the closest version to the lost original of Peter's Life of Matthew of Abano. The text is preceded by a liturgical section containing a solemn Office for the celebration of the Transfiguration (Aug. 6) (illustrated by a magnificent painting on fol. 7v), a religious Office that Peter the Venerable introduced into France. It is followed by a series of responses and proses in honor of the Virgin also attributed to Peter the Venerable. In fact, the growing practice and deeper understanding of Marian devotion in France may be chiefly attributed not only to Bernard of Clairvaux but also to Peter himself. He had prescribed for his monks, over and above the two solemn conventual masses, a daily mass in honor of the Virgin at her "matutinal" altar. Decorating fol. 23, in a setting reminiscent of the portal of the great abbey, a Cluniac monk wearing his black frock and displaying the tonsure of choir monks is kneeling at the Virgin's feet. He begs her to intercede with her son: "Mater misericordie, spes et via venie, pia pium pro nobis exora

filium" (Mother of mercy, hope, and way of pardon, virtuous one, implore your holy son on our behalf). The hieratic pose of the Virgin seated on a throne, Christ holding a scroll in his hand, the looping and fluted folds of the garments, the undulating decoration of the arcade, and the vivid yet delicate colors (beige, pale blue highlighted with white, vermillion, and green) all combine to make this one of the most beautiful and well preserved examples of Cluniac illumination from the end of the 12th century.

Exactly when it was given to the abbey of Saint-Martin-des-Champs is unknown. It does not appear on the monastery's first inventory dating from the beginning of the 13th century. The manuscripts of Saint-Martin-des-Champs entered the national collection during the Revolution in 1797. The remaining Cluniac manuscripts followed them there in the 19th century.

Marie-Hélène Tesnière

Léopold Delisle, *Le Cabinet des Manuscrits de la Bibliothèque Impériale,* 3 vols. (Paris, 1868–1881), 2:235–41. L. Delisle, *Inventaire des manuscrits de la Bibliothèque Nationale, Fonds Cluny* (Paris, 1884), 223–27, no. 129. André Wilmart, "Le poème apologétique de Pierre le Vénérable et les poèmes connexes," *Revue bénédictine* 51 (1939): 53–69. Charles Samaran and Robert Marichal, *Catalogue des manuscrits en écriture latine portant des indications de date, de lieu ou de copiste...,* vol. 3 (Paris, 1974), 589 and pl. XXXVIII. *Pierre Abélard et Pierre le Vénérable: Les courants philosophiques, littéraires, et artistiques en Occident au milieu du XIIe siècle* (Paris, 1975); see articles by Robert Folz and Marie-Louise Thérel. Denise Bouthillier, "La tradition manuscrite du 'De Miraculis' de Pierre le Vénérable: Bilan d'une première recherche," in *Revue d'histoire des textes* 6 (1976): 99–142. Jean-Pierre Torrell, O. P. Bouthillier, and Denise Bouthillier, *Pierre le Vénérable et sa vision du monde,* Spicilegium Sacrum Lovianense, Etudes et Documents, fasc. 42 (Leuven, 1986).

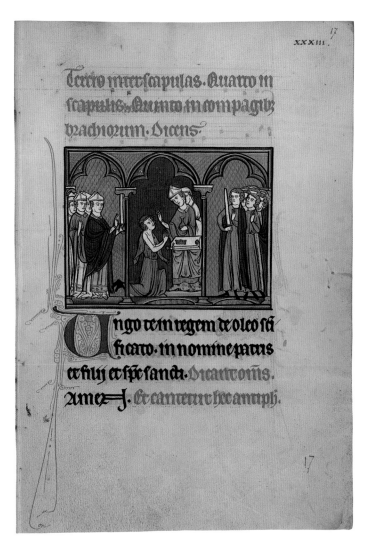

15

Coronation Ordinal of 1250

Département des Manuscrits, Lat. 1246, fol. 17

*Parchment; IV + 44 + 1 fols.; 215 × 150 mm. Bound
in parchment. Paris, mid-13th century. Vie de Saint-
Denis and Guines workshops. Probably became
part of the royal collections in the 16th century.*

The fifteen miniatures of the coronation
ordinal of 1250 present the oldest known
iconographic cycle showing the coronation
of a French king–no less than Saint Louis–
at the moment when the ritual had virtually
assumed the definitive form it was to retain
until the coronation of Charles X in 1825.

The coronation ceremony traditionally
took place in the cathedral of Reims in the
presence of the ecclesiastic and lay peers of
the realm. The archbishop of Reims officiat-
ed, assisted by the abbot of Saint-Remi of
Reims, whose abbey kept the Holy Ampulla,
and by the abbot of Saint-Denis, who

brought with him for the occasion the regalia
or insignia of royalty which were conserved
by his abbey. The anointment affirmed the
supremacy (by divine right) of the *Very
Christian King* over the other monarchs of the
Occident and invested the person of the king
with a quasi-priestly character.

The progress of the ceremony as proposed by this coronation ordinal produced
in Paris in the middle of the 13th century is
pictured as follows: The archbishop of Reims
greets the monarch at the entrance of his
cathedral. He seats him on a high platform,
visible to all, in the center of the nave (fol. 1).
A procession conducted by the abbot of
Saint-Remi then brings forth the Holy
Ampulla, ceremoniously displayed under a
silken canopy (fol. 4). The king swears several
oaths promising to protect the church in its
properties and its persons. He then receives
the chivalric insignia which the abbot of
Saint-Denis had laid upon the altar: silken
breeches woven with golden fleurs-de-lis, the
gold spurs (fol. 16), and the sword. Next, the
ceremony of anointment made the king of
France, the Lord's anointed, in reference to
the Old Testament kings, a miracle-working
king endowed with the power to cure scrofula. With a golden needle the archbishop
extracts a small amount of holy oil from the
Holy Ampulla and performs seven anoint-
ments on the body of the king, simply clad in
a red silken tunic cut open in front and
back, fastened by silver clasps (fol. 17). The
tunic is refastened and the *grand chambellan*
helps him slip on the hyacinth-colored dalmatic (fol. 26). He receives the insignia of his
power: the ring, the scepter in the right
hand, and the hand of justice in the left (fol.
28). Then the king is ready for the coronation
ceremony. The great crown, brought from the
abbey of Saint-Denis, is set on the king's
head in a ritual requiring the hands of the
archbishop and the peers. All respectfully
give him the kiss of peace and fidelity (fol.
26). The king then takes communion in both
forms. The great crown is replaced with a
smaller one. Finally, preceded by the *grand
connétable* who holds the sword, the king
returns to the palace for the banquet (fol. 42).

It is not known for whom this manuscript
was made, but it probably entered the royal

collections in the 16th century. It is known, however, that it was consulted for the coronations of Francis I and Henry IV.

Marie-Hélène Tesnière

Robert Branner, *Manuscript Painting in Paris During the Reign of Saint Louis* (Berkeley, 1977), esp. 211, 225 and figs. 133, 135, 249C. Richard A. Jackson, *Vive le Roi! A History of the French Coronation Ceremony from Charles V to Charles X* (Chapel Hill, N.C., 1984). Richard A. Jackson, "Les 'Ordines' des couronnements royaux au moyen-âge," in *Le sacre des rois* (Paris, 1985), 63–74. Jacques Le Goff, "Reims, ville du sacre," in *Les lieux de mémoire*, ed. Pierre Nora, vol. 2, *La Nation* (Paris, 1986), 115–23. Danielle Gaborit-Chopin, *Regalia: Les instruments du sacre des rois de France; Les "honneurs de Charlemagne"* exhibition at the Musée du Louvre, Oct. 14, 1987–Jan. 11, 1988 (Paris, 1987). Richard A. Jackson, "Manuscripts, Texts, and Enigmas of Medieval French Coronation," *Viator* 23 (1992): 35–71, esp. 56–58.

16
Latin Psalter with the Arms of France and Castile
Département des Manuscrits, Lat. 10434, fols. 13v–14 and binding, fore-edge, top (detail)

Parchment; 185 fols.; 213 × 151 mm. Bound in green morocco with gilt tooling, 18th century; trace of red velvet(?) on the inside covers. Paris, mid-13th century. According to Branner, this artist belongs to the workshop of Dominican Bibles moralisées *from Toledo and Oxford. The arms of France and Castile painted on the edges are contemporary with the manuscript; this could be the Psalter with the arms of France and Castile which during the reign of Charles V was reserved at Saint-Germain-en-Laye (Deslisle,* Recherches sur la librairie de Charles V, *vol. 2 [Paris, 1907], no. 48). According to a note (fol. 184v) dated 1426, this Psalter seems to have been lent by a London priest to a Carthusian brother. On the upper inside cover is the engraved bookplate of a Venetian bookseller, Amadeo Svajer (d. 1792); stamp of the Bibliothèque Nationale during the Revolution (1792–1801) on fol. 9.*

The only prayer book available to lay persons in the 13th century was the Psalter. It was one of the first books one learned how to read. A Psalter in the University Library of Leiden (MS 313) was known to have been used by Saint Louis to learn his alphabet. The pictorial summary of the Old and New Testaments by which the Psalter was frequently introduced after the calendar made it an ideal manual for religious instruction.

The arms of France and Castile on the edges of this Psalter attest to its royal origin (gold fleurs-de-lis on azure background and gold castles on red background, in a diamond-patterned border). Indeed, these were the arms of Blanche of Castile, Saint Louis's mother. The same motif is found on the edges of at least two manuscripts believed to have been donated by Saint Louis, one to the Sainte-Chapelle (Gospels of the Sainte-Chapelle, Lat. 8851) and the other to the royal abbey of Saint-Corneille de Compiègne (Missal, Lat. 18009). According to abbé Leroquais, the calendar of this manuscript may link it to the church of Saint-Germain l'Auxerrois, a royal parish since Philip Augustus built the castle of the Louvre. Yet it is also known that Charles V kept a Psalter at

61

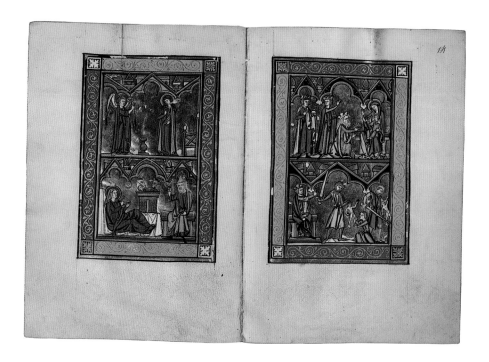

Saint-Germain-en-Laye (the same patron saint) with the arms of France and Castile. If that was the manuscript displayed here–which is very likely–would it not rather have been given directly by Saint Louis to the chapel of Saint-Germain-en-Laye, in the château of which he was so fond? Between 1230 and 1238, Saint Louis built this beautiful Gothic chapel, whose boss in the apse vault displays one of his earliest known portraits. The actual Psalter is preceded by a pictorial summary of eight leaves which presents sixteen remarkable paintings that retrace the story of the Creation and the life of Christ from the fall of the angels to the Last Judgment (fols. 13v-14: the Annunciation, the Nativity, Epiphany, the Massacre of the Innocents). Especially noteworthy are the two scenes from the life of Saint John the Baptist (fol. 12), reflecting Louis's veneration for the saint whose relics he had taken to the holy chapel at Saint-Germain. The fact that the chapel was dedicated to Saint John the Baptist serves to reinforce the link between this Psalter and Saint-Germain-en-Laye.

These paintings are typical of Parisian illumination in the mid-13th century. The borders of gilt foliated scrolls on blue and salmon-rose background are still Romanesque. The superimposed registers of biblical scenes, the thick layers of gold, the distinct blue and red ocher colors, and the schematic designs underscored by a thick black line are all inspired by the technique used in stained glass windows. The Psalter proper, with its litanies and its prayers, is decorated with seven historiated initials for the days of the week, and with filigree and endline ornament delightful in its refinement and inventiveness.

The turbulent life of this manuscript can be followed episodically. By 1426 it had come into the hands of a certain Robertus Lucas, a London priest, who lent it to one of his friends, a Carthusian monk at the Charter House of the Salutation of the Blessed Virgin Mary in London. In the 18th century it was in the possession of a Venetian bookseller, Amadeo Svajer. The library of San Marco in Venice (1794) purchased a major part of his manuscript collection. This Psalter was very likely sent in 1797 from Italy to France and to the Bibliothèque Nationale by Monge and Berthollet, "Commissaire de la République."

Marie-Hélène Tesnière

Léopold Delisle, *Le Cabinet des Manuscrits de la Bibliothèque Impériale*, vol. 1 (Paris, 1868), 6–10. Carol Frati, *Dizionario Bio-bibliografico dei Bibliotecari e Bibliofili italiani dal sec. XIV al XIX...* (Florence, 1934), 528–29. Chanoine Victor Leroquais, *Les Psautiers manuscrits latins des bibliothèques publiques de France*, vol. 2 (Mâcon, 1940–1941), 95–97, no. 327. *Les manuscrits à peintures en France du XIIIe au XVIe siècle*, exhibition at the Bibliothèque Nationale (Paris, 1955), 12, no. 10. Jean Porcher, *L'enluminure française* (Paris, 1959), 45–46, pl. XLIV. *Le livre*, exhibition at the Bibliothèque Nationale (Paris, 1972), 121, no. 362. Robert Branner, *Manuscript Painting in Paris during the Reign of Saint Louis...* (Berkeley, 1977), 60, 65, 208, fig. 101

17
French Bible of Acre
Bibliothèque de l'Arsenal, MS 5211 Rés.,
fol. 4

Parchment; 368 fols.; 285 × 200 mm. Bound in red morocco with gilt fillets (18th century). Acre, third quarter of the 13th century. Probably made for Saint Louis, king of France, ca. 1250–1254; in the 15th century, it belonged to a bibliophile from Dauphiné, Louis de Grolée, abbot of Bonnevaux and of Saint-Pierre in Vienna; in the 18th century, it was part of the collection of Antoine René d'Argenson, marquis de Paulmy.

The history of French biblical translation is long and complicated. It began in the 12th century in northern France and in England with abridged versions, in verse, of biblical tales. About the year 1200, prose translations were made of certain books of the Bible, leading to what today is called the "Bible of the 13th Century." Scholars disagree on whether it was composed in the second quarter or at the end of the 13th century. Whatever the case, the second half of the 13th century appears to have been the critical period for the circulation of a more or less complete French translation. The text of this Bible from Acre is an abridged compilation, inspired by Pierre Comestor, which provides testimony of the various stages in the development of a Bible in French. That it circulated to a certain degree is known from evidence in other manuscripts, but it was not known to those who composed the Bible of the 13th Century and it had no direct successors.

Copied in the Holy Land around 1250–1254, the "Bible française de Saint-Jean d'Acre" not only provides an interesting example of biblical translation but is also probably the oldest and most beautiful illuminated manuscript to come out of the Latin Kingdom of Jerusalem. Acre, a port on the Palestine coast, was conquered by the crusaders in 1104, lost, and then retaken by Richard the Lion-Hearted and Philip Augustus in 1191. After the loss of Jerusalem in 1187, it became the de facto capital of the Latin Kingdom and the Patriarchal See. Pilgrims and merchants passed through it,

63

el comence
ment

AU COMENCEMENT

crea deu le ciel ⁊ la terre. La
terre estoit vaine ⁊ vuide. ⁊
tenebres estoient sur la face
del abisme. ⁊ li esperiz de deu
estoit porte sur les aigues.
E deu dist. Soit faite lumi
naire. E fu faite. E deu vit
le luminaire que il estoit
bon. ⁊ departi la lumiere des
tenebres. Lors apela la lumie
re ior. ⁊ les tenebres nuit.
E vespres ⁊ matin. est faiz
un ior. E deu dist. Soit faiz
li firmamenz en mi les ai
gues. ⁊ departe les aigues des
aigues. Donc fist deu le fir
mament. ⁊ departi les aigues
qui estoient desouz le firma
ment. de celes qui estoient
sur le firmament. ⁊ ensi est
fait. E apela le firmament
ciel. E fait est vespres ⁊ ma
tin le segunt ior. Lors dist
deu. Soient assemblees les ai
gues qui sunt desouz le firma
ment en un leu. ⁊ aparoisse
la sechere. ⁊ ensi est fait. E deu
apela la sechere la terre. ⁊ les
assemblees des aigues apela
mers. Donc vit deu que bon
estoit. ⁊ dist. Germe la terre
herbe verdoiant. ⁊ faisant se
mence. ⁊ arbres faisanz fruiz
selonc lor maniere. dont quel
soit la semence en soi meisme
sur terre. E ensi est fait.
Adonques mist fors la terre
herbe verdoiant. ⁊ semence
portant selonc sa maniere.
⁊ arbres fruiz faisanz. Lors
vit deu que bon estoit. E fait
est vespres ⁊ matin le tiers
ior. E deu dist. Soient fait
luminaire el firmament dou
ciel. ⁊ departent le ior de la
nuit. ⁊ soient en signes. ⁊
tens. ⁊ iors. ⁊ ans. ⁊ luisent
el firmament. et enluminent
la terre. E ensi est fait. Donc
fist deu deus granz luminai
res. Le plus grant luisist
au ior. ⁊ le meindre a la nuit
⁊ les esteiles. ⁊ les mist el fir
mament por enluminer la
terre. ⁊ por departir la lumie
re des tenebres. E vit deu q̄
bon estoit. E vespre ⁊ matin
est fait li quarz iors. Adonqs

and it became the scene of a flourishing commercial and cosmopolitan society. Significant cultural activity seems to have been stimulated by European nobles, the church, and the religious orders, as well as by Christians from the East. Saint Louis sojourned at Acre a number of times between 1250 and 1254, and the scriptorium there may have been founded under his patronage. Whatever the case, the workshop has been credited with some ten manuscripts in an impressively homogeneous style produced between 1250 and 1291.

Contemporaneous with Saint Louis's stay in Acre, this Bible was probably commissioned by the king. Richly decorated, it includes twenty miniatures, for the most part full pages, which illustrate each of the twenty books of the Old Testament. Each miniature is composed of a number of small scenes in a decorative and highly varied arrangement much favored in the 13th century. Two different artistic styles are clearly evident: one close to contemporary Parisian work, the other obviously influenced by Byzantine art of the 9th and 10th centuries. The painter's keen sense of observation, seen in the illuminated page illustrating Genesis (fol. 3v), is reflected in the depiction of Saracen dress and of local animals such as camels. There seems to be a definite affinity between the miniatures in the French Bible of Acre and the frescoes of Saint Francis of Assisi in the chapel of Kalenderhane Camii in Constantinople, suggesting that the artist also worked in that city. Possibly the king took this Bible back to France with him.

By the late 15th century, the manuscript belonged to Louis de Grolée, abbot of Bonnevaux and of Saint-Pierre of Vienna, who had his arms painted on the first leaf. Four manuscripts owned by this bibliophile from the Dauphiné region came to the Bibliothèque de l'Arsenal through the intermediary of the marquis de Paulmy, the library's founder in the 18th century.

Danielle Muzerelle

S. Berger, *La Bible française au moyen-âge* (Paris, 1884). H. Martin and P. Lauer, *Les principaux manuscrits à peintures de la Bibliothèque de l'Arsenal à Paris* (Paris, 1929). H. Buchthal, *Miniature Painting in the Latin Kingdom of Jerusalem* (Oxford, 1957). J. Folda, *Crusader Manuscript Illumination at Saint-Jean d'Acre, 1275–1291* (Princeton, 1976). C. L. Striker and Y. Dogan Kuban, "Work at Kalenderhane Camii in Istambul," *Dumbarton Oaks Papers* 22 (1968) and 25 (1971). *Trésors de la Bibliothèque de l'Arsenal,* exhibition at the Bibliothèque de l'Arsenal (Paris, 1980), no. 87. *Les Bibles en français: Histoire illustrée du moyen-âge à nos jours,* ed. P. M. Bogaert (Turnhout, 1991). M. Lefèvre and D. Muzerelle, "La bibliothèque du marquis de Paulmy," in *Histoire des bibliothèques françaises,* vol. 3, *Les bibliothèques de l'Ancien Régime, 1530–1789,* ed. Claude Jolly (Paris, 1988), 302–15.

65

18

TIBAUT

Roman de la poire

(Romance of the pear)

Département des Manuscrits, Fr. 2186,

fols. 8v–9

*Parchment; II + 83 + 1 fols.; 206 × 135 mm. Paris,
ca. 1250–1260. Illustrated in the workshop of the so-
called Bari Master. From the collection of Cardinal
Mazarin (Mazarin 963); purchased by the
Bibliothèque Royale in 1668.*

A truly exquisite little Psalter dedicated to
love, this manuscript is supposed to have
been offered to a princess of royal blood
known as Agnès in Paris about 1250–1260.
The identical arms which she and the knight
bear on their *bliaud* (azur studded with gold-
en fleurs-de-lis, crossed with gilt bands decorated in red diamond shapes) have retained
their mystery to the present day. And mystery
also surrounds the author of this long poem,
who is known only by his first name, Tibaut.

The *Roman de la poire* is a long allegorization of a man's falling in love with his lady. They share a pear together, giving the story its name. The romance blends a delightful lyric song, refrains, acrostics, enigmas, and paintings that breathe life into the banality of the central theme. The romance was largely inspired by the first part of the *Roman de la rose* by Guillaume de Lorris. The lover utters in a sigh ("Han! Nes!") the name of his lady, Agnès. In another allusion toward the end of the text, the medieval script of the phrase *tua sit* (Let her be thine) mirrors the name of the lover, Tibaut. The succession of embellished initials in the refrains composes the names of the three protagonists of this courtly poem: ANNES–TIBAUT–AMORS.

The iconographical cycle (nine full-page illuminated paintings, which was unusual for the period, and eighteen historiated initials) complete the understanding of the text. They clearly demonstrate the relationship between the courtly service undertaken by the lover for his lady and the feudal service which the knight owed his lord. The prologue of the *Roman* therefore takes the form of a long oath of fidelity by the lover to his lady. She receives him as a vassal and liege man (ll. 14–15, 89–90); he places his hands, joined, in hers (fol. 1). This is the traditional *immixtio manuum* for homage. She gives him next the *osculum*, the kiss on the mouth (fol. 4v). Then comes the double investiture: that of action as symbolized by the ring (l. 88) and that of feoffment symbolized by veil and lance (ll. 186–91). The second investiture is represented here (fol. 8v): the lady entrusts the knight with the veil that he will wear on his helmet, and with the standard that will wave from his lance on his departure for the tournament against the slanderers, the *losengiers*:

. . . s'ai mis en votre lance
qui n'est pas entamee cest panon qui balance.
Seur gent mal renommee ferez sanz
    demorance!
Amis, cest cuevrechief qui est biax et plesanz
portez sur vostre chief: contre les mesdisanz,
cui Diex envoit meschief, s'aidiez as fins amanz!

(I have attached to your virgin lance this fluttering standard. Strike without hesitation those individuals of evil fame! Wear on your helmet this fine and beautiful veil. In opposing the slanderers—may God call down curses upon them!—give succor to elegant lovers!)

Unusually, the manuscript has retained its original binding decorated with cold-stamped ornaments. It belonged in the 17th century to Cardinal Mazarin (1602–1661), who had one of the largest libraries in Europe (40,000 printed volumes); his collection of 2,156 manuscripts was bought by the Bibliothèque Royale in 1668.

Marie-Hélène Tesnière

Hans Robert Jauss, "Entstehung und Strukturwandel der Allegorie Dichtung," in *La littérature didactique, allégorique et satirique: Grundriss der romanischen Literaturen des Mittelalters*, vol. 6, no. 1 (Heidelberg, 1968), 235–36, and no. 2 (Heidelberg, 1970), no. 4708. M. Alison Stones, "Secular Manuscript Illumination in France," in *Medieval Manuscripts and Textual Criticism* (Chapel Hill, 1976), 83–102. Robert Branner, *Manuscript Painting in Paris during the Reign of Saint Louis: A Study of Styles* (Berkeley, 1977), 102–06, figs. 287 and 289. Christiane Marcello-Nizia, ed., *Le Roman de la poire by Tibaut* (Paris, 1984). Marie-Hélène Tesnière, review of the preceding book in *Bibliothèque de l'Ecole des Chartes* 145 (1987): 451–53.

19

Breviary of Philip the Fair

Département des Manuscrits, Lat. 1023,
fol. 7v

*Parchment; II + 577 + III fols.; 205 × 125 mm.
Paris, late 13th century. Bound in red shagreen, 19th
century. Made for Philip the Fair; was in the
library of Charles V in the keep of the château de
Vincennes.*

Léopold Delisle deserves credit for having
determined more than a century ago the
royal origin of this precious manuscript by
identifying it with a breviary that followed
the use (local rites) of Paris "très bien escript
et ystorié" (very well written and decorated)
and that was described in an inventory of
King Charles V's possessions at the Château
de Vincennes in 1380. At that date, the volume was still in a binding with the arms of
France. The image of a king praying to the
Virgin in the first initial of the manuscript
(fol. 8) confirms the royal destination of this
manuscript. The special feasts noted in the
calendar (dedication of the Sainte Chapelle,
commemoration of the crusaders who died
in Egypt, the death of Philip Augustus) clearly indicate an association with a descendent
of Saint Louis who Delisle suggested was
Philip IV the Fair. We know from an
accounting of 1296 that Philip the Fair
directed that the sum of 107 *livres tournois* be
paid for the making of a breviary. The painted decoration fits perfectly with this date.
The same style appears in the first illustration of a copy of Gratian's *Decretales* in the
municipal library in Tours, a manuscript

bought in 1288 from the Parisian illuminator
Honoré. Furthermore, it is known from the
royal account of 1296 cited above that Master
Honoré was working at that date on the decoration of the king's books. The breviary
artist's technique is evident once again in a
Somme le roi in the British Library (Add.
54180), a manuscript which also leads us back
to Philip the Fair's entourage, since the
author of this moral compilation, Brother
Laurent, was the king's confessor.

The sole large painting in the breviary
(fol. 7v) depicts, on two registers, the anointing of David and the combat of David and
Goliath. It displays certain stylistic similarities to works painted and illuminated for the
English court about the same period
(Westminster retable, Psalter of Alfonso). The
extraordinary linear refinement, identical in
the 164 ornamented initials illustrating the
body of the breviary, constitutes the culmination of the elegant Gothic graphic style so
characteristic of the Paris School in the second half of the 13th century.

François Avril

L. Delisle, *Notice de douze livres royaux du XIIIe et du XIVe siè-
cles* (Paris, 1902), 57–63. L. Delisle, *Recherches sur la librairie de
Charles V* (Paris, 1907), 1: 178–181 and 2: 25, n. 128. G. Vitztum,
*Die Pariser Miniaturmalerei von der Zeit des hl. Ludwig bis zu
Philipp von Valois* (Leipzig, 1907), 39–46, pls. VII–VIII. V.
Leroquais, *Les bréviaires manuscrits des bibliothèques de France*
(Paris, 1934), 3: 465–75, pls. XII–XVII. J. Porcher, *Les manuscrits
à peintures en France du XIIIe au XVIe siècle* (Paris, 1955), 21, no.
29. E. G. Millar, *An Illuminated Manuscript of "La Somme le
Roy" attributed to the Parisian Miniaturist Honoré* (Oxford, 1953).
La librairie de Charles V, exhibition at the Bibliothèque
Nationale (Paris, 1968), 64, no. 128.

20

GOSSOUIN DE METZ

Image du Monde

(Picture of the world)

Département des Manuscrits, Fr. 574,

fols. 27v–28

Parchment; VI + 142 + IV fols.; 388 × 260 mm.
Bound in marbled calf, on the spine the arms of
Charles X; gilt edges bearing traces of the arms of
the House of Revel (six horizontal bands in azur
and gold). Paris, ca. 1315–1320. Illustrated by the
Master of the Roman de Fauvel (BNF Fr. 146),
Geoffroy de Saint-Léger. Written and illuminated
for Guillaume Flote, lord of Revel and chancelier
de France (ex libris on fol. VIv), later in the posses-
sion of Duke Jean de Berry (d. 1416), who affixed
his signature as owner (fols. VI, 139v, 141); described
in the inventories of 1402 and 1416, when it still had
silver clasps with the arms of the house of Revel. In
1416 it was valued at 12 livres and 10 sous tournois,
and was given to the daughter of the duke, Marie
de Berry, duchess of Bourbonnais. On fol. 141, a
note concerning ownership reads: "Dominique de
Bourgoingne, philozophe du Thoison d'or, roy de
Frise et referendaire de l'Apocalipse" with the
motto "J'ay quis honneur" and a D *and an* M *inter-*
twined in a love knot. On fol. 142 is a bouquet of
flowers in a jar with the motto "Tou se me fait leson
venir" and the letter G. *Acquired by the*
Bibliothèque Nationale in the 16th century
(Fontainebleau 527).

The 13th century, a century of order and
learning, saw the development of the great
Latin encyclopedias (by Barthélemy
l'Anglais, Thomas de Cantimpré, Vincent de
Beauvais), vast compilations of knowledge,
with commentaries, moral reflections, and
arrangement according to a Christian
scheme of things, starting with God and
finishing with the description of nature. But
laymen unfamiliar with Latin were also interested in the philosophy of nature. Gossouin
de Metz's *Image du Monde* apparently is the
oldest encyclopedic treatise written in a vernacular language. Composed in verse in the
dialect of Lorraine, it was written in 1246 for
Saint Louis's brother Robert d'Artois, who
wanted to know how the world had been
"constructed."

The manuscript displayed here gives a
prose version, written in the late 13th or early
14th century. The author divided his treatise
into three parts: God and human intelligence; nature and the elements of the cos-
mos; and, finally, physical phenomena and
astronomy. *Clergie* ("scholarship"), claimed
the author, henceforth reigned in Paris the
way it once reigned in Athens. The king
could rightfully be proud of this but was
advised to remain vigilant to ensure that
clergie survives. Clergie was in some ways a
synonym for culture in the Middle Ages. By
learning the seven liberal arts—Grammar,
Logic, Rhetoric, Arithmetic, Geometry, Music,
and Astronomy—men learned the "science de
clergie." It was by this system of classification
that knowledge was transmitted in medieval
schools. After Grammar, which is "the gateway to knowledge" since it governs speech,
comes Logic. Logic, represented here by a
group of clerics and monks in discussion
(fol. 27v), establishes truth and falsehood and
allows us to distinguish good from evil.
Rhetoric, which organizes speech, provides
the foundations for the laws of the kingdom,
and is represented here by the king and his
chancelier, who holds a sealed parchment in
his hand (fol. 27v). Arithmetic allows us to
understand the world in which everything is
number; here a cleric points to some figures
on a disc representing the world (fol. 28).

In both content and illustration, this manuscript is perfectly representative of the cultivation that prevailed in the king's entourage and administration in the first half of
the 14th century. The manuscript was illustrated with very fine paintings around
1315–1320 by the Master of the Roman de

Fauvel, for Guillaume Flote, one of the most influential counselors at the royal court from Louis X to Charles V, and chancelier of France between 1338 and 1348. The Master of the Roman de Fauvel, whom François Avril has identified as a *libraire* (copyist) named Geoffroy de Saint-Léger, was the accredited illuminator to the king's aristocratic entourage. This manuscript's illustration was then copied about 1320–1330, probably for the king of France (BNF Fr. 25344).

The manuscript subsequently belonged to Duke Jean de Berry, who kept it among his most precious manuscripts in his château at Mehun-sur-Yèvre. He affixed his signature to three pages. At his death in 1416, the manuscript passed with forty of the duke's most beautiful manuscripts to his daughter, Marie de Berry, duchess of Bourbonnais. It turned up again about the middle of the century in the hands of a certain "Dominique de Bourgoigne, philosophe du Toison d'or" (Dominic of Burgundy, sage of the Golden Fleece). Then in Bruges the libraire Jean le Clerc had it copied in 1464. William Caxton would use that copy (British Library Royal 19 A IX) for his English translation. The manuscript shown here became part of the French royal collection in the 16th century.

Marie-Hélène Tesnière

Jules Guiffrey, *Inventaires de Jean duc de Berry (1401–1416)* (Paris, 1894), 235–36, no. 908; 135, no. 1064; 237, no. 485. Léopold Delisle, *Le Cabinet des Manuscrits de la Bibliothèque Impériale*, vol. 1 (Paris, 1868), 58, 66, 167. O. H. Prior, *L'Image du monde de maître Gossouin: Rédaction en prose, texte du manuscrit de la Bibliothèque Nationale, Fonds Français 574, avec corrections d'après d'autres manuscrits, notes et introduction...* (Lausanne, 1913). Raymond Cazelles, *La société politique et la crise de la royauté sous Philippe de Valois* (Paris, 1958), esp. 92. *Le Roman de Fauvel in the Edition of Messire Chaillou de Pesstain: A Reproduction in Facsimilé of the Complete Manuscript, Paris, Bibliothèque Nationale, Fonds Français 146*, with an introduction by Edward H. Roesner, François Avril, and Nancy Freeman Regalado (New York, 1990), 45–48. M. T. Gousset and R. M. Rouse, *Richard et Jeanne de Montbaston, libraires parisiens du second quart du XIVe siècle* (chap. 4 about the collaborators of Richard and Jeanne de Montbaston), forthcoming.

21

FRÈRE LAURENT

La Somme le Roi (The royal summa)
Bibliothèque de l'Arsenal, MS 6329, fol. 2

*Parchment; 213 fols.; 215 × 150 mm. Northern
France, 1311. Velvet binding of the 18th century, with
remnants of medieval embroidered cloth on the
boards. Made for Countess Jeanne d'Eu and de
Guines (d. 1330); belonged in the 15th century to
Jacques d'Armagnac, duke of Nemours (d. 1477);
was in Charles A. Picard's collection, which was
sold in 1780 to Antoine René de Voyer d'Argenson,
marquis of Paulmy, founder of the Bibliothèque
de l'Arsenal.*

In 1279–1280, at the request of King Philip
the Bold, Friar Laurent, a Dominican from
Orléans who was prior of the convent of
Saint-Jacques in Paris and the king's confessor, composed a manual of moral instruction.
This book of vices and virtues is known as
La Somme le Roi. The author drew his inspiration in great measure from earlier texts,
and in particular from a treatise on vices and
virtues entitled *Miroir du monde* (Mirror of
the world). *La Somme le Roi* achieved great
success and a wide circulation. This is attested by the numerous translations in diverse
languages and dialects and by the consider-

able number of manuscripts which have survived. Frequently, they were ornately illuminated by a cycle of fifteen miniatures whose
subjects never varied. The colophon of this
manuscript states that Lambert le Petit
copied it in 1311 at the request of Countess
Jeanne d'Eu and de Guines, widow of Jean
de Brienne, who was killed at the battle of
Courtrai in 1302.

The manual is lavishly illustrated. In addition to the usual fifteen full-page miniatures
(lacking only the leaf depicting the garden of
virtues), there are at the front five miniatures
depicting the lives of Christ and the Virgin;
especially noteworthy is a portrait of the
countess kneeling before the Virgin (fol. IV),
possibly one of the first medieval portraits.
The Eu-Guines family arms are visible in the
corners. The rich decoration is enhanced by
numerous historiated initials and borders of
floral scrollwork dotted with animals, monsters, and grotesque figures. The manuscript's style links it to the region of Amiens
or Arras.

In the 15th century the manuscript
belonged to the famous bibliophile Jacques
d'Armagnac, duke of Nemours, whose autograph ex libris appears on folio 214: "This
book of vices and virtues belongs to the duke
of Nemours, count de la Marche, Jacques. For
Carlat." After he was executed for high treason in 1477 in the reign of Louis XI, his
property was seized and his manuscripts,
especially those kept in the castle of Carlat,
were given to his accusers. By the 18th century the manuscript was owned by Charles
Adrien Picard, from whom the marquis of
Paulmy obtained it.

Danielle Muzerelle

H. Martin and P. Lauer, *Les principaux manuscrits à peintures de
la Bibliothèque de l'Arsenal à Paris* (Paris, 1929). E. Brayer, "'La
Somme le Roi' de Frère Laurent," in *Positions des thèses de
l'Ecole des Chartes* (Paris, 1940), pp. 27–35. E. G. Miller, *An
Illuminated Manuscript of "La Somme le Roi"* (Oxford, 1953).
L'art et la cour, exhibition at the National Gallery of Canada
(Ottawa, 1972), no. 16. *Trésors de la Bibliothèque de l'Arsenal*,
exhibition at the Bibliothèque de l'Arsenal (Paris, 1980), no.
90. S. Blackman, "The Manuscripts and Patronage of Jacques
d'Armagnac" (Ph.D. diss., University of Pittsburgh, 1993). M.
Lefèvre and D. Muzerelle, *La bibliothèque du marquis de
Paulmy*, in *Histoire des bibliothèques françaises*, vol. 3, *Les bibliothèques de l'Ancien Régime, 1530–1789*, ed. Claude Jolly (Paris,
1988), 302–15.

22

Liber de Kalila et Dimna
(Book of Kalila and Dimna),
translated from Spanish into Latin
by Raymond de Béziers
Département des Manuscrits, Lat. 8504,
fol. IV

*Parchment; III + a-b + 168 + IV fols.; 278 × 187
mm. Offered to Philip the Fair on June 3, 1313,
probably by the chancellor of France, Pierre de
Latilly, on the occasion of the conferring of knight-
hood on Philip's sons. Belonged in the 16th century
to Cardinal Georges d'Amboise (shelfmark D8 of
his library) and then to Cardinal Mazarin, before
entering the royal collection in 1668.*

Having learned that there were mountains in
India where plants grew endowed with the
power of resuscitating the dead, Burzoe,
physician of the 6th-century king of Persia,
Khursaw, set out to find them. Actually, the
plants were only a symbolic image to designate a book containing precepts of wisdom
capable of arousing the ignorant. This book
in Sanskrit, *Pantchatantra*, was a collection
of Indian fables intended for the moral education of princes. It dramatized the lessons
with animals; two jackals were cast in the
roles of the heroes Karataka (who would
become Kalila) and Damanaka (Dimna). The
book was translated from Sanskrit into
Pehlevi, from Pehlevi into Arabic, and finally
from Arabic into Castilian in the mid-13th
century in Toledo for the infante of Spain,
Alphonse the Wise.

   At the request of Queen Jeanne de
Navarre, wife of Philip IV the Fair, Raymond
de Béziers undertook to translate a copy of
the Spanish text which had been brought to
Paris. He translated the text into Latin and
complemented it with a Latin translation by
Jean de Capoue, which probably had come
to his attention in the meantime. He inserted
into the text aphorisms and maxims, under-
lined in red, which he drew from a variety of
ancient and Christian poets. In so doing he
made an interesting attempt to juxtapose, if
not to assimilate, two sources of wisdom
from two cultures, the Oriental and the
classical.

73

After the death of his patroness in 1305, Raymond de Béziers offered this royal book (intended for the royal princes) to the "royal majesty of the fleur-de-lis" (*liliate regie majestati*), Philip the Fair and his children, for Pentecost on June 3, 1313. This coincided with the entertainments held to celebrate the knighting of the king's son, Louis de Navarre. The festivities are represented at the front of the volume by five miniatures glued onto the manuscript. At the beginning of the prologue (fol. iv), the royal family is represented by a veritable heraldic portrait, with each of the participants identifiable by the arms decorating their clothing. In the center, King Philip the Fair is seated on his throne. Seated on his left are his eldest son, Louis, king of Navarre, the future Louis X (the Quarrelsome), who would succeed him in 1315, and Philip's uncle Charles, count of Valois. Seated on his right are his daughter, Isabelle, queen of England, wife of Edward II, and his two younger sons: Philip, the future Philip V (the Tall), and Charles, the future Charles IV (the Fair). As fate would have it, all the kings who would rule France from 1315 to 1328 are shown here, as well as the woman who in a sense was the cause of the Hundred Years War—Isabelle, mother of the future Edward III of England.

It is likely that this manuscript was a presentation copy offered to the king himself through the intermediary of the chancellor of France, Pierre de Latilly. The manuscript belonged in the 16th century to Cardinal Georges d'Amboise (1460–1510) and in the following century to Cardinal Mazarin (1602–1661) before entering the royal collection in 1668.

Marie-Hélène Tesnière

Léopold Hervieux, *Les fabulistes latins depuis le siècle d'Auguste jusqu'à la fin du Moyen Age*, vol. 5, *Jean de Capoue et ses dérivés* (Paris, 1899), 379–775. Léopold Delisle, review of preceding book in *Journal des savants* 1898: 158–73. Gaston Paris, "Raimond de Béziers: Traducteur et compilateur," in *Histoire littéraire de la France*, vol. 33 (Paris, 1906), 191–253. Charles Samaran and Marie-Louis Concasty, "Christophe Auer: Copiste de grec et de latin au XVIe siècle," in *Scriptorium* 23 (1969): 212. Charles Samaran and Robert Marichal, *Catalogue des manuscrits en écriture latine portant des indications de date, de lieu ou de copiste...*, vol. 3 (Paris, 1974), 59 and pl. LXXXVII. Pascale Bourgain, "Les contes," in *Mise en page et mise en texte du livre manuscrit*, ed. Henri-Jean Martin and Jean Vezin (Paris, 1990), 163–64.

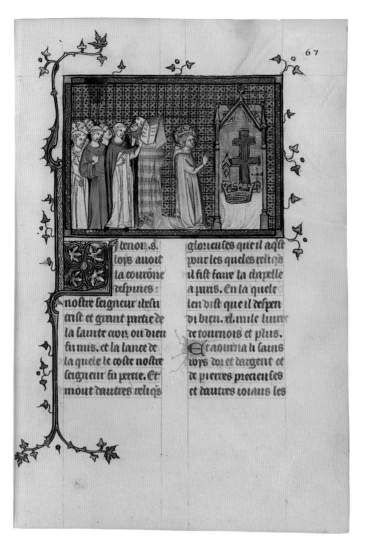

23

GUILLAUME DE SAINT-PATHUS
Vie et miracles de Saint Louis
(Life and miracles of Saint Louis)
Département des Manuscrits, Fr. 5716,
pp. 62–63

*Parchment; 666 pp.; 225 × 150 mm. Bound in dark
green morocco with the monogram of Roger de
Gaignières, late 17th–early 18th century. Paris, ca.
1330–1340. Until 1424, part of the library assembled
by Charles V in the Louvre. Owned by Roger de
Gaignières; acquired for the Bibliothèque Royale in
1733 with the manuscripts of Châtre de Cangé.*

This text is the French translation of a lost
Latin original used in the canonization proceedings of the saintly King Louis. It was
composed for Blanche of France, Saint
Louis's daughter, who died in 1320 in the
Franciscan convent of Lourcine, which she
had founded in the Faubourg Saint Marcel.

As early as 1368, this copy figured among
the books Charles V brought together in one

of the towers of the Louvre. Its presence
there can be documented until 1424, when
the Royal Library was purchased en bloc by
John of Lancaster, duke of Bedford. He at
that time was regent of France for his
nephew Henry VI, who then held Paris.

The manuscript's ninety illustrations are
divided into two distinct series: the first
relates to the king's edifying actions; the second, beginning with folio 285, consists of
sixty-five supplementary miniatures illustrating the miracles that occurred at the sovereigns' tomb in the abbey of Saint-Denis.
Drawn with a sharp line and standing out in
vivid colors on conventional checkered backgrounds, these scenes date from 1320–1340 at
the earliest. This eliminates the possibility
that the manuscript was Blanche's personal
copy, as was long thought.

The painter of these miniatures was obviously a contemporary of the famous Jean
Pucelle, whose hand is evident in many manuscripts that can be dated to the second
quarter of the 14th century. Among them are
the final illustrations of the Hours of Jeanne
de Navarre (BNF NAL 3145), one of the most
beautiful works of court illumination from
this period. The artist is probably an illuminator named Mahiet, who about 1323–1326
worked under Pucelle's direction on the secondary decoration of the Breviary of
Belleville (BNF Lat. 10483–10484). Beginning
in the 1330s, Mahiet must have supervised a
flourishing workshop. He may have been the
Norman cleric, Mathieu Le Vavasseur, who
was admitted as *libraire juré*, or accredited
bookseller, to the University of Paris in 1342.

François Avril

H.-F. Delaborde, ed., *Vie de saint Louis par Guillaume de Saint-Pathus* (Paris, 1899). L. Delisle, *Recherches sur la librairie de Charles V*, vol. 1 (Paris, 1907), 319. J. Porcher, *Les manuscrits à peintures en France du XIIIe au XVIe siècle* (Paris, 1955), 97, no. 199. K. Morand, *Jean Pucelle* (Oxford, 1962), 49. *La librairie de Charles V* (Paris, 1968), 81, no. 152. *Les fastes du gothique: Le siè-cle de Charles V* (Paris, 1981), 299–300, no. 247.

24

GUILLAUME DE MACHAUT

Oeuvres (Works)

Département des Manuscrits, Fr. 1586,
fols. 56v–57

*Parchment; II + 321 + II fols.; 300 × 210 mm. Paris,
ca. 1350–1355. Bound in brown calf, 19th century,
with the monogram of Napoléon III. Former royal
collection.*

An innovative poet and composer, Guillaume
de Machaut from the Champagne region of
France is a figure of major importance in
French literature and music of the 14th century. Apart from his celebrated Coronation
Mass, his art was essentially of secular inspiration and found its most finished expression
in a series of *dits,* narrative stories in verse,
interspersed with lyric and musical pieces
(lays, virelays, ballades, and rondeaux). In
them the author successfully celebrated the
traditional themes of courtly love for which
he assumed a tone that is free and direct,
unencumbered with rhetoric. Although he
ended his life in Reims, where he had
obtained a canonry, Machaut spent most of
his career in the service of different influen-

tial patrons, notably the king of Bohemia, John of Luxembourg; John's daughter and son-in-law, Bonne of Luxembourg and John the Good, king of France; and even John the Good's sworn enemy, Charles the Bad, king of Navarre.

Very early on, Machaut seems to have taken an interest in the material presentation of his works. A number of collections made in his lifetime have survived whose preparation and perhaps even illustration he must have overseen closely. The oldest known such collection is the remarkable manuscript exhibited here. Apart from some lyrical pieces copied at the end of the volume, none of the works is apparently later than 1350. Despite the exceptionally fine craftsmanship, there is nothing to throw light on the manuscript's origin. One can only suspect that it was intended for some important individual in the French court, indeed a member of the royal family. Ursula Günther has hypothesized that it could be a copy intended for Bonne of Luxembourg, wife of the future king, Jean the Good, and mother of Charles V–this because of the inclusion of the *Judgment of the King of Bohemia* (a work dedicated to Bonne's father, John of Luxembourg) at the beginning of the volume.

Despite the homogeneity of the style, the 104 illustrations, all in grisaille, are the work of three different artists. Of these the workshop foreman is the illustrator of the most important text in the collection, the *Remède de Fortune* (Fortune's remedy). This painter is one of the leading representatives of the stylistic renewal which began to assert itself in Parisian illumination in the third quarter of the 14th century and which is distinguished by a realistic depiction of people and nature. It was a clear break with the elegant and somewhat artificial style which prevailed at court until then. The illustrator's interest in exact observation extended even to clothing details, which he rendered faithfully and which make his miniatures one of the most useful sources for our knowledge of fashion in this period. The two collaborators with the Master of the Remède de Fortune display a style closely related to his and must have been trained by him. The closer to the workshop foreman is the painter of the scenes from the *Jugement du roi de Bohême* (fols. 1–22) and from the *Dit du lion* (Story of the lion, fols. 103–120). The second artist distances himself from the Master of the Remède with his more spare and angular drawing, the pale complexion and sickly cast of his figures. He was responsible for the illustrations of the *Dit de l'alérion* (Story of the little eagle) and the *Dit du verger* (Story of the orchard, fols. 59–102), and of the ballades and rondeaux in the final musical section (fols. 121–196). It is indeed possible that the artist may be the Master of the Coronation Book of Charles V (British Library Tib. B VIII), an illuminator who can be traced until the end of the 1370s in the service of the "Sage roi" (wise king) and his court.

François Avril

F. Avril, "Un chef-d'oeuvre de l'enluminure sous le règne de Jean le Bon: La Bible moralisée, manuscrit Fr. 167 de la Bibliothèque Nationale," *Fondation Eugène Piot: Monuments et mémoires* 58 (1972): 112–14.F. Avril, *L'enluminure du XIVe siècle à la cour de France* (Paris, 1978), 25–26, pl. 23–26. U. Günther, "Contribution de la musicologie à la biographie et à la chronologie de Guillaume de Machaut," in *Guillaume de Machaut*, colloquium and roundtable organized by the Université de Reims, April 19–22, 1978 (Paris, 1982), 95–115. F. Avril, "Les manuscrits enluminés de Guillaume de Machaut: Essai de chronologie," in *Guillaume de Machaut*, 118–24. *Les fastes du gothique: Le siècle de Charles V* (Paris, 1981), 318–19, no. 271. L. Earp, "Scribal Practice," *Manuscript Production and the Transmission of Music in Late Medieval France* (Ann Arbor, Mich., 1983). L. Earp, "Machaut's Role in the Production of Manuscripts of His Works," *Journal of the American Musicological Society* 62 (1989): 461–503.

25

DENIS FOULECHAT

Translation of John of Salisbury's *Policraticus*

Département des Manuscrits, Fr. 24287, fol. 2

Parchment; II + 296 + II fols.; 312 × 215 mm. Paris, ca. 1372. Copied by Henri de Trévou (fols. 1–82, except 78) and Raoulet d'Orléans (fols. 83–270) and illustrated by the Master of the Policraticus of John of Salisbury, the Master of the Travels of Mandeville, and a collaborator of the Master of the Coronation of Charles VI. Bound in red morocco with the arms of Cardinal de Richelieu, gilt edges. Very likely the presentation copy to King Charles V; borrowed from the Royal Library on Oct. 7, 1380, by the duke of Anjou; belonged to Cardinal Richelieu (d. 1642), whose manuscripts were deposited at the Sorbonne in 1660; acquired by the Bibliothèque Nationale in 1792.

Charles V was a great lover of books. In 1368 he transferred and brought together on the three floors of the Falconry Tower of the Louvre a research library of more than a thousand volumes, which he apparently made fairly accessible to his counselors. The king consulted books when meditating on politics and the practice of government, as is evident from the numerous political treatises that were translated on his order into French. In 1372 he entrusted the Franciscan Denis Foulechat with the task of translating one of the most important texts about political theory to be produced in the Middle Ages, John of Salisbury's *Policraticus sive de nugis curialium et vestigiis philosophorum.* Written in 1159 by the eminently well read English humanist, who was the secretary and friend of Thomas à Becket, the book projected a quite theocratic vision of the state and posed for the first time the question of monarchical legitimacy and tyrannicide. More than one hundred Latin manuscripts of this text are known; it was a source for medieval political theorists and was widely read by members of Charles V's entourage (Raoul de Presles, Nicole Oresme, Simon de Hesdin, and others). However, only three complete manuscripts of Foulechat's translation have survived–the translation seems not to have gone much beyond the royal entourage.

François Avril has identified in the present manuscript the hand of two copyists accredited to Charles V: Henri de Trévou and Raoulet d'Orléans. The manuscript lacks the customary dedicatory miniature of the author offering his book to the king: this is probably because the author had been reproved for associating with the Fraticelli heretics. He was therefore not present in Paris to offer his translation to the king and wished to retain his anonymity. He discreetly revealed his name, however, in an acrostic in the translation of *Entheticus,* a kind of summary at the front of *Policraticus.*

The quality of the work as a whole makes it very clear that the manuscript is indeed the presentation copy for the king. The painting on fol. 2 is a remarkable synthesis that perfectly illustrates one of the paragraphs of the translator's prologue. The Latin text can be read from the manuscript open before the king: "Beatus vir qui in sapiencia morabitur et in justicia meditabitur et in sensu cogitabit circonspectionem Dei" (Blessed is the man who dwells in wisdom and meditates on justice and considers God's comprehensive vision). Seated on one of the chairs from which justice was meted out, the wise king Charles V, identifiable by his high forehead and large nose, wearing gloves, points with his finger to the manuscript placed on a bookwheel. He is the very picture of the learned and just king–later the term would be "enlightened"–blessed by the hand of God. It is from Him that the king wields the *potestas,* or power. The apologia for royal wisdom is continued on fol. 12, which illustrates the theme "Benedicta terra cujus rex sapiens" (Blessed is the land whose king is wise–a conflation of Ecclesiastes 10.17 and Ecclesiasticus 10.3).

This manuscript is mentioned, without indication of the incipit of the second leaf, in the Royal Library inventory drawn up in 1373 by Gilles Malet, "garde de la Librairie" (keeper of the library); a marginal note indicates that it was borrowed on Oct. 7, 1380, by the duke of Anjou, one of King Charles V's brothers. It was probably not returned, since it does not appear in the succeeding inventories. In the 17th century it belonged to

Cardinal Richelieu, whose arms are on the binding. Deposited with the cardinal's collection at the Sorbonne in 1660, it became part of the national collection in 1792.

Marie-Hélène Tesnière

Léopold Delisle, *Le Cabinet des Manuscrits de la Bibliothèque Impériale*, vol. 2 (Paris, 1907), 204–07. L. Delisle, *Recherches sur la librairie de Charles V* (Paris, 1907), 1:85–88 and 2:85, no. 501. *La librairie de Charles V*, exhibition catalogue with entries by François Avril (Paris, 1968), no. 206. Claire Richter Sherman, *The Portraits of Charles V of France (1338–1380)* (New York, 1969). Claire Richter Sherman, "Representations of Charles V of France (1338–1380) as a Wise Ruler," *Medievalia et Humanistica: Studies in Medieval and Renaissance Culture*, n.s. 2 (1971): 83–96. Charles Brucker, *Le "Policratique": Un fragment de manuscrit dans le ms. B.N., fr. 24287*, in *Bibliothèque d'Humanisme et de Renaissance* 34 (1972): 269–73. Ammon Linder, "The Knowledge of John of Salisbury in the Late Middle Ages," *Studi medievali* 18 (1977): 315–66. Charles Brucker, ed., *Tyrans, princes et prêtres*, bks. 4 and 8 of the translation of *Policraticus* of John of Salisbury by Denis Foulechat, in *Le Moyen français* (Paris, 1987), 1–223.

26

NICOLE ORESME

Translation of Aristotle's *Politics, Economics,* and *Ethics*

Département des Manuscrits, Fr. 204, fol. 347 (detail)

Livre des Politiques with *Table des notables* and Glossary (fols. 1–326); *Livre de Yconomique* (fols. 326v–346v); *Livre des Éthiques,* with Prologue common to the *Éthiques* and *Politiques,* and Glossary (fols. 347–584).

Parchment; IV + 584 + II fols.; 425 × 315 mm. Paris, ca. 1380–1390. On fol. 584, after the explicit and in the same hand, the initials G p p. Perhaps done for Blanche of Savoy (d. 1387), wife of Galeazzo II Visconti (d. 1378), founder of the library in Pavia; listed in the inventories of the library of the dukes of Milan in Pavia in 1426 and 1459; brought to France by Louis XII in 1499 for his library at Blois; note on fol. 584: "De Pavye au roy Loys XIIe." On the inside of the front cover, there is a reference to the manuscript's location in the library at Blois; "Des hystoires et livres en françoys. Au pulpistre troysieme par terre du cousté devers la court" (Some histories and books in French. At the third desk at ground level on the side toward the courtyard).

Charles V had surrounded himself with a team of translators, drawn usually from clerics close to the chancery. In the forefront was Nicole Oresme, one of the most remarkable figures of the 14th century. Astrologer, mathematician, and economist, enlightened and influential, he notably persuaded the king of the need for a stable and fixed currency. While Oresme was dean of the Cathedral of Rouen, King Charles V entrusted him with the translation of all those texts by or attributed to Aristotle deemed relevant for the conduct of government and for morality (the *Ethics, Politics, Economics*). This body of texts had been known in France since the second half of the 13th century thanks to Arab-Latin and Greek-Latin translations. Oresme completed his task between 1370 and 1374 and revised his translation a number of times, as can be seen from the original manuscript now at Avranches (Bibliothèque Municipale 223). In his letters King Charles V insisted

79

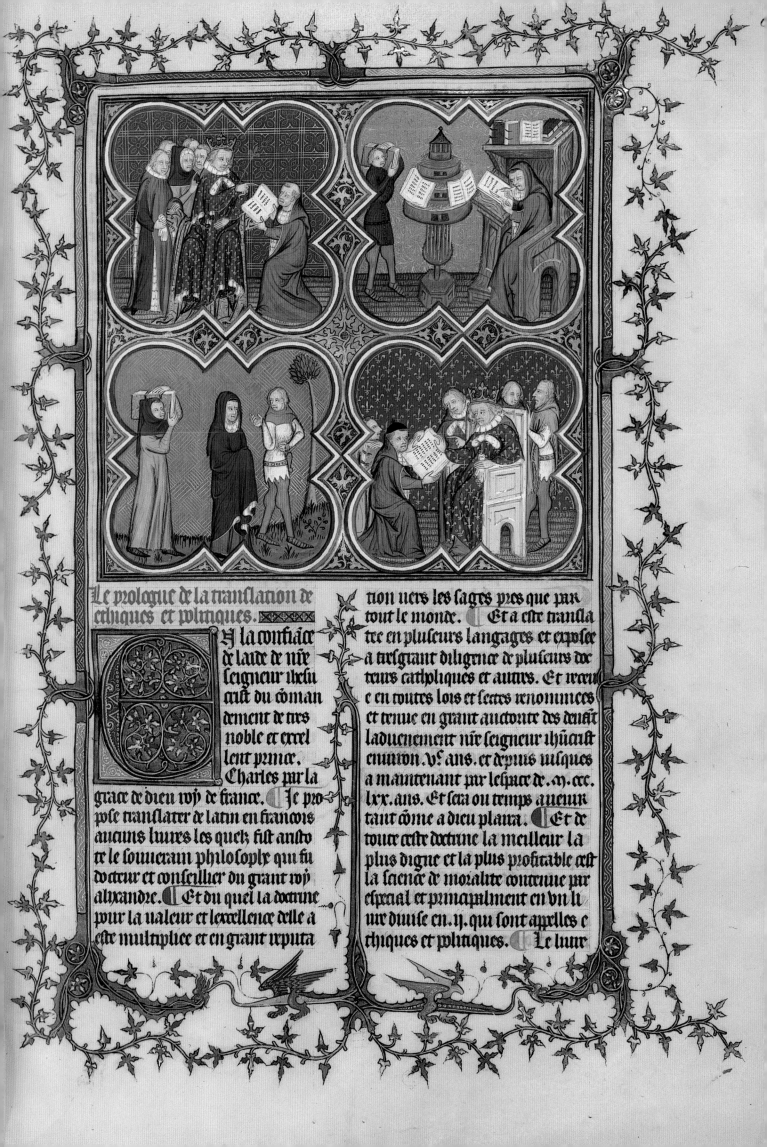

Le prologue de la translation de ethiques et politiques.

A la confidace de laude de nře seigneur ihesu crist du coman dement de trs noble et excel lent prince . Charles par la grace de dieu roy de france . ¶ Je pro pose translater de latin en francois aucuns liures les quelz fist aristo te le souuerain philosophe qui fu docteur et conseillier du grant roy alixandre . ¶ Et du quel la doctrine pour la valeur et lexcellence delle a este multipliee et en grant reputa

tion uers les sages pres que par tout le monde . ¶ Et a este transla tee en pluseurs langages et exposee a tresgrant diligence de pluseurs doc teurs catholiques et autres . Et receu e en toutes lois et sectes renommees et tenue en grant auctorite des deuant ladueneument nře seigneur ihucrist enuiron . vc . ans . et depuis iusques a maintenant par lespace de . m . ccc . lxx . ans . Et sera ou temps auenir tant come a dieu plaira . ¶ Et de toute ceste doctrine la meilleur la plus digne et la plus profitable est la science de moralite contenue par especial et principalment en vn li ure diuise en . ij . qui sont appellees e thiques et politiques . ¶ Le liure that "ces traductions... lui sont très néces-saires et pour cause" (these translations... are very necessary to [me], and for good rea-son). His insistence becomes clearer when we realize that Aristotle's principles (in the *Politics*) were followed on two occasions when the post of *chancelier* was filled by a process of election–a highly rare occur-rence–in 1372 for Guillaume de Dormans and in 1373 for Pierre d'Orgemont.

This monumental manuscript, which con-tains Oresme's entire translation in a single volume, is typical of Parisian manuscripts in Charles V's time. Written in a large, highly legible script known as *littera cursiva formata*, somewhat unusual for manuscripts of this kind (compare Brussels, Bibliothèque Royale 9091, Epîtres de Sénèque en français), it was illuminated by an artist who worked on a large number of manuscripts produced for Charles V (compare BNF Fr. 437, *Rational des divins offices*). The manuscript did not figure in the library at the Louvre but must have belonged to someone very close to the royal entourage. Apart from the decoration, it con-tains the copy of the latest version of Oresme's translation. The painting on fol. 347, which ought to be at the front, rein-forces the impression that it was produced for someone in the royal circle. The minia-ture is a perfect illustration of Oresme's pro-logue to his translation of the *Ethics* and the *Politics:* "The consideration and the resolu-tion of our good King Charles, who has had good and excellent books translated into French, are to be recommended." Surrounded by his counselors, and notably by the *chancelier* who holds his gloves, Charles V, arrayed in a jurist's robe, requests a kneeling Oresme to translate Aristotle; Oresme, at work in his study, examines a number of books for his translation; in the company of one of his clerics, he goes to the palace; he reads his translation to the king and his counselors. More than a simple depiction of the translation, this painting is what might be termed a material representa-tion of the ambitious cultural transfer so desired by Charles V and to which Oresme referred in his Prologue as *translatio studii:* the language of culture, having been first Greek, then Latin, henceforth will be French.

The manuscript may have been prepared for Blanche of Savoy, the wife of Galeazzo II Visconti (founder of the library of the dukes of Milan in Pavia). An inventory of 1426 listed the manuscript along with a half-dozen Parisian manuscripts of identical style as "deposited" at the library. It was then bound in embossed red leather. In 1499, Louis XII took possession of certain volumes from the library and had them brought to his castle at Blois. On fol. 594 the manuscript bears the following note in the king's hand: "De Pavye au roy Loys XIIe" (From Pavia to King Louis XII).

Marie-Hélène Tesnière

Léopold Delisle, "Les *Ethiques*, les *Politiques* et les *Economiques* d'Aristote: Traduites et copiées pour le roi Charles V," in *Mélanges de paléographie et de bibliographie* (Paris, 1880), 257–282. Siméon Luce, "Le principe électif, les traductions d'Aristote et les parvenus au XIVe siècle," in *La France pendant la Guerre de Cent Ans: Episodes historiques et vie privée aux XIVe et XVe siècles*, 2d ed. (Paris, 1890), 179–202. L. Delisle, *Recherches sur la librairie de Charles V* (Paris, 1907), 1:104–07 and 2: 81–83. Antoine Thomas, "Les manuscrits français et provençaux des ducs de Milan au château de Pavie," *Romania* 40 (1911): 571–609. Albert Douglas Menut, ed., *Maistre Nicole Oresme, Le Livre de Ethique d'Aristote, published from the text of manuscript 2902, Bibliothèque Royale de Belgique* (New York, 1940). Elizabeth Pellegrin, *La bibliothèque des Visconti et des Sforza, ducs de Milan au XVe siècle* (Paris, 1955), esp. 118 and supplement with 175 plates (Paris, 1969). A. D. Menut, "Maistre Nicole Oresme, *Le Livre de Yconomique d'Aristote*: Critical Edition of the French Text from the Avranches Manuscript with the Original Latin Version, Introduction and English Translation," *Transactions of the American Philosophical Society*, n.s. 47, pt. 5 (1957). A. D. Menut, "Maistre Nicole Oresme, Le Livre des Politiques d'Aristote, published from the text of Avranches manuscript 223 with a critical introduction and notes...," *Transactions of the American Philosophical Society*, n.s. 60, pt. 6 (1970). Serge Lusignan, "La topique de la 'Translatio Studii' et les traductions françaises de textes savants au XIVe siècle," in *Traduction et traducteurs au moyen-âge*, ed. Geneviève Contamine (Paris, 1989), 303–15.

81

Le pmi chapitre parole ant
fiacois descedur des troys.
Quatre cens z .iiij. ans auant
que romme fust fondee
regnoit prians e troye
la grant. Il enuoia paris lamsne de
ses filz en grece pour rauir la royne
helene feme du roi menelas pour soi
uegier dune honte que li grec li orent fa
faitte. Li greiois qui mult furet cour
rouce de ceste chose se simuirent grande
ment z vindrent assegier troye.

ce siege qui .x. ans dura
furent occis tuit li filz
le roi prians et la roy
ne ecuba sa feme. La cite
fu arse z destruite le peu
ple z li baron occis. Mes aucuns escha
perent de celle pestilence z pluis des
princes de la cite qui sespandurent en
diuerses parties du monde pour que
rir nouuelles habitations. come he
lenus eneas anthenor z maint au
tre. Cilz helenus fu li vns des filz au

27

Les Croniques de France selon ce qu'elles sont composées en l'église Saint-Denis en France (The Chronicles of France as composed in the church of Saint-Denis in France)

Département des Manuscrits, Fr. 10135, fol. 3

Parchment; III + 450 + II fols.; 330 × 218 mm. Paris, ca. 1370. First gathering illustrated by the Master of the Coronation of Charles VI, the rest by his followers. Bound in red morocco with the royal arms and monogram (18th century). Manuscript probably produced for Charles V; on fol. 450v, signature of Charles VI (after 1393); was part of the library of the dukes of Burgundy, at least from 1420 to 1487; entered the royal collections in the second half of the 18th century.

The abbey of Saint-Denis, where French kings were buried and the royal regalia were housed, was the place where the "official" history of France first emerged. Indeed, by the late 12th century, monks like Rigord and Guillaume le Breton—who were also historians—had drawn up short Latin texts for the benefit of the faithful who came in ever greater numbers to visit the royal tombs; each tomb had a text describing the king's life, major deeds, and the state of his soul. The intense historical activity undertaken by the abbey in the two centuries starting with Suger's abbacy (1122–1151) resulted in the constitution, by the mid-13th century, of a major corpus of Latin texts recounting the history of the kings of France. Then King Louis IX (later Saint Louis), having ordered the rearrangement of his predecessor's tombs in order to highlight dynastic continuity and royal grandeur more clearly for visitors, also asked the abbey to write a history of the kings of France in the vernacular French. The monk Primat ultimately delivered the completed text to Louis's successor, Philip III, in 1274. The account was later expanded and continued, notably by Richard Lescot, so that by 1360 the abbey possessed a written history of the kings of France from their mythical Trojan origins right up to 1350. From that date onward, however, the official history of France would no longer be written at Saint-Denis but rather at the royal chancery.

The manuscript on display, titled *Les Croniques de France selon ce qu'elles sont composées en l'église Saint-Denis en France*, contains the French-language version of the royal chronicles up to the death of Philip VI of Valois in 1350, as they were composed at the abbey of Saint-Denis. This volume was probably produced around 1370 for Charles V, as suggested by the style of the paintings and by the two lions with long tails supporting an empty escutcheon, an emblem found in many manuscripts and formal charters drawn up for Charles V. It does not, however, include the textual and iconographic modifications carried out under Charles V, designed notably to legitimize dynastic continuity and stress the sacred nature of the monarchy (compare BNF Fr. 2813). Indeed, although this text is a history of kings, it is still a history with a primarily religious and baronial slant, recounting the story of the abbey and of various nobles. Whatever the case, the chronicles were designed to "mirror the lives of princes" and to serve as examples, and it is likely that Charles had this copy made for a close acquaintance or relation.

The manuscript opens with a painting that depicts the legend of the Trojan origins of the Franks in four quatrefoil compartments (fol. 3), featuring the colors blue, white, and red. According to the legend, Francio, one of Hector's sons, fled the burning city of Troy alongside Aeneas. After a long period of wandering and numerous conquests, Francio and his men built the city of Sycambria on the Danube. They defeated the Alani tribe and were exonerated from paying tribute to Rome, which earned them the name "Franks" ("free"). Then they crossed the Rhine and founded Paris. The four miniatures that make up the painting (the Greeks landing in Asia Minor, the attack on Troy, the founding of Sycambria by Francio, and the victory of the king of Franks over the emperor of the Alani) illustrate the key features of the myth: the ancientness and nobility of the Franks (notice the fleurs-de-lis on the battlements of Troy), the cultural prestige of being founders of cities (like the Romans), and their supremacy, as a nation,

83

over the empire, whose chief they once vanquished (note the imperial crown fallen to the ground).

This manuscript naturally passed from Charles V to his son, Charles VI, who placed his signature on fol. 450v. It was one of the numerous manuscripts that, probably lent to the king's uncles, disappeared from the Royal Library during the reign of Charles VI. It was later part of the collection of the dukes of Burgundy, from the death of John the Fearless in 1419 until 1487. It found its way back into the royal collection in the second half of the 18th century.

Marie-Hélène Tesnière

Léon Lacabane, "Recherches sur les auteurs des Grandes Chroniques de France dites de Saint-Denys," in *Bibliothèque de l'Ecole des Chartes*, vol. 2 (1840– 1841), 57–74. Léopold Delisle, "Une fausse lettre de Charles VI," in *Bibliothèque de l'Ecole des Chartes*, vol. 51 (1890), 87–92. L. Delisle, *Recherches sur la librairie de Charles V* (Paris, 1907), 1:318 and 2:162–64. Colette Beaune, *Naissance de la Nation France* (Paris, 1985), esp. 15–54. Bernard Guénée, "Les Grandes Chroniques de France, Le Roman aux roys (1274–1518)," in Pierre Nora, ed., *Les lieux de mémoire*, vol. 2, *La Nation*, vol. 1 (Paris, 1986), 189–214. François Avril, Marie-Thérèse Gousset, and Bernard Guénée, *Les Grandes Chroniques de France: Reproduction intégrale en fac-similé des miniatures de Fouquet, manuscrit français 6465 de la Bibliothèque Nationale de Paris* (Paris, 1987). Anne D. Hedeman, *The Royal Image: Illustrations of the "Grandes Chroniques de France," 1274–1422* (Berkeley, 1991), esp. 96–144 and 251–52. Gabrielle M. Spiegel, *The Chronicle Tradition of Saint-Denis: A Survey* (Brookline, Mass., and Leiden, 1978).

28

PIERRE LE FRUITIER,
CALLED SALMON
Réponses à Charles VI and *Lamentations* (Replies to Charles VI and Lamentations)
Département des Manuscrits, Fr. 23279, fol. 53

Parchment; II + 121 + II fols.; 280 × 205 mm. Paris, 1409. Bound in red morocco with gold fillets, 18th century. Presentation copy to Charles VI; purchased in 1784 for the Bibliothèque Royale at the La Vallière sale.

Although he had received an excellent education, King Charles VI does not seem to have been an ardent book lover. In this he was quite unlike his uncles and especially his father, the well-read Charles V, who, it was said, regretted to see his heir attracted more to weaponry than to intellectual matters. Indeed, it was beginning with Charles VI's reign that the collections his father had painstakingly assembled began to be dispersed. From 1392 on, this break-up quickened when the unfortunate king suffered his first attacks of madness. By a strange paradox, it was during his troubled reign that the Parisian book trade, supported by other patrons and notably by the king's uncles Jean de Berry and Philip the Bold, as well as by his own son, Louis de Guyenne, enjoyed its most fertile activity. In another paradox, in about 1409 one of the most beautiful manuscripts to leave the Parisian workshops during this period was illuminated for none other than this king who had little time for books: Pierre Salmon's *Réponses à Charles VI.* Salmon, a political agent in the service of John the Fearless, duke of Burgundy, composed this strange text as a dialogue between the king and himself concerning the duties

y senſuuient les lamentations Salmon pour au
cunes merueilles a sun auennes ou pelermage
de ce monde z les epiſtres pour ce par sin baillees
et enuorees A treſexcellent z treſpuiſſant prince

imposed upon the king and his servants. The dialogue is followed by a commentary on various passages of Scripture related to the same subject. A final part, the *Lamentations*, recounts the somewhat mysterious missions that Salmon undertook in behalf of Charles VI in England, the Low Countries, and Avignon.

The quality of the twenty-seven miniatures accompanying these texts measures up to the royal station of their recipient. They represent the best of Parisian craftsmanship from that time and are the work of a number of illuminators each with a distinct style of his own. Of these the most remarkable is beyond any doubt the Boucicaut Master, the artist responsible for the manuscript's two presentation scenes. The scene on fol. 53, the most intricate and animated, demonstrates the artist's skill in embellishing this classic presentation scene with a multitude of anecdotal details, keenly observed and arranged in convincing spatial volume. Some years later Salmon did a new version of his work, augmented by a pastiche of Boethius's *Consolation of Philosophy*. A part of the illustration for this second manuscript, now in the public and university library of Geneva (MS Fr. 165), was also entrusted to the Boucicaut Master.

François Avril

P. Durrieu, "Le Maître des Heures du Maréchal de Boucicaut," *Revue de l'art ancien et moderne* 20 (1906): 22. J. Porcher, *Les manuscrits à peintures en France du XIIIe au XVIe siècle* (Paris, 1955), 96, no. 197, pl. XXV. M. Meiss, *French Painting in the Time of Jean de Berry: The Boucicaut Master* (London, 1968), 37, 87–88, 124–25, figs. 67, 68, 70, 71. C. Beaune and F. Avril, *Le miroir du pouvoir* (Paris, 1989), 23–25. B. Guénée, *Un meurtre, une société: L'assassinat du duc d'Orléans: 23 novembre 1407* (Paris, 1992), 210–16. A. D. Hedeman, "Pierre Salmon's Advice for a King," *Gesta* 32, no. 2 (1993): 113–23.

29
Psalter of Jean de Berry

Département des Manuscrits, Fr. 13091, fols. 9v–10

Parchment; 272 + VII fols.; 250 × 177 mm. Bourges, ca. 1386–1390. Bound in olive morocco with the monogram CCP, 17th century. Copy made for Jean de France, duke of Berry. At fol. 1, ex libris of the duke by his secretary, Jean Flamel: "Ce Psaultier qui est en latin et en françois est a Jehan, filz de roy de France, duc de Berry et d'Auvergne, conte de Poitou, d'Estampes, de Bouloingne et d'Auvergne. J. Flamel" (This Psalter which is in Latin and French belongs to Jean, son of the king of France, duke of Berry and of Auvergne, count of Poitou, of Estampes, of Boulogne, and of Auvergne. J. Flamel). Signature of the duke on fol. 272v; acquired for the royal collection in the second half of the 18th century.

Jean de France, duke of Berry (1340–1416), was the third of John the Good's four sons, all equally famous for their ostentatious lifestyles. His name is associated with some of the most beautiful illuminated creations from the end of the Middle Ages. Ordered by the duke from a number of outstanding artists whom he adroitly attracted to his service, these works bear the mark of the personal tastes of this extraordinary patron—without doubt the most refined connoisseur of his time.

One of the manuscripts that best exemplifies his involvement is his celebrated Psalter. Over and above the series of miniatures which illustrate in traditional fashion the eight textual divisions of the psalms—some of those miniatures can be credited to Jacquemart de Hesdin, the duke's official illuminator—the manuscript text is preceded by a cycle of twenty-four paintings in grisaille which constitutes one of the most remarkable interpretations of the Apostle's

Creed, an iconographic theme that was extremely popular at the end of the Middle Ages. Twelve Apostle figures, each captioned with an article of the Creed, alternate with an equal number of prophets identified with prophetic passages of parallel meaning (for example, fols. 9v–10: David and Saint Andrew). The very plastic treatment of the figures and their strongly individualized physiognomies are exceptional for this period—and for good reason: according to the entry for this manuscript in Jean de Berry's inventories, the painting of these grisailles was entrusted not to an illuminator but to the famous André Beauneveu, the great sculptor from Valenciennes. In 1386 Jean de Berry summoned Beauneveu to Bourges, where he ended his career working on Mehun-sur-Yèvre castle, the luxurious residence, today virtually entirely destroyed, that the duke had had built not far from Bourges.

François Avril

L. Delisle, "Les Livres d'heures du duc de Berry," *Gazette des Beaux-arts* 29 (1884): 392–97. P. Durrieu, "Les miniatures d'André Beauneveu," in *Le manuscrit*, vol. 1 (Paris, 1894), 51–56, 83–95. R. de Lasteyrie, "Les miniatures d'André Beauneveu et de Jacquemart de Hesdin," in Fondation Eugène Piot, *Monuments et mémoires publiés par l'Académie des Inscriptions et Belles-Lettres*, vol. 3 (Paris, 1896), 71–119. V. Leroquais, *Les Psautiers manuscrits des bibliothèques publiques de France*, vol. 2 (Paris, 1941), 144–46, pls. CXVIII–CXXVII. J. Porcher, *Les manuscrits à peintures en France du XIIIe au XVIe siècle* (Paris, 1955), 87, no. 180, pl. XX. K. Morand, *Jean Pucelle* (London, 1962), 29–30, pl. XXVIII. M. Meiss, *French Painting in the Time of Jean de Berry: The Late XIVth Century and the Patronage of the Duke* (London, 1967), 135–54, 331–32, figs. 51–82. *Les fastes du gothique; Le siècle de Charles V* (Paris, 1981), 181–82, no. 296.

30

CHRISTINE DE PISAN
Le livre de la Cité des Dames
(The book of the City of Women)
Département des Manuscrits, Fr. 607,
fol. 2

Parchment; III + 79 + III fols.; 347 × 262 mm.
Paris, ca. 1405. Illustrated by the Master of the Cité
des Dames. Bound in lemon-colored morocco with
the royal arms (17th century). Presented by the
author to the duke of Berry, whose ex libris and
signature it bears (fol. 79). Probably belonged to
Jacques d'Armagnac, duke of Nemours; entered the
royal collection in 1477.

The first female writer to earn a living with
her pen, Christine de Pisan (1364–after 1429),
defender of the position of women, looms
like a mythical figure. Her father had been an
astrologer and physician to Charles V. A
widow at thirty, Christine de Pisan wrote
extensively, most of her books being commissions that she presented princes of the royal
family.

At the very beginning of the century she
had already voiced her opposition to the part
of the *Roman de la rose* (The romance of the
rose) written by Jean de Meun, condemning
it as insulting to women. Her *Dit de la rose*
(Story of the rose) immortalized the celebration held in 1402 at Louis d'Orléans's resi
dence to establish the Order of the Rose, a
chivalric order which, in the courtly tradition
of Guillaume de Lorris's part of the *Roman
de la rose*, claimed the defense of women as
its goal. Some time later, between December
13, 1404, and April 1405, Christine wrote the
Livre de la Cité des Dames, a book inspired by
Boccaccio's *De claris mulieribus* (About
famous women), newly translated into
French (1401). In it she defended with striking
modernity the position of women. As in
Saint Augustine's *City of God*, the Cité des
Dames is a fortress, "a combative work aimed
at the heresy and barbary that in her eyes
was the fate reserved for women" (Hicks and
Moreau).

While the author is writing in her study,
three beautiful crowned ladies present themselves before her (fol. 2). They are Reason
with her shining mirror, in which people can
peer into the depths of their souls;
Rectitude, with her rule which traces limits;
and Justice, the chosen daughter of God,
into whose face one cannot look and who
holds in her hand a cup with which she
metes out to everyone their due. These three
virtues will help her lay the foundations of a
city whose stones are composed of the emi-
nent accomplishments of women. Only
women of virtuous renown will reside in this
city–those whose virtue, wisdom, and good
works have been of greatest service in the
cause of women (female warriors, politicians,
good wives, lovers, those who have prophe-
sied or been creative). Certain Ladies of
France will also be admitted; in the front
rank appear Ysabeau de Bavière (the wife of
Charles VI), Jeanne (the young duchess of
Berry), and many other princesses from

France and abroad. The city will be crowned by the glory of the Virgin and sainted women.

Christine closely supervised the copying and illustration of her works. The artist known as the Master of the Cité des Dames illustrated at least four identical copies of it about 1405 in accordance with her instructions. One was offered to the duke of Burgundy, John the Fearless (Brussels, Bibliothèque Royale 9393); the present manuscript was offered to the duke of Berry, who affixed his signature and asserted his ownership (fol. 79). The manuscript does not figure in any of the duke's inventories, however. Probably it was given to one of his daughters, perhaps to Bonne, the wife of Bernard d'Armagnac. The manuscript then would have passed naturally enough into the library of his grandson Jacques d'Armagnac, duke of Nemours (1437–1477). On the inside of the front cover, a note indicates the number of leaves and of miniatures in the volume, typical for this experienced bibliophile's manuscripts (compare cat. 21). Armagnac's properties were confiscated in 1477 by Louis XI (for having conspired with the Ligue du Bien Public,) and his manuscripts became part of the royal collection.

Marie-Hélène Tesnière

Léopold Delisle, *Le Cabinet des Manuscrits de la Bibliothèque Impériale*, vol. 1 (Paris, 1868), 86–90. Millard Meiss, *French Painting in the Time of Jean de Berry*, vol. 1, *The Late Fourteenth Century...* (New York, 1967), 219, 313, 356; and vol. 3, *The Limbourgs and Their Contemporaries* (New York, 1974), 12–15, 290, 378–82, figs. 34–45. Suzanne Solente, "Christine de Pizan," in *Histoire littéraire de la France*, vol. 40 (Paris, 1974), 335–442. Eric Hicks and Thérèse Moreau, ed. and trans., Christine de Pisan, *Le livre de la Cité des Dames*, (Paris, 1986). Charles Sterling, *La peinture médiévale à Paris, 1300–1500* (Paris, 1987), 1:286–95, fig. 191.

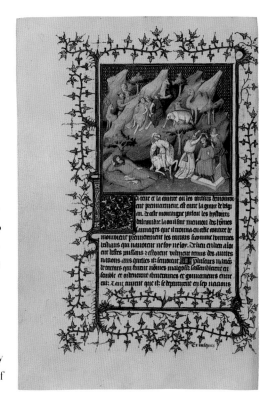

31

FRÈRE HAYTON
Fleur des histoires de la Terre d'Orient
(Flower of the stories of the land of the Orient)
Département des Manuscrits, Fr. 12201, fol. 17v

Hayton, Fleur des histoires de la Terre d'Orient *(fols. 1–65v)*; Liber de toto orbe terrarum *(fols. 66–82v)*; Jean IV, archbishop of Sultanieh, Ordonnances de Thermibey *(fols. 83–97)*.

Parchment; IV + 97 + II fols.; 310 × 213 mm. Paris, first half of 1403 (between July 28, 1402, and May 24, 1403). Illustrated by the workshop of the Master of the Clères femmes of the Duke of Burgundy. Made for Philip the Bold; described regularly in all the inventories of the library of the dukes of Burgundy until the Revolution; transferred between 1794 and 1796 from the Bibliothèque Royale of Brussels to Paris, where it became part of the national collection.

On May 24, 1403, the duke of Burgundy, Philip the Bold (1342–1404), paid Jacques Raponde (an Italian merchant residing in Paris who acted as the duke's financial agent, book dealer, and counselor) 300 gold francs for three manuscripts. The manuscripts included copies of Hayton's *Fleur des histoires de la Terre d'Orient.* They were illuminated, bound in velvet, and adorned with the coat of arms of Burgundy. The duke kept one copy for himself and offered the other two to his brother, the duke of Berry, and to his nephew, the duke of Orléans. The only surviving volume, the one belonging to the duke of Burgundy, is noteworthy for several reasons. The book testifies to the interest taken by the dukes of Burgundy in Oriental matters and especially in the crusades against the Turks. It should perhaps be pointed out that Philip the Bold's son, the future John the Fearless, commanded the French troops in the crusade against the Ottomans and was taken prisoner in a disastrous battle at Nicopolis on the Danube (1396) while helping King Sigismond of Hungary defend his kingdom against the Turkish invasion led by Sultan Bajazet. John's liberation was a complicated affair, and this manuscript contains, among other things, one of the principal French accounts of the victory at Ankara on July 28, 1402, in which Tamerlane, the great khan of Mongolia, vanquished Bajazet–a victory that temporarily ended the Ottoman threat to Constantinople and incidentally freed many French knights captured at Nicopolis. Thus Tamerlane appeared as a savior of Western Christendom. The author of this short text on Tamerlane's kingdom and court was a certain Jean, archbishop of Sultanieh (Persia). He arrived in Paris in 1403 bearing a letter from Tamerlane inviting King Charles VI to engage in trade. That is why the manuscript can be dated with certainty from the first three months of 1403.

The manuscript's illumination represents one of the first examples of the Flemish influence that revitalized Parisian painting at the beginning of the 15th century. The artist, originally from the Low Countries, worked in Paris between 1400 and 1405 and painted the lovely illustrations for a copy of Boccaccio's *Clères femmes* (Lives of famous women) which was offered to the duke of Burgundy in 1404 (BNF Fr. 12420). His work is characterized by the juxtaposition of acid colors (green-orange), the use of perspective space still cut off by a geometric background, and a supple and mannered handling of physical postures. Fol. 17v depicts the "coronation" of Gengis-Khan. In the background the Tartars are shown living in the mountains among wild beasts like bears, elephants, and camels. Gengis dreams of a white knight who announces Christ's will that Gengis should be made khan. Despite the accuracy of the textual descriptions, these depictions of the Oriental world have distinctly Western features.

The manuscript remained in the library of the dukes of Burgundy until the French Revolution. It was then transferred from Brussels to Paris between 1794 and 1796 and became part of the national collection.

Marie-Hélène Tesnière

Henri de Moranvillé, "Mémoire sur Tamerlan et sa cour par un dominicain, en 1403," *Bibliothèque de l'Ecole des Chartes,* vol. 55 (1894), 433–64. Millard Meiss, *French Painting in the Time of Jean de Berry: The Late Fourteenth Century and the Patronage of the Duke* (New York, 1967). M. Meiss, *The Boucicaut Master* (New York, 1967). M. Meiss, *The Limbourgs and Their Contemporaries* (New York, 1974), 345, 383, 415, 418. Jean Richard, "La croisade bourguignonne dans la politique européenne," *Publications du Centre Européen d'Etudes Burgondo-médianes* 10 (Geneva, 1968), 42–44. J. Richard, *Les récits de voyage et de pélerinage* (Turnhout, 1981). Patrick M. De Winter, *La bibliothèque de Philippe le Hardi, duc de Bourgogne (1364–1404): Etude sur les manuscrits à peintures d'une collection princière à l'époque du "style gothique international"* (Paris, 1985), esp. 99, 208–210, and figs. 208–10.

32

LAURENT DE PREMIERFAIT

Translation of Boccaccio's *De casibus virorum illustrium* (On the fates of famous men)

Département des Manuscrits, Fr. 226, fol. 6v

Parchment; I + 276 + III fols.; 350 × 430 mm. Paris, ca. 1415–1420. Illustrated by the Master of the Bedford Hours, the Master of the Rohan Hours, and the Master of the Cité des Dames. Bound in red morocco with the royal arms and monogram. May have belonged to a member of the House of Savoy; was in the royal collections by the time of Francis I.

During the Middle Ages, Boccaccio was more widely read and illustrated in France than anywhere else. What the French appreciated, however, was not the racy tales of the *Decameron* (which would gain popularity only in the 16th century) but rather the austere accounts of ancient wisdom and morality found in *De casibus virorum illustrium*, in which Boccaccio recounted the tragic fates of eighty kings and other powerful figures subjected to Fortune's capricious wheel from antiquity to the 14th century.

On April 15, 1409, Laurent de Premierfait presented a translation–the second he attempted–to Jean, duke of Berry. Laurent was one of those men who enabled royal circles in Paris to keep abreast of Avignon-based humanism, and his intelligent translation was accompanied by a full historical commentary. He also conceived the major iconographic cycle (up to two hundred miniatures), unequaled in Latin manuscripts, which greatly contributed to the popularity of the work in French aristocratic circles. No fewer than eighty manuscripts and several printed editions of the work are known to exist.

This manuscript is one of the oldest. Stylistic criteria make it possible to date the volume to 1415–1420. The iconography follows the tradition of the earliest manuscripts of this translation (Paris, Bibliothèque de l'Arsenal 5193; Vienna, Österreichische Nationalbibliothek SN 12766; and Geneva, Bibliothèque Publique et Universitaire 190).

The manuscript opens with a magnificent vision of a verdant paradise featuring a Fountain of Life around which unfold five episodes from Genesis: an angel carries Adam to heaven, God creates Eve, God forbids Adam and Eve to eat the fruit of the tree of knowledge, they transgress and are cast out by the archangel. In the margins, five medallions set among foliate scrollwork illustrate other biblical incidents: the creation of Adam, Eve spinning, the discovery of Abel's murder, the murder of Abel, the apocryphal murder of Cain. The large painting, identical to one found in a manuscript in the former Kettaneh collection (now in a private collection in the United States), serves as a frontispiece to the volume, setting the tone for the rest. It conveys the idea that it was the fault of our original ancestors that humankind was subjected to Fortune's "taunts" ("moqueries de Fortune") to suffering, and to death. It was therefore the source of a veritable catalogue of horrors and quasi-infernal tortures–all fully illustrated–that were guaranteed to impress readers and incite them to good behavior.

Although the miniature on fol. 1 constitutes a veritable portrait of the duke, recognizable by his wide face and flat nose as well as by the arms woven into the cloth covering his chair (azure with gold fleurs-de-lis and red engrailed border), the manuscript was not executed until after Jean's death and was not part of his collection. Nothing is known of its origin. The coat of arms painted on the shield of the archangel Michael driving Adam and Eve from Eden (fol. 6v) suggest that the manuscript once belonged the ducal House of Savoy, but it was part of the French royal collections by the reign of Francis I.

Marie-Hélène Tesnière

M. Meiss, *French Painting in the Time of Jean de Berry: The Late Fourteenth Century*, 2 vols. (London, 1967), 1:93, 318, 356, fig. 503; and *French Painting in the Time of Jean de Berry: The Limbourgs and Their Contemporaries*, 2 vols. (New York, 1974), 1:367, 378, 405, figs. 65, 828, 848, 850, 851. F. Simone, "La présence de Boccace dans la culture française du XVe siècle," *Journal of Mediaeval and Renaissance Studies* 1 (1971): 17–32. C. Bozzolo, *Manuscrits des traductions françaises d'oeuvres de Boccace* (Padua, 1973), 16–23. *Boccace en France*, exhibition at the Bibliothèque Nationale, 1975, no. 103. M.-H. Tesnière, "Lectures illustrées de Boccace en France: Les manuscrits français du 'De casibus virorum illustrium' dans les bibliothèques parisiennes," *Studi sul Boccaccio* 18 (1989): 175–280, esp. 179–85 and 215–23. *Boccaccio Visualizzato,* forthcoming.

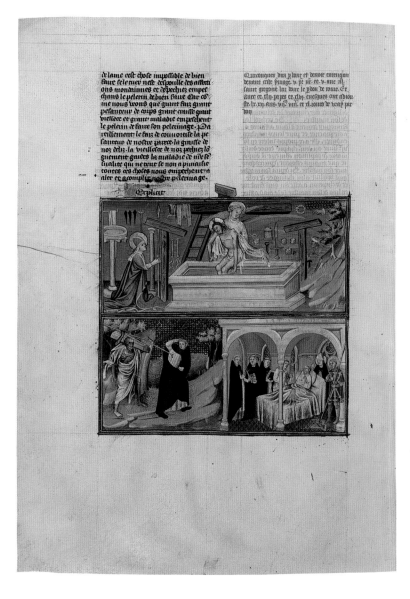

33

JEAN GERSON

La médecine de l'âme, ou La science de bien mourir (Medecine for the soul, or The science of dying well)

Département des Manuscrits, Lat. 14245, fol. 191v

Jacques Legrand, *Livre des bonnes moeurs* (Book of good morals), without the final treatise on death (fols. 158–191v); Questions in Latin to ask the dying (fol. 192); Jean Gerson, *La science de bien mourir* (fols. 192–193); Gerson, *L'A.B.C. des simples gens* (Cathechism for simple people) (fols. 193–194); Gerson, *Examens de conscience* (Examinations of conscience) (fols. 194–196).

Parchment; fols. 157–196; 393 × 285 mm. Paris, 1st quarter of the 15th century, between 1404 (date when the Livre des bonnes moeurs *of Legrand was first composed) and 1415 (terminus ante quem for the illustration). Fol. 158: illustration by the workshop of the Master of Rohan; fol. 191v: illustration by an assistant of the Master of the Apocalypse of the Duke of Berry, called the Master of Boethius (BNF Fr. 12459). Made in Paris for the infirmary of the abbey of Saint-Victor of Paris; classification number EEE 15 in the catalogue of Claude de Grandrue (description on fol. 156); acquired by the Bibliothèque Nationale in 1796 with the manuscripts of Saint-Victor.*

The forty leaves (fols. 157–196) which now form the last section of this manuscript were joined to the preceding texts (biblical and patristic Latin texts copied in the 12th and 13th centuries) in the course of the 15th century, when the whole manuscript was chained in the reading room of the famous abbey of Saint-Victor in Paris. In the early 15th century, however, the last section, containing French-language texts by two of the most famous preachers of that century, Jacques Legrand and Jean Gerson, had been kept in the abbey's infirmary. Indeed, this precocious handbook on the "art of living and dying well" seems to have been designed for use by patients there. Written in French for monks whose knowledge of Latin was scanty, it was intended to accompany those near death in their passage to the otherworld

93

as well as to incite them to live a "good" life. Following Jacques Legrand's *Livre des bonnes moeurs*, which taught them how to avoid committing mortal sins and how to conduct their lives according to their station, there came a set of French texts written by Jean Gerson which constituted an "ecclesiastical directory" for those on the point of death. *La médecine de l'âme, ou La science de bien mourir* prepared the dying person to receive the last sacraments. The *A.B.C. des simples gens*, first catechism in French, reminded him of the principal prayers. Finally, the three *Examens de conscience*, especially *Selon les péchés capitaux* (According to the deadly sins), prepared him for confession.

In front of this set is a painting (fol. 191v) executed by an assistant of the Master of the Apocalypse of the Duke of Berry, inciting the dying to meditation and prayer. In the upper register is the famous vision of Saint Gregory: the crucified Christ appears, half-risen from his tomb, propped up by an angel, surrounded by the instruments of the Passion and symbols of his life (on the right, the coins of Judas, the crown of thorns, the sword of Saint Peter, the ear of Malachus; on the left, the column, the nails, the sponge at the end of a pike, the seamless tunic, and so on). In the lower register a monk from the abbey of Saint-Victor is dying. His brothers bring the last rites to his bedside. He is aided by Saint Victor himself, who slays a demon, and by Saint Augustine, bishop of Hippo, whose rule governs the abbey. A rubricated note mentions that Saint Gregory and the other popes will grant an indulgence of 7,840 days of true pardon to whomsoever will say five "Paters" and five "Aves" before this picture. Given the relationship between text and image, this indeed represents an early and very interesting primitive version of the *Arts de bien vivre et bien mourir* that enjoyed such success beginning in 1480 in the form of woodcut-illustrated pamphlets depicting the combat which raged around the dying man's bed between the Devil's troops and the celestial legions who wrestled for his soul.

This manuscript bears the classification number EEE 15 from the catalogue prepared by the abbey's librarian, Claude de Grandrue, in 1514. As was customary, the manuscript's contents were detailed on fol. 156. It entered the Bibliothèque Nationale in 1796 with the collections of the abbey of Saint-Victor.

Marie-Hélène Tesnière

Emile Mâle, *L'art religieux de la fin du moyen-âge*, 4th ed. (Paris, 1931), 1:91–108. Mgr. Palémon Glorieux, ed., *Oeuvres complètes de Jean Gerson*, vol. 7. *L'oeuvre française*, no. 310, pp. 154–57 (*A.B.C. des simples gens*); no. 330, pp. 393–400 (*Examens de conscience*); no. 332, pp. 404–07 (*La médecine de l'âme*). Millard Meiss, *French Painting in the Time of Jean de Berry: The Late Fourteenth Century and the Patronage of the Duke* (New York, 1967), 354. M. Meiss, *The Limbourgs and Their Contemporaries* (New York, 1974), 372, 403, 475, no. 30. Geneviève Hasenhor, "La littérature religieuse," in *La littérature française des XIVe et XVe siècles*, vol. 8, pt. 1, *Grundriss der romanischen Literaturen des Mittelalters* (Heidelberg, 1992), esp. 266–83. Evencio Beltran, ed., Jacques Legrand, *L'Archiloge Sophie, Le Livre de bonnes moeurs* (Paris, 1991), 49. Danièle Calvot and Gilbert Ouy, *L'oeuvre de Gerson à Saint-Victor de Paris: Catalogue des manuscrits* (Paris, 1991), no. 40, pp. 189–92.

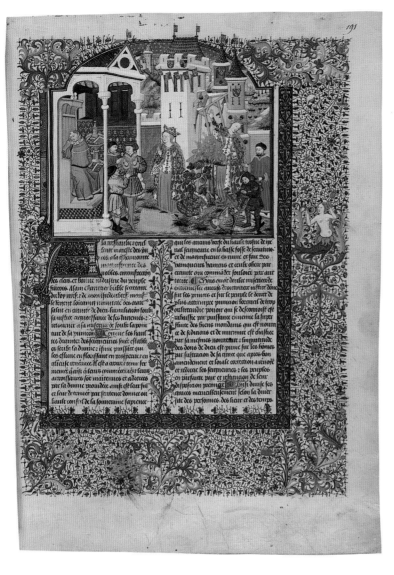

34

GILLES DE ROME
Le Régime des princes
(The government of princes)

LAURENT DE PREMIERFAIT
Translation of Cicero's *De amicitia*
(On friendship) and *De senectute*
(On old age)

ALAIN CHARTIER
Le Quadriloge invectif, Dialogus super deploratione Galliae calamitatis, and *Le Curial*
Département des Manuscrits, Fr. 126, fol. 191

Parchment; V + 263 + III fols.; 430 × 310 mm. Rouen, a little after 1450. Painted by the Talbot Master. Bound in red morocco with the royal arms, late 17th–early 18th century. Made for the hôtel de ville of Rouen; offered to Colbert in 1682 by the councillors of the city of Rouen; acquired by the Bibliothèque Royale in 1732 with the manuscripts of Colbert.

This manuscript is probably the oldest surviving example of bibliophilic patronage by the city councillors of Rouen during the 15th century. When and under what circumstances the councillors first got the idea to establish a collection of precious books in their city hall is unknown. The oldest records relating to the production of manuscripts for the councillors' library date from 1454, but the first orders must have originated from about 1450. Perhaps the collection of books was planned to celebrate the city's recent liberation from English occupation, while at the same time demonstrating its refound prosperity. The three last works in the present collection are indicative of that patriotic state of mind; two of them were written by Alain Chartier, secretary to Charles VII and Norman to boot. *Le Quadriloge invectif* and *Dialogus super deploratione Galliae calamitatis* recount the miserable state to which the kingdom was reduced in the 1420s and make a vibrant appeal for French unity. On folio 191, exhibited here, France in heraldic robe lectures the three estates, which are fighting among themselves.

95

With the exception of the scene from fol. 121, the manuscript illustration is entirely the work of an illuminator already active in Rouen at the time of the English occupation. Called the Talbot Master after one of his most prominent clients, Lord John Talbot, the earl of Shrewsbury, he filled a number of commissions from the earl. The most important was for a collection of romances in French which the earl offered to Marguerite d'Anjou on the occasion of her marriage with Henry IV of England in 1445 (British Library, Royal 15 E VI). The Talbot Master's production was divided between books in large format with secular content like the London manuscript and the present manuscript, to which it is possible to add a Valerius Maximus preserved in Brussels (Bibliothèque Royale 9078), two Boccaccios in the British Library (Royal 16 G V and 18 D VII), and the inevitable books of hours, sometimes according to the usage of Rouen, sometimes of Paris, Thérouanne, or Sarum. Three other books of hours intended for Talbot and his wife, Marguerite Beauchamp, also came from the master's workshop. His ties with the English milieu are further illustrated by the manuscript copy of Saint Bonaventure's *Méditations sur la vie du Christ* in the Jean Galopes translation dedicated to Henry V of England, in which he painted the dedication scene (BNF NAF 6529). Also of interest was his collaboration about 1430–1440 on a Rouen book of hours now preserved in Naples (Biblioteca Nazionale I.B.27) with the Master of the Légende Dorée of Munich, an artist who would play a deciding role in the training of the Master of the Echevinage de Rouen, the leading figure in Rouen illumination from the second half of the 15th century.

Manuscript Fr. 126, whose municipal destination is emphasized by a shield with the city arms at the bottom of the first miniature, rivals the London volume in the care with which it was painted and in its marginal decoration. It is the artist's masterpiece. The two manuscripts, in large format and essentially similar size, present a number of similarities. The illuminator has placed the dedication scene to Louis de Bourbon which precedes the translation of Cicero's *De senectute* (fol. 153) in an architectural structure that can almost be superimposed on that of the frontispiece painting for the collection Talbot offered Marguerite d'Anjou. The artist's elaborate style is evident throughout the Paris volume – shimmering colors studded with pure, barely modeled hues, stylized landscapes surmounted by starry skies with a curiously archaic flavor for the mid-15th century. Stylistically, the Talbot Master gives every appearance of having followed the Falstolf Master from whom he adopted the dry and graphic interpretation of the Boucicaut group models. The artist received a more modest order from the Rouen councillors, for whom he painted the miniature of Aristotle's *Politiques* (Politics), still preserved in Rouen.

A single miniature in Fr. 126 – on folio 121, at the beginning of the *De l'Amitié (De amicitia)* – is the work of a separate artist working in a style related to that of the Bedford Master. This scene, showing Laurent de Premierfait giving the text of his translation to Duke Louis de Bourbon, obviously served as model for the one in a copy of the same text which was illuminated about 1470 by a successor to the Master of the Echevinage de Rouen and painted for Jean II de Hangest, Louis XI's bailiff of Evreux, and later of Rouen (British Library Harley 4917, fol. 1). The copy points up in a particularly striking way how the manuscripts in the city councillors' library supplied a pool of models that played an important role at that time.

François Avril

C. Gaspar and F. Lyna, *Les principaux manuscrits à peintures de la Bibliothèque Royale de Belgique*, pt. 2 (Paris, 1947), 40. C. Rabel, "Artiste et clientèle à la fin du Moyen Age: Les manuscrits profanes du Maître de l'Echevinage de Rouen," in *Revue de l'art* 84 (1989): 59, no. 14. C. Beaune and F. Avril, *Le miroir du pouvoir* (Paris, 1989), 84, 163. F. Avril and N. Reynaud, *Les manuscrits à peintures en France, 1450–1520* (Paris, 1993), 170–71, no. 88.

35

Book of Hours of Marguerite d'Orléans
Département des Manuscrits, Lat. 1156B,
fol. 25

*Parchment; 207 fols.; 209 × 148 mm. Western
France, ca. 1430. 18th-century binding with mosaic
decoration. Marguerite d'Orléans; acquired in 1733
by the Bibliothèque Royale with the manuscripts
belonging to Jean-Baptiste Châtre de Cangé.*

The combined arms of Brittany and Orléans
that appear behind the lady praying in the
Obsecro te illustration (fol. 25) are repeated
elsewhere in the manuscript and indicate
that this book of hours was produced for
Marguerite d'Orléans (sister of the poet-
prince Charles d'Orléans), shown in prayer
before the Virgin. In 1426 Marguerite married
Richard, count of Etampes and member of
the House of Brittany. She was the mother of
Duke Francis II of Brittany and paternal
grandmother of Anne de Bretagne (see cat.
60). Perhaps begun in expectation of
Marguerite's marriage, this book of hours is
one of the most exquisite examples of 15th-
century French illumination. It was executed
in a complex series of stages recently
retraced by Eberhard König, who argues that
while the text may be the one for which the
copyist Yvonnet de La Mote from Blois was
paid in 1421, the decoration would have been
executed later, in several successive phases.
The calendar was probably painted around
1426, in Rennes, in a strangely provincial
manner. The chief miniaturist, known as the
Master of the Marguerite d'Orléans Hours
after this manuscript, only did the bulk of

the illumination sometime around 1430, perhaps also in Rennes. A final artist at some
later point added various heraldic motifs and
even little scenes in the margins of folios 13,
17, 102, and 154. He was probably a Parisian
illustrator, and his work has been identified
in several other contemporary productions,
notably a Bartholomaeus Anglicus manuscript copied for Jean de Chalon, governor of
Auxerre, in 1447 (Amiens, Bibliothèque
Municipale 399).

The forty-one miniatures here reflect the
influence exercised by the Boucicaut Master
over the Master of the Marguerite d'Orléans
Hours. Many of the compositions are based
on Boucicaut's models; highly revealing in
this regard is the scene of the Visitation (fol.
58) which reuses motifs typical of the old
Paris master – an angel carrying the Virgin's
train, the little landscape in the distance, and
the rays of sunshine darting over the horizon. Saint Mark on folio 17 is directly borrowed from the Hours of Jeanne
Bessonnelle, wife of Macé de Beauvau (BNF
Lat. 1411), one of the finest books of hours by
the Boucicaut workshop, whose early arrival
in Angers was of crucial importance in the
development of illumination in western
France. But the sources for the paintings in
the Marguerite d'Orléans Hours are more
complex still, as König's research reveals. For
the artist did not merely mimic the style of
the master with whom he had studied in
Paris, he also borrowed elements from a
highly varied range of manuscripts. These
included the Limbourg *Belles Heures* (a man-

97

O bſcao te domina
ſancta maria ma
ter dei pietate ple
niſſima ſummi regis filia ma

uscript then in the Angers region and al
fruitfully used by the Rohan Master and his
workshop, now in New York, Metropolitan
Museum, Cloisters), Jean de Berry's *Grandes
Heures* (BNF Lat. 919), the *Roman de la rose* in
Valencia (Biblioteca Universitaria 1372), and
even one of his own earlier works, the *Secrets
de l'histoire naturelle* (BNF Fr. 1377–1379). One
of the strangest influences appears in the
scene illustrating the canonical hour of
Nones of the Holy Ghost (fol. 150), in which
the two cripples in the foreground imitate
the figures in a drawing of the Bethesda miracle (Brunswick, Herzog-Ulrich Museum),
which Millard Meiss attributes to the Rohan
Master.

These various models were reinterpreted
with sharp, incisive draftsmanship and
meticulous pictorial execution accompanied
by a harmonious use of rich and varied colors that lend an enameled appearance to
each painting. But the artist's decorative
genius is affirmed most strongly in the imag-
inative borders–a whole range of little
figures, bursting with vitality, enlivens the
margins. These scenes are marked by
unmatched inventiveness and dynamism,
though their meanings are clear only to varying degrees. This microcosm nevertheless
brings to life a whole facet of medieval culture. The battle scene accompanying the
martyrdom of Saint Lawrence (fol. 171) has
been interpreted by König as depicting the
retaking of Orléans by the French in 1429.

François Avril

C. Couderc, *Album de portraits tirés des manuscrits de la
Bibliothèque nationale* (Paris, [1908]), 29, pl. LXV. V. Leroquais,
Les livres d'heures manuscrits de la Bibliothèque Nationale (Paris,
1927), 1:67–70, pls. XLVI–L. J. Porcher, *Les manuscrits à peintures en France du XIIIe au XVIe siècle* (Paris, 1955), 113, no. 241.
E. König, *Französische Buchmalerei* (Berlin, 1982), 53–56,
64–66, 72, 116–17, 122–24, 134, 217, 255, figs. 116, 118–19, 251, 273,
297–98. E. König, *Les Heures de Marguerite d'Orléans* (Paris,
1991). F. Avril and N. Reynaud, *Les manuscrits à peintures en
France, 1440–1520* (Paris, 1993), 28–29, no. 5.

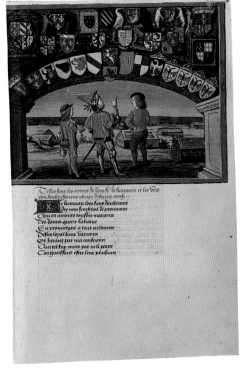

36

RENÉ D'ANJOU
Le Livre du Coeur d'amour épris
(The book of the heart in love)
Département des Manuscrits, Fr. 24399,
fol. 91

*Parchment; 138 fols.; 310 × 215 mm. Provence, 1460.
Illustrated ca. 1480–1485. Red morocco binding.
Was part of the Gaignat collection and the collec-
tion of the duke of La Vallière; purchased at the
sale of that collection in 1784 for the Bibliothèque
Royale.*

Posterity remembers the second son of the
House of Anjou as "Good King René"
(1409–1480). His reputation as a remarkable
patron and a generous and well-read prince
completely overshadowed the vicissitudes of
his rather infelicitous political career.
Between 1420 and 1435, René inherited a
number of titles. He was duke of Bar,

99

Lorraine, and Anjou, and king of Jerusalem, Naples, and Sicily—realms he governed first from Anjou and then from Provence, where he finally made his home in 1471.

René's keen aesthetic sense, evident in a taste for lavish display, elaborate entertainments, and the visual arts, can be discerned as well in his love for painting and books. René was not only a bibliophile but a writer: in 1457 he composed the *Livre du Coeur d'amour épris*, pure fiction or poetic tale drawing its inspiration from a brief love story. Strongly permeated with the spirit of the Arthurian legends, the work borrowed its allegorical form from the *Roman de la rose* (Romance of the rose). While asleep, the author dreams that ardent desire has just seized his heart and conferred upon it knightly arms to lead it into the quest for his lady, a prisoner in the Castle of Rebellion. After he has braved numerous dangers, a brief meeting dashes the hero's hopes. Filled with resignation, he is condemned to end his days in the Hospital of Love. In one episode, Heart and his companions visit the cemetery occupied by famous lovers whose coats of arms decorate the facade (fol. 91): these include mythical, biblical, and antique figures, as well as contemporaries. At the top center the duke of Berry's coat of arms is flanked by a bear and a swan; below are the arms of Gaston Phoebus, count of Foix and the winged white stag, emblem of King Charles VII, brother-in-law of the author; in the upper right-hand corner are those of René himself.

Copied around 1460 by a skilled calligrapher who embellished certain initials with iconographic features—such as the crest of Heart surrounded by "amorous thoughts" (fol. 8)—the manuscript was illustrated by a little-known Provençal illuminator active between 1480 and 1485. This book presents a complete cycle of paintings, as distinct from the famous copy (ca. 1460) preserved in Vienna (Österreichische Nationalbibliothek 2597), which Barthélemy d'Eyck, King René's favorite painter, never completed.

Marie-Thérèse Gousset

O. Smital and E. Winkler, *René, duc d'Anjou: Livre du Cuers d'amour espris/Herzog René von Anjou: Buch von liebenbrannten Herzen* (Vienna, 1926), 38, 61–88. O. Pächt, *René d'Anjou-Studien*, vols. 1 and 2, *Jahrbuch der kunsthistorischen Sammlungen in Wien* 69 (1973). O. Pächt and D. Thoss, *Die illuminierten Handschriften und Inkunabeln der Österreichischen Nationalbibliothek: Französische Schule I* (Vienna, 1974), 38, 42–477, figs. 7, 10–16. René d'Anjou, *Le livre du cuer d'amours espris*, S. Wharton, ed. (Paris, 1980). M.-T. Gousset, D. Poirion, and F. Unterkircher, eds., *Le coeur d'amour épris* (Paris, 1981), 110–31. A. Châtelet, "Le problème du Maître du Coeur d'Amour Epris: René d'Anjou ou Guillaume Porchier?" in *Bulletin de la Société de l'Histoire de l'Art Français* 1980 (1982): 12. F. Robin, *La cour d'Anjou-Provence: La vie artistique sous le règne de René* (Paris, 1985), 183–84, figs. 108–10. C. de Mérindol, *Le Roi René et la seconde maison d'Anjou: Emblématique, art, histoire* (Paris, 1987). F. Avril and N. Reynaud, *Les manuscrits à peintures en France, 1440–1520*, exhibition at the Bibliothèque Nationale (Paris, 1993), no. 209, pp. 370–71.

37

LOUIS DE BEAUVAU
Translation of Boccaccio's *Filostrato*
Département des Manuscrits, Fr. 25228,
fol. 85v

Parchment; III + 93 + III fols.; 224 × 160 mm.
Copied at Blois, ca. 1455–1456, by Pierre d'Amboise
for Marie de Clèves, third wife of Charles
d'Orléans; her arms and emblems are on fol. 1.
Listed in the 1487 inventory of Marie's possessions
at the château de Chauny following her death;
belonged in the 17th century to Eustache de La
Salle, a bibliophile from Reims; in the 18th century
to Louis-César de La Baume Le Blanc, duke of La
Vallière; purchased at the 1784 sale of his collection
by the Bibliothèque Royale.

This little manuscript provides tangible
proof of the cultural exchange between the
courts of Blois and Anjou-Provence during
the era of the two famous poet-princes
Charles d'Orléans (1364–1465) and René
d'Anjou (1409–1480), creating a refined literary society in which Italian influences blended into the local poetic ambience of amorous
melancholy.

Sometime around 1453–1455, Louis de
Beauvau (d. 1462), seneschal of Anjou from
1445 to 1458 and member of the Order of the
Crescent, discovered a copy of Boccaccio's
Filostrato in the library of his master, René
d'Anjou. Beauvau took delight in translating
into French the story of the unrequited love
of Troilus, abandoned by the fickle Cressida
(daughter of the soothsayer Calchas), who
not only went over to the Greeks but also
preferred Hector to Troilus. Beauvau's translation, the first to be made directly from
Italian, was fairly reliable and full of charm;
it enjoyed notable success, as evidenced by
the fourteen manuscript copies that have
survived.

The manuscript displayed here is the oldest known copy. It was executed in Blois by a
certain Pierre d'Amboise about 1455–1456 for
Marie de Clèves, the young wife whom
Charles d'Orléans had married upon his
return from captivity in 1440. The manuscript, adorned with some fifteen grisaille
miniatures highlighted in gold, bears on fol. 1
the princess's arms and emblems. These
emblems–adopted from those of her mother-
in-law, Valentina Visconti–included a
chantepleure (a watering can that dispensed
tears), tears, pansies, her motto "Riens ne
m'est plus" (Nothing more matters to me),
and the letters *h* and *m* linked by a love-knot,
alluding to the couple's first names, Charles
and Marie (compare BNF Fr. 20026, fol. 1). The
young woman apparently did shed some
tears, because in one of his rondeaux Charles
gently reproached her for reading a tale that
made her sad.

Lire vous voy fais merencolïeux
De Troïlus, plains de compassïon;
D'Amour martir fu en sa nascïon:
Laissez l'en paix, il n'en est plus de tieux!
Repaissez-vous en parler gracieux.

(Rondeau 202 [Paris: Champion, 1971, p. 406])

(I see you reading the melancholy story of
Troilus, who merits pity; he was a martyr to
Love in his own country. Leave him in peace,
there are no more like him! Restore yourself
with pleasing speech.)

By a strange osmosis, the fine depiction (fol. 85v) of the wretched Troilus soothed by the music of Trojan woman (Helen, Andromache, Cassandra) becomes a wonderful symbol of the sorrowful, almost despairing, poetry of the poet-prince Charles d'Orléans.

After the death of Marie de Clèves, the inventory of her possessions in the château de Chauny, drawn up in 1487, reveals that she owned twenty manuscripts of religious, poetic, and chivalric content, including this one. But subsequent trace of this volume was lost, and it was notably absent from the Blois library of her son, the future Louis XII. It reappeared in the 17th century in the hands of Eustache de La Salle, a bibliophile from Reims, and was owned by the duke of La Vallière in the 18th century. It entered the Royal Library in 1784 along with part of La Vallière's manuscript collection.

Marie-Hélène Tesnière

Pierre Champion, *La librairie de Charles d'Orléans* (Paris, 1910), 115–17. Alfred Coville, *La vie intellectuelle dans les domaines d'Anjou-Provence, de 1380 à 1435* (Paris, 1941), 140–83. Carla Bozzolo, *Manuscrits des traductions françaises des oeuvres de Boccace* (Padua, 1973), 116–17. *Boccace en France,* exhibition at the Bibliothèque Nationale, entries by F. Avril and F. Callu (Paris, 1975), 63–64. no. 110. Gabriel Bianciotto, "Recherches sur Louis de Beauvau et le Roman de Troyle," in *Les Angevins et la littérature* (Angers, 1979), 28–46. G. Bianciotto, "Edition critique et commentée du 'Roman de Troyle': Traduction française du XVe siècle du 'Filostrato' de Boccace," *Perspectives médiévales* 7 (June 1981): 15–22. François Avril and Nicole Reynaud, *Les manuscrits à peintures en France, 1440–1450,* exhibition at the Bibliothèque Nationale (Paris, 1993), 247, no. 134.

38

*Equestrian Armorial of the
Golden Fleece*

Bibliothèque de l'Arsenal, MS 4790, fol. 51

*Paper; 167 fols.; 290 × 210 mm. Flanders, 1433–1435
(?). Bound in brown calf with gold-tooled fleurons
(16th century). Belonged to the Discalced
Augustinians of Lyon, then to Joseph-Louis, baron
d'Heiss, who sold his collection in 1781 to Antoine
René de Voyer d'Argenson, marquis of Paulmy, the
true founder of the Bibliothèque de l'Arsenal.*

Faced with the decline of chivalry and the
Christian ideal of the warrior defending his
faith, Christian nobles in the late Middle
Ages strove to revive the crusading spirit by
establishing chivalric orders like the Order
of the Garter in 1348 and the Order of Saint
Michael in 1469 (see cat. 44). The duke of
Burgundy, Philip the Bold (1342–1404),
influenced by the ideas of Philippe de
Maizières, planned to create a new chivalric
order following the disastrous expedition led

by his son, John the Fearless (then duke of
Nevers), smashed by the Ottomans at
Nicopolis in 1396. But it was only Philip's
grandson, Philip III the Good (a staunch
defender of Christianity), who managed to
actually found the brilliant Order of the
Golden Fleece, with the aim of liberating the
Holy Land. On January 10, 1430, in Bruges,
during the celebrations of his marriage to
Isabelle of Portugal, Philip III announced
the establishment of the order. The statutes,
comprising sixty-six articles, were solemnly
ratified in Lille on November 22, 1431, during
the first chapter meeting, where twenty-four
knights were named. The total number of
members was set at thirty-one, with the
House of Burgundy maintaining perpetual
sovereignty, since the order was designed to
enhance the prestige of the powerful duke.

The crusading order's symbol was the
Golden Fleece, alluding to the expedition of
Jason and the Argonauts. The four officers of
the order included a "king of arms" who was
the grand master of ceremonies and had to
be well versed in the science of heraldry. The
Burgundian herald Jean Lefèvre de Saint-
Rémy was named the first Herald of the
Golden Fleece. He has therefore long been
credited–despite the absence of any
proof–with compiling the order's grand
equestrian armorial (book of heraldry),
although this attribution is now questioned.

The grand equestrian armorial of the
Golden Fleece is still one of the most glamorous of medieval armorials, even though
incomplete (various owners and binders have
mistreated it by trimming edges, or mixing
up and even losing pages). It is composed on
the one hand of seventy-nine full-page
equestrian portraits, beginning with the
emperor, the king of France and his twelve
peers (including, of course, the duke of
Burgundy on fol. 51), and several European
monarchs, followed by the knights admitted
to the order between 1431 and 1433, wonderfully depicted in jousting poses. On the other
hand, the volume contains a European armorial of 942 coats of arms arranged by country
and armorial region, with names and sketchy
portraits dating up to 1461. The main part is
thought to date from 1433–1435, a period

103

when Spain had made equestrian armorials highly fashionable, and to be the work of a single artist, probably from northern France or Flanders. The vigorous draftsmanship, underscored by black lines and the use of pure bodycolor, is spectacular, and the highly stylized equestrian figures are unique in 15th-century art.

This manuscript belonged to the Discalced (or "Barefoot") Augustinian friars in Lyon, then to Baron d'Heiss, before being acquired in 1781 by the marquis of Paulmy, the true founder of the Bibliothèque de l'Arsenal.

Danielle Muzerelle

L. Archey, *L'ancien Armorial équestre de la Toison d'or* (Paris, 1890). *La Toison d'or,* exhibition, Bruges, 1962. R. Pinches and A. Wood, *A European Armorial of Knights of the Golden Fleece* (London, 1971). *Trésors de la Bibliothèque de l'Arsenal,* exhibition at the Bibliothèque de l'Arsenal (Paris, 1980), no. 111. M. Pastoureau, "Le grand Armorial équestre de la Toison d'or," *Revue de la Bibliothèque Nationale* 8 (June 1983): 34–38. C. de Mérindol and M. Pastoureau, *Chevaliers de la Toison d'or* (Paris, 1986). M. Lefèvre and D. Muzerelle, "La bibliothèque du marquis de Paulmy," in *Histoire des bibliothèques françaises,* vol. 3, *Les bibliothèques de l'Ancien Régime, 1530–1789,* ed. Claude Jolly (Paris, 1988), 302–15.

39

JEAN FROISSART
Chroniques, Livre II
(Chronicles, book II)
Département des Manuscrits NAF 9606, fol. 1

Book II of Froissart's Chroniques *(published by Gaston Raynaud, vol. 9 [1895] to p. 313 of vol. 11 [1899]), followed by two letters from the duke of Orléans, dated Aug. 7, 1402, and March 27, 1403, ending his alliance with the duke of Lancaster, plus the king of England's reply, dated May 31, 1403.*

Parchment; I + 227 + II fols.; 440 × 317 mm. Ca. 1455–1460. By the workshop of the Master of Jouvenel des Ursins and the Master of Boethius. These three volumes (NAF 9604–9606) were copied from a manuscript produced for Arnaud de Corbie, later owned by his son, Philippe (BnF Fr. 6474; Brussels, Bibliothèque Royale IV 1102; BnF Fr. 6475). Belonged to the earl of Ashburnham in the 19th century. Purchased in 1899.

Jean Froissart's *Chroniques* are a key source for 14th-century European history, particularly concerning the wars that pitted France against England from 1327 to 1400. Froissart was an admirable storyteller, providing a lively and colorful picture of aristocratic society with its wars, sudden attacks, duels, knightly jousts, and solemn processions. He wrote for and about elite nobles, leaving a wonderful account of their culture. Froissart traveled throughout Europe, questioning, investigating, taking notes, and gathering testimony and reports from the main participants themselves–princes, knights, and heralds. He constantly classified, organized, and revised his text, probably to take new sources into account, but perhaps also to accommodate shifting political loyalties.

Froissart was born in Valenciennes in 1337 and always remained a man of the north. He was summoned to the court of Edward III of England by the queen, Philippa of Hainaut, who became his patroness. He remained there for ten years or so, frequenting and interrogating English knights and French knights taken prisoner at the battle of Poitiers (1356). After the death of his patroness in 1369, Froissart returned to Flanders, where he became the protégé, in

Et commence le second volume
des cronicques de france z dengleterre
et de plueure qui y sont aduenuce Et
auffi purillement de autre guerres
qui sont aduenuce en pluc desquesme
Ditalie de guienne et de bretaigne fitee
et compilees par noble perfonne meff
Jehan froiffart

OUS AUEZ bien
a deffus ouy parler
et recorder comment
le duc de lancladen
se tourna francoie
par la prinfe ou il
fut a rniet en gafcoigne Et comment
Il vint en france veoir le roy de france
Et fejourna bien vn an ou plus a
parie et tant y fut que il y print
trefgrant defplaifance. Car il auda
au commencement et auffi au diff
nement twuier o fe roy charlec tele
chofe quil ny twuua mie dont Il fe
mezncolia et fe repentit moult tre
dement de ce quil eftoit tourne francoie
maie Il difoit bien que ce auoit efte
pir contrainte et non mie par autre
voie. Si faufa quil fe amblewit de

pivie ou Il auoit twp fejourne et re
tournewit en fon pue et plue fe tour
newit anlloie Car meulx ou coun
te luy plaifoit le fcuue du roy dengle
terre que du roy de france Et fift am
fi comme il ozdonna et donna a ente
de a toue ceulx dont Il auoit la cognoif
fance excepte a ceulx de fon confeil quil
eftoit tout defhaitie. Et monta vnej
four a cheual luy quatrefme tout de
coinea et fe parti de pivie et cheual
ta vie fon pue et fee gent petit a
petit le furuoient Et exploecta tant
pir fee fournece quil vint a bordeaulx
Et twuua la monfeigneur Jehan de
neufuille fenefchal de bordeaulx a
qui il recoza toute fon auenture Et
fe twuua bon anlloie et dift quil
auoit twp plue chier a mentir fa foy
enuere le roy de france que enuere le
roy dengleterre qui eft fon naturel
feigneur A inft demourat le fiece de
lancladen bon anlloie tant comme il
vefquit de quoy le duc danlou fut molt
duuement courouce Et dift bien et
jura que fe iamaie Il le tenoit Il luy
fewit ofter la tefte de deffue lec efpaulec

turn, of the dukes of Hainaut (Robert de Namur) and Brabant (Wenceslas de Luxembourg), then of Gui de Blois.

Froissart's text survives in over one hundred manuscript copies but only became widespread in France at a relatively late date, starting in the second half of the 15th century. The manuscript displayed here, based on a copy (Brussels, Bibliothèque Royale IV 1102) made for Arnaud de Corbie (d. 1414; chancellor of France, notably under Charles VI), is a very rare example of a pro-French version, strongly suggesting that it might have been "edited" in the chancery itself (which had become the key place where "official" French history was written). Book II, covering the years 1375 to 1386, relates the social unrest, urban rivalries, and wars that tore apart a Flanders divided between France and England. The castle of the count of Flanders, Louis II de Mâle, was burned in the midst of a conflict with the inhabitants of Ghent, and so the count appealed in 1382 to his natural liege lord, the king of France; the cities of Ghent and Bruges, meanwhile, sent representatives to seek help from Richard II of England. This is the incident illustrated here (fol. 1), framed by a delightful flowered border. Philip the Bold, duke of Burgundy, and Louis de Mâle, present themselves to the young King Charles VI, who wears a cloak with his coat of arms and bearing the scepter. The duke of Burgundy, the king's uncle, is identifiable by the heraldic emblem on the short tunic covering his breastplate: a pattern of six gold and azure bands combined with a pattern of gold fleurs-de-lis against an azure ground (*parti coticé d'or et d'azur de six pièces, parti d'azur semé de fleurs de lys d'or*). The emblem worn by the count of Flanders, meanwhile, is gold with a red-tongued sable lion rampant (*d'or au lion de sable armé et lampassé de gueules*). Both have their characteristic red caps. Behind the king, Olivier de Clisson, the royal *connétable*, raises his sword in a sign of fealty. On the right, representatives of the Flemish towns, wearing lavish doublets, petition Richard II, whose cloak is adorned with the combined emblems of France and England.

The exact provenance of the manuscript is unknown. It may have been copied for a member of the entourage of René d'Anjou.

Marie-Hélène Tesnière

Léopold Delisle, "Vente des manuscrits du comte d'Ashburnham," *Journal des savants* 1899: 493–500. Eberhard König, *Französische Buchmalerei um 1450* (Berlin, 1982), esp. 201–03. Marie-Hélène Tesnière, "Les manuscrits copiés par Raoul Tainguy: Un aspect de la culture des grands officiers royaux au début du XVe siècle," *Romania* 107 (1986): 301–08, 324–25, 354–61. Charles Sterling, *La peinture médiévale à Paris, 1300–1500*, vol. 2 (Paris, 1990), 116–31 and figs. 114 and 115.

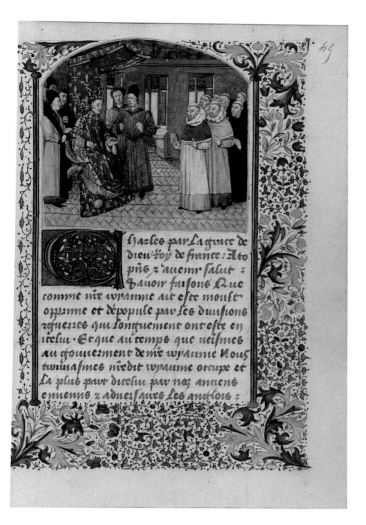

40

Ordonnances royaulx pour la Réformation de la justice, avril 1454 (Royal ordonnances for the reformation of justice, April 1454)

Département des Manuscrits, Lat. 1577A, fol. 45

Pragmatique sanction de Bourges *in Latin, 1438 (fols. 1–43v), copied Nov. 20, 1457; Ordonnances royaulx pour la Réformation de la justice, Montils-lès-Tours, April 1454 (fols. 45–102v), copied Nov. 18, 1457.*

Parchment; II + 104 + III fols.; in two parts (former numeration: 43 and 58 fols.), brought together early on; 175 × 133 mm. Workshop of the Master of the Boccaccio of Geneva. Bound in red morocco with the arms of J.-B. Colbert; edges speckled in red and green ink. Was part of the manuscript collection of J.-B. Colbert; became part of the royal collection in 1732 along with the Colbert collection.

The famous *Ordonnances royaulx* for the "reform of justice," drawn up at Montils-lès-Tours in April 1454, mark the reestablishment of the monarchy's administrative and judicial institutions at the end of the Hundred Years War. At the same time, they represent the birth certificate of a modern state since they constitute in a very real sense France's first codification of legal proceedings.

In 1418 the young Charles VII fled English-occupied Paris, taking refuge in his personal fief in Bourges. He endowed his "kingdom of Bourges" with an administration and a Parlement at Poitiers (becoming the only legitimate legal body, since the Parlement that remained in Paris recognized Henry VI of England in 1422 and became an organ of the English government). Paris was reconquered in 1436 and the administration reunified. It was not until 1454, however, that political conditions and the issuing of these ordonnances (or legal decrees) made it possible to restore Parlement to its normal function, that is, to a full complement of members divided into three chambers.

This modest and rare little manuscript is an almost contemporary copy, dated Nov. 18, 1457. It is illustrated by one of the greatest artists of the time, the Master of the

107

Boccaccio of Geneva, who produced numerous richly decorated manuscripts for the entourage of René d'Anjou. Although the *Ordonnances* had been drawn up at Montils-lès-Tours, the favorite residence of Charles VII in the Loire Valley, the artist has chosen to draw a fictitious royal séance at the Parlement of Paris (fol. 45). The king is seated under a canopy decorated with fleurs-de-lis representing the *lit de justice* (the divan from which the monarch presided over Parlement). He is wearing the coronation coat, edged in orphrey decorated with gems, attached at the left shoulder by a clasp. In his right hand the king holds the golden scepter topped by a fleur-de-lis. His close counsellors are grouped around him. Two high magistrates from the Court of Parlement, identifiable by their long robes and their white hoods lined with ermine, present themselves respectfully before him, holding their bonnets in their hands and apparently indicating their fealty. The floor of the Parlement chamber is covered with a mat, as was customary in wintertime.

It is not known who commissioned this manuscript. But everything (especially the script) suggests that it was produced for one of the high-ranking members of Charles VII's entourage, probably someone from the parlementary milieu. For it also contains the text of the *Pragmatic Sanction of Bourges*, which, insofar as it might be perceived as having established the liberties of the Gallican church with respect to the Holy See, was primarily defended by members of Parlement and royal jurists.

Marie-Hélène Tesnière

Ordonnances des roys de France de la troisième race (Paris, 1723–1849), 13: 267–91 (*Pragmatique sanction de Bourges*, juillet 1438) and 14: 284–314 (*Ordonnances de Montils-lès-Tours "pour la réformation de la justice,"* avril 1454). Françoise Autrand, "Rétablir l'Etat: L'année 1454, au Parlement de Paris," in *La reconstruction après la Guerre de Cent Ans* (Bordeaux, 1979), 1:7–21. Eberhard König, *Französische Buchmalerei um 1450: Der Jouvenel-Maler, der Maler des Genfer Boccaccio und die Anfänge Jean Fouquets* (Berlin, 1982), 211–13. Charles Sterling, *La peinture médiévale à Paris, 1300–1500*, vol. 2 (Paris, 1990), 133–65.

41

Translation of Boethius's *De consolatione philosophiae* (Consolation of philosophy)

Département des Manuscrits, Fr. 809, fol. 40

Jean de Meun, Testament (fols. 1–26); French translation (Jean de Meun and anonymous) of De consolatione philosophiae *(fols. 27–96)*

Parchment; IV + 96 + III fols. Ca. 1460. Illustrated by the artist known, based on this manuscript, as the Master of Boethius. Originally joined with BnF Fr. 19153. Belonged in the 16th century (signature on fol. 96) to Françoise d'Alençon (d. 1550), granddaughter of the notorious Jean d'Alençon, who was sentenced to death (but later reprieved) at Vendôme in 1456; purchased by the Bibliothèque Royale in the 18th century.

Boethius's *De consolatione philosophiae*, read in the light of Holy Scripture and Christianized first by the Carolingian commentators and then by the School of Chartres, was one of the classic books of medieval education. While awaiting execution in his prison, Boethius received the visit of Philosophy who, summoning him to self-knowledge, disclosed to him the absurdity of Fortune and her false riches.

The text thus became the principal literary source for the iconography of Fortune and her wheel, generating an image that was very popular in the Middle Ages, especially in the 15th century. No longer was Fortune pictured, as in antiquity, as an inconstant woman perched over her wheel. Instead she is two-faced, one who spins her wheel rapidly and malevolently, turning a man into a king, then hurling him into adversity and death, at her whim. She was represented as early as the 11th century in a Boethius manuscript at Monte Cassino, accompanied by the words that punctuated, and would continue to punctuate throughout the Middle Ages, the rise and the fall of the powerful: *Regno* (I reign), *Regnabo* (I will reign), *Regnavi* (I have reigned), *Sum sine regno* (I am without a kingdom). During the Romanesque period, the wheel was carved in stone or the tympanums of cathedrals like Beauvais and Amiens. The motif was also widely used in richly decorat-

venerable old man's only riches consist of Philosophy (who, at his side, spurs him to wisdom) and some books saved from his fine library, here placed flat in a wall recess. On the other side the somber and emaciated face of "Fortune adverse" (bad Fortune) turns toward the wheel on which are firmly seated the ephemeral and external riches that accompany her: Wealth, Honor, Youth, and Glory. Wealth is the old man wearing a robe and tightly clasping his purse; Honor is the emperor on his throne with his scepter and his globe; Youth is the young noble gazing at himself in a mirror and holding a falcon on his fist; Glory is the soldier armed with a long pike, larger than all the others, since glory is everyone's dream.

Originally this manuscript formed the second part of a volume that included the *Roman de la rose* (BNF Fr. 19153), according to the recent discovery of François Avril. The second part at least, which is exhibited here, belonged in the 16th century to Françoise d'Alençon, granddaughter of the notorious Jean d'Alençon (d. 1482).

Marie-Hélène Tesnière

V. L. Dedeck-Héry, ed., "Boethius' 'De Consolatione' by Jean de Meun," *Mediaeval Studies* 14 (1952): 165–275. Pierre Courcelle, *La Consolation de philosophie dans la tradition littéraire: Antécédents et postérité de Boèce* (Paris, 1967). Tamotsu Kurose, *Miniatures of Goddess Fortune in Medieval Manuscripts* (Tokyo, 1977). Eberhard König, *Französische Buchmalerei um 1450: Der Jouvenel-Maler, der Maler des Genfer Boccaccio and die Anfänge Jean Fouquets* (Berlin, 1982), 189–91. Glynnis N. Cropp, "Les manuscrits du 'Livre de Boece De Consolacion,'" *Revue d'histoire des textes* 12–13, no. 59 (1982–1983): 335–37. Charles Sterling, *La peinture médiévale à Paris, 1300–1500*, vol. 2 (Paris, 1990), 166–75, figs. 166 and 173. François Avril and Nicole Reynaud, *Les Manuscrits à peintures en France, 1440–1520*, exhibition at the Bibliothèque Nationale, 1993, p. 120, no. 60.

ed manuscripts of the 15th century and appeared in the numerous French translations of Boethius (thirteen), in the second part of the *Roman de la rose* which was inspired by them, in the writings of Petrarch and Boccaccio, and in Martin Lefranc's *Estrif de Fortune et Vertu.*

The manuscript displayed here contains a rare compilation of two of the most widely circulated French translations of Boethius in the Middle Ages—the one that Jean de Meun offered to King Philip the Fair, and an anonymous glossed translation entitled *Le livre de Boece De consolacion.* Its light and refined illustration, which dates from about 1460, presents a thoroughly new iconography. Particularly at the beginning of Book II (fol. 40), it offers an original synthesis of the persona of Fortune seen through the perspective of Philosophy. The true "Fortune propice," or good Fortune, is the one that allows man to turn toward inner well-being: it is the young and candid face of Fortune which seems to bless Boethius in his prison. The

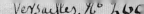

ne plaist a par
ler en vne partie
de mon œuure
de ce dont plus
autres escriptu
res ont parle au
commencement
de la leur Cest
a dire de la guerre plus memorable

qui onques encore furent faictes
Laquelle eulx de autant eurent
auec les Rommains soubz hanibal
leur duc et empereur Car point voir
onques mais tens ou ates de plu
seurs mains Richesses ou ny ne plus
eussent de poissance ou de force ne
de qui plus sceussent dire ne desub
alite de batesllier neurent a faire

42

PIERRE BERSUIRE

Translation of Livy's Decade III

Département des Manuscrits, Fr. 274, fol. 1

Parchment; III + 298 + VI fols.; 405 × 293 mm. Paris, last quarter of the 15th century (after 1480). Workshop of a follower of Fouquet. Bound in red morocco with gold fillets, spine with the arms and emblem of Charles III de Bourbon, archbishop of Rouen (d. 1594). Transferred from the library of Gaillon Castle (summer residence of the archbishops of Rouen) to the Cabinet du Roi in the Louvre during the reign of Henry IV; entered the Bibliothèque Royale at the beginning of Louis XV's reign (ca. 1732).

Between 1354 and 1356, at the request of King John the Good, the Benedictine monk Pierre Bersuire translated into French the three *Decades* by Livy that were then known (1, 3, and 4). Bersuire thus inaugurated the long series of translations commissioned during the reigns of Charles V and Charles VI (1364–1422), which made a substantial number of ancient Latin texts available to a wider public, providing aristocratic circles with a cultural model established by the royal entourage, a model which in certain instances persisted into the mid-16th century.

Bersuire's translation survives in more than sixty manuscript copies and three printed editions, making it a key medieval reference work on antiquity. As the first major literal translation of Livy into French, it was preceded by an annotated glossary of roughly sixty terms specific to ancient civilization. In his prologue, Bersuire wrote that he intended it for those who wished "to know the art of chivalry and to follow the example of ancient virtues." Fifteenth-century humanists were particularly interested in drawing political and institutional models from the text.

The opening illustration of *Decade III* (fol. 1) dresses Carthage in the urban trappings of Ile-de-la-Cité in Paris, where France's legal and administrative institutions were located. The young Hannibal begs his father, Hamilcar, to take him to Spain, while Livy writes his *History* in a study that is already Renaissance in style. In the background is the tip of Ile-de-la-Cité and the royal palace complex: just behind the low ramparts is Saint-Louis Hall and the Grand Courtyard that gave onto the palace garden, while further back is the Grand Chamber (where the Parlement met), flanked by its two towers (the Tour d'Argent and the Tour Bonbec). On the right are the two gables of the Great Hall, the state reception room where the king received distinguished visitors and where the famous statues of the kings of France were housed. This view of Paris in the late Middle Ages imitates a miniature executed by Jean Fouquet for the *Grandes Chroniques de France* (BNF Fr. 6465, fol. 25) and recalls the famous depiction of Paris in the calendar (month of June) in the duke of Berry's *Très Riches Heures*, illustrated by the Limbourg brothers.

It is not known for whom this manuscript was produced. In the 16th century, it was part of the rich library of the archbishops of Rouen, at Gaillon Castle. It was taken to the Cabinet du Roi under Henry IV, and became part of the royal collections early in the reign of Louis XV.

Marie-Hélène Tesnière

Léopold Delisle, *Le Cabinet des Manuscrits de la Bibliothèque Impériale*, vol. 1 (Paris, 1868), 258–60. Henri Omont, *Histoire romaine de Tite-Live: Traduction française de Pierre Bersuire, reproduction des 63 miniatures des manuscrits français 273 et 274 de la Bibliothèque Nationale* (Paris, n.d.). Charles Samaran and Jacques Monfrin, "Pierre Bersuire, prieur de Saint-Eloi de Paris (fin XIIIe s.–1362)," in *Histoire littéraire de France*, vol. 39 (Paris, 1962), 259–450. François Avril, Bernard Guénée, and Marie-Thérèse Gousset, *Les Grandes Chroniques de France: Reproduction intégrale en fac-similé des miniatures de Fouquet, manuscrit français 6465 de la Bibliothèque Nationale de Paris* (Paris, 1987), 19–21.

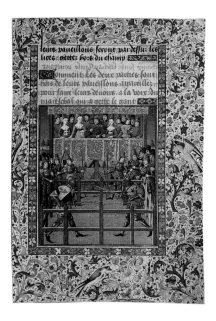

43

Cérémonies et ordonnances à gage de bataille (Ceremonies and edicts for trial by combat)

Département des Manuscrits, Fr. 2258, fol. 22

Parchment; I + 47 + II fols.; 235 × 160 mm. Paris, ca. 1460–1465. Bound in red morocco with the arms and monogram of Philippe de Béthune. François II, duke of Brittany; Philippe de Béthune (d. 1649); transferred to the Bibliothèque Royale in the late 18th century.

This little book contains the procedures to be followed when settling a quarrel by trial by combat. This lavishly decorated copy was made for François II, duke of Brittany, as evidenced by the heraldic decoration of the initials: the two principal initials contain the ermined escutcheon of Brittany, and the others display the knotted-rope emblem instituted by François II.

The scenes of the trial by combat are presented according to a predictable formula. The confrontation of the combatants takes place in an enclosed space, in front of *juges d'armes*, the referees who monitor the legality of the blows exchanged. On the observers' stand at the rear of the miniature an elegant audience of lords and ladies witnesses the combat (fol. 22). Despite its secular subject matter, the diminutive format, presentation of miniatures, and lavish decoration link this manuscript to books of hours rather than to treatises. Each of the eleven miniatures describing the phases of the encounter is

surrounded by a lovely dense border covered with light blue and gold acanthus leaves, flowers, and birds, and a decorative flowered band on burnished gold in light, fresh hues in which blue prevails. For a long time these scenes were attributed to the great Parisian illuminator Master François. Now, however, they are attributed to an artist of a slightly earlier generation who was also active in the capital, known as the Master of Jean Rolin, so called after his principal client, Cardinal Jean Rolin, bishop of Autun, son of the famous Nicolas Rolin, chancellor of Philip the Good, duke of Burgundy. This work, from the 1460s, serves as a good illustration of the transition between the two artists.

Nicole Reynaud

C. Coudere, "Cérémonies des gages de bataille: Reproduction des miniatures du ms. Fr. 2258 de la Bibliothèque Nationale," in *Trésors des bibliothèques de France*, vol. 1 (Paris, 1926), 3–9, pls. I–X. J. Porcher, *Les manuscrits à peintures en France du XIIIe au XVIe siècle* (Paris, 1955), 129, no. 269. C. Sterling, *La peinture médiévale à Paris, 1300–1500*, vol. 2 (Paris, 1990), 200–204, fig. 195. P. R. Monks, "The Master of Jean Rolin II as the Illuminator of the Gages de bataille in Paris, Bibl. nat., Fr. 2258," *Scriptorium* 46 (1992): 50–60, pls. 1–4. F. Avril and N. Reynaud, *Les manuscrits à peintures en France, 1440–1520* (Paris, 1993), 44–45, no. 13.

44

Statuts de l'ordre de Saint-Michel (Statutes of the Order of Saint Michael)

Département des Manuscrits, Fr. 19819, fol. 1

Parchment; III + 29 + II fols.; 205 × 150 mm. Tours, 1470. Painted by Jean Fouquet (ca. 1420–1478/1481). Bound in parchment. From the Achille de Harlay and Chauvelin collections; acquired in 1755 by the abbey of Saint-Germain-des-Prés; entered the Bibliothèque Nationale along with the Saint-Germain-des-Prés collection in 1795–1796.

In an effort to guarantee the allegiance of ranking nobles by establishing a chivalric order that could rival the duke of Burgundy's Order of the Golden Fleece, Louis XI decided to found the Order of Saint Michael in August 1469. The order's insignia was to be a piece of jewelry that depicted the archangel on a rock slaying the devil; it hung from a neck-chain of golden shells linked by dou-

ble-knotted cords. The founding charter stip
ulated the production of two copies of the
statutes, preceded by a miniature showing
the king and the first fifteen knights named
to the order. Each knight was to receive a
booklet illuminated with his coat of arms. In
1470, Jean Fouquet, the king's official painter,
was paid for having painted panels with the
arms of these knights.

The book of statutes exhibited here–the
king's own copy and by far the finest of all
extant copies–should also be attributed to
Fouquet. It contains only one large miniature, taking up three-quarters of the page,
showing the king surrounded by the fifteen
knights, as stipulated. The four officers of the
order are also shown in the background.

This page is striking for the majesty of its
conception and the simple beauty of its composition, marked by an extreme economy of
means and the absence of extraneous lavishness. The coloring represents a prodigious
tour de force. The composition is entirely
built around shades of white (a composition

that historian Henri Focillon compared to
cathedral portals where standing figures
were "grouped on two sides in sharp perspective that focused on a central figure in
the rear"). Indeed, white was Fouquet's preferred color, and his virtuosity conveys the
variety of fabrics and the play of light, with
only a few highlights in red and black on the
knights' ceremonial robes, plus the discreet
shimmer of gold in the open shutter, the
painting, and the king's chair. These light
touches of gold are picked up again in the
golden lettering of the text and the gold
monochrome decoration at the bottom of the
page (another technique favored by
Fouquet). Two angels in gold, shell-like
armor hold the neck-chain just below the
royal escutcheon. The initial *L* of the text
(with shell and double-knot motifs) is also in
monochrome gold.

Most striking perhaps are the strong mod-
eling of volumes in shadow, the full folds of
white damask and ermine, and the artist's
synthesizing vision of this gallery of portraits.
In what Contamine called a "masterpiece
depicting an imaginary scene" (since the
order never actually met), Fouquet used the
power of composition to convey his profound sense of royal majesty and authority.

Nicole Reynaud

P. Durrieu, "Les manuscrits des Statuts de l'ordre de Saint-
Michel," *Bulletin de la Société Française de Reproduction des
Manuscrits à Peintures* 1 (1911): 17–21. H. Focillon, "Le style
monumental dans l'art de Jean Fouquet," *Gazette des Beaux-
Arts* 1 (1936): 26. J. Porcher, *Les manuscrits à peintures en France
du XIIIe au XVIe siècle* (Paris, 1955), no. 252. P. Contamine,
"L'ordre de Saint-Michel au temps de Louis XI et de Charles
VIII," *Bulletin de la Société Nationale des Antiquaires de France*
1976: 212–38. N. Reynaud, *Jean Fouquet* (Paris, 1981), 63–65. F.
Avril, *La passion des manuscrits enluminés* (Paris, 1991), 62–63. F.
Avril and N. Reynaud, *Les manuscrits à peintures en France,
1440–1520* (Paris, 1993), 143–44, no. 72. C. Schaefer, *Jean Fouquet
an der Schwelle zur Renaissance* (Dresden, Basel, 1994), 240–43,
264, fig. 160.

113

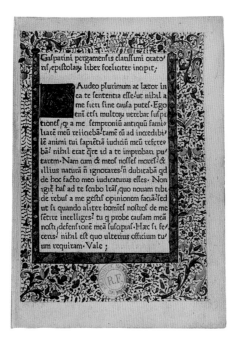

45

GASPARINO BARZIZZA

Epistolae (Letters)

Réserve des livres rares, Rés. Z. 1986, fol. 2

Paris: Ulrich Gering, Martin Crantz, and Michael Friburger (1470). 118 fols., 4⁰. Bound in mottled calf, 18th century. From the Collège de Sorbonne library; transferred to the Bibliothèque Nationale in 1796.

Born about 1360 in Bergamo, Gasparino Barzizza was one of the first Italian humanists. He taught rhetoric, grammar, and moral philosophy in Pavia, Padua, and Milan, hoping above all to revive Latin literature. His *Epistolae* were based on Cicero's model and were designed to teach students prose composition by supplying them with examples of epistolary art. The 1470 edition displayed here is not only a first edition but also the first book printed in France.

Following Italy (where German printers had installed presses at the Santa Scolastica monastery in Subiaco, near Rome, in 1464), France became the second country to import the new technology which by the late 1450s had already spread from Mainz to other Germanic cities such as Strasbourg, Bamberg, Cologne, Eltville, Basel, Augsburg, and Nuremburg. The first French press was set up on the premises of the Sorbonne at the initiative of Guillaume Fichet from Savoy

and Johannes Heynlin from the Rhineland, both professors of theology and *socii* (fellows) at the Sorbonne. While it was Heynlin who recruited three printers from Germany (Michael Friburger, Martin Crantz, and Ulrich Gering), both professors supervised the Sorbonne print shop, selecting texts, verifying manuscripts, preparing copy for printing, and correcting proofs. The humanist tastes of the two Sorbonne socii, who shared an admiration for classical eloquence and style, can be seen in their choice of the first book that they had printed—Barzizza's model letters, which were intended for their own students and which Fichet dedicated to Heynlin. Other authors whose work came off the Sorbonne press (Sallust, Florus, Cicero, Valerius Maximus, and Lorenzo Valla, to name just a few) confirmed this humanist orientation, as did the adoption of Roman type used in Italy for literary works in Latin. Contemporary authors, however, were not excluded from the publishing program—Fichet printed his own *Rhetorica* as well as Greek cardinal Jean Bessarion's *Orationes*, which preached a crusade against the Turks.

Although an advocate of the newly invented printing press, Guillaume Fichet preferred to offer handwritten and illuminated manuscripts to persons of distinguished rank, following medieval tradition. This was the case when he presented a copy of Cardinal Bessarion's *Orationes* to Louis XI in 1472. Thus no book from the first French printing press is known to have been offered to the king. Louis XI nevertheless granted letters of naturalization to the three printers in 1475, who had left the Sorbonne two years earlier to set up shop on rue Saint-Jacques, at the sign of the "Golden Sun," where they published other, more conventional, texts.

Ursula Baurmeister

Gesamtkatalog der Wiegendrucke, no. 3675. J. Veyrin-Forrer, *La lettre et le texte: Trente années de recherches sur l'histoire du livre* (Paris, 1987), 161–87.

46
Mirouer de la Redempcion de l'umain lygnage (Mirror of redemption of the human race)

Réserve des livres rares, Rés. A. 1241 bis, fols. t5v–t6

Lyon: Martin Huss, Aug. 26, 1478. 204 fols.; folio. Bound in green parchment with the coat of arms of the abbey of Saint-Victor in Paris, 18th century. Acquired by confiscation during the Revolution.

The *Mirouer de la Redempcion* is a translation of the *Speculum humanae salvationis*, a well-known Latin work written in the early 14th century, probably by a Dominican monk from Strasbourg, though sometimes attributed to Ludolphe de Saxe. More precisely, it is a translation of a German adaptation that greatly expanded the forty-two initial chapters of the *Speculum* and was published in Basel by Bernhard Richel in 1476. The *Speculum* circulated widely in many versions – Latin text, translation and/or adaptation in various languages – in both manuscript and printed form.

The *Speculum* recounts the story of the Fall and Redemption using the typological method, which assumed that every event in the New Testament (antitype) was prefigured by an episode in the Old Testament (type). A typological reading of the Scriptures revealed a mysterious concordance between the two Testaments that was attributed to divine inspiration. To avoid the risk of faulty typological interpretation, Chancellor Jean Gerson vainly attempted to forbid it to laymen and poorly educated clerics. It was nevertheless precisely to this group that numerous translations of the *Speculum* were apparently aimed several decades later. The large number of editions testifies to the revival of allegorical exegesis in the tradition of the 13th-century *Bibles moralisées* (illuminated Bibles that depicted allegorical concordances).

The *Mirouer de la Redempcion* was translated by Julien Macho, an Augustinian monk from Lyon. All of Macho's work as author, translator, and publisher was entirely aimed at the dissemination of religious books in French, providing material for reflection and prayer for a public able to read but not able to understand Latin. The use of pictures even made it possible to reach the illiterate.

115

Everyone could recognize the story of the prodigal son, depicted here in almost comic-strip form, whose ultimate banquet is prefigured by those of Ahasuerus and the children of Job. Such banquets symbolized the bliss awaiting the Elect in the hereafter.

For this first French edition, Martin Huss (a German printer established in Lyon as early as 1478) reused the woodblocks employed for the Basel edition that Macho had translated. As the first illustrated book to be published in France, it underscores the intellectual and artistic links that were rapidly being established between German-language printing towns and intellectual centers in France.

Denise Hillard

Bibliothèque Nationale: Catalogue des incunables, vol. 2 (Paris, 1981–1985), no. S-353. J. Lutz and P. Perdrizet, *Speculum humanae salvationis. Texte critique, traduction de Jean Mielot (1448)*, 2 vols. (Mulhouse and Leipzig, 1907–1909). P. Perdrizet, *Etude sur le Speculum humanae salvationis* (Paris, 1908). A. Wilson and J. Lancaster-Wilson, *A Medieval Mirror: Speculum humanae salvationis, 1324–1500* (Berkeley, 1984).

47

JEAN D'ARRAS
Le livre de Mélusine
(The book of Mélusine)
Réserve des livres rares, Rés. Y². 400, fol. 142

Geneva: Adam Steinschaber, August 1478. 192 fols.; folio. Purchased late 17th or early 18th century.

At the close of the 14th century, Jean, duke of Berry (who was also count of Poitou and brother of King Charles V), commissioned Jean d'Arras to compose a genealogical romance glorifying the Lusignan family from Poitou. According to a very old legend, the Lusignans' origins could be traced back to a fairy named Mélusine (that is, Mère-Lusine, or "Mother Lusignan").

Mélusine, daughter of the fairy Présine, was fated to change into a serpent every Saturday. The only way she could become a mortal again was to forbid her husband, Raimondin, son of the count of Forez, to see her on that day. At first their union was fruitful, thriving until the day when, despite the ban, Raimondin spied on Mélusine at her bath. There he saw that Mélusine's body ended in a large serpent's tail. Once found out, Mélusine had to flee forever.

Jean d'Arras was able to weave his tale around two elements traditionally found in oral, folk literature–a mother-goddess and the breaking of a taboo–thereby making them a part of learned, written literature.

These sources of inspiration enabled Jean d'Arras to create an entirely new and original type of romance, totally different from the many contemporary prose renderings of the tales of Charlemagne or King Arthur.

The Mélusine story appeared in print form at an early date; a German prose adaptation of a version in verse was published in 1474, and Jean d'Arras's book dates from 1478. The first edition displayed here was published in Geneva by the first printer to set up there, Adam Steinschaber (originally from Schweinfurt, Germany). *Mélusine* was also the first illustrated book to be published in Geneva and, along with *Mirouer de la Redempcion* (see cat. 46), one of the first illustrated French texts to appear. Printers in both Geneva and Lyon were more open to less scholarly forms of culture than their colleagues in Paris, and did not hesitate to produce books that were not only in the vernacular but also illustrated.

The Mélusine romance lent itself particularly well to illustration, which helped make mythical aspects of the story more explicit and gave visual form to supernatural events. The Geneva edition included sixty-three engravings copied from the Basel edition of the German adaptation, which in turn closely followed a manuscript copy. Flat washes of color were added by hand to the woodcuts, lending them a great deal of charm.

Denise Hillard

Bibliothèque Nationale: Catalogue des incunables, 4 vols. (Paris, 1981–1985), vol. 2, no. J-150. W. J. Meyer, ed., *L'histoire de la belle Mélusine de Jean d'Arras: Reproduction en fac-similé de l'édition de Genève* (Bern, 1923–1924). Jean d'Arras, *Mélusine*, ed. L. Stouff (Dijon, 1932; repr. Geneva, 1974). A. Lökkös, *Catalogue des incunables imprimés à Genève, 1478–1500* (Geneva, 1978), no. 2. L. Harf-Lancner, "L'illustration du roman de Mélusine de Jean d'Arras dans les éditions du XVe et du XVIe siècles," in *Le livre et l'image en France au XVIe siècle* (Paris, 1989), 29–55.

48

GIOVANNI SIMONETTA

Commentarii rerum gestarum Francisci Sfortiae (Commentary on the deeds of Francesco Sforza), edited by Francesco Puteolano

Réserve des livres rares, Rés. Vélins 723, fol. 2

Milan: Antonio Zarotto, Jan. 23, [1482]. 292 fols.; folio. Binding by Derôme the Younger, 1789; green morocco gilt, on sides neoclassical borders, liners and endleaves of rosewatered silk, gilt edges. Presentation copy, printed on vellum, intended at first for Louis XI, then for Charles VIII; Charles de Rohan, prince de Soubise; Count MacCarthy Reagh; acquired at its sale in 1817.

This account of the life and exploits of Francesco Sforza (who took the duchy of Milan by force in 1470) was written to affirm the legitimacy of the Sforza dynasty—whose claims the Holy Roman emperor had refused to confirm. Its author, Giovanni Simonetta, secretary in the ducal chancellery, was arrested and exiled in 1479 when Ludovico il Moro, the younger brother of Galeazzo Maria Sforza, who had been assassinated in 1476, made himself guardian of his nephew Gian Galeazzo. Ludovico il Moro then decided to use the *Commentaries* as an instrument of propaganda and asked Francesco Puteolano to revise the text, adapting it to his own political ends. Publication was entrusted to Antonio Zarotto, the first printer to operate a press in Milan. On Jan. 6, 1481, Zarotto was granted a six-year privilege for the book. When it came time to distribute the book in the reigning circles of Europe, Pietro Gallarati undertook to introduce it to the French court.

Pietro Gallarati was a *camerarius* of Francesco Sforza and had been a member of the Consiglio Segreto since 1477, conducting numerous diplomatic missions on behalf of the dukes of Milan. In 1466 he was sent to the court of France to negotiate the marriage of Galeazzo Maria Sforza with Bonne de Savoy. At that time, Louis XI referred to him in a letter to the duke of Milan as "nostre chier et amé compère" (our dear and beloved friend). He also had family connections in the entourage of the French king through his brother-in-law Francesco Roero, a native of Asti in Piedmont, who, under his French name François Royer, had belonged to Louis's household before Louis became king and had been named bailiff of Lyon and seneschal of the Lyon region in 1462.

Gallarati had a copy of the *Commentaries* printed on vellum for the king, inserting a letter of his own composition dedicated to Louis XI and dated Feb. 3, 1482, in place of the dedication that had been addressed by Francesco Puteolano to Ludovico il Moro.

The book was illuminated in an anonymous Milanese workshop and the decoration consists of initials painted on a gold background and borders decorated with flowers and pomegranate ornaments in Ferrarese style; at the bottom of the page, the arms of France are surmounted by a crown and flanked by the letters *L* and *O* for Ludovico.

For reasons unknown, the deluxe copy–the first extant printed book intended for a king of France–could not be presented to Louis XI before he died on Aug. 30, 1483. Pietro Gallarati therefore added a second dedicatory epistle, this one in manuscript, addressed to Charles VIII. The volume seems to have been removed from the royal collection sometime before 1518, however, because it does not figure in the inventory drawn up at that time of the Royal Library in Blois, where the books of Charles VIII had been deposited in 1500. There is no subsequent trace of it until the 18th century and it only reentered the collections of the Bibliothèque Nationale in 1817.

Ursula Baurmeister

Bibliothèque Nationale: Catalogue des incunables, vol. 2 (Paris, 1985), no. S-278. *Lettres de Louis XI, roi de France*, ed. J. Vaesen, E. Charavay, and B. de Mandrot (Paris, 1883-1909). *Dépêches des ambassadeurs milanais en France sous Louis XI et Francesco Sforza*, ed. B. de Mandrot (Paris, 1916-1923). L. Cerioni, *La diplomazia sforzesca nella seconda metà del quattrocento e i suoi cifrari segreti* (Rome, 1970). *Dispatches with Related Documents of Milanese Ambassadors in France and Burgundy, 1450-1483*, ed. P. M. Kendall and V. Ilardi, vols. 1 and 2 (Athens, Ohio, 1970-1981). G. Ianziti, *Humanistic Historiography under the Sforzas* (Oxford, 1988), 127-23

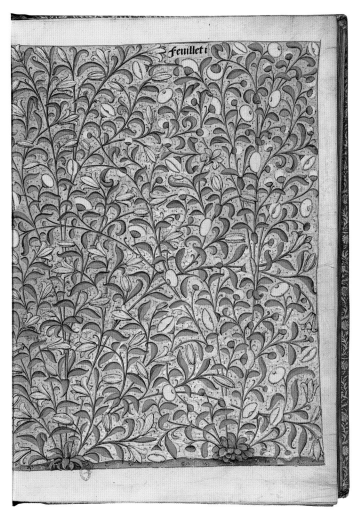

49

La Mer des hystoires.
Le martirologe des sainctz
(The ocean of histories.
The martyrology of the saints)
Réserve des livres rares, Rés. Vélins 677,
fols. A1, ss8v

*Paris: Pierre le Rouge for Vincent Commin,
1488–1489. 270 + 310 fols.; folio; 2 vols. (Rés. Vélins
676–677). Binding signed by Bradel, red morocco,
neoclassical border, gilt edges painted with the
French royal arms. Vellum copy presented to
Charles VIII.*

Printed by Pierre le Rouge, the first official
printer and bookseller to the king, *La Mer des
hystoires* is considered one of the most beautiful illustrated French books of the 15th century. Its title was taken from Giovanni
Colonna's *Mare historiarum,* but the text is a
translation of a universal chronicle entitled
Rudimentum novitiorum. An anonymous cleric
from Lübeck compiled the *Rudimentum*
between 1470 and 1474 and Lucas Brandis
printed it there about 1475. Beginning with
the creation of the world and ending in 1473,
the *Rudimentum* adopted the traditional division into six ages and drew from a wide variety of sources: the Bible, the Church Fathers,
and many authors from antiquity and the
Middle Ages. A number of disparate texts,
including a list of pagan gods, a geographic
dictionary, the *Description de la Terre Sainte*
(Description of the Holy Land) by the
German Dominican Burchardus de Monte
Sion, and thirty of Aesop's fables are inserted into the chronological account. The
anonymous translator, a native of the region
of Beauvais who enjoyed the patronage of a
certain André de La Haye, lord of Chaumont,
added a history of the kings of France adapted from extracts of the *Chroniques de France.*
The account ends with the coronation of
Charles VIII in 1484.

Intended for King Charles VIII, this copy
was printed on exceptionally fine vellum. The
borders, initials, and numerous woodcuts
were hand-colored with miniatures, and
some of the cuts were overpainted. The second volume, which contains the history of

119

the kings of France and is on exhibition here, begins with two large full-page paintings. On the left is the panoply of French royal heraldry, surmounted by the motto "Saint Denis Monioye" – "Montjoie" being the war cry of Frankish kings, to which was added the name of the patron saint of France in the 12th century. On the right-hand page, lilies and marguerites intertwined on a gold background symbolize the union between Charles VIII and Marguerite of Austria, to whom he was betrothed in 1483, before he ascended the throne, and whom he repudiated in 1491 in order to marry Anne of Brittany.

This is the first of some thirty Parisian editions, for each of which a vellum copy was presented to Charles VIII, the first king of France to own printed books. After his death in 1498, his collection was transferred from the castle of Amboise to the Royal Library created by his successor, Louis XII, in the castle of Blois. Since that time, these books have always been part of the royal – later national – collection.

Ursula Baurmeister

Bibliothèque Nationale: Catalogue des incunables, vol. 2 (Paris, 1985), no. R-221. Th. Schwarz, *Über den Verfasser und die Quellen des Rudimentum novitiorum* (Rostock, 1888). E. A. Wright, "*La Mer des hystoires,* Paris, 1488," in *Boston Public Library Quarterly* 11 (1959): 59–74. R. Brun, "'La Mer des histoires' de Pierre le Rouge offerte à Charles VIII," in *Humanisme actif: Mélanges... offerts à Julien Cain,* vol. 2 (Paris, 1968), 191–97. U. Baurmeister and M.-P. Laffitte, *Des livres et des rois: La Bibliothèque Royale de Blois* (Paris, 1992), no. 17.

50

FRANÇOIS VILLON

Le Grant Testament Villon et le Petit. Son Codicille. Le Jargon et ses Balades (Villon's large testament and his small one. His codicil. The jargon and his ballads)
Réserve des livres rares, Rés. Ye. 245, fols. g2v–g3

Paris: Pierre Levet, 1489. 58 fols.; 4to. Binding by Bozérian the Younger, in red straight-grained morocco, early 19th century. Acquired late 18th or early 19th century.

"Mais priez Dieu que tous nous veuille absoudre" (But pray God that He may forgive us all). The throbbing refrain of the *Ballade des pendus* (Ballad of the hanged), the most famous of Villon's ballads, plunges us immediately into the very heart of his poetry. It poses the eternal query about life and death, far removed from the traditional allegories of courtly poetry, and five hundred years later it is still moving. The first edition of Villon, published in 1489, was illustrated with engravings whose naive simplicity fit well with the sincerity of the poems.

Born about 1431, Villon studied in Paris and became master of arts in 1452. But in this troubled period he led a difficult and tumultuous life. He was implicated in a good many shady affairs, including thefts or brawls that occasionally ended in someone's death. Associating with the disreputable characters of Paris, known as the Coquillards, he was so

familiar with their "jargon" that he even composed some ballads using their slang. At the same time Villon was involved in the life at court and sought the patronage of Duke Charles d'Orléans, a poet himself and organizer of the poetry contests at Blois. At Moulins, Villon enjoyed the patronage of another duke-poet, Jean de Bourbon. Released from prison a number of times, he was finally condemned to be hanged in 1463. His sentence was commuted to ten years of exile outside Paris, and from that point on the poet disappeared from view. His mysterious end has lent a special resonance to his poems. The verses seem to hold a tragic foreknowledge of his fate, translating as they do his fear of an ignominious and terrible death.

Villon's work consists essentially of two *Testaments*, written in octaves interspersed by ballads. In the *Petit Testament*, or *Lais*, Villon bequeaths ridiculous objects and goods he did not own. Some of the bequests in the *Grand Testament* proceed from the same vein of parody and irony but are mixed with more serious themes. The poet prefaces them with a long meditation on his lost youth, his downfall, his sufferings, and death. Villon's art, employing every poetic register, enables readers to grasp human truth in all its forms. He juxtaposes melancholy with burlesque and satiric poetry, lyricism with drole or mocking caricature, obscene portraiture of fallen women with pious evocations of his mother and the Holy Virgin. The profound contradictions of Villon the man are reflected in the multiple facets of Villon the poet.

Denise Hillard

Bibliothèque Nationale: Catalogue des incunables, vol. 2 (Paris, 1981–1985), no. V-179. *Le Testament Villon. Le Lais Villon et les poèmes variés*, ed. J. Rychner and A. Henry, 5 vols. (Geneva, 1974–1985). *The Poems of François Villon*, trans. G. Kinnell (Boston, 1977; repr. 1982). R. R. Peckham, *François Villon: A Bibliography* (New York and London, 1990). R. Sturm, *François Villon: Bibliographie et matériaux littéraires–Bibliographie und Materialen (1488–1988)* (Munich, 1990).

51

La Danse Macabre

(The dance of death)

Réserve des livres rares, Rés. Ye. 189, fol. a3v

La Danse Macabre nouvelle (The new dance of death); *Les Dis des trois mors et des trois vifs* (The stories of three living and three dead); *La Danse Macabre des femmes* (The women's dance of death); *Le Débat du corps et de l'ame* (The debate of body and soul); *La Complainte de l'ame damnée* (The complaint of the damned soul)

Paris: Guy Marchant, June 7–July 7, 1486. 32 fols.; folio. Bound in red morocco, 18th century. From the collection of Louis-Jean Gaignat; later from the collection of the duke of La Vallière; acquired from the sale of his collection in 1784.

52

La Danse Macabre
(The dance of death)
Département des Manuscrits, Fr. 995,
fols. 2v–3

La Danse Macabre (fols. 1–17); *Le Dit des trois morts et des trois vifs* (fols. 17v–22v); *La Danse des femmes* (fols. 23–43v); *La Reine morte* (fols. 44, 44v)

Parchment; IV + 44 + III fols.; 314 × 198 mm. Paris, 1490–1500, workshop in the style of Rouen. Bound in red morocco with the arms of Jean-Baptiste Colbert. It is not known for whom this manuscript was made. It belonged in the 16th century to a Deroiliefort-Bruille family; in the 17th century to the academician Ballesdens, who at his death (1675) bequeathed it to Colbert (MS Colbert 1849). It was acquired for the royal collection in 1732 with Colbert's manuscripts.

Uncertainty still surrounds the origin of *La Danse Macabre*, or *La Danse des morts*, which appeared in the second half of the 14th century and enjoyed great success throughout Europe until the mid-18th century. Did it spring from the legend of the three horrible cadavers that appear in the evening to three young people in the cemetery to remind them of man's fate, the inexorability of death, and to exhort them to be good? Or was it initially a kind of mimed spectacle intended to stir the faithful at the end of a sermon on death? We do not know. Hierarchical representation of society, equality before death, brevity of life—these are the themes it developed. The dance of death was long said to be an upshot of the plague. According to Jacques Chiffoleau, it demonstrated the existential solitude of 15th-century men when contemplating their ancestors and their rulers.

The oldest visual representation (1424) of a *danse macabre* was in Paris on the walls of the Cemetery of the Innocents, a meeting place for strollers and street merchants. It was the source of numerous European representations, especially in London (for example, in Pardon Churchyard). The fresco in the Cemetery of the Innocents was destroyed in 1663, but the woodcuts published in an edition of 1485 by the Parisian printer Guy Marchant provide a reasonably exact picture. The work enjoyed such success that Marchant printed two other editions in quick succession, one a copy of the first edition and published without date, the other (cat. 51) dated 1486 and augmented with a number of other texts. The latter *Danse* also includes a number of supplementary characters. The

Latin verses of "Vado mori" (I go off to die) were added at the top of the woodcuts.

The manuscript exhibited here (cat. 52), dating from 1490–1500, was very likely copied from one of these editions and was produced in Paris, but in a style typical of Rouen. Thirty couples, consisting of one who is dead and one who is living, succeed one another in this dance that all must learn: from the pope, emperor, cardinal, king, archbishop, and constable to the hermit and little child. The half-skeleton, half-mummy that drags the living character away by the hand is not Death but the character himself in death; it is a mirror image, the future double of the living character, draped in his shroud, a spade on his shoulder for digging his grave. The king may well point to his scepter; it makes no difference. Death is the same for all. So is it that he laments (fol. 3):

Las, on peult bien veoir et penser
que vault orgueil, force et lignage.
Mort destruit tout, c'est son usage,
aussi tost le grant que le mendre,
Qui moins se prise plus est sage.
En la fin fault devenir cendre.

(Alas! The value of pride, strength, and lineage can well be imagined. Death destroys all, that is its custom, as much for the great as for the smallest. Whoever thinks himself least is all the wiser. At the end, we must turn to ashes.)

Marie-Hélène Tesnière

Gesamtkatalog des Wiegendrucke, no. 7945. *La Danse Macabre de Guy Marchant*, ed. Pierre Champion with facsimile of the edition of Guy Marchant, Paris, 1486 (Paris, 1925). Emile Mâle, *L'art religieux de la fin du moyen âge en France* (Paris, 1931), 347–89. André Corvisier, "La représentation de la société dans les Danses des morts du XVe au XVIIIe siècle," *Revue d'histoire moderne et contemporaine* 16 (1969): 489–539. Pierre Vaillant, "La Danse Macabre de 1485 et les fresques du Charnier des Innocents," in *La mort au moyen-âge* (Strasbourg, 1977), 81–86. Jean Batany, "Les 'Danses Macabres': Une image négative du fonctionnalisme social" and Jane H. M. Taylor, "Un miroer salutaire," in *Dies illa: Death in the Middle Ages*, ed. Jane H. M. Taylor (Manchester, 1984), 15–27 and 29–43. Jacques Chiffoleau, "Du Christianisme flamboyant à l'aube des Lumières," in *Histoire de la France religieuse*, ed. Jacques le Goff and René Rémond, 4 vols. (Paris, 1988–1992), 2:149–60. *The Danse Macabre of Women, MS Fr. 995 of the Bibliothèque Nationale*, ed. Ann Tukey Harrison (Kent, 1994).

53

Lancelot du Lac. La Quête du Saint Graal. La Mort le roi Artu
(Lancelot of the lake. The quest for the Holy Grail. The death of King Arthur)
Réserve des livres rares, Rés. Vélins 614, fol. 3

Paris: For Antoine Vérard, 1494. 250 + 192 + 240 fols.; folio; 3 vols. (Rés. Vélins 614–616). Bound in red morocco gilt, French royal arms on covers, 18th-century. Vellum copy presented to Charles VIII.

Written about 1220 by an anonymous author, *Lancelot du lac*, grouped here with *La Quête du Saint Graal* and *La Mort le roi Artu*, is the undisputed masterpiece of medieval prose romance. It is a tale of adventure about the quests of the knights of the Round Table, the love of Launcelot for Queen Guinevere, and the Holy Grail, whose quest is forbidden to Launcelot because of his sinful love but whose secrets will be revealed to his son Galahad. This vast work enjoyed great popularity, as the numerous extant 13th-, 14th-, and 15th-century manuscripts testify.

A first edition was published as early as 1488; the present copy belongs to the second edition. It was offered to Charles VIII by Antoine Vérard, a Parisian bookseller who specialized in the publication of deluxe copies on vellum intended for the kings of France and England, great lords such as Charles d'Angoulême, father of the future Francis I, and a wealthy clientele of high officials and financial officers. After the death in 1493 of Pierre Le Rouge, official bookseller and printer to the king (see cat. 49), Vérard became the accredited supplier to the court,

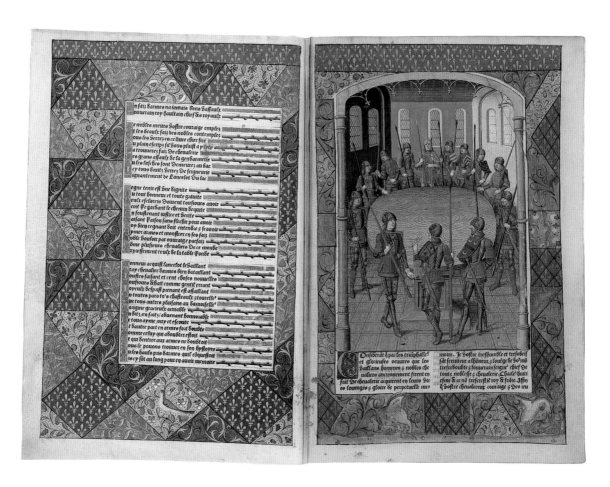

though he never officially held the title of bookseller to the king.

The deluxe copies underwent more or less important modification according to the social status of the person for whom they were intended and the price that was paid. Here the large woodcuts are overpainted with miniatures more closely related to the text. Numerous small miniatures replaced the chapter summaries, which, instead of being printed as in the regular copies, were added by hand in the margins. Charles VIII's copy is the only one to contain an additional leaf inserted at the front of the first volume. On the recto is a large painting representing a tournament, and on a raised platform in the background Vérard can be seen presenting the king with a copy of the work. There begins a long acrostic dedication, perhaps written by the bookseller himself. Read vertically, the initial letters of these verses reveal: CHARLES DE VALOIS ROY DE FRANCE HUITIESME DE CE NOM (Charles de Valois, king of France, the eighth of this name). On the following folio, the knights of the Round Table are grouped around King Arthur. Below begins Vérard's epistle to the king, copied in large part from the anonymous prologue in the first edition. These two paintings are the work of the Master of Jacques de Besançon, reputedly the most prolific and sought after French illuminator of the 15th century, who worked regularly for Vérard from 1492 onward.

Ursula Baurmeister

Bibliothèque Nationale, *Catalogue des incunables*, vol. 2 (Paris, 1985), no. L-31. P. Durrieu, *Un grand enlumineur parisien au XVe siècle: Jacques de Besançon et son oeuvre* (Paris, 1892), no. XLVIII. C. E. Pickford, "Antoine Vérard: Editeur du Lancelot et du Tristan," in *Mélanges de langue et littérature françaises du moyen âge et de la Renaissance offerts à... Charles Foulon*, vol. 1 (Rennes, 1980), 280–84. U. Baurmeister and M.-P. Laffitte, *Des livres et des rois: La Bibliothèque Royale de Blois* (Paris, 1992), no. 20. F. Avril and N. Reynaud, *Les manuscrits à peintures en France, 1440–1520* (Paris, 1993), 256–62.

9

10

54

Coins of the 8th–16th Centuries

Pictured: nos. 9 and 10

1 *Charlemagne,* denier, *Toulouse, 794–812*
Cabinet des Médailles, 800
Silver; diameter: 21 mm; weight: 1.63 g
Obverse: + CARLVS REX FR, *cross*
Reverse: + TOLVSA *monogram of* KAROLVS

2 *Louis the Pious,* solidus, *Duurstede(?), 814–840*
Cabinet des Médailles, 1072
Gold; diameter: 200 mm; weight: 4.32 g
Obverse: + DN HLVDOVVICVS IMP AVC, *laureate
bust, draped on the right*
Reverse: + MVNVS DIVINVM, *cross in a crown of
foliage*

3 *Charles the Bald,* denier, *Bourges, 840–866*
Cabinet des Médailles, 736
Silver; diameter: 20 mm; weight: 1.45 g
Obverse: + CARLVS PI, *laureate bust with cuirass
on the left*
Reverse: BITV-RICES *in two lines*

4 *Hugh Capet,* denier, *Beauvais, 987–996*
Cabinet des Médailles, 178
Silver; diameter: 22 mm; weight: 1.22 g
Obverse: HER[VE]VUS HVGO REX, *cross decorated
with two bezants*
Reverse: BELVACVS CIVITAS, *monogram of*
KAROLVS

5 *Philip II,* denier parisis, *Paris, 1180–1223*
Cabinet de Médailles, 285
Silver; diameter: 20 mm; weight: 1.00 g
Obverse: PHILIPVS REX, *in the field* FRA-NCO, *in
two lines, the second retrograde*
Reverse: + PARISII CIVIS, *cross*

6 *Philip II,* denier tournois, *Tours, 1204–1223*
Cabinet de Médailles, 354B
Silver; diameter: 19 mm; weight: 0.90 g
Obverse: PHILIPVS REX, *cross*
Reverse: + TVRONVS CIVI, *châtel tournois*

7 *Louis IX,* gros tournois, *1266(?)–1270*
Cabinet de Médailles, 18
Silver; diameter: 26 mm; weight: 4.10 g
Obverse: + LVDOVICVS REX; *in the exterior legend:*
+ BNDICTV:SIT:NOME:DNI:NRI:DEI:IHV:XPI, *cross*
Reverse: + TVRONVS CIVIS, *châtel tournois: bor-
der of twelve lilies*

8 *Philip IV,* gold florin called *"à la Reine," 1305*
Cabinet de Médailles, 233
Gold; diameter: 27 mm; weight: 4.75 g
Obverse: PHILIPP:DEI:GRA:FRACHORV:REX, *the
king seated holding a scepter and a fleur-de-lis,
between two lilies*

Reverse: + XPC:VICIT:XPC:REGNAT:XPC:IMPERAT, *cross in quadrilobes leafy and ornamented with flowers and decorated by four lilies*

9 *Charles VII*, royal d'or, *Lyon, 1429–1431*
Cabinet de Médailles, 1378
Gold; diameter: 30 mm; weight: 3.72 g
Obverse: + KAROLVS:DI:GRA:FRANCORV:REX *clover, the king standing holding two scepters; background sprinkled with lilies*
Reverse: + XPC:VINCIT:XPC:REGNAT:XPC:INPERAT, *cross clover and leafy in a quadrilobe with fleur-de-lis ornamented by four crowns*

10 *Charles VIII*, écu d'or de Bretagne, *Rennes, 1491–1498*
Cabinet des Médailles, 1862
Gold; diameter: 28 mm; weight: 3.41 g
Obverse: : KAROLVS:DEI:GRA:FRANCORVM:REX: R, *écu de France between two ermine tails crowned; above: sun*
Reverse: : XPS:VINCIT:XPS:REGNAT:XPS:IMPERAT:R *cross with fleur-de-lis ornamented with four ermine tails crowned*

11 *Louis XII*, teston, *Paris, 1514*
Cabinet de Médailles, 2081
Silver; diameter: 28 mm; weight: 9.53 g
Obverse: +: LVDOVICVS:I:G:FRANCORV:REX: *bust on the right, head covering of crown on a hood*
Reverse: + XPS:VINCIT:XPS:REGNAT:XPS:INPT: *écu de France crowned in a polylobe*

This selection of eleven coins documents the principal stages of French coinage between the late 8th and early 16th centuries. Charlemagne's reform of 794 created a new denarius (1) whose appearance would hardly change until the 10th century, although its weight diminished and its fineness deteriorated: the denarius of Charles the Bald (3) was still very close to that of Charlemagne. Alongside the almost exclusive use of silver that lasted until about 1270, some very specific gold strikings did exist, like the solidi of Louis the Pious intended for commerce with peoples in the north (2). The absence of a purely royal coinage under Hugh Capet shows the weakness of the Capetian dynasty in its beginnings: only some denarii and oboles issued by Hervé, bishop of Beauvais (4), and a unique denarius of Laon survive. Philip II instituted the double system of the denier parisis (5) north of the Loire and the denier tournois to the south, whose distinctive marks (FRA-NCO in the north, the châtel

in the south) would endure until the second half of the 14th century. Under Louis IX appeared the first multiple of the denarius: the *gros denier* was worth twelve denarii and enjoyed international success, unlike the first royal gold coin, the écu, issued probably in 1270. The period which extended from Philip IV to Philip VI saw the flowering of a multitude of gold coins of extremely varied and artistic types. Of these the gold florin "à la Reine" (8) is one of the purest examples. The Hundred Years War would provoke a deterioration of coinage that was spectacular in its scope and swiftness: the royal d'or, ordered Oct. 9, 1429 (9), represents Charles VII shortly after his coronation (July 17, 1429) and marks the return to a coinage of pure gold, after the issues of gold of poor fineness (as low as 750 parts per thousand). In the 15th century various provinces were united into the kingdom of France. Among them was Brittany, which nonetheless retained some issues of a special type (10) until the mid-16th century. The king's portrait appeared for the first time under Louis XII on heavy silver coins, called testons (11), which opened a new chapter in the history of French coins.

Michel Dhénin

M. Prou, *Catalogue des monnaies françaises de la Bibliothèque Nationale: Les monnaies carolingiennes* (Paris, 1896). A. Dieudonné, *Catalogue des monnaies françaises de la Bibliothèque Nationale: Les monnaies capétiennes ou royales françaises*, vol. 1, *De Hugues Capet à la réforme de Saint Louis;* vol. 2, *De Louis IX (Saint Louis) à Louis XII* (Paris, 1923–1932). J. Lafaurie, *Les monnaies des rois de France*, vol. 1, *De Hugues Capet à Louis XII* (Paris, 1951). J. Duplessy, *Les monnaies françaises royales de Hugues Capet à Louis XVI (987–1793)*, vol. 1, *Hugues Capet à Louis XII* (Paris, 1988).

II

From Royal Collections to National Patrimony

3 The Religion of Royalty

From Saint Louis to Henry IV (1226–1589)

Elizabeth A. R. Brown

A glowing red comet swept over France a month before the death of King Philip Augustus in 1223, signifying the celestial jubilation at Philip's approaching arrival in heaven and the salvation he had won through his deeds, pleasing in the eyes "of the supernal Lord of the stars." The king died on July 14. The following day, at the moment of his burial at the abbey church of Saint-Denis, Saint Denis himself, patron of the kings of France, appeared, shining with light, accompanied by white-clad angels and escorting the king to "an honorable man named James" who lay mortally ill in Italy, in the house of the pope's chief penitential officer. The saint ordered James to tell the pope to celebrate a mass so that the king would be absolved of his venial sins. Restored to health, James carried out Denis's instructions and the pope fulfilled the divine mandate—presumably making possible Philip's immediate entry into heaven. These stories appear in a Latin epic poem written by the royal cleric Guillaume le Breton. The tales, which circulated widely, elevated the virtues of the king and made him the celestial companion of Saint Denis and all God's angels.[1]

Guillaume and his narrative reflect the shift in the locus of French power and culture that had taken place in the preceding century. Authority had begun to pass, decisively, from monastic centers, generally located in the countryside, to cities and the royal court. One of the harbingers and architects of this change was himself a monk: Suger, abbot of Saint-Denis (1122–1151), the church where Philip Augustus was interred and where many of the king's predecessors lay buried. Aiming to benefit himself and his abbey, Suger allied himself with the monarchy and in his writings exalted the king as sovereign over the realm's other lords and as the supreme defender of France and her churches.[2] The future lay with the kings and their entourage, and if Rigord, another monk of Saint-Denis, composed a laudatory but traditionally straightforward history of the deeds of Philip Augustus (1180–1223), it was the royal servant Guillaume le Breton who produced the epic work glorifying his king as "three and four times blessed, so that in body and soul he might rise to the stars." The victories of Philip Augustus over the English and of his son, Louis VIII (1223–1226), over the southern Albigensians provided the material foundations, the territory and wealth, that permitted the monarchy to enlist apologists, artists, architects, and builders in its service. The kings' administrative and judicial reforms, their protection of the realm's churches, gained their subjects' loyalty. These accomplishments go far to explain the impassioned rhetoric of the Majorcan visionary Ramón Lull, who in 1311 addressed King Philip the Fair (1285–1314) as "most glorious, most illustrious, magnificent champion of the Church and defender of the Christian faith," and declared that in him, "beyond the other rulers of the world, singularly shine forth today justice, truth, faith, charity, unswerving hope in beatitude, beauty with fortitude, magnanimity with temperance, largesse with prudence, humility and devotion and Christian religion, piety, benignity, wisdom, chastity, and, in brief, many, many gifts of nature and infused grace."³ Such veneration of the kings of France would flower in succeeding centuries and remain strong even when, in the sixteenth century, the Catholic religion, bulwark of the monarchy, was challenged by the heresies of the Protestants.

"Un roi, une foi"

The canonization of Louis IX (1226–1270) in 1297 and the miracles wrought by his remains (see cat. 23) magnified and strengthened the monarchy's prestige and force, buttressing the belief that all members of the royal family—not merely the king— were distinguished by holy blood.⁴ Through his saintly life and deeds, his faith in and courageous implementation of the church's teachings, his two crusades, and his lavish endowment of religious foundations, King Louis gave special luster to the dignity of the French crown. In accomplishing his canonization, his grandson Philip the Fair ensured to his descendants, direct and indirect, an ancestor whose renown elevated them and confirmed the kings' most Christian status. The popularity of the name Louis (and Louise) among the king's progeny is understandable, for all who bore it were considered the saint's spiritual godchildren. Prior to Louis's canonization, the legitimacy of his house's rule was defended by contrived arguments explaining away the embarrassing disjunctions among the three lines of kings (Merovingian, Carolingian, and Capetian) that had governed France—justifications which recalled the Bible's unsettling pronouncement that God transfers kingdoms as he wishes. The image of the sainted Louis forcefully supplemented such justifications. At four critical moments (in 1328, 1498, 1515, and 1589), blood-ties to Saint Louis would smooth the transition from the direct line of the Capetians to other branches when the reigning kings failed to produce heirs capable of ascending the throne.⁵

When the twelve-year-old Louis IX became king in 1226, France was threatened by the Albigensian heresy, and his foreign-born mother, the regent Blanche of Castile, soon had to confront a conspiracy of nobles thirsty for the power they hoped to seize from a child king and his mother. The circumstances were strikingly similar in 1559, when Henry II (1547–1559) died suddenly and unexpectedly, leaving a fifteen-year-old son, Francis II (1559–1560), and a foreign-born widow, Catherine de

Médicis, to confront pertinacious Huguenots and antagonistic princes. The ultra-Catholics sternly reminded Catherine de Médicis of the likeness of their age to the days of Louis IX and hoped that she, like Blanche of Castile, would wage unremitting warfare and force unconditional surrender on her opponents, political and religious.[6] The queen mother herself recognized the likeness between her situation and the crises Blanche had confronted, and although she did not want to be thought Blanche's imitator, she hoped to be able to make peace and preserve it, as Blanche had done, until her own son, Charles (IX), was old enough to govern.[7] But for forty years attempts to placate and compromise simply inflamed the opposition, and in 1590 a servant of the crown denounced the "worldly prudence" of the "empirical" and called for the application of the same harsh and repressive remedies that Louis and his mother had used "to cure the plague that afflicted the realm,... to restore health to this kingdom, half-dead and languishing."[8] Times had changed, however, and it was the limited toleration granted in 1598 in the Edict of Nantes, not the massacre of Protestants in Paris on Saint Bartholomew's Day 1572 or the murder of the Guises at Blois in 1588, that brought a measure of peace, however troubled, to France.

From the time of the Albigensians until 1598, the principle "one king, one faith" (un roi, une foi), however threatened, reigned supreme in France. In 1567 Charles IX proclaimed that justice and religion (which he equated with Catholicism, the one true faith) were the columns, indissolubly linked, on which the kingdom rested; as divine providence had established one sun and one king in the realm, so, by similitude of reason, there should be only one religion, followed by God-fearing people who honored their king.[9] Yet after the Edict of Nantes, as before, another religion, the religion of monarchy, was as important a force for French strength and unity as justice and the Catholic faith. The kingdom considered itself (and was widely believed to be) the most Christian nation of all, a second Israel; its rulers were viewed as second Davids, defenders of orthodoxy, and they commanded veneration that rivaled devotion to papal Rome and Protestant Geneva. This loyalty goes far to explain the success of the kings of France in dealing not only with the disruptions caused by heresy, but also with those resulting from the wars with England that raged for more than a century, and from the bitter rivalries of landed princes in the fifteenth century. The doctrines of the royal religion, forged by the kings and their supporters, were disseminated through ceremonies and symbols whose traces are preserved in manuscripts and artifacts the kings commissioned. It seems no accident that the first of the three surviving illustrated French coronation books, the *ordo* of 1250 (cat. 15), was created during Louis IX's reign, its miniatures reflecting and testifying to the exaltation of the royal office that he accomplished.[10] Of all the influences that affected French culture from the thirteenth through the sixteenth centuries, this religion, the religion of royalty, was the most potent.

Royal Ceremonial and Royal Power

The central ritual of the monarchy was the installation ceremony that transformed the ruler from a merely human being to a creature priestly and semidivine. The learned arguments of theologians who sharply distinguished the king's status from the cleric's were unpersuasive in the face of the ceremony of consecration and the king's subsequent admission, priestlike, to communion in both kinds, as he received not only the wafer but also the wine reserved to the clergy. As had been true since Carolingian times, a central feature of the coronation was the anointment of the new ruler with holy oil. From the beginning of the thirteenth century special stress was laid on the nature of the oil used for the ritual, believed to have been brought from heaven by the Holy Spirit for Clovis's consecration (in fact, baptism) in 496 and to have been miraculously replenished ever since. It is little wonder that in 1793 the Holy Ampulla that held this holy chrism was ceremoniously broken to bits, sarcastically decried as "a sacred bauble of ninnies" (ce hochet sacré des sots).[11] Nor, in view of the belief's long history, is it surprising that many faithful were still convinced, with a late fourteenth-century apologist, that the king of France was anointed "more nobly and more sacredly than any king. . . and thus is called the most noble, the very Christian defender of the faith and the church, nor does he recognize any temporal sovereign over him" (see cat. 15).[12] Each anointing recalled that of King David, the ruler's Old Testament prototype, and every depiction of David, in prayer books and churches, recalled the king's similarity to him (see cat. 19). Royal authority was symbolized by the regalia with which the new king was invested after his anointing: the ring, the spurs, the sword, the crown, the scepter, the rod with hand. The participation of the peers of the realm in the coronation emphasized the ties that bound the king to France's magnates, the ceremonial acclamation the realm's acceptance of their hereditary monarch. The coronation raised the ruler above his subjects and made him mediator between them and God.

The king's exercise of the royal touch testified to his preeminence over other mortals. Since at least 1100 the kings of France were believed able to heal by their touch a variety of glandular and purulent diseases referred to as "the king's evil," and the godlike power they claimed remained a prized attribute for centuries, abandoned only after the coronation of Charles X in 1825.[13] Because of the anointment with heaven-sent oil, and the power that thereby flowed through their hands, by the mid-fourteenth century kings washed their hands no more than necessary and kept them covered.[14] Thus, in a family portrait of Philip the Fair with his children and his brother, Philip alone is portrayed clasping gloves in his right hand (cat. 22; compare cat. 25).[15] Louis IX had formalized the ceremony of the royal touch by using a special blessing and the sign of the cross, thus heightening the king's priestliness. Louis's grandson, Philip the Fair, saw that the ceremony was advertised, attracting pilgrims from many lands; in 1315 Louis's great-grandson, Louis X, to buttress his power and self-confidence, made the first post-consecration pilgrimage to Corbeny, the shrine of Saint Marcoul, particularly associated with the power to heal. More than two centuries later, the image of Henry II exercising the royal touch at Corbeny was added to a devotional book given to the king by the noble Dinteville brothers, seeking to regain the royal favor they had forfeited during the reign of the king's father, Francis I (1515–1547) (see cat. 80). In this context the power of the king to heal was endowed with significance beyond the literal, revealing the importance his subjects accorded to this attribute. Not only could he cure physical disease, he could also remedy the evils that beset both the kingdom and his individual subjects.

In France, anointment with the miraculous, heaven-sent oil and the ritual of the royal touch remained exclusively male. At their coronations queens were anointed with the consecrated oil ordinarily used in liturgical ceremonies; the queen's throne was less impressive than the king's and was situated at the left of the choir, a position considered inferior to the right-hand position occupied by the king's; her scepter was smaller than her husband's.[16] Queens, like kings, nonetheless enjoyed the special privilege of taking both wine and bread at communion, and the prayers said at their coronations emphasized their roles as mothers of future rulers, as protectors of the needy, and as defenders of the faith. They were looked to as intercessors, and they and other aristocratic and royal women exercised considerable power, particularly when they survived their husbands.[17] Still, the debarment of women from the throne was established after the death of Louis X in 1316 and later accorded theoretical justification through an obscure law of the Salian Franks.[18] This impediment gave a Gallic twist to the misogyny that was as widespread and deep-rooted in France as elsewhere, but such notions did not prevent individual women from assuming roles as patrons, as molders of cultural and moral values, or as powers behind the throne—or even, as in the notable case of Joan of Arc, as warrior-savior of the realm and architect of the coronation of Charles VII (1422–1461) at Reims. Christine de Pisan rose to the defense of women, ancient and modern (see cat. 30), but her impressive accomplishments, like those of the regents Blanche of Castile, Louise of Savoy (mother of Francis I), and Catherine de Médicis, were condescendingly termed "virile" and said to make her "truly a man."[19]

Coronation and the exercise of the royal touch were only two of the many ceremonies that demonstrated the loftiness of the royal office and permitted subjects to participate in celebrating their rulers' glory. Some, like coronation and the first demonstration of the power to heal, were associated with specific sites, and Reims and Corbeny set special value on their prerogatives. So too did Saint-Denis, the royal abbey north of Paris, which by the thirteenth century had become the royal mausoleum, and which guarded the regalia and the oriflamme (the crimson banner linked with Clovis and Charlemagne that accompanied the kings to battle). There the kings journeyed before leading France's armies to war; there the monarchs' remains were borne and interred to cries of "The king is dead; long live the king," before their successors set forth to be crowned at Reims. Entry ceremonies to these and other cities bound rulers to their subjects, who witnessed their devotion to the monarch by accompanying him into their cities and offering him and his family rich gifts.

Royal marriages provided other occasions for festivity, as subjects joined their rulers in celebrating the carefully negotiated unions that were designed to add lands to the kingdom or transform rivals and foes into friends and allies. Solemn religious processions held to win God's favor at times of crisis or to appease divine anger joined king and people as common suppliants and penitents. Such ceremonies as the knighting of the king's three sons in 1313 at the week-long *grand feste* that Philip the Fair mounted in Paris (see cat. 22) provided the occasion for feasting, parading, and staging dramatic tableaux that showed Paradise filled with angels, Hell with its stinking brimstone, and scenes from the Bible and the fables of the crafty Renard

135

the Fox. On this occasion princes, nobles, and commoners massed to take the Cross and vow to drive the heathen from Jerusalem, thus witnessing French dedication to crusading. Each royal ceremony was a carefully staged and orchestrated performance, designed to impress those who witnessed it. Reports of such festivities, initially laconic, became lengthier and more vivid as rulers and their admirers sought to preserve in written and pictorial form the splendor of events that were of their very nature evanescent, but whose substance would be repeated and elaborated as ruler succeeded ruler. With the introduction of printing in the late fifteenth century, richly illustrated booklets commemorating coronations and entry ceremonies made possible the wide dissemination of images of royal power which until then had been witnessed only by actual spectators or the privileged few with access to the manuscripts containing descriptions of the celebrations.

Paris and Royal Culture

Under Philip the Fair, Paris was thought another Rome; in 1323 Jean of Jandun likened it to Paradise (see cat. 42).[20] Whatever the prerogatives of other cities, Paris was a special seat of solemnity and celebration, sheltering the king's body before its burial at Saint-Denis, welcoming him as he returned from Reims and Corbeny, witnessing the display of precious relics of Jesus and his saints. Although they could be and were held in other cities, Parisian entry ceremonies, knightings, royal marriages, and processions were somehow finer and more awe-inspiring than those celebrated elsewhere. By the reign of Philip Augustus (who was praised for ordering its streets paved, and who had a huge wall and the fortress of the Louvre created to defend it), Paris, the largest and richest city in the realm, and indeed in northern Europe, was the kingdom's capital and its heart. In the middle of the Ile de la Cité, Saint Louis had by 1248 built the Sainte-Chapelle to house the Crown of Thorns and other precious relics of Christ and the Passion that he had purchased from Emperor Baldwin of Constantinople; the chapel and its relics endowed both the city and, especially, the nearby quarters of the Parlement of Paris, the realm's highest court, with special holiness. In the first decades of the fourteenth century, Philip the Fair constructed the huge and impressive royal palace on the Ile that signified his grandeur, part of which still survives in the present-day Conciergerie. The Grand'Salle of the palace (destroyed by fire in 1618) was adorned with statues of the kings of France stretching back to the legendary Pharamond, reminding the crowds who thronged its precincts of the unbroken line of their rulers, recalled as well by earlier monuments—the gallery of kings on the facade of nearby Notre-Dame and the kings arrayed in homage to Saint Denis on the northern portal of the abbey church of Saint-Denis.

Paris was the artistic and commercial hub of the kingdom, as well as its administrative center. There nobles and princes, women as well as men, came to shop and order clothing and manuscripts. At the beginning of the fifteenth century, Christine de Pisan declared that the sovereign manuscript painters of the world worked in Paris (and lavished praise on her own, a woman called Anastaise, for the "sweetness" of her borders and backgrounds).[21] It is not surprising that a century later an artist closely linked to Paris was commissioned to add the major illuminations to a French version with commentary of Petrarch's *Triumphs,* the text of which had been translated, copied, and otherwise embellished in Rouen (cat. 55). The kings sometimes favored the residences and palaces outside Paris that they constructed and adorned, but these preferences varied from reign to reign. Paris was a constant, the center from which royal justice and authority emanated, where the rulers' majesty was most dramatically displayed. Throughout the dark days of the wars against the English and the internecine conflicts that pitted the princes of the blood against one another, Paris remained, as Eustache Deschamps wrote at the end of the fourteenth century, a city without equal: "Riens ne se puet comparer à Paris."[22]

To Paris, it was said, the emperor Charlemagne had transferred from Rome the seat of the world's learning, linked with the city's university, which jealously guarded the privileges that the kings, beginning with Philip Augustus in 1200, bestowed on its scholars. The monarch, considered the protector of the realm's learning and the guarantor of its orthodoxy, was expected to be a font of wisdom to his subjects. As a legend in the copy of the translation of John of Salisbury's *Policraticus* (cat. 25) offered to Charles V (1364–1380) proclaimed, "Blessed is the land whose king is wise" (Benedicta terra cuius rex sapiens).[23] No land was thought to deserve this blessing more than the most Christian realm of France, and many kings took seriously their duty to advance study of God, the universe, the past, and human nature, through their own efforts and through the institutions of learning they supported. Saint Louis promoted the research of the polymath Vincent de Beauvais, *lector* (literally, reader) at the Cistercian monastery the king had founded at Royaumont near Paris, and he listened attentively to the texts that Vincent and other ecclesiastics discussed in his presence.[24] Charles V had philosophical works he hoped would make him a better ruler read to him each day (see cat. 26). Francis I gloried in his reputation as "Father of Arts and Letters." He had his personal "readers" and, prompted by Guillaume Budé (see cat. 68), encouraged the diffusion of humane letters and science by naming "royal readers" to lecture publicly at Paris on Greek, Hebrew, and mathematics, thus augmenting the teachings of the faculties of the university.[25] Nor was Francis I the first French king to patronize such studies in Paris. Two hundred years earlier, Ramón Lull, admittedly dedicated to crusading and aiming to convert the heathen rather than to advance liberal studies, had called on Philip the Fair and the pope to establish centers for the study of eastern languages, and professors of Hebrew and Arabic were actually named at Paris in 1319.[26]

The kings' alliance with the Parlement of Paris and the Faculty of Theology of the city's university enabled the kings to exert control over ideas believed to threaten the monarchy, the realm, and the Catholic faith and, increasingly, to determine what notions would be tolerated and which condemned. Visionaries and philosophers whose ideas touched sensitive theological issues were the earliest victims of repression; in the sixteenth century the doctrines of Luther and his followers and the writings of Rabelais (cat. 70) were condemned—although Francis I protected his sister Marguerite of Angoulême, queen of Navarre (and grandmother of Henry IV [1589–1610]), whose courageous advocacy of reform of the Catholic church attracted suspicions of heresy (see cat. 71). The advent of printing in the middle of the fifteenth century made dissemination of controversial doctrines far easier—and more difficult to regulate, particularly when copies of handbills and books printed outside

Paris could be smuggled in for distribution (see cat. 72). Thus a conspiracy that threatened Francis II in 1560 was blamed not only on preachers from Switzerland but also on "a malicious dispersal of damnable books brought from Geneva, infecting people who through want of learning and judgment have no ability to understand the teachings of the Church."[27] The futility of the monarchy's efforts to throttle dissent foreshadowed the equally fruitless actions of the revolutionaries' ruthless attack on the press before Danton's fall.

The Kings of France and the Power of the Past

"Before he went to bed," Joinville reported, "Saint Louis had his children brought before him and recounted to them the deeds of good kings and emperors, and told them that they should learn from the examples of such men. He also recounted to them the deeds of the bad princes who, by their lewdness, depredations, and avarice, lost their kingdoms, saying 'I remind you of these things so that you will act as you should, so that God will not be angry with you.'"[28] It was Louis who commissioned Primat, monk of Saint-Denis, to compose the vernacular history of the French that came to be known as the *Grandes Chroniques de France*. Completed in 1274, Primat's work popularized a vision of the monarchy rooted in the Trojan past, whose three royal lines (Merovingian, Carolingian, and Capetian) enjoyed special divine favor and protection. It included not only stories glorifying kings but also admonitory accounts of evil, do-nothing rulers. Over time, it was extended and modified; changing tastes, politics, and patrons affected the choice of images to illustrate it, which powerfully influenced the way the text was read. The stories and myths it recorded were sources of French unity and pride. The Trojan origin of the French, Turpin's tale of Charlemagne's exploits in Spain, and the story of the emperor's alleged pilgrimage to Constantinople and Jerusalem were universally accepted until skeptical scholars in the sixteenth century denounced and suppressed them. In the frontispiece of a copy of the *Grandes Chroniques* made for Charles V and treasured by Charles VI (1380–1422), the fleurs-de-lis of France adorn the towers of Troy (cat. 27).[29] At first copied virtually exclusively for royal and princely audiences, in the late fifteenth century the *Grandes Chroniques* was more widely diffused and served as the basis and inspiration for the *Annales et chroniques de France* of Nicole Gilles (d. 1503), published posthumously (with an extravagantly elaborate title) in 1525 and issued in expanded, revised, and expurgated editions for almost a century.[30]

Following Saint Louis's example, his successors encouraged investigation of the past, which they harnessed to their purposes. They were not solely interested in the history of France but increasingly looked to ancient history and also to ancient philosophy for guides to conduct. The history of Rome was particularly compelling and grew more so as interest in and contact with Italy and humane letters increased. The antique past was no longer perceived as a threat to Christianity and the Catholic faith, as it had once been. In a world in which the boundaries between past and present were far less rigid than they are today, ancient heroes joined biblical and medieval giants as prefigurations of contemporary luminaries. The past was projected into the present, the present into the past; Carthage assumed the guise of Paris in a fifteenth-century illustration of Livy's history of Rome (cat. 42). This was no new phenomenon. In the *Roman de la poire,* written in the middle of the thirteenth century, famed lovers of ancient and early medieval legend were prototypes of the poem's protagonists, whose garb adorned with fleurs-de-lis links them to contemporary France (cat. 18). From early on the realm's leaders identified themselves and were identified with heroes (and villains) of the past; kings were seen as virtual reincarnations of figures both secular and biblical—Charlemagne, David, and sometimes Pharaoh. In the curious (to our eyes) portrait of Francis I as composite pagan god (cat. 62), whose significance is fully delineated in the accompanying verse, the king appears as the embodiment of the furious Mars in war, Minerva in peace, Diana at the hunt, Mercury in prosperity, and Amor (Love) full of grace. "In honoring your great king, who surpasses Nature," the French are admonished, "you honor all these gods."

Such antique images complemented but did not efface the Christian. Identification with ancient gods and heroes was subordinated to the monarch's position as most Christian king, as was forcefully shown by the persecutions launched in the wake of the appearance in 1534 of posters denouncing "the horrible, great, and insufferable abuses of the papal Mass" (cat. 72). Henry II may have been portrayed crowned with a laurel wreath, his breastplate recalling the gods of mythology, but he wore the emblem of Saint Michael (cat. 78), who vanquished the dragon of evil and disbelief. Classical images abounded at the king's glorious entry to Paris in 1549, but so too did services at Notre-Dame, and the festivities culminated in the burning, live, of "heretical sacramentarians" who had contravened the ordonnances his father had issued "for the extirpation and grave punishment of such pernicious and damnable opinions."[31]

Hierarchies of Power and Culture

In a world in which ever-increasing attention was paid to precedence and distinctions of rank, the king was seen (particularly by those who looked to him for advancement) like God at the center of the universe, ordaining differences and distinctions, recognizing and rewarding merit by creating and bestowing offices, pensions, and noble rank—as well as honors like the Order of Saint Michael, a superillustrious chivalric order founded by Louis XI (1461–1483) in 1469, when the renown of the princely orders established earlier was waning (see cat. 44). It was thought the king's prerogative and duty to decree and enforce order so that charity, peace, and concord would reign among his subjects.[32] Adapting an antique and early Christian theme, writers often likened the kingdom to a body, the king being its head; they also divided his subjects into three orders, or estates—those who prayed, those who fought, and those who labored with their hands. The wheel of fortune was commonly thought to govern the rise and decline of individuals within the universe, but those who pinned their hopes to the service of the king believed, often rightly but sometimes at their peril, that they were more likely to flourish than to fall (cat. 41). The king controlled advancement in the church as well as the state, and Nicole Oresme was not the first or last royal servant to be rewarded with ecclesiastical preferment for his efforts on the king's behalf (see cat. 26).

The often-voiced notion that true nobility was manifested in deeds and manners rather than springing from birth and land was honored more in theory than in prac-

139

tice. In the last decades of the twelfth century the clerk Andreas Capellanus announced that social orders had existed since the dawn of time and were immutable, and declared that no one should exceed or attempt to escape the boundaries of his status.[33] Philip III (1270–1285) and his son Philip IV transformed his exhortation into mandate in sumptuary ordonnances issued in 1279 and 1294. The statute of 1294 decreed not only what different social orders should wear but also what and from what they should eat; dukes, counts, and barons were distinguished from knights, and nobles with less than six thousand *livres* in income from those of greater wealth.[34] Kings and nobles, glorying in the armorial bearings that linked them with their lineages, displayed them on hangings, tapestries, and even bed covers. Most important, they used them to adorn their clothing, the most public manifestation of such outward and visible signs of rank, status, and dignity, which set their bearers off from others. In a family portrait of Philip the Fair the robes of the king and his younger sons are adorned with the fleurs-de-lis of France, those of his brother Charles of Valois distinguished by bars of gules, whereas his daughter Isabelle, wife of Edward II of England (1307–1327), wears the leopards of England, and his eldest son Louis the golden chains of Navarre, the realm he had inherited from his mother (cat. 22; compare cat. 25). Such princely display was undeniably prideful. After his failed first crusade, Joinville tells us, Saint Louis eschewed the expensive furs, cloth, and golden spurs he had worn before.[35] In 1292, lying on her deathbed, his daughter-in-law Jeanne, countess of Alençon, bemoaned the fleurs-de-lis "painted and displayed on all [her] trappings"; castigating herself for the royal adornments that had covered her "stinking flesh," she cried out to the Blessed Virgin Mary, "Where do we read that you placed on your clothes the arms and emblems of Solomon, David, and other earthly kings?"[36] Nonetheless, royalty and nobility continued to wear such garments, and servants' liveries sported their masters' arms. Whatever Jeanne of Alençon thought of the Blessed Virgin's humility, Mary was sometimes depicted in robes garnished with fleurs-de-lis, which, to be sure, designated her as lily flower incarnate but also linked her to the royal lineage of France. Armorial bearings were potent signs: the English Edward III (1327–1377) publicized his claim to France by adding the French arms to his own (see cat. 39); the pretensions of Louis XII (1498–1515) to Milan, Lombardy, Naples, and Jerusalem were signified by arms and other devices he joined to those of France (see cats. 55, 58). On another level, the Dintevilles, a noble family of middling status, had the arms of Henry II and Catherine de Médicis depicted with their own in a book of hours, to witness their allegiance to the crown and the service they had rendered to the king (see cat. 80).

As if to assert their individuality and defend themselves against the engulfing embrace of lineage signified by the ubiquitous armorial bearings, members of the elite, beginning in the fourteenth century, chose for themselves special devices, mottoes, and even colors which were theirs and theirs alone.[37] An early fifteenth-century depiction of Pierre Salmon presenting a manuscript to Charles VI (cat. 28; compare cat. 34) shows the king enthroned and garbed in robes with fleurs-de-lis, but the hanging behind him displays the peacocks that were his emblem, and the canopy above carries his motto, "James" (*jamais*: never). These personal motifs and others (the broom plant and tigers with crowns encircling their throats) predominate in the illuminations that show the king in private; the personal emblems of the princes who attend him place their identity beyond dispute.[38] In the late fifteenth and sixteenth centuries, initials joined devices and mottoes as particularizing emblems of the well-born. Those of Marie of Clèves are found with her device and symbols on her copy of Boccaccio's *Filostrato* (cat. 37). The interlaced initials on bindings created for Henry II are more enigmatic, probably designedly so, since if read as *H* and *D* they could designate the king and his mistress, Diane de Poitiers—or "*H*enri *Deuxième*"; if read as *H* and *C*, the king and his wife, Catherine de Médicis (see cat. 81). These symbols betokened ownership, and as such could prove an embarrassment. The intertwined lily flowers and daisies (marguerites) that with the royal arms adorn the illuminations added to the first and most luxurious printed book (on vellum) acquired by Charles VIII, clearly show that it was intended for him and his fiancée, Marguerite of Austria, who had been raised at the court of France as his future bride, only to be repudiated for Anne of Brittany in 1491. Substituting Anne's name for Marguerite's in the genealogical chart was easy enough, but the daisies that remained identified the spurned queen-elect as clearly as did her name (see cats. 49 and 71).[39]

Nobility, Chivalry, and Crusading

The princes and nobles of the realm basked in the radiance reflected from the king. They figured prominently at royal ceremonies and festivities, and they imitated royal ways. The pride they took in their proximity to and blood-ties with the king, and their hope of gaining royal largesse and favor, generally overbalanced impulses to challenge monarchical authority—although they sometimes appropriated royal ceremonies, practices, and devices to magnify their own glory. Many became patrons in their own right, enlisting the services of authors, copyists, illuminators, and translators, whom they often shared with the king; their manuscripts sometimes rivaled the king's in splendor. The works the books contained were usually the same as those that filled the royal collections, and the princes identified themselves strongly with the same symbols of French glory that the kings promoted.

Like royal celebrations, those held at princely and noble courts grew increasingly elaborate. Tournaments and other passages of arms, which most French kings eschewed, became the special purview of the aristocracy.[40] In the fifteenth century the dukes of Burgundy and Anjou sponsored and dramatized such events, which attracted nobles anxious (like the classical and Arthurian heroes they adopted as their models) to prove their valor in an age when warfare was becoming increasingly professionalized. There and at assemblies of chivalric orders, nobles sported themselves like peacocks, displaying their brilliant trappings, distinguished by armorial bearings and devices that the orders' heralds meticulously recorded (see cat. 38).[41] The luckless René, duke of Anjou and count of Provence, great-grandson of King John II (1350–1364) and claimant of (among other lands) Naples, Sicily, Jerusalem, and Aragon, took refuge from political and military defeat (and vainly attempted to rouse support for his ambitious ventures) by founding the Order of the Crescent in 1448, and by sponsoring and participating in jousts and tournaments (see cat. 36; compare cat. 53).[42]

The chivalric ethos and feats of arms associated with tournaments had long been linked to crusading.[43] Many of Saint Louis's descendants, inspired by his fame as a crusader, took the Cross, but Louis was the last king of France to lead a crusade and dwell in the Holy Land. A French chronicler's comment regarding Philip the Fair's crusading zeal applies equally to his successors: "sed nihil fecit"—but he did nothing.[44] Charles V had Godfrey of Bouillon's capture of Jerusalem in 1099 lavishly reenacted when the Emperor Charles IV visited Paris in 1378, but this was for entertainment and to rouse enthusiasm for attacking the English, not the infidels.[45]

In the late fourteenth and fifteenth centuries, with royal attention diverted to war with the English, French princes and nobles took up the cause of Jerusalem and a few actually fought the heathen—generally unsuccessfully. There was no lack of fervor and good intentions. When Philip the Good, duke of Burgundy, founded the Order of the Golden Fleece in 1429, he did so "for the reverence of God and support of the Christian faith, and to honor and exalt the noble order of chivalry." The chivalric aims received special emphasis: honoring the deeds of ancient knights and promoting the noble feats of the living, who were powerful and strong. Yet Philip the Good's dedication to God and crusading was profound, and at the Feast of the Pheasant at Lille in 1435, members of the Order of the Golden Fleece swore extravagant vows binding them to gallant displays of arms against the Turks.[46] Talk of crusading continued sporadically for a century, but Francis I's alliance in 1536 with Suleiman the Magnificent, leader of the Turks and enemy of Christendom, showed that the days of crusading had given way to an age of political calculation (see cat. 67), as French zeal for conquering Italy eclipsed ardor for combating the heathen. Likewise, Henry II's death in 1559 from a wound suffered in a latter-day celebratory tournament dampened enthusiasm for such encounters, which survived as antiquated relics of the chivalric splendor they had once evoked.[47] In the sixteenth century the warriors who fought in God's name, Catholics and Protestants, battled one another on France's own soil, Christian against Christian, each side proclaiming the advent of Antichrist once associated with heathen possession of Jerusalem.[48] Noble and chivalric ideals retained romantic appeal for centuries, but they were outmoded vestiges of an era that had disappeared.

The Artisans of Culture

The identities of those who crafted the works through which the cultural values of kings and nobles were diffused were usually eclipsed by the names and lineal symbols of their patrons. The respective roles played by artists and patrons in designing monuments and manuscripts are often difficult to determine and doubtless varied, but some patrons are known to have taken proprietary and controlling interest in the themes and iconography of the works they commissioned. Scribes sometimes recorded their names at the end of manuscripts they copied—and occasionally their relief at completing their task. But the names of most artists, decorators, and binders, whose identities and styles were evidently known to the contemporaries who hired them and bought their works, are preserved not in signatures on their creations but rather in records of the payments they received. This is true not only of those who worked for numerous patrons and entrepreneurs but also of those who were designated as royal artisans. The works attributable to the sculptor André Beauneveu, who served noble and civic patrons and made Charles V's funeral effigy at Saint-Denis, reveal him as a consummate artist, but his name can be attached to the paintings of monumental prophets and apostles at the beginning of the duke of Berry's Psalter (cat. 29) only because it appears in a catalogue of the ducal library. Just a handful of manuscripts and one painting can be assigned to Jean Bourdichon of Tours, royal painter to Louis XI, Charles VIII, Louis XII, and Francis I, although accounts reveal that he executed a host of religious images and portraits (of towns as well as individuals)–as well as designing coins and clothes and painting statues, banners, and armorial shields. Such artists seem to have been more concerned with the pensions and payments they received than with their future fame. They frequently worked collaboratively. A splendid Bible produced for Charles V was said to have made many journeys through Paris, in rain and shine, before it was completed.[49] The glamor and celebrity of individual artists increased in the sixteenth century, particularly when Francis I summoned masters from Italy to his court. These artists' renowned names added luster to the reputation of their patron, but it is still not always easy to determine whether a work was created by, for instance, Primaticcio or Rosso, or under their inspiration or direction.

Authors and even translators were special cases, and their names were ordinarily preserved with their works, although it took some six hundred years for the confessor whom Saint Louis's daughter Blanche commissioned to write her father's life to be identified as Guillaume de Saint-Pathus (cat. 23). With the advent of printing, the names of those who produced and sold books became familiar, and such entrepreneurs (successors of the less well known and less powerful *libraires*) played an important role in marketing authors, whose works brought them the financial gain they sought. Before this, authors sometimes directed or participated in the preparation and illustration of the first generation of manuscripts containing their creations.[50] Publishers and printers, pursuing profit, did their best to make authors' works salable. The woodcuts that, in 1489, the printer Pierre Levet included in his edition of François Villon's poems (the first to be published) increased the verses' vividness and drama (cat. 50). Almost half a century later, in 1532, the generally respected publisher Galiot du Pré fattened his edition not with pictures but with apocryphal lyrics that many took to be Villon's own work, and he accorded the impressive title *Oeuvres* to the poet's production, an early appearance of a title on which publishers have capitalized ever since. Francis I, apparently displeased, charged the poet Clement Marot with preparing a better edition, and little more than a year later Du Pré published a soberer and improved collection, pruned of the additions–and still called Villon's *Oeuvres*.

The Popular Diffusion of the Royal Mystique

The images of majesty displayed on the coinage (see cat. 54) and on the great seals appended to royal mandates and ordonnances reminded subjects of the illustrious status of the ruler who presided over and dispensed laws and justice to them (see cat. 40). The motto "Christus vincit, Christus regnat, Christus imperat" (Christ conquers, Christ reigns, Christ rules), prominently featured on gold coins minted from

143

the time of Saint Louis on, suggested the proximity of the monarchs to God and their superiority to other rulers, as well as the Christ-like virtues and powers to which the kings aspired.[31] From the mid-twelfth until the late fifteenth century, the seal (and some of these coins) showed the king in majesty on a throne modeled on the regal seat that Abbot Suger of Saint-Denis associated with the Merovingian Dagobert and proudly kept at the abbey church (see cat. 5; compare cat. 22);[32] like other images it reminded those who saw it of the king's ties with the royal past. The seal, the oriflamme, the golden fleurs-de-lis on field of blue, the battle cry "Montjoie–Saint Denis," wondrous tales of royal healing and Saint Louis's miracles, solemn prayers for the ruler intoned in churches, pride in royal guardianship of the precious relics of the Passion that held material promise of salvation–all fortified subjects' loyalty to and pride in their rulers, effacing barriers of rank and hierarchy. Such respect was not unquestioning, nor did the virtuous king expect it to be. If the realm was a body politic, the limbs and other organs–the king's subjects, high and low–would suffer when the head ailed, and it was in the subjects' interest and also their duty to strive to bring him and his counsellors back to health. Subjects seeking reform assumed they could persuade their ruler that their counsel deserved an audience. When in France's bleakest moments Pierre Salmon (cat. 28), Christine de Pisan, and Alain Chartier (cat. 34) lamented the realm's plight, they did so not to counsel revolt but rather to offer positive remedies they believed the king and his advisers would adopt. The wisest rulers, imitating Saint Louis, responded by rectifying the abuses brought to their notice. Such actions, even when judiciously calculated, enabled the monarchy to survive and flourish, its authority unscathed, through and after the nightmarish days of internal strife and conflict with England that marked the fourteenth and fifteenth centuries. A series of kings who ruled majestically and for the most part responsibly acquired a precious stock of power and authority that a headstrong and imprudent monarch might squander but could not–as yet–exhaust.

The impressive treasury of images, symbols, and texts amassed by the medieval and early modern kings of France inspired and challenged their successors, who employed and elaborated them. Their effectiveness and potent impact on the people of France were witnessed by the fury that the opponents of the monarchy and the Catholic faith–the Huguenots in the sixteenth century, the revolutionaries in the eighteenth–vented on manuscripts, relics, statues, regalia, and even royal remains, as if believing they could destroy the power of both church and kingship by eradicating the material traces and representations of their authority. The repeated restorations and revivals of the vestiges of the religion of royalty in the nineteenth century–by Napoléon as well as by royal descendants–demonstrated both the inefficacy of these savage campaigns of destruction and the enduring power of the ideals the earlier kings had promoted.

For their generous counsel I should like to thank Neithard Bulst, William W. Clark, Michael W. Cothren, Richard C. Famiglietti, Carla Lord, Myra Dickman Orth, Nancy Freeman Regalado, Mary A. Rouse, and particularly Ralph S. Brown, Jr., and Paula Lieber Gerson.

1 Guillaume le Breton, *Philippidos libri XII*, in *Oeuvres de Rigord et de Guillaume le Breton, historiens de Philippe-Auguste*, 2 vols., ed. François Delaborde (Paris, 1882–1885), 2:265–66, 375–77, esp. 377n2 (other sources that relate the story of the miraculous vision); Raymonde Foreville, "L'image de Philippe Auguste dans les sources contemporaines," in *La France de Philippe Auguste: Le temps des mutations* (Paris, 1982), 115–32, at 127; John W. Baldwin, *The Government of Philip Augustus: Foundations of French Royal Power in the Middle Ages* (Berkeley, 1986), 390–92; Alain Erlande-Brandenburg, *Le roi est mort: Etude sur les funérailles, les sépultures et les tombeaux des rois de France jusqu'à la fin du XIIIe siècle* (Geneva, 1975), 18.

2 See Andrew W. Lewis, "Suger's Views on Kingship," in *Abbot Suger and Saint-Denis: A Symposium*, ed. Paula Lieber Gerson (New York, 1986), 49–54.

3 BNF Lat. 3323, fols. 2r, 22v (*Liber natalis pueri parvuli Iesu Christi*); Jocelyn N. Hillgarth, *Ramon Lull and Lullism in Fourteenth-Century France* (Oxford, 1971), 114–17, 342, no. 113.

4 Andrew W. Lewis, *Royal Succession in Capetian France: Studies on Familial Order and the State* (Cambridge, Mass., 1981), 122–39; trans. Jeannie Carlier as *Le sang royal: La famille capétienne et l'Etat, France, X^e–XIVe siècle* (Paris, 1986), 165–82; Elizabeth A. R. Brown, "Kings Like Semi-Gods: The Case of Louis X of France," *Majestas* 1 (1993): 5–37.

5 In 1328 Charles IV, third son and successor of Philip the Fair and the last direct Capetian, was followed by Philip of Valois, son of Philip the Fair's brother Charles. In 1498 Louis XII, grandson of Charles VI's brother, Louis of Orléans, and husband of Louis XI's daughter, Jeanne, succeeded his father-in-law. Similarly, on Louis XII's death in 1515, the crown passed to his son-in-law, Francis I of Angoulême, great-grandson of Louis of Orléans. The right of Henry II's son-in-law, Henry IV of Bourbon and Navarre, who succeeded Henry II's three sons in 1589, was based on his descent from Saint Louis's son Robert, count of Clermont and lord of Bourbon through his wife.

6 *Relations des ambassadeurs vénitiens sur les affaires de France au XVIe siècle*, ed. Nicolò Tommaseo, 2 vols. (Paris, 1838), 2:108–10 (report of Giovanni Correro, Venetian ambassador to France, 1569).

7 Charles IX ruled from 1560 to 1574. Elizabeth A. R. Brown, *Jean du Tillet and the French Wars of Religion: Five Tracts, 1562–1569* (Binghamton, N.Y., 1994), 19–20, 22.

8 "…les mesmes remedes qui furent lors appliquez à guerir la playe qui affligeoit ce Royaume (sinon en tout) au moins en la pluspart sont maintenant fort a propos, pour donner la guarison a la mesme maladie de laquelle ce Royaume est a present tourmenté;… n'ont esté preferez pour en vser plustost que de ceux des empiriques, qui par leurs prudences mondaines, pensants remedier a la maladie l'ont enflammee & empiree;… a restituer la santé a ce Royaume demy mort & languissant": Helie du Tillet, dedication (1590) added to Jean du Tillet, *Sommaire de l'Histoire de la gverre faicte contre les heretiques Albigeois, extraicte du Tresor des Chartres du Roy* (Paris, 1590), [2]r, [3]v; on the work, see Brown, *Jean du Tillet*, 23–24.

9 *Les Edicts et Ordonnances des Roys de France depvis S. Loys ivsqves a present*, ed. Antoine Fontanon, 4 vols. (Paris, 1580), 4:1811, no. 32 (Nov. 8, 1567).

10 Jean-Claude Bonne, "The Manuscript of the Ordo of 1250 and Its Illuminations," 58–71, at 69; Jacques Le Goff, "A Coronation Program for the Age of Saint Louis: The Ordo of 1250," 46–57, both in *Coronations: Medieval and Early Modern Monarchic Ritual*, ed. János M. Bak (Berkeley, 1990); Richard A. Jackson, "Manuscripts, Texts, and Enigmas of Medieval French Coronation Ordines," *Viator* 23 (1992): 35–71, at 56–58, 65–68.

11 Danielle Gaborit-Chopin, *Regalia: Les instruments du sacre des rois de France, les "Honneurs de Charlemagne"* (Paris, 1987), 46.

12 Richard A. Jackson, ed., "The *Traité du sacre* of Jean Golein [1374]," *Proceedings of the American Philosophical Society* 113, part 4 (1969): 305–24, at 309. The ritual of the royal touch profoundly impressed Venetian dignitaries who spent time in France in the mid-16th century: *Relations des ambassadeurs vénitiens*, 1:289 (Marino Cavalli, 1546), 2:542–43 (Giovanni Michel, 1575).

13 Marc Bloch, *Les rois thaumaturges: Etude sur le caractère surnaturel attribué à la puissance royale, particulièrement en France et en Angleterre* (Paris and Strasbourg, 1924; repr. Paris, 1961); trans. J. E. Anderson as *The Royal Touch: Sacred Monarchy and Scrofula in England and France* (London, 1973); Frank Barlow, "The King's Evil," *English Historical Review* 95 (1980): 3–27.

14 Jackson, "*Traité du sacre* of Jean Golein," 317–18.

15 Note the gloves, prominently displayed, in two late representations of Saint Louis: Pierre-Marie Auzas, "Essai d'un répertoire iconographique de saint Louis," in *Septième centenaire de la mort de saint Louis: Actes des colloques de Royaumont et de Paris (21–27 mai 1970)* (Paris, 1976), 3–22, figs. 4 and 6. See also Claire Richter Sherman, *The Portraits of Charles V of France (1338–1380)* (New York, 1969), 25–27, 35, 74, and figs. 10 and 71.

145

16 Claire Richter Sherman, "The Queen in Charles V's 'Coronation Book': Jeanne de Bourbon and the 'Ordo ad Reginam Benedicendam,'" *Viator* 8 (1977): 255–98, and the accompanying plates; and Sherman, "Taking a Second Look: Notes on the Iconography of a French Queen, Jeanne de Bourbon, 1338–1378," in *Feminism and Art History: Questioning the Litany*, ed. Norma Broude and Mary D. Garrard (New York, 1982), 100–117.

17 Particularly useful on the activities and authority of French queens are the essays by André Poulet ("Capetian Women and the Regency: The Genesis of a Vocation") and Elizabeth McCartney ("The King's Mother and Royal Prerogative in Early-Sixteenth-Century France") in *Medieval Queenship*, ed. John Carmi Parsons (New York, 1993), 93–141.

18 Kathleen Daly and Ralph E. Giesey, "Noël de Fribois et la loi salique," *Bibliothèque de l'Ecole des Chartes* 151 (1993): 5–36, discuss Fribois's role in disseminating the Salic myth; Giesey will consider the myth in greater detail in a forthcoming revision of his study *The Juristic Basis of Dynastic Right to the French Throne* (Philadelphia, 1961), published in the *Transactions of the American Philosophical Society*, n.s. 51, no. 5 (1961).

19 Natalie Zemon Davis, "Gender and Genre: Women as Historical Writers, 1400–1820," in *Beyond Their Sex: Learned Women of the European Past*, ed. Patricia H. Labalme (New York, 1980), 153–82, esp. 158. Cf. Etienne le Blanc's statement in the *Gestes* of Blanche of Castile, dedicated to Francis I's mother, the influential Louise of Savoy: "Virtue has been seen in enough cases reigning and abounding in the hearts of some women more than in many men, and when this happens they deserve to be called not only women but [rather] men; thus clerks say that *man* is a common noun" (Et assez a on veu vertu regner et abonder au cueur daucunes dames plus que en beaucoup dhommes. Et quant ce aduient/elles meritent non seullement estre appellees femmes/mais hommes. Et aussy les clercs dyent que la declinaison dhomme est commune): BNF Fr. 5715, fol. 7r.

20 Hillgarth, *Ramon Lull*, 106–07, 110, esp. n. 262; Charlotte Lacaze, "Parisius–Paradisus, an Aspect of the Vie de St. Denis Manuscript of 1317," *Marsyas: Studies in the History of Art* 16 (1972–1973): 60–66.

21 Gilbert Ouy and Christine M. Reno, "Identification des autographes de Christine de Pizan," *Scriptorium* 34 (1980): 221–38, at 222; Sandra L. Hindman, *Christine de Pizan's "Epistre Othéa": Painting and Politics at the Court of Charles VI* (Toronto, 1986), 69–70.

22 Eustache Deschamps, "Balade (sur Paris) [1394]," in *Oeuvres complètes . . .*, ed. Le Marquis de Queux de Saint-Hilaire and Gaston Raynaud, 11 vols. (Paris, 1858–1903), 1:301–2. See Willibald Sauerländer, "Medieval Paris, Center of European Taste: Fame and Realities," in *Paris: Center of Artistic Enlightenment*, ed.

George Mauner et al. (University Park, Pa., 1988), 13–25; and also Raymond Cazelles, "Le Parisien au temps de saint Louis," in *Septième centenaire*, 97–104.

23 BNF Fr. 24287, fol. 12; Sherman, *Portraits*, 76–77, fig. 73. As Sherman notes, the citation reworks Eccles. 10.17, "Beata terra cuius rex nobilis est." Cf. the frontispiece (pp. 74–75, fig. 71), where the king is shown in his library, crowned, pointing to a book open to the verse from Eccles. 14.22, "Beatus vir qui in sapientia morabitur, et qui in iustitia sua meditabitur" (Blessed is the man who shall dwell in wisdom and meditate in his justice).

24 Serge Lusignan, *Préface au "Speculum maius" de Vincent de Beauvais: Réfraction et diffraction* (Montreal, 1979), 19, 51–53, 56–57; Léopold Delisle, *Le Cabinet des Manuscrits de la Bibliothèque Impériale: Etude sur la formation de ce dépôt comprenant les éléments d'une histoire de la calligraphie, de la miniature, de la reliure, et du commerce des livres à Paris avant l'invention de l'imprimerie*, 3 vols. (Paris, 1868–1881), 1:7–8; Jean, lord of Joinville, *Oeuvres*, ed. Natalis de Wailly (Paris: Adrien Le Clere, 1867), 20–26 (chap. 5: Robert de Sorbonne) and 30–34 (chap. 9: Guillaume d'Auvergne, bishop of Paris).

25 James K. Farge, *Le parti conservateur au XVIe siècle: Université et Parlement de Paris à l'époque de la Renaissance et de la Réforme* (Paris, 1992), 35–41, 45.

26 Hillgarth, *Ramon Lull*, 49–50, 115, 125–28.

27 Francis II, edict of March 1560, in *Mémoires de Condé . . .*, ed. Denis-François Secousse, 6 vols. (Paris, 1743–45), 1:9–10.

28 Joinville, *Oeuvres*, 464 (chap. 139).

29 Anne D. Hedeman, *The Royal Image: Illustrations of the* Grandes Chroniques de France, *1274–1422* (Berkeley, 1991), 96, 99, 139–40, 143, 251–52, fig. 72; Hedeman considers the emphasis on crusading in John II's copy (pp. 63–67) and studies the carefully edited and illustrated copy executed for Charles V (BNF Fr. 2813), on which his son's was modeled (pp. 93–133, esp. 97–98). Bernard Guenée discusses the creation and diffusion of the *Grandes Chroniques* in "Les *Grandes Chroniques de France*: Le Roman aux roys (1274–1518)," in *Les lieux de mémoire*, pt. 2, *La Nation*, ed. Pierre Nora, 3 vols. (Paris, 1986), 1:189–214.

30 Jacques Riche, "L'historien Nicole Gilles (14..?–1503)," *Positions des thèses de l'Ecole des Chartes* (1930): 135–40. The two-volume edition published by Galliot du Pré in Paris in 1525 was entitled *Les treselegantes Tresveridiques et copieuses Annalles Des trespreux/ tresnobles/treschrestiens et tresexcellens moderateurs des belliqueuses Gaules. Depuis la triste desolation de la tresinclyte & tresfameuse cite de Troye Iusques au regne du tresvertueux roy Francois a present regnant. Compilees par feu treseloquent & noble Historiographe en son viuant Indiciaire et secretaire du Roy et Contreroleur de son tresor maistre Nicole gilles iusques au temps de tresprudent &*

victorieux roy Loys onziesme. Et depuis additionnees selon les modernes hystoriens iusques en L'an Mil cinq cens et vingt. The simplification of the title began with the edition of 1536, when, significantly, the word *Tresveridiques* was dropped, but the short title *Annales et chroniques de France* was not used until 1553. This edition retained a reference to Troy that was not dropped until 1573, when the title insisted that the work had been revised "selon la verité des Registres & Pancartes anciennes, & suyuant la foy des vieux Exemplaires."

31 I. D. McFarlane, *The Entry of Henri II into Paris, 16 June 1549* (Binghamton, N.Y., 1982), esp. 68–70. For Francis I, see R. J. Knecht, *Francis I* (Cambridge, 1982), 235–36, 248–52, 390–91; idem, "Francis I, 'Defender of the Faith'?" in *Wealth and Power in Tudor England: Essays Presented to S. T. Bindoff*, ed. E. W. Ives, R. J. Knecht, and J. J. Scarisbrick (London, 1978), 106–27; and Farge, *Parti conservateur*, 95–116.

32 Jean du Tillet, *Recveil des rangs des grands de France*, in his *Recveil des Roys de France . . .* (Paris, 1618), 3–5.

33 "Non enim otiose vel sine causa fuit ab aevi primordio inter homines ordinum reperta distinctio, sed ut quisque intra generis saepta permaneat et per omnia sui ordinis finibus contentus existat, et ea, quae maioris sunt ordinis stabilita natura, sibi nullus usurpare praesumat, sed ipsa tanquam aliena relinquat. . . . Ideoque firmiter assero, neminem sui ordinis debere metas excedere, sed intra suum ordinem quemque probum alicuius probae feminae amorem perquirere": Andreas Capellanus, *Trattato d'amore. Andreae Capellani regii Francorum "De amore" libri tres. Testo latino del sec. XII con due traduzione toscane inedite del sec. XIV*, ed. Salvatore Battaglia (Rome, 1947), 46, 58 (responses of the *nobilis mulier* to the *plebeius*). On the other hand, Andreas also suggested that with the sanction of the prince *probitas* (uprightness) can alter *ordo* and warrant the transformation of plebeians into knights or vavasors. See ibid., 68, a declaration of the *nobilior femina* to the *plebeius*, "Quamvis probitas possit nobilitare plebeium, ei tamen ordinem mutare non potest, ut plebeius procer efficiatur sive vavassor, nisi principis ei forsan potentia tribuatur, qui potest quibuslibet bonis moribus nobilitatem adiungere"; and ibid., 70, the response of the *plebeius*, "Si propter suos mores et probitatem aliquis plebeius dignus a principe nobilitari inveniatur, cur nobili non dignus sit amore, non video."

34 Henri Duplès-Agier, "Ordonnance somptuaire inédite de Philippe le Hardi," *Bibliothèque de l'Ecole des Chartes*, 3d ser. 5 [15] (1854): 176–99 (1279); *Ordonnances des roys de France . . .*, ed. Eusèbe-Jacob de Laurière, et al. 22 vols. and *Supplément* (Paris, 1723–1849), 1:541–43; see also Paul Lacroix, *Recueil curieux de pièces originales rares ou inédites en prose et en vers sur le costume et les révolutions de la mode en France . . .* (Paris, [1852]), 3–60.

35 Joinville, *Oeuvres*, 448 (chap. 135); Yvonne Deslandres, "Le costume du roi saint Louis: Etude iconographique et technique," in *Septième centenaire*, 105–14.

36 "Haa doulce Vierge Marie, par ta grant humilité tu voulsise que nom royal feust en toy oblié du très grant & puissant roy Salemon, duquel lignaige tu estois estraite; & j'ai voulu tout mon lignaige surmonter, & les poures petit prisier, les fleurs de lys de France en mes paremens peindre & démonstrer. Haa, Madame, en quel lieu list-on qu'en vos paremens vous meissiés les armes & les signes du roy Salemon, de David, ne des autres roys mondains. Et je, qui suis si miserable par dehors, estoie si royamment aournée, & par dedans estoie charoigne puante de si riches aournemens & atours enveloppée": from the anonymous *De felici obitu Johannæ comitissæ Alenconii et Blesensis*, edited from a Premonstratensian manuscript, in *Veterum scriptorum, et monumentorum historicorum, dogmaticorum, moralium; amplissima collectio*, ed. Edmond Martène and Ursin Durand, 9 vols. (Paris, 1724–33), 6:1219–38, at 1223.

37 Elizabeth A. R. Brown, "The Ceremonial of Royal Succession in Capetian France: The Funeral of Philip V," *Speculum* 55 (1980): 266–93, at 280 (repr. in Brown, *The Monarchy of Capetian France and Royal Ceremonial* [Aldershot, 1991], VIII). Particularly useful are the studies by Christian de Mérindol, "Signes de hiérarchie sociale à la fin du Moyen Age d'après le vêtement: Méthodes et recherches," in *Le vêtement: Histoire, archéologie et symbolique vestimentaires au moyen âge*, vol. 1 of *Cahiers du Léopard d'Or* (1989), 161–223; and *Le roi René et la seconde maison d'Anjou: Emblématique, art, histoire* (Paris, 1987), 167–213.

38 Richard C. Famiglietti, *Royal Intrigue: Crisis at the Court of Charles VI, 1392–1420* (New York, 1986), xv–xviii; Famiglietti, *Tales of the Marriage Bed from Medieval France (1300–1500)* (Providence, 1992), 67, and cf. 74; Marcel Thomas, *The Golden Age: Manuscript Painting at the Time of Jean, Duke of Berry* (New York, 1979), 96–99; Millard Meiss, *French Painting in the Time of Jean de Berry: The Boucicaut Master* (London, 1968), 25, 37, 87–88, 124–25, figs. 69–72; Anne D. Hedeman, "Pierre Salmon's Advice for a King," *Gesta: International Center of Medieval Art* 32 (1993): 113–23.

39 Ursula Baurmeister and Marie-Pierre Laffitte, *Des livres et des rois: La Bibliothèque Royale de Blois* (Paris, 1992), 96–99; Patrick Van Kerrebrouck, with Christophe Brun and Christian de Mérindol, *Les Valois* (Villeneuve d'Ascq, 1990), 156, 158–59n7.

40 Richard Barber and Juliet Barker, *Tournaments: Jousts, Chivalry, and Pageants in the Middle Ages* (New York, 1989), 38–44, 107–25, 132–35.

41 Maurice Keen, *Chivalry* (New Haven, 1984), 102–42, presents a particularly useful discussion of the mythology of chivalry and the development of heralds, heraldry, and armorials.

147

42 Van Kerrebrouck, *Les Valois*, 292–306; Michael T. Reynolds, "René of Anjou, King of Sicily, and the Order of the *Croissant*," *Journal of Medieval History* 19 (1993): 125–61. Emile G. Léonard summarizes the chief events of René's life in *Les Angevins de Naples* (Paris, 1954), 487–91; for René's writings, see Barber and Barker, *Tournaments*, 114–17, who reproduce a number of illustrations from the copy of his treatise on the tournament owned by Louis of Bruges, for many years a servant of the duke of Burgundy (BNF Fr. 2693), ibid., 170–71, 174–75, 178–79, 181–84, 187; see also Baurmeister and Laffitte, *Livres*, 202–3, no. 51 (also 193–94, on Louis of Bruges). Louis de Beauvau, seneschal of Anjou, who translated Boccaccio's *Filostrato*, learned Italian when he was in Italy with René.

43 Keen, *Chivalry*, 44–63, 214–15.

44 Christopher J. Tyerman, "Sed Nihil Fecit? The Last Capetians and the Recovery of the Holy Land," in *War and Government in the Middle Ages: Essays in Honour of J. P. Prestwich*, ed. John Gillingham and J. S. Holt (Cambridge, 1984), 170–81.

45 Hedeman, *Royal Image*, 128–33. Similarly, those admitted to John II's short-lived Order of the Star, founded in 1351, were clearly expected to demonstrate their loyalty and bravery against the English; they had to receive special royal authorization to undertake such "distant voyages" as crusading required: Raymond Cazelles, *Société politique, noblesse et couronne sous Jean le Bon et Charles V* (Geneva, 1982), 144–46; Hedeman, *Royal Image*, 107–10.

46 Keen, *Chivalry*, 179, 214–15; for the foundation of the order in 1429, see *Chronique de Jean le Févre, seigneur de Saint-Remy, transcrite d'un manuscrit appartenant à la Bibliothèque de Boulogne-sur-Mer*, ed. François Morand, 2 vols. (Paris, 1876–81), 2:172–73.

47 Barber and Barker, *Tournaments*, 135, 209–11; Keen, *Chivalry*, 238–43.

48 Denis Crouzet, *Les guerriers de Dieu: La violence au temps des troubles de religion, vers 1525–vers 1610*, 2 vols. (Seyssel, 1990).

49 The inscription in the so-called Vaudetar Bible is quoted in *Les fastes du gothique: Le siècle de Charles V*, exhibition catalogue, Galeries Nationales du Grand Palais (Paris, 1981), 331, no. 185. Robert Branner's hypotheses regarding the creation of manuscripts in Paris in the 13th century provide useful guides to earlier and later practice: *Manuscript Painting in Paris during the Reign of Saint Louis: A Study of Styles* (Berkeley, 1977), 1–21. See also Richard H. Rouse and Mary A. Rouse, "The Commercial Production of Manuscript Books in Late-Thirteenth- and Early-Fourteenth-Century Paris," in *A Potencie of Life: Books in Society, The Clark Lectures, 1986–1987*, ed. Nicolas Barker (London, 1993), 45–61. Patricia Stirnemann and Marie-Thérèse Gousset caution against the anachronistic application of the notion of the full-fledged workshop or atelier to a period when production was familial and artisanal, in "Marques, mots, pratiques: Leur signification et leurs liens dans le travail des enlumineurs," *CIVICIMA: Etudes sur le vocabulaire intellectuel du moyen âge*, vol. 2, *Vocabulaire du livre et de l'écriture au moyen âge* (Turnhout, 1989), 34–55, at 39–40.

50 Sylvia Huot discusses Guillaume de Machaut's possible supervision of the production of the collection of his works in BNF Fr. 1586, in *From Song to Book: The Poetics of Writing in Old French Lyric and Lyrical Narrative Poetry* (Ithaca, 1987), 242–73.

51 Ernst H. Kantorowicz, with Manfred F. Bukofzer, *Laudes Regiae: A Study in Liturgical Acclamations and Mediaeval Ruler Worship* (Berkeley, 1958), esp. 1–5. The 14th-century dukes of Brittany Charles of Blois and Jean IV considered themselves sovereigns in their duchy, and they proudly used this motto on their coins, which also proclaimed them dukes "by grace of God": *La Bretagne au temps des Ducs* (Daoulas, 1991), 38–39, no. 23.3; 53, nos 50.2 and 50.5; 54, no. 50.7; and the article by Jean Kerhervé, "Idéologie et appareil d'Etat dans la Bretagne des Montforts: XIVe–IVe siècles," ibid., 72–80.

52 *Abbot Suger on the Abbey Church of St.-Denis and Its Art Treasures*, 2d ed., ed. Erwin Panofsky and Gerda Panofsky Soergel (Princeton, 1979), 72–73 (*De administratione*, chap. 34), 200–201, fig. 22; Brigitte Bedos-Rezak, "Suger and the Symbolism of Royal Power: The Seal of Louis VII," in Gerson, *Abbot Suger and Saint-Denis*, 95–103; Bedos-Rezak, "Idéologie royale, ambitions princières et rivalités politiques d'après le témoignage des sceaux (France, 1380–1461)," in *La "France anglaise" au moyen âge: Colloque des historiens médiévistes français et britanniques* (Paris, 1988), 483–511, esp. 507; Martine Dalas, *Corpus des sceaux français du moyen âge*, vol. 2, *Les sceaux des rois et de régence* (Paris, 1991), esp. 248–50, 261–63 (seals of Charles VII and Henry VI), 272–73, 281–83, 297 (the different forms of the seals of Louis XI, Charles VIII, and Louis XII).

149

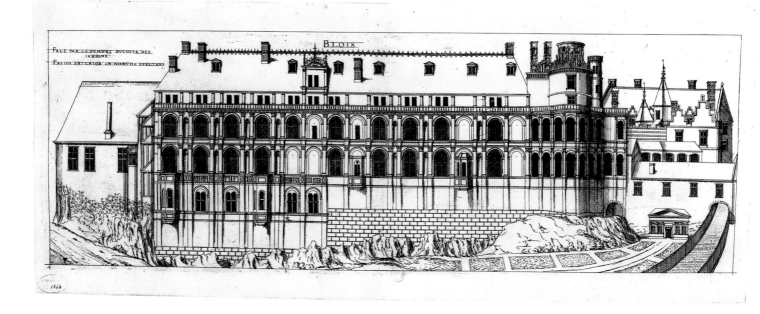

BLOIS

FACE PAR LE DEHORS DV COSTÉ DES
IARDINS
FACIES EXTERIOR IN HORTOS SPECTANS

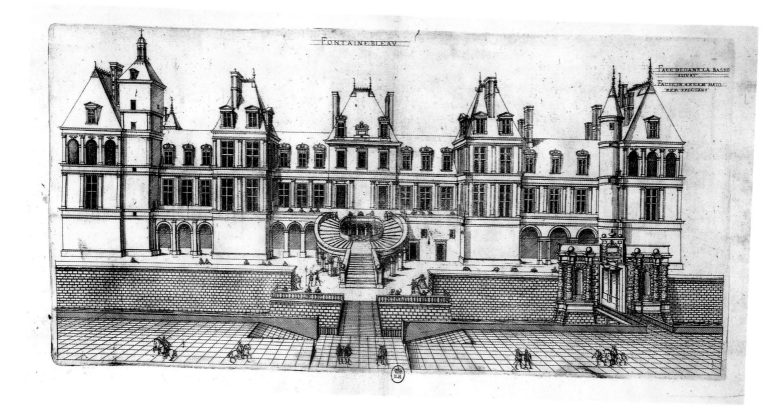

FONTAINEBLEAV

FACE DEDANS LA BASSE
COVRT
FACIES IN AREAM MAIO-
REM SPECTANS

4 The First Libraries

Blois, Fontainebleau, Paris

Antoine Coron

The political and cultural history of France during the period between Louis XII's accession to the throne and Louis XIV's personal assumption of power (1498–1661) can be divided into three major phases. The first, up to the death of Henry II in 1559, looked to Italy as a land to be conquered and as inspiration for France's own Renaissance (embodied by the ongoing construction of Fontainebleau château). There then followed, between 1562 and 1598, eight civil wars and a dozen shaky "truces" during which factions tore each other apart and the monarchy was weakened to the point of being obliged to reconquer Paris (1594), drive the Spanish from the kingdom (1597), and finally reestablish its legitimacy in the minds of all Frenchmen by publishing the "perpetual and irrevocable" treaty of religious peace known as the Edict of Nantes (1598). The sixty years that followed were characterized by the royal government's regaining of domestic control, the main architect of which was Cardinal Richelieu. Government monitoring of printing was reinforced and its stranglehold over the emerging press became total–even the French language itself became an object of government concern. Once the last rebellion by feudal nobility was suppressed, the framework and mechanisms of absolute monarchy were in place, awaiting the arrival of Louis XIV on the scene.

These three historical phases nevertheless correlate poorly to the development of the Royal Library. Although three successive library locations suggest parallel divisions, it is impossible to attribute the same significance and chronological framework to them.[1] So three distinct libraries must be identified according to where they were housed–Blois, Fontainebleau, and Paris–each one having its own specific role and status. Blois (1498–1544) has been studied the most closely, thanks to a remarkable exhibition in 1992 which was seen both at the Bibliothèque nationale de France and in Blois.[2] Fontainebleau (1544–1567) is the most famous because of its setting, the artistic "school" with which it is associated, and the book bindings crafted there. In contrast, although the Bibliothèque Royale was located in the Latin Quarter of Paris for nearly a century (1567-1666), the early Parisian period is by far the most obscure.[3]

There would never have been a Royal Library at Blois if Louis de Touraine, the younger brother of King Charles V, had not married the rich Milanese Valentina Visconti. The Italian marriages of the French princes were anything but disinterested. Thanks to his wife's dowry, the future duke of Orléans rounded out his domain in the west by buying the *comté* of Blois and its powerful castle from Guy II de Châtillon. After the assassination of her husband, Valentina took refuge there with their children. In 1409 Charles d'Orléans, heir to the duchy, ordered that his father's library in Paris and a selection of his mother's manuscripts be brought within the castle's protective walls. The first inventory of the library at Blois in 1417 lists 91 volumes.

Although its establishment had begun sumptuously under the patronage of Louis d'Orléans, the library at Blois later encountered serious setbacks. Charles d'Orléans was taken prisoner by the English after the French defeat at Agincourt and lived in London, where he set about creating a second library containing a little more than 60 volumes. Not until 1440 did he recover his manuscripts at Blois, where they had been stored for safekeeping in the tower of the Treasury. Two years later an inventory by Jean de Tuillières listed 188 manuscripts, a number which increased regularly during the last twenty-five years of the prince's life.

When Charles d'Orléans, one of the most appealing French poets of the fifteenth century,[4] died in 1465, his son Louis was only three years old. All the young duke's properties, including the castle library, were held in guardianship. The books received proper care, there were a few loans and some occasional purchases, but Louis II d'Orléans at first showed little interest in the library. Like his father, he acquired his taste for books during captivity. A plotter and a rebel during Charles VIII's minority, he underwent a harsh imprisonment from 1489 to 1491, in the course of which he became studious and learned Latin. Thus, when he succeeded Charles VIII in 1498 as Louis XII, he was a remarkably cultivated monarch.

Louis XII was familiar with Italy, having accompanied his predecessor to Naples, and he kept in his employ Hellenists like Guillaume Budé and Janus Lascaris, and the historian Claude de Seyssel. He looked to the Roman emperor Marcus Aurelius as his model. He was also a patron of printers, being the first French king to grant them privileges. It was during his reign that Josse Bade, the principal humanist printer in Paris, received support from Guillaume Petit, the king's confessor and the inquisitor general of France, a fascinating individual who later served as royal librarian.

Early in Louis XII's reign, the library at Blois grew to a size that startled visitors, little accustomed to finding such a large number of books–many of them new–in a northern noble's library. On November 11, 1501, the Orléans family collection, which had lain dormant for thirty-six years, was reinstalled in the castle. In the same period, Charles VIII's library at Amboise was added to that of Louis XII and augmented with books which the dukes of Milan had collected in Pavia.

The thirty volumes that Charlotte of Savoy set aside for her son Charles VIII following Louis XI's death in 1483, though limited in number, were the first to be handed down from one king of France to another since Charles V had ascended the throne a century before. Although he knew Latin and Italian, Louis XI preferred hunting to books, and so it was the queen who developed bookish tastes, especially for illuminated manuscripts. Jean Fouquet and Jean Bourdichon, who later took Fouquet's place as painter to the king, also worked for her. Charlotte of Savoy had her own librarian, Martin l'Uillier, and counted in her collection the *Grandes Heures du duc de Berry* (Great book of hours of the duke of Berry), which she passed on to Charles VIII.[5]

Charles VIII had received only a rudimentary education, but he had an appreciation for art and allowed the development of a nascent humanism, especially requesting French translations to add to his library. Above all, he was reputed to like chivalric romances, books of history, and astrological treatises, which fed his dreams of crusades and Italian conquests. These "backward" tastes were typical of the French nobility,[6] even though Charles surrounded himself with learned Italians: Fausto Andrelini was his official poet and Paolo Emili and Giovanni di Candida his historiographers. As for painters, he remained loyal to the Master of Moulins, to Jean Perréal, and to Jean Bourdichon.

Although printing had been introduced into the kingdom in his father's reign,[7] no printed work had found its way into Louis XI's library. Things changed with Charles VIII, who in 1483 received from the hands of a Milanese diplomat the Latin version of Giovanni Simonetta's history of Francesco Sforza (cat. 48). Both Pierre le Rouge, the first to hold the title of bookseller and printer to the king (cat. 49), and later Antoine Vérard, an important publisher-printer who specialized in French translations which were often accompanied by illustrations, furnished the king with deluxe copies printed on vellum (cat. 53), lavishly illuminated.

All of this, however, would not have resulted in such a remarkable library without the books that Charles VIII brought back from Italy. After months of campaigning, he had entered Naples on February 22, 1495, claiming to be its legitimate king by virtue of a series of inheritances going back to Queen Jeanne I. The conquest was short-lived, but Charles did succeed in bringing back to France spoils of war consisting not only of a sizable number of paintings, pieces of furniture, and objets d'art, but of an important collection of manuscripts and printed books which the Aragonese kings had accumulated.

The library in Naples had been founded by Alphonse V the Magnanimous. His successor, Ferdinand I (1458–1494), turned it into one of the five great Italian collections of the fifteenth century, ranking with the Visconti library in Pavia, the Vatican at Rome, the Marciana in Venice, and the Laurenziana in Florence. Ferdinand was largely responsible for the introduction of printing into his realm,[8] and his collection was generously stocked with the first Italian printings, especially imprints from Rome. It was thanks to Ferdinand that Latin antiquity made its appearance in the French Royal Library. The first Greek manuscripts, some of them dating from the eleventh century, also came from the Neapolitan collection. In all, by 1498 more than 1,140 volumes from Naples were held by Charles VIII's widow, Anne de Bretagne, in Amboise. She would probably have kept them separate from the royal collection had she not become queen once again by marrying Louis XII.

153

Louis XII was preoccupied with the same Italian dreams as his predecessor. Tracing his rights back to his grandmother, he asserted a claim to be duke of Milan. A double campaign in 1499 and 1500 resulted in the conquest of the duchy, capture of Ludovico il Moro, and seizure of the Visconti library in the ducal castle in Pavia. The library had been founded by Galeazzo II in the second half of the fourteenth century, when Petrarch resided in the city, and the Visconti gave it their constant attention. The Sforza family later fostered its growth with book purchases, gifts, and conquests of war. A first inventory in 1426 listed 1,000 items. By 1500 the library had apparently grown no further, but Ludovico il Moro, pupil of the Italian humanist Francesco Filelfo, devoted himself to it, entrusting Bartolomeo Calvo with its reorganization. The predominance of manuscripts made the collection a humanist library of major importance, if only for the items it had acquired from Petrarch's library.[9] Finally, it is worth noting the relatively high proportion of French manuscripts and manuscripts in French (cat. 26), which attested to an intensity of exchange from both sides of the Alps, as well as to the aristocratic nature of this library (some four hundred volumes of which remained in the royal collection at Blois).

Such swift and substantial expansion of the library amounted to a metamorphosis. Thanks to the Italian wars, what had been a family collection, composed of random personal contributions from successive kings and princes, became a library which, though certainly diverse in its composition, was clearly "Renaissance" in nature. The sole addition to the library made under Louis XII that countered this italianization was the acquisition of the library of Louis of Bruges, lord of Gruthuyse, a wealthy Flemish noble in the service of the dukes of Burgundy. Although it is not clear when or how Louis XII acquired a hundred or so volumes from Bruges, the presence of the arms of Anne de Bretagne suggests that it occurred prior to 1514.

Francis I succeeded Louis XII on January 1, 1515. The Royal Library at Blois was almost complete. Apparently nothing worthy of note was added at the beginning of the new reign. The 1,626 items in the inventory drawn up by Guillaume Petit in 1518 tallied closely with the number of volumes assembled by the "Father of the People," as Louis XII was called. Until 1544, then, the library was kept at Blois and was administered by librarians—first Adam Laisgre, then Guillaume Petit until 1536, and finally Mellin de Saint-Gelais and Jean de la Barre. In 1530 Jacques Lefèvre d'Étaples restored order to the library and perhaps, as Henri Omont suggests, drew up the Latin part of the catalogue, the so-called inventory of 1518.[10] Yet the library barely increased in size. The roughly 270 additional volumes listed in the 1544 inventory largely correspond to books brought back from Naples but not catalogued until then. The new king contributed only a few dedication copies and volumes transferred from his own personal library, thereby relieving it of what interested him least, notably scientific works on geometry, medicine, and geography.

Although early in his reign Francis I spent more time in Amboise, it was Blois that he transformed into the first French château profoundly marked by Italian influence. Distinguished visitors were inevitably shown the library. It occupied a large room on the second floor of a wing later rebuilt in the seventeenth century by Gaston d'Orléans. A door, three windows, and a chimney are the only surviving features permitting a reconstitution of the arrangement of books according to the old shelfmarks, based on a "courtyard-side" and "moat-side" system; the books were placed on shelves along the walls or on stands perpendicular to the walls, each stand holding as many as eighty volumes, according to the 1544 inventory.[11] Strangely, although royal collections did not distinguish printed books from manuscripts in the sixteenth century, at Blois a distinction was made between volumes "covered in leather" and those "covered in velvet" or other cloth (which seem to have been shelved separately within each of the room's thematic divisions). In 1518, some of the most valuable books were stored separately in cabinets underneath certain stands, or in a pine chest. In 1544, some 141 select volumes were being kept in two "cases," one of which contained the *Grandes heures du duc de Berry* and numerous presentation copies, often by Italian authors. The other case had a copy of Petrarch's *Triumphs* illuminated in Rouen for Louis XII (cat. 55), plus a set of mostly French volumes.

The nearly 1,900 volumes in the royal collection at Blois thus made up the core of the 5,000 books constituting the "old" Bibliothèque Royale (prior to Colbert's reorganization). In its way the library reflected Louis XII's "ordered and controlled" monarchy, as praised by Claude de Seyssel. It was a king's library, reserved for the monarch and those close to him. It retained its aristocratic character by virtue of the sources of the acquisitions and the historic and "courtly" tone of a substantial part of the books. The collection was also, however, clearly humanist, dedicated to the values of the new urban elites while serving as a storehouse of "sources" to satisfy their thirst for knowledge. Finally, it was unquestionably Christian—books on theology accounted for roughly a quarter of the collection. That fragile balance collapsed when Francis I imparted a new direction to the library transferred to Fontainebleau.

The Library at Fontainebleau

Francis I had not just been heir to the throne, like his predecessors, but had been a far more pampered heir than they. He had lost his father as a young boy and had been raised by his mother, Louise de Savoie, for whom he was "Caesar," and his sister, the refined Marguerite d'Angoulême, author of the *Heptaméron*. Both, in Michelet's words, gazed upon him in an "ecstasy of worship and devotion." Francis combined traditional chivalric values with intense curiosity about the arts beyond the Alps. He read Latin, composed verse on occasion, and knew something about everything. As soon as he came to the throne, he turned his attention to Italy. His victory at Marignano brought Leonardo da Vinci to his court, and his defeat at Pavia marked the end of far-flung ambitions and the veritable start of a Renaissance rooted in the French kingdom itself. Rabelais could write in 1532, "Now all the disciplines of learning are restored, the study of languages introduced. . . ."[12]

As he mounted the throne, Francis I had at his disposal a family library begun a century before by his grandfather, Jean d'Angoulême, the brother and companion in captivity of Charles d'Orléans. Francis I's father, Charles d'Angoulême, shared with Charles VIII a liking for books beautifully printed on vellum and acquired many, adding them to the family's library at Cognac. So it was that Francis I inherited 200 books and a bibliophile tradition which Louise de Savoie carefully nurtured. She herself collected illuminated manuscripts and employed in her service the painter

Robinet Testard (cat. 56). The king acquired from her and her entourage a taste for highly refined books, such as those his tutor François Demoulins had illustrated by Godefroy le Batave and Jean Clouet.

After the death of Louise of Savoy in 1531, her books were combined with those of the Angoulême family and with volumes offered to the king or acquired by him. This already substantial collection grew further with the addition of the Moulins library, which had been seized in 1523 along with all the properties of the traitorous *Connétable* de Bourbon. The confiscation comprised 100 volumes whose history went back roughly two centuries to the reign of Charles V (brother-in-law of Louis II de Bourbon). Some manuscripts from the libraries of Jean de Berry and the dukes of Burgundy had entered the Bourbon collection as a result of a series of marriages. Nearly all these books were in French, as were most of the books that Francis I acquired in the first half of his reign.

Care of the books was assigned to selected officers of the royal household. Some of these "librarians of the Chamber" are known to us today: Guillaume de Sauzay, who had already held the office during the reign of Louis XII; his son, Jean de Sauzay; Jean Verdurier; and the poet Claude Chappuis (from 1532 to 1560). These librarians, who were distinct from the staff at Blois, followed the king in his constant moves. It must be supposed that the books in their charge were equally nomadic or that they were divided among the king's principal residences: the Louvre, Saint-Germain-en-Laye, Amboise, Chambord, Blois (where certain books ended up), and Fontainebleau. A payment order to Chappuis in January 1539 for transporting the books that had come from Turin for deposit at Fontainebleau, Paris, and Saint-Germain-en-Laye[13] confirms the existence of at least three libraries which Francis I maintained in addition to the old library at Blois. The choice of Fontainebleau as the principal, or even the only, site for the royal collections of books evidently occurred later and was probably less premeditated than has been claimed. It needs to be understood in the context of the establishment of a new library quite distinct from earlier private collections.

Tradition, coupled with a natural tendency to place the earliest possible date on the emergence of the literary Renaissance in France, have resulted in dating Francis I's first acquisitions of Greek books to the very beginning of his reign. By this reckoning, the creation of the library at Fontainebleau could be seen as the culmination of a fully matured plan. But long-term continuity was foreign to Francis I's thinking, and it is not at all certain that the library was planned from the outset.

Contrary to assertions by Jean Boivin, Léopold Delisle (who cites Boivin),[14] and Henri Omont,[15] the main historical sources on the subject—Francis I's acquisitions of Greek books began neither in 1515 (when Janus Lascaris allegedly established at Fontainebleau "a library specially devoted to Greek manuscripts") nor even in 1529 (when the king reportedly dispatched Girolamo Fondulo to Italy to buy such manuscripts). The first assertion apparently has no basis in fact whatsoever, and the second entails an error in dates.[16]

Now it so happened that, as a result of his education, Francis I had found himself in a situation shared with many others at the beginning of the sixteenth century. His professed interest in Greek authors depended on translations—which, incidentally, he promoted during the whole of his reign. To gain access to them he needed the help of intermediaries. Guillaume Budé performed that role for several years in order to further *bonae litterae* at court. Later the king employed his own private readers, Jacques Colin and Pierre Duchastel, both Hellenists.[17]

For a long time the king's personal collections contained no Greek books other than the two or three that Janus Lascaris had presented to him at the beginning of his reign. Until 1538, the only important group of Greek manuscripts in any of the royal libraries was at Blois—some 40 volumes, most of which had come from Naples. By about 1550 the number of Greek books in the royal collection had increased more than tenfold to 540 items, according to the catalogue drawn up by Angelos Vergikios and Constantin Palaeocappa. Thus, in a very short time (since few of the acquisitions postdate 1545), Francis I's collection of Greek books had become the largest in the world, surpassing that of Saint Mark's in Venice.[18]

The sudden arrival of so many Greek books in Fontainebleau around 1540 understandably arouses curiosity. What purpose did they serve so far from Paris and its university? Furthermore, what was the significance of such luxurious and sturdy bindings on working manuscripts that so few in the château entourage were likely to use? The usual response to the first question argues the case for royal ambition and the desire to rival the most famous libraries of the age. Since Greek was considered the foremost language, superiority in that field would be enough to assure preeminence to the king's collection. As for the bindings, their sturdiness supposedly demonstrated the "public" character of the library at Fontainebleau, and their lavishness mirrored the library's elegant interior.

It is unlikely that Francis I ever conceived of the library at Fontainebleau as a demonstration of cultural hegemony. His effort to assemble such a collection was motivated not by the concept of a new kind of royal library but by the aim to create a scholarly reference library—a library intended to underpin the new college to be built in Paris.

In 1530 new instruction was offered in Greek, Hebrew, and mathematics (Latin was only added in 1534) by a handful of professors in Paris appointed and paid by the king, the so-called *professores regii*, or "royal readers."[19] This modest group of teachers incarnated hopes for a revival of *bonnes lettres* (that is, classical culture), beginning with Greek. The idea of founding a college to teach ancient languages—at first only Greek, then Hebrew and Latin as well—had been gestating, somewhat erratically, ever since 1518. Further development rested on the unflagging efforts of Budé. The appointing of professores regii was seen as just the first step toward establishing a new college and constructing a vast new building, as confirmed by repeated allusions in subsequent years. Right up to his death (around 1540), the fulfillment of this plan had been Budé's most fervent wish, one shared by the royal readers.

Credit for finally getting the college under way nearly fell to Pierre Duchastel. Prior to coming to the king's attention, the remarkable Duchastel had lived near Erasmus in Basel, then worked as a corrector of Greek texts for the printer Froben.[20] Duchastel subsequently traveled to Rome and Venice, made a living as a translator in Cyprus, and spent time in Egypt before traveling up to Constantinople via Jerusalem and Damascus. On his return to France, this four-year tour earned Duchastel a certain esteem at court, and he was named reader to the king around 1537.

The professores regii were directly answerable to the reader to the king, who saw the monarch daily and who indeed read to him during meals. Right from his appointment, Duchastel took his new responsibilities seriously, defending the royal readers from attacks by Sorbonne professors and obtaining several significant improvements in status for his protégés. Above all, in 1538 Duchastel convinced the king finally to build the promised college on the site of the old Nesle mansion opposite the Louvre (where the Institut de France is now located). A royal document dated December 19, 1539, made generous provisions for the administration and construction of a "fine and grand college" designed to host six hundred scholarship students and their professors.[21] There were notably plans for what the king himself termed a "fine and magnificent library,"[22] which Duchastel was instructed to fill with books in Greek.

All the French ambassadors in Italy, themselves infatuated with Hellenism, endeavored to carry out the king's plan. In Rome, Georges d'Armagnac was particularly active from 1541 to 1545. And above all, Guillaume Pellicier in Venice collaborated closely with Duchastel in hunting down Greek manuscripts, then engaging as many as twelve copyists in the king's service. When naming Pellicier ambassador in 1539, Francis I had told him of the importance of the task. Pellicier was thus one of the best-informed people concerning the king's plans when he specified, in a letter to Antoine Rincon dated September 1, 1540, the destination of the manuscripts he was instructed to collect at great expense. After having informed Rincon–ambassador in Constantinople–of the imminent founding of the college, Pellicier explicitly stated that, since it need to be "endowed with a library, [the king] is having books sought on every side, mostly especially Greek."[23]

Girolamo Fondulo, mentioned above, had already returned with some fifty volumes the year before. Duchastel himself, with alacrity, purchased books in Greek from the heirs of two former ambassadors, one of whom, Georges de Selve, had been the patron of Angelos Vergikios at Venice. Vergikios, from Crete, entered the service of Francis I in 1539 as an "expert writer in Greek letters" and was swiftly included among the royal readers, on whose lists he would still be found twenty years later.

Although numerous Greek books flowed into France between 1539 and 1544, the Collège des Trois Langues for which they were destined remained, alas, in the planning stage. As was often the case, Francis I did not carry out his intentions. The fault has been laid at the door of Chancellor Poyet, who was all-powerful until the summer of 1542. The war which then broke out and lasted four years was a further obstacle. As late as spring 1544, however, certain professors still believed that their college would be built. On May 1 of that year, royal reader in medicine Guido Guidi, in the dedicatory epistle to the king in his volume on surgery, praised Duchastel's efforts to constitute the future library (cats. 65 and 66).

On May 22, 1544, Francis I decided to move the Royal Library from Blois to Fontainebleau. The transfer, which took place in June, temporarily postponed plans for the creation of a research library dedicated to the three languages of antiquity and open to the professors of the royal college as a source of studies and publications. Duchastel, who was appointed master of the king's library (maître de la Librairie) upon Guillaume Budé's death in August 1540, had been a fervent promoter of the new Royal Library. He had conceived of it not as a library turned in upon itself–a characteristic in many respects of the library at Blois–but as one intended for scholars and even accessible to a distant readership through a publication program to be undertaken by the printer Robert Estienne. So that the printings might be as attractive as possible, Duchastel had on November 2, 1540, ordered type punches from Jean Garamond, based on designs by Angelos Vergikios.[24] From 1544 to 1551 Estienne used them exclusively in all his Greek printings. All the texts, save one, were published from copies in the Royal Library–*ex Bibliotheca Regia*, as the title pages proudly announced. After Estienne's departure for Geneva, Adrien Turnèbe and later the Morel family pursued this venture. The subsequent masters of the library, like Pierre Montdoré, Jacques Amyot, and even Jacques-Auguste de Thou, were intent on encouraging this undertaking as the most vital vestige of a scholarly project which ought not to be completely abandoned.

The amalgamation at Fontainebleau of the principal royal libraries–those of Blois, the Collège des Trois Langues, and the king's personal or family collections–represents the last stage in a process that for fifty years molded the library of the kings of France from an aggregate of disparate libraries having virtually nothing in common. The humanist collection was spawned by fascination with Italy, worship of bonae litterae, and concern to procure a research tool for the royal readers comprising works of Greek and Latin antiquity, the writings of the Church Fathers in their original language, and their most learned commentators. Meanwhile, a second, more varied class of material emerged from the personal nature of each monarch's "family" library; it comprised not only works on canon law and classics of theology and medieval piety in Latin but also numerous chivalric romances, chronicles, and a quantity of "old" poetry in French.

The humanist evolution in the content of the Royal Library must be qualified, however, even when the king's initiatives seem to point in the same direction. The content of most of the books printed in Venice between 1501 and 1530 indicates that they were acquired for the future royal college, where they were supposed to swell the Greek collections. On the other hand, the interesting library of printed books that Francis I obtained for his personal use from Venice in 1539, which he instructed Etienne Roffet to bind in dark calf, throws light on the king's own tastes. The selection was encyclopedic, with two sorts of material predominating: poetry (notably Ariosto) and history. It is interesting to note that Herodotus, Xenophon, Julius Caesar, Valerius Maximus, Dio Cassius, and even Virgil and Ovid were all read in Italian. The French king's culture changed languages, became more refined (he acquired the 1528 edition of Castiglione's *Il cortegiano* [The courtier]), but remained eminently *chivalric.*

In the last panel of the famous gallery that Francis I built at Fontainebleau, a fresco by Rosso Fiorentino depicts "l'Ignorance chassée" (Ignorance cast out). Francis I is shown with a book in his hand entering the temple of Jupiter, its entrance seemingly closed off to a blind and frightened crowd outside. The library was located just

159

above this allusion to the king's efforts on behalf of the royal college. As at Blois, the books were probably arranged on shelves along the walls and on desks. Although their number scarcely exceeded 3,600 volumes, they took up much more space than they presently do in the Bibliothèque nationale de France because they were normally laid flat on shelves.

Some 900 of these volumes were the object of a major sixteen-year binding program that was begun in 1544 and lasted until the accession of Francis II in 1559.[25] Credit must go to the king's successive binders, Etienne Roffet, Gommar Estienne, and Claude Picques, craftsmen who turned Henry II into what Louis-Marie Michon termed "the greatest bibliophile of his day." Indeed, 750 bindings from the Fontainebleau library bear Henry II's arms and monogram.

This magnificent set of morocco bindings—sometimes decorated with inlay, fillets, and gold and silver tooling—drew admiring visitors' attention to the core of the library originally destined for the royal college. The Greek and Oriental manuscripts acquired by Francis I were bound on boards *alla greca* (except for a few that retained their Italian bindings[26]), over wooden boards, with flat spines and raised headcaps. These manuscripts were joined by 250 printed books, either recently acquired or drawn from the collection of first editions at Blois. The initial intention was clearly to constitute an ideal library around the Greek collection, featuring major writers of pagan and Christian antiquity in their original languages. Subsequently, the person who made the selection (perhaps Mellin de Saint-Gelais or Mathieu La Bisse) complemented it with polemical, anti-Lutheran texts, scientific books, a French version of Machiavelli's *Art of War*, and even two large vellum volumes illuminated at Antoine Vérard's workshop.

In the late 1550s, although the binder to the king was crafting masterpieces, the Royal Library grew ever more slowly until in the next decade it failed to record a single new acquisition. This state of affairs endured for sixty years and then improved but slightly. The catalogue which the Dupuy brothers used until 1650 indicates that the library had acquired only some 20 printed volumes between 1561 and 1650. This occurred in spite of the fact that France prided itself on having a copyright deposit requirement (*dépôt légal*) ever since Francis I issued a decree at Montpellier on December 28, 1537.

Because of its context, as well as its purposes and declared goals, the king's edict reflected the intellectual euphoria which colored the last period of peace in his reign between the summers of 1537 and 1542. But it testified also to an increased distrust of the writings of the religious reformers. It was therefore an ambiguous document, liberal and at the same time wary, imposing controls on books entering France and ordering French printers to provide Mellin de Saint-Gelais, keeper of the library of Blois, with a copy of each new publication. What he was supposed to do with those publications is not very clear. The king wanted to add to his library only "works worthy of being seen." The librarian enjoyed complete freedom of choice, but his selection criteria must have been relatively severe: from 1538 to 1561, no more than 118 French imprints entered the Royal Library, an average of roughly 5 a year. Approximately 300 titles were printed in Paris alone about 1535. So Fontainebleau was not a library of record. Neither was it any longer really the king's library. Henry

II endowed it with only a few dozen books; his successors, none. It was the most luxurious of the research libraries but unfortunately quite far from those who could make use of it.

Pierre de La Ramée (Ramus), the most brilliant of the *professores regii* in Charles IX's time, a secret Protestant but one who enjoyed the king's patronage, found a safe haven at Fontainebleau in 1562–1563. He had the leisure then to appreciate both the library and its total isolation. In 1567 this dean of royal readers, then at the peak of his influence with the queen mother, implored her in a long Latin preface[27] to found at last in the Latin Quarter the royal college for which Francis I had "oft laid the plans" and which Henry II also envisaged but which was prevented by "unforeseen wars and deaths." To accomplish this, he pointed out that the library must first be moved from Fontainebleau and placed near the university in the heart of the Latin Quarter.[28] It was for this reason—and not to protect it from civil disturbances—that the Royal Library was moved from what Ramus called "the woods and fields" of Fontainebleau to Paris.

The Royal Library in the Latin Quarter

At this point begins the most obscure period in the history of the Royal Library. Exactly where its books were transported initially is unknown—probably to a house in the Latin Quarter, though there is no supporting evidence. As for the date, the man in charge of the move, Jean Gosselin,[29] affirms simply that it took place under Charles IX. Very likely the move occurred in the months following Ramus's preface, for civil war broke out again in September 1567. With the return of peace, Ramus, having lost his principal supporters, was forced to leave Paris. Forbidden to teach thereafter, he was assassinated two days after the Saint Bartholomew Massacre (August 26, 1572).

The plan for a royal college, presented to Catherine de Médicis as the only project worthy of her name, failed for the second time. In the next twenty years, among the darkest in French history, the weakening of central government, the division of the country, and the isolation of Paris deprived the project of any hope of realization. However, Jacques Amyot (1513–1593), who succeeded the Protestant Pierre Montdoré in 1567 as master of the king's library, was also "grand almoner" and therefore oversaw the royal readers. This meant that a single officer once again had responsibility over both the *professores regii* and the collections intended for their use, which probably facilitated the loan of books, though little else. At the end of this period the Royal Library was reduced to a woeful state, buried in dust and prey to insects. Amyot—who was a Hellenist like Budé and was held in esteem by the last Valois kings, whom he had served as tutor—even felt compelled to join the Catholic League. That party, hostile to Henry IV, ruled over Paris; and the Royal Library, under threat a number of times, was even at its mercy for some months in 1593–1594. Gosselin has left us a curious account of that period when, fearful for his own safety, he prudently abandoned the books that had been entrusted to his care.[30] Fortunately, the ensuing pillage was limited.

With the return of royal government to Paris in the spring of 1594, the status of the library improved. Upon Amyot's death, the position of master of the king's library had been bestowed on Jacques-Auguste De Thou (1553–1617). This loyalist and Gallican member of the Parlement, with useful Protestant friends, was one of the most learned men in Paris. His own library was already famous and became the finest printed book collection of his day. (Given the growing cultural domination of the Jesuits, it was a bastion of what Budé would have called "bonnes lettres.") In his first decision, De Thou moved the Royal Library in 1595 into the Collège de Clermont in the rue Saint-Jacques. The Jesuits had been expelled from it following Châtel's assassination attempt against Henry IV. The two-part catalogue that Gosselin compiled, arranged by item location,[31] probably dates from this period: half of the books, most in French, were stored in the "upper library" and the other part, including those in Italian, Spanish, and Greek, in the "lower library of the king." In all, they totaled 3,650 volumes, including 723 Greek books (a mixture of manuscripts and printed books). The Royal Library held fast to its scholarly goals, and the project for a royal college was taken up again as soon as peace returned.

On November 14, 1594, Henri Monantheuil, a royal reader in mathematics, opened the academic year with a lecture in Latin on the need to fulfill Francis I's plans by at last building the college that had been on the drawing boards for more than fifty years. Monantheuil went into a long description of the various buildings, staff, and roles, as though the plans had just been laid. There were to be ten subjects (including Arabic, political science, and theology), twenty professors, a botanist, a surgeon, and naturally a "keeper of the Royal Library" (*bibliothecophylax*). The library, to be located above the classrooms, was to be open not only to royal readers but to all scholars, on the model of libraries in Heidelberg and Ingolstadt.

De Thou also accentuated the library's scholarly aims by acquiring a group of Greek manuscripts more numerous than those at Fontainebleau and, in the opinion of Henri Omont, superior in value and antiquity. The collection of Cardinal Niccolò Ridolfi, a nephew of Pope Leo X, had been gathered in part by Janus Lascaris. Acquired in 1550 by Marshal Strozzi, an Italian in the service of Henry II, the collection had been unscrupulously "appropriated" by Catherine de Médicis. Ever since creditors had tied up Catherine's property upon her death in 1589, De Thou had made every effort to persuade the king to purchase the manuscripts. The affair was long and difficult, but finally, on May 16, 1599, nearly 800 volumes–three-quarters of them Greek–found their place in the "room adjoining the upstairs hall" in the Collège de Clermont. Acquisition of the Ridolfi manuscripts made Greek the library's second language and Greek books its principal scholarly attraction. It underscored the now more urgent need for a librarian capable of taking full advantage of such a large collection. Jean Gosselin was not the man for the job. Out of consideration for his advanced years, however, Isaac Casaubon, the foremost Hellenist of the time, who had been lured first by a stipend as royal reader, had to await his predecessor's death in November 1604 before he could succeed to the title of librarian.[32]

Casaubon's first task was to organize the Royal Library's fourth move in sixty years. The Jesuits had, in fact, just received authorization to reopen their colleges in Paris–except for Clermont, which they nevertheless reoccupied and where it is reported they readily kept the king's books in compensation for those lost ten years earlier. A new library location had to be found and De Thou, who also acted as agent for the Cordeliers, naturally hit on the idea of transporting the Royal Library to their monastery, where it was at first placed in the outbuildings of the infirmary.[33] Such an odd location would seem astonishing had it not been for De Thou's need for a temporary library while awaiting construction of the royal college, which he assumed was imminent.

Two days before Christmas 1609, Sully, De Thou, and Cardinal Du Perron, grand almoner to the king, visited the buildings where the royal readers normally gave their courses.[34] That was where Henry IV had finally decided to build the long-awaited college. Claude Chatillon drew up the plans for the building, which was designed to be imposing.[35] The central section was to be flanked by two sixty-meter-long, forty-meter-deep wings. At each end would be two classrooms, over which was to be installed "His Majesty's library, the finest in the world for manuscripts."[36]

This third attempt, coming after those in 1539 and 1567, should have been the good one. Even the assassination of Henry IV on May 14, 1610, did not bring things to a halt. On July 28, the young Louis XIII, wielding a silver trowel that Sully gave him, mortared the first stone. Unfortunately, the college's three promoters did not remain his counsellors for long—Sully was soon dismissed, and De Thou and du Perron died in 1617 and 1618, respectively. Slowed by various constraints, construction came to a halt in 1619. In 1634 one of the wings was completed. And then nothing more happened until the 1770s.

These vagaries necessarily affected the Royal Library. Casaubon, fearing a Catholic reaction after Henry IV's death, accepted James I's invitation to go to London, combining the responsibilities of librarian and royal professor of Greek literature. Casaubon had at any rate spent most of his time reading the books in his care. His successor, Nicolas Rigault, was the first librarian in the modern sense of the word. A learned jurist who was close to De Thou, he, along with Claude Saumaise and J.-B. Hautin, began in 1619 to prepare a catalogue in two parts, organized according to location. Each item was assigned a shelf number—the first "call numbers"—systematically placed at the beginning of each volume.

The task of putting things in order seems to have culminated about 1622, when Rigault finished a fair copy of his catalogue. It was then, in fact, that the Royal Library left the Cordeliers infirmary for a large renovated house on the monastery grounds fronting the rue de la Harpe. Rigault, who lodged there, also personally shelved the manuscripts of Philippe Hurault de Cheverny, a nephew of De Thou manuscripts which the king had purchased the same year.

Of the more than 400 manuscripts in this collection, a third were in Greek and came from Jean Hurault de Boistaillé, Charles IX's ambassador to Venice and Constantinople. Other, rarer items reflected the taste of leading members of Parlement—Philippe Hurault's father had been chancellor of France—for manuscripts from the early Middles Ages. These had become available through the pillage of monastic libraries by Protestant troops.[37]

From then until the library's last move in 1666, not a single acquisition of Latin, Greek, or Oriental "sources" found its way into the Royal Library. The manuscripts of Savary de Brèves, another ambassador to Rome and Constantinople, which the king had purchased in 1632, were appropriated by Richelieu. The historic collection of Antoine de Loménie, sold to the king in 1638, was diverted in the same way, before winding up in the palace of another cardinal, Mazarin. The only collection to be added to the Royal Library was the one bequeathed in 1656 by Jacques, the younger of the two Dupuy brothers. For forty years the Dupuys had exercised veritable intellectual sway over the republic of letters. They were originally based at the De Thou residence; then, beginning in 1645, Pierre Dupuy, successor of Nicolas Rigault, and his brother Jacques settled down with their many books into the house in the rue de la Harpe.

A certain amount of information is available concerning the respective arrangements of the two libraries housed there. The king's library was physically split in two, according to the division of Rigault's catalogue. There was a "large room," the *bibliotheca major*, containing 2,450 manuscripts which made up the "humanist" collection of Greek and Latin materials; in an adjacent *galerie médiocre*,[38] there were 1,532 "modern" (we would say "medieval") manuscripts and 1,329 printed books—all but about 20 of them published before 1562.

The library of the Dupuy brothers—along with that of their De Thou relatives and the library that Naudé had started to assemble for Mazarin—was one of the largest nonroyal and nonmonastic libraries in Paris.[39] Its content was probably the most scholarly. In addition to 260 ancient manuscripts, the spacious eighteen-meter-long gallery boasted 9,225 printed books, nearly all dated after 1561.

The very appearance of the volumes in each of the two libraries denoted two different worlds or, more precisely, two different eras. Books from the Royal Library, bound so that they could be stored flat, were often fitted with metallic *bossettes*, or bosses, to protect the leather from the rough surfaces of the shelves. In deciding to forgo this hardware, Pierre Dupuy ordered that all volumes be shelved upright in his library, the only way to store a large number of volumes in a limited space.

A century had gone by since the Francis I's libraries had been consolidated at Fontainebleau. This initiative is customarily described as the founding act of the Royal Library and Francis credited as the "father of letters" by making books permanently available to the literati. His edict of Montpellier, by mandating deposit of all new publications, is also seen as the first move to safeguard intellectual output from the ravages of time. Furthermore, the king's patronage and his bookbinders' skill are perceived as endowing this grand intellectual enterprise with artistic beauty.

But, as demonstrated here, the library at Fontainebleau in no way prefigured the Royal Library of the eighteenth century, much less the comprehensive library of *dépôt légal* that succeeded it. Nor did the edict of Montpellier have any impact on the library. Until the second half of the seventeenth century, printed books were clearly in the minority at the Royal Library, where Italian imprints still outnumbered French. The fashionableness of Greek which Budé skillfully instilled in the court of Francis I—especially the project for a trilingual college that was never implemented as planned—encouraged the library to develop in a direction which in the long run alienated it from the court.

The successors of Henry II bypassed the Royal Library at Fontainebleau by setting up their personal collections. Except for the nine-year-old Louis XIII, they simply did not visit it any more. It was in the Louvre, in his study "decorated with a large number of paintings, antiques, and old books and manuscripts," that Henry IV conducted the landgrave of Hesse through "his" library.[40] Ignored by the monarchy, perpetually tied to a project whose realization was always on the distant horizon, the Royal Library finally became sclerotic.

One may wonder what the Royal Library meant to visitors to the Dupuy "study" on rue de la Harpe. People seeking recent scientific publications, pitting their minds against new philosophic systems, debating controversial points—what could such people find in the old books of the Bibliothèque Royale? The answer lies in the guide to its riches that Philippe Labbe drew up in 1653. This Jesuit's discerning appraisal is filled with a new excitement. The select list of printed books he append-ed to his *Nova bibliotheca*[41] was replete with unknown treasures to be discovered. They were all incunabula. Labbe's list indeed constitutes the first published cata-logue of books printed in the fifteenth century.

A new word was born, and with it the history of printed books took its first steps.

1 In terms of a chronology specific to the royal libraries, for example, the period 1501–1664 would be preferable to 1498–1661.

2 Ursula Baurmeister and Marie-Pierre Laffitte, *Des livres et des rois: La Bibliothèque Royale de Blois*, exhibi-tion at the Bibliothèque Nationale (Paris, 1992). See also Denise Bloch, "La formation de la Bibliothèque du Roi," in *Histoire des bibliothèques françaises*, vol. 1, *Les bibliothèques médiévales, du VIe siècle à 1530* (Paris, 1989), 311–31.

3 Simon Balayé devotes a mere 26 of the 546 pages of *La Bibliothèque Nationale des origines à 1800* (Geneva, 1988) to its first century in Paris.

4 Charles liked to surround himself with literary figures and poets: François Villon was his dining com-panion.

5 Baurmeister and Laffitte, *Des livres et des rois*, no. 14.

6 On the tastes of the French nobility in the 16th century, see André Chastel, *Cultures et demeures en France au XVIe siècle* (Paris, 1989).

7 Gasparino Barzizza, *Epistolae* (Paris, [1470]). See cat. 45.

8 In 1471 he offered a bishopric to the Strasbourger Sixtus Riessinger, the early printer of Naples, accord-ing to L. Delisle (*Le Cabinet des Manuscrits de la Bibliothèque Impériale* [Paris, 1868], 1:228).

9 Taken by Gian Galeazzo I Visconti from Francesco Carrara, Petrarch's heir.

10 Henri Omont, *Anciens inventaires et catalogues de la Bibliothèque Nationale* (Paris, 1921), 11–12.

11 According to a description of the library by Antonio de Beatis, secretary to Cardinal Louis of Aragon, who visited Blois in 1517; cited in Bloch, "Formation," 323.

12 Letter of Gargantua to Pantagruel in chap. 8 of *Pantagruel.*

13 *Catalogue des actes de François Ier* (Paris, 1905), 8:171, no. 30840.

14 Delisle, *Cabinet des Manuscrits*, 1:151–62.

15 H. Omont, *Catalogues des manuscrits grecs de Fontainebleau sous François Ier et Henri II* (Paris, 1889), iv–viii, 371–72.

16 Contrary to what Boivin, Delisle, and Omont thought they read (or didn't bother to verify), the note accompanying the list of the 50 Greek manuscripts that Fondulo purchased for the king in Italy is dated not 1529 but 1539 (BNF Grec 3064, fol. 68v).

17 In 1527 Francis I granted Colin a license to publish Claude de Seyssel's inferior manuscript translations of Greek authors, which were gathering dust in the Royal Library of Blois.

18 The collection of Greek manuscripts in the BNF is still extraordinary.

19 On the origins of what would become the Collège de France, see Abel Lefranc, "La fondation et les com-mencements du Collège de France (1530–1930), in *Le Collège de France (1530–1930): Livre jubilaire* (Paris, 1932), 27–58.

20 For a biography of Duchastel, see Pierre Doucet, "Pierre Du Chastel, grand aumônier de France," *Revue historique* 133 (1920): 212–57; 134 (1920): 1–57.

21 Document reproduced in Pierre Galland, *Petri Castellani. . . vita*, ed. Etienne Baluze (Paris, 1674), 154–57. Jean Grolier, treasurer of France and a great collector of books, was placed in charge of contracts for the planned building.

22 Letter from Francis I to the duke of Ferrara, Sept. 18, 1538, published in Abel Lefranc, *Histoire du Collège de France* (Paris, 1893), 153–54.

23 Guillaume Pellicier, *Correspondance politique (1540–1542)*, ed. Alexandre Tausserat-Radel (Paris, 1889), 78.

24 Annie Parent, "Les 'Grecs du Roi,'" in *L'art du livre à l'Imprimerie Nationale* (Paris, 1973), 55–65.

25 Anthony Hobson, *Humanists and Bookbinders* (Cambridge, 1989), 172–213 and 263–66.

26 Anthony Hobson, "Les reliures de la bibliothèque de François Ier," *Revue française d'histoire du livre* 36 (1982): 409–26.

27 In the *Proemium mathematicum ad Catharinam Mediceam* (Paris, 1567). A French translation was published the same year.

28 The library was moved before the death of Charles IX on May 30, 1574 (if Jean Gosselin, who was responsible for this operation as master of the library, is to be believed) and after November 1573, date of Origen's *Opera* edited by Gilbert Génébrard, royal reader in Hebrew who celebrated the library of Fontainebleau again in an epistle to the king.

29 J. Gosselin, *Remonstrance touchant la garde de la Librairie du Roy* (Paris, 1594). Charles IX died on May 30, 1574.

30 In the *Remonstrance*, Gosselin recalled that he had taken care to bar the door securely before leaving, but the Ligueurs had broken through the wall.

31 See Omont, *Anciens inventaires*, 1:265–437. He wrongly dates the Gosselin catalogue 1560.

32 Gosselin, who had greater enthusiasm for the occult sciences than for Greek, was almost 100 years old when he died.

33 See Laure Beaumont-Maillet, *Le grand couvent des Cordeliers de Paris* (Paris, 1975), 118–19 and 199–206.

34 See Lefranc, *Histoire*, 234–43.

35 Chastillon had already designed Place Royale (now Place des Vosges) in Paris. For his plans for the royal college, see his *Topographie française* (1641–1647), pl. 8.

36 *Le Mercure Français* (Paris, 1609–1610), fol. 407; quoted in Lefranc, *Histoire*, 233–35.

37 In this exhibition, cats. 3 and 6 came from Philippe Hurault's collection.

38 According to Claude du Molinet, cited by Omont, and other sources.

39 The two Jesuit libraries in Paris, especially that of the Collège de Clermont, directed by Fronton du Duc, were larger.

40 In October 1602. See C. de Rommel, ed., *Correspondance inédite de Henri IV . . . avec Maurice-le-Savant* (Paris, 1840), 65.

41 The complete title is *Nova Bibliotheca mss. librorum, sive specimen antiquarum lectionum* (Paris, 1653). See the ninth *supplementum*.

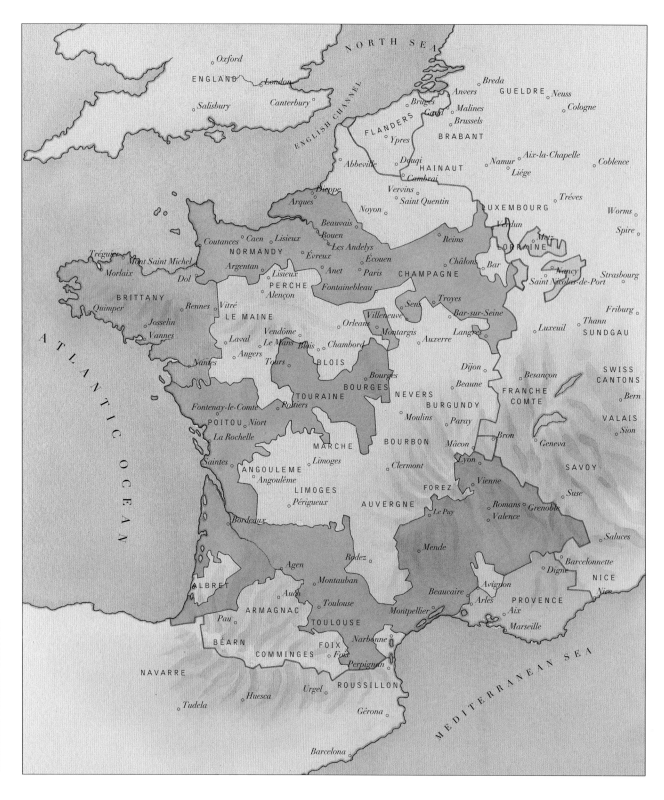

NORTH SEA

Oxford
ENGLAND
London
Salisbury
Canterbury

ENGLISH CHANNEL

Bruges
Gand
Anvers
Breda
GUELDRE
Neuss
Cologne
Malines
Brussels
FLANDERS
Ypres
BRABANT

Abbeville
Douai
HAINAUT
Cambrai
Namur
Liège
Aix-la-Chapelle
Coblence

Dieppe
Arques
Vervins
Saint Quentin
LUXEMBOURG
Tréves
Worms

Beauvais
Rouen
Reims
Verdun
Metz
Spire

Coutances
Caen
Lisieux
Les Andelys
Châlons
Bar
LORRAINE

Tréguier
Mont Saint Michel
NORMANDY
Évreux
Écouen
Nancy
Strasbourg

Morlaix
Dol
Argentan
Anet
Paris
CHAMPAGNE
Saint Nicolas-de-Port

BRITTANY
Lisieux
PERCHE
Fontainebleau
Troyes
Friburg

Quimper
Rennes
Vitré
Alençon
Sens
Bar-sur-Seine
Langres
Luxeuil
Thann
SUNDGAU

Josselin
Vannes
LE MAINE
Orléans
Villeneuve
Montargis
Auxerre
Dijon
Besançon
SWISS CANTONS

Laval
Vendôme
Le Mans
Blois
Chambord
Beaune
FRANCHE COMTÉ
Bern

Nantes
Angers
Tours
BLOIS
Bourges
BOURGES
NEVERS
BURGUNDY
Paray
Mâcon
Bron
Geneva
VALAIS
Sion

ATLANTIC OCEAN

Fontenay-le-Comte
Rottiers
TOURAINE
Moulins
BOURBON

POITOU
Niort
MARCHE
Limoges
Clermont
Lyon
Vienne
SAVOY
Suse

La Rochelle
Saintes
ANGOULEME
Angoulême
LIMOGES
Périgueux
AUVERGNE
FOREZ
Le Puy
Romans
Valence
Grenoble
Saluces

Bordeaux
Mende
Barcelonnette
Digne
NICE

Agen
Rodez
Beaucaire
Avignon
Arles
PROVENCE
Aix
Nice

ALBRET
Auch
Montauban
Montpellier
Marseille

Pau
ARMAGNAC
Toulouse
Narbonne
MEDITERRANEAN SEA

BÉARN
COMMINGES
TOULOUSE
FOIX
Foix
Perpignan

NAVARRE
Urgel
ROUSSILLON

Tudela
Huesca
Gérona

Barcelona

FRANCE IN THE 15TH AND 16TH CENTURIES

Borders of the kingdom in 1461

Borders of the kingdom in 1589

Area permanently added to the kingdom

Royal domain in 1461

Area permanently added to the royal domain

Catalogue Numbers 55–105

55

PETRARCH

Les Triomphes (The triumphs),
anonymous French translation with
the commentary by Bernardo Illicino
Département des Manuscrits, Fr. 594,
fols. 178v–179

*Parchment; III + 404 + II fols.; 370 × 260 mm.
Rouen, ca. 1503. Painted by the Master of the
Triumphs. 19th-century binding in violet shagreen
on wooden boards, with a double border of wax-
based pigment; remains of violet velvet on the
boards; tooled gilt edges. Louis XII; figured in the
royal inventories from the inventory of the library
of Blois in 1518 (no. 324; no. 1816 in the inventory of
1544).*

The Rouen origin of this manuscript, explicitly indicated by the heading to the text: "Les
triumphes du poethe messire Françoys
Petrarche translatez à Rouen de volgaire ytal-
ien en françoys" (The triumphs by the the
poet Master Francis Petrarch, translated in
Rouen from the Italian vulgate into French),
is confirmed by certain characteristics of the
script as well as by the style of illumination.
This was the second very lavish work to
come from Rouen's workshops, following
another manuscript by Petrarch, *Remèdes de
Fortune* (Fortune's remedies; BNF Fr. 225),
which was offered to Louis XII. There is no
indication of date, but it must be very close
to that of the *Remèdes*, whose translation was
completed in 1503. The monarch's coat of
arms appears on the frontispiece (fol. 2v) in a
full-page heraldic painting whose peculiarities Robert Scheller has pointed out. They
reflect the broad themes of royal propaganda
during the reign: the porcupines supporting
the shield of France were the emblem of
Louis d'Orléans, brother of Charles VI, and
are repeated for that reason by his grandson.
The two serpents coiled around a tree on
each side of the central group are an allusion
to Louis XII's ties with the Visconti dynasty
of Milan, from whom the king claimed
descent through his grandmother, Valentina
Visconti—family ties which served as pretext
for French claims to Milan and Lombardy.
Finally, two angels hold a closed crown over
the helmet surmounting the shield—a crown

of an absolutely new kind in the royal
emblematic arsenal, reflecting the monarchy's imperial pretensions, affirmed as early
as 1498, when Louis XII entered Paris.

The magnificent cycle of illustrations
accompanying the *Triomphes* represents the
first serious attempt on the part of a French
artist to illustrate the Petrarch poem, already
the subject of a well-established iconographic tradition in Italy. It was inspired largely by
Bernardo Illicino's commentary. Rather than
employing the frontal view so readily adopted by Italian illuminators, notably the
Florentine Francesco di Antonio del Cherico,
the French miniaturist preferred a lateral disposition of the different processions that
evoked successively the triumphs of Love, of
Chastity and Reason, of Death, of Fame (fols.
178v–179), of Time, and of the Trinity. The
processions move before the spectator's gaze,
generally from left to right, with the exception of the triumph of Love, which goes in
the opposite direction. But the artist introduced a considerable innovation as well by
dividing his compositions in two, forming
diptychs, in which the figure to be supplant-
ed is succeeded by the following one. The
only other case in which this panoramic
technique was employed to illustrate the
Petrarch poem is to be found in the little
manuscript in the Bibliothèque de l'Arsenal
(MS 6480), painted about 1524–1526 by
Godefroid Le Batave, who may have gotten
the idea from Louis XII's manuscript.

The paintings, of uniform technique, are
certainly the product of a single artist and
are of a quality comparable to those in the
volume of the *Remèdes*, to which they are
generally linked because of their shared
place of origin and highly similar style. The
two cycles reflect the same culture that
emerged from the first French Renaissance,
stemming from masters like Bourdichon and
Poyet. The coloring is also very similar in
both manuscripts, with hues that are intense,
contrasting, and cold. But the figures of the
Triomphes have a statuesque character and a
pronounced static verticality which denote a
temperament distinct from that of Jean
Pichore, the more spirited and dramatic

painter of the *Remèdes*. Just like Pichore, of whom he was doubtless the privileged associate, the Master of the Triumphs was a Parisian and not a Rouennais. His ties with the milieu of Parisian book illustration are evident in the first French printed edition of Petrarch's poem, published by Barthélémy Vérard in 1514, the illustrations for which reflect a number of the miniatures found in the *Triomphes*. The miniature of the triumph of Death, for instance, is literally reproduced from the manuscript of Louis XII (fol. 135), but reversed.

François Avril

A. Masséna, prince d'Essling, and Eugène Müntz, *Pétrarque: Ses études d'art, son influence sur les artistes, ses portraits et ceux de Laure, l'illustration de ses écrits* (Paris, 1902), 226–31. G. Ritter and J. Lafond, *Manuscrits à miniatures de l'Ecole de Rouen* (Paris, 1913), 15–17, 33–37, pls. I–XIV. J. Porcher, *Manuscrits à peintures du XIIIe au XVIe siècle* (Paris, 1955), no. 356. E. Pellegrin, *Manuscrits de Pétrarque dans les bibliothèques de France* (Padua, 1966), 219–20. S. Cohen, *The Image of Time in Renaissance Depiction of Petrarch's Trionfo del Tempo* (Tel Aviv, 1982), 147–48, fig. 105. J. Plummer, *The Last Flowering: French Painting in Manuscript, 1420–1530* (New York, 1982), 90. R. W. Scheller, "Ensigns of Authority: French Royal Symbolism in the Age of Louis XII," *Simiolus* 13 (1983): 104, fig. 17. A.-M. Lecoq, *François Ier imaginaire: Symbolique et politique à l'aube de la Renaissance française* (Paris, 1987), 25–34. M.-P. Laffitte and U. Baurmeister, *Des livres et des rois: La bibliothèque royale de Blois* (Paris, 1992), 169–71, no. 39. F. Avril and N. Reynaud, *Les manuscrits à peintures en France, 1440–1520* (Paris, 1993), 414–15, no. 236.

56

OCTOVIEN DE SAINT-GELAIS
Translation of Ovid's *Epistulae heroidum* (Letters of heroines)
Département des Manuscrits, Fr. 875, fol. 36

Parchment; II + 138 + III fols.; 360 × 250 mm. Cognac, between 1496 and 1498. Bound in lemon-colored morocco with the royal arms, late 17th to early 18th century. Copy owned by Louise of Savoy, acquired later by the library of Fontainebleau.

In 1496 Octovien de Saint-Gelais, bishop of Angoulême, young court prelate who flattered himself that he knew much about literature and humanism, finished translating in decasyllables Ovid's *Epistulae Heroidum*, a collection of twenty-one letters which the Latin poet had fictitiously attributed to various heroines of antiquity grieving over their unrequited loves. The work enjoyed an immediate success and has been preserved in fourteen manuscripts, many very sumptuous and richly illuminated. Two editions were printed in the course of the 16th century. Saint-Gelais owed his fortune to the Angoulême family and probably hastened to submit his translation to Louise of Savoy, the very young widow of his patron, Charles d'Angoulême. Very quickly Louise dispatched her *escrivain* (writer) in ordinary, Jean Michel, to purchase the necessary parchment to make a highly finished copy of Ovid's letters. The transcription and illumination of the volume was probably completed as early as 1498, for upon Louis XII's accession to the throne Louise, as countess d'Angoulême and mother of a potential and serious candidate to the succession, was obliged by the king to leave Cognac and settle down with her children, first in Blois and later in Amboise.

We have before us the fruit of the combined efforts of copyist Jean Michel and the accredited artist of the Angoulême couple, Robinet Testard. The latter's illustrations are surprising in their monumental format, marking a break with what he had painted up until then. They consist of a series of large miniatures representing the heroines, plus a few masculine figures mentioned in the text, shown half-length; the first six lines of each letter are placed under the image, the whole

173

Comme le cisne quant mort luy est prochaine
Doulcement chante a voix tresseraine.
Pareillement ie dido pour tout voir.
Qui ne te puis par pryere esmouvoir.
Et qui plus nay en ta veule esperance.
Dxes te fais scavoir ma doleance.

thing being framed by a border of very restrained motifs. As always with Testard, the execution is very sharp and graphic, yet the faces–too large in proportion to the rest of the body and very carefully modeled–denote a certain quest for individuality and give the appearance of being authentic portraits. Maulde de La Clavière has even suggested that the Laodamia of fol. 71v is a portrait of Louise of Savoy herself. The characters are shown in the act of writing, most often in the privacy of an enclosed space (fol. 1, Penelope writing to Ulysses; fol. 36, Dido writing to Aeneas), occasionally in a landscape (fol. 30, Hypsipylé, queen of Lemnos, writing to Jason, in which case features are stylized in the extreme, as with fol. 101v, the melancholy Leander seated in a white tunic, his feet in the water of the Hellespont, contemplating the palace of Hero on the other side of the strait). Dress is alternately exotic or inspired by the fashion of the day. Although in general all dramatic effect is avoided (contrary to the copies of this work illuminated later in the circle of Jean Pichore [BNF Fr. 873 and 874; Assemblée Nationale MS 1466; Vienna, Österreichische Nationalbibliothek 2624]), Testard nevertheless occasionally succeeds in stirring emotion through the simple play of line and color, as seen in the highly expressive and tragic figure of Canacé, daughter of Aeolus, staining with her blood the letter of farewell she is writing to Macareus, her incestuous brother (fol. 58v). About the same period the artist illuminated another copy of Ovid's work in smaller format (San Marino, Huntington Library, HM 60): the heroines shown there are, as here, half-length, but their faces were often retouched in the 18th century.

François Avril

P. Durrieu and J.-J. Marquet de Vasselot, *Les manuscrits à miniatures des Héroïdes d'Ovide, traduites par Saint-Gelais, et un grand miniaturiste français du XVIe siècle* (Paris, 1894), 5–7. R. Maulde de La Clavière, *Louise de Savoie et François Ier* (Paris, 1895), 50–52. C. Couderc, *Album de portraits d'après les collections du Département des Manuscrits* (Paris, 1908), 55, pl. CXX. J. Porcher, *Les manuscrits à peintures en France du XIIIe au XVIe siècle* (Paris, 1955), 163, no. 346. D. Thoss, *Publius Ovidius Naso: Héroïdes traduites en français par Octovien de Saint-Gelais (Österreichische Nationalbibliothek Wien, Cod. 2624)* (Munich, 1986), 10. F. Avril and N. Reynaud, *Les manuscrits à peintures en France, 1440–1520* (Paris, 1993), 407–08, no. 231.

57

Louenge de la victoire et conqueste du royaume de Napples, avec les piteux regretz et lamentacions du roy Alphonce
(Praise for the victory and conquest of the Kingdom of Naples, with the piteous regrets and lamentations of King Alphonse)
Reserve des livres rares, Rés. Ye. 1055, verso of title page

Lyon: Printer of the Louange de la victoire de Naples *(Matthias Huss?), ca. 1495. 6 fols.; 4to. Molded revorim binding by Jean de Gonet, 1986 (no. 170/200 of the first subscription). Was part of a collection broken up in the 19th century whose provenance is no longer known.*

Wearing his crown, Alphonse II of Aragon, king of Naples, is on board ship ready to flee his kingdom, which the army of King Charles VIII of France has invaded. The illustration for this little poem pertains to one of the outstanding incidents of the Wars of Italy. Upon Queen Jeanne's death in 1435, the Kingdom of Naples passed from the House of Anjou to that of Aragon, but legally the king of France had a claim to it. When Ferdinand I of Aragon, king of Naples, died in 1494, Charles VIII undertook to assert his claim with military force. His expedition moved across Italy and arrived in Rome, where it remained until Jan. 28, 1495. Alphonse II, son and successor of Ferdinand, was terrorized and abdicated on Jan. 23 in favor of his son Ferdinand II. On Feb. 3 he sailed for Sicily, at that time held by the Spanish. On Feb. 22 Charles VIII entered Naples. The French camp was

euphoric, as this *Louenge* (praise), written for the occasion, confirms.

With Charles VIII's reign began the circulation of printed news accounts which preceded the periodical press by a century and a half. The principal subjects were taken from official acts or from accounts of incidents either by a witness or elaborated from firsthand reports. Information and propaganda were inextricably interwoven and French royal power quickly became adept in its use of the printing press to influence public opinion. The costly Wars of Italy, which kept the king far from home, required popular approval.

The well-informed anonymous author of the *Louenge* skillfully described the abdication of Alphonse II "à l'appetit et volonté du vent" (by the caprices of the wind) and gave a legitimate coloring to the French victory. Right had triumphed, naturally, and so Charles VIII could fulfill the highest duty of a Christian king by leaving for the crusade. From the first stanzas, the Italian expedition was recast in this perspective. While it was of course pro-French propaganda, it reflected a viewpoint widely held throughout Europe.

Unlike the majority of 15th-century news sheets, the *Louenge* was printed not in Paris but in Lyon, point of convergence for mail at the time of the Wars of Italy. It is illustrated by an original engraving specially adapted to the subject, which was also unusual for material of this kind.

Denise Hillard

Bibliothèque Nationale, *Catalogue des incunables*, vol. 2 (Paris, 1985), no. L-216. J. P. Seguin, "L'information à la fin du XVe siècle en France: Pièces d'actualité imprimées sous le règne de Charles VIII," in *Arts et traditions populaires* (1956): 309–30 and (1957): 47–74. Y. Labande-Mailfert, *Charles VIII et son milieu (1470–1498): La jeunesse au pouvoir* (Paris, 1975).

58

Golden Bull of Louis XII, King of France, Naples, and Jerusalem and Duke of Milan

Cabinet des Médailles, Chabouillet 2913 (Inventaire des Monuments d'Or et d'Argent 439)

Gold; diameter: 100 mm; weight: 303.50 g. Paris(?), November 1500–1503. Purchased in 1803.

Obverse: LVDOVICVS.DEI.GRA.FRANCORVM.NEAPOLIS. ET.HIERVSALEM.REX. DVX.MEDIOLANI., *the king with crown, seated full-face on a throne, wearing a dalmatic with the arms of France and a cloak with the arms of Naples (quartered Anjou–Sicily/Jerusalem), wearing the chain of the Order of Saint Michel, holding a scepter and a globe, with feet on a cushion covered with fleurs-de-lis, in front of a tapestry with the combined arms of France and Naples. The central part providing the representation of the king is set inside the crown bearing the legend. The scepter is a separate piece.*

Reverse: Without legend, two shields crowned and conjoined: the shield of France surrounded by the chain of the Order of Saint Michel, and the shield of Naples placed on the crescent of the Order of the Crescent, bearing the motto LOS.EN CROSSA... *(Los en croissant). The whole inside a wide striped band which has been set between the central element and the edge formed by the obverse.*

Edge: Trace of two large holes, filled, located symmetrically at 11 o'clock and at 1 o'clock.

Objects comparable to this one are rare, but enough have survived to establish its nature and authenticity. This is a gold bulla used to seal a particularly solemn act by which Louis XII (it can only be he) acted in his capacity as king of France and of Naples. The legend is explicit: Louis XII is provided with his titles of king of France, king of Naples, king of Jerusalem, and duke of Milan.

The iconography differs from that of Louis XII's seal as king of France (Dalas, no. 217). In the bulla Louis XII carries a scepter and a globe, not a scepter and the hand of justice; he is not under a canopy but in front of a hanging and lacks the two lions at his feet. Furthermore, unlike the royal seal, on which the figure of the king is shown more official than individual, the representation of Louis XII on this bulla is a veritable portrait. His features are quite individualized and are comparable with other sculpted or painted portraits and with those figuring on Italian and French medals and coins.

Louis XII used the aforementioned combined titles only between Nov. 11, 1500, and September 1504. By November 1500 he had assumed the title king of Sicily; and in 1504 he gave up the duchy of Milan in favor of his daughter Claude. Thanks to heraldry, M. Pastoureau has succeeded in establishing a more precise dating: the arms of Anjou-Sicily, quartered here with the arms of Jerusalem to form those of the kingdom of Naples, are represented by a *semé* (scattered pattern) of lilies and a label (horizontal device denoting eldest son); in 1503 they were modified and henceforth displayed three lilies and a label. Therefore this bulla has to predate 1503.

The bulla should be compared with the seal known from an impression appended to

177

an act of Sept. 14, 1501 preserved at Monte Cassino (Dalas, nos. 229–229*bis*): both have points in common but also differences. On the obverse the representation of the king is the same, with the scepter and the globe, but the throne is different and, especially, the background is the combined arms of France and Jerusalem; however, the legend LVDOVICVS DEI GRA FR[ANCO]RV REX . . . NEAPOLI indicates clearly that this is a seal of the kingdom of Naples. The counterseal supplies the confirmation: LVDOVICVS.DEI.GRA.FRANCOR.IERVSALEM. ET.NEAPOLI.REX: the type or design of the counterseal accords with that of the obverse: under a crown two shields conjoined, the one with the arms of France, the other with those of Jerusalem. Another impression of this same seal appended to an act of March 12, 1502, is known from a drawing. This seal, engraved in Paris, was sent to Italy during the summer of 1501.

The gold bulla could only have been used to seal an important treaty between November 1500 and 1503. The only one that meets these conditions is the secret treaty of Granada of Nov. 11, 1500, signed with Ferdinand the Catholic and concerning the partition of Italy.

The bulla was deposited on 6 floréal, year XI (April 26, 1803) in the Cabinet des Antiques, Médailles and Pierres Gravées of the Bibliothèque Nationale by Citizen Gosselin, curator of the cabinet. It had been purchased "by order of the First Consul [Napoléon Bonaparte]" for 1,200 francs. It had belonged to a prince of Monaco, who in 1803 had been dead but a few years. That means the prince in question must have been Honoré III, who died in 1795. The bulla then became the property of an individual whose name is unknown. It might be supposed that the Monaco provenance of this bulla would supply a trail leading to the act to which it was appended. Indeed, it was Louis XII who recognized Monaco as a sovereign principality by an act in favor of Lucien Grimaldi. However, this document, retained in the principality's archives, is posterior to our gold bulla, since it is dated 1512 and carries the wax seal of Louis XII, king of France. It is amusing to note that Millin gave successively two different versions of France's purchase of the bulla. Both versions were anachronistic and were determined by the government in power when he published them. In 1808 he wrote: "His Majesty the Emperor of the French ordered its purchase for the Cabinet of the Bibliothèque impériale." Then in 1814, in a pamphlet in which he celebrates the return of Louis XVIII, who "returns to France like another Louis XII," he wrote: "It was purchased for the Cabinet of the Bibliothèque du Roi." The bulla was stolen from the Cabinet des Médailles in 1831 but found in the Seine with some other objects the thieves had hidden. A copy of the bulla in gilded bronze (weight 325.08 g) is preserved also in the Cabinet des Médailles. There are also casts in the Archives Nationales (Collection de Sceaux D91 and 91*bis*) and some casts in pewter (sale no. 68 of Kunst und Münzen, Lugano, December 1993, no. 1658).

Michel Dhénin

A. L. Millin, "Description d'un sceau d'or de Louis XII qui appartient au Cabinet de la Bibliothèque Impériale. . . ," extract from *Magasin encyclopédique* (Paris, 1808), vol. 4. Millin, *Description d'un sceau d'or de Louis XII. . .* (Paris, 1814). *Trésor de numismatique et de glyptique. . . : Sceaux des rois et reines de France* (Paris, 1834), 13, pl. XIV, no. 2. N. de Wailly, *Eléments de paléographie*, vol. 2 (Paris, 1838), 356, pl. K, no. 2, and p. 385, no. XLVIII. M. de Robiano, "Variétés numismatiques," pt. 2, "Sceau de Louis XII comme duc de Milan," *Revue de la numismatique belge* 1853: 32–34, pl. II,2. A. Chabouillet, *Catalogue général et raisonné des camées et pierres gravées de la Bibliothèque Impériale, suivi de la description des autres monuments exposés dans le Cabinet des Médailles et Antiques. . .* (Paris, [1858]), 483–84, no. 2913. L.-C. Douët d'Arcq, *Collection de sceaux* (*Ministère d'Etat. Archives de l'Empire. Inventaires et documents. . . .*), vol. 1 (Paris, 1863), no. 91. E. Babelon, *Guide illustré du Cabinet des Médailles. . . : Les antiques et les objets d'art* (Paris, 1900), 303–04. M. Pastoureau, "Médaille ou sceau? Note sur une prétendue bulle d'or de Louis XII," *Bulletin de la Société Française de Numismatique*, January 1981: 5–6, and 4, fig. 2. M. Dalas, *Corpus des sceaux français du moyen âge*, vol. 2, *Les sceaux des rois et de régence* (Paris, 1991), 308–9, nos. 228–228*bis*.

59

JEAN MAROT

Le Voyage de Gênes (Voyage to Genoa)

Département des Manuscrits, Fr. 5091, fol. 22v

Parchment; V + 40 + VI fols.; 307 × 210 mm. Tours, ca. 1508. Painted by Jean Bourdichon (ca. 1457–1521). Bound in red morocco with gold fillets, late 17th or early 18th century. Copy dedicated to Anne de Bretagne; seen by Peiresc at the home of a certain M. Desneux in the early 17th century (cf. Carpentras, MS 1793, fol. 31); a note (fol. Av) by Abbé Claude Sallier (keeper at the Département des Livres Imprimés from 1726 to 1761) indicates that the manuscript was taken from the Versailles repository and handed over to the Bibliothèque Royale by Jacques Hardion (keeper of books at the Cabinet du Roi in Versailles from 1730 to 1766).

Louis XII's rapid and almost unimpeded conquest of the city of Genoa in April 1507 struck public opinion as an unheard-of feat of arms, sparking many rapturous accounts by court chroniclers and poets who vied with one another to extol the king's greatness and fame. Jean Marot, the king's official poet, composed a verse account of the victorious expedition, copied in a fine manuscript intended for the triumphant monarch's wife, Anne de Bretagne (shown on fol. 1 receiving the book from the poet, accompanied by her ladies-in-waiting and other courtiers). The eleven superb full-page paintings illustrating the text can be attributed to Jean Bourdichon, a follower of the famous Jean Fouquet and official court illuminator under Louis XI, Charles VIII, and Louis XII. Bourdichon's masterpiece, *Les Grandes Heures d'Anne de Bretagne* (BNF Lat. 9474) is documented by a receipt for payment dated 1508.

Scenes depicting the various episodes of the campaign alternate with complex allegorical scenes in which Genoa, personified as a young Italian woman, converses with Merchandise and the People (fol. 6v), weeps with Despair, Suffering, and Rage (fol. 34v), and then sees Reason appear, naively depicted as Regina Coeli (the Queen of Heaven, that is, the Virgin Mary, fol. 37v). The narrative scenes display greater inspiration, for Bourdichon made good use of picturesque armor and plumed helmets, tunics embroidered with porcupines (the emblem of the Orléans family, adopted by Louis XII), decorative equestrian trappings, Italian dress, and all the heraldic devices associated with triumphal entries. Louis XII is shown in various paraphernalia bearing various crests, either when leaving Alexandria followed by the duke of Bourbon (fol. 15v) or when receiving Genoese burghers who beg for mercy (fol. 21v), where the king is bedecked in white feathers and a tunic embroidered with gold bees and hives, as is his horse's blanket, bearing on the border the magnanimous motto "Non utitur aculeo Rex" (Our king does not use his spur). In another illustration (fol. 22v), he makes a triumphal entry into Genoa under a red-and-gold-striped canopy wearing a tunic woven with letter *A* in gold.

Two years later, in May 1509, a victory at Agnadel in Lombardy provided another excuse for a similar manuscript, this time in the form of a collection of various poems rather than a verse chronicle, illustrated in the same spirit of courtly praise. This latter manuscript, *Epîtres des poètes royaux* (Letters by royal poets), is now at St. Petersburg (National Library of Russia MS Fr. F.v. XIV, 8).

Nicole Reynaud

C. Couderc, "Les miniatures du Voyage de Gênes de Jean Marot d'après le ms. fr. 5091 de la Bibliothèque Nationale," in *Trésors des bibliothèques de France*, vol. 2 (Paris, 1929), 39–55. J. Porcher, *Les manuscrits à peintures en France du XIIIe au XVIe siècle* (Paris, 1955), no. 352. *Jehan Marot: Le voyage de Gênes*, ed. G. Trisolini (Geneva, 1974). R. W. Scheller, "Gallia cisalpina: Louis XII and Italy 1499–1508," *Simiolus* 15 (1985): 37–40. F. Avril, *La passion des manuscrits enluminés* (Paris, 1991), 104–5, no. 42. F. Avril and N. Reynaud, *Les manuscrits à peintures en France, 1440–1520* (Paris, 1993), 303, no. 167.

60

Petites Heures d'Anne de Bretagne
(Little book of hours of Anne de
Bretagne)
Département des Manuscrits, NAL 3027,
fols. 13v–14

*Parchment; 11 + 78 fols.; 172 × 120 mm. Rouen(?),
ca. 1503. Painted by the Master of the Triumphs of
Petrarch. Binding, probably the original, in red
velvet with clasps. Made for Anne de Bretagne(?);
Catherine de Médicis (her arms and her emblem
"Ardorem extincta testantur vivere flamma" illumi-
nated on an added double-leaf, fols. Av and B);
collections Norzy; Ambroise Firmin-Didot, Gaston-
Noël des Vergers; bequeathed in 1935 to the
Bibliothèque Nationale by Marquise Hélène de
Toulongeon, née des Vergers.*

It is possible, though not at all certain, that
this little book of hours from the early 16th
century may have been produced for Queen
Anne de Bretagne. The arguments favoring
that traditional attribution, based on a note
in the Firmin-Didot sale catalogue devoted to
the manuscript, are the following: the repeated mention of Saint Anne (mother of Mary)

on the calendar (Jan. 30, Feb. 26) and in the
litanies, as well as in the intercessory prayers
(fol. 77v). Right after an intercessory prayer to
Saint Louis, the monogram of the name *Anne*
is repeated in the borders of the side margins, accompanied by an ermine, the emblematic animal of the ducal house of Bretagne.
Furthermore, disguised portraits of Louis XII
can supposedly be detected in the paintings
on folios 29, 31v, and 77*bis*, portraying
Gideon, Benaiah (one of the three Jewish soldiers who brought water back to David from
the well in Bethlehem), and Saint Louis. In
König's view, the text's adherence to the use
(or local rites) of Rouen, disconcerting for a
book of hours intended for the queen of
France, could be explained by the fact that
Cardinal Georges d'Amboise, archbishop of
Rouen, may have ordered the manuscript for
presentation to the queen (König 1992). It is
an appealing hypothesis supported by the
existence of two Petrarchs of similar style
copied and in part decorated in Rouen for
Louis XII around 1503 (cat. 55). But the arguments identifying the person to whom it was
addressed as Anne de Bretagne are far from

181

conclusive: the supposed monogram of the queen in this book of hours is a combination of the letters *A* and *E*, which are not found in other manuscripts that certainly belonged to her; and the animal identified as an ermine is usually only a civet with brownish spotted fur. The commonplace figures thought to represent Louis XII correspond only slightly to the king's well-known features. Finally, if this manuscript was a gift intended for the queen, it is surprising that so little account was taken of all the saints for whom she felt particular devotion and who were to be found not only in her prayerbook now in the Pierpont Morgan Library (M. 50) but also, fifteen years later, in the *Grandes Heures* (Great book of hours, BNF Lat. 9474).

For the Office of the Virgin, the painter seems to have hesitated between two different types of layout, some sections being introduced by a single image, others by two pictures arranged as a diptych, the one on the left being a biblical scene or a complementary scene to the episode from Christ's infancy shown on the opposite leaf. This latter arrangement is used for Prime (the third section of the Office), where a scene of Moses before the Burning Bush is paired with the Nativity (fols. 25v–26); for Sext, where the Three Mighty Ones bringing water from Bethlehem to David are paired with the Adoration of the Magi (fols. 31v–32); and for Compline, where the Assumption is complemented on the left by the group of the Apostles attending the event (fols. 37v–38).

The presentation in diptych form seems to derive from earlier attempts by Jean Poyet, who adopted a similar typological iconography in one of his earliest works, the Hours in the Teyler Museum in Haarlem (MS 78). The subject matter of individual miniatures is alternately evangelical (fol. 14, the Annunciation exhibited here) or typological. The scenes for Lauds and Tierce (fol. 19v, Augustus and the Tiburtine Sibyl; fol. 29, the Fleece of Gideon) belong to the second category. The only saint to be honored with a miniature in the section of intercessory prayers is Saint Louis, shown here serving the poor at the table (fol. 77*bis*). The decoration is completed by a remarkable series of marginal borders with extremely varied geo-metrical motifs, in dark hues of black or blackish-brown, sometimes alternating with gold backgrounds and on which ermines or civets and the monogram *AE* mentioned earlier stand out. It is one of the most meticulous works of the Master of the Triumphs of Petrarch—one in which his extraordinarily fine and concise pictorial technique, his slow and almost static compositions, contrast with Pichore's animation and emotivity in the large paintings of the *Remèdes de Fortune*. As in the three other books of hours that are attributable to him, the Master of the Triumphs is fond of the grisaille technique, which he uses here in his double-pages, as counterpoint to colored scenes, to contrast biblical or typological themes with evangelical themes.

François Avril

L. Delisle, *Les Grandes Heures d'Anne de Bretagne et l'atelier de Jean Bourdichon* (Paris, 1913), 29–34, 112–15, pls. 69–70. V. Leroquais, *Supplément aux livres d'heures manuscrits de la Bibliothèque Nationale (acquisitions récentes et donation Smith-Lesouëf)* (Mâcon, 1943), 1–5, pls. XVII–XXVIII. J. Porcher, *Les manuscrits à peintures en France du XIIIe au XVIe siècle* (Paris, 1955), 169, no. 358. E. König, *Stundenbuch des Markgraf Christoph I. von Baden, Codex Durlach I des Badischen Landesbibliothek* (Karlsruhe, 1977), 163–95, 213, figs. 16–21, 39. König, *Das Stundenbuch der Maria Stuart, Handschrift aus dem Besitz der herzoglichen Hauses Württemberg* (Darmstadt, 1988), 52, 53–54, 59, 62, 64, 67, figs. 2, 3, 6, 10. König, *Leuchtendes Mittelalter*, vol. 4, *Grosse Buchmalerei zwischen Rouen und Paris: Der Froissart des Kardinals d'Amboise aus der Sammlung des Fürsten Pückler-Muskau mit 200 Miniaturen* (Rotthalmünster, 1992). F. Avril and N. Reynaud, *Les manuscrits à peintures en France, 1440–1520* (Paris, 1993), 417–18, no. 238.

61

GIOVANNI FRANCESCO CONTI
(ALIAS QUINTIANUS STOA)
*De celeberrimae Parrhisiorum urbis
laudibus sylva cui titulus [est] Cleopolis*
(Abundance of praise for the highly
celebrated city of Paris, titled
Cleopolis)
Réserve des livres rares, Rés. Vélins 2125,
binding (upper cover)

*Paris: Jean de Gourmont, Aug. 2, 1514. 42 fols.; 4to.
Bound in brown calf, silver and blind tooling, gilt
edges, early 16th century. From the collection of the
count of Palm, then of the baron of Neuenstein, purchased at its sale in Regensburg in 1815.*

The Italian humanist Giovanni Francesco
Conti is better known by his nom de plume,
Quintianus Stoa—Quintianus from Quinzano
d'Oglio (his hometown in the province of
Brescia), and Stoa from the Greek word for
portico or gate. Thus he styled himself the
"Gateway of the Muses," thanks to his art of
composing in Latin verse.

The start of his career was marked by the
conquest of the duchy of Milan by Louis XII,
king of France and grandson of Valentina
Visconti. Attracted like many Italians to the
French court, Quintianus Stoa managed to
win royal favor—in 1507 he obtained a chair
at the University of Pavia and in 1509 he received a poet's laurels from Louis XII himself. When the French lost the duchy in
December 1512, Quintianus followed his

patron, and it was in Paris that in 1514 he
published a long poem glorifying the capital
of the kingdom, titled *Cleopolis*. The poem
was unstinting in its praise, rhapsodic about
everything from geographical location and
climate to buildings, customs, art, trades, and
productions of every sort. Quintianus, as a
humanist who was also a courtier, dedicated
Cleopolis to Antoine Duprat, who presided
over the Paris Parlement and would become
chancellor of France in 1515.

The remarkable binding is one of a group
of "Louis XII bindings" that were probably
made in Paris between 1503 and 1520 in the
bindery of Simon Vostre, who was *libraire et
relieur-juré* (accredited bookseller and binder)
at the university. These bindings are characterized by a number of decorative features,
such as parallel bands within a rectangular
frame adorned with both blind and gold (or
silver) tooling. The blind stamps were typically French, whereas Italian influence is evident in the motifs of the other stamps as well
as in the use of heat to impress them. In the
more elaborate central band, a porcupine
(emblem of Louis XII) alternates with the
royal coat of arms (with painted field) and the
arms of the queen, Anne de Bretagne (even
though she had died in early 1514). The presence of such arms was more a gesture of
homage to royalty than a sign of possession;
although some of the bindings in the group
can be directly linked to the king, most of
them belonged to other people of high rank.
The volume exhibited here is a copy printed
on vellum (whose contents and title page differ from paper copies) and may well be the
dedicatory copy given by Stoa to Antoine
Duprat himself.

Denise Hillard

J. Van Praet, *Catalogue des livres imprimés sur vélin de la
Bibliothèque du Roi*, vol. 4 (Paris, 1822), 112, no. 143. P. Lacombe,
"'Cleopolis': Description et éloge de Paris par Stoa (1514),"
Bulletin de la Société de l'histoire de Paris et de l'Ile de France 17
(1890): 114–17. J. Guignard, "L'atelier des reliures Louis XII
(Blois ou Paris) et l'atelier de Simon Vostre," in *Studia biblio-
graphica in honorem Herman de la Fontaine Verwey* (Amsterdam,
1968), 209–39. *Dizionario biografico degli Italiani*, vol. 28
(Rome, 1983), 429–31 (article "Conti" by R. Ricciardi).

62

François Ier en déité

(Francis I as a god)

Cabinet des Estampes, Na 255 Rés.

Parchment glued on oak panel. 23.4 × 13.4 cm.
France(?), mid-16th century. Given by the count of
Caylus to the Cabinet des Estampes, June 15, 1765,
in homage to Francis I, believed to be the founder
of the Bibliothèque Royale.

The allegory is explained by the verses on
the pedestal of the king's statue:

> Françoys en guerre est un Mars furieux
> En paix Minerve et Diane à la chasse
> A bien parlé Mercure copieux
> A bien aymer vray Amour plein de grâce.
> O France heureuse honore donc la face
> De ton grand Roy qui surpasse Nature,

Car l'honorant tu sers en mesme place
Minerve, Mars, Diane, Amour, Mercure.

(Francis in war is a furious Mars; in peace,
Minerva and Diana at the hunt; in speaking
well, eloquent Mercury; in loving well, true
Cupid full of grace. O happy France, honor
therefore the face of your great King who surpasses Nature, for in honoring him you serve
alike Minerva, Mars, Diana, Cupid, Mercury.)

The king wears Minerva's helmet, Mars's
armor, Mercury's winged sandals and staff,
Diana's hunting horn, and Cupid's bow and
quiver; a Medusa's head adorns his breastplate. This elevation of the monarch into a
superman with the attributes of the Olympian gods was typical of royal iconography in
the 16th and 17th centuries.

The painting was long considered the
work of the Italian artist Niccolò dell'Abate
(ca. 1512–1571), invited to Henry II's court in
1552; more recently, it has been attributed to
the royal portraitist Nicoletto da Modena (ca.
1490–1569). Neither hypothesis can be correct.
Since the octave was written in the present
tense, the portrait must have been painted
before Francis I died in 1547. However,
Niccolò dell'Abate did not arrive in France
until 1552, and Nicoletto da Modena had
departed for England by 1537. Recently,
Thierry Crépin-Leblond saw in this painting
"a miniature cut from a manuscript intended
for Francis I," painted by the Master of the
Hours of Henry II. The vividness of the colors, the expert arrangement of the drapery,
and the sharply defined profile support this
hypothesis. The ascribed date remains 1545.

Françoise Jestaz

Livres d'heures royaux: La peinture de manuscrits à la Cour de
France au temps d'Henri II, catalogue of the exhibition by
Thierry Crépin-Leblond, Ecouen, Musée de la Renaissance,
Sept. 23–Dec. 13, 1993, 30, no. 2.

63

L'Eléphant fleurdelisé
(Elephant with fleurs-de-lis)
Cabinet des Estampes, Eb 14d

Etching by Antonio Fantuzzi (active at Fontainebleau between 1537 and 1550) after Rosso Fiorentino. 29.3 × 42.8 cm. Monogram halfway up on the right.

The Bolognese painter and etcher Antonio Fantuzzi worked at the château of Fontainebleau as Primaticcio's assistant from at least 1537, the date when his name appeared in the *Comptes des bâtiments du Roi* (royal building accounts). He produced etchings of the principal motifs of the so-called gallery of Francis I, whose decoration had been entrusted to Rosso in 1532. This cycle of paintings is an obscure and erudite panegyric of the monarchy and of the sovereign. The painter depicts the fortunes, good and bad, of the king in peace and in war.

In each of the gallery's twelve bays, the principal painting is surrounded by a sumptuous stucco and painted frame whose significance is linked to that of the central painting. At the top of each appears the king's personal emblem, the crowned salamander, sometimes accompanied by the king's monogram, the letter *F*.

L'Eléphant fleurdelisé was on the north wall in the gallery's fourth bay. The elephant was thought to be superior to all other creatures and became the symbol of piety, wisdom, invincible power, and infallible memory. This one exhibits the royal *F*, the fleur-de-lis, and the salamander, showing that it represents Francis I. The gods Zeus (air), Neptune (water), and Pluto (earth), having first laid down their arms, come respectfully to greet him. He is the master of the world, and no ordinary mortal approaches him.

Françoise Jestaz

Erwin and Dora Panofsky, "The Iconography of the Galerie François Ier at Fontainebleau," *Gazette des Beaux-Arts* 1958, no. 2: 113–90. Henri Zerner, *Ecole de Fontainebleau: Gravures* (Paris, 1969). *Ecole de Fontainebleau,* exhibition, Paris, Grand Palais (Paris, 1972). Eugene A. Caroll, *Rosso Fiorentino: Drawings, Prints, and Decorative Art,* exhibition, Washington, D.C., National Gallery of Art, Oct. 25, 1987–Jan. 3, 1988.

185

64

La Nymphe de Fontainebleau
(The nymph of Fontainebleau)
Cabinet des Estampes, Ed 1

Engraved by Pierre Milan, completed by René Boyvin, after a drawing by Giovanni Batista Rosso. 1544–1545. Line engraving, 30.7 × 51.4 cm. Latin inscription on three lines: "O Phidias, O Apelles, Quidquamne ornatius vestris temporibus excogitari potuit ea sculptura, cujus hic picturam cernitis, Quam Franciscus primus, Francorum Rex potentissimus bonarum artium ac litterarum pater, sub Dianae, a venatu conquiescentis, atque Urnam Fontisbellaquae effundentis statua, Domi suae inchoatam reliquit." On the lower left, "cum privilegio Regis," and on the right, "Rous. Floren. inven."

The Latin inscription can be translated as follows: "Oh Phidias, oh Apelles, was it possible in your day to conceive of anything more beautiful than the sculpture you see represented here in the form of Diana resting after the hunt and pouring forth the waters of Fontaine Belle-Eau, which Francis I, most powerful king of France and father to fine arts and letters, left uncompleted in his house?" Pierre Milan's engraving – one of the most famous of the 16th century – therefore reproduces a carved relief begun for King Francis I, showing Diana, goddess of the hunt, seated near her dogs and leaning on an urn from which water pours abundantly. The text presents this spring as the fountain called Belle-Eau (Beautiful Water) which, according to popular etymology, lent its name to Fontainebleau. Another explanation for the name, however, was recorded in the 17th century by Father Dan, the first historian of

Fontainebleau château, according to which the spring was discovered by a hunting dog named Bliaut (presumably the one shown just in front of Diana). Despite the mention of Diana in the inscription, the figure became famous under the name of the Nymph of Fontainebleau.

Framing the central motif are two groups of caryatids holding baskets overflowing with fruit, below which are singing children and musicians. These figures are identical to ones on the fresco *Danaé* that Primaticcio painted over the central bay of the south wall of Francis I's gallery in the château.

It is not known where the relief carving of Diana was to have been placed, nor has any trace of it survived. It might have been set in one of the *cabinets hors-d'oeuvre* (rooms adjacent to the main gallery), perhaps the southern one demolished as early as 1534 to make way for a terrace where Primaticcio painted *Danaé*. That would explain why the relief was never completed or installed in the château, and why Father Dan made no mention of it in *Le trésor des merveilles de la maison royale de Fontainebleau*, published in 1642.

The legend associated with the subject made this a popular image, and it became even more famous around 1850 when the engraving was used as a model by J. P. Alaux for his painting on the middle bay of the north wall of the gallery.

Françoise Jestaz

Françoise Bardon, *Diane de Poitiers et le mythe de Diane* (Paris, 1963). See also the bibliography for cat. 63.

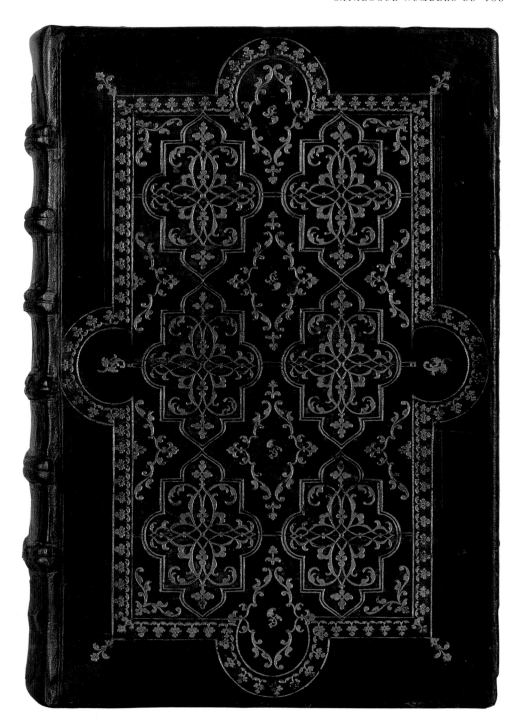

65

Chirurgia (Surgery), translated from
the Greek by Vidus Vidius
Département des Manuscrits, Lat. 6866,
binding

*Paper; III + 351 + III fols.; 345 × 250 mm. Rome,
between 1539 and 1542; copied by Christoph Auer.
Bistre and wash drawings by Francesco Salviati.
Binding attributed to Etienne Roffet, ca. 1542, black
morocco, gold-tooled, gilt edges. Presentation copy
for Francis I.*

66

Chirurgia (Surgery), translated from the Greek and annotated by Vidus Vidius

Réserve des livres rares, Rés. fol. Td⁷⁴. 2, p. 235

Paris: Pierre Gaultier, April 30, 1544. [34], 533 pp.; folio. Bound in olive morocco with triple gilt fillet, round sides, arms and emblem of Charles III de Bourbon, archbishop of Rouen (d. 1594), on spine, gilt edges. Transferred from the castle of Gaillon, summer residence of the archbishops of Rouen, to the King's Cabinet in the Louvre under Henry IV, and then at the beginning of Louis XV's reign about 1732 to the Bibliothèque Royale.

Among the treasures in the celebrated library of Cardinal Niccolò Ridolfi, a great 16th-century collector, was a precious 10th-century Greek manuscript containing texts on surgery by twenty-four physicians from antiquity. The texts had been assembled by the Greek physician Nicetas and were illustrated by paintings (Florence, Laurentianus 74.7). It was at the suggestion of Cardinal Ridolfi that the respected Florentine physician Guido Guidi, alias Vidus Vidius, translated several extracts into Latin around 1540: Galen's *De fasciis* and his commentaries on three texts of Hippocrates, as well as the *De laqueis* and *De machinamentis* by Oribasius. Christoph Auer, a scribe presumably from Austria who had settled in Rome, made the present copy. The bistre and wash drawings, some of which were inspired by the paintings in the original Greek manuscript, were long attributed to Primaticcio. Today, however, Francesco Salviati and one of his students have been identified as the artists.

In 1542 Vidius came to France at the invitation of Francis I, who named him his personal physician and appointed him professor regius (royal lecturer). Probably it was upon Vidius's arrival at court that he offered the king his manuscript along with a copy of the original Greek texts, also transcribed by Auer and illustrated by Salviati (BNF Grec 2246). The binding in black morocco, with gilt decoration composed of six large arabesque stamps and smaller foliate tools, the whole within a border with semicircular projections, is attributed to Etienne Roffet, the king's binder. Another presentation binding made for Francis I, which covers the first volume of the Bible printed by Robert Estienne (Paris, 1538–1540), bears the same arabesque stamp and is now generally assigned to Etienne Roffet.

In Paris, Vidius formed a friendship with his compatriot Benvenuto Cellini, the famous goldsmith and sculptor who not long before had also taken up residence in France. Cellini suggested that Vidius come live in the castle of the Petit Nesle that the king had just granted him in lifetime gift. Le Petit Nesle also housed some artisan workshops, including that of the printer Pierre Gaultier. It was to Gaultier that Vidius entrusted the printing of his *Chirurgia.* Although a slightly revised version of the text served as copy, the woodcuts for this edition are in fact reversed copies of Francesco Salviati's drawings. At the front of the volume Vidius had inserted three supplemental texts of Hippocrates that he himself had translated and annotated: *De ulceribus, De fistulis,* and *De vulneribus capitis.* He also offered a manuscript of the last text to the king (BNF Lat. 6861). The drawings of surgical instruments in the manuscript wouldalso serve as models for the woodcuts in the printed edition.

Ursula Baurmeister

L. Deslisle, *Le Cabinet des Manuscrits de la Bibliothèque Impériale,* vol. 1 (Paris, 1868), 154, 163, 183. L.-M. Michon, "Les reliures exécutées pour François Ier," *Gazette des beaux-arts,* 6th ser., 7 (1932): 320. B. Cellini, *Mémoires* (Paris, 1951), 219–20, 224. W. Brockbank, "The Man Who Was Vidius," *Annals of the Royal College of Surgeons of England* 19 (1956): 269–95. J. Guignard, "Premières reliures parisiennes à décor doré: De l'atelier des reliures Louis XII à l'atelier du Maître d'Estienne ou de Simon Vostre à Pierre Roffet," in *Humanisme actif: Mélanges... offerts à Julien Cain,* vol. 2 (Paris, 1968), 248–49. M. Hirst, "Salviati illustrateur de Vidus Vidius," *Revue de l'art* 6 (1969): 19–28. Ch. Samaran and M.-L. Concasty, "Christophe Auer, copiste de grec et de latin au XVIe siècle," *Scriptorium* 23 (1969): 211, no. 54. *La médecine médiévale à travers les manuscrits de la Bibliothèque Nationale,* exhibition catalogue (Paris, 1982), nos. 29–31.

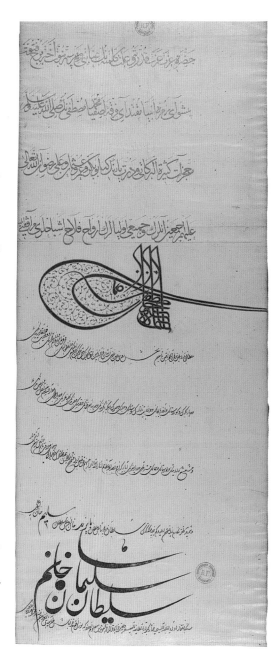

67
Letter of Süleyman the Magnificent to Francis I, King of France
Département des Manuscrits, Division Orientale, Supplément Turc 822
Istanbul, 14 šewal 942 of the Hegira
(April 6, 1536)

*Scroll. Cream-colored paper with cloth backing; invocation (*sülüs *script in gold ink;* tuğra *in blue and gold ink; text (*divanî *script) in black ink; traces of gold powder; name of Sultan Süleyman (large* nesih *script in blue ink). Length: 2.040 m; width: 0.355 m.*

189

As proof of the budding alliance between the kings of France and the Ottoman sultans in the early 16th century, this letter (a *feṭḥ-nâma*, or "victory letter") was addressed by Süleyman the Magnificent to Francis I in 1536. Infused with the solemnity and the magnificence appropriate to this type of document, as well as to the rank of the person to whom it was addressed, it was calligraphed with great care in a number of scripts by the same hand, using inks of different colors. After the usual invocation and full list of the sultan's titles came the *tuğra*, the illuminated imperial monogram (which includes the name "Süleyman," his ancestry, and the words "ever victorious"). This constituted the sovereign's true mark, drawn by a special official of the *divan*, or council of viziers, and contributed to the document's artistic value. It received the same esthetic treatment given to imperial decrees, *firmans* (edicts), and other archival documents. This letter is comparable to those addressed in the same period to the doge of Venice, to Emperor Charles V, and to King Sigismond of Poland.

The alliance between France and the Ottoman Empire, which had been forged after the French defeat at Pavia and the captivity of Francis I in 1525, entered a more active phase in 1533, when war broke out again between Francis and Charles V. The document is important because it marks the beginning of a permanent French embassy at the Sublime Porte, as the Ottoman court was called. After recounting his victories in the so-called Two-Iraqs campaign, Süleyman informed Francis I that his divan had received the French ambassador, Jean de la Forêt. He went on to refer to the "the friendship and concord which unites us" and said he would accept a permanent French ambassador at Constantinople, as the king of France wished.

Annie Berthier

J.-L. Bacqué-Grammont, "Deux lettres de Soliman le Magnifique à François Ier," in *Actes du XXIXe Congrès des orientalistes, Etudes Turques* (Paris, 1976), 13–20. *Vers l'Orient,* exhibition at the Bibliothèque Nationale (Paris, 1983), no. 69. *Soliman le Magnifique,* exhibition at the Grand Palais (Paris, 1990), no. 24.

68

GUILLAUME BUDÉ
De l'Institution du prince
(The school of the prince)
Bibliothèque de l'Arsenal, MS 5103, fols. 1V–2

Parchment; 118 fols.; 252 × 174 mm. Paris, ca. 1517–1518. Bound in brown calf. Made for Francis I; in the 18th century belonged to Antoine René Voyer d'Argenson, marquis de Paulmy, founder of the Bibliothèque de l'Arsenal.

Guillaume Budé, born in Paris on Jan. 26, 1468, was descended from an important family of royal officials which can be traced back to the end of the 14th century, when one of its members was ennobled by Charles VI. His father, Jean Budé, a royal counsellor, was a bibliophile with a rich library. After the young Guillaume Budé completed his studies in civil law, he devoted himself with a passion to studying Latin and especially Greek literature, and took lessons in Greek from the famous Georges Hermonyme of Sparta. Even before he had actually published anything himself, he enjoyed a great scholarly reputation in humanist circles. He continued, however, to fill the offices of royal notary and secretary. From the beginning of Francis I's reign, he pleaded the cause of belles lettres and philology, his great passion, and fought mightily for the creation of a college dedicated to teaching Latin, Greek, and Hebrew, the languages of antiquity.

To realize that goal, in 1517 or 1518 Guillaume composed and dedicated to King Francis a collection of apothegms drawn from Plutarch. Better known by the title under which it was published in 1547,

L'Institution du prince throws interesting light on the relationship between humanism and royal power. Budé argued for an absolute monarchy, enlightened by well-educated counsellors. The text survives in a number of manuscript copies, but this one, prepared for presentation to the king and perhaps revised by Budé himself, is the most accurate. Later printed editions are often far removed from Budé's original text.

The manuscript opens to a full-page miniature (fol. ıv) composed of two registers in a Renaissance frame. On the upper register, the author is writing in his study, protected by Mercury and Philology, since, as he remarks on fol. 34v, "fault que tout home mercurial... ayt pour sa campaigne de jour et de nuict une dame qui s'apelle Philologie. C'est à dire amour des bonnes lettres et inclination à l'étude" (every just man should have as his companion day and night a lady called Philology. That is to say, a love of good literature and a desire for study). In the lower register he presents his book to King Francis I; on the left is a woman clothed in a black dress covered with gold coins, which may symbolize Budé's *De asse* (a study of the weights of ancient coins, which at that time was Budé's best-known work). In the frame on the right-hand page (fol. 2) are the royal *F*, the lily, and the salamander, the personal emblems of Francis I.

Danielle Muzerelle

L. Delaruelle, *Guillaume Budé* (Paris, 1907). *Guillaume Budé*, exhibition, Paris, Bibliothèque Nationale, 1968, no. 76. Cl. Bontems, *Le prince dans la France des XVIème et XVIIème siècles* (Paris, 1965). D. McNeil, *Guillaume Budé and Humanism* (Geneva, 1975). M. Lefèvre and D. Muzerelle, "La bibliothèque du marquis de Paulmy," in *Histoire des bibliothèques françaises*, vol. 3, *Les bibliothèques de l'Ancien Régime, 1530–1789*, ed. Claude Jolly (Paris, 1988), 302–15.

191

69

Collection of Roman Coins Illustrating Guillaume Budé's De asse

Pictured: no. 1 below

The Renaissance set a high price on knowledge about antiquity, to the great benefit of numismatics, the science of medals and coins. Great interest was shown in the classification of ancient coins. Guillaume Budé (1467–1540), Hellenist scholar and friend of Francis I, published in Paris in 1514 a work on metrology, or the study of weights of ancient coins, entitled *De asse et partibus ejus libri quinque* (Five books about the *as* and its divisions). The audience for this treatise, a long and ponderous precursor of metrology, filled with numerous digressions, was limited to a small circle of scholars. The ten Roman coins displayed here illustrate the work of the individual whom Erasmus called "the French prodigy." (The terms *aes signatum* and *aes grave* are explained below.)

1 *Aes signatum*, Rome, 1st half of 3d century B.C. Ox, right./Ox, left, RRC 5/1, BNF Fonds Général 3, 1,376.60 g.

2 *Aes grave*, Rome, ca. 225–220, *triens*, helmeted head of Minerva, left./Prow, right, RRC 35/3a, BNF Ailly 88, 87.47 g.

3 *Aes grave*, Rome, ca. 225–220, *quadrans*, head of Hercules, left./Prow, right, RRC 35/4, BNF Ailly 89, 68.65 g.

4 *Aes grave*, Rome, ca. 225–220, *sextans*, head of Mercury, left./Prow, right, RRC 35/5, BNF Ailly 97, 51.64 g.

5 *Aes grave*, Rome, ca. 225–220, *uncia*, helmeted head of Roma, left./Prow, right, RRC 35/6, BNF Ailly 108, 25.92 g.

6 *Aes grave*, Rome, ca. 225–220, *as*, laureate head of bearded Janus, right./Prow, left, RRC 36/1, BNF Ailly 44, 254.64 g.

7 *Aes grave*, Rome, ca. 225–220, *semis*, laureate head of Saturn, left./Prow, left, RRC 36/2, BNF Ailly 54, 136.74 g.

8 *Aes grave*, Rome, ca. 225–220, *triens*, helmeted head of Minerva, left./Prow, left, RRC 36/3, BNF Ailly 60, 78.07 g.

9 *Aes grave*, Rome, ca. 225–220, *as*, head of Mercury, left./Prow, left, RRC 36/5, BNF Ailly 111, 40.03 g.

10 *Aes grave*, Rome, ca. 220, *dupondius*, helmeted head of Minerva, left./Prow, left, RRC 41/4, BNF Ailly 114, 219.35 g.

Roman coinage did not appear until about 300 B.C.—a late date given the fact that Greek cities in southern Italy had been striking coins since the 6th century B.C. In the course of the 3d century, when, after the defeat of Pyrrhus, Rome brought these Greek cities under its power and warred victoriously against Carthage, two types of bronze coinage were issued: the bronze ingot, or *aes signatum*, and the large, round, cast-bronze disk, or *aes grave*.

1 The ingots of varied stamps or designs (eagle/Pegasus, bull/bull, shield/wheel, sword/sheath, stalk of wheat/tripod stool, anchor/tripod stool, trident/caduceus, hens/rostra, elephant/sow) weighed about 1,400–1,600 grams, or about five Roman pounds, and may have served as money. The idea behind them can be found in Etruria, where ingots of a type called *ramo secco* had been fabricated since the 6th century. These ingots, which present a fixed typology, differ in their metallic composition from the aes signatum and seem totally unrelated to any system of weights. They must have been intended to serve the same purpose as the aes signatum, however, since the two types of ingots are found together in ancient hoards.

2 The *aes grave*, or heavy bronze, existed in a number of different denominations:
dupondius (two units, weighing 24 oz. and marked "II")
as (one unit, weighing 12 oz. and marked "I")
semis (one-half unit, weighing 6 oz. and marked "S")
triens (one-third unit, weighing 4 oz. and marked "....")
quadrans (one-fourth unit, weighing 3 oz. and marked "...")
sextans (one-sixth unit, weighing 2 oz. and marked "..")
uncia (one-twelfth unit, weighing 1 oz. and marked "."

In the beginning, an *as* weighed the same as a Roman pound, 324.72 grams. This coining served as a model for the cast bronze of Volterra, Ariminium(?), Iguvium(?), Tuder, Hatria, Luceria(?), and Venusia. When the head of Janus appeared on the obverse of the *as*, about 225 B.C., it weighed no more than 10 ounces. The Second Punic War (218–201 B.C.) accelerated the process of weight reduction. The financing of the war and the enormous military expenses caused by it had catastrophic effects on Roman finances and on the issue of Roman money. The weight of the *as* dropped to a half-pound (162.36 g) and subsequently entered a phase when its weight was a mere sixth of the pound's (54.12 g)—at the same time that Roman authorities began issuing the denarius in 214/213 B.C.

The collection of Republican coins in the Cabinet des Médailles is the largest in the world, thanks to a bequest in 1877 by Pierre-Philippe Bourlier, baron d'Ailly (inv. no. F 2799). His collection included 17,348 coins: 42 gold, 11,371 silver, and 5,935 bronze. In 1877 there were fewer than 4,000 Republican coins in the general collection of the cabinet. Baron d'Ailly, who died in Nice on April 16, 1877, left an incomplete four-volume work entitled *Recherches sur la monnaie romaine depuis son origine jusqu'à la mort d'Auguste* (Lyon, 1864–1869).

Michel Amandry

Revue numismatique 1874–1877: 474–76. M. Crawford, *Roman Republican Coinage*, 2 vols. (Cambridge, 1974; rev. eds. 1983–1989).

70

FRANÇOIS RABELAIS
Pantagruel. Les horribles et espoventables faictz et prouesses du tres renommé Pantagruel roy des Dipsodes, filz du grand geant Gargantua. Composez nouvellement par maistre Alcofrybas Nasier. (Pantagruel. The horrible and terrible deeds and feats of the infamous Pantagruel, king of the Dipsodes, son of the great giant Gargantua. Newly composed by Master Alcofrybas Nasier)
Réserve des livres rares, Rés. Y². 2146, title page

Lyon: Claude Nourry dict [called] Le Prince, [1532].

[64] fols.; 8ᵛᵒ. Sold at the De Bure brothers' auction, Paris, Jan. 22, 1835, lot 2273, for 60 francs. Purchased by the Bibliothèque Nationale at the Prince d'Essling sale, Paris, May 3, 1847, for 660 francs.

In 1532, François Rabelais apparently embarked upon a new career as a physician. Having spent years in travel and study, the former monk was appointed doctor at the hospital of Lyon. That same year he edited

193

and published the second volume of *Epistolarum medicinalium* by G. Manardo (a doctor from Ferrara), as well as commentaries on Galen and Hippocrates. Nothing indicated that this learned physician was none other than the Alcofrybas Nasier mentioned on the title page of *Pantagruel,* a novel aimed at the general public that was probably placed on sale at the Lyon fair in the autumn of 1532.

The book was an instant hit and was reprinted several times in Lyon and Paris. However, the tiny number of surviving copies makes it difficult to classify and accurately establish publication details. The volume presented here is the only remaining copy from the edition published by Claude Nourry, a Lyon printer who specialized in popular booklets and works of fiction. It currently represents the oldest extant version of the text, even though some scholars postulate that an earlier edition, of which no copies survive, was printed by François Juste.

The book recounts the childhood, experiences, and exploits of a hero, Pantagruel, in the fashion of a medieval romance. Various themes are interwoven, the main inspiration apparently being *Les grandes et inestimables cronicques du grant et enorme geant Gargantua* (The great and inestimable chronicles of the great and enormous giant Gargantua), a cheap pamphlet of poor literary quality whose popularity at the summer fair inspired Rabelais to exploit the subject of giants by inventing Pantagruel, son of Gargantua. The character of Pantagruel can be traced back to a figure in 15th-century mystery plays—the sprite of thirst who incited people to drink by throwing them salt. Rabelais's entire book celebrates wine, love, and mortal pleasures. Contemporaries fully understood this—in October 1533 a theologian denounced the book for obscenity before the Faculty of Theology in Paris, and all the coarse passages in the copy exhibited here were inked out in the 16th century. But the text also reflects the enthusiasm of humanists of the day, and the most famous passage now is the letter from Gargantua to Pantagruel conveying the excitement of rediscovering ancient civilization.

Encouraged by the success of *Pantagruel,* in 1534 Rabelais wrote *La vie inestimable du grand Gargantua, père de Pantagruel,* which thereby became the first book of the cycle, extended in 1546 by *Tiers livre* (Third book) and completed in 1548 by *Quart livre* (Fourth book). After being reworked, *Pantagruel* and *Gargantua* were republished in a definitive edition in 1542, which featured prominently on the first Index (list of forbidden books) issued by the Paris Faculty of Theology in 1543.

Geneviève Guilleminot-Chrétien

François Rabelais, *Pantagruel: Première édition critique sur le texte original,* ed. V.-L. Saulnier (Geneva, 1965). S. Rawles and M. A. Screech, *A New Rabelais Bibliography: Editions of Rabelais before 1626* (Geneva, 1987), 65–72, no. 1.

71

*Initiatoire instruction en la Religion
chrestienne pour les enffans*
(Beginning instruction in the
Christian religion for children)
Bibliothèque de l'Arsenal, MS 5096, fols. Av–1

*Parchment; 57 fols.; 226 × 152 mm. France, ca. 1527.
Bound in red velvet (16th century). Made for
Marguerite de Navarre (1492–1549); belonged in the
17th century to Roger de Gaignières (1642–1751);
acquired in 1763 by Charles-Adrien Picard, then in
1780 by Antoine René de Voyer d'Argenson, marquis
de Paulmy, founder of the Bibliothèque de
l'Arsenal.*

In 1527 Marguerite d'Angoulême, Francis I's
sister and widow of the duke d'Alençon,
married Henri d'Albret, king of Navarre.
Marguerite, the "pearl" of princesses, poetess,
storyteller, and very well read, achieved fame
as much from her literary work (*Heptaméron*,
etc.) as from the role she played with her
brother and the important part she took in
the beginnings of the Reformation in France.
Deeply concerned by questions relating to

spiritual life and mysticism, she gave protection to the first reformers, especially Bishop
Briçonnet and the group at Meaux. When
Lefèvre d'Etaples and Gérard Roussel (who
would become her chaplain and bishop
d'Oloron) took refuge in Strasbourg, she corresponded regularly with them, as she did
with Sigismond de Hohenlohe, dean of the
Strasbourg chapter and responsible for the
spread of Luther's ideas in France. Although
she never broke with the Catholic church,
she was nonetheless accused of Lutheranism.
It is in this context that this very lovely manuscript must be viewed.

Written for the queen of Navarre at the
time of her marriage (1527), the manuscript is
a sort of catechism that has been attributed
to the Württemberg reformer Johannes
Brenz. The text was introduced into France,
probably by refugees from Strasbourg, well
before the translation of the catechism that
Christophe, duke of Württemberg, had
ordered in 1562 for the region of
Montbéliard. We know also that Marguerite
had studied the writings of Brenz and other

German reformers, as she revealed in her *Miroir de l'âme pécheresse* (Mirror of the sinful soul). That work, published in 1531, brought an outcry against her from the Sorbonne.

The decoration of the manuscript is also of great interest. The script is meticulous, and on every leaf there are richly ornamented borders in gold and in color, with birds, insects, and marguerites (daisies). The manuscript opens with two large miniatures. On folio Av the arms of the princess are presented in a golden wreath against an azure background sprinkled with stars and daisies (marguerites). On folio 1 Henri d'Albret, king of Navarre, the grandfather of the future Henry IV, is shown in the middle of a garden holding a daisy in his hand. One can also identify Marguerite with several courtiers in the middle ground and in the distance is the Temple of Love. At the bottom of the miniature is the Latin caption "Inveni unam preciosam margaritam quam intimo corde collegi" (I have found one precious daisy, which I have gathered to my inmost heart). The other miniatures depict scenes from the Bible. Folio 2v also features portraits of Henri d'Albret, his brother Charles, and Marguerite accompanying Christ carrying the cross.

The remarkable character of these portraits did not escape Montfaucon. After he saw the manuscript at the home of the bibliophile Gaignières (who had obtained it from Boucot, keeper of the rolls of officials and a collector), he reproduced folio 2 in his *Monumens de la monarchie françoise* (vol. 4, p. 260) in 1723. In 1763 the manuscript came into the possession of C.-A. Picard, and then at the sale of his books in 1780 was acquired by the marquis de Paulmy.

Danielle Muzerelle

A. J. V. le Roux de Lincy, *Essai sur la vie et les ouvrages de Marguerite d'Angoulême*, taken from the *Heptaméron des nouvelles* (Paris, 1853). H. Martin and P. Lauer, *Les principaux manuscrits à peintures de la Bibliothèque de l'Arsenal à Paris* (Paris, 1929). P. Jourda, *Marguerite d'Angoulême* (Paris, 1930). W. G. Moore, *La réforme allemande et la littérature française* (Strasbourg, 1930). *Trésors de la Bibliothèque de l'Arsenal*, exhibition at the Bibliothèque de l'Arsenal (Paris, 1980), no. 119. M. Lefèvre and D. Muzerelle, "La bibliothèque du marquis de Paulmy," in *Histoire des bibliothèques françaises*, vol. 3, *Les bibliothèques de l'Ancien Régime, 1530-1789*, ed. Claude Jolly (Paris, 1988), 302-15.

72

ANTOINE MARCOURT

Articles veritables sur les horribles, grandz et importables abuz de la Messe papalle (True articles on the horrible, great, and insufferable abuses of the papal Mass)

Réserve des livres rares, Rés. D². 453

[Neuchâtel: Pierre de Vingle, 1534]. Plano; 25 × 37 cm. Acquired in 1957 from the Stadt- und Universitätsbibliothek of Bern.

Lutheran ideas began gaining ground in France about 1520 and quickly led to punishment and even executions. Francis I, though loyal to Catholic doctrine, nevertheless displayed an apparent tolerance at various times, for political reasons. The year 1534 was marked by a halt to persecution against Parisian reformers because the king was negotiating with German Lutheran princes. Part of the Protestant community in Paris chose that moment to demonstrate its faith by posting a proclamation, in a tactic already used on several occasions, notably in Geneva and in Neuchâtel. From Neuchâtel they brought some posterlike broadsheets printed by Pierre de Vingle, the text of which was composed of four theses against the mass by Antoine Marcourt, a pastor in Neuchâtel who had come originally from Picardy.

In the night of Oct. 17–18, the broadsheets were put up at street corners in Paris, in a number of cities in the Loire Valley, and even on the door of the king's chamber. Francis I perceived it as an organized plot and was furious. Prodded by his entourage of intransigent Catholics (while his sister Marguerite de Navarre, who openly protected the reformers, was absent), he ordered Parlement to crack down. Following accusations and investigations, more than two hundred persons were said to have been arrested in Paris and some twenty were publicly burned. Several hundred fled. On Jan. 21, 1535, a procession of considerable importance took place in the king's presence to demonstrate the kingdom's devotion to the Holy Sacrament.

The consequences for the French Reformation were severe. Advocates of a harsh policy definitely carried the day in the council and repressive measures were strengthened. Many moderate sympathizers with the Reformation returned to the Catholic church, whether from conviction or from fear, while the most determined reformers would follow Calvin, whose *Christianae religionis institutio* was published in Basel in 1536.

No copy of these broadsheets was preserved in France. For centuries historians used a version published in 1564 by Jean Crespin, which was in fact based on a different broadsheet distributed in 1560 in Normandy. In 1943 fragments of the broadsheet were discovered in the Bern Stadtbibliothek. They had been used to make the boards of a contemporary binding done at Neuchâtel, perhaps in the bindery of Pierre de Vingle. From these pieces, it was possible to reconstitute a few copies, including this one and the one exhibited in the Musée de l'Imprimerie in Lyon. Their use as bindings (to which they owe their survival) explains the color of the paper and the traces of trimming.

Geneviève Guilleminot-Chrétien

R. Hari, "Les placards de 1534," in *Aspects de la propagande religieuse* (Geneva, 1957), 79–142. G. Berthoud, *Antoine Marcourt: Réformateur et pamphlétaire* (Geneva, 1973).

73

MICHEL SERVET
(MICHAEL SERVETUS)
Christianismi restitutio
(The restoration of Christianity)
Réserve des livres rares, Rés. D². 11274,
title page

[Vienne: Balthazar Arnoullet and Guillaume Guéroult,] 1553. 734 pp.; 8ᵛᵒ. 18th-century English binding, in red morocco decorated with a pattern of squares highlighted in green paint and gilt radiating motifs. Copy owned by Germain Colladon; Richard Mead, before 1740–1745; Claude-Gabriel Gros de Boze, d. 1753; Président de Cotte; Louis-Jean Gaignat (sale, 1769, no. 569); purchased by the Bibliothèque Royale at the duke de la Vallière sale (1784, no. 913).

Michael Servetus, Spanish-born physician and theologian, was convicted of heresy and burned in Geneva on Oct. 27, 1553, with a copy of the *Christianismi restitutio* hanging

197

from his belt. In this, his last treatise, the author was anxious to show the fluctuations affecting the soul and the mind, and in the course of it came up with the first known description of blood circulating through the lungs—well before Harvey. This important scientific discovery, unappreciated in his own time, though publicly mentioned by William Wotton in the late 17th century in *Reflections upon Ancient and Modern Learning*, was not the cause of Servetus's tragic fate. Rather, the Anabaptist and Trinitarian ideas presented in his text incited the hostility of Catholics as well as Lutherans and Calvinists. In this book Servetus, who had become known about 1531 with the publication at Haguenau of writings denying the dogma of the Trinity, accused Rome and the Reformation of having falsified original Christian doctrine—and he tried to reconstitute it from Plato and Plotinus. He retained the liturgy and Purgatory but rejected original sin and the Trinity. He rehabilitated charity and preached in favor of adult baptism.

Servetus finished writing *Christianismi restitutio* in 1546. At that date, having completed his legal and medical studies, having traveled in Italy and Germany, and having worked as proofreader in a Lyon print shop, he settled down in Vienne in the Dauphiné region to become physician to the archbishop. Having vainly offered his manuscript to printers in Basel, Servetus persuaded two printers from Lyon, Balthazar Arnoullet and Guillaume Guéroult, to come to Vienne. He pledged to cover printing expenses, correct the proof himself, assume responsibility for selling the book, and pay 100 écus as a bonus.

The work was printed in greatest secrecy from Sept. 25, 1552 to Jan. 3, 1553. It bore no address and was signed only by the initials M. S. V. (Michel Servet de Villanueva, the village of Servetus's birth). This precaution did not prevent Calvin, who had received excerpts of the manuscript, from easily detecting the identity of the author. Documents sent from Geneva with Calvin's approval permitted officials in Vienne to arrest Servetus. He escaped from prison, but while en route to Naples rashly decided to pass through Geneva. There he was recognized, arrested, sentenced, and burned.

Almost all of the 800 to 1,000 copies of *Christianismi restitutio* were destroyed, including those which had been entrusted to the agent of Sebastien Gryphe at Frankfurt and those intended for sale in Lyon. Only three copies have survived: one in Edinburgh, one in Vienna, and one in Paris. The Paris copy belonged to Colladon, the jurist who assisted Calvin throughout Servetus's trial. In it are two leaves of handwritten notes in Latin intended as an index of ideas in the book that violated orthodoxy. In fact, though, they merely constitute a list of the chapters. The book was saved just in time from the fire of which it still bears traces.

Annie Charon

R. H. Bainton, *Michel Servet, hérétique et martyr* (Geneva, 1953). J. F. Fulton, *Michael Servetus: Humanist and Martyr* (New York, 1953). J. Lecler, *Histoire de la tolérance au siècle de la Réforme* (Paris, 1955). H. Baudrier, *Bibliographie lyonnaise*, 12 vols. (1895–1921; repr. Paris, 1964), 10:91–102. J. Delumeau, *Naissance et affirmation de la Réforme* (Paris, 1965), 115–16. J. Aiguader, *Miguel Servet* (Barcelona, 1981).

74

ORONCE FINE

Map of the World

Département des Cartes et Plans, Rés. Ge DD 2987 (63)

Paper; wood engraving; 2 sheets gathered, hand-colored; 520 × 595 mm. Paris, 1534–1536. From the collection of the geographer Jean-Baptiste Bourguignon d'Anville; acquired by Louis XVI on Feb. 18, 1782.

In the Renaissance, maps of the world prepared by French geographers were still rare. The work of Oronce Fine is for that reason all the more interesting. Fine assumed his place in the great European movement that followed the rediscovery of Ptolemy's *Geography*. His work gave expression to a world perception that combined reality with hypothesis. Fine covered the uncertainties of the cosmographer with the cloak of science—a science which still remained mainly theoretical. Son and grandson of physicians, Oronce Fine was born in Briançon (Dauphiné) in 1494 and died in Paris in 1555. Mathematician and astronomer, he lectured in mathematics in 1531 at the Collège de France, which Francis I had just founded on the advice of Guillaume Budé. Fine wrote particularly about astronomy and astronomical instruments. In a treatise which has remained in manuscript, he explains how to determine geographic coordinates with the aid of an instrument he calls a *méthéoroscope*, an astrolabe modified by the addition of a compass. The manuscript copy of the treatise, with a dedication intended for Francis I, has been preserved.

Oronce Fine was also a cartographer. He published in particular a map of France and

199

two maps of the world. In order to prepare those maps, he strove to bring together the largest possible number of geographic coordinates. He thereby completed and corrected the information transmitted by the Greek geographer Ptolemy. He likewise studied cartographic projections. In 1531 he produced a bicordiform map of the world. The map of the world of 1534–1536, however, uses cordiform projection, as did Apian's map of the world published in Ingolstadt (Bavaria) in 1530. Apian could in fact have copied Fine, who noted on the map of the world of 1534–1536 that he had drawn it fifteen years earlier for Francis I and that he had been obliged to bring the original draft up to date.

A second copy of the map of the world of 1534–1536 is preserved in Nuremberg. It is this copy which gives dates for the map engraved by Fine.

The map of the world of 1534–1536 is bordered with a handsome Renaissance decoration: two columns support a pediment bearing the Latin inscription "Recens et Integra Orbis Descriptio" (A new and complete description of the world), interrupted in the middle by the coat of arms of France. The author's name appears in the lower part of the border.

In the northern part of the world map, Fine has drawn the name *Asia* running on each side of the central meridian to cover both present-day North America and Asia, the name *America* then being reserved for South America. As a consequence, *Catay* and *Mangi*, which Columbus had hoped to reach, appear to the west of the Gulf of Mexico.

Also to be noted is the presence of a vast southern land mass (*Terra Australis*), "recently discovered but not yet explored." Indeed, the discovery of Tierra del Fuego by Magellan suggested that the southern continent hypothesized by geographers had at last been reached.

Monique Pelletier

L. Gallois, *De Orontio Finaeo* (Paris, 1890). D. Hillard and E. Poulle, "Oronce Fine et l'horloge planétaire de la Bibliothèque Sainte-Geneviève," in *Bibliothèque d'Humanisme et Renaissance: Travaux et documents*, vol. 33 (Geneva, 1971), 311–51. G. Kish, "The Cosmographic Heart: Cordiform Maps of the Sixteenth Century," *Imago mundi* 19 (1965): 13–21. G. Schilder, *Australia Unveiled* (Amsterdam, 1976). R. W. Shirley, *The Mapping of the World* (London, 1983).

75

Anonymous Terrestrial Globe

Département des Cartes et Plans, Rés. Ge A 340

Engraved copper; diameter of sphere: 250 mm. Rouen, [late 16th century]. Purchased in 1861; the purchase register notes: "found at Lignière [Lignières] (Cher) with provenance from the Abbé de Lecuy" (Abbot Lécuy, vicar general of Paris, d. 1834).

Nearly all Renaissance globes were of German origin. This Rouen globe, in engraved copper, is an exception. It cannot, however, be attributed to French production of the day, since its geographic markings resemble those of an Italian map which is itself the only one of its kind.

This is the only metal globe known to have been engraved in Rouen in the 16th century. Unfortunately, the work is unsigned. It may have been done for some Rouen shipowner, who would certainly have been interested in an object with such lovely marine-inspired decoration: Neptune's chariot, tritons, and ships. Abbé Anthiaume has demonstrated that information provided by the globe was unrelated to the flourishing school of hydrography at Dieppe. The globe has a graduated horizon and meridian. The horizon rests on four quadrants which are connected by a pivot leg and whose upper parts are formed by men represented from the waist up, probably tritons. Indeed, three of the men are bearded, while the fourth is surmounted by a skull.

This globe resembles the world map in two hemispheres engraved in Venice by

Giulio de Musi and published by Michele Tramezzino (Département des Cartes et Plans, Rés. Ge B 1113). Both items clearly separated North America (*Novus Orbis*) from Asia. Japan (*Sipago*) was reduced to a small island that is named only on the globe. Although the maker of the sphere pointed out that the west coast of North America had not yet been discovered, the peninsula of California was taking shape. In South America (*America*), the Amazon and the Rio de la Plata stood out with exaggerated enlargement as on the 1544 world map of Sebastian Cabot (Département des Cartes et Plans, Rés. Ge AA 582). In imitation of the Venetian map, the globe showed a large band of land to the south which encompasses three-quarters of the Antarctic circle. It ends below the cartouche bearing the globe's title, *Nova et Integra Universi Orbis Descriptio, Rothomagi*, above which is depicted Neptune's chariot.

Perhaps the globe's maker was influenced by López de Gómara, whose work began to appear in 1552. Gómara is thought to have generated at least two additions to the Venetian map. First, the globe calls attention to the voyage of Jean de Kolno, a Pole in the service of the King of Denmark, who, according to Gómara, had preceded Sebastian Cabot to the coasts of Labrador. Second, an inscription focuses attention on the gold resources of the province of Collao, south of the Amazon: Gómara spoke about temples made of gold "depuis le hault jusques en bas" (from top to bottom), and the globe's maker also stresses the discovery of a house all of gold. Abbé Anthiaume has pointed out that the place-names on the globe are primarily Spanish, which prompts him to identify the maker as one of the numerous Spaniards residing in Rouen. He notes, further, that the name *Lusitania* (Portugal) on the Venetian map was replaced on the globe by *Galicia*. He therefore deduces that the globe could not predate 1580, when Philip II added the Portuguese crown to that of Spain.

Monique Pelletier

Gabriel Marcel, "Note sur une sphère terrestre en cuivre faite à Rouen à la fin du XVIe siècle," *Bulletin de la Société Normande de Géographie* 1891. A. Anthiaume, *Cartes marines, constructions navales, voyages de découvertes chez les Normands, 1500–1650*, 2 vols. (Paris, 1916). R. Hervé, "Essai de classement d'ensemble, par type géographique, des cartes générales du monde (1487–1644)," *Globusfreund* 25–27 (1978): 63–74. R. W. Shirley, *The Mapping of the World* (London, 1983).

76

GUILLAUME BROUSCON

*Manual of Navigation for the Use of
Breton Sailors*

Département des Manuscrits, Fr. 25374, fol. 4

*Parchment; 1 folded map (310 × 275 mm) followed
by 25 leaves foliated 5–29 (175 × 140 mm). Bound in
stamped calf. [Le Conquet,] 1548. From the library
of the chapter at Notre-Dame de Paris, transferred
to Louis XV in 1756.*

Although France is endowed with an extensive coastline, royal governments seem to
have been slow to recognize it, due no doubt
to the kingdom's feudal structure and the
prolonged autonomy enjoyed by the maritime princedoms. The first documents that
provided a sketch of French coasts were produced by foreigners (Italian and Catalan *portulans*, or charts). Direct state involvement in
such matters goes back no farther than the
government of Richelieu (1626–1642). Indeed,
French maritime history has to be examined

first within a provincial framework. In the 1 6th century, the two principalities with the greatest maritime activity were Normandy and Brittany. Both became sites of important hydrographic schools, at Dieppe and Le Conquet, respectively. The first French maritime charts were drawn up there, as much in response to the needs of maritime trade along the western coast of Europe as for expansion to the other side of the Atlantic (for example, the voyages of exploration undertaken by G. Verrazano in 1524–1529 and by Jacques Cartier between 1534 and 1543).

Guillaume Brouscon from Le Conquet, a port of call on Brittany's western tip, is the first known member of a line of hydrographers who earned distinction between approximately 1543 and 1650 by drafting highly original piloting manuals. Reduced to a small format, sometimes in manuscript and sometimes produced from woodcuts, these works contributed significantly to navigation in northwestern Europe for two reasons. First, they provided information about the tides, which was essential for knowing when to enter and leave the western ports. They were composed of calendars, map-cards, and tidal charts that made it possible to determine the time of high and low tide in every port of the region covered for any day of the month. Yet they did not require the user to do any calculations. Furthermore, rather than being useful only for educated Breton sailors, they employed a most ingenious system of cartographic and iconographic representation (notably depicting patron saints on calendars), to make scientific data accessible to all sailors in the West, whether literate or not and regardless of mother tongue. Significantly, the examples known to us have been preserved in Great Britain as well as in France.

These manuals generally contained a detailed map of Europe's Atlantic coasts from Norway to the straits of Gibraltar, and included the British Isles. Such was Guillaume Brouscon's manual, dated 1548 and entirely in manuscript, which is exhibited here. Decorated with eleven flags to identify the different countries and five vignettes for port cities on the Continent, this map (fol. 4), despite its inaccurate tracings–especially in the Cotentin region–and despite the inaccuracy of some of the latitudes shown, was a real navigational tool that helped its possessor fix his position. That becomes clear from the area mapped–the area with which Breton sailors needed to be familiar–and from the presence of a latitude scale. The manual consisted additionally of five chapters of text and drawings that explained various astronomical procedures for determining latitude at sea. It constituted a veritable little treatise on astronomical navigation along the lines of the Portuguese "libros de marinharia" and the Spanish "arte de navigar" from the same period. However, it may be asked whether these latter were intended for the same sailor readership. Portuguese progress in the nautical arts notwithstanding, we know that the tradition of navigating by dead reckoning without calculating latitude continued.

Catherine Hofmann

E. G. R. Taylor, *The Haven-finding Art: A History of Navigation from Odysseus to Captain Cook* (London, 1956; rev. ed. 1971). L. Dujardin-Troadec, *Les cartographes bretons du Conquet: La navigation en images, 1543–1650* (Brest, 1966). H. D. Howse, "Some Early Tidal Diagrams," in *Centro de Estudos de Historia e Cartografia Antiga, serie separatas 173* (Lisbon, 1985). H. Michéa, "Les cartographes du Conquet et le début de l'imprimerie: Guillaume Brouscon, une vie pleine de mystère," *Bulletin de la Société Archéologique du Finistère 140* (1986). M. de La Roncière and M. Mollat du Jourdin, *Les portulans: Cartes marines du XIIIe au XVIIe siècle* (Fribourg and Paris, 1984). Monique Pelletier, "La France dans L'Europe des clercs et des marchands," in *Mémoire de l'espace français: Cartes de France du IVe au XVIIIe siècle* (forthcoming).

DESCRIPTION NOVVELLE DES MERVEILLES de ce mõde, & de la dignite de lhomme, compofee en rithme francoyfe en maniere de exhortation, par Ian parmentier, faifant fa derniere nauigation, auec Raoul fon frere, en lifle Tapro bane, aultrement dicte Sama tra.

Item Vn champ royal fpecialement cõpofe par maniere de paraphrafe fur foraifon dominicale.

Item plufieurs chãps royaulx faictz par fedit Jan Parmentier foubz termes aftronomiques & geographiques & maritimes/ a fhonneur de fa trefheureufe Vierge Marie mere de Dieu.

Item Moralite trefelegante/ compofee par fe fufdit Jan parmentier/a dix perfonnaiges/a fhonneur de faffumption de fa Vierge Marie.

Deploration fur fa mort defditz Parmentiers compofee par Pierre crignon/compaignon defditz Parmentiers en fadicte nauigation.

77

JEAN PARMENTIER

Description nouvelle des merveilles de ce monde, & de la dignité de l'homme (New description of the marvels of this world, and of the dignity of man), and other texts by Pierre Crignon and Geert Morrhe

Réserve des livres rares, Rés. Ye. 205, title page

Paris: Geert Morrhe, Jan. 7, 1531 [1532 n.s.]. [96] pp.; 8vo. First edition. Bound in brown calf [1994] as a replacement for the 17th-century binding. Acquired by the Bibliothèque Royale ca. 1730.

Although French attempts to colonize the New World failed or ended in disappointment at the outset, this does not mean that French navigators had no interest in distant voyages. On the contrary, the first half of the 16th century counted a substantial number of bold initiatives. The Basques, the Bretons, and the Normans early on sailed across the Atlantic with sufficient presence to force Christopher Columbus to alter the route of his third voyage in 1498. Six years later, Paulmier de Gonneville became the first known Frenchman to reach Brazil. In 1509 the citizens of Rouen were more astonished by the sight of seven Indians in costume, with their weapons and canoes, than by the mariners' exploit in having brought them home from Newfoundland.

Jean Parmentier (1494–1529), who sailed over the Atlantic from Cape Breton Island to Recife, from Guinea to Santo Domingo, was probably the first Frenchman to compete with the Portuguese on the route for the Spice Islands. He had been planning to go there when he died of fever in Sumatra on Dec. 3, 1529. Since the preceding Easter he had commanded an expedition of two ships, the larger of which, *La Pensée,* had been the first vessel in Jean Ango's fleet to reach North America in 1508.

For over thirty years this shipowner controlled the majority of French commercial enterprises overseas. He made a fortune from it. In Dieppe he built a palace (burned by the English in 1694) and in Varengeville a summer house, where he had the honor of receiving the court of Francis I. Ango was also a patron of the arts and surrounded himself with Italian artists. Even his pilots could be poets. This was the case with Pierre Crignon, the editor of the *Description nouvelle,* and especially with Jean Parmentier, in whose memory this collection was published.

Astrologer (that is, astronomer, cosmographer, and geographer) Parmentier earned as much respect in his lifetime for his maps as for his *rondeaux* and *chants royaux* (royal songs), which won him five major prizes in Norman poetry contests. His social standing and linguistic virtuosity made him a typical member of the poetic school of *grands rhétoriqueurs,* yet his work is distinctive in its original use of maritime metaphors. With Parmentier, French poetry suddenly broadened its domain to include the new worlds discovered with enthusiasm, celebrated in songs of unusual sincerity. Nowhere is this cosmic lyricism better expressed than in the *Traité en forme d'exhortation contenant les merveilles de Dieu et la dignité de l'homme* (Treatise in the form of an exhortation containing the marvels of God and the dignity of man), which he composed during his last voyage, when his companions were for a time discouraged by the vastness of the Indian Ocean. Published two years after his death along with the core of his poetic work and prefaced by Pierre Crignon's biographical notes, so that the name Parmentier might survive "by fame and immortal praise," it would certainly have disappeared from the collective memory if two copies had not been preserved. This first printed book dedicated to a French navigator was protected by its proximity to the almost equally rare first edition of Marguerite d'Angoulême's *Miroir de l'âme pécheresse* (Mirror of the sinful soul, 1531), with which it had been bound.

Antoine Coron

Le discours de la navigation de Jean et Raoul Parmentier de Dieppe; Voyage à Sumatra en 1529; Description de l'île de Sainct-Domingo, ed. Ch. Schefer (Paris, 1883; repr. Geneva, 1971). Jean Parmentier, *Oeuvres poétiques*, ed. Françoise Ferrand (Geneva, 1971). Jean Garapon, "Jean Parmentier, poète de l'immensité," in *Mélanges Jeanne Lods* (Paris, 1978), 671–78. A. L. Boers, "The Editorial Practice of a Sixteenth-century Scholar-Printer," *Quaerendo* 14, no. 1 (Winter 1984): 43–62. Brigitte Moreau, *Inventaire chronologique des éditions parisiennes du XVIe siècle*, vol. 4, 1531–1535 (Paris, 1992), no. 256.

78

NICOLO DELLA CASA
Henricus II Francor. Rex Eta XXVIII, 1547
(Henri II, king of the French, age twenty-eight, 1547)
Cabinet des Estampes, N2

Engraving; 41 × 29.3 cm. Unsigned.

Nicolo della Casa, despite his Italianate name, came from Lorraine—he modified his name when he went to Rome in the 1540s with a compatriot, the engraver Nicolas Béatrizet. Rome, of course, was an artistic center of prime importance in the 16th and 17th centuries, and it attracted young artists from all across Europe. Until the 18th century Rome would remain the crucible of international art.

During della Casa's stay in Rome, between 1543 and 1545, he copied Michelangelo's *Last Judgment* in eleven engravings, his most famous works. He probably left Rome for Florence to work in the studio of the sculptor Baccio Bandinelli (1493–1560); there he engraved a portrait of the sculptor and a picture of his workshop, as well as a striking portrait of Cosimo I de' Medici (1544).

Comparing this portrait with an engraved depiction of Henry II, Robert Dumesnil hypothesized that the latter was also engraved by della Casa. Henry II was presented as an antique hero, endowed by the engraver with a profile suitable for a medal, and crowned with laurels like a Roman emperor. He wears armor identified as ancient by the mantling and the form of the helmet and by the shield. Its finely incised decoration, however, typified the taste of the French court, with delicate engraving covering the breastplate and the armlets, as in the models of Etienne Delaune (ca. 1518–1583), whose sketchbook is preserved in Munich.

205

HENRICVS Ⅱ FRANÇOR·
REX ETA XXVIII 1547·

Here, the historiated decoration focuses
on two themes that evoke the sea, with sea-
horses, mermaids, combats of tritons in the
style of Mantegna (1431–1506), and Perseus
delivering Andromeda. On the shield are displayed crescent moons, the personal emblem
of the king, which illustrate his motto "Donec
totum impleat orbis" (Until it fills the globe).
The motifs were perhaps intended to emphasize the influence of the moon on earthly
affairs, since lunar cycles are so closely
linked to the sea.

Françoise Jestaz

André Linzeler, *Inventaire du fonds français: Graveurs du XVIe
siècle*, vol. 1 (Paris, 1932). Johannes Schobel, *Princely Arms and
Armour: A Selection from the Dresden Collection*, trans. M. O. A.
Stanton (London, 1975).

79

JEAN DUVET

La Licorne purifie une source
(The unicorn purifies a spring)
Cabinet des Estampes, Ed 1b Rés.

*Engraving; 22.5 × 39.5 cm. Inventoried in 1779 by
Hugues-Adrien Joly as no. 52. Thirsty animals
gather at the bank of a river poisoned by a serpent.
They are waiting for the unicorn to dip its horn into
the water and purify it.*

This engraving illustrates the power—analo-
gous to that of Christ—possessed by the
mythical unicorn, a cross between a rhinoceros and a narwhal, whose horn was thought
to have curative and purifying powers. Rulers
collected and preserved the powdered horn
in reliquaries (themselves objets d'art), for it
was thought to work as detector of and anti-
dote to poison. The late Middle Ages and the
Renaissance, when poisoning was rampant in
many European courts, glorified the unicorn.

The engraving is striking for the modernity of its perspective, its stylized motifs, and
the contrast between the vertical lines of the
plant kingdom and the rounded forms of the
animal kingdom. The *Histoire de la licorne*, of
which "La licorne purifie une source" is a
part, was engraved with a great spontaneity
of etching techniques, and with a fully emo-
tive style that links Duvet to the School of
Fontainebleau.

The first French engraver of international
importance, Jean Duvet (b. Langres, 1485; d.
ca. 1570) began his career as a goldsmith.
After executing a number of attention-getting
works for Langres Cathedral, he received the
title of goldsmith to the king. Engraver of
coins and decorator as well, he worked on
the "solemn entries" made by Kings Francis I
(1515–1547) and Henry II (1547–1559) into
Langres and later Dijon. Influenced by

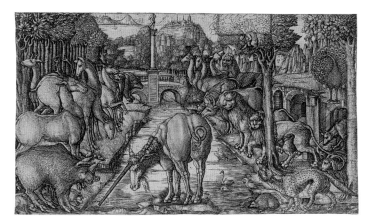

Dürer, Mantegna, and Raimondi, he began to engrave in 1519. Colin Eisler attributes seventy-three engravings to him. The best-known series, *Apocalypse figurée*, was a royal commission (1545–1556) consisting of twenty plates, the text of which he typeset himself and the imagery of which thoroughly reinvigorates Dürer's iconographic ideas.

Duvet also was responsible for a series of six large horizontal plates, unsigned, whose iconography has remained mysterious to the present day. The series was the *Histoire de la licorne*, immediately thought to allude to the love between Henry II and Diane de Poitiers. In any case, it was for this series that he was given the title Master of the Unicorn.

Françoise Jestaz

Jean-Eugène Bersier, *Jean Duvet: Le maître à la licorne, 1485–1570?* (Paris, 1977). Colin Eisler, *The Master of the Licorne: The Life and Work of Jean Duvet* (New York, 1979).

80

Hours of Henri II

Département des Manuscrits, Lat. 1429, fol. 107v

Vellum; 124 fols.; 182 × 122mm. 1547–1550. Illustrations by the Master of the Getty Epistles (fols. 3v, 5, 6, 7, 40, 73, 107v); by the Master of Henri II (fols. 8, 15v, 28, 38v, 54, 58v, 65v); and by the Master of the Henri II Grisailles (fols. 37, 45, 49v, 87). Binding (probably original) in fawn-colored morocco, marbled, with gold-stamped fillets outlining covers and spine. Gilt edges. Holes for laces. Royal collections; Musée des Souverains, 1866; returned to the Bibliothèque Nationale.

In the reign of Henry II (1547–1559), the arts of the book prospered alongside monumental architecture and the decorative arts. French printing had reached a sophisticated maturity, leaving the medium of illuminated manuscripts as the exclusive preserve of the aristocracy.

Manuscripts such as the Hours of Henry II need to be understood as works of art with a commemorative significance. This finely crafted prayer book, meant for private devotion and delectation, was painted by at least three artists. Their work can be traced in two other contemporary manuscripts, the Hours of Montmorency and the Hours of Dinteville, in which their fully developed Renaissance style is set off by *maniera* frames of rich complexity.

Traditional in text and layout, Henry II's book is nevertheless innovative in its Old Testament miniatures, which echo metaphorically the cares and duties of Henry's new reign.

The last miniature in the book shows Henry II in the church of Saint-Marcoul at Corbény, healing the scrofulous with his touch (fol. 107v). This ceremony took place a few days after Henry's coronation at Reims Cathedral on July 26, 1547. The folios that follow contain Latin antiphons and responses to Saint Marcoul headed in French: "The prayers which the kings of France are accustomed to say when they wish to touch those sick from scrofula." These healing powers were bestowed upon French kings by unction from the holy ampulla at the coronation ceremony. While the royal touch could be exer-

cised at any time or place that pleased the king, the tradition of the immediate post-coronation ceremony had begun at Corbény in the mid-14th century with John the Good. The tradition of royal healing had converged only gradually with the healing powers attributed to Saint Marcoul, and by the 15th century the king's ability to heal was believed to derive more from the saint's intercession than from the annointing at the coronation.

The miniature reaffirms the king's own powers, while the prayers maintain the link with Saint Marcoul. Codicological irregularities within the manuscript suggest that this section was altered to commemorate Henry II's coronation. Identical prayers, without the French preface, also appear in a book of hours made for Francis I, Henry's father (Christie's, June 24, 1987, lot 265, dated

1532–1540). The accompanying miniature, however, gives all the credit to Saint Marcoul: Francis kneels before the saint, whose healing is seen in the background. The Saint Marcoul prayers and preface, unillustrated, are also found in Henry's own fleur-de-lis–shaped hours (Amiens, Lescalopier 22) and in the now-lost Hours of Francis I, both dating from the 1550s.

In the miniature displayed here, the afflicted wait in patient devotion, lining the nave of an imaginary church of Gothic proportions and classical detailing. The newly crowned king is garbed symbolically in his gold fleur-de-lis–embroidered regalia; on the far right in profile stands the new cardinal, Charles of Lorraine, who, as archbishop of Reims, had presided at Henry's coronation. The man next to him, holding a mace, is probably Charles's older brother, Francis.

The artist of this miniature, the Getty Master, has painted elongated, elegant figures with characteristic delicacy and minute detail. The image of Henry II healing the scrofulous with his touch may allude to the power of the monarch to heal all his subjects through his declared intention to reestablish the power of the French church. Thus, like the miniatures throughout the book, this image asserts the greater rights and duties of kingship.

Myra D. Orth

Henri Omont, ed., *Livres d'heures de Henri II* (Paris, 1905). Victor Leroquais, *Les livres d'heures manuscrits de la Bibliothèque Nationale*, 3 vols. (Macon, 1927), 1:276–79, no. 139. Marc Bloch, *Les rois thaumaturges: Etude sur le caractère surnaturel attribué à la puissance royale particulièrement en France et en Angleterre*, 2d ed. (Paris, 1983), 286, 316, 453. Richard Jackson, *Vive le Roi! A History of the French Coronation from Charles V to Charles X* (Chapel Hill, N.C., 1984). Frederic J. Baumgartner, *Henry II, King of France, 1547–1559* (Durham, N.C., 1988). *Livres d'heures royaux: La peinture de manuscrits à la cour de France au temps de Henri II*, exhibition at Ecouen, Musée de la Renaissance (Paris, 1993), 33–35, no. 4 (full bibliography).

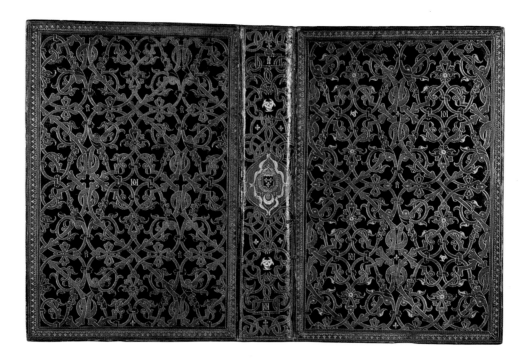

81

Bible Hébraïque (Hebrew Bible)

Département des Manuscrits, Division
Orientale, Hébreu 16, binding

*Parchment; 318 fols.; 520 × 370 mm. Anonymous
German copy from the end of the 13th century.
Incomplete at the beginning and end. Parisian
binding, ca. 1555. Was in Henry II's library at
Fontainebleau.*

"Codex membranaceus, characteribus
Hebraeo-Germanicis scriptus, quo continen-
tur Josue, Judices, libri Regum, Jeremias,
Ezechiel, Isaïas, Oseas, Prophetae Minores,
Psalmi, Job, Proverbia Salomonis, Daniel,
Esdras, Paralipomena..." (Parchment codex
written in Hebraeo-Germanic characters, in
which are contained Joshua, Judges, the
Books of Kings, Jeremiah, Ezekiel, Isaiah,
Hosea, the Minor Prophets, the Psalms, Job,
the Proverbs of Solomon, Daniel, Esdras,
Paralipomena...). Such is the basic description of this manuscript in the first printed
catalogue of the Bibliothèque Royale (Paris,
1739).

The Latin catalogue entry, however,
remains silent on the most interesting aspect
of the codex, namely, its binding, one of the
most beautiful French bindings of the 16th
century. It is the elegant handiwork of

Claude Picques, who was binder to three
kings: Henry II, Francis II, and Charles IX.
On a ground of black morocco, the boards
present a magnificent ensemble of interlacing and ornamental foliage of light tan
morocco, with certain geometric and foliate
patterns painted in green. The spine bears
the traditional royal arms. The matching doublures have black interlacing and white bows
on a background of dark tan, in a composition resembling marble. Indeed, the insides
of the covers strangely evoke certain decorative motifs in the château d'Anet, where
Diane de Poitiers, the king's paramour,
resided. It would not be surprising if the
preparatory sketch for the binding was drawn
in the workshops of Philibert de l'Orme,
architect of the château from 1552 to 1556.

Of Henry II's thirty-one Hebrew manuscripts, this volume stands out in extravagant
richness. No doubt the monumental format
of the volume explains why it received this
highly ornamental mosaic covering.

Michel Garel

E. Quentin-Bauchart, *La bibliothèque de Fontainebleau et les
livres des derniers Valois (1515–1589)* (Paris, 1891), 77–100. M.
Garel, "Une reliure oubliée de Claude Picques," *Revue de la
Bibliothèque Nationale* 7 (1983): 39–41. Garel, *D'une main forte:
Manuscrits hébreux des collections françaises*, exhibition at the
Bibliothèque Nationale (Paris, 1991), 112–13, no. 78.

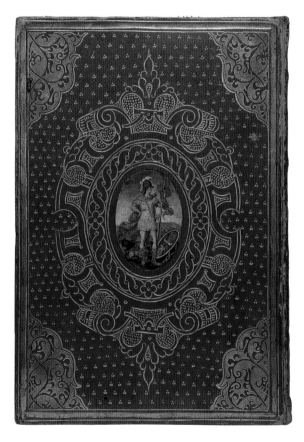

82

Recueil de tacticiens grecs
(Miscellany of Greek tacticians)
Département des Manuscrits, Grec 2523,
fol. 35 and binding

*Paper; 76 fols.; 253 × 160 mm. Paris, 1564. Copied
by Ange Vergèce. 16th-century binding, probably
original, in red morocco with gilded and azure decoration in the center and corners, and a painted
medallion in the center, showing Minerva on front
cover back and Mars on the other. Apparently
belonged in 1598 to Frédéric Morel the Younger,
professor of Greek and royal printer. Purchased by
the Bibliothèque Royale in 1732 (see note on endpa-
per: "Achepté en 1732, au mois de mars. Payé deux
louis dor, valant 48 sous" [Purchased in March 1732.
Bought for two gold louis, worth 48 sous]).*

Executed by one of the most famous
Renaissance copyists, Ange Vergèce (who
signed and dated the manuscript in 1564),
this thin, precious volume brings together
two treatises on military science written by
two Greek authors in the 1st century A.D. The
first, a certain Aelian, concentrated on tactics
and on troop maneuvers on the battlefield,
and dedicated his tract to Emperor Trajan.
The second, Onesandros, discussed strategy.
These two highly technical texts were composed by theoreticians who had never fought
a battle, but they were astonishingly popular
for centuries. The treatises were transmitted
from Graeco-Roman antiquity through
Byzantium to Renaissance Europe, where in
the intellectual excitement of the period the
Greek manuscript copies continued to exist
side by side with Latin translations and the
first printed editions.

Vergèce (first quarter of the 16th century–1569) himself completed at least ten copies
of Aelian. None of these, not even the one he
executed for the king in 1559, was as well
done as this masterpiece of calligraphy, whose
sponsor—whether scholar or rich patron—

cannot be identified. The script of the volume is elegant, and the refined decoration includes meticulously drawn and watercolored little archers, hoplites, and cavalry in various battle formations. Inspired by the recent Venetian edition of philologist Francesco Robortello (the "editio princeps" of 1553), these delicate miniatures replaced the schematic and purely utilitarian diagrams found in previous manuscripts. Unperturbed by anachronism, the artist shows the soldiers in 16th-century costumes with helmets, halberds, and plumes. The camp of the Cloth of Gold can be seen behind the ancient encampments.

The same high quality of work is to be found in each of 130-odd manuscripts copied by Vergèce. The erudite Cretan resided first in Venice, then in Rome, and finally in Paris, where Francis I entrusted him with organizing the Greek collections of the library at Fontainebleau. Humanists of his time so prized his script that it became the model for the Greek font which Garamond created on the king's order and which was used for Greek books in France for nearly two centuries.

Marie-Odile Germain

Alphonse Dain, *Les manuscrits d'Onésandros* (Paris, 1930). Dain, *Histoire du texte d'Élien le tacticien* (Paris, 1946). Dain, "Les stratégistes byzantins," in *Travaux et mémoires* (Paris, 1967), 317–92. A. Hobson, *Humanists and Bookbinders* (Cambridge, 1989), 194.

83

FRANÇOIS CLOUET
Catherine de Médicis en veuve
(Catherine de Médicis as a widow)
Cabinet des Estampes, Na 22 Rés., boîte 4

Black and red chalk on vellum (sheet trimmed on three sides); 33.1 × 22.3 cm. Inscribed: "La reine mère du roi" (the Queen Mother). Ca. 1560. From the collection of the abbey of Sainte-Geneviève, no. 23.

The collection of drawings apparently held by the former abbey of Sainte-Geneviève since 1753 entered the Cabinet des Estampes (Print Department) of the Bibliothèque Nationale in 1861. The most notable feature of the collection was a somewhat disparate set of 16th-century portraits acquired directly from the descendants of the Dumonstier family. Along with the Brisacier collection (acquired a little later), the Sainte-Geneviève collection represents an anthology of 16th-century portraiture of a quality that bears comparison with the finest Clouets in Chantilly, the more refined Foulons from the Lécurieux album, and the Quesnel plates in the Gaignières album.

211

The portrait in black and red chalk exhibited here is probably one of finest achievements of François Clouet (before 1522–1572) during the last years of his career. Dimier has suggested that it is a sketch for a lost oil painting, copies of which, drawn or painted in miniature, still exist (notably at Chantilly). Queen Catherine, widowed at forty, was overcome with grief and dressed in black for the rest of her life. Ambassadors were struck by her pale complexion and stoutness as much as by her intelligence and stubbornness, the two aspects of her personality that Clouet strove to render. Also evident is the sad resignation of the woman who in 1560 wrote to her daughter, the queen of Spain, "Recommend yourself well to God, because you once saw me as happy as yourself, never thinking of any other tribulation than not being loved enough by the king, your father, who honored me more than I merited."

Catherine was also known for what we would today call patriotism when in her later years she staunchly exclaimed, "All my life I have kept in mind the goal of doing well and, with no respect for anything whatsoever, of procuring everything I thought liable to help and serve the maintenance of the kingdom." Another portrait from the same period, also in the Sainte-Geneviève collection, shows Catherine with a fleshier face and an introspective gaze, as though lost in some nostalgic reverie; not only does it fail to convey the resoluteness of the female politician, but it also lacks the interest of the twin psychological insights of the first portrait, perhaps one of Clouet's finest masterpieces.

François Fossier

J. Niel, *Portraits des personnages français les plus illustres du XVIe siècle* (Paris, 1848), 1:234. H. Bouchot, *Les portraits aux crayons des XVIe et XVIIe siècles conservés à la Bibliothèque Nationale...* (Paris, 1884), 153. L. Dimier, *Histoire de la peinture de portrait en France au XVIe siècle* (Paris and Brussels, 1924), vol. 2, no. 460. *De François Ier à Henri IV: Les Clouet et la cour des rois de France*, exhibition at the Bibliothèque Nationale (Paris, 1970), no. 42. J. Adhémar, "Les portraits dessinés du XVIe siècle au Cabinet des Estampes," *Gazette des Beaux-Arts*, September 1973, no. 399.

84

La reine Artémise et son fils se rendent au tombeau du roi Mausole
(Queen Artemisia and her son going to King Mausolus's tomb)
Cabinet des Estampes, Ad 105 Rés., fol. 45

Pen, pencil, and wash; 40.5 × 54.6 cm. Given to the Cabinet des Estampes by M. Roussel, fermier général (tax collector), Jan. 27, 1765.

L'Histoire de la reine Artémise, written from 1560 onward by Nicolas Houel, a learned apothecary and connoisseur of art, is a collection of poems constituting a disguised defense of Catherine de Médicis and her government, based on the similar fates of the two queens. Houel dedicated the work to Catherine, widowed upon the accidental death of Henry II in 1559, who found herself invested with the regency of the French kingdom during the minority of her son Charles IX. To illustrate his lessons, Houel compared the life of Catherine with that of Queen Artemisia, the inconsolable widow of King Mausolus who had been obliged to take up the education of her young son Lygdamis. The book, never published, is known from the original manuscript preserved in the Cabinet des Estampes.

The *Histoire* comprises four books, of which only the first two were illustrated. Houel turned for illustrations to a painter who had already worked at the Fontainebleau court, Antoine Caron, and to his assistants.

The text appears in the form of handsomely lettered sonnets, opposite which are drawings in monochrome using India ink or sepia highlighted in white. In the upper border, two scrolls contain Catherine de Médicis's motto, "Ardorem testantur" (They witness the fire) and "Extincta vivere flamma" (To live while the flame is extinguished), between which is an escutcheon with the

combined arms of France and the Médicis, flanked by foliage and figures of children. The side borders contain the monogram *K* for Catherine and various emblems recalling her undying love for her husband and her inconsolable sorrow. The lower border, which remains empty, was meant to contain the title of the work.

The cycle is divided into four parts: the first glorifies the reign of Mausolus and describes his funeral procession and the construction—as ordered by his widow—of the extraordinary Mausoleum at Halicarnassus, one of the seven wonders of the ancient world. The second book sets forth the rules of good government, using both ancient queens and queens of France as examples. After her son's coronation, Artemisia is charged with the physical and intellectual education of the king. The third and fourth

books—not illustrated—reinforce the examples given by the first two.

Henry IV was to select some of these drawings at the beginning of the 17th century to serve as *modelli* for the Flemish weavers summoned to Paris to weave tapestries. In so doing, Henry wanted to honor his wife, Marie de Médicis, cousin of Catherine, by likening her to that brilliant queen. The parallel between these two famous women would become still clearer after Henry IV's death (1610), when Marie became regent upon the accession to the throne of the young Louis XIII.

Françoise Jestaz

Maurice Fenaille, *État général des tapisseries de la manufacture des Gobelins depuis son origine jusqu'à nos jours, 1600–1900*, vol. 1, *Les ateliers parisiens au XVIIe siècle* (Paris, 1923), 109–212. *Images of a Queen's Power: The Artemisia Tapestries*, exhibition at the Minneapolis Institute of Arts (Minneapolis, 1993), 1–42 and ills.

213

85

MICHEL DE MONTAIGNE
Essais (Essays)
Réserve des livres rares, Rés. 8° Z. Payen 2,
upper cover of the binding

*Bordeaux: Simon Millanges, 1580. 650 pp.; 8ᵛᵒ.
Bound in fawn-colored morocco with gilt decoration; leafy oval cartouche with the initials E.R. in
the center, surmounted by a royal crown, cornucopia at the corners, with semés of fleurs-de-lis and
roses. Ca. 1580. Purchased in 1870 along with the
collection of Jean-François Payen.*

"Je suis moi-même la matière de mon livre"
(I myself am the subject of my book). That is
how Michel de Montaigne described his work
in the brief foreword to his *Essais*, initially
written for his family and friends in the
belief that his death was near. These were in
no way family, political, or military memoirs
like those his contemporaries were writing.
Montaigne's was an original enterprise that
he initiated in a series of chapters of varying
length in which he delivered his reflections—
the fruit of his observations and his reading
on diverse themes—on idleness, on liars, on
the education of children, on friendship, on
cannibals, on the conventions of dress, on
prayers, on books, on freedom of conscience,
and so on.

These essays became his life's work.
Montaigne had begun writing them as early
as 1572, when he gave up his office in the
Parlement of Bordeaux to withdraw to his
castle in the Périgord region. Although he
could then spend long hours in his library,

he had also to meet the obligations of a
country nobleman and from time to time
rejoin the ranks of the royal army or appear
at court. After publication of the first edition
in 1580, he also undertook a long trip in Italy.
Later he became mayor of Bordeaux, before
bringing out a new edition of the *Essais*, to
which he had added book 3 in 1588, and
which he continued to revise until his death
in 1592.

Although Montaigne personally presented
his *Essais* to Henry III in July 1580, the circumstances in which the volume illustrated
here was offered to Queen Elizabeth of
England are unknown. The binding bearing
the queen's monogram, *E R*, surmounted by a
royal crown depicted in the French manner,
was apparently made in France. The semé (or
overall pattern) of fleurs-de-lis and roses
(which should be interpreted as the Tudor
rose, even though it does not match the
English design) represents the royal English
heraldic emblems. The simplest hypothesis
suggests that Montaigne sent it to the queen,
but it is legitimate to ask whether the fleur-
de-lis pattern simply evokes the queen's arms
or whether it had another meaning. The duke
of Anjou, brother of the king and heir apparent to the French crown, was staying with the
queen of England in late 1581 and early 1582,
and their engagement had even been
announced. It is therefore tempting to speculate—though with no proof, of course—that
this volume figured among the many presents that the duke offered the queen, in
which case the fleur-de-lis would represent
his own heraldic emblem.

The volume came into the possession of
the Dawnay de Downe family and then into
the hands of a collector, M. Edwards. It was
shown in 1814 to Van Praet, the curator of
printed books at the Bibliothèque Royale. In
1858 it was acquired by Dr. Payen, a great collector of Montaigne's editions.

Geneviève Guilleminot-Chrétien

J. Marchand, "Le Montaigne de la reine Elisabeth
d'Angleterre," *Bulletin de la Société des Amis de Montaigne*, 3d
ser., no. 22 (April–June 1962): 23–27. D. M. Frame, *Montaigne: A
Biography* (New York, 1965). R. A. Sayce and D. Maskell, *A
Descriptive Bibliography of Montaigne's Essais* (London, 1983),
no. 1. M. Lazard, *Michel de Montaigne* (Paris, 1992).

86

*Les Pénitents blancs et bleus du roy
Henri IIIe* (The blue and white
penitents of King Henry III)
Réserve des livres rares, Rés. La²⁵. 6,
fols. IV–V–VI

*[Paris, between 1583 and 1589]. One plate engraved
in three pieces; 35 × 29 cm each. Excerpt from* Les
belles figures et drolleries de la Ligue, *compiled
by Pierre de l'Estoile (Paris, 1589–1590); album of
49 fols.; folio. Acquired in 1824.*

Descended from a family of Parisian officials
and closely associated with legal circles and
members of Parlement, Pierre de l'Estoile
pursued a career in the royal chancellery. A
sincere royalist, he remained steadfastly loyal
to the Catholic religion in spite of his sympa-
thy for numerous reformers and his condemnation of certain church abuses. Profoundly
moderate, he lived through the civil wars
under Henry III and the beginnings of Henry
IV's reign without openly taking sides. He
was a born observer, forever curious, and jot-
ted down day by day all the news he could
gather from 1574 until his death in 1611. His
interests encompassed every sphere, from
domestic and foreign politics to court gossip
and human-interest stories.

L'Estoile's passion for gathering information reached its peak during the dangerous
months when Paris was in the hands of the
Catholic League and other Catholic extremists, from the end of 1588 to Henry IV's ultimate victory. He collected everything that circulated in that period in the streets–satirical
posters, pamphlets, poems, and songs. It is
known that he assembled more than three
hundred items about the League "printed in

Paris and publicly hawked in the streets," but
only the collection that he called *Les belles
figures et drolleries de la Ligue* has survived–a
collection intended to show posterity the
"wickedness, vanity, folly, and deception of
this infernal league."

This album, in which the pieces with
l'Estoile's annotations are glued recto-verso
and sometimes overlap, primarily follows a
chronological order. It supplies examples,
often unique now, of the lively character and
narrative quality of these large engraved
woodcuts by Parisian illustrators that retrace
the principal events of the civil wars. The
woodcut illustrated here, probably from
slightly before 1589 and placed by l'Estoile at
the beginning of the collection, recalls the
great processions through the streets of Paris
by "blue and white penitents" (so called from
their habits), which the king instituted in
1583 and in which the king and his nobles
marched.

This album, along with l'Estoile's other
manuscripts, became the property of the
abbey of Saint-Acheul near Amiens when its
abbot, Pierre de Poussemothe de l'Estoile,
who was the compiler's heir, died in 1718. It
escaped confiscation by national authorities
during the Revolution, but the Bibliothèque
Royale was able to purchase it in 1824 from
M. de Mongie. Often consulted by historians,
the collection has helped form our historical
image of the League.

Geneviève Guilleminot-Chrétien

Mémoires-journaux de Pierre de l'Estoile, vol. 4, *Les belles figures
et drolleries de la Ligue* (Paris, 1876; facsimile with reproductions of the plates, Paris, 1982). P. de l'Estoile, *Registre-journal
du règne de Henri III,* vol. 1, ed. M. Lazard and G. Schrenck
(Geneva, 1992), 7–50.

215

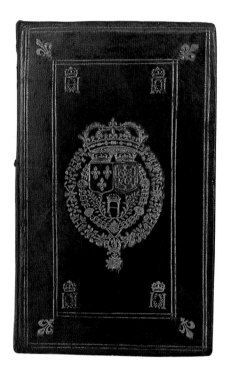

87

MARC LESCARBOT

Histoire de la Nouvelle France

Réserve des livres rares, Rés. 8º. LK¹² 724, binding, upper cover

Paris: Jean Milot, 1609. 888 pp. and 3 maps; 8ᵛᵒ. Maps engraved by Swedelinck after drawings by Lescarbot. Contemporary green leather gilt, with arms and monogram of Henri IV. Removed from the King's Cabinet in the Louvre to the Bibliothèque Royale in the early 18th century.

In the early 17th century the French were still behind in the race across the Atlantic to the North American continent. In 1604 Pierre du Gua de Monts, a former companion of Henry IV, established a new settlement in Acadia. He was accompanied by Champlain, cartographer on an earlier expedition to Quebec, and by another of Henry IV's companions, Biencourt de Poutrincourt.

De Monts returned to France to replenish his supplies, and when he set sail again from La Rochelle in 1606, he had with him new companions, among them Marc Lescarbot. Born about 1570, this pleasant and resourceful young lawyer who courted the Muses made up his mind in twenty-four hours to join the expedition. The expedition would last only a year and three months but it brought him enduring fame.

On his return, he published a sort of epic poem, a parody of the *Iliad*, recounting the "défaite des sauvages armouchiquois" (defeat of the savage armouchiquois) and, more important, the *Histoire de la Nouvelle France* (History of New France), in which he assumed the role of historian and defended the need for a settlement—which Sully opposed. The beginning of the book is a clever and intelligent summary of attempts at settlement in the 16th century, for which Lescarbot did not fail to consult Cartier's manuscript "relié en velours bleu" (bound in blue velvet) kept in the king's library. The lively chapters devoted to his own travels constitute a source of major importance for early 17th-century expeditions in terms of ocean crossings, the life of the colonists, the landscapes experienced, or relations with the natives. The last part treats the manners and customs of the American Indians and is the equal of the ethnological comments made by his contemporary Champlain.

At the same time, Lescarbot published *Muses de la Nouvelle France* (Muses of New France), which contains not only poems he composed on board ship or while on American soil but also a description of a naumachia, a nautical spectacle organized by a group of colonists and considered to be the first theatrical performance in North America. Lescarbot never returned to America but continued to be interested in it. The *Histoire de la Nouvelle France* was immediately translated and published in England and editions were published in France in 1611 and 1617. In 1627 Richelieu finally laid the foundation for French political expansion in North America.

The copy displayed here was bound for Henry IV. In the early 18th century it was kept along with the dauphin's copy (now in the library of Versailles) in the King's Cabinet in the Louvre.

Isabelle de Conihout

H. Harisse, *Notes pour servir à l'histoire... de la Nouvelle-France* (Paris, 1872), 19–25. Marcel Trudel, *Histoire de la Nouvelle-France*, vol. 2, *Le comptoir, 1608–1627* (Montreal, 1966). René Baudry, *Marc Lescarbot* (Montreal, 1968). Bibliothèque Nationale du Québec, *Laurentiana parus avant 1821* (Montreal, 1976), 256–57.

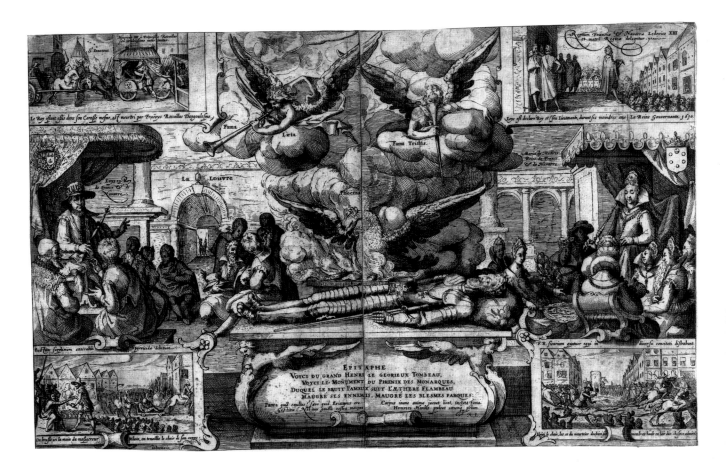

88

Allégorie sur la mort du roi Henri IV
(Allegory on the death of King
Henry IV)

Cabinet des Estampes, Collection Hennin
no. 1580

*Engraving; anonymous; 39.5 × 64.5 cm. Paris,
ca. 1610.*

This engraving is one of the numerous
portrayals published after King Henry IV was
stabbed to death by François Ravaillac on
May 14, 1610, in the rue de la Ferronnerie. The
king was on his way to visit his minister
Sully, who was sick, at the Arsenal. Henry
was a very controversial ruler during his lifetime, and his tragic death helped him go
down in history as an ideal monarch,
mourned by an inconsolable people. Two
weeks later the assassin was tortured before
being quartered in the Place de Grève.

217

In the foreground of the engraving is a tomb on which the body of the king, clothed in armor and crowned with laurel, is stretched out like a recumbent funeral figure. On the tomb appears the following engraved inscription:

Epitaphe
Voyci du Grand Henri le glorieux tombeau
Voyci le monument du Phoenix des Monarques
Duquel le bruit fameux suit l'aethéré flambeau
Maugré ses ennemis, maugré les blesmes
Parques.

(Epitaph: Here is the glorious tomb of Great Henry. Here is the monument to the Phoenix of Monarchs, who will be heard from, following heavenly fire, in spite of his enemies, in spite of the ghastly Fates.)

Behind the tomb, a phoenix is burning on a pyre. The phoenix was a mythical bird which, after being consumed by flames, was reborn from its own ashes. It symbolizes here the immortality of the king. In the curls of smoke, two personifications of Fame blow their trumpets: Fama Laeta (Joyous Fame) and Fama Tristis (Sad Fame).

The scene is set in front of the Louvre. Canopies are symmetrically placed on each side. On the left is Louis XIII enthroned and holding the scepter surrounded by his ministers: "Louis XIII, roy de France et de Navarre." His canopy is decorated with the arms of France and of Navarre. On the right his mother, "Marie de Médicis, reine de France et de Navarre," is seated opposite him, flanked by her ladies-in-waiting.

In the four corners, cartouches depict four scenes concerning Henry IV's assassination and its immediate aftermath. At the top left, "Henricus IIII a Francisco Ravaillac/Sica crudeliter interimitur" (Henry IV is cruelly killed with a dagger by François Ravaillac). Below, the legend indicates: "Le Roy estant assis dans son carosse mesme est meurtri par

Françoys Ravaillac d'Angoulesme" (The king, seated in his carriage, is assassinated by François Ravaillac from Angoulême). The action occurs in front of a church designated as "Saint-Innocent."

At top right, "Regnum Franciae et Navarrae Ludovico XIII/et matri Reginae delagatur" (The kingdom of France and Navarre is entrusted to Louis XIII and to the queen mother). The legend explains: "Loys est déclaré Roy et (son lieutenante durant ses moindres ans) la Reine gouvernante, 1610" (Louis is declared king and [his lieutenant, during his minority] the queen regent). At bottom left: "Justum supplicium execrabili parricidae debitum" (The just torture that an execrable regicide deserves). The legend notes: "On brusle ici la main du massacreur vilain, on tenaillie le chair de son corps inhumain" (Here the hand of the evil assassin is burned, the flesh of his inhuman body is torn). In the foreground, Ravaillac is tortured on the scaffold. In middle background he can be seen on a cart being taken to the place of torture.

Finally, bottom right: "F. R. Sicarium quatuor equi in diversa concitati distrahunt" (Four horses set in opposite directions pull the assassin F. Ravaillac apart). The legend says: "Voiici le chair, les os du meurtrier déchiré, ses membres hault en lair dun chascun admiré" (Here are the flesh and bones of the mutilated assassin, his limbs held high for all to admire).

The engraver has not been identified. He was probably one of the Flemish artists active in Paris in the early 17th century.

Laure Beaumont-Maillet

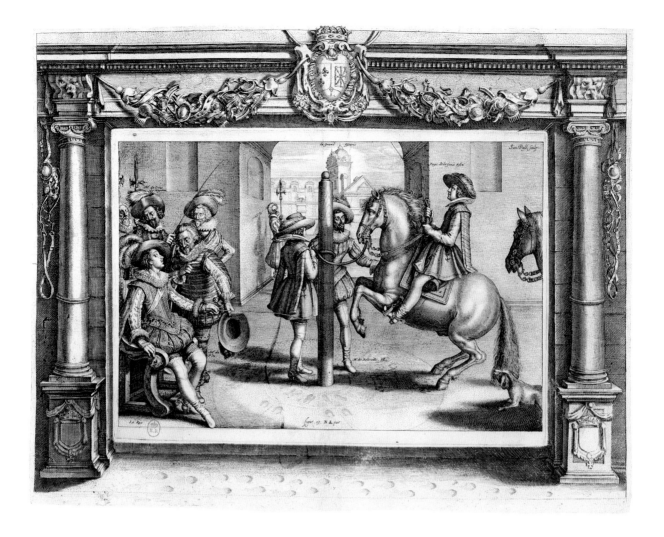

89

ANTOINE DE PLUVINEL

Maneige royal. . . gravé et représenté par Crispian de Pas, flamand
(Royal horsemanship. . . engraved and illustrated by Crispian de Pas, Fleming)

Réserve des livres rares, Rés. S. 151, planche 13n

Paris: Guillaume le Noir for Crispian de Pas, 1623. Twenty-three fols., of which 18 are double-column numbered 1–69; title engraved; and 64 plates; in-folio oblong. Contemporary citron morocco gilt, sides covered with a semé of fleurs-de-lis, with arms and monogram of Louis XIII. Removed from the King's Cabinet in the Louvre and placed in the Bibliothèque Royale in the early 18th century.

Antoine de Pluvinel, a member of the gentry from Dauphiné, was one of the greatest horsemen of his time. To save young French nobles the expensive and dangerous trip to Italy to complete their training, with Henry IV's support he founded an academy in Paris about 1595 to give instruction in horsemanship as well as dancing, fencing, and painting. Pluvinel's instruction marked the beginning of the revival of equestrian art in France in the 17th century. Pluvinel, who was assistant tutor to the dauphin, gave him lessons in horsemanship which were so successful that his royal pupil asked him to note down the principal rules of his method. Pluvinel died, having made his fortune, in 1620, leaving his uncompleted manuscript to his friend and pupil René Menou de Charnizay.

Pluvinel had approached Crispin II de Pas to engrave the plates for his work. Crispin de Pas belonged to a famous line of Dutch engravers and spent long periods in Paris between 1617 and 1630, notably to teach in Pluvinel's academy. No doubt under some pressure to recover his expenses, in 1623 Crispin de Pas published *Maneige royal* (Royal horsemanship), in an edition based on the uncompleted manuscript, furnished to him by one of Pluvinel's relatives, Jean-Daniel Peyrol. The edition was divided between a number of Parisian booksellers and print dealers.

Maneige royal presents a dialogue between young Louis XIII and the royal Master of the Horse. It is remarkable for the quality of its engravings, which make it one of the most handsome illustrated French books of the early 17th century. The clarity and accuracy with which such places as the gallery of the Louvre, the garden of the Tuileries, and the Grandes Ecuries (stables), now gone, are depicted, the portrayals of the young Louis XIII, Pluvinel, and members of the court who are engaged in equestrian demonstrations, and the paces of the horses justify the considerable popularity that Dutch and Flemish engravings enjoyed in the decade 1620–1630 and the influence they had on French book production.

The presentation copy to Louis XIII contains all the engravings of Crispin II de Pas highlighted in gold (the lovely engraved title, the portrait of Louis XIII, and the sixty-four plates). The binding in citron-colored morocco with smooth spine and semé of fleurs-de-lis exhibits a decoration characteristic of French royal bindings in the early 17th century.

In 1625 Menou de Charnizay published a completely revised edition under the title *Instruction du roy en l'exercice de monter à cheval* (Instruction for the king in the exercise of riding a horse). More faithful to the text left by Pluvinel, it reuses the 1623 plates, which had lost their original crispness.

Isabelle de Conihout

D. Franken, *L'oeuvre gravé des Van de Passe* (Amsterdam and Paris, 1881), nos. 717, 822, 1360. Henri de Terrebasse, *Antoine de Pluvinel, dauphinois* (Lyon, 1911), 50. Jeanne Duportal, *Contribution au catalogue général des livres à figures du XVIIème siècle* (Paris, 1914), 147. Duportal, *Etude sur les livres à figures édités en France de 1601 à 1660* (Paris, 1914), 283. G. Mennessier de la Lance, *Essai de bibliographie hippique*, vol. 2 (Paris, 1917), 325. *Hollstein's Dutch and Flemish Etchings...*, vol. 16 (Amsterdam, 1974), nos. 75, 105, 175. E. B. Wells, *Horsemanship: A Bibliography* (New York and London, 1985), no. 5855. Jean Héroard, *Journal* (Paris, 1989), 121–23.

90

DANIEL DUMONSTIER

George Villers, premier duc de Buckingham (George Villers, first duke of Buckingham)

Cabinet des Estampes, Na 24 Rés., fol. 13

Trois crayons (black, red, and white chalk) with pastel highlights on backed paper; 42.1 × 33.2 cm. Inscribed "Le duc de Boukinkan 1625." Originally in Philippe de Béthune's collection, then acquired by the abbey of Sainte-Geneviève.

Daniel was the last Dumonstier (or Dumoustier), a dynasty of court portraitists that distinguished itself throughout the 16th century. Although an illegitimate child, Daniel (ca. 1574–1646) obtained in 1603 the reversion of the title of painter and valet to the king that his uncle Etienne had held. In spite of Daniel's affectation of coarseness (which Tallemant des Réaux evoked when describing him as beastly in speech but good-natured), he was in touch with the best minds of his generation (notably Peiresc and Malherbe), collected books and medals, and was considered by the abbé de Marolles to be one of the glories of his age.

> Daniel Du Moutier eut une âme sincère.
> Travaillant en crayon, il s'en fit de l'honneur.
> En cela son savoir fut rempli de bonheur
> Sa parole était douce et sa piqure amère.
>
> (Daniel Du Moutier was sincere of soul.
> Working with chalk, he met with much honor.
> In that, his skills found a happy goal. His words
> were soft-spoken but his sting, bitter.)

Daniel was granted lodgings in the Louvre galleries, near the engraver Michel Lasne, to whom he taught much. There Dumonstier was better placed than anyone to draw all the individuals peopling the brilliant court of

Henry IV and Marie de Médicis, and later at the court of Anne of Austria (who commissioned Dumonstier to do the portrait of the young Louis XIII, as recounted in the diary kept by the royal physician Héroard). The scholar and art connoisseur Nicolas de Peiresc himself admitted that he "could not get Dumonstier to do anything, because for two months he scarcely budged from the Louvre for having done portraits of queens, princess, and ladies of the courts with such diligence that he almost died." Dumonstier's style was a little old-fashioned for the day, and he used only lead point and black chalk, with a few pastel highlights. He tended to flatter his models – "They are so stupid," he claimed, "that they think they are just the way I draw them, and they pay me better." His art thus lacked the realism that inspired subsequent engravings, which contributed to the greater glory of artists like Robert Nanteuil.

In any event, this 1625 portrait of the duke of Buckingham (1592–1628), then aged thirty-two, is probably accurate and is very similar to the large portrait painted by Van Dyck the same year (Florence, Pitti Museum). James I's former favorite was in Paris for the second time, in order to confirm the marriage contract between the young King Charles I and Princess Henriette; this was the historical setting exploited by Alexandre Dumas in *The Three Musketeers* for the famous incident of Anne of Austria's gift of diamond aglets. C. Dulong has demonstrated, moreover, the veracity of this incident, spiritedly describing the lady-killing duke's "slender waist, athletic shoulders, and soft gaze. It is rare to encounter such a felicitous marriage of gracefulness and virility, which were exactly the qualities appreciated during an age of lace-wearing warriors. "Buckingham's lace collar," continues Dulong, "makes a fine setting for his perfect face–thin, triangular, and imposing, lit by a little smile that speaks volumes. The eyes are brown [here Dumonstier is more accurate, for the duke's eyes were light-colored] and the hair tawny, as is the fine moustache. The only things British about this handsome, sombre hero are his complexion and build. Physically and mentally he effervesces." It is unlikely that Dumonstier ever saw either Van Dyck's painting or the anonymous 1616 portrait of Buckingham in his Order of the Garter apparel (London, National Portrait Gallery). He certainly must have drawn the seductive ambassador from life, with a veracity that testifies to his real talent.

François Fossier

221

H. Bouchot, *Les portraits aux crayons des XVIe et XVIIe siècles conservés à la Bibliothèque Nationale...* (Paris, 1884), 150. J. Adhémar, "Les dessins de Daniel Dumonstier du Cabinet des Estampes," *Gazette des beaux-arts,* March 1970: no. 27. *Marie de Médicis et le palais du Luxembourg,* exhibition at the Palais du Luxembourg (Paris, 1991), no. 153.

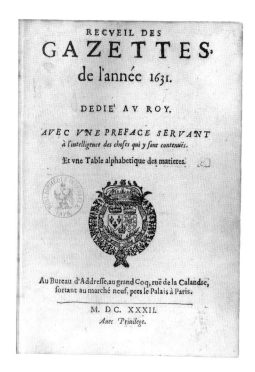

RECVEIL DES
GAZETTES.
de l'année 1631.

DEDIE' AV ROY.

AVEC VNE PREFACE SERVANT
à l'intelligence des chofes qui y font contenuës.
Et vne Table alphabetique des matieres.

Au Bureau d'Addreſſe, au grand Coq, ruë de la Calandre,
ſortant au marché neuf, pres le Palais à Paris.

M. DC. XXXII.
Auec Priuilege.

91
Recueil de "Gazettes"
(Collection of *Gazettes*) for the
year 1631
Réserve des livres rares, Rés. 4to Lc^2. 1,
title page and portrait

Paris: Au bureau d'adresses au Grand Coq, 1632.
Quarto; bound in red morocco with the arms of
Rochechouart Mortemart (the family of marquise de
Montespan). Portrait of Théophraste Renaudot
engraved by Michel Lasnes in 1644. Probably
acquired by the Bibliothèque Nationale between
1792 and 1837.

Generally considered as the first evidence of
a French newspaper, the *Gazette* was published on May 30, 1631, in Paris by Théophraste Renaudot's "bureau d'adresse," a
kind of news agency. Renaudot, who was
physician in ordinary to Louis XIII, was anxious to help the poor obtain employment. He
created a "bureau d'adresse" where advertise-
ments were not only feverishly consulted on
the spot but were also printed and sold as
lists. Imitating commercial English broadsheets and Dutch and Venetian gazettes,
Renaudot added worldwide news to his lists
and gave them the title *Gazette*. The word is
derived from the Italian *gazetta*, which itself
came from the Venetian *gazeta*, a little coin
given in exchange for a news sheet. Later the
word *journal* (newspaper) gradually replaced
gazette.

Cardinal Richelieu, who worked assiduously to restore royal authority, understood
the advantage the government could take of
news circulated in this way. A gazette could
hush up rumors and produce an idealized
image of the king. Louis XIII granted
Renaudot (1586–1653) exclusive rights to publish news. The *Gazette* appeared every Friday
as a four-page in quarto booklet. It immediately won great popularity, and at the end of
the year the operation doubled in size with
the publication of a second four-page booklet
entitled *Nouvelles ordinaires de divers endroits*
(General news from various places).

Like foreign gazettes of the time,
Renaudot's news sheet was a newspaper in
epistolary style. It contained a series of
reports from various European cities and
from France, the older news preceding more
recent events. A perfect instrument of government, the *Gazette* received contributions
written in their entirety by the king or
Richelieu, which were hastily inserted for
publication.

On Louis XIII's death in 1643, Renaudot
obtained an extension of his privilege from
the queen regent, Anne of Austria, and support from Cardinal Mazarin, so the *Gazette*
remained a government organ right up to the
end of the monarchy.

When Renaudot died in 1653, his sons
continued his work. In 1762 the *Gazette*
changed its title to *Gazette de France*, and in
1792 it became a daily newspaper. The *Gazette*
de France was published until 1915, and thus
it was not only the first French newspaper
but the one that had the longest run, almost
three hundred years.

This collection of *Gazettes* from 1631 is
bound in red morocco with the arms of the
Rochechouart de Mortemart family, related to
the marquise Montespan, proving the interest
of the nobility in this periodical news sheet.
The provincial nobility and middle classes
could also satisfy their thirst for news thanks
to the many reprints of the *Gazette* in Lyon,
Rouen, Strasbourg, and elsewhere.

Laurence Varret

Eugène Hatin, *Bibliographie historique et critique de la presse*
périodique française (Paris, 1866), 3–12. Gilles Feyel, "Gazette
[de France]," in *Dictionnaire des journaux, 1600–1789* (Paris,
1991), 443–49.

92

JACQUES CALLOT

Obsidio Rupellae. Siège de La Rochelle
(Siege of La Rochelle)

Cabinet des Estampes, Ed 25

223

Etching and drypoint; 146 × 167 cm; 1629–1630

Jacques Callot (ca. 1592–1635) was an etcher
from Lorraine who served an apprenticeship
with a goldsmith in Nancy. At age fifteen, like
many other artists from Lorraine, he set off
for Italy and studied burin and etching techniques under Antonio Tempesta in Florence.
Callot then created a new technique by
engraving on a hard ground that made it pos-

sible to etch with the precision and the freedom of drawing in pen and ink. This enabled him to achieve extraordinary miniature engravings and to represent crowds of people in small areas. *Siège de La Rochelle* is a good example in a very large format. Here Callot describes in a single picture the principal events that took place from the beginning of the siege of the city in September 1627 until its surrender on Nov. 1, 1628.

The engraving was ordered by King Louis XIII immediately after the city's capitulation. Callot executed it in 1629–1630 and received for his work the enormous sum of 12,000 livres. Six plates in juxtaposition form a vast map showing the town, the coast, and the hinterland. The work is completed by ten framing borders given over to captions, dedications, and listings of the principal incidents of the siege, with portraits of Louis XIII and his brother, Gaston d'Orléans. Callot actually engraved only two of the plates; the remaining borders were done by his Parisian collaborators, Michel Lasne, Abraham Bosse, and perhaps Israël Henriet. The six large copperplates used for the engraving have been at the Chalcography Department of the Louvre since 1861.

When La Rochelle, a center of Protestant resistance, was besieged in 1627, Richelieu, to block English aid, closed off access from the sea by a gigantic dike, shown in the middle of the engraving with all the details of its construction. After holding out for more than a year, the town surrendered, an event that can be seen at the bottom of the upper-left plate, where Louis XIII receives the deputies from La Rochelle who have come to beg his pardon. The king's triumphal entry in the conquered town is detailed in the adjacent plate.

Françoise Jestaz

J. Lieure, *Jacques Callot: Catalogue de l'oeuvre gravé*, 5 vols. (Paris, 1927), 660–61, no. 655. *Jacques Callot*, exhibition at the Musée Historique Lorrain, Nancy (Paris, 1992).

93
La Guirlande de Julie
(Julie's garland)
Département des Manuscrits, NAF 19735, fol. 2

Vellum; III + 100 + II fols.; 300 × 220 mm. Bound in red morocco decorated here and there with an interlaced L *and* J *by Le Gascon. Paris, 1641. Painted by Nicolas Robert. Offered May 22, 1641, to Lucine-Julie d'Angennes; purchased in Paris in 1726 at the sale of books belonging to the chevalier de B. by the abbé de Rothelin, who gave it to M. de Boze; acquired at the sale of de Boze's collection in 1753 by President De Cotte. In 1769 the volume passed into the collections of Gaignat and la Vallière; acquired by the London bookseller Payne, it became the property of the duke of Uzès; purchased in 1989 from the Ganay family by the Bibliothèque Nationale.*

From the moment in 1631 when Charles de Sainte-Maure, future duke of Montausier (1610–1690), was first introduced to the eldest daughter of the marquise de Rambouillet, Lucine-Julie d'Angennes (1607–1671), he fell madly in love with her. Mother and daughter had made the "chambre bleue" in the Rambouillet residence the most sought-after salon of the Parisian literary and fashionable world, a place where the self-important mingled with individuals of real talent. It was the center of a society that Molière would later immortalize in comedies like *Les Précieuses ridicules*, *Le Misanthrope*, and *Les Femmes savantes*.

As early as 1632 the young Montausier conceived the notion of preparing for his "mortal goddess" a collection of verses that would take as its theme flowers to exalt allegorically Julie's beauty and other qualities. To weave this symbolic garland, Montausier collaborated with the most fashionable poets of his time, including Chapelain, Ménage, Tallemant des Réaux, and Scudéry. Julie received the collected verses in 1634 and expressed thanks to the authors, though without undue emotion. During the next six years, Montausier was caught up in the turmoil of the Thirty Years War (1618–1648), winning fame for his heroism and consoling himself during his absence by writing sonnets to Julie and letters to his friends.

Faced with the apparent indifference of a lady whose heart was more difficult to con-

LA
GVIRLANDE
DE
IVLIE.

quer than a fortress, the marquis returned to his notion of the garland, but this time in a version the lavishness of which matched the extravagance of his fictional passion. The result was the masterpiece exhibited here.

Montausier entrusted the calligraphy of the text to Nicolas Jarry (ca. 1620–before 1674), the most skillful specialist of the period and one who excelled in imitating actual printing. The job of illustrating the book was given to artist of prodigious talent, Nicolas Robert (1614–1685). The crown of flowers on folio 2, decorating the title page, definitively justifies the painter's renown. The depiction of variegated tulip petals, pulpy and at the same time silky, on folio 46, reveals the level of perfection Robert had attained even before he reached the height of his fame with the much-admired botanical plates he painted for Gaston d'Orléans, brother of Louis XIII. The artist's scientific rigor in his work for scholars did not exclude elegance from his compositions, as is particularly noticeable in the bouquet of violets on folio 34.

On May 22, 1641, the feast day of Sainte Julie, Montausier offered his superb gift to Mademoiselle d'Angennes. Three years later he married her. Thanks to the art of Jarry and Robert, the sixty-two verses, the picture of the crown, the portrait of Zephyrus (fol. 4), and the twenty-nine flowers form a garland that blooms forever.

Marie-Thérèse Gousset

Abbé J.-J. de Rive, *Notices historiques et critiques de deux manuscrits uniques et très précieux de la bibliothèque de M. le duc de La Vallière dont l'un a pour titre: "La guirlande de Julie," et l'autre, "Recueil de fleurs et insectes peints par Daniel Rabel en 1624"* (Paris, 1779), 1–36. J.-C. Brunet, *Manuel du libraire et de l'amateur de livres*, 2d ed., vol. 2 (Paris, 1814), 172. M. de Marolles, *Le livre des peintres et graveurs*, 2d ed., ed. G. Duplessis (Paris, 1872; repr. Geneva, 1973), 39. A. Schnapper, *Le Géant, la licorne et la tulipe: Collections françaises au XVIIème siècle* (Paris, 1988), 58, color ill. on front cover. A. Schnapper and G. Aymonin, *Daniel Rabel: Cent fleurs et insectes* (Paris, 1991), 14. I. Frain, *La Guirlande de Julie* (Paris, 1991).

94

MADELEINE DE SCUDÉRY

Clélie: Histoire romaine, première partie
(Clélie: A Roman story, part 1)
Réserve des livres rares, Rés. Y². 1496,
Carte du tendre

Paris: Augustin Courbé, 1654. 602 pp.; 8ᵛᵒ. Bound in red morocco with gold fillets and flat tooled spine, 17th century. Confiscated from Gilbert de Voisins during the Revolution.

The publication from 1654 to 1660 of *Clélie* represented the high point of Madeleine de Scudéry's career as a fiction writer. Although the book bore the name of Georges de Scudéry, there was never any doubt at the time that his sister Madeleine had written it. Born in 1607, orphaned young with little wealth, Madeleine was nevertheless able to acquire a refined education and to enter Parisian high-society circles alongside her brother, who was also a literary figure. She was a regular at the sophisticated salons hosted by the marquise de Rambouillet, where she met scholars and members of the Académie Française. After sojourning in Marseille from 1644 to 1646, Madeleine de Scudéry encountered great success with a long novel, *Le grand Cyrus*, published from 1649 on. A new circle formed around her (more literary and less purely social than the one around the marquise de Rambouillet), in which the ideals of preciosity and Platonic love were carried to an extreme.

Scudéry depicted the regulars at her Saturday gatherings in a new novel, *Clélie*, that she began writing in 1653. The story, set in Rome, served as pretext for the description of numerous acquaintances, hôtels, and palaces, as well as long dialogues on worldliness, heroism, and morality in love, all based on actual conversations held among her entourage. The book's success notably stems from the pleasure contemporary readers took in trying to identify the players in the little world she portrayed. But Scudéry refused to divulge the key to this roman à clef, so precise identification remains uncertain, even though some of the characters are recognizable, such as the writer Paul Pellisson (then in love with Madeleine), Madame de Sévigné,

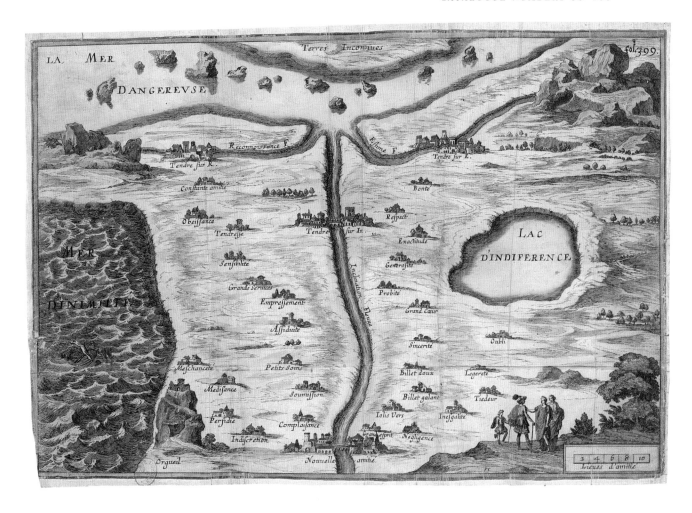

the superintendent of finances Nicolas Fouquet (to whom Madeleine would remain loyal even after his arrest), and the writer Paul Scarron and his wife (the future Madame de Maintenon).

But the most immediate stir was created by the *Carte du tendre*, or Map of Affection, engraved by François Chauveau and inserted in the first part of the novel. It was a salon game invented during the winter of 1653–1654 to retrace the progress of Pellisson's affection, and it sparked a fad for "amorous geography" that took the form of allegorical almanacs and imaginary maps.

Geneviève Guilleminot-Chrétien

227

G. Mongrédien, *Mademoiselle de Scudéry et son salon* (Paris, 1946). A.-M. Bassy, "Supplément au Voyage de Tendre," *Bulletin du Bibliophile* 1982: 13–33. R. Godenne, *Les romans de Mademoiselle de Scudéry* (Geneva, 1983), 195–299. N. Aronson, *Mademoiselle de Scudéry, ou le voyage au Pays de tendre* (Paris, 1986).

95

*Le cardinal Mazarin dans la galerie
haute de son palais*
(Cardinal Mazarin in the upper
gallery of his palace)
Cabinet des Estampes, AA4 Rés.

*Engraving by Robert Nanteuil and Pierre Van
Schuppen, after François Chauveau. Signed bottom
left: "Nanteuil 1659, F. Chauveau delineavit." 47.6 ×
56.9 cm.*

Cardinal Mazarin, trusted counsellor of
Richelieu and later prime minister under
Anne of Austria during the minority of Louis
XIV (1643–1661), is pictured in the upper
gallery of his Parisian residence (the future
Bibliothèque Royale, later the Bibliothèque
Nationale), surrounded by his collection of
paintings and antiquities. The engraving by
Nanteuil and Van Schuppen was intended to
decorate the top section of the thesis defend-

ed by Charles-Maurice Le Tellier, the future archbishop of Reims. It shows statues and busts set in shell-shaped niches, with paintings hung on walls "tendus de damas rouge cramoisi semé des armes et chiffre du cardinal" (covered in a crimson damask patterned with the cardinal's arms and monogram). In the rear of the gallery is Guido Reni's *David*, now in the Louvre. An immense carpet more than forty meters long covers the floor, and in the foreground Mazarin, clad in cardinal purple, poses with several objects from his collection.

In 1643 Mazarin rented from a high magistrate named Tubeuf a residence located at the intersection of rue Neuve des Petits-Champs and rue Vivienne, which he purchased in 1649. This palace Mazarin never considered to be other than a showcase for his collections and a decorative setting for his entertainments. In fact, he only resided there for a few days just before his death in 1661. From the time he took the palace over in 1643, he found it too confining, and though he was only a tenant, he obliged the landlord to go to the considerable expense of remodeling it.

Although the architect François Mansart began the work, he fell out with Tubeuf and Pierre Le Muet succeeded him in May 1646. To exhibit the cardinal's rich collections, two galleries, one above the other, were planned. These have been almost wholly preserved and are now the Gallerie Mansart and the Gallerie Mazarine of the Bibliothèque nationale de France. The taste for galleries, which dated from the 16th century, was launched by Francis I at Fontainebleau, then introduced in the great palaces of Rome, and subsequently flowered once again in France, especially in Paris (as in the Hôtels Bullion and Séguier).

Loyal to his Italian taste, Mazarin stubbornly sought artists from his country of origin to decorate his Paris residence. Thus he invited Giovanni Francesco Romanelli (ca. 1610–1662), the pupil of Pietro da Cortona, to execute the frescoes of the upper gallery: mythological and pseudohistorical subjects are painted on the vault, with landscapes by Giovanni Francesco Grimaldi (1606–1680), pupil of the Carraccis, in the ceiling arches over the windows and the niches facing them. The lower gallery, reserved for ancient and modern statuary, was decorated by the same Grimaldi in grisaille with false architectural effects and stuccos framing the *M* and the cardinal's hat.

The 1661 inventory of the collection listed 450 paintings (most by Italian painters, with a few from the northern schools and even fewer French paintings), 78 tapestries and hangings, 120 Greek and Roman antiquities, and 126 busts, not counting the furniture, jewelry, table service, and the incomparable library richly furnished with more than 30,000 books.

This was the largest fortune in the whole of the 17th century, and Mazarin during his lifetime refused to have it inventoried. The executors of his will, however, were obliged to do so. A part of the inheritance, the smallest portion, was assigned to his nephew by marriage, the duke de Mazarin, husband of Hortense Mancini. The largest part was dispersed among the galleries, the libraries, and the palace of Louis XIV and Colbert. Thus "a goodly part was preserved" (P. Goubert).

Françoise Jestaz

229

G. J. de Cosnac, *Les richesses du Palais Mazarin* (Paris, 1884). *Mazarin, homme d'Etat et collectionneur, 1602–1661,* exhibition at the Bibliothèque Nationale (Paris, 1961). Roger-Armand Weigert, "Le Palais Mazarin: Architectes et décorateurs," *Art de France* 2: 147–65. Simone Balayé, *La Bibliothèque Nationale des origines à 1800* (Geneva, 1988), 174–81. Claude Dulong, *La fortune de Mazarin* (Paris, 1990). Pierre Goubert, *Mazarin* (Paris, 1990).

96

RASHÎD AL-DÎN

Recueil d'oeuvres théologiques
(Collection of theological works)

Département des Manuscrits, Division
Orientale, Arabe 2324, fol. 168

Fadl Allâh ibn Abî l-Khayr Alî Rashîd
al-Dîn, *al-Madjmû'a al-Rashîdiyya*

Paper; 375 fols.; 535 × 385 mm. Ottoman overlapping binding (end of 16th century). Made at Tabriz (Iran), between A.H. 707 and 170 (A.D. 1307–1310). Calligraphed by Muhammad ibn Mahmûd al-Baghdâdî and illuminated by Muhammad ibn al-'Af'îf al-Kâshî. Passed from the Bibliothèque de Mazarin into the royal collection in 1668.

Among the many manuscripts from Mazarin's library that entered the royal collection in 1668 were 343 Oriental books, many of which were Arabic manuscripts dispatched from Istanbul by the ambassador Denys de la Haye. By virtue of its content, physical appearance, and composition, this manuscript is an especially important monument

for the period of the Il-Khâns, the Mongol dynasty that reigned in Persia in the 13th and 14th centuries.

Rashîd al-Dîn played a key role when the dynasty converted to Islam. Physician to King Abaqa (1265–1282), he rapidly rose to become vizier. A man of Persian culture who succeeded in mastering Arabic, Rashîd al-Dîn accompanied Abaqa's successor, King Ghâzan (1295–1394), as his translator at the surrender of Rahba (Syria). In the same way that monarchs built magnificent palaces, Rashîd built a new neighborhood in the city of Tabriz that bore his name, Rab' Rashîdî. He erected student residences, founded a library with sixty thousand volumes, and promoted artisans of the book trade: papermakers, copyists who worked under the careful supervision of scholars, illuminators, and binders.

Encouraged by the sultan Uljaytu (1304–1316), Rashîd al-Dîn published a collection of his own theological writings. At the beginning of the work were attestations by seventy scholars concerning its conformity to the Koran. The work itself was divided into four books: the Book of Explanations (Tawdîhât), the Book of the Key to the Commentaries (Miftâh al-tafâsîr), the Book of Prophecy (Al-Sultâniyya), and the Book of Verities That Attract Grace (Latâ'if al haqâ'iq). In his preface, Rashîd asked that a copy on large leaves, called "Baghdâdî," be made and deposited at the mosque at Rab' Rashîdî and that other copies be disseminated to various places.

The names of the calligraphers and illuminators of this carefully decorated volume appear in the marginal floral ornaments of the two tapestrylike frontispieces (fols. 3v–4). The pattern is based on tapered fleurons that define lobed quatrefoils with shaded background. Each treatise is preceded by a frontispiece that features the title and table of chapters in cartouches ornamented by floral motifs in different colors (especially brick red). The corners of the frame are decorated by trelliswork. At the beginning of each treatise, a rosette (fols. 167v–168) bears the author's name, Rashîd, and the title.

Certain decorative elements on these pages link this manuscript, executed at Tabriz, with the Koran calligraphed at Baghdad by Yâqût al Musta'sîmî (BNF Arabe 6716). Both use the same colors in the floral ornaments: sea-green, carmine, and carmine wash.

According to the *Dharî'a*, the best Korans–including six by the famous Baghdad calligrapher Yâqût al Musta'sîmî–were given as *waqf*, pious founder's gifts, to the mosque Rab' Rashîdî. The mosque founded by Rashîd al-Dîn, influenced by Baghdad and Iran, became a center of important editorial production and cultural exchange.

Yvette Sauvan

E. M. Quatremère, *Histoire des Mongols de la Perse écrite par Rashîd Eldin* (Paris, 1836), preface. I. Stchoukine, *La peinture iranienne sous les derniers abbasides et les Il-Khâns* (Bruges, 1936). R. Ettinghausen, "Manuscript Illuminations," in *Survey of Persian Art*, ed. A. U. Pope (Oxford, 1939). *Mazarin, homme d'Etat et collectionneur, 1602–1661,* exhibition at the Bibliothèque Nationale (Paris, 1961). Muhammad Muhsin al-Tahrâni, *Darî'a ilâ tasanîf al'Shî'a* (Najaf-Téhéran, 1936–1978). B. Gray, ed., *Arts of the Book in Central Asia* (Paris and London, 1979).

97
Evangiles éthiopiens (Ethiopian Gospels)

Département des Manuscrits, Division Orientale, Ethiopien 32, fols. 7v–8, 6v–7

Parchment; 207 fols.; 290 × 210 mm. Ethiopia, 14th century. Acquired for Chancellor Séguier (1588–1672) in Egypt. Gift of Mgr de Coislin, bishop of Metz (1697–1732), to the abbey of Saint-Germain-des-Prés. Deposited in the Bibliothèque Nationale in 1796 with the abbey's collections.

This is one of the oldest Ethiopian manuscripts in the Bibliothèque Nationale. Its decoration and script suggest a date in the 14th century. The book was given to the monastery of the Apostles of Mount Qwesqwam by Sayfa Ar'ad, king of Ethiopia (1344–1371), but it is not possible to determine whether Sayfa Ar'ad had it copied and illustrated or whether he simply gave it to the monastery as a gift.

Dayr al-Muharraqa, in Egypt, which the Ethiopians called Qwesqwam, was a Coptic monastery where an important community of forty Ethiopian monks resided during the 14th century after receiving pilgrims en route to Jerusalem. The last leaves of the manuscript contain rules and documents, dating

231

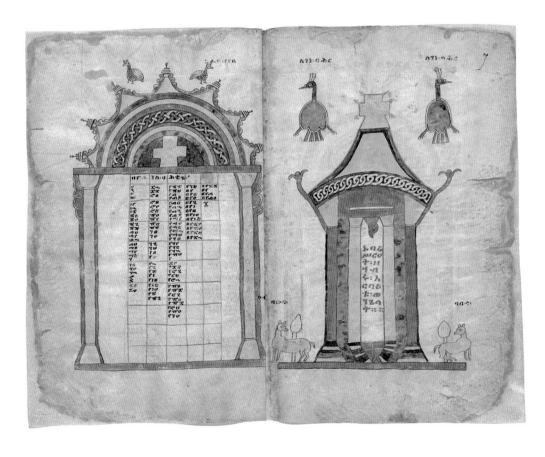

from the 14th to 16th centuries, concerning the monastery.

In this manuscript, as in most Coptic, Armenian, and Jacobite Syrian Gospel manuscripts, the Four Gospels are preceded by the Epistle from Eusebius to Carpianus, the Canon tables of Eusebius of Caesarea, and a brief treatise on the harmony of the Gospels. The manuscript is decorated with paintings that represent the Crucifixion (fol. 7v), Resurrection (fol. 8), Christ in Majesty (fol. 8v), and the Evangelists Matthew (fol. 11v), Mark (68v), Luke (104v), and John (162v), and are among the oldest known Ethiopian illuminations.

On the left (fol. 6v) is displayed the last page of the Canon tables of Eusebius, decorated with peacocks–the symbol of eternity–as often found both in Oriental copies (Armenia, Syria, Egypt, etc.) and in the Western copies of this text (see cat. 6). On the right (fol. 7) is a representation of the "Fountain of Life," a theme whose origin here seems to be Syrian and which is often found at the end of the tables. Deer symbolizing the faithful drink from a spring covered by a simple structure, symbolizing the word of God.

The manuscript was purchased in Egypt for Chancellor Pierre Séguier (1588–1672) and shipped from Cairo around 1646 by Jean Magy the merchant, whose wax seal is visible on folio 1. Subsequently, it entered the library of Mgr de Coislin, bishop of Metz from 1697 to 1732, who bequeathed it to the library of the abbey of Saint-Germain-des-Prés in Paris. In 1796 it was deposited in the Bibliothèque Nationale when the abbey's property was confiscated.

Francis Richard

H. Zotenberg, *Catalogue des manuscrits éthiopiens (Gheez et amharique) de la Bibliothèque Nationale* (Paris, 1877), 24–29. J. Leroy, *Les manuscrits à peintures: Ethiopie* (Paris and New York, 1961), 8. *Trésors d'Orient*, exhibition at the Bibliothèque Nationale, Paris, 1973, no. 112. *D'Axoum à Gondar: Monnaies et manuscrits éthiopiens de la Bibliothèque Nationale*, exhibition at the Bibliothèque Nationale (Paris, 1988), 5, no. 1. S. Uhlig, *Athiopische Paläographie* (Stuttgart, 1988), 249–51.

98

ISRAËL SILVESTRE

Veue et perspective de Vaux-le-Vicomte du costé du jardin
(Perspective view of Vaux-le-Vicomte from the garden side)

Cabinet des Estampes, Va 420

Etching; 42.4 × 73 cm ("traits carrés"); 47.2 × 73.5 cm (plate); bottom left, signature: "Israël Silvestre delineavit et sculpsit"; on the right: "cum privilegio Regis."

Vaux (now Vaux-le-Vicomte, fifty kilometers southeast of Paris) was the domain of Nicolas Fouquet, superintendent of finance for Louis XIV from 1653 to 1661. When he purchased it in 1641, it was only a modest castle with outbuildings and property consisting of a park, some arable farmland, and peasant houses. Fouquet enlarged it first by buying the hamlets of Maison-Rouge and Jumeaux, but for fifteen years he was too busy with his career to give any thought to Vaux's renovation. Only when he became minister of state and superintendent of finance did he decide to develop the property on an order of magnificence appropriate to his rank.

To meet his objective, he invited the best artists of the crown: Louis Le Vau, chief architect for the Bâtiments du Roi (royal buildings) since the death of Lemercier (1654), then busily modernizing the château of Vincennes for the king; Charles Le Brun, painter in ordinary to the king since 1646 (and actually first painter designate, though not declared out of consideration for Poussin, the holder of the title); and André Le Nôtre, the landscape architect of the Tuileries. Contrary to an accepted notion, Fouquet cannot be credited with discovering the masters who were soon to create Louis XIV's Versailles; he borrowed them from the king's service.

Le Vau drew up the plans for the château at Vaux and construction began in 1656. Its

233

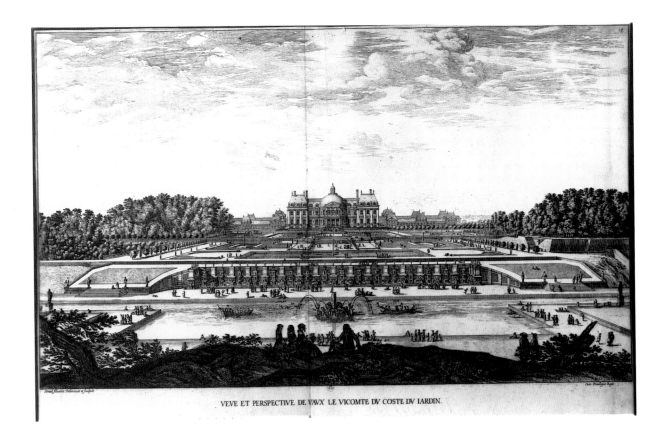

VEVE ET PERSPECTIVE DE VAVX LE VICOMTE DV COSTE DV IARDIN.

most original feature is the central grand salon "à l'italienne," that is, a salon two stories high in a rotunda-style building projecting out sharply on the garden façade and covered by a dome of obvious baroque inspiration. The salon separates two symmetrical apartments on the ground floor: on the right, one intended for the king and on the left, the splendid apartment for the master of the house. Contrary to tradition, in this château the *piano nobile* (literally, grand floor) is the ground floor and the second floor is given over to private apartments. The castle was built of stone from Creil, considered nobler (and also more costly) than the brick that was customarily employed in the construction of French châteaux and that originally had been planned; this was reserved for the outbuildings. In September 1657, the masonry and roof were almost finished; Fouquet's haste to see his residence completed was such that he spent money lavishly.

Le Brun, who had already worked for Fouquet in his house at Saint-Mandé near Paris, was entrusted with the decoration of the château and directed a team of painters and sculptors, just as he would soon do at Versailles for Louis XIV. He glorified the minister without stint, employing mythology and ancient history whose symbolic meaning was clearly understood at that time: Hercules

illustrates Fouquet's power, Apollo his intellect and taste for the arts.

The garden laid out at the foot of the castle was one of Le Nôtre's first major creations, and in it the principles that would dominate all his work can already be discerned. He transformed all the natural aspects of the site, for example, streams and the slope of the terrain, using them to full advantage and arranging natural resources in a masterful hierarchy. A great central axis traverses the whole composition extending from the entry through the middle of the château and descending through the flowerbeds to the transverse valley transformed into a canal, then rising to the top of the hill.

This is the vantage point of the engraver. The château, wholly free and unconstrained on its terrace, dominates the landscape with a commanding view on all sides, all the more so since tall wooded plantings were kept at a distance. The effect of the principal view is accentuated by the regular slope of the land, and at the same time compensated for by the progressive widening of water basins. The minor transversal axes conclude with special landscaping effects, the most important, at the bottom of the hill, being the Grand Canal (in the foreground of the engraving), which is nine hundred meters long and which ties in with the natural landscape.

Here, then, is the expression of the classic concept of a French garden, which implies an absolute domination of site by means of perspectives. The French tradition differs from the Italian, which had reigned all-powerful until then and which consisted of juxtaposing enclosed gardens centered on some special landscaping effect or on a fountain.

Because of the scope, the beauty, and the unity of its construction, Vaux became the universal masterpiece of French art in Mazarin's time. When Fouquet was foolish enough to invite Louis XIV on Aug. 17, 1661, to a magnificent entertainment recorded in the poem by La Fontaine (cat. 99), he sealed his fate in the mind of a king already worried about the power of his minister and the origin of his fortune and who was, to boot, jealous of Vaux's splendor. Fouquet was arrested, judged, convicted for embezzlement, and sentenced to life in prison. His collections were confiscated by the king and the construction work at Vaux was abruptly halted. Its artists were brought into the king's service. Vaux represents a decisive step in the formation of the *style Louis XIV* and an important moment in the history of French art.

Israël Silvestre (1621–1691) took as the vantage point for his engraving the hilltop that closes off the view from the château, where a colossal replica of the *Hercule Farnèse* statue stands today, which provides a perfect view of the château's scenic site but downplays the impression of its architecturally baroque character by making almost imperceptible the forceful projection of the central rotunda. Although the engraving is undated, it is unlikely that it could have been done after Fouquet's disgrace and should be dated from the year of the king's visit, when the estate had reached a state of virtual perfection.

Françoise Jestaz

Jean Cordey, *Le château de Vaux-le-Vicomte* (Paris, 1927). Daniel Dessert, *Fouquet* (Paris, 1987).

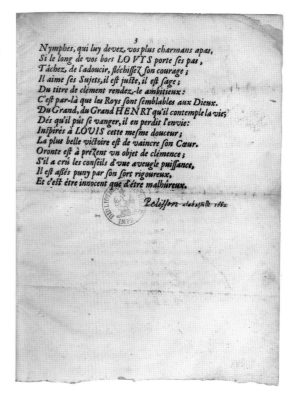

99

JEAN DE LA FONTAINE

Elégie [aux nymphes de Vaux]
(Elegy [to the nymphs of Vaux])
Réserve des livres rares, Rés. Ye. 1031, p. 3

Paris, ca. 1662. Three pp.; 4to.

On Aug. 17, 1661, Nicolas Fouquet, marquis de Belle-Isle, superintendent of finance, gave a sumptuous entertainment in honor of Louis XIV in his new residence, Vaux-le-Vicomte, built between 1656 and 1661 by the architect Louis Le Vau. Surrounded by writers and poets like Molière, Perrault, Ménage, and Racine, and by artists and scholars, Fouquet knew how to reward talent in a pleasant and agreeable way.

In 1661 Jean de La Fontaine was forty years old. The future author of the *Fables* was still an unknown. His sole work, a comedy in imitation of Terence, *L'Eunuque* (The eunuch), published in 1654, had been a failure. In a letter to François de Maucroix, an old friend who was then in Rome on business for Fouquet, La Fontaine extolled the festivities that had so bedazzled him. Moving rapidly over the splendor of the dinners and the walks in the gardens and park designed by

André Le Nôtre, he lingered over Molière's play *Les Fâcheux* (The bores), which Molière himself called the first comedy-ballet to be "conceived, written, learned, and performed in fifteen days." He was fascinated by this art of depicting characters from life.

Fouquet, however, wound up by sealing his fate with this extravaganza. The individual whose motto was "To what will I not rise?" learned to his chagrin that it was unwise to rival the king, even if the king was only twenty-three years old. Indeed, the display of such luxury did displease Louis XIV. The king had already been convinced by Colbert that Fouquet was administering the royal finances dishonestly and was using his office for personal enrichment at the king's expense. On Sept. 5, 1661, Fouquet was arrested in Nantes, and on Dec. 31 he was imprisoned in the château of Vincennes.

La Fontaine was so upset that he became ill. The arrest forced him to realize that he had accomplished nothing of importance. He who had wished to equal Terence had merely written flattery of the mighty.

About March 1662 the *Elégie aux nymphes de Vaux* was published clandestinely and without indication of authorship, a short poem of three loose pages printed in italics. La Fontaine did not sign it until 1671. In the verse La Fontaine did not demand justice but rather appealed for the king's mercy in behalf of Fouquet.

> Nymphes, qui lui devez vos plus charmants
>   appas,
> Si le long de vos bords Louis porte ses pas,
> Tâchez de l'adoucir; fléchissez son courage.
> Il aime ses sujets, il est juste, il est sage,
> Du titre de clément rendez-le ambitieux:
> C'est par là que les rois sont semblables aux
>   dieux.

> (Nymphs, who owe him your most appealing charms, / If Louis makes his way along your shores / Try to soften him up; try to sway his will. / He is fond of his subjects, he is just, he is wise. / Make him long to be called merciful: / It is in clemency that kings most resemble the gods.)

Though written under the cloak of anonymity, his plea lacked neither courage nor beauty. Others, like Perrault, hastened to make people forget they had been Fouquet's friends. La Fontaine's verse was known first in manuscript, a copy of which is preserved in the Bibliothèque de l'Arsenal, but its circulation increased after it was printed. This edition is extremely rare. Only three copies are known, two of which are preserved in the Bibliothèque nationale de France.

This copy bears an inscription from the period on the first page: "Plainte sur les malheurs d'Oronte. M. Fouquet" (Complaint about the misfortunes of Oronte. M. Fouquet), and at the end of the poem in the same hand: "Pelisson à la Bastille 1662." This suggests that at first the *Elégie* was attributed to Paul Pellisson, Fouquet's principal agent, who was imprisoned in the Bastille because of his friendship with Fouquet.

Marie-Françoise Quignard

Roger Duchêne, *La Fontaine* (Paris, 1990). Jean de La Fontaine, *Oeuvres complètes*, vol. 2, *Oeuvres diverses*, ed. Pierre Clarac (Paris, 1991).

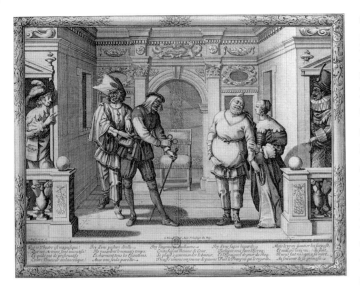

100

ABRAHAM BOSSE

L'Hôtel de Bourgogne

Cabinet des Estampes, Ed 30 Rés (G. D. 1268)

Etching; 25.4 × 31.5 cm; 1633–1634. Signed in the lower left-hand corner: "A. Bosse in et fe"; noted in the middle: "Le Blond excud. Avec privilège du Roy."

Abraham Bosse (1602–1676) has enabled us to glimpse a performance of a play by the Royal Company at the Hôtel de Bourgogne, a theater not far from the Louvre. Early in the 17th century, Paris had no permanent theater. To put on a show in Paris, a company could rent this hall in the Hôtel de Bourgogne, which belonged to the Confrérie de la Passion (a theatrical confraternity initially formed to present Passion plays). Otherwise, plays were performed in makeshift theaters such as halls used for playing tennis. Among the twenty or thirty short-lived companies for which records survive, the troupe of Robert Guérin, known as Gros-Guillaume, seems to have surpassed all the others. Established in 1615, it gave itself the title of Royal Company in 1629 and settled into the Hôtel de Bourgogne permanently after a decree was published by the King's Council that gave the members of the cast the title of King's Players.

Gros-Guillaume had two inseparable companions: Gaultier-Garguille and Turlupin. Masters of the art of farce, they were immensely enjoyed by Parisian audiences, and engravers made numerous grotesque portraits of them. The engraving by Abraham Bosse evokes a scene in which all three are represented: Turlupin on the left, playing the boastful, cowardly, and greedy valet; Gaultier-Garguille in the middle, dressed all in black, always playing old men and very much liked by audiences because his specialty was ribald songs; and Gros-Guillaume on the right, who played men's roles as well as women's, with a reputation for being irresistible. His belly, held in place between two belts, was a major attraction. A woman, probably Gaultier-Garguille's wife, also an actress in the same company, is beside him.

What play are they performing? It is very difficult to say. Few of these farces were written down, and the actors used only a summary outline while they improvised, inventing rejoinders from their imaginations, using rather rude and offensive language in scandalous situations.

The famous trio simply vanished when Gaultier-Garguille died in 1633, Gros-Guillaume in 1634, and Turlupin in 1637. Their demise marked the end of coarse Gallic farce, and the Hôtel de Bourgogne then devoted itself to literary theater, as a new repertory and style emerged with Racan, Rotrou, and Molière.

Bosse was one of the first engravers who brought to life French society under the reign of Louis XIII by depicting characters from every social class, and particularly from the petite bourgeoisie of the towns and countryside, who had not served as inspiration for artists until that time. This realistic portrayal of contemporary life was something new. Accurate descriptions of men's and women's dress, domestic habits, incidents from daily life, and urban and rural furnishings make the approximately fifteen hundred engravings left by this prolific artist infinitely precious. In his precision in drawing what he saw, Bosse was a most original engraver, not to mention a historian.

Françoise Jestaz

André Blum, *Abraham Bosse et la société française au XVIIe siècle* (Paris, 1924). Georges Mongrédien, *La vie quotidienne des comédiens au temps de Molière* (Paris, 1992).

237

IOI

PIERRE CORNEILLE

Andromède (Andromeda)

Réserve des livres rares, Rés. Yf. 604, fol. 57

Rouen: Laurens Maurry, near the Palace, 1651. [5] fols.; [1] fol. of plates. 124 pp. [6] fols. of folding set; 4ᵗᵒ. Copy from the Paris Monastery of the "Augustins déchaussés," confiscated in the Revolution and acquired during that period by the Bibliothèque Nationale.

After its last performance in 1693, Corneille's *Andromède* was forgotten. A simple fashionable entertainment, written to fulfill an official request, the subject was doubtless imposed on Corneille. The play appears incidental or even a mistake in the oeuvre of a dramatist whose work was consistently rooted in history.

For carnival time in 1647 Mazarin had arranged for the performance of *Orfeo*, an Italian opera written by abbé Buti, set to music by Luigi Rossi, with scenery and theatrical effects by Giacomo Torelli. Torelli, an Italian architect and painter whom Mazarin had brought to Paris, was the first to take advantage of mechanical contrivances to change scenery. In spite of the feeble libretto, Torelli scored a triumph. The dissatisfaction

that erupted against the cardinal, however, and which would result in the Fronde, rebounded against Italian opera. Under pressure of events, Mazarin requested Corneille, who was considered the leading dramatic poet in France since the triumph of his *Le Cid* in 1637, to compose a musical tragedy based on mythology which would be a gorgeous production reusing the scenery and stage effects constructed by Torelli for *Orfeo*.

Louis XIV's illness from smallpox, followed by the turmoil of the Fronde, delayed *Andromède*'s performance, which had been planned for the carnival festivities in 1648. It was performed by Molière's company at the end of January 1650 in the Petit-Bourbon Theater, which opened for the first time to the public. Charles Coypeau d'Assoucy's music, now partly lost, figured in only a limited way in the show.

On March 3, 1650, Corneille published the *Dessein de la tragédie d'Andromède*, a program intended to accompany the performances. The immense success the production enjoyed was described by Théophraste Renaudot in his *Gazette* of Feb. 18, 1650.

Printing of the original edition of the play was completed on Aug. 13, 1650, but its sale was delayed until 1651, probably because of the agitation caused by the Fronde. The second edition, completed on Aug. 13, 1651, contains six large plates and a frontispiece engraved by François Chauveau. The plates, twice the dimensions of the book's pages, bear the number of the page to which they correspond and were designed to be mounted on a binding strip. "Chaque acte aussi bien que le prologue a sa décoration particulière et du moins une machine volante" (Each act as well as the prologue has its special scenery and at least one flying machine). Because of the interest actors had in its depictions of scenery and stage machinery, this edition seems to have found constant use in 17th-century theater. The text of the second edition contains some unique variations in the series of editions Corneille corrected. This is one of the rare copies to contain all the plates.

Corneille penned a tribute to Torelli, nicknamed "the great magician," in the Argument: "Cette pièce n'est que pour les yeux" (This play is only for the eyes). These words allow us to place *Andromède* in the movement that was bringing French theater closer to opera and in which poetry, music, architecture, and painting all intertwined.

Marie-Françoise Quignard

E. Picot, *Bibliographie cornélienne* (Paris, 1876), 60–67. P. Bjurström, *Giacomo Torelli and the Baroque Stage* (Stockholm, 1961). Pierre Corneille, *Andromède*, ed. Christian Delmas (Paris, 1974).

102
Costumes for the Ballet royal de la Nuit (Royal ballet of the night)
Cabinet des Estampes, Collection Hennin no. 3674 (Warrior, Apollo, Lute Player)

Anonymous, ca. 1650. Drawings in gouache with gold highlights. 1. Warrior, 255 × 185 mm. 2. Apollo, 260 × 167 mm. 3. Lute Player, 270 × 185 mm.

The *Ballet royal de la Nuit* was first performed on Feb. 23, 1653, at the Petit-Bourbon Theater. The best artists of the day participated in a performance that recalled the sumptuous period that had preceded the somber years of the Fronde. Two composers, Jean de Cambefort and Jean-Baptiste de Boesset, wrote the required tunes and solos to verses by Isaac de Benserade (who would soon collaborate with the young Lully). The ballet also brought together the best ballet masters—Chancy, Mazuel, and Vertpré. Scenery and stage effects by Giacomo Torelli and costumes by Henry de Gissey contributed to the brilliance of this dazzling entertainment—as an exceptionally rich collection of iconographic sources reminds us. Four compilations contain numerous costumes and settings, two of them in Paris (the BnF and the Bibliothèque de l'Institut) and two in Great Britain (at Windsor Castle and at Waddesdon Manor, in the Rothschild collection). The Rothschild compilation was owned by Louis Hesselin, famous for the entertainments he organized in his home in Essonne (south of Paris), where in 1656 he received Queen Christine of Sweden.

The theme of the ballet was designed, as Marie-Françoise Christout has put it so well, "to allow for the alternation of poetic and farcical scenes, a constant switching from noble mythology to lively burlesque, from magical inspiration to allegory." Composed of forty-five entrées, or scenes divided into four

239

parts (corresponding to their performance in four lengthy sections throughout the night), it called for all the changes of scenery and the proliferation of characters of every variety that so dazzled the crowd of spectators. The fourth and last part ends with the appearance of Aurora, who soon yields her place to the rising Sun, Apollo, played the first time by King Louis XIV. The drawing of Apollo does indeed seem to resemble the young ruler. Here the king is performing the final ballet surrounded by various spirits, including Peace and Victory, so that all will realize what his future role will be. This tableaulike grand finale should not obscure the importance that Louis XIV gave to ballet as an activity. He danced this role of Apollo again for the last time on Feb. 4, 1670, in the *Divertissement royal des Amants magnifiques* (Royal divertissement of the magnificent lovers), but he also performed a wide range of roles—including plebeian characters— alongside dancers like Beauchamp and Raynal and musicians such as Lambert and Lully.

Many attributions have been proposed for these anonymous drawings—Henri de Beaubrun; the miniaturist Louis Van der Bruggen, nicknamed Hans; and the pastellist Nicolas Du Monstier—all of whom figure in the cast and credit lists in the librettos of court ballets of the period.

Catherine Massip

Marie-Françoise Christout, *Le ballet de cour de Louis XIV, 1643–1672: Mises en scène* (Paris, 1967), 68–71. Christout, *Le ballet de cour au XVIIe siècle* (Geneva, 1987). *Lully: Musicien soleil*, exhibition at Versailles, 1987, no. 21 (note by M.-F. Christout).

103

NICOLAS SANSON
Map of France
(showing fiscal districts)
Département des Cartes et Plans, Ge A 592

Paper; colored copper engraving; 1710 × 1790 mm.
Paris, 1652–1653. Purchased Aug. 23, 1872.

The name Nicolas Sanson of Abbeville is synonymous with the emergence of French cartographic publications in the face of Dutch supremacy in the field. He was the author of numerous printed maps (348 of which are signed) from 1627 until his death in 1667. Sanson was a "deskbound" geographer who consulted primarily bookish documents (ancient authors, travel accounts, missionary reports, and so forth) and had only limited resources available for publishing his work.

His superiority stemmed from neither his sources nor the decorative features of his maps, but rather from his methodic zeal to clarify and classify. A series of geographic tables published in 1644–1645 containing the nomenclature of countries and regions categorized according to their importance assured his reputation and illustrate his method, providing a glimpse of what would become his hallmark—the almost obsessive tracing of all political and administrative boundaries.

241

Known above all for his world atlas (1658)– the first of its kind to be produced by a Frenchman–he contributed in a major way also to the revitalization of the cartography of France. He had already attracted Richelieu's notice in 1627 with his map of historic Gaul. At first Sanson limited himself to maps of a general character, the most novel of which were two thematic maps published in 1632 and 1634 (a map of postal relay stations and a map of rivers). In the 1640s after he had moved to Paris, he imagined projects of greater breadth, aimed at improving the administration of the kingdom and for which he solicited official commissions. His goal was to produce a homogeneous series of maps showing the civil and religious administrative districts for the entire country.

The wall map of the *généralités* (fiscal districts) of the French kingdom followed the same logic. It was compiled by assembling approximately ten individual maps of the local governments or provinces of France that had been published separately between 1648 and 1652 at a scale of 1:880,000, plus maps of bordering regimes. This impressive overview served as a sort of preface to a map of France on multiple sheets arranged by fiscal districts. In the foliate border that contains details about the fiscal administration of the kingdom, Sanson set out his cartographic objectives: "Et à présent, il n'y a presque plus d'*Election* ou de *Recette* en France dont je ne puisse donner la carte particulière;... Celle-ci en est un abrégé" (At present, there is hardly any subdivision of a fiscal district for which I do not have a specific map;... This is an abbreviated version).

After producing a map of France in thirty hand-drawn sheets for Richelieu, he turned to Chancelier Séguier and to Colbert. Colbert, who probably believed more in collective endeavors than in individual ones, merely entrusted Sanson with the centralization of cartographic data within the framework of the investigations undertaken in 1663 by the *intendants* (local administrators). In 1664 Colbert asked him to prepare a hand-drawn atlas of the districts of the salt tax (*Grande Gabelle*), composed of a general map and twenty-one individual maps. Beginning in 1645 Sanson presented a proposal to the Assembly of the Clergy for detailed maps of the dioceses of France. The first of these did not appear until 1653 and Sanson had neither the time nor the means to finish the project. More than a hundred maps at a scale of approximately 1:234,000 had been published, however, and were collected in 1776 by his son Guillaume to form an atlas.

Catherine Hofmann

M. Pastoureau, "Les Sanson: Un siècle de cartographie française (1630–1730)" (thesis, University of Paris, 1981). Pastoureau, *Les atlas français, XVI–XVIIe siècles: Répertoire bibliographique et étude* (Paris, 1984). Pastoureau, "Les premiers atlas administratifs de la France, XVIe–XVIIIe siècles," in *Actes du colloque "Le fait départemental"* (Chaumont, 1984), 125–37. Pastoureau, ed., *Nicolas Sanson d'Abbeville: Atlas du monde, 1665* (Paris, 1988). M. Pelletier, "Des cartes pour partager: Divisions administratives, frontières, pays, plans terriers du 16e au 18e siècle," in *La cartographie française* (forthcoming).

104

JACQUES MARETZ
Coast of Provence
Département des Cartes et Plans, SH Pf. 71, div. 3, p. 2

Vellum; 4 assembled, hand-drawn sheets, gathered; 800 × 2,800 mm. [1633]. From the map collection of the Service Hydrographique de la Marine; deposited in 1947 in the Bibliothèque Nationale.

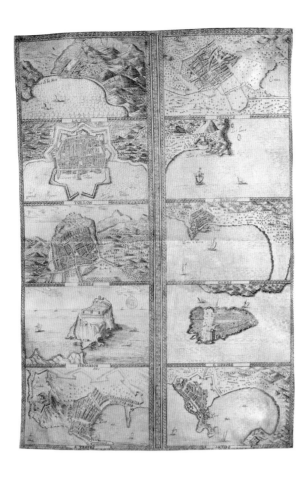

105

JACQUES MARETZ
Aerial Views of the Ports of Provence
Département des Cartes et Plans, SH Pf. 71,
div. 3, p. 2, 1–2

Vellum; 2 hand-drawn sheets originally intended to frame the coastal map of Provence by the same cartographer; each, 800 × 597 mm. [1633]. From the map collection of the Service Hydrographique de la Marine; deposited in 1947 in the Bibliothèque Nationale.

With its international borders and maritime coast, Provence was a favorite subject of military mapmakers starting in the second half of the 16th century. Jacques Maretz's map is a glamorous example of the maps traditionally produced for the absolute monarchy. Drawn in pen and ink and highlighted in gold, it has a title scroll with a dedication to Cardinal Richelieu and a baroque decoration of mythological and allegorical figures bearing the arms of Richelieu on the left, of Louis XIII in the middle, and of Provence on the right. The delicacy of the workmanship and the richness of the gilding further attest to the map's prestige, as does the elaborate decoration featuring an arabesque border, mariners' compass, marine monsters, and ships of all kinds (galleys, tartans, fishing boats), depicting the sea as an intensely lively place.

The making of this superb map reflects Richelieu's dual concerns upon coming to power. As "grand master, chief, and superintendent of the trade and navigation of France" since 1626, he had set himself the goal (as Colbert would do later with more lasting success) of reaffirming French maritime ambitions in the face of English and especially Dutch sea power. Mastery of the Mediterranean in the context of a European diplomacy still dominated by the Habsburgs of Spain and of Vienna was a major challenge. Strengthening the coastal defenses of Provence was essential not only to cut off the great supply route between Catalonia and Genoa, but also to ward off the constant and formidable Barbary pirates. Successive inquiries into the condition of the coasts beginning in 1626 demonstrated their vulnerability. Louis XIII's visit to Montpellier in 1632 saw the appointment of Henri de Séguiran as the new lieutenant general of the Seas of Levant, with the mission of conducting a new inspection. To "tirer le plan de la côte de la mer et de toutes les villes, ports, châteaux qui y sont" (draw a coastal map with all the towns, ports, and castles situated on it), Séguiran arranged for Maretz to accompany him. Maretz, "professor of mathematics and engineer to His Majesty," had made the first flat-projection map of Aix (1624). Two other engineers, Augier and Flour, assisted Maretz during the brief survey trip, from Jan. 11 to March 17, 1633.

Drawn to a large scale (1:117,300), this map of the coast of Provence (cat. 104) marks a real improvement over the first printed map of Provence drawn by Pierre-Jean Bompar around 1592 and constantly plagiarized thereafter. First, the cartographic advances of Maretz's map included narrowing the difference in longitude between Nice and Saintes-Maries to 3°, a distance much closer to the actual one (2°42′) than Bompar's, whose map stretched the provincial coast by presenting a longitudinal difference of 4°30′. Although inland areas were still represented by non-naturalistic conventions (notably with the relief depicted by numerous wavy peaks), as a result of observations limited to the shoreline, Maretz's drawing of the coast constitutes a great advance in accuracy and precision.

The ultimate purpose of the document and its military interest are evident from the attention given to defensive strength and to the vulnerability of the region to maritime attacks. Thus, thanks to the representation of coastal relief, the distinction between rocky coasts and low-lying coasts (of highest interest to the military) appeared for the first time on a general map of the coast of Provence. The depiction of the principal ports or defensive sites of Provence on a double series of plates (cat. 105), designed from the start to flank the map, completed the overall view in useful fashion by providing local information for the evaluation of the defensive capabilities of the province. Bird's-eye views of the great port cities (for instance, Marseille, Arles, and Toulon) revealed their capacities for self-defense, while the "lifelike portrayals" (Nostre Dame de la Mer, Tour de Bouc, Château d'If, and so on) took general topographic features into account, highlighting the defensive potential of certain coastal sites.

All depictions of the coast of Provence would be derived from this remarkable map for more than fifty years. In 1634 Charles Tassin, imitated later by Sanson and Jaillot, brought out a printed version in three sheets in his *Cartes générales de toutes les Provinces*. In the 1660s at Colbert's urging the chevalier de Clerville would undertake new surveys of the shoreline, though all things considered they were less satisfactory than those of 1633. Not until the 18th century and the work of G. Delisle would maps of Provence correct Maretz's drawings on certain points.

Catherine Hofmann

H. Méthivier, "Richelieu et le front de mer de Provence," *Revue historique* 185 (1939): 123–41. D. J. Buisseret, "Les ingénieurs du roi au temps de Henri IV," *Bulletin de la section de géographie du Comité des Travaux Historiques et Scientifiques: Histoire de la cartographie et géographie historique* 77 (1964): 13–84. M. Foncin and M. de la Roncière, "Jacques Maretz et la cartographie des côtes de Provence au XVIIe siècle," in *Actes du 90e congrès national des Sociétés Savantes: Section de Géographie* (Paris, 1966), 9–29. M. Pastoureau, J. M. Homet, and G. Pichard, *Rivages et terres de Provence: Cartographie d'une province* (Avignon, 1991).

245

III

The Kings Collect for the Savants

5 "It's for the King"

Sacred and Absolute Monarchy (1600–1789)

Orest Ranum

The shop was in Paris, on the rue Saint-Honoré, and the year was 1699, but it might have been centuries earlier, or in any other great French city. Ever so carefully, an artisan was fashioning red and green cording into a stunningly beautiful braid. A fellow craftsman came into the shop and immediately noticed the braid maker's intense concentration. Was it for a military uniform, a bishop's vestment, or a luxurious bed? Turning without stopping his work, the braid maker uttered one short phrase: "It's for the king." It mattered little what the king was going to do with the braid–it was to be his and it had to be the best. Pride in his royal commission radiated from the braid maker's work.

Multiplied hundreds of times, little stories of this sort are found in the contracts surviving from the Ancien Régime. Every single manufactured product, no matter how banal or how unique, and every type of creative endeavor inspired this intensity of purpose. The royal presence was pervasive in studies, shops, gardens, libraries, and laboratories all over the realm. Such a high degree of royal inspiration for creative and highly skilled work might be expected in far-off Bali or some other exotic culture, but hardly, or so it would seem to us, in France. Certainly there were other sources than the monarchy for inspiring creativity and skilled craftsmanship, for example, well-to-do clergy and aristocratic patrons. But in the Ancien Régime, the monarch's gaze over what we call the creative dimension in the culture–in the arts, literature, scientific research, technological development, and even commercial activity–became truly all-pervasive. It had not always been so. The attitude expressed in "It's for the king" permeated French culture in ways that helped ensure social, religious, and political stability. These had been in very short supply during the Wars of Religion that racked France almost without interruption from the early 1560s to the late 1590s.

Personal and psychological relations with the king, if only in the imagination, were strong in all European monarchies, but in France these intensified through cultural expression, as a result of fears about strife and heresy. Culture in the early modern centuries had something lofty or transcendental about it. Through culture, mortals reached toward the divine, and the king. Proclaiming in a dedication that the inspiration for a poem, a painting, or a scientific discovery came from the king was absolutely natural in the Ancien Régime, and it did not imply some loss of personal self-fulfillment or credit. Such direct, one-to-one relations between the creative individual and the prince intensified when royally founded institutions supported virtually every form of creative cultural expression. Monarchs were flattered, honestly appreciated, and, of course, harshly criticized for what they did or did not do; but above all they increasingly became the focus for persons undertaking a task that was especially fine or out of the ordinary.

To be sure, insincerity and hyperbole often studded these dedications to the king, for, like braid makers, poets and historians needed the money that a royal thank-you was sure to bring. Still, although royal payments were slow and never as generous as the recipients hoped, they were certainly more frequent and sizable than what aristocrats and merchants could pay. But more important than the money was the quite sincere, sometimes humorous crediting of royalism for almost every type of creative activity in the realm.

Veiled behind bevies of official culture brokers and inspectors, the king awarded titles to the chosen few whose creative works particularly pleased him or his advisors. Guilds and other "quality controllers" pervaded the literary, scientific, and artistic communities, not only in Paris but throughout the realm. The king's first braid maker—like the first poet, first painter, first composer, first harness maker, and first almost anything else—was therefore a person highly trained in his or her craft and the work produced was submitted to the critical review of those who did not hesitate to be ruled by their jealousy about the title "first," and the royal pension that went with it. Not only merit but hierarchy in society thus were harnessed for the glory of Louis XIV, the French Apollo who drove his creative steeds across the golden heavens. Not a few of the king's most creative subjects actually lived in the royal residence of the Louvre. Like the annual pension to the braid maker, the money given a poet, an explorer, or a philosopher came directly from the royal household accounts. Illustrations showing an author presenting his creative work to the king in the form of a book, which had become so commonplace in the sixteenth century, became flesh and blood when the king founded companies of scholars and literati to foster research and to improve the French language.

Creativity in the arts and sciences was believed to be divine in origin and humanity's highest expression. To have spirit, *esprit*, signified possessing intelligence that could, it was believed, only come from God. Kings were adored as vice-regents of both the Christian and the pagan gods, with the distinctions between the two sometimes being left unclear. Responding to doctrinal battles between Catholics and Protestants, to civil wars and to the challenge of interpreting discoveries about ancient Egyptian, Greek, and Roman civilizations, in the mid-sixteenth century the Council of Trent had decreed limits to the fusion and confusion between sacred and pagan religious beliefs and symbols. The church, with all its saints, distanced itself from the antique gods and goddesses, but the French kings did not follow its lead.

All in one, yet each unique, in a bewildering array of symbols, attributes, and metaphors, biblical accounts and ancient pagan beliefs undergirded French kings. This diversity of antique cultures enriched the king-centered creative impulses of the Ancien Régime. Kings were the fount of creativity and of "Right Reason"—the two pillars on which royal power rested, through the arts and the law. The monarchy placed itself squarely in a position to solve the religious and political problems of the sixteenth century by claiming ultimate authority over both. In a climate of fear and violence, the censorship exercised by royal officials in the king's name was accepted, because of fears about civil war and doctrinal strife.

By accepting to be the source of both creativity and law, the monarchy slowly restored internal stability by 1652, but this was accomplished at a high price. Like the church, the monarchy came to be held responsible for the morality and the patriotism of every impulse within the cultural sphere. Habits that seemed innocent at the beginning, and that were indeed innocent—for example, the weekly meetings of the creative and the witty in *salons*—would be seen as dangerous encounters in the late eighteenth century, because of the expectation that all creative energy be channeled through the established institutions founded by past kings. Still more disquieting, theological disputes about such things as the frequency with which the faithful should take communion engendered theological and even philosophical arguments questioning the Right Reason of royal authority. The Jansenists, like the salons, escaped their assigned spheres of creativity and eventually created opinions—and opportunities for debate and contestation—that would completely undermine kingly power and institutions among the middle and wealthier classes. Almost like a time bomb, the sources of authority that the monarchy developed to overcome civil war in the late sixteenth century would be the cause of its downfall in the 1790s. The heavy shadows of the Roman imperial age—of Augustus, Virgil, Seneca, Tacitus, and Hadrian—haunted not only the statesmen but also the moralists and poets of the seventeenth century, forcing esprit into established channels and institutions.

In law and in temporal religious matters, the king and his world were considered sacred and absolute. Taking his name in vain—that is, swearing an obscenity in the name of Louis XIV—was a crime punishable by death. Anyone who attacked the king's sacred person was drawn and quartered and his body burned, as happened to Ravaillac, Henry IV's assassin (cat. 88), and Damiens, the would-be assassin of Louis XV. That both words and actions could incur the death sentence provides an important clue to the character of the Ancien Régime as it consolidated its power in society with the help of jurists, priests, poets, and engineers in the royal service.

251

To the very end of the Bourbon monarchy in 1830, French kings continued to manifest their divinity by using the royal touch to cure their subjects of the dreaded disease called scrofula. "The king touches you, God heals you," was the liturgical formula (cat. 80). Did his subjects believe in these powers? The answer is not a straightforward yes or no. Individuals, like large crowds, participate in rituals that they may comprehend only dimly and believe still less. Those who failed to be cured continued to believe that in their bodies lurked an evil that had prevented a divine/royal cure.

The king had nearly priestly rank in the church. He was the only layman to take both the bread and the wine during the communion services that accompanied his coronation. When he traveled about, subjects continually tried to touch his clothes, hoping that some of his power would flow into them. As protector against foreign enemies, plagues, and revolutions, the king was worked for, prayed for, and loved and hated like a somewhat distant but influential family member. As a last resort, the desperately poor or sick would write him and ask for help. Etchings of the king, perhaps purchased from a street vendor, are typically found in inventories of the pictures that hung on the walls of modest merchant and professional households.

Nor was it just the "ignorant" peasants or the "ill-educated" artisans who sustained the royal religion with their faith. Indeed, it was among the more educated that loyalty to and love for the king infused every aspect of creative life. The more energetic professionals, especially the lawyers, judges, and rural nobility, continually elaborated and believed in the royal religion. There were, of course, religious and political factions in French society that could inspire not only criticism of but even rebellion against a particular king, or against the excessive force exerted by his troops. Opposition came from religious leaders, who gave their loyalty to papal Rome and tended to see the royal religion as sacrilegious, and from nobles, whose historical claims to independence were undermined by the obligatory fawning on the monarch at Versailles.

How could so much of the cultural power—in literature, the arts, philosophy, and science—be incarnated in a single human body? This question, like the causes of Rome's decline, remains a perennial subject of debate not only in French history but in European and world history as well. The political phenomenon known as monarchy, be it absolutist or constitutionalist, with all its military, theatrical, and intellectual force, pervades world history from the earliest to the most recent centuries. Reading about Louis XIV or about the monarchs of the eighteenth century immediately prompts reflections about similar cultural and political moments in European, Asian, American, and African states. This is as it should be. Persons living in democratic political cultures tend to view the monarchical phenomenon as just another "peculiar institution," but in fact the processes of building self-esteem in individuals, of harnessing creative energies and assuring domestic tranquility, are not all that different over time, as Montesquieu was to point out in his *Spirit of the Laws* (cat. 145).

In the mid-seventeenth century, after decades of violence and civil war had shaken France, the deeply religious mathematician and philosopher Blaise Pascal (cat. 122) achieved an understanding of monarchy that at least went beyond what the ancient philosophers and saints had said about it. "Why do kings come to have so much power?" he asked. If cannons, crowns, and flags were to be blotted out on royal portraits and coins, kings (and queens) would look just like other human beings. Why, then, do people tremble in the presence of the king, who is only flesh and blood? Reflecting on human nature after the manner of Saint Augustine, Pascal concluded that all humans want to have power over others. A desire to acquire power, property, and recognition is human nature: we discern in kings only what we ourselves are.

This reflection led Pascal to two conclusions. The first was that although God may give kings authority to rule over their subjects, it is actually the human condition, and our desire to be little kings or queens in our dealings with others, that explain royal power. Fearing for the king's life is nothing more than fearing for one's own life. Pascal's second conclusion was that a king's power must be absolute in order to control the tendencies toward wildness and violence in the hearts of his subjects. To people living in a democratic political culture, these conclusions seem not only wrong but patently inapplicable. Still, no other writer rent the veil of psychology, hermeneutics, and myth that was French kingship more completely than did Pascal. Yet his thought on the subject was not particularly influential. The French, like any other people, do not particularly like to be told that they are individually power-hungry and vain. Indeed, for Pascal, the tendency of all peoples to believe themselves morally upright and superior to others was merely collective individual vanity. Better, it was thought, to praise the king and in this way to sustain claims to collective greatness and glory. The little secret self was king every bit as much as Louis XIV.

The religion of royalism thus had its critics, but they were like so many voices crying in the wilderness. Until 1652 the shattering effects of religious controversy and civil war generated a yearning for stability at almost any price, and stability meant absolute monarchy. It is important to elucidate the images of the wise, all-powerful, conquering, and just monarch created by generations of writers, artists, architects, philosophers, and even fireworks makers in the Ancien Régime. Kings as persons struggled to live up to the roles created for them by their most creative subjects. These mythologers—like the dancing master, the philosopher, the fencing master, and the tailor in Molière's *Bourgeois gentilhomme* (each of whom claims that his particular art plays a prime role in the making of a gentleman)—and the royalism of the talented and creative who shaped kingship must be scrutinized (cat. 109).

The royal residences—the Louvre, Versailles, Fontainebleau, and, later, Marly—as well as the Royal Library, the various academies, and the Observatory, were filled with complex symbolic and verbal allusions to the greatness of France and her kings. On coins, on stamped paper, on city gates, on barracks and customs houses, on the Mint, and on each ship of the royal fleet were to be found royal portraits and the arms of France: three fleurs-de-lis on a blue field accompanied by the binding chains on their red field (a stylized "carbuncle") that constituted the arms of the kingdom of Navarre. Here, in sign and word, culture and royal power appeared perpetually and universally bound together.

The commonplace belief held, of course, that the muses either suffered or fell silent during years of civil and foreign wars. Yet in Ronsard's mid-sixteenth-century verses and in Malherbe's early seventeenth-century ones, a hearty, immortalizing, and intellectual royalism sustained the monarchy in its darkest days. Educated persons believed that great poetic creativity occurred only rarely in the history of the world, and that when it did arise, it was under the aegis of a conquering and just monarch. As the seventeenth century progressed, hopes for a new golden age slowly turned into a belief that it *was* at the very least a silver age.

Jean Bodin, in his *Six Books of the Republic* (1576), responded to the disorder of war by offering a new, more profoundly philosophical foundation for state sover-

253

eignty. The older religious principles had become contested by Protestants, hence the task of coming up with a new, secular foundation for state power. Civil and religious strife not only unleashed a popular movement for stability but also laid the philosophical foundation for modern state powers that would gradually be diffused over much of the world during the succeeding centuries.

While never giving up in his efforts to help his king bring peace to France, Bodin's contemporary, Michel de Montaigne, withdrew to his tower to read and to reflect on every aspect of human nature and of individual responsibility for order (cat. 85). The more he appeared to be retreating into his studies, the more intensely the power of his pen brought him to the very center of every Frenchman's political life. Asking, "What do I know?" Montaigne addressed the news from Brazil about the habits of the cannibalistic natives who customarily devoured the enemies they slew in battle. Some commentators were already asserting that these Brazilians were not really people but represented a subhuman species previously unknown to Europeans. The claims of the French and their European neighbors to a superior "human" status seemed ironic if not ridiculous to Montaigne, as he contemplated the atrocities committed against innocent and defenseless civilians (including women and children) in the name of religion. Montaigne, Jean de Léry, the pioneering observer of the Brazilians, and the devoted communities of nuns and monks who set off for the New World to bring medical attention, literacy, and a new faith to the Amerindians—it was these who paved the way for a less ethnocentric France and Europe, albeit at a heavy price for the autonomy of the Amerindians.

Henry IV's conversion to Catholicism in 1594, and the subsequent defeat and decline of the Ultra-Catholic forces, inaugurated a new era and a new dynasty of French kings, the Bourbons. The forces for stability supported Henry IV. Through a governance as militaristic and absolutist as that of any of his predecessors, Henry censored writers and preachers in the name of assuring public peace. He needed to quell the violence, yet he personally remained a target of that violence for having changed his religion too many times. For the first Bourbon, power would always be essentially military and built upon a male-to-male fidelity, rather than upon a royal apotheosis in paint and in verse.

Guided by Sully and by projectors such as Laffemas, Henry's most important cultural achievement would be the launching of a new and monumental Paris. He had a precocious sense of how building not only enhances pride but creates employment. In the mid-sixteenth century Henry II had approved the pulling down of most of the big old castle that was the Louvre, and he, his Florentine wife (cat. 83), and his frail sons accomplished a brilliant, but only partial rebuilding. The Pont Neuf, a new bridge across the Seine, would be completed under Henry IV, as would parts of the Louvre, among them the Grand Gallery that linked the Louvre to the Tuileries Palace. The rapid construction of residential squares—the first, known as the Place Dauphine, was situated at the point where the Ile de la Cité joins the Pont Neuf, and the second, originally called the Place Royale but now known as the Place des Vosges, occupies a former marsh along the eastern edge of the capital—suddenly transformed the old city into a vast theatrical space. With straight streets, regular fenestration of house facades, and uniform roof lines designed to enhance the effect of these geometric vistas, a new and monumental Paris was born, and that new Paris celebrated royalism. Poets, painters, and engravers virtually fell over one another as they attempted to capture this "new Rome" in verse, cityscapes, and etchings. The grand vista and arches that served as the setting for Pluvinel's riding lessons were none other than the Place Royale (cat. 89). Never mind that the verses and engravings exaggerated the beauty and expanse of these new spaces and focused on the many courtly love trysts that supposedly took place under the arches of the Place Royale: northern and eastern Europeans tingled over the magnetism of the new city. The Seine River and the new squares and royal residences (among them the Luxembourg Palace) became staging areas for grandiose processions, games, fireworks, boating events and log-rolling parties, and royal fanfares and receptions. All this increased the theatrical dimension of French monarchical power and helped integrate thousands of humbler urbanites into the royal religion. The cheering Parisians loved a spectacle and would trek across the city to gawk at the beautiful horses and gilded coaches that bore the royal family and their court across the square and to stare open-mouthed at the precious gems and sumptuous clothes worn by these "gods," "heroes," and "heroines."

The French preoccupation with grand urban projects that simultaneously created monuments and employment dates from Henry IV's reign. The new Paris, with its ordered vistas that centered on royal residences or equestrian statues, brought about an unquenchable thirst for ever more lofty and grandiose spaces, spaces which satisfied a need to be proud of something that stood above religious turmoil and which expressed both control over nature *and* the almost geometric stability of the society.

Henry IV's elder son, Louis XIII (1610–1643), the stuttering and authoritarian monarch who relentlessly pursued nobles and Protestants (cat. 92) for breaking "his" laws, never inspired the same awe or creative imagination as his father and son did. His reign shows how the royal religion could flourish almost in spite of, rather than because of, a personal royal inspiration for creative imagination. Aside from participating in a few ballets, Louis the Just expressed no interest in scholarship or the creative arts. Additions to the Louvre during his reign had routine administrative inspiration.

The absence of royal involvement in the arts and learning had haunted the talented ever since the death of Francis I in 1547. Working for the king or writing about him in the abstract was one thing; being directly inspired by his words and presence was another. For centuries, prominent clergymen had been great cultural patrons, usually (but not always) in accord with royal policies. In Cardinal Richelieu, Louis XIII found not only a great minister but an inspirer and a legislator for virtually all the creative energies in the realm. Well educated and sensitive to the cosmopolitan (Hispanic and Italianate) artistic, literary, and scientific trends of high culture, the cardinal did everything he could to bring the French along on the road to greatness and to cultural as well as political superiority in Europe. Henry IV had chiefly insisted on quiet and majestic urban spaces; Richelieu, by contrast, focused on a vast and spiritual program of renewal and of coherence in every aspect of state politics and culture.

Striking deep emotional chords, the poets and essayists of the seventeenth century assumed roles in society hitherto occupied only by saints and nobles. In the great
cultural moment of the 1630s, Louis XIII would be praised for inspiring poets,
philosophers, and scholars, but he was really a sort of "dummy king," while Richelieu was the ventriloquist who gave him speech and authority. Louis XIII's stuttering
inability to speak the lofty and refined French that Richelieu was sponsoring may
actually have prompted his creative subjects to speak ever more eloquently in his
name.

Richelieu listened to every word that was said to him and measured every defer-
ential gesture to see if it was appropriate. Vulgar and sensual innuendo in speech
became politically incorrect. Then, just as they gained Richelieu's ear, men of letters
assumed the serious task of creating a regular and plainer (that is, less convoluted)
sentence structure, an ordered French language in which each word would have its
unique cultural and social force in a grand hierarchy of eloquence. Surrounded by
administrators with literary and intensely political and religious sensitivities, the cardinal knew about almost every literary and artistic trend in the realm virtually as
soon as it arose. In his presence conversation became not only political but literary,
though it retained undercurrents of state control over what was said and, more
important, *how* it was said. Slowly but surely Parisian elite society aped the subject
matter, the choice of words, the tone of voice, and the gestures that characterized the
little literary circle surrounding the cardinal—and the scripts recited by the actors
who performed in the private theater he had built.

Instead of merely shaping the literary and artistic culture of France, Richelieu
went on the offensive to increase state power. The trend toward stability was still
overpowering, and it permitted Richelieu's program to become the norm in elite
society. But in defining and extending the power of the state, the cardinal set in
motion forces that would prove the state's undoing in 1789. Not for nothing was he a
prince of the church. His strategy of bringing the Huguenots back into the fold (separating religious orthodoxy from obedience to the state) would be used to build new
foundations for monarchical power. The cardinal also kept a wary eye on the Jesuits
and their schools. Gallican to the core, he feared that France might become too educated and that, as a result, there would be too many people idly writing and too few
working the fields. Esprit had to be channeled: it could be dangerous. When the theologian Saint-Cyran disagreed with the cardinal about the powers of divine grace, he
was imprisoned for life. The Jansenist thorn that Saint-Cyran stuck into the side of
the Richelieu state would go deeper and deeper into the body politic and destabilize
the monarchy long before the French Revolution.

Richelieu's ideal monarchy was inspired by Counter-Reformation visions of the
Roman Catholic church—totally ordered, French, hierarchical, and aspiring to the
heavens. Four major innovations sustained and extended this vision. First, in sponsoring the country's earliest regularly published newspaper, the *Gazette de France*
(cat. 91), the cardinal sought to create opinion where there was none, and especially
to convince that opinion of the rightness of his policies before someone could challenge them. The Richelieu cultural program was launched under clouds of religious
strife, foreign war, and aristocratic plotting. Aiming to enlarge the opinion sphere in

the realm by linking kingship, French patriotism, godliness, and the cultural pursuit of glory, his majesty and his collaborators themselves wrote for the paper. By inflated prose, royal military victories were raised to world-class events and defeats were couched as appeals for still greater sacrifice. The French reader was brought to feel a part of a great renewal in the state and to take pride in his king. When dissenters were heard, the cardinal tried to answer them; if they persisted, he simply had them arrested in order not to spoil the overall theatrical illusion of great political and cultural achievement.

Second, Richelieu's personal love of words and of the theater coincided with several cultural currents waiting to be brought into prominence by his initiatives. Throughout France the Jesuits were rapidly expanding their highly successful secondary schools, and one of the features of their education program was theatrical performances by the pupils. The boys not only learned how to overcome stage fright, they learned noble postures and gestures through acting and elocution, and moral principles through performing in adaptations of Plutarch's and Livy's writings. Prior to the 1630s, French theater had been the street-corner and market type: raucous, popular, and full of sarcastically treated stock characters, notably at the Théâtre de Bourgogne (cat. 100). Several playwrights led by Pierre Corneille developed a morally and politically edifying theater in which the principal characters almost always belonged to imperial or noble families and entered into conflict about wars, lands, women, courage, and duty. Richelieu had a theater built in his palace and sponsored this sort of play. These performances left the spectator thinking that he had not only learned a great deal about politics but had actually been a participant; in reality, he had neither been consulted nor had he uttered a single word about the political issues of the day. Plays were quickly published and, like the *Gazette,* were read all over the realm. This led to the diffusion of a feeling that one could participate in politics by attending the theater, and to the discovery that being French meant being able to recite Rodrigue's *tirade* from the *Cid.* The theater in Richelieu's day articulated hitherto unknown or barely perceived notions about words, power, and feelings.

Third, when a number of writers began meeting to read their works aloud and to discuss literary theory, Richelieu offered to "protect" them by founding an institution whose primary duty would be the creation of a more eloquent French language that was capable of expressing edifying thoughts. Conceived of as an arena where the members would fashion purity of style and praise for the king and then diffuse them throughout the realm, the Académie Française met writers' professional and civic need for a place in the state. Unlike earlier academies, Richelieu's would not advise the monarch, nor would the cardinal attend. Existing solely to elevate French to the lofty rank of Ciceronian Latin and make it a medium for noble thought, the Académie became a self-perpetuating corporation of forty "immortals" who undertook the implementation of the Richelieu cultural program to unify French patriotism, absolute royal power, and literary achievement. Even today it is de rigueur for newly elected academicians to insert a word of praise for the cardinal into their maiden speeches. Work on the Académie's official dictionary of the French language began soon after the foundation in 1637, and it continues today, a testimony to the belief that it is through proper usage and clear, grammatical prose that humans can achieve personal and collective fulfillment in conformity with state and nation. To think otherwise would have been almost heretical, as the royal religion received its greatest and most coherent linguistic cultural impulse under Richelieu.

Fourth, as Richelieu himself recognizes in the *Political Testament,* philosophy, literature, and propaganda are never enough to sustain the state. Scientific knowledge, technological advances, and precise information about past political and religious conditions were needed in order to defend French interests and rights abroad and at home. The state had to generate new knowledge and assure the preservation of what was already known. Cartography would flourish in this heady world of representing things and spaces. The Italians had long since developed practical maps for military and navigational purposes; they had even decorated the walls of their galleries with maps that visually conveyed ideas about their possessions and self-fulfillment through accumulating titles and lands. Whether they showed estates, realms, or uncharted seas, maps gave their owners a power over things and empires. Sanson's maps of fiscal districts (cat. 103) functioned in exactly the same way as the maps of newly claimed possessions in the New World: both made Frenchness public by presenting names and spaces. For the French monarchy, imperialism began at home as enhanced power over the king's subjects. Making maps more scientific did not change their character as talismans of power.

For centuries there had been tiny circles of clerkly scholars in royal service, but since the monarchy's very survival in the Wars of Religion had been challenged by claims about its past nature and limits, precise historic fact would always be needed to supplement divine-right principles of governance. France as a state was little more than an idea and an accumulation of royal rights—each requiring or authorizing some royal service. The administrative memory of all these rights was so enormous that special guardians of charters and books had to be appointed. The royal library in Richelieu's day was staffed by the Dupuy brothers, learned, almost "on-line" resource scholars who supplied information about points of historical fact to the cardinal. What exactly did the pope say about the archbishop of Reims in 978? What baptismal names were given to sons born into the Orléans branch of the royal family in the fifteenth century? Strange as these questions may seem, they had political repercussions and the state required the answers.

Despite all their duties, the Dupuy brothers found time to research and write very important treatises about royal rights, especially in regard to the Roman Catholic church's claims to exercise power within France. Richelieu relied on the Dupuys to provide the facts needed to sustain state power in any controversy, and today the notes taken by these brothers are part of the massive manuscript collections of the Bibliothèque nationale de France. These notes are perhaps not valued as treasures, but they nonetheless embody the knowledge that is the collective memory of the French state and nation. The Richelieu–Louis XIII state had a remarkably abstract, almost impersonal cultural force at its center. It rested on the power of words, law, force, history, and the royal religion. When the cardinal and the monarch died, a reaction took place that broke down some of the high-minded and principled powers that had been developed in French culture.

Still, culture, especially elite culture, changes individual lives and social groups at their deepest levels of identity, especially when nourished by feelings of inferiority and fears of disorder. The civil war known as the Fronde (1648–1652) was less violent than the Wars of Religion in the sixteenth century, but it was threatening enough to nourish the impulses for controlling and inspiring culture following Richelieu's example. The need to overcome feelings of inferiority vis-à-vis the Italians, the Spanish, and the ancient Greeks and Romans continued to nourish the ideal of greatness and nobility through literature, art, and courtly manners. Lest the French seem peculiar, a glance across the English Channel suggests that there, too, powerful religious and political principles were at work to propel England toward a new conformity. The Puritans had distinctly different aims from those of Richelieu and the statist culture he launched, but they shared overpowering impulses to reshape the individual, society, and culture. The French looked on in disbelief as the English put their king to death. All the more did theirs—Louis XIV, a handsome boy of ten— seem an inestimable treasure to be revered and obeyed.

Louis XIV matured into a vigorous, thoughtful, majestic, even absolutist king who marked every aspect of French culture with his name. A master observer and listener, the king practiced the same arts of governance as Richelieu, but with the more secular, indeed profane emphasis that resulted inevitably from the fact that he was not a priest or a bishop. The young king's principal minister, Cardinal Mazarin (cat. 95), was Richelieu's hand-picked successor. The totally faithful ministers, Jean-Baptiste Colbert and Michel Le Tellier, acquired the administrative brilliance and sangfroid of those rare statesmen, the survivors of revolution and civil war who remain in office to build state power out of aggressive counterrevolutionary impulses in society.

Colbert legislated and channeled the creative forces in French elite culture into still more academies, luxury goods, industries, technology, engineering projects, imperial expansion in Canada, the West and the East Indies, and, last but not least, urban squares, waterworks, and boulevards in Paris and the provincial capitals. To be sure, everything was done in Louis's name, but it was the post-Fronde political stability and the driving force of experienced royal officials that created what came to be known as the Century of Louis XIV.

Royal patronage of learning and of the arts—architecture, the theater, opera, and the decorative arts—became less personal in the 1660s, as still more academies were established and pensions increasingly came to be distributed on the basis of merit and by "peer review." Could France become as great as Rome had been in the time of Caesar Augustus? And, as in Richelieu's day, the overall distinction and recognition of French creativity in the arts, literature, and science were an integral part of Louis XIV's aim to dominate European culture. Nowadays we may think of science and the arts as simply liberating and expressive for the human spirit. This liberal view of culture is a recent development; it prevails largely in elite circles and is questioned by persons from non-Western cultures who may see Americanism or Europeanism behind the mask of cosmopolitan or Western labels. Louis XIV and his subjects were like the non-Westerners; they saw that political power lay in the arts, literature, and science, and their non-French contemporaries would eventually resist and even fight French claims to cultural superiority. First the Italian and then the Spanish cultural achievements had caused the French to feel inferior. After 1660,

259

the Richelieu–Louis XIV cultural program began to attract favorable European attention. True, the great Roman artist-architect Bernini could still scoff at French buildings and urban plans, but French power, both military and cultural, clearly was increasing on the European stage of nations.

Richelieu's Académie Française became the model for a series of academies founded in the 1660s that increased the social value of creativity by recognizing talent and supporting it financially. The Academy of Inscriptions was created in 1663, initially to immortalize the king through phrases of praise to be engraved on monuments and coins (cat. 114, no. 4). After the royal library, no other scholarly center would be as influential in defining the learned, pagan-divine, and heroic characteristics of the royal religion as manifested in the persona of the Sun King. When Louis and his army first led a military operation to cross the Rhine, the parallel between his reign and that of various Roman emperors became a cause for celebration and propaganda. The members of the Academy of Inscriptions concerted their reflections on history and rhetoric to find just the right phrase to engrave on a medal depicting the king at the head of his troops. One academician suggested: "The marvelous crossing of the Rhine." Another, Jean Racine, the tragedian, suggested simply: "The crossing of the Rhine," and his more economical phrase was selected because it adhered to the classicizing rhetorical principles that enhanced glory through simplicity and clarity. This is what French classicism would be as a process or cultural strategy in the late seventeenth century: careful reflection about antique precedents and rules, followed by a decision grounded on a rationalist principle such as "less is more," thereby delineating French literary, architectural, and artistic styles and setting them apart from the more baroque style emanating from Italy.

The Academy of Painting and Sculpture had received its first charter in 1648, but not until 1663 did its vague and stormy autonomy from the painters' guild become established (cat. 114, no. 2). While guild-like training in technique and an apprenticeship in Rome still seemed essential to young painters, and would continue to be so down through the centuries, under Charles Le Brun's leadership the academy began to offer a rigorous and rationally constructed curriculum in which Poussin's paintings were the ideal for young artists first to imitate and then to surpass. The academicians competed to celebrate, by their brushstrokes, Louis XIV, patron of the arts, conqueror and hero, just as their colleagues in the Académie Française celebrated him in verse.

Accompanying these formal attempts to channel creative impulses into royal service was an increasingly official policing of books. Censorship lay heavily not only on the so-called scandalous writings (for example, pornography) but also on the political advice offered by such loyal state servants as Vauban, who in his *Dîme royale* attempted to warn the king about the disastrous effects of his foreign policy on his people (cat. 121).

Feeling the competition from the Royal Society in London, Colbert chartered an Academy of Sciences in 1666. The savants immediately undertook ambitious research projects in botany, astronomy, cartography, chemistry, and mathematics, and they made assurances that their findings would be very useful to the Ludovician state. Over the next century, the Academy of Sciences gained immense prestige—

perhaps more than it deserved—as a result of the authority the monarchy had given it to shape research, not only in natural philosophy but in the validation of technological inventions and discoveries. Sébastien Leclerc's masterpiece *Louis XIV's Visit to the Academy of Sciences* not only depicts all the scientific projects that interested its members but also shows the royal botanical gardens and the Observatory in the distance. The burning mirror before the king reflects the sun onto him, capturing Apollonian creative power for him and, through him, for his subjects. Scholarship, literature, the arts, and the sciences attained a remarkable symbolic and historical unity as a result of antique inspiration and of the passion to create French greatness. Along with the pursuit of immortality in the Heaven of the New Testament came a patriotic and royalist quest for *gloire* that would place Ludovician France on the short roster of truly golden ages. Like the Académie Française, the "sovereign court" in all matters of grammar and usage, the new academies founded in the 1660s played roles as validators and judges of almost every type of creative initiative in the arts and sciences.

In 1671 Colbert founded an Academy of Architecture, whose aim once again was to master all the knowledge of the ancients and then expand it by creating something equally creative but French. Would a French column designed by Claude Perrault ever be considered the equal of ancient Greek and Tuscan columns? It is tempting to smile condescendingly at so much pretentiousness, but the impulse to equal and then, if possible, surpass the great achievements of the Greeks and the Romans would be an all-pervading force in French culture throughout the Ancien Régime, as it had been in Renaissance Italy and as it would be in eighteenth-century Britain.

And what could be closer to architecture than typography, where each segment of a letter was designed according to the same classical proportions as a building? The creation of a Roman-inspired but now distinctly French typography also received royal sponsorship. The royal printing works that had been founded late in the reign of Louis XIII and that were housed in the royal palace of the Louvre were given the mission of creating distinctly French characters for new type fonts that would be cut and cast, enabling the French printers to produce books that would survive the test of time. The results were very impressive—unique, yet inspired by great Roman models—and the fonts are still widely used today. Whether represented by a Poussin etching, a column, or the letter *Q*, the Roman-inspired classicism of the seventeenth century can easily be dated, yet it also has timeless and timely qualities.

If Paris was the sun of this academic support movement for channeling and championing creativity and royalism, the provincial cities were the moons. Soissons, Nîmes, Arles, Angers, Villefranche in the Beaujolais, Montpellier, and Caen all had academies of one type or another whose members assembled weekly to discuss their research and writing and to report on their readings from the flow of scholarly journals that first began to crisscross the realm, and all of Europe, in the late seventeenth century. Whether they belonged to a prestigious Parisian institution or a provincial one, academicians benefited from the prestige conferred by their membership and, for the most part, considered themselves to be deeply royalist state servants.

Colbert's ideas were so literally antique-revivalist that he sponsored the design and building of still more public squares dominated by triumphal arches and equestrian statues of Louis XIV. To Henry IV's monumental theater—Paris—the elliptical Place des Victoires and the hexagonal Place Louis XIV (now the Place Vendôme) were added, creating additional geometrical vistas and grandeur. The sober façade of the new wing of the Louvre—with its columns designed by Perrault—captured something of the essence of the classical ideal: it has repose, monumentality, and such grandeur that huge columns and pilasters seem small. Again, Leclerc's print of the construction of the Louvre inspired awe about what the French could accomplish in technology, despite the obviously exaggerated transcendental aspect so characteristic of Ludovician culture. The triumphal arches built to celebrate Louis XIV's military victories seem small by comparison with some of the massive late-Roman ones, or with the Grande Arche that is their descendant and that is yet one more attempt to demarcate monumentally the city of light.

Though the royal library had been collecting manuscripts since the reign of Charles V, only under Francis I did French kings become true collectors of works of art, relics, and *curiosités*. Paintings, bronzes, rock-crystal vases and ewers, agates, enamels, and precious stones were part of the royal collections, along with such artifacts as a strigil dug up by a peasant near Lyons, a horn from a narwhal, ancient coins, and saintly relics. These objects had the power to stimulate the imagination about how humans had lived in the past. The curious and the scholarly alike began wondering about the divine meanings hieroglyphs conveyed.

During the reign of Louis XIV, under Colbert's impetus (again!) the crown developed a program for purchasing artifacts and treasures not only from ancient (cat. 127) and modern cultures but from civilizations throughout the world. Competition was strong among European collectors as each state and its culture enhanced its prestige by gaining possession of recognizably beautiful and rare objets d'art and of curiosities from far-off regions.

Following the lead of a handful of private collectors led by Roger de Gaignières, the crown began to buy the paintings, sculptures, tapestries, musical scores, manuscript poems, and luxury editions that the French had produced during the seventeenth century. Academies began to collect instruments, experimental scientific equipment, scientific notes and papers, sketches—in short, everything produced by the creative imagination. The idea that all these items were part of the *patrimoine* was born only after the habit of collecting these treasures had become well established. This movement was a logical result of defining creativity as the expression of esprit working "for the king," a patrimoine of the mind that was passed down through revolutions and different governments to become very strong in our day.

The Sun King approved of all this, but he never really made the capital his own. The royal heart beat more forcefully in the countryside, and especially at a small hunting retreat near a village west of Paris called Versailles. By replacing it with a château and government buildings, Louis echoed the cultural preferences of his ancestors, the builders of Saint-Germain-en-Laye, Fontainebleau, and Chambord. Versailles permitted expanded fêtes and hunts and increased isolation from protest and from general urban disagreeableness. Surrounded by people he chose to have near him, the king could savor the plays of Molière (cat. 109), the operas of Lully (cat. 107), the motets of Delalande, and the paintings and furnishings produced by his academies. The cultural tension that would develop between Paris and Versailles is often exaggerated: in the first decades, the court in the country was like a colony set up by the capital and highly dependent upon it for design, entertainment, and luxury goods. The fêtes at Versailles were cleverly publicized and communicated to all of Europe via news reports and engravings (cat. 108), making them yet another instrument of prestige, if not of intimidation, in the French program to dominate European diplomacy and culture.

Louis may not have consciously realized that the Parisian standards for taste and politeness—even the salons—had something vaguely "new-money" about them. The whole cultural program launched by Richelieu, the new monumental city of Henry IV, and the classicizing impulse that was taken so literally had something common or nonaristocratic about them. In fact, was not writing itself, and the emphasis on learning rather than on waging war and hunting, still a bit too urban for the French aristocracy? Molière's comedies captured the ridiculous aspects of social climbing via self-fashioning in accordance with high culture, and these plays were very well received at Versailles. The king's own taste, and the courtly culture that he established at Versailles, had baroque and cosmopolitan features that were more clearly aristocratic than the Parisian literary-based culture of the 1660s.

Along with their unique presence in the salon movement, women also created distinct literary and cultural spheres that were their own in the last half of the seventeenth century. Aristocratic and courtly in manners, if not always in rank, the *précieuses* created a special vocabulary to talk about love and friendship by using this vocabulary in their conversation, poems, and novels. Thus a heritage left by a powerful queen, Anne of Austria, who had quashed the rebellions of the Fronde, provided a stimulus for a cultural feminism that pervades the novels of such writers as Madame de Lafayette, Madame de Sévigné, the famous letter writer, and Mademoiselle de Montpensier, the memorialist. Be the setting contemporary France or the tumultuous court of the late sixteenth century, these writings gave force to the private and the intimate in human relations.

In such novels, political power often turns on passionate love, betrayal, and impossible or oppressive marriage. By creating a new social and cultural space for women and enhancing the dignity of women as writers, despite the shrill ridicule heaped on them by such writers as Boileau, this feminism had powerful implications for the hitherto unexamined nature of patriarchal power. The feminism was not, of course, hostile to the monarchy; but, like the salons, the Jansenist movement, and the coffeehouse culture of the eighteenth century, the novels unleashed possibilities for exploring relations between the sexes and how they functioned at the foundation of society. These relations became charged with power in the novels of the Ancien Régime, for the family could be interpreted as the microcosm for society. The structures of love and power in the seventeenth century were explored over and over again, not only in Choderlos de Laclos's *Liaisons dangereuses* (cat. 153) but in the political philosophy of Rousseau. The fact that Rousseau's father had read him the great novels written by late seventeenth-century women no doubt embold-

263

ened the young man to express his most intimate feelings and thoughts in a limpid and direct style.

The final decades of the Sun King's life were filled with humiliating diplomatic reversals, military defeats, and the deaths of heirs to the throne and other close family members. The spontaneity that had characterized the early decades of the reign slowly turned into unbearably boring routine, broken now and then by funerals. The little circles of young talent that always gathered around the powerful—the poets, the "petits abbés," and the wits who had coalesced first around the dauphin and then, when he died, around the duke of Burgundy, who also died—had spent years planning for power under the coattails of a handful of prominent conspiratorial aristocrats who complained about their loss of power at Versailles. Some of these alienated aristocrats became highly effective ideologues and were able to communicate their powerlessness by posing as civic activists. The aristocratically inspired play *Turcaret*, by Lesage, and still more *The Persian Letters* of Montesquieu, unleashed a "countercultural" revolution that would have devastating consequences for the royal religion. Molière's ironic critique of new wealth behind a veneer of courtly manners was replaced by a harsh, somewhat paranoid picture of the tax official as completely grasping and corrupt. From the distance of an imagined oriental and despotic culture, Montesquieu's Persians, Usbek and Rica, made parallels to the spineless courtiers of Versailles who confused ceremony with real power over budgets and armies. Aristocratic political activism took the guise of social and even racial superiority, undergirded with feelings of "enslavement" by the monarch. Like ripples from a pebble thrown into a pool, Boulainvilliers's and Montesquieu's ideas (cat. 145) tore away at the theatrical and courtly foundations that Richelieu and Louis XIV had given the state. And, very important, the underlying fear of disorder that had prevailed in the seventeenth century dissipated. In fact, the mood of the 1710s and 1720s held that society was so stable that it oppressed the individual spirit.

While Louis XV was maturing, France was governed by an elderly cardinal, Fleury, who guided foreign policy masterfully until his death in 1740 but who had not been trained to keep a surveillant's eye on literary, operatic, and theatrical circles. The little storms created by aristocrats hardly seemed important enough to merit his attention. True, Jansenist ideas about grace, especially since they had gained support in judicial circles, were perceived as opposition to the royal religion; but these ideas might well have been accommodated to the absolute monarch if the original alliances between the state and the Jesuits had been redefined. This was not to be the case.

The eighteenth century was fond of mechanistic, indeed clock-like metaphors about virtually everything, and these metaphors were never more appropriate than when used to describe the cultural politics of the century. The wheels and gears went round and round, but always in the same direction, tearing away the intellectual, religious, and cultural foundations of the Richelieu state by means of theological and philosophical writing, satire, and wit.

That Louis XV was personally inclined to privacy has often been mentioned as a reason for the tensions and the gaps that would develop between the monarchy and elite society during the 1740s; but his distance from court functions was more a sign than a cause of deeper sources of disenchantment. No better evidence for the changed mood than Saint-Simon's *Memoirs* (cat. 155) could be found to confirm the fact that the Camelot-like moment at the Versailles of the 1670s was not repeated under Louis XV. The great ministries kept up and expanded their paperwork; the gardens were not only maintained but replanted; but the magical theatricality of royal power that had prevailed during the Sun King's reign became a catacomb of memories.

The cultural vitality of the realm in the eighteenth century centered unabashedly and forcefully in the capital. To be sure, some of the larger provincial cities, especially those with great law courts and local academies, complemented and extended Parisian literary, artistic, and scientific projects, but it was Paris that radiated French culture throughout the eighteenth century. The increased role of the press—the scholarly journals for the academies, the plays and the novels for polite society, and, of course, the newspapers and women's magazines—contributed to a sense of movement and vitality in French culture. The monarchy of Louis XIV had harnessed creative energies to express itself through ideas about immortality, and through a timeless classicism sustained by court routine. Eighteenth-century Paris, by contrast, radiated timeliness that stimulated creative expectation. Well before there were any political projects to undertake, activism gained momentum. Provincials and foreigners alike continually wondered about what the Parisians would come up with next. Indeed, some elements of what we call today the "culture of shock" were beginning to appear in the most stylish aristocratic and artistic circles after 1775.

Creativity in the sense of producing something different from what had been obtainable before became a commercial necessity in the elite luxury market that Paris became during the eighteenth century. To hold their provincial and foreign readers, weekly newspapers and newsletters had to print stories about inventions, articles of clothing, or theatrical performances. Indeed, the tempo of eighteenth-century Parisian culture came to be governed by a weekly printing schedule, a surprisingly rapid rhythm for a society used to the church calendar. Reporting and gossiping about the weekly meetings of the various academies or salons and weekly reports about commercial and fiscal activities energized Parisian elite, literary, artistic, and artisanal circles to produce not only the new but the new and different or the new and better. Reports of scientific experiments and new inventions were in the vanguard of this movement; accounts of explorations in the Pacific or of the discovery of still more fossils were not far behind. Descriptions of increasingly precise clock escapements vied with the latest news about diet, miasmas, canal building, and the antique sculpture just unearthed at Paestum in Italy. In the salons, the poems, stories, and conversations that were exchanged exuded excitement about the new and the experimental.

The invention of the designer dress (Françoise Leclerc, a pioneering *haute couturière*, comes immediately to mind) attracted a great deal of attention, thanks to women's magazines that featured these styles in their pages. As the European capital for ribbons, wigs, luxury cloth, and satin shoes, Paris boasted couturières who created dresses whose cut was often more important than the quality of the fabric. When clever young seamstresses began to imitate these *coquette* styles, they created

265

a leveling effect in urban society. And, for the first time, the great couturières dared to wear the clothes they had designed,which had previously been reserved for the well-to-do. Indeed, the empire of French clothing extended from Mount Vernon to St. Petersburg and would prove far less ephemeral than Napoléon's.

In this burgeoning creative environment the older Richelieu–Louis XIV state was not so much challenged as taken for granted. The royalism of the academies that had centered on the person of the king slowly became more institutional and passive, as expressed in the routine academic administration. Talk about jealousies and competitiveness over elections to the academies or about the reputations of guests at salons, and news that a director for the royal theater and opera had been appointed, attracted younger writers to a participatory elitist culture that imagined a writer's or a scientist's visibility made him as powerful as a judge or general. Since the king did not wish to express his taste to any but his most intimate courtiers, his ministers competed with aristocrats in the dangerous game of launching plays, operas, and writers, much as nineteenth-century English lords would compete over horses.

The royal imprint on the Parisian urban setting followed in the lines first traced during the reign of Henry IV. The Place Louis XV (now the Place de la Concorde) enhanced the grandeur of the Tuileries; the new Saint-Geneviève Church (now the Panthéon) and the Royal Mint show distinctive eighteenth-century ornamentation, but the fundamental ordering of spaces and of building masses so as to heighten the impression of majesty remained firmly in place. But now these structures were understood to be by-products of what could almost be called "royalism by committee," as contrasted with direct kingly initiative.

Beneath the apparent stability of royal institutions, ominous signs of weakness lurked just where Richelieu had feared. The Roman Catholic church of the eighteenth century continued to wield enormous institutional if not cultural power. Ever critical, churchmen—and the Jesuits in particular—pressed royal officials to use all the king's powers to stamp out Jansenist thought, as if this were a totally dangerous or alien phenomenon. Why, the priests asked, did the police not do more to ban "immoral" writing, etchings, plays, and prostitution? The powers that the institutionalized church had over French society, and over the monarchy, remained formidable throughout the century, despite the church's declining success in recruiting the talented writers and administrators upon which its vitality depended. Through its administration of the sacraments, the church married or buried those whom it deemed Roman Catholic and Christian. For someone who wished to live "philosophically" or like an "old Roman"—that is, privately and without an institutional religious affiliation—the question of burial inevitably led to frustration and a feeling of powerlessness.

The anticlericalism of the philosophes, and of Voltaire in particular (cat. 148), can only be understood if the power of the church as a political and administrative force is kept in mind. Battles over Jansenist charges that the Jesuits were subservient to Rome, miscarriages of royal justice in cases involving Huguenots, and, above all, censorship of books on ethics, politics, and psychology, loomed very large in a culture that was rapidly fragmenting and attracting an increasing number of readers and interested participants. Since the sixteenth century, political activism had been at least partially expressed in writing. After 1720 it seemed as though science, literature, and the arts were all imbued with an intense, creative, civic-duty intent, as new knowledge and writing became increasingly activist.

Competition for literary repute became so intense that the cultural and financial significance of the older centers of recognition—royal patronage—paled before the reputation to be acquired in salons and coffeehouses and through book sales. Elections to academies were won or lost in the salons, those weekly "conversation" meetings held under the aegis of various highly competitive women. Literary production increased enormously as Dutch and Swiss publishers flooded Paris with illegal books. Royal censors read on and on, searching for Jansenist heresy, while the whole culture was shifting toward Enlightenment activism. Competition in conversation, being witty and urbane and up-to-date, fueled the overheated furnace of participatory social relations that undermined the spectatorial politics inherited from the seventeenth century.

The seventeenth century had been the age of the theater, of Corneille, Molière, and Racine; the eighteenth century certainly had a lot of theater and a standard operatic repertory, but it became the first great age of the philosophical tale and the novel, the distinction between the two not always being clear to the reader. Clearly written and usually short, such works as Voltaire's *Candide,* Diderot's *D'Alembert's Dream* (cat. 147) and *Rameau's Nephew,* and Rousseau's *Emile,* to mention only four, communicated the most abstract philosophical, scientific, and pedagogical theories of the century to nonspecialist and specialist alike. Precedents for these philosophical stories existed, of course; one has only to recall the ones by Erasmus and More or, more recently, by Fontenelle and Fénelon (cat. 125), all of whom produced some of their most profound and creative work in novelistic form. But after about 1720 it became almost unthinkable for writers in Paris to address their works exclusively to specialists and scholars. Scholarly publication intended solely for other scholars was certainly a flourishing aspect of eighteenth-century culture, but publications addressed simply "to the reader" established the trends in French culture, and the relation of that culture to the monarchy.

To discern trends in patronage and to measure for whom or for what creative energies are expended, it is always interesting to examine the careers of brilliant autodidacts, that is, persons lacking a university education and family connections to elite institutions. Their career trajectories are revealing of the prevailing forces in a culture. When the Swiss immigrant and autodidact Rousseau arrived in Paris and began to savor its literary and salon culture, he brought something new, a way of notating music numerically. Rousseau was soon swept up into writing on ethical topics for the prize competitions that the various provincial academies organized. In Rousseau's writings a kingly presence is never really manifest in personal terms, and this did not result from his foreign-republican origins. The king-person, loved or hated, on whom social stability had been thought to depend, and from whom literary and other creative energies flowed, had faded. A century earlier, even in the height of the revolutionary Fronde, such an absence would have been unthinkable.

Another example is the son of the Huguenot clockmaker Caron, who changed his name to Beaumarchais and made a career of gunrunning to the insurgent American colonists before he turned to writing plays. Not once does Beaumarchais imagine that his character Count Almaviva in *The Marriage of Figaro* (cat. 154) is undermining respect for social privilege and the entire "feudal" legal system that supports it. Almaviva manipulates the legal system in order to seduce a housemaid. Brid'orson, the magistrate, is ridiculous. And Figaro, in prose as forceful as the Alexandrine verses that Corneille gave Roderigue, cries out: "No, monsieur le Comte, you shall not have her. Just because you are a great nobleman does not mean that you are a great genius. Nobility, fortune, rank, jobs, all these give pride! What have you done in order to have so much wealth? You took the trouble to be born, nothing more" (act 5, scene 3). These were sentiments that everyone could understand. The government had tried to suppress the play, using its antiquated police powers that dated from the seventeenth century; but the only result was to make the play and its author famous. Beaumarchais's characters were undermining the social order in a devastating way, and this in a monarchy that had already become more of a bureaucratic machine than a paternalist psychological power capable of inspiring respect.

The writer, the savant who made discoveries about nature, and the philosopher who inspired confidence in humanity's capacities to build a new and better social order—that is, a Newton, a Voltaire, a Franklin, a Rousseau, a Lavoisier—were the geniuses who offered direction to a culture that was enthusiastic about itself and eager for change. Some writers and artists, and some government officials, attempted to stem the tide of opinion and activism, but wasn't Voltaire just as much an activist when he was defending the monarchy as when he attacked magistrates for their injustice toward a Huguenot in the Calas Affair? French power, French culture? In his personal and cultural identity, the writer had evolved from a royal servant to a moral authority in his own right. No longer did he resemble the artisan braid maker who said, "It's for the king." The literary culture of eighteenth-century Paris did not have the royal gaze at its center. Indeed, we of a later century can interpret Watteau's great painting for Gersaint, the art dealer, as an indication of how that century looked to the future: a portrait of Louis XIV is being packed up for storage. The Richelieu state would easily be dismantled during the early summer of 1789, only to be put back together again in 1792 to counter the military incursions of foreign powers. This time, however, the revived state centered on the Jacobin political and cultural program and on Foucher's police.

POVR LA BONTE',
DANS LA PIECE DE L'ELEMENT DE L'EAV.

Vn Grand Fleuve, avec ce mot **FACIT OMNIA LÆTA.** Les grands Fleuves portent l'abondance & la fertilité par tout où ils paſſent ; De meſme les bons Princes tels que Sa Majeſté, font le bonheur & la richeſſe des peuples qui leur obeïſſent.

Loin de moy tout perit, tout languit de foibleſſe,
Et ſeiche de triſteſſe
Faute de mon ſecours ;
Prés de moy tout fleurit, tout profite & s'áuance,
Et l'on me voit porter la joye & l'abondance
Par tout où je porte mon cours.

Perrault.

VUÉ-PERSPECTIVE DE LA PLACE DE LOUIS LE GRAND,
avec la Représentation des Salles construites à l'occasion du Mariage de
MONSEIGNEUR LE DAUPHIN.

6 The Grand Siècle to the French Revolution (1661–1799)

Emmanuel Le Roy Ladurie

The period 1661–1799 is extraordinarily significant for the evolution of the Bibliothèque Nationale and for its relationships with power, state, and culture. Credit for reviving the Royal Library in the seventeenth century unquestionably goes to Louis XIV and of course to Colbert, who was not the unimaginative gangster that Gabriel Désert has portrayed in his recently published works (works which, incidentally, have great merits). As Colbert saw it, a royal library ought to contribute to the king's glory, that is, to what now we would call his image. From a "political" standpoint certain things have remained more or less permanent!

Of the improvements that Colbert introduced, or that occurred during his lifetime, special mention should be made of the cataloguing system which the great scholar Nicolas Clément perfected and which would be continued along some of the principles he devised virtually to the end of the twentieth century. Only the impending move of the Bibliothèque nationale de France to Tolbiac has made a cataloguing system of a different sort unavoidable. Moreover, using the strong-arm tactics of the recently deceased Henry IV, Colbert took advantage of monasteries unable to resist royal pressure in the age of classicism and bought up their most precious manuscripts at bargain prices (cat. 11). He also encouraged the establishment of medal and print collections. During the time Colbert was in office, the king purchased the collection of 120,000 engravings amassed by abbé de Marolles, which formed the nucleus of our present Department of Prints and Engravings.

Following Colbert, the minister of war, Louvois, more or less directly took in hand the destiny of the library. Louis XIV had been presented with some exquisite imperial Chinese editions and, with the help of the Jesuits implanted in China, the first purchases of Chinese works began (cat. 129). Paris even had a Chinese librarian, married to a French woman, who was supposed to draw up the first catalogue of Chinese books. In general, the acquisition of manuscripts from distant countries was in full swing in private libraries. In 1700 the archbishop of Reims, a member of the

Louvois-Letellier family, gave the library its first Aztec manuscript, the *Codex Tellerianus.*[1]

It was in the eighteenth century that the Royal Library enjoyed its most remarkable development thanks to its great director, abbé Bignon.[2] He came from a noble family *(noblesse de la robe)* that was on familiar terms with the Ponchartrain family (the same family that gave its name to the famous lake near New Orleans). Bignon's activity covered several areas. To begin with, he moved the library into the principal building of the present complex, Mazarin's former palace. (Mazarin had wanted a pied-à-terre near the residence of his friend—perhaps Platonic—Anne of Austria, who, after the death of her husband, Louis XIII, resided in what is now the Palais Royal.) Moreover, since Bignon wanted to keep a firm grip on his institution, he placed *commis*—a type of civil servant in modern parlance—in administrative posts. They were preferable to the traditional *officiers,* who were more difficult to control because they owned their offices.

One of Bignon's great contributions lay in further refining the library's cataloguing system. But enrichment of the collections interested him fully as much. Purchases of private collections quickened in the most varied fields (manuscripts, medals, musical scores, maps, posters). His finest acquisition was the huge library of the recently deceased Colbert, which he bought for the equivalent of twelve million francs, or about 2.4 million dollars, in today's money (now the price of some very fine illuminated manuscripts!). The acquisition of foreign and especially Oriental works continued as before through diplomats as intermediaries. Furthermore, Bignon maintained personal contacts with distinguished foreign librarians of his time, such as Sir Hans Sloane in London, to whom the English are indebted for part of the early holdings of the present British Library, and Garelli, who supervised the library of the Austrian emperor. The abbé corresponded as well with Russian scholars who were themselves interested in books and manuscripts preserved in St. Petersburg.

To a small extent under Louis XIV, and then especially under Louis XV, the library was opened up not just to privileged scholars but to a wider public, a policy which the librarians and the staff as a whole took in stride with their customary graciousness.

In the history of the library, as in other aspects of French life, the Revolution is a fascinating phenomenon. The Royal Library under Louis XVI (1774–1793) contained three hundred thousand volumes and was served by seventy employees, a staff scarcely larger than when the library had housed a mere seventy thousand volumes around 1720. Individual productivity necessarily had to keep pace with the growth of the collections, sometimes putting the salaried staff into a less gracious humor and prompting complaints from contemporaries. The work was not only absorbing but sometimes dangerous. Ladders had to be climbed constantly, resulting in broken bones and other mishaps. Moreover, the library was unheated for fear it might catch on fire, an anxiety that persisted during the following centuries. A single room was provided with a small fireplace, and in wintertime staff members popped in from time to time to warm up. The same concern for fire prevention ruled out the use of candles; the sun was the only source of illumination.

The Revolution was hard on earlier directors of the Bibliothèque Nationale. One of them, Pierre Le Noir, was falsely accused by a subordinate of having stored barrels of gunpowder in the library cellars—a distant echo of England's Gunpowder Plot. Later, two of my predecessors were guillotined. The first was Anne-Louis Lefèvre d'Ormesson, an excellent man who had added substantially to the library's acquisitions, was compensated with a meager salary, and wanted to make the library accessible to the people. His guilt consisted in belonging to a great family of the noblesse de robe in the Ancien Régime. The second director to come under the guillotine was Jean-Louis Carra, d'Ormesson's successor. He had masterminded the despicable campaign against Le Noir but, as a Girondist, was himself later overtaken and even devoured by the Revolution, which considered him much too moderate in his politics.

After Carra, the directorship went to Sébastien Chamfort, an important writer whose *Maximes* can still be read with pleasure and interest. Though of modest beginnings, Chamfort had nonetheless benefited from the Ancien Régime—which did not prevent him from joining the extremist Jacobin wing of the Revolution. He scarcely had time to display his administrative talents, which appear to have been mediocre in any case. In 1794, during the Robespierrist dictatorship, Chamfort too was overtaken by events. A "dove" rather than a "hawk," he was placed under house arrest. Panic-stricken at the idea of going to prison, Chamfort tried unsuccessfully to commit suicide, first with a pistol, then with a razor blade. He died some months later from his self-inflicted wounds. The directorship of the Bibliothèque Nationale has always been a risky job! As if that weren't enough, the entire library staff was denounced to the Robespierrist police by an employee named Duby (no relation to our great historian of the Middle Ages). He accused them of being aristocrats, which was enough to get them all fired, although in fact many of those dismissed came from modest backgrounds.

But every picture of the French Revolution is painted in chiaroscuro. After recalling such painful episodes, may I be permitted to point to the Revolution's more agreeable effects on the Bibliothèque Nationale? Paradoxically, I am alluding to the innumerable legal confiscations made at the expense of the clergy and the aristocratic *émigrés*. Whatever objections may be raised to these despoilments, they were in fact carried out in conformity to (revolutionary) law. It is to this seizure of manuscripts, books, and medals that the Bibliothèque nationale de France owes its ultimate and most opulent development. Entire cartloads of material were unloaded in our courtyard, sometimes in the rain. Splendid collections from monasteries, churches, and private houses were transported in carts from which works that had been piled up helter-skelter sometimes fell to the ground. Report has it that a curator, La Porte du Teil—from a family of the Robe and ancestor of a mustachioed general of the Vichy régime—discovered an enormous Bible in Carolingian gilt script, which we still have,[3] while rummaging in the sweepers' room—where an overburdened employee had no doubt put (or hid) it "temporarily." The "booty" from these confiscations was enormous: 250,000 books, 85,000 prints, 15,000 manuscripts, many of them illuminated, along with precious maps and coins.

Some examples: In May 1793, at the height of the Terror, 18,000 coins or medals, including 7,000 of Roman origin, were brought from the monastery of Sainte-

Geneviève (the present Panthéon). In December 1795 the abbey of Saint-Germain-des-Prés "furnished," if I dare use that word, 9,000 manuscripts to the Bibliothèque Nationale; more than one of them would bring a fortune today at Sotheby's or Christie's. In 1796 the Sorbonne was "relieved" of 1,900 manuscripts, an action which the curators of that institution still hold against us, though in a friendly way. In September 1798 the turn came for 33,000 prints to be "imported" at one fell swoop from the Palais Mazarin; 5,000 maps, including some magnificent and very old specimens, also arrived, many of them taken from the famous Parisian abbey of Saint-Victor (cat. 33). Many other individual items deserve to be described and have their histories told. I will single out only one, the astonishing manuscript of the Hours of Anne de Bretagne—still among our treasures today, with its exquisite illuminated pages like so many paintings, and its decoration composed of a host of flowers and insects framing the written portions.

The history of the Revolution yields anecdotes worthy of a counterrevolutionary anthology or a Guinness book of records for stupidity in the 1790s. Some very beautiful manuscripts were burned in the public square simply because they belonged to the Ordre du Saint-Esprit. It is even reported that General Hanriot, a Jacobin extremist, talked of burning down the Bibliothèque Nationale because it was the former library of the kings of France. Fortunately, no serious thought was given to acceding to such eccentricity. Clearly, the relations between the Revolution and the library, and more generally between the library and those in power, can assume sharp contrasts over time and even in the present.

These forced transfers took the Bibliothèque Nationale nearly a century to "digest," classify, itemize, and index. Gradually the library would be able to assure these treasures the safety, the convenience of scientifically tested facilities, and then the readers and the exhibitions they deserved. To that end, our curators would benefit from valuable state aid, aid sometimes grudgingly apportioned, sometimes generous.

1 The University of Texas Press, by the way, has just brought out the first faithful reproduction of it: Eloise Quinones Keber, *Codex Telleriano-Remensis: Ritual, Divination, and History in a Pictorial Aztec Manuscript* (Austin, 1995).

2 On abbé Bignon, see Françoise Bléchet in *Histoire des bibliothèques françaises*, vol. 2, *Les bibliothèques sous l'Ancien Régime, 1530–1789*, ed. Claude Jolly (Paris, 1988), 215–21.

FRANCE IN THE 18TH CENTURY

—————— Principal administrative units

"Pays d'élections"

"Pays d'états"

Catalogue Numbers 106–61

106

ROBERT NANTEUIL

Louis XIV

Cabinet des Estampes, AA5 Rés. Nanteuil

Robert Nanteuil (1623–1678). Signed and dated bottom center: "Nanteuil pingebat et sculpebat cum privilegio Regis, 1672." First state: 69.3 × 59.5 cm.

The king, shown in bust turned three-quarters to the left, wears a breastplate with a lace ruffle and a draped scarf, within a laurel wreath. Above is arranged the skin of the Nemean lion (the traditional attribute of Hercules); the two forepaws, adorned with a fleur-de-lis, fall over the upper corners of the frame. In the lower corners appear two emblematic medals; the one on the left bears the motto "Increscunt obice vires" (Strength is increased by the obstacle) and is illustrated by a sun whose rays reflect in a mirror, the better to set ablaze a sheaf of seven arrows, symbol of the United Provinces (Holland); the medal on the right bears the motto "Somnum abrupisse dolebitur" (He who interrupts his sleep will suffer), illustrated by Hercules dozing after his combat with Antaeus and tied up by the Pygmies who hope to capture him. This is again an allusion to Louis XIV's struggle against the Dutch in 1672, the year in which the monarch had just won a number of victories, forcing his way into some forty cities as conqueror.

A ribbon connecting the two medals bears the inscription: "Offerebat humilissimus subditus Jac. Nicolaus Colbert abbas" (Offered by the most humble servant, abbot Jacques-Nicolas Colbert). Indeed, like the ten other portraits Nanteuil engraved of Louis XIV, it was commissioned to embellish a thesis, in this case one defended by Jacques-Nicolas Colbert, abbot of Le Bec and future archbishop of Rouen. The full thesis, including the text of the propositions defended which were engraved on a second plate below the king's portrait, has survived in only a single copy. It was part of the Edmond de Rothschild collection, now in the Louvre. Nanteuil engraved the portrait from a pastel done between Feb. 5 and 17, 1672. "Je prétends exprimer toute sa majesté" (I mean to express all his majesty), he is supposed to have said about the portrait.

Of the eleven portraits he engraved of the king, ten were made from life; only one, the first, was a copy of a painting, by Pierre Mignard (Petitjean and Wickert, no. 133). Nanteuil, who was drawer and engraver in ordinary to the king, began his career of portraitist in Paris by executing pencil and pastel portraits which he then engraved on copper. Unfortunately, only a tiny number of the portraits he drew still exist. He made four pastels of Louis XIV at different ages, altering them to reflect the king's aging appearance with retouches primarily to the wig and the moustache and accentuation of the wrinkles. He customarily posed all his models for representation at three-quarters and at rest. The head and top of the bust are seen slightly from the side, while the gaze is directed to the front toward the viewer. The background is often rather dark and devoid of unnecessary ornamentation. Daylight arrives from the side in such a way as to permit the play of some shadows, allowing the features to stand out. Without ever seeking to flatter his sitters, he nonetheless presented them in a favorable way. He had the gift of breathing life into a portrait by the radiance of a look or by the half-smile that arrests the viewer's attention. On seeing one of Nanteuil's portraits offered to Queen Marie-Thérèse, Anne of Austria, the king's mother, is supposed to have exclaimed, "Venez, Madame, voir votre mari en peinture, il vit" (Come, Madame, and see your husband in paint; he's alive).

Nanteuil engraved only the face and entrusted the rest to an assistant. It was unusual for him to draw dress, hair, or frame. He determined the general pose, oversaw the execution, and reserved to himself "les proportions et la liaison de toutes les parties" (the proportions and the union of all the parts), as he observed in his *Maximes sur la gravure*. He left behind 221 portraits, listed in the Petitjean and Wickert catalogue in 1925.

Françoise Jestaz

E. Bouvy, *Le portrait gravé et ses maîtres: Robert Nanteuil* (Paris, 1924). Charles Petitjean and Charles Wickert, *Catalogue de l'oeuvre gravée de Robert Nanteuil* (Paris, 1925), no. 142. Josèphe Jacquiot, *Médailles et jetons de Louis XIV, d'après le manuscrit de Londres*, 4 vols. (Paris, 1968), 2:273–78. Véronique Meyer, "Les thèses: leur Soutenance et leurs illustrations dans les universités françaises sous l'Ancien Régime," in *Eléments pour une histoire de la thèse*, ed. Claude Jolly and Bruno Neveu, *Mélanges de la Bibliothèque de la Sorbonne* 12 (Paris, 1993), 45–111.

279

107

FRANCESCO CAVALLI

Xerse (Xerxes)

Département de la Musique, Vm⁴ 2, p. 121

*Xerxes opera italien orné d'entrées de ballet repre-
senté dans la grande gallerie des peintures du
Louvre devant le Roy apres son mariage avec
Marie-Therese d'Autriche infante d'Espagne l'an
1660. Le Seigneur Francesco Cavalli en a fait la
Musique et les Airs de Ballet ont esté composez par
Jean Baptiste de Lully Surintendant de la Musique
de la Chambre/Recueilly par le Sr Fossard ordinaire de la Musique du Roy. L'an 1695.*

*General score, 1695. Handwritten copy by François
Fossard; 336 pp.; 440 × 290 mm.*

Xerxes by Francesco Cavalli (1602–1676) was
performed for the first time in Paris in the
Gallery of Paintings at the Louvre on Nov. 22,
1660. The opera had its premiere in Venice in
1654 at the ss Giovanni e Paolo Theater and
was already well known throughout Italy.
Mazarin selected this opera because the
preparation of *L'Ercole amante*, an original
commission for the wedding celebrations of
Louis XIV and Marie-Thérèse, was behind
schedule. In an effort to accommodate
French tastes, Lully was asked to add a
French-style overture to Cavalli's opera, considered to be the first of its kind, with six
ballet scenes that had no connection with the
plot, although some felt they made an allusion to the political situation (first scene:
The Basques, half French, half Spanish).

Mazarin's efforts to transplant Italian
opera to France were one of the most inventive features of his patronage. For two
decades, the cardinal-minister unstintingly
employed financial resources and networks
of influence to get the most talented male as
well as female singers, musicians, and composers from Italy to come to France. The fruit
of this policy, often greeted with little enthusiasm by its French detractors, was the creation of three original commissions: *Orfeo* by
Luigi Rossi (1647), an undeniable masterpiece; *Les Noces de Thétis et de Pélée* by Carlo
Caproli (1654); and *L'Ercole amante* by
Francesco Cavalli (1662).

François Fossard (1642–1702), "petit violon"
with the King's Musicians, for a time shared
the position of royal music copier with André
Danican Philidor. His collection of engravings and drawings illustrates festivals and
celebrations of the French court and is currently dispersed among Paris, Stockholm (the
Tessin collection), and Copenhagen.

The juxtaposition of the Italian and
French styles gives Cavalli's score of *Xerxes* a
curious look, because Fossard had prepared
the pages for an instrumental arrangement
with several parts, and he had to transcribe
long Italian recitatives for voice and figured
bass. Loret the journalist complained about
the length:

> Enfin, je l'ay vû le Xerxès
> Que je trouvay long, par excès;
> Mes yeux pourtant, et mes oreilles
> Y remarquèrent cent merveilles,
> Sans compter mille autres apas,
> Lesquels je ne comprenois pas,
> N'entendant que la langue mienne,
> Et, point du tout, l'Italienne

(I finally saw *Xerxes*. I found it excessively
long. But my eyes and my ears found a
hundred wonders without even mentioning a thousand other pleasures, because I
understand no language other than my
own and certainly do not understand
Italian).

Catherine Massip

Henry Prunières, *L'opéra italien en France avant Lulli* (Paris,
1913), 252–61.

Rupture du Palais et des enchantemens de l'Ysle · Troisiesme Journée · d'Alcine representeé par un feu d'Artifice

Israel Silvestre del, et sculps.

108

ISRAËL SILVESTRE

*Les Plaisirs de l'Isle Enchantée.
Troisième journée: Rupture du Palais
et des enchantemens de l'Isle d'Alcine
représentée par un feu d'artifice*
(Pleasures of the Enchanted Isle.
Third day: Blow-up of the palace and
of the enchantments of the Isle of
Alcina represented by fireworks)
Cabinet des Estampes, Collection Hennin
no. 4215

*Etching signed at bottom left: "Israël Silvestre del.,
et sculpsit"; on the right: "g." 28.5 × 43.2 cm.
Published in 1673.*

"The pleasures of the Enchanted Isle, or the
entertainments and divertissements of the
king at Versailles, divided into three days and
begun the seventh day of May in the year
1664" form a series of nine plates. Louis XIV
ordered them from Israël Silvestre (1621–1691)
to memorialize the spectacular entertainments that took place at Versailles May 7–12,
1664.

281

After the showy fête of Aug. 17, 1661, which his former minister Nicolas Fouquet had offered him at Vaux-le-Vicomte (see cat. 98), the young king would brook no rivals and aspired to be the only one able to offer such extraordinary spectacles, enhancing his fame and projecting an image of magnificence in France and abroad. He called upon the most famous artists of the age: the decorator Carlo Vigarani, summoned from Italy by Mazarin in 1659, created the ingenious and astonishing stage contrivances and effects in the midst of which dancers and musicians would perform; Molière and Lully (superintendent of the music of the King's Chamber from 1661 onward) collaborated to compose ten comedy-ballets on themes from antiquity or based on fantasy.

From May 7 to 12, 1664, there took place *Les Plaisirs de l'Isle Enchantée*, which included, according to André Félibien in his *Description du Château de Versailles* of 1674, "course de bagues, collation ornée de machines, comédie mélée de danse et de musique, ballet du Palais d'Alcine, feu d'artifice et autres fêtes galantes et magnifiques" (tilting at rings, collation from amid wonderful devices, comedy interspersed with dance and music, ballet of the palace of Alcina, fireworks, and other elegant and magnificent entertainments). On May 7 there was the tournament and an elaborate buffet; May 8 saw Vigarani's presentation of Molière's comedy *Princesse d'Elide* performed in a temporary theater erected by Vigarani and with music by Lully; on May 9, "the third day," came the turn for the *Ballet d'Alcine,* a subject drawn from Ariosto's *Orlando furioso.* An evil queen,

Alcina, casts her magic charms to detain the knight Ruggerio and his valiant companions. As Félibien notes, "Ils en furent délivrés après beaucoup de temps consommé dans le délices par la bague qui détruisait les enchantements" (After much time passed in revels, they were freed by the ring which destroyed the spells). Then the palace of Alcina was destroyed with a great crash of thunder and fire, in the form of the grandiose fireworks illustrated here by Silvestre. In the foreground, Louis XIV can be glimpsed from the back under a canopy along with his wife Marie-Thérèse and some great lords surrounded by a crowd of courtiers. The spectacle unfolded in front of what would become the parterre of Latone, on which the palace of Alcina was erected. All around, landscaped greenery hints at the immense vistas of the great park of Versailles.

The art of the court ballet attained exceptional brilliance in France from 1645 to 1672. The total spectacle, a blend of dance, song, and acting, reached its apotheosis with these royal entertainments. Musicians, dancing masters, scene painters, and authors of librettos gravitated around the young king and his court. The king's inclination to go on stage himself and to be acclaimed by his subjects certainly had something to do with the success of this art.

Françoise Jestaz

Pierre de Nolhac, *La création de Versailles* (Paris, 1925). Pierre Verlet, *Versailles* (Paris, 1961). *Lully: Musicien soleil,* exhibition at Versailles (Versailles, 1987).

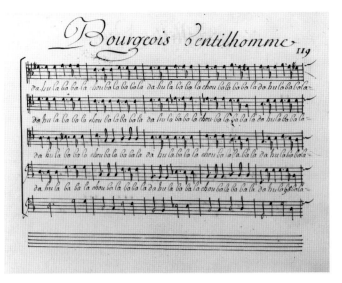

109
JEAN-BAPTISTE POQUELIN, KNOWN AS MOLIÈRE, AND JEAN-BAPTISTE LULLY

Le Bourgeois gentilhomme (LWV 43)
Département de la Musique, Rés. F. 578, p. 119
(detail)

*Le Bourgeois Gentil homme Comedie Ballet Donné
par le Roy a toutte sa Cour dans le chasteau de
Chambord au Mois D'octobre 1670 fait par
Monsieur de Lully Sur Intendant de la Musique du
Roy et par Le Sieur Molliere.*

*Orchestra score; 3 fols.; 183 pp.; 435 × 290 mm.
Handwritten copy by André Danican Philidor the
Elder with notes by others, ca. 1690. Probably from
the Philidor Collection.*

The collaboration between Molière and Lully
which produced nine comedy-ballets from
1664 to 1670 was largely the result of royal
design. A good pupil of Mazarin, the young
Louis XIV understood that a rich and brilliant court life was of major importance for
the development of the royal image.

Of these nine works–*Le Mariage forcé*
(1664), *Les Plaisirs de l'Isle Enchantée* (1664; see
cat. 108), *L'Amour médecin* (1665), *La Pastorale
comique* (1667), *Le Sicilien* (1667), *Le Grand
divertissement royal de Versailles* (*Georges
Dandin*) (1668), *Le Divertissement de Chambord
(Monsieur de Pourceaugnac)* (1669), *Les Amants
magnifiques* (1670), and *Le Bourgeois gentilhomme* (1670)–eight belong to the Philidor

Collection either as scores alone or as scores
that also contain the full text of the theatrical
play. In the preface to *L'Amour médecin*,
Molière himself paid tribute to the splendor
of these productions, though a theatrical performance alone does not do justice to the
work: "Il seroit à souhaiter que ces sortes
d'ouvrages pussent toujours se montrer à
vous avec les ornements qui les accompag-
nent chez le Roi... et les airs et les symphonies de l'incomparable Monsieur Lully,
mêlés à la beauté des voix et à l'adresse des
danseurs, leur donnent sans doute les grâces
dont ils ont toutes les peines du monde à se
passer" (We should hope that such works
could always be performed with the embell-
ishments used when performed before the
king... and the arias and symphonies of the
incomparable Monsieur Lully, combined with
the beauty of the voices and the agility of the
dancers, probably lend them graces without
which they suffer greatly).

The Philidor Collection is one of the most
important sources of music in the royal musical repertory of the 17th century. Particularly
well represented are the instrumental music
and court ballets created for Louis XIII, the
court ballets and entertainment for the
Régence of Anne of Austria, and Lully's ballets. During the revolutionary confiscations
and the transfer from the royal libraries, the
collection included fifty-nine volumes, of
which only thirty-eight still exist. Most were
gathered by André Danican Philidor the
Elder (ca. 1652–1730), the musician of the
King's Ecurie and the founder of a "dynasty"
of artists which included among its members
François-André Philidor, a brilliant composer
of *opéras-comiques*.

This manuscript, used by Henry Prunières
when publishing Lully's complete works,
contains instructions for performance and
the names of dancers–Messieurs Laval,
Duval, Dumoulin, and so on–who were
active in the 18th century.

Catherine Massip

Jean-Baptiste Lully, *Oeuvres: Les comédies-ballets*, vol. 3, ed.
Henry Prunières (Paris, 1938). Maurice Pellisson, *Les comédies-
ballets de Molière* (Paris, 1914; repr. 1976).

283

Veüe du fonds de la Grotte de Versailles, orné de trois Grouppes de marbre blanc, qui representent le Soleil au milieu des Nymphes de Thetis, et ses chevaux pensez par des Tritons.

Prospectus Cryptæ Interioris Versaliarum, ubi Sol inter Nymphas Thetidis, et ejus equi cum Tritonibus, statuis marmoreis exhibentur.

110

JEAN LEPAUTRE

Veue du fond de la grotte de Versailles, orné de trois grouppes de marbre blanc, qui représentent le Soleil au milieu des Nymphes de Thétis; et ses chevaux pensez par des Tritons

(View of the back of the grotto of Versailles, decorated with three groups of white marble, showing the Sun amid the Nymphs of Thetis, and his horses groomed by Tritons)

Cabinet des Estampes, Hc 17 fol. pl. 109

To the right, the same title in Latin. Etching; 37.2 × 56.4 cm. Signed at bottom right: "le Potre sculps 1676." Seventh plate of the Description de la grotte de Versailles *by André Félibien (Paris: Imprimerie Royale, 1676).*

Le Soleil apres avoir achevé son cours descend chez Thetis, ou six de ses Nymphes sont occupées a le servir, et à luy offrir toutes sortes de rafraichissemens

Groupe de sept figures de marbre blanc, dont celles marquées 1. 2. 3 et 4 sont de François Girardon de Troye, et celles marquées 5. 6. et 7 sont de Thomas Regnaudin de Moulins, dessiné par P. Monier et gravé par Jean Edelinck

Signum Solis apud Thetidem orbe peragrato diuersantis: ad sunt sex Nymphæ specie ministrantium, quæ defessum Deum tepidis et odoratis aquis refouent

Signum Statuarum Marmorearum septenarii, quarum I. II. III. et IV. opus sunt f. Gerardi Trecensis V. VI. et VII. sunt Tho. Regnaudini Ordeninensi opus. P. Monier. Inuenit. Edelinck Sculpsit. 1678

III

JEAN EDELINCK

Le soleil après avoir achevé son cours descend chez Thétis, ou six de ses nymphes sont occupées à le servir, et à luy offrir toutes sortes de rafraichissemens, grouppe de sept figures de marbre blanc, dont celles marquées 1, 2, 3 et 4 sont de François Girardon de Troyes et celles marquées 5, 6 et 7 sont de Thomas Regnaudin de Moulins. Désigné par P. Monier et gravé par Jean Edelinck
(The Sun, after having completed his course, visits Thetis, where six of her nymphs are busy serving him, offering him all sorts of refreshments, a group of seven figures in white marble, those marked 1, 2, 3, and 4 being by François Girardon of Troyes, and those marked 5, 6, and 7 by Thomas Regnaudin of Moulins. Drawn by P. Monier and engraved by Jean Edelinck)

Cabinet des Estampes, Hc 17 fol. pl. 118
To the right, the same text in Latin and the number 16. Etching; 42.5 × 57.5 cm. Sixth plate of the Description de la grotte de Versailles.

The grotto of Thetis, no longer in existence, was a small, almost cubical house behind the wing of outbuildings at the north of the park of Versailles. Its upper part served as a reservoir. The ground floor enclosed a grotto conforming to 16th-century taste with interior decoration composed of shells, mother of pearl, amber, coral, marble, and gilded bronze. Three recesses were filled by the famous groups of sculpture *Apollon servi par les nymphes* and the *Chevaux du Soleil*, by Girardon, Tuby, the Marsy brothers, and Regnaudin. Behind them, hydraulic organs imitated murmuring fountains and singing birds.

Thanks to the *Comptes des Bâtiments du roi*, which records everything planned or built for the king, it is possible to follow year by year the progress of the building works that Louis XIV had wanted done at Versailles. Starting with an unpromising lay of land, surrounded by marshes, with no view and merely featuring a knoll upon which Louis

285

XIII had constructed a hunting pavilion, Louis XIV, assisted by architect Louis Le Vau followed by Jules Hardouin-Mansart, as well as landscape gardener André Le Nôtre, produced grandiose results. He turned Versailles into a setting for the most famous royal residence in France, and the most brilliant image of the monarchy.

By 1665 the park had assumed the general appearance it would retain until the end of the reign. The massive landscaping effort was accompanied by a program of sculptural decoration. A whole series of artworks populated the gardens. Louis XIV, intent on seeing to it that the gardens were admired, had them reproduced in prints and disseminated. Thanks to the engravings designed to illustrate André Félibien's *Description de la grotte de Versailles* in 1676, we have an accurate idea of the grotto of Thetis, considered the most important work of sculpture of the day.

The grotto was intended to celebrate the sun, which Louis had adopted as his emblem: "Comme le soleil est la devise du Roi et que les poètes confondent le soleil et Apolon, il n'y a rien dans cette superbe maison qui n'ait rapport à cette divinité" (Since the sun is the emblem of the king and since the poets identify the sun with Apollo, there is nothing in this superb house which is unrelated to that divinity) (Félibien, p. 11).

Charles Perrault, Colbert's principal assistant, conceived the subject. "Il serait bon de mettre Apollon qui va se coucher chez Thétys après avoir fait le tour de la terre, pour représenter que le Roi vient se reposer à Versailles après avoir travaillé à faire du bien à tout le monde" (It would be well to have Apollo go to the abode of Thetis to sleep after having traveled around the world, representing the king who goes to Versailles to rest after having worked to bring about the common good).

Obviously, an overall program had been established for the statuary in the royal residences. Colbert, who had been entrusted with the job of building superintendent, busied himself with all matters relating to the king's artistic enterprises, with the help of the Académie des Inscriptions: "Rien n'échappe plus à sa vigilance, depuis les thèmes des statues du parc de Versailles jusques à ceux des livrets des opéras de Quinault" (Nothing escapes his vigilance, from the subjects of the statues in the park at Versailles to those of Quinault's librettos for the operas) (R.-A. Weigert, *Le Style Louis XIV* [Paris, 1941]).

Research by Liliane Lange shows that the idea of the grotto and its decoration must be attributed to Charles and Claude Perrault, but that the concept was partially modified later by Charles Le Brun.

In its day the grotto was one of the most visited and most admired of all of Versailles's marvels; the king gave elaborate buffets there, as well as theatrical shows and suppers. This famous building was demolished twenty years later, when Jules Hardouin-Mansart constructed the north wing of the palace. The sculptures were removed first to the Bosquet des Dômes, then to the Bosquet des Bains d'Apollon in a setting conceived by Hubert Robert in the romantic vein in 1781.

Françoise Jestaz

Pierre Verlet, *Versailles* (Paris, 1961). Liliane Lange, "La grotte de Thétis et le premier Versailles de Louis XIV," in *Art de France* 1 (1961): 133–48. Jean-Marie Pérouse de Montclos, *Histoire de l'architecture française de la Renaissance à la Révolution* (Paris, 1989).

112

CHARLES LE BRUN
*Louis XIV recevant l'hommage de
l'Eloquence* (Louis XIV receiving the
homage of Eloquence)
Cabinet des Estampes, B6 Rés., boîte 4

*Black chalk, gray wash drawing, squared with a
style on beige paper; 27.8 × 22.2 cm. Ca. 1678.*

This drawing, of unknown provenance, is a
first sketch for one of the ovals placed at the
springing of the vault in the Grande Galerie
of Versailles. The date 1663, suggested by J.
Thuillier, links it to the period when Louis
XIV revitalized the Academy of Painting and
Sculpture and appointed Charles Le Brun
(1619–1690) director of the Gobelins tapestry
factory. This date, however, is questionable,
since all of the approximately three hundred
preparatory studies for the paintings of the
gallery date from 1678, after Jules Hardouin-
Mansart's plan won approval, and the technique of squaring by use of a style was typical of the gallery drawings by Le Brun that
were designed to be engraved.

Whereas the decoration on the barrel
vault was devoted to the king's military campaigns, the "six camayeux rangés en bandeau

dans l'architecture feinte. . . et douze médail-
lons ovales placés sur les retombées ou cour-
bures de la voûte" (six monochromes in a
row along the imitation architecture. . . and
twelve oval medallions placed on the vault's
springings or curves), in the description provided by Massé in 1753, were intended to
illustrate the administrative reorganization of
the kingdom, the major construction projects, and the monarch's acts of benevolence.
A certain monotony in the composition,
almost identical to the painting that adorns
the ceiling of the Ambassadors' Staircase
(*Louis XIV Reforming Justice*), or again in several of the medallions in the gallery (such as
Restoring Financial Order and *Navigation
Reestablished*), demonstrates that this was a
minor work in the artist's eyes.

The king, in antique dress and seated
under a makeshift canopy, receives the
homage of a kneeling figure and is flanked by
a god or allegorical figure. The most interesting aspect of this drawing is the iconography,
since it gives unusual attributes both to
Minerva, protector of architecture, who
strangely is holding the drawings for a
church in her right hand, and to kneeling
Eloquence, who holds the caduceus associated with Mercury (who only rarely, and at a
late date, is shown as the god of eloquence).
A famous 1514 drawing by Dürer similarly
depicted the Celtic character Ogmios, known
as the Gallic Hercules, which may suggest
that Le Brun's represents an initial plan for
decorating the Grande Galerie with themes
from the Herculean myth.

François Fossier

H. Jouin, *Charles Le Brun et les Arts sous Louis XIV* (Paris, 1889),
575. *Charles Le Brun: Peintre et dessinateur,* exhibition at
Versailles (Versailles, 1963), no. 160; *Le Brun à Versailles,* exhibition at Versailles (Paris, 1985).

POVR LA BONTE',
DANS LA PIECE DE L'ELEMENT DE L'EAV.

Vn Grand Fleuve, avec ce mot FACIT OMNIA LÆTA. Les
grands Fleuves portent l'abondance & la fertilité par tout où
ils paſſent; De meſme les bons Princes tels que Sa Majeſté,
font le bonheur & la richeſſe des peuples qui leur obeïſſent.

FACIT OMNIA LÆTA

Loin de moy tout perit, tout languit de foibleſſe,
Et ſeiche de triſteſſe
Faute de mon ſecours;
Prés de moy tout fleurit, tout profite & s'auance,
Et l'on me voit porter la joye & l'abondance
Par tout où je porte mon cours.

Perrault.

113

*Devises pour les tapisseries du Roy, où
sont representez les Quatre Elemens et
les Quatre Saisons de l'année*
(Emblematic figures for the king's
tapestries, on which are represented
the Four Elements and the Four
Seasons of the year)
Département des Manuscrits, Fr. 7819,
planche 16

*Vellum, 35 fols., and paper, 8 double-pages; 400 ×
265 mm. Paris, 1664–1672. Bound in green morocco,
18th century. Transferred from the Cabinet du Roi
in Versailles to the Bibliothèque Nationale on 25
messidor, year III (July 13, 1795).*

In 1663 Colbert founded the Petite Académie
(Little Academy), the future Académie des
Inscriptions et Belles-Lettres. Composed of
Jean Chapelain, the abbé de Bourzeis, the
abbé de Cassagnes (all members of the
Académie Française), and Charles Perrault,
future author of the *Contes* (see cat. 126), who
served as secretary, the Petite Académie
devised an epigraphic system designed to
perpetuate the glory of the king in the manner of classical antiquity. The academy's collaboration with the Gobelins tapestry factory,
headed by the king's principal painter,
Charles Le Brun, led to the 1664 production
of tapestries representing the Elements and
the Seasons—two series of four independent
hangings for use in the royal châteaux. All
follow the same model: in the center scene,
the traditional classical divinities are set
against a landscape; in the top center, the
ornamental border contains a medallion with
the royal arms, surmounted by a crown; on
both sides of the composition, a view evokes
an important event of the reign (in the
Elements) or Louis XIV's monogram appears
(in the Seasons); and in the four corners, a
medallion with an allegorical theme symbol-

izes the king's cardinal virtues: Piety, Magnanimity, Munificence, and Valor.

While the tapestries were still on the loom, Colbert ordered that Le Brun's designs for the medallions be painted in gouache on vellum. To execute this first manuscript of paintings commissioned directly for the Bibliothèque Royale, he turned to Jacques Bailly. Bailly was a miniaturist painter and "faiseur d'ouvrages en façon de la Chine" (maker of books in the manner of China), a specialist in painting flowers and fruit in the style of Nicolas Robert, who had just been admitted to the Royal Academy of Painting and Sculpture in June 1663.

The manuscript, painted for Louis XIV's personal pleasure, freely interprets the thirty-two border medallions of the tapestries, and is preceded by a frontispiece and two introductions in a lavishly ornamented frame. The manuscript was begun and completed in 1664 and Jacques Bailly received 1,551 livres for its execution. Each page of the manuscript, bordered with a gilt fillet, contains a title, several lines of prose explanation, and a motto on a decorative frame, below which is a sestet usually composed by Charles Perrault. The gold lettering was the work of the celebrated master calligrapher Nicolas Jarry (see cat. 93). Upon completion, the manuscript was set in a chased silver-gilt frame, the work of the goldsmith Thomas Le Roy.

At Bailly's request, in 1668 an engraved version of the royal manuscript was made by the printmaker Sébastien Leclerc, who did not stop with the emblematic figures but went on to etch the tapestries. It was then decided to imitate the collection of etchings and Bailly was asked to complete his manuscript. In 1672 he added eight full-page miniatures depicting the tapestries. Painted on paper in a more conventional style, they lack the freshness of the emblematic figures and betray the spirit of the manuscript.

For far from having produced a volume of reproductions, Bailly had created one of the most original books of mottos and emblems of the 17th century. The king's bounteous virtues are depicted through the ethereal fantasy of the monkeys with soap bubbles for *Magnanimité* (Magnanimity) (pl. 10), the poetic limpidity of the dolphins and nautiluses for *Valeur* (Valor) (pl. 17), the supreme elegance of the *Bastimens de l'Eté* (Summer buildings), which recall the classicism of the Perrault brothers' architectural projects (pl. 32), the vivacity of the hunt scene in *Automne* (Autumn) (pl. 37), and the humor of the arabesque decoration for *Hiver* (Winter) that prefigures Bérain (pl. 40). "Grâce à lui, tout est joie" (Thanks to him, all is joy), croak smiling frogs, dwellers in the river of royal *Bonté* (Munificence) (pl. 16). With these poetic recreations, Bailly established himself as the talented heir of Paul Jove in the courtly art of the heroic emblematic figure.

Marianne Grivel

Jean Cordey, "Un manuscrit à miniatures du XVIIe siècle: Devises pour les tapisseries du Roy." *Bulletin de la Société de l'Histoire de l'Art Français* 1926: 84–90. *Le siècle de Louis XIV*, exhibition at the Bibliothèque Nationale (Paris, 1927), 54, no. 134. *Collections de Louis XIV: Dessins, albums, manuscrits*, exhibition at the Orangerie des Tuileries (Paris, 1978), 238, no. 233. *Colbert, 1619–1683*, exhibition at the Hôtel de la Monnaie (Paris, 1983), 153, no. 653. Marc Fumaroli and Marianne Grivel, *Devises pour les tapisseries du Roi* (Paris, 1988). Jean-Marc Chatelain, *Livres d'emblèmes et de devises: Une anthologie (1531–1735)* (Paris, 1993), 125–26. Charles Perrault, *Mémoires de ma vie* (Paris, 1993), 28–29 and 132–33.

4

II

II

10

114

*Eleven Medals from Louis XIV's
"Histoire métallique"*
(History in medals)
Pictured: nos. 4 (obverse and reverse),
5 (obverse and reverse), 10, and 11 (obverse
and reverse)

1 The Birth of Louis XIV, 1638
*Cabinet des Médailles, série royale 482 (silver;
diam. 73 mm)*

Obverse: LVDOVICVS . MAGNVS . REX . CHRIS-
TIANISS. *The bust of Louis XIV from the right,
clothed in armor with lilies and the* paludamentum
*(general's cloak). He is crowned with a laurel
wreath. The initial* R *of the engraver's name
(Jérôme Roussel). Reverse:* ORTVS . SOLIS . GALLI-
CI. *The "lever du soleil sur les Français" (sun rising
over the people of France) is illustrated by a gallop-
ing quadriga drawing a chariot in which the
dauphin is riding. Exergue:* SEPT. V. MIN. XXXVIII/
HOR. XI. MIN. XXII. ANTE./MERID. M.DCXXXVIII.
/D. *(initial of the engraver, Dufour). On the edge
are the twelve signs of the Zodiac in their position
at the time the dauphin was born, 11:22 A.M.
Sunday, Sept. 5, 1638. It should be noted that, at the
new Saint-Germain château, Anne of Austria gave
birth to a "long hoped-for" son after twenty-two
years of wedlock. The son was immediately given
the name Dieudonné ("God-given").*

*MLG 1702, no. 2, with Louis XIII's portrait on the obverse.
MLG 1723, not indicated. Divo, no. 2, for the reverse. F.
Bluche, Louis XIV (Paris, 1986). Bluche, Dictionnaire du Grand
Siècle (Paris, 1990).*

*2 Founding of the Royal Academy of Painting
and Sculpture, 1647.*

*Cabinet des Médailles, série royale 523 (silver;
diam. 70 mm).*

Obverse: LVDOVICVS *(Rose).* XIIII *(Rose).* REX *(Rose).*
CHRISTIANISSIMVS. *The bust of Louis XIV as an
adolescent from the right, head uncovered, long and
flowing hair, wearing a breastplate and the* paludamentum. *The embroidered collar is turned
down. The king is wearing the cross of the Order of
the Holy Spirit. The signature of the engraver,*
MOLART F., *is engraved under the king's shoulder.*
Reverse: SCHOLAE AVGVSTAE. *In a sculpture and
painting workshop, two busy geniuses prefigure the
founding of the Academy of Rome. Exergue:* ACAD .
REG . PICT . ET . SCVLPT . LVTETIAE/ET . ROMAE .

5

5

4

INSTITVT / M.DC.XLVII. *The engraver's signature* MOLART *appears on the horizontal bar of the easel.*

MLG 1723, no. 76 variant. J.-J. Guiffrey, *Revue numismatique* 1889. Blanchet et Dieudonné, *Manuel de numismatique française* (Paris, 1930), 111. J. Jacquiot, *La médaille au temps de Louis XIV* (Paris, 1970), no. 333.

3 Dueling Abolished

Cabinet des Médailles, série royale 597

(gold; diam. 72 mm)

Obverse: LVDOVICVS . MAGNVS . REX . CHRIST-IANISS. *The bust of the king from the right, clothed in the armor and with the* paludamentum *held on the shoulder by a clasp decorated with a lion's head. The king's wig is crowned with a laurel wreath. Signature of the engraver R[oettiers].* *Reverse:* SINGVLARIVM. CERTAMINVM. FVRORE. COERCITO. *The semicircular legend stating that "la fureur des combats singuliers est abolie" (the frenzy of single combat has been abolished) crowns the main scene that includes three disheveled people holding daggers and swords, lying at the foot of Justice, who is brandishing a scale and a long sword. Exergue:* IVSTITIA / OPTIMI . PRINCIPIS *praises the justice of the best of princes. Engraver's signature R[oettiers].*

MLG 1702, no. 67. *MLG* 1723, no. 178. Forrer, vol. 5, 175. Divo, no. 67 var.

4 Royal Academy of Inscriptions and Medals, 1663. Cabinet des Médailles, série royale 625

(silver; diam. 70 mm)

Obverse: LVDOVICVS . MAGNVS . REX . CHRIS-TIANISSIMVS. *The bust of Louis XIV from the right, wearing armor decorated with a Gorgon's head and the* paludamentum *tied on the shoulder. Under the bust there is the signature of the engraver R[oettiers]. Reverse:* RERVM . GESTARVM . FIDES. *Right profile of Mercury seated on a stone block, carrying the caduceus in his left hand and holding a stylet in his right hand with which he is engraving on a bronze plaque the laudatory epitaph* LVD. MAG. / PIO.FELICI. / P.PATRIAE. / TRIVMPH. *Behind him is a vessel filled with medals. Trays garnished with medals up against the base of the two columns are in front of him. Exergue:* ACADEMIA . REGIA . INSCRIPT ./ ET . NVMIS . INSTITVTA / M.DC.LXIII. *Engraver's signature R[oettiers].*

The Petite Académie, founded on Feb. 3, 1663, adopted the name Royal Academy of Inscriptions and Medals in 1701.

MLG 1702, no. 73 var. *MLG* 1723, no. 75. J. Jacquiot, *La médaille au temps de Louis XIV* (Paris, 1970), no. 333. Divo, no. 72 var.

5 *Paris Embellished and Expanded*
Cabinet des Médailles, série royale 702
(silver; diam. 73 mm)

Obverse: LVDOVICVS . MAGNVS . REX . CHRIST-
IANISS. *The bust of Louis XIV from the right, wear-*
ing the armor with shoulder decoration of lilies and
the paludamentum *tied on the shoulder with a*
round clasp decorated with a Gorgon's head. Under
the bust there is the signature of the engraver R[ous-
sel]. Reverse: ORNATA * ET * AMPLIATA * VRBE.
Flanked by the two new city gates of Saint-Martin
and Saint-Denis, a turreted personification of the
city holds the ship of Paris, seated on a stone deco-
rated with a cornucopia. At its feet, the figure of the
Seine holds a jar from which a ribbon of water is
flowing. Exergue: * LVTETIA * *under which there is*
the engraver's signature, .MOLART.F.

MLG 1702, no. 116; the medal is dated M.DC.LXX. *MLG* 1723, no.
115. *TNG*, vol. 15, no. 6. Forrer, vol. 4, no. 119. Divo, no. 116.

6 *Rewards Granted to Writers, 1666*
Cabinet des Médailles, série royale 976
(gold; diam. 72 mm)

Obverse: LVDOVICVS . MAGNVS . REX . CHRIS-
TIANISSIMVS. *The bust of the king, right profile,*
draped, crowned with a laurel wreath. The signa-
ture of the engraver M. MOLLART F. *appears under*
the bust. Reverse: BONARVM * ARTIVM * REMVNER-
ATORI. *Liberality is standing in the center holding a*
cornucopia overflowing with fruits and flowers. At
her feet, four figures represent the Arts. Eloquence
is holding a lyre; Poetry holds up a trumpet and
places a laurel wreath on his head; Astronomy is
measuring a globe; the genius of History is writing,
seated on a pile of books. Exergue: LIBERALITAS.
On the exergue is the engraver's signature, MOL-
LART FECIT.

MLG 1702, no. 87. *MLG* 1723, no. 83. Both medals are dated
M.DC.LXVI. Forrer, vol. 4, p. 119., J. Jacquiot, *Médailles et jetons*
de Louis XIV (Paris, 1968), 183–87, pl. XXXV. Divo, no. 87.

7 *Founding of the Royal School of Saint-Cyr,*
1686
Cabinet des Médailles, série royale 946
(silver; diam. 72 mm)

Obverse: LVDOVICVS . MAGNVS . REX . CHRIS-
TIANISSIMVS. *A right profile of the king, crowned*
with a laurel wreath. Under the neck is the
engraver's initial R[oettiers]. Reverse: CCC PVELLAE
. NOBILES . SANCIRIANAE. *In front of the facade of*
a building featuring with a central pediment, built
by Mansart, Piety is holding the hands and encour-
aging two nuns while the young ladies stand by in

their uniform clothing and coiffures. The nuns are
wearing the golden cross sprinkled with lilies, with
Christ on the one side and Saint Louis on the other.
The central figure with the veiled head personifies
the king's piety. Exergue: PIETAS / M.DC.LXXXVII.
Engraver's signature, T. BERNARD F. *(Thomas*
Bernard fecit).

It was in response to Mme de Maintenon's
wish that Louis XIV set up this aristocratic
convent school bearing the name of Saint
Louis, dedicated to the education of the
"trois cents Demoiselles nobles" (three hundred noble misses). Mme de Maintenon
directed the house and retired there after the
death of Louis XIV. She is buried in the
chapel choir.

MLG 1702, no. 220. *MLG* 1723, no. 217. *TNG*, pl. XXVI. J.
Jacquiot, *Médailles et jetons de Louis XIV* (Paris, 1968), 455–60.
Guiffrey, *Revue numismatique* 1887: 286. *Club Français de la*
Médaille 24–25 (1969): 15. Divo, no. 220. B. Neveu in *Journal des*
Savants, July–December 1988: 277–80.

8 *Generosity of the King, 1685*
Cabinet des Médailles, série royale 922
(gold; diam. 70 mm)

Obverse: LVDOVICVS . MAGNVS . REX . CHRIS-
TIANISSIMVS. *Head of the king, right profile.*
Signed by the engraver R[oettiers]. Reverse: LIBER-
ALITAS ITINERVM SOCIA. *The king is on horseback,*
dressed as imperator, *advancing in step to the*
right, preceded by Liberalitas *holding a cornu-*
copia filled with fruits and flowers in her right
hand. From her left hand, she is sowing coins on the
ground from a second cornucopia. In exergue there
are two crisscrossed cornucopias. The initial of the
engraver R[oettiers] appears on the right.

MLG 1702, no. 208. *MLG* 1723, no. 208. Forrer, vol. 5, p. 175.
TNG, not indicated. Divo, no. 208.

9 *Submission of Luxembourg, 1684*
Cabinet des Médailles, série royale 2840
(gold; diam. 83 mm)

Obverse: LVDOVICVS MAGNVS–REX CHRISTIANIS-
SIMVS. *Three-quarter bust of Louis XIV from the*
right and a profile of his face. The sovereign, whose
long wig is falling in curls onto his shoulders, is
wearing armor decorated with a radiant Helios
(sun), trimmed with cloth. Under the bust, the
engraver's signature, Mollart, is in cursive script.
The medal's smooth field, bordered by the legend,
has a wide milled edge with lilies.

The portrait is in low relief, which contrasts
with the considerable attention to detail of the orna-

mental effects of the breastplate, while the handling of the detailed curls rises from a wavy and dense mass. The handling of the face is slightly heavier and falls between two extremes, as if to position itself in a third plane through an admirable sense of relief, probably inspired by an engraving. The engraver seems more inspired by drawing than by sculpture, giving the portrait a haughty dimension reminiscent of the spirit of Italian classicism.

This represents a completely original aspect of the art of engraving by Mollart, who was asked to produce "medallions" commemorating the military victories to the east of the kingdom, in particular the submission of Luxembourg in 1684.

MLG 1702, no. 203, with var. on reverse. MLG 1723, no. 203, with var. on reverse. TNG, p. 33, no. 1, for the obverse.

10 *Nec pluribus impar, 1674*
Cabinet des Médailles, série royale 2830
(silver; diam. 81 mm)

Obverse: LVD . MAGNVS. – FRAN . ET . NAV . REX . P[ATER] . P[ATRIAE]. *The bust of the king in armor decorated with Helios, seen from three-quarters to the right and the profile of his head, on top of which is a decorated, plumed helmet. The raised headband of the helmet shows a bearded mask. Signature,* F. WARIN F., *under the bust. Reverse:* NEC PLVRIBVS IMPAR. *The radiant sun above the puffs of clouds illustrates Louis XIV's motto. Exergue: 1674.*

This type of radiant sun–a sort of heraldic emblem–dominating the universe and floating in space was selected by Mauger the engraver in 1647 and again in 1663. The perfect symmetry in the composition reveals the significant mastery of the artist and engraver. As on the obverse, the smooth and bare field accentuates the direct relationship between the sun, capable of separating the clouds, and the universe, which becomes easily accessible to it. The work presented here may be the only known signed and medal by François Warin.

MLG 1702, no. 74 var. MLG 1723, not indicated. TNG, p. 11, no. 3 var. for the reverse and p. 25, no. 2. Forrer, vol. 6, pl. 359. Divo, no. 74 var.

11 *Bernini's Proposal for the Colonnade of the Louvre, 1665*
Cabinet des Médailles, série royale 3080
(gold; diam. 112 mm)

Obverse: LVDOVICO . XIV . REGNANTE . ET . AEDI-FICANTE. *Sumptuously clothed bust of Louis XIV, "ruler and builder," seen from three-quarters to the right, wearing breastplate decorated with a sun. His head, a profile seen from the right, is uncovered. Reverse:* MAIESTATI . AC. AETERNIT . GALL . IMPERII . SACRVM. *Under a sky darkened by massive clouds in the process of breaking up appears the facade of the Louvre as the Italian artist Giovanni-Lorenzo Bernini, known as Le Cavalier Bernin, had planned it. Exergue:* M.DC.LXV. *Engraver's signature hollowed out on the recessed portion used as a base for the decoration of the architecture:* IOAN[NES] . VARIN.FECIT.

In the foreground of this majestic composition is a wall made of bonded stones that makes it possible to see beyond a trench that underlines the sequencing of the facade, with its recesses and protuberances. The imposing building, on top of which is a railing interspersed with sculptures, is very much in the sumptuous taste of Italian classicism, but an elevation more similar to that of ancient temples was chosen over this exuberant project, moderating the Italianate decoration of twinned columns with the classical severity of a central pediment (see cat. 115). This unique medallion, formed by two single sides then joined, presents the king's portrait, in high relief, emphasizing Jean Varin's exceptional talents as a sculptor and engraver.

TNG, pl. 10, nos. 7 and 8, and pl. 14, no. 5. Forrer, vol. 6: 372., J. Jacquiot, *La Médaille au temps de Louis XIV* (Paris, 1970), nos. 450, 451, 452.

To publicize the positive effects of his government and the utility of the institutions he founded, Louis XIV did not hesitate to call on the art of minting and, in particular, the advertising potential offered by medals. Artists, meanwhile, by linking art with classical literature, were able to elevate the technique of metal engraving to a new type of sculpture.

Borrowing a suggestion made as early as 1602 by Rassas de Bagarris, the keeper of Henry IV's Cabinet des Médailles, to mint a series of "historical medallions," Louis XIV

293

founded the Petite Académie in 1663; under Colbert's supervision, this academy was to oversee the invention and development of mottos and emblematic figures, as well as the proper execution of drawings and their transfer to metal (no. 4 above). The Sun King's *Histoire métallique* includes a uniform series (41 mm) and a royal historical series (70–83 mm). The eleven medals presented here, made of gold, silver, or bronze, are part of the *série royale*. They were often minted after the events that were being commemorated. Thus the medal commemorating the birth of the king has a portrait of the already-adult sovereign on the front (no. 1). Conversely, the Royal School of Saint-Cyr was commemorated as soon as it was founded in 1686 (no. 7). Meanwhile, the king's motto, "Nec pluribus impar" (Not unequal to many), was used on several occasions on medals marking military successes (no. 10). Finally, a motto was developed in 1682 to reinforce the authoritarian ban on the practice of dueling (no. 3). Louis XIV was also a patron of architecture (nos. 5 and 11), and there was no limit to his generosity (no. 8) in supporting literary (no. 6) and artistic creativity.

Thomas Bernard, Michel Molart, Joseph Roettiers, Jérôme Roussel, and François and Jean Varin created this handful of masterpieces that not only extol the king but also provide original testimony concerning the artistic influences in France in the 17th century.

Sylvie de Turckheim Pey

Abbreviations

MLG 1702   *Médailles sur les principaux événements du règne de Louis le Grand...* (Paris, 1702)

MLG 1723   *Médailles sur les principaux événements du règne entier de Louis le Grand...* (Paris, 1723)

TNG   *Trésor de Numismatique et de glyptique françaises* (Paris, 1834)

Forrer   Leonard Forrer, *Biographical Dictionary of Medallists*, 8 vols. (London, 1902–1930)

Divo   J.-P. Divo, *Catalogue des médailles de Louis XIV* (Paris, 1982)

115

SÉBASTIEN LECLERC

Représentation des Machines qui ont servi a eslever les deux grandes pierres qui couvrent le fronton de la principale entrée du Louvre (Illustration of devices used to lift the two large stones of the pediment over the main entrance of the Louvre)

Cabinet des Estampes, Ed 59 b

Caption in Latin, lower right-hand margin. Etching; 38 × 62.5 cm. Signed bottom center: "S. Le Clerc fe. 1677."

Sébastien Leclerc's etching shows the laying of the two large sloping stones that made up the pediment over the east façade of the Louvre, known as the colonnade wing, in 1672. Colbert, named superintendent of the king's buildings in 1664, knew that Louis XIV's attention was shifting from Paris to Versailles, but he nevertheless wrote that same year to Poussin apropos of the Louvre that "we should perfect the most beautiful building in the world and make it worthy, if possible, of the grandeur and magnificence of the monarch who must reside there." That is why, despite the king's distaste for Paris, Colbert decided to terminate the east façade of the royal palace, calling upon the best architects in France and Italy. He himself wrote to Bernini in 1664: "The priceless products of your mind that make the entire world admire you . . . will not allow him [the king] to finish his superb and magnificent Louvre palace without showing drawings of it to a man of such high caliber as yourself."

Several months later, Bernini submitted a first proposal for completing the wing. Colbert then urged him to come to Paris, where, from March to October 1665, the Italian architect was treated like a monarch. Bernini designed a second plan that won the

Representation des Machines qui ont servi a esleuer les deux grandes pierres qui couurent le fronton de la principale entrée du Louure. *S. le Clerc fe. 1677* *Icon Machinarum quibus subleuati sunt ingentes duo Lapides tympano majoris portæ Luparæ incumbentes.*

king's favor, and construction even began; but it was soon halted owing to the enormous cost it would have entailed (cat. 114, no. 11). The French architects who had initially been bypassed were solicited once again. Louis Le Vau and François Mansart submitted proposals, but these were rejected. So in April 1667 Colbert summoned Le Brun, Perrault, and Le Vau, ordering them "to work together incessantly to devise a plan and elevation of the facade of the entrance facing Saint-Germain." On Nov. 26, 1667, the first foundation stone was laid, and construction work continued into 1678, when it was abandoned in favor of Versailles.

One of the high points of construction was the laying of the two huge sloping stones that constituted the pediment; the special equipment and technical prowess required were considered worthy of being recorded for posterity. Colbert, who realized that engravings were the best way to publicize and record the triumphs and splendor of the reign, commissioned talented engravers to immortalize the major events and construction projects associated with the French monarchy, including "the plans and eleva-

tions of royal residences, decorative painting and sculpture found therein, the paintings and figures in the Cabinet of His Majesty. . . as well as the figures of plants and animals of all species, and other rare and singular things" (Council of State, decree dated Dec. 22, 1667). The engravings thus commissioned formed the basis of the collection traditionally known as the Cabinet du Roi, or King's Cabinet. Leclerc was one of the mainstays of the project, having engraved almost every possible subject, as demonstrated by the 1980 catalogue of his work by Maxime Préaud. Concerning the etching displayed here, the 18th-century publisher Pierre-Jean Mariette judged it "one of the most perfect works by Sébastien le Clerc, who did it for the King of France" (*Notes manuscrites* [1710–1725], 4:213).

Françoise Jestaz

Marianne Grivel, "Le Cabinet du Roi," in *Revue de la Bibliothèque Nationale* 18 (1985): 36–57. Antoine Picon, *Claude Perrault, 1613–1688, ou La curiosité d'un classique* (Paris, 1988). Robert W. Berger, *The Palace of the Sun: The Louvre of Louis XIV* (University Park, Penn., 1993).

Illustrissimo viro Domino D. Joanni Baptistæ Colbert

116

ROBERT NANTEUIL

Jean-Baptiste Colbert

Cabinet des Estampes, AA5 Rés. Nanteuil

Drypoint by Robert Nanteuil (1623–1678). Etching by Gilles Rousselet (1610–1686). Proof before all letters: 51.6 × 74 cm; 1668.

Jean-Baptiste Colbert (1619–1683), Louis XIV's devoted minister, was "toujours plein du Roi"—always concerned about the glory of his sovereign—as the abbé de Choisy put it, yet he did not totally neglect his own glory. Numerous pictures of Colbert exist, though their iconography does not match the richness of those of Richelieu or Mazarin. Colbert's iconography was based on four successive portraits done by Philippe de Champaigne, Claude Lefebvre, Robert Nanteuil, and Pierre Mignard.

Nanteuil (1623–1678) produced engravings from his own drawing, whereas the portraits from the other three artists were copied and widely circulated by numerous engravers. This portrait of Colbert is typical of the por-

traits sketched from life that Nanteuil had made his speciality. There were two reasons why Colbert chose Nanteuil: Nanteuil was originally from Reims, as was Colbert, and he was a fashionable portraitist who had already had Mazarin and even the king pose for him (see cats. 95 and 106).

Colbert's portrait is framed in an oval medallion held against an obelisk by two women. The figure standing on the left, her hair ablaze, personifies Piety; the one on the right, seated, with a key in her hand and a dog lying on a safe at her feet, personifies Loyalty. At the foot of the figure on the left, the cock with an hourglass in its claw symbolizes Diligence and Assiduity. Under the oval, on a pedestal, Colbert's coat of arms is shown ringed by the chains of the Orders of Saint-Michel and of the Holy Spirit.

The obelisk stands in the middle of a vast court bordered in the rear by the Grande Galerie of the Louvre and on the right by the Tuileries. The sight of busy workers recalls the work undertaken at Colbert's own request in the Tuileries. On each side of the

obelisk, two groups of putti symbolize
Architecture, Astronomy, and Painting on the
left, and Sculpture on the right.

The choice of the Louvre and the Tuileries
as settings for Colbert's portrait was highly
symbolic. Colbert never stopped trying to
convince Louis XIV to reside in Paris, even
though the king eschewed the Louvre palace,
where his mother died in 1666. He preferred
to live in Saint-Germain and had already
begun work on Versailles.

The sketch engraved in drypoint by
Nanteuil suggests a rather sober portrait.
Indeed, the finished likeness displayed the
impassive expression of the man whom the
abbé de Choisy described as having "yeux
creux" (sunken eyes) and "sourcils épais et
noirs" (thick black eyebrows), the same whom
Mme de Sévigné nicknamed the "Nord"
(North). The group of allegorical figures was
engraved by Gilles Rousselet, after a drawing
by Charles Le Brun. The view of the Louvre
and the Tuileries was probably etched by
another artist.

Following the usual 17th-century practice,
the plate was engraved to decorate the upper

part of a thesis by Louis Béchameil, which he
defended on Jan. 21, 1668. It was an emphatic
tribute to Colbert, not only for the multiple
posts he held (director general of buildings,
arts, tapestries, and manufactures of France
from 1664 on, and controller general of
finance from 1665) but also for his personal
qualities: work, faith, and loyalty to his king.

Jacqueline Melet-Sanson

Eugène Bouvy, *Le portrait gravé et ses maîtres: Robert Nanteuil*
(Paris, 1924). Charles Petitjean and Charles Wickert, *Catalogue
de l'oeuvre gravé de Robert Nanteuil* (Paris, 1925), no. 53.
Jacqueline Melet-Sanson, "L'image de Colbert vue par ses
contemporains," in *Colbert*, exhibition at the Hôtel de la
Monnaie (Paris, 1983), 485–531.

L'ACADEMIE DES SCIENCES ET DES BEAUX ARTS
DÉDIÉE AU ROY.
Par son très humble très obéissant et très fidèle Serviteur et sujet Seb. le Clerc.

117

SÉBASTIEN LECLERC

L'Académie des Sciences et des Beaux-Arts. Dédiée au Roy. Par son très humble très obéissant et très fidèle Serviteur et sujet Sébastien le Clerc (The Academy of Sciences and Fine Arts. Dedicated to the king by his very humble, very obedient, very loyal servant and subject Sébastien Leclerc)

Cabinet des Estampes, Ed 59 c

Etching; 24.8 × 38.4 cm. Sixth state, 1698.

This print, one of the most beautiful and widely known by Sébastien Leclerc, depicts the inner courtyard of a colonnaded palace where representatives of all the Arts and Sciences can be seen with their instruments as they go about their business before their students. One hundred and sixty-two people have been counted and nearly as many devices, tools, and various other objects.

In the foreground on the left, two men are observing the behavior of a bird they are in the process of asphyxiating under a bell jar, in an experiment on the composition of air.

Another man is solving a problem in optics, and a group of students is attending a geometry session while a palm reader is predicting the future of an awestruck young man. Engineers are studying plans of fortifications, while before them lies a pile of various instruments, including anamorphic apparatus and objects used to study and teach perspective and optics.

In the background, an astronomer uses a chart to explain how the universe is organized, to an attentive audience seated in a semicircle around him. At the bottom of the stairs are a celestial sphere and a terrestrial sphere.

In the middle, several people are involved in numismatology and heraldry, and Pythagoras is demonstrating his theorem on the right. Behind him there is an Archimedean screw, and Vilette's mirror bursts into flame before an enraptured onlooker.

In the center of the composition, Rhetoric is represented by an orator and a large group of people listening enthusiastically to the speech. Just to the left, an orchestra seated on a terrace symbolizes Music. Drawing, painting, and sculpture lessons are being given under the arcades to the right. In the rear, the interior of another courtyard is visible through the colonnade, where men are operating several stone-lifting machines and cranes, while four architects study a drawing. The Science of God has not been forgotten, as a theology course is being taught in the palace library.

Sébastien Leclerc (1637–1714), the engraver with a universal mind, as he liked to say, was named a member of the Academy of Painting and Sculpture in 1672 and taught geometry, perspective, and mathematics from 1680 to 1699. He himself wrote scientific treatises: *Pratique de la géométrie* (1682); *Discours touchant le point de veue dans lequel il est prouvé que les choses qu'on voit distinctement ne sont veues que d'un oeil* (1679), a contribution to the teaching of perspective; *Divers habillemens des anciens Grecs et Romains* (1706); *Traité d'architecture* (1714); and *Nouveau système du monde conforme à l'Ecriture Sainte* (1706). Above all, with the accuracy of a scientist, he illustrated a number of scientific treatises written by academy members with whom he met each week. His oeuvre includes more than three thousand engravings.

Leclerc's qualities earned him exceptional fame even in his own time. Aficionados snapped up the first engravings as soon as they came off his press and their popularity continued until the end of the Ancien Régime. When he died in October 1714, he was the object of much glory and honor as the chief engraver during the century associated with Louis XIV.

Françoise Jestaz

Maxime Préaud, *Inventaire des graveurs français du XVIIe siècle*, vols. 8 and 9, *Sébastien Leclerc* (Paris, 1980). Maxime Préaud, "L'Académie des Sciences et des Beaux-Arts: Le testament graphique de Sébastien Leclerc," *Racar* 10, no. 1 (1983): 73–81. *Colbert (1619–1683)*, exhibition at the Hôtel de la Monnaie (Paris, 1983).

118

JOHANNES HEVELIUS

Selenographia sive Lunae description
(Selenographia, or a description of the moon)
Réserve des livres rares, Rés. V. 244, figure R

Danzig: Andreas Hünefeld at the author's expense, 1647. [24]–563 pp.; folio. Bound by Andreas Hünefeld(?), red morocco over wooden board, gold-tooled, gilt edges. Presentation copy for Louis XIV.

The *Selenographia* by the astronomer Johannes Hevelius is the first lunar atlas, but it also deals with the construction of lenses and telescopes and with the observation of celestial bodies in general as well as the planets and the sun. The author himself engraved the numerous text illustrations and plates, including the three large double-page maps of the moon and forty descriptions of the lunar phases.

The son of a brewer, Hevelius was born in 1611 in Danzig, Poland, and while very young began his studies of mathematics and astronomy. In 1630 he left for Holland to study law in Leiden, then traveled to England and France, where he met the greatest scientists and scholars of the day, including John Wallis, James Usher, and Samuel Hartlieb in England and Pierre Gassendi in Paris. Hevelius returned to Danzig in 1634, but only in 1639 did he respond to the last wishes of his former teacher, the astronomer Peter Crüger, and resume his astronomical observations.

299

Hevelius, who constructed his own instruments and set up an observatory on a large platform which he had built on the rooftops of three adjoining houses, became so famous that scholars, ambassadors, and princes from all over Europe came to visit him. He kept up active correspondence with numerous scholars, such as Marin Mersenne and Ismaël Boulliau in Paris. In 1664 he was elected a member of the Royal Society in London.

To finance his work, Hevelius was obliged to look for patrons, and it was for that reason that in 1654 he sent his *Epistolae IV* to Louis XIII's brother Gaston d'Orléans. In 1663 Colbert, the king's minister, asked the poet and academician Chapelain to draw up a list of scholars and scientists worthy of receiving a pension from the king. Chapelain, who had heard about Hevelius from Gassendi, put Hevelius's name on the list. As a token of his gratitude, the astronomer sent the king the present copy of the *Selenographia,* wonderfully embellished in gold and color and bearing an autographed dedication dated Sept. 21, 1663, from Danzig.

The profusely gilt red morocco binding decorated with filigree was probably done either by Andreas Hünefeld, who printed the work and who was also a binder, or by one of his successors. At least three other copies of the *Selenographia* were bound in the same bindery. One was presented by the author to the Bodleian Library in Oxford in 1649, and a second to the University Library of Cambridge in 1650. The original owner of the third copy, which was recently offered for sale, is unknown.

Ursula Baurmeister

L. C. Béziat, "La vie et les travaux de Jean Hévélius," *Bulletino di bibliografia e di storia delle scienze matematiche e fisiche* 8 (1875): 497–558, 589–669. E. Zinner, *Deutsche und niederländische astronomische Instrumente des 11.–18. Jahrhunderts* (Munich, 1956), 375–82. *Collections de Louis XIV: Dessins, albums, manuscrits,* exhibition catalogue (Paris, 1977), no. 343. K. Targosz, "Johannes Hevelius et ses démarches pour trouver des mécènes en France," *Revue d'histoire des sciences* 30 (1977): 25–41. H. M. Nixon, "Quelques reliures d'un intérêt particulier pour les Polonais dans les bibliothèques anglaises," in *VIIIe Congrès international des bibliophiles, Varsovie, 23–29 juillet 1973* (Warsaw, 1985), 68–69. *Fine Books and Manuscripts in Fine Bindings from the Fifteenth to the Present Century,* Martin Breslauer, catalogue 110 (New York, 1992), no. 86.

119

Les Campagnes de Louis XIV.
Campagne du Roy pendant l'année
M.DC.LXXVI.
(The campaigns of Louis XIV. The king's campaign during the year 1676)
Département des Manuscrits, Fr. 7892, fol. 1

Parchment; 161 fols. (fols. 159–161 are blank); 380 × 295 mm. Green leather binding. After 1678. Fol. 1: Portrait of Louis XIV dressed as a Roman emperor in front of his tent.

"S'agrandir est la plus digne et la plus agréable occupation des souverains" (Expansion is the most worthy and pleasant occupation of monarchs), wrote Louis XIV to the marquis de Villars on Jan. 8, 1688. The Dutch War (1672–1678) perfectly illustrates this vainglorious affirmation, since the Nijmegen Treaty gave France northern possessions such as Aire, Saint-Omer, Cambrai, Bouchain, Condé, and Valenciennes and, above all, in the eastern region of the Kingdom. This profitable war was probably also "pleasant" for the French monarch since the Sun King, then in the prime of his forties, unhesitantly broke away from the arms of Mme de Montespan to spend 641 days on the battlefields, where he demonstrated genuine strategic and tactical capabilities that won the admiration of his subjects.

The war was less glorious than royal panegyrists claimed, because the small Calvinist republic foiled the army of the Sun King for a long time. But it provided the occasion for a skillful propaganda campaign conducted by Louis's historian-poets Boileau and Racine (Racine published a *Précis historique des guerres de Louis XIV depuis 1672 jusqu'en 1678*). They were charged with celebrating the glory of "Louis-le-Grand," the king of "a fortunate nation, a model for other nations" (according to Voltaire in *Le Siècle de Louis XIV*), although

by 1679 Europe was already preparing its revenge.

The four volumes known as the *Campagnes de Louis XIV* contain a series of maps that make it possible to follow the progress of the operations and movements of French troops. Each of the forty-four maps in the manuscript exhibited here (two of which fold out) is set in a cartouche composed of various figures borrowed from Greek mythology. Two pages are incomplete, containing only the painted cartouche for a map that was never made. Louis XIV is illustrated at the beginning of the volume dressed as a Roman emperor (fol. 1). This portrait, perhaps based on a painting by Mignard, is not signed but is similar in handling to an equestrian portrait of Louis attributed to Petitot.

The king was enamored of beautiful manuscripts. He owned the *Livre de la Chasse* by Gaston Phoebus and the Book of Hours of Anne de Bretagne illuminated by Bourdichon. Alongside these two treasures of medieval illumination, his collection included several compilations produced for his own honor and glory. The *Campagnes* are particularly prestigious examples, representing the ultimate triumph of illuminated manuscripts as "total" art: illustrations with remarkable finesse and life were entrusted to such first-rate artists as Jean Cotelle, F. Bedau, Jean Petitot, and Sylvain Bonnet, whereas the text of the marching orders, in batarde and initials painted in gold, is the work of Charles Gilbert (1642–1728), the best student of the renowned Nicolas Jarry, the calligrapher of *La Guirlande de Julie* (see cat. 93).

The original bindings, probably destroyed during the Revolution, were worthy of the content, according to the *Catalogue des livres du Cabinet du Roi à Versailles* (1775, NAF, 2622), which describes the manuscript as "relié en chagrin noir et enrichi sur le plat de la Devise du Roy, de son médaillon couronné par la Victoire et par la Renommée, de Trophées, de Festons &a. Le tout en or. in folio avec étiquettes, bordures et fermoirs d'or" (bound in black grain leather and embellished on the board with the king's device, his medallion crowned by Victory and by Fame, Trophies, Festoons, and so forth, all in gold. Folio, with gilt labels, borders, and clasps).

Michèle Sacquin

John B. Wolf, *Louis XIV* (New York, 1968). Ragnhild Hatton, *Louis XIV and Europe* (London, 1976). J. Klaits, *Printed Propaganda under Louis XIV: Absolute Monarchy and Public Opinion* (Princeton, 1976). William James, *The Age of Louis XIV: The Rise of Modern Diplomacy* (Cambridge, Mass., 1976). Joseph Konwitz, *Cartography in France, 1660–1848: Science, Engineering, and Statecraft* (Chicago, 1987). François Bluche, *Louis XIV* (Paris, 1987). Paul Sonnino, *Louis XIV and the Origins of the Dutch War* (Cambridge, 1988). Lucien Bély, Jean Béranger, and André Corvisier, *Guerre et paix dans l'Europe du XVIIe siècle*, 2 vols. (Paris, 1991). Emmanuel Le Roy Ladurie, *L'Ancien Régime* (Paris, 1991). François Robichon, "La campagne de Hollande, 1676–1678," *Tradition magazine, armes-uniformes-figurines* 84 (January 1994): 10–15.

120

Almanach royal pour l'année MDCLXXVII. La levée du siège de Mastric ou La Retraite du Prince d'Orange et des ses alliez à l'approche de l'armée du Roy commandée par le Maréchal Duc de Schomberg. Avec la disposition du Camps des Ennemis suivant le Plan qui en a esté levé exactement par un officier présent aux actions.

Cabinet des Estampes, Qb⁵ 1677

In the lower left-hand margin: With the king's privilege. On the right: In Paris, at N. Langlois, rue Saint-Jacques à la Victoire (first state). In the second state, dedication to the maréchal duke of Schomberg. Engraving and etching; 81.2 × 53.2 cm.

In 1672, the very Christian king Louis XIV decided to "annihilate" the Protestant Republic of Holland that was too openly hosting France's enemies and was speaking disparagingly of the king's actions in its newspapers. The years 1672–1678 were marked by numerous military operations and diplomatic failures. In 1676, the main effort of the French armies was directed against Flanders, a territory of Spain. In April, the king went with his brother, Monsieur, and took the town of Condé (upper left-hand vignette); Monsieur attacked Bouchain on May 10 (upper right-hand vignette). The prince of Orange, governor of the Netherlands, attacked Maastricht, which had recently become a French possession, and the French laid siege to Aire-sur-la-Lys, which they took on July 31, 1676 (lower right-hand vignette).

William of Orange realized he could not take Maastricht, so he retreated when the French army attacked. The etching shows the maréchal duke of Schomberg arriving at the fortified city and, to the left, the Dutch army fleeing. At the same time, naval battles were taking place in the Mediterranean, and Colbert reorganized the French navy, which distinguished itself by winning several spectacular victories against the Spanish fleet, particularly off the coast of Palermo on June 2, 1676 (lower left-hand vignette). In the upper-middle medallion, Louis XIV is obviously the dominant figure in the almanac.

The term *almanac* describes a work that contains not only temporal divisions and astronomical observations but also all sorts of scientific, historical, literary, and other information. It differs from a *calendar*, which is simply a table of the days of the year. Almanacs became large illustrated folios at the end of the 16th century and the size became standardized under Louis XIV, with fixed dimensions approximately 85–90 cm high and 50–55 cm wide. Because of its large size, an almanac must be engraved on two plates and printed on two folios that are connected. In the lower portion, a small space is set aside for the calendar. The rest of the plate is devoted to a large composition often surrounded by medallions, cartouches, and ornaments. The subjects are extremely varied and deal with the events of the previous year, including scenes of popular customs, social, political, or religious satires, military events, court entertainment, receptions for ambassadors, allegories in the king's honor, or the building of a monument.

Between 1640 and 1740 five or six almanacs were published each year. The deluxe copies, given to the king or the lords in his entourage, were done on satin. The Cabinet des Estampes has a few copies. Those almanacs that deal with the glorification of the king are most numerous. All important events are included.

No item can better document the iconography of Louis XIV's reign from his childhood to his death in 1715.

Françoise Jestaz

Victor Champier, *Les anciens almanachs illustrés: Histoire du calendrier depuis les temps anciens jusqu'à nos jours* (Paris, 1886). Ernest Lavisse, *Histoire de France illustrée des origines jusqu'à la Revolution,* vol. 7, *Louis XIV* (Paris, 1911).

121

SÉBASTIEN DE VAUBAN
Projet d'une Dixme royale
(Proposal for a royal tithe)
Réserve des livres rares, Rés. R. 1556

[Rouen: Antoine II Maurry,] 1707 [1706]. 204–20 pp.; folio. Bound by Widow Fétil in calfskin, 1707. Gift from the author to the "Augustins déchaussés" monks at Place des Victoires, Paris. Probably confiscated during the Revolution.

Born in 1633, Sébastien Le Prestre de Vauban was an engineer in the royal army. He participated in all the wars waged during Louis XIV's reign, contributing to the success of the many sieges laid by royal troops and considerably strengthening the fortifications of borders and ports. He was made maréchal de France (field marshal) in 1703. Endowed with a curious and inventive mind and an immense capacity for work, he was constantly observing the state of affairs in the kingdom, its potential wealth, and the poverty of the masses during his travels around France. Between the wars and the pomp and ceremony of state, the chronic government deficit was on a steady rise. Taxes were not imposed equitably on the various social classes and the revenues collected were very limited.

In 1697 Vauban began working on a proposal for tax reform, which he wrote up in late 1699 or early 1700. He presented it to the king at three evening meetings, and a few

305

handwritten copies were circulated. In 1706, probably because of the enormous economic difficulties France was experiencing as a result of its involvement in the War of Spanish Succession, Vauban decided to have the text printed and distributed among some of his friends to get their reactions. The text was in no way meant to create a social disturbance but was merely an attempt to improve tax revenues. Vauban recommended that existing taxes be replaced by a maximum assessment of one-tenth of income in kind from all landholdings and of cash income on all other goods. He presented forms to be used to establish the statistical bases and, as a first step, to count the population and livestock.

Controls on the book trade forced Vauban to publish his text clandestinely. The book was given to a printer in Rouen, Antoine Maurry, whose printing equipment has recently been identified beyond doubt. In December 1706, packages of one hundred copies each were sent to the gates of Paris, and Vauban went to pick them up in his official carriage to avoid the checkpoints at the Paris gates. He immediately gave some of the books to his regular binder, the Widow Fétil, who bound them in morocco or calf-skin, or simply covered them with marbled paper. Vauban refused to hand over any copies to booksellers and gave the first copies instead to visitors and friends. The volume displayed here, for instance, is marked "gift of the author" and belonged to a religious community in Paris.

But the secret was not to be kept for long. On Feb. 14, 1707, the Privy Council, which was responsible for handling violations of laws governing the book trade, discovered that the book was in circulation but had been printed without permission and ordered it seized and destroyed. On March 14, the police chief was ordered to find the publisher. It appears that Vauban was not warned of the legal action until March 24, whereupon he proceeded to gather up all the copies still at the binder's.

Already ailing, he was severely affected by this affair. His health took a rapid turn for the worse, and he died on March 30. There is no truth, however, in the account given in Saint-Simon's *Mémoires*, which spawned the grim legend of the king's great servant who died in royal disgrace. On March 28, Louis XIV publicly praised Vauban for his personal qualities and his services as field marshal. Vauban's fame, though, was not enough to prevent the posthumous search of his residence and the arrest of his personal valet—all to no avail, since the police never found the rest of the books.

Geneviève Guilleminot-Chrétien

Michel Morineau, "Tombeau pour un maréchal de France: La dîme royale de Vauban," in *Vauban réformateur* (Paris, 1983), 231–95. "Vauban, *Projet d'une dixme royale*," presentation by Jean-François Pernot, Association des Amis de la Maison Vauban, 1988. "Vauban, *La dîme royale*," presentation by Emmanuel Le Roy Ladurie, Paris, 1992. Jean-Dominique Mellot, "Dynamisme provincial et centralisme parisien: L'édition rouennaise et ses marchés (vers 1600–vers 1730)" (doctoral diss., University of Paris I, 1991–1992).

PENSÉES
DE
M. PASCAL
SUR LA RELIGION,
ET SUR QUELQUES
AUTRES SUJETS.

❦❦❦❦❦❦❦❦❦❦

I.
Contre l'Indifference des Athées.

 U E ceux qui combattent
la Religion apprennent au
moins quelle elle eſt avant
que de la combattre. Si
cette Religion ſe vantoit d'avoir une
A

122

BLAISE PASCAL

Pensées sur la religion, et sur quelques autres sujets...

(Thoughts on religion and other subjects...)
Réserve des livres rares, Rés. D. 21374, p. 1

Paris: Guillaume Desprez, 1669. [32] fols.+ 365 pp. + [1] fol.; 12mo. Purchased in 1851 from M. Salacroux.

Blaise Pascal was born June 19, 1623. From childhood he showed, as Chateaubriand put it, "terrifying genius." At sixteen, his *Essai sur les coniques* (Essay on conical sections) filled with admiration the mathematicians with whom his father associated. At nineteen he devised and built an arithmetic machine, ancestor of the calculator, which was his greatest claim to fame during his lifetime.

Until 1654 Pascal was essentially a scientist, a mathematician-physicist (in 1647 he published *Traité sur le vide*, a treatise on the vacuum). But religion filled him with torment. The night of Nov. 23, 1654, was decisive. About this night of ecstasy, he wrote, "Oubli du monde total et de tout, hormis Dieu" (Oblivious to the world, totally, and to everything save God). From then on he was converted to Jansenism, an austere and exacting Christian doctrine which had been adopted by the abbey of Port Royal.

The controversy over divine grace and free will that had broken out in the second half of the 16th century between the Jesuits and the Jansenists became more acrimonious. Pascal threw himself into the battle with irony, passion, and eloquence. In the *Provinciales* (Provincial letters), eighteen letters published anonymously and separately from January 1656 to May 1657, he lashed out against the laxity of Jesuit morality.

At the same time, when not prevented by illness, he prepared a defense of the Christian religion that he addressed to everyone: Christians, libertines, and skeptics. His death on Aug. 19, 1662, at thirty-nine interrupted this project. Only scattered notes—about a thousand fragments on bits of paper of every size, partly classified by Pascal—

survived from it. These are the *Pensées* (Thoughts on religion and other subjects).

Two copies made immediately after his death give us his papers as they were found. As for the originals, they have come down to us incomplete, with some fragments missing, and gathered together and bound in great disorder. The Port Royal authorities used one of the copies to prepare the *Pensées* for publication. Choosing from among the most finished and the least compromising of the fragments, rearranging them in a new order, and adding some glosses, the editorial committee issued this edition in January 1670.

The copy of *Pensées* in the BNF, in its original brown calf binding, is one of two known copies that bear the date 1669. It lacks the "approbation des prélats" (approval of the prelates), the "privilège" (license), the errata, and the "table des titres" (table of headings). The "table des matières" (table of contents) at the end has only its first leaf. The edition was a limited one intended for the family and the committee of Port Royal to be submitted for approval by the bishops. The bishops insisted on some changes in the text; the offending passages were corrected, reprinted, and leaves substituted in the faulty copies. This copy, like the one in the library in Troyes, provides precious testimony on the uncensored text.

For more than three centuries the numerous editions of the *Pensées* have questioned the accuracy of preceding editions and each time given assurances that they were faithful to Pascal's intentions. All have been admirable exercises, but the wealth of ideas in the work and the very fact that it was unfinished rules out any possibility of a definitive edition.

Marie-Françoise Quignard

J. Le Petit, *Bibliographie des principales éditions originales d'écrivains français du XVe au XVIIIe siècles* (Paris, 1927), 207–13. Louis Lafuma, *Histoire des "Pensées" de Pascal (1656–1952)* (Paris, 1954). Jean Anglade, *Pascal l'insoumis* (Paris, 1988). Antony McKenna, *Entre Descartes et Gassendi: La première édition des "Pensées" de Pascal* (Paris, 1993).

123

MOLIÈRE

Les Oeuvres posthumes, volume 7
(Dom Juan, ou Le Festin de Pierre)
Réserve des livres rares, Rés. Yf. 3167,
"Le Festin de Pierre"

Paris: Denis Thierry, Claude Barbin, Pierre Trabouillet, 1682. 261–3 pp.; 12mo. Bound by Thouvenin in green morocco, after 1819. Acquired by the Bibliothèque Royale in 1819.

Dom Juan, first performed on Feb. 15, 1665, met with resounding popular success. But this play, which features a debauched and hypocritical member of the nobility who even dares to defy God, caused such a scandal that it was canceled after fifteen performances. Unlike other plays by Molière, usually printed after their first performance on stage, *Dom Juan* was not published at all during the author's lifetime.

In 1682 La Grange and Vivot, two comedians in his company, published the first edition of Molière's complete works and included *Dom Juan*, according to a manuscript left by Molière but now lost. They did not, however, respect the original script but instead shortened the "poor man's scene," which had caused the most uproar.

Following regulations, the printed text was submitted to Nicolas de La Reynie, police lieutenant, who acted as censor. He demanded further changes and the complete deletion of the dialogue in which Sganarelle, the valet, claims to convert Dom Juan, and the whole of the ensuing poor man's scene. The publishers complied and changed the text by reprinting some sections and replacing certain pages. The deletion of long passages changed the balance of the page format and left a number of blank spaces in the rewritten parts.

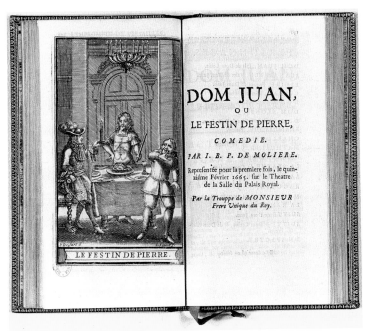

The revised 1682 text was reproduced in later editions during the 17th and 18th centuries, even though some people, such as Voltaire, still remembered another version. Yet another version, but one probably closer to the original, was used for foreign publication. *Dom Juan* sparked renewed interest around 1810, when bibliographers discovered a copy largely in precensorship condition, with the exception of one section. The Bibliothèque Royale managed to acquire this copy in 1819, on the death of its owner, bookseller Regnauld Bretel, but its provenance was unknown. One other copy of the exact, uncensored text remains in circulation: it was the personal copy of La Reynie, who kept the text submitted to him and even had it bound with his coat of arms.

During the 19th century, Molière's publishers finally had the means to produce a text as close as possible to the original one, and the theater was able to stage productions more faithful to the original play. Yet we still do not know the play as it was written and produced by Molière.

Geneviève Guilleminot-Chrétien

A. J. Guibert, *Bibliographie des oeuvres de Molière publiées au XVIIe siècle* (Paris, 1961), 2:609–12 and 631–41. Molière, *Oeuvres complètes*, ed. G. Couton (Paris, 1971), vol. 2. *Don Juan*, exhibition at the Bibliothèque Nationale (Paris, 1991), 65–83.

124
Portrait of Jean Racine by His Eldest Son, Jean-Baptiste
Réserve des livres rares, Rés. p. Yc. 558(2)

Ink drawing, after 1714; 140 × 180 mm. Sheet found in the binding of an annotated Horace, Poemata. *Paris: H. Estienne, 1575. Acquired after the Louis Racine bequest (1756) but already present at the Bibliothèque Nationale by 1848.*

Jean Racine (1639–1699), a leading tragedian of the classical period on a par with Pierre Corneille, was received in high places and was part of the intimate circle of Louis XIV, whom he served as historiographer for twenty years.

Racine's eldest son, Jean-Baptiste, was totally dedicated to his father, and collected books and documents with a view to publishing Racine's works and a biography, which he never completed. In 1747 Jean-Baptiste died a bachelor in Paris, leaving this legacy to his brother Louis.

Jean-Baptiste was known to have some artistic talent, as this sketch purportedly drawn by him suggests—if the note "Racine dessiné par son fils aîné" (Racine drawn by his eldest son), which appears on the sheet, is to be believed. This sketch decorated the cover of a volume of an incomplete copy of Horace's *Poemata* (Paris: Henri Estienne, 1575), which contained many notes in different handwriting styles and belonged to Louis Racine. The portrait—an ink wash drawing highlighted in pencil—depicts a courtier of about fifty years of age. It is a quick sketch. As a result of hesitation or in an attempt to create a more honest rendition, the relatively thin mouth was redrawn. The correction was not erased and so a double image appears. As a whole, however, it is a solid, attractively drawn picture. The features are very close to those of Racine's portrait engraved by Edelinck for Charles Perrault's work, *Des Hommes illustres qui ont paru en France* (Paris, 1696–1700), and patterned after Jean Baptiste Santerre's painting, regarded as the official historiographic portrait of Racine. This fact cannot be reasonably contested, despite the recurring and often lively arguments over which portraits of Racine are true and which are false.

309

125

FRANÇOIS DE SALIGNAC
DE LA MOTHE-FÉNELON
Les Aventures de Télémaque
(The adventures of Telemachus)
Département des Manuscrits, Fr. 14944,
fols. Av–1

*Paper; 505 fols.; 240 × 180 mm. Red morocco bind-
ing. Autograph manuscript [1694]. The volume
opens with a portrait of Fénelon on a sheet of vellum.*

A sketch similar to the drawing in question
was discovered in 1949 by Jacques Masson-
Forestier in the cover of a collection of Saint
Basile's works translated by Racine (*Le
Monde,* Sept. 17 and Dec. 10, 1949). This discovery led experts to take a closer look at the
bound volume of Horace, which was found to
contain seven more sketches of the same portrait intermingled with various family documents. The features appearing in these drawings are nearly identical, with only minor differences, and appear to be drawn by the
same hand.

What were the circumstances surrounding
these drawings? On the back of the document is a personal note written to Jean-
Baptiste Racine by his mother, Catherine de
Romanet, in December 1714. Thus this later
drawing could not have been a sketch for J.-
B. Santerre's painting or for Edelinck's
engraving. Was it meant to correct these
works, according to Jean-Baptiste Racine's
memory of his father, with the thought of a
new portrait? Whatever the case, this document provides an exceptionally lifelike portrait of the poet.

Catherine Allix

Frantz Calot, *Les portraits de Racine: Vrais et faux visages du
poète* (Paris, 1941). Jacques Masson-Forestier, "Les portraits de
Racine: Dessins retrouvés," *Cahiers raciniens* 4 (1958): 179–90.
Roger Reboussin, "Les portraits de Racine: Dessins retrou-
vés," pt. 2, *Cahiers raciniens* 5 (1959): 302–5. Masson-Forestier,
"Le portrait de Racine par Santerre," *Cahiers raciniens* 7
(1960): 395–96. Masson-Forestier, "Les portraits de Racine,"
Cahiers raciniens 8 (1960): 551–58.

In 1699 the first five books of *Télémaque* were
published anonymously in Paris in a volume
entitled *Suite du quatrième livre de l'Odyssée
d'Homère, ou Les aventures de Télémaque, fils
d'Ulysse* (The continuation of the fourth book
of Homer's Odyssey, or The adventures of
Telemachus, son of Odysseus). By the time
the next five books were published that same
year, royal approbation had been withdrawn.

Publication had probably occurred against
the wishes of Fénelon (1651–1715), who that
very year had fallen into disgrace due to his
sympathies with the mystical religious movement known as quietism. He lost his position
as tutor to the duke of Burgundy (Louis
XIV's grandson) and was banished to his
archdiocese of Cambrai. But *Télémaque* had
probably already been written by 1694 ("I did
it at at time when I was entranced by the
signs of munificence and confidence with
which the king showered me...": letter of
1710 to P. Le Tellier, in *Oeuvres,* 7:166).

Télémaque, in fact, was a pedagogical treatise based on the fourth book of the *Odyssey*
and was part of an extensive educational curriculum designed to last several years. "It is a
fabulous tale in the form of a heroic poem,
like those of Homer and Virgil, in which I set
out the principal teachings appropriate to a
prince whose birth destines him to reign"
(letter to Le Tellier).

Télémaque was also a manual of eloquence and taste. The education of the prince takes place in a timeless, polished maritime Greece where mythology is employed to graft royal glory onto antique civilization. The fluid style of Fénelon's gentle persuasion is somewhat weighed down, however, by the admonishments and lectures placed in the mouth of Mentor. The basic theme is the son's quest for his father, and the trials undergone by Telemachus teach him both self-control and the art of governing, while Mentor, his tutor, combines a statesman's ambition with the wisdom of Minerva.

The political exposition culminates in the utopia of Salente, where Idomeneus (Louis XIV) reigns with justice but must cure himself of despotic tendencies and a penchant for lavishness and war. He applies the reforms advocated by Mentor, which include not only a return to the land and a reduction in expenditures but also–more troubling–a rigid society that monitors personal mobility. In fact, Fénelon was expressing a reactionary agricultural and aristocratic trend within what deserves to be read and analyzed as one of the great reformist systems at the end of Louis XIV's reign.

This "livre singulier" (exceptional book), in Voltaire's words, enjoyed immediate and long-lasting, if ambivalent, popularity. Contemporaries saw it as a roman à clef with satirical portraits targeting king, court, and bigots as well as Fénelon's adversary, Bossuet. Enlightenment philosophers, meanwhile, flagrantly misinterpreted *Télémaque* to their own ends–they saw it as a glorification of nature that converged with Rousseau's ideas. Even more mistakenly, they read it as a progressive critique of absolutism. That was the basis of the myth of gentle Fénelon, the swan of Cambrai, as opposed to Bossuet, the eagle of Meaux.

Michèle Sacquin

Jean Orcibal, "L'influence de Fénelon dans les pays anglo-saxons au XVIIIe siècle," *Revue du XVIIIe siècle* 12–14 (1951–1952): 276–87. Charles Dedeyan, *Le Télémaque de Fénelon* (Paris, 1958). Priscilla P. Clark, "Leçons du Grand Siècle: The Aesthetics of Education in *Télémaque*," in *Papers on French Seventeenth-Century Literature* 6 (1976–1977): 23–36. Volker Kapp, *Télémaque de Fénelon: La signification d'une oeuvre littéraire à la fin du siècle classique* (Tübingen and Paris, 1982). *Papers on French Seventeenth-Century Literature* 17 (1982) (issue dedicated to Fénelon). Marguerite Haillant, *Culture et imagination dans les oeuvres de Fénelon "ad usum delphini"* (Paris, 1982–1983). Fénelon, *Oeuvres*, ed. J. Le Brun (Paris, 1983). *Papers on French Seventeenth-Century Literature* 13 (1986) (articles by Claire-Lise Malarte and Philip Wolfe).

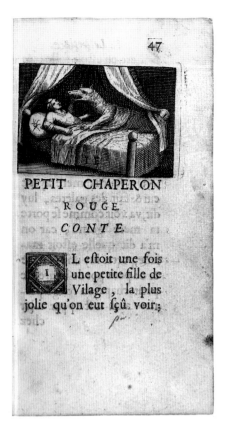

126

CHARLES PERRAULT

Histoires ou Contes du temps passé
(Stories or tales of bygone times)
Réserve des livres rares, Rés. p. Y². 263, p. 47

*Paris: Claude Barbin, 1697. [8] + 225 + [4] pp.; [1]
fol. of plates (frontispiece); 12ᵐᵒ. Purchased in 1898.*

Charles Perrault was born on Jan. 12, 1628,
into a family belonging to the parliamentary
haute bourgeoisie. Together with his
brothers—one of whom, Claude, became the
architect of the Louvre's colonnade—he
wrote, at the height of the unrest known as
the Fronde, a burlesque entitled *Enéide trav-
estie*, in which he already took a stand against
Homer and Virgil.

From 1663 to 1683, as a senior civil servant, general inspector at the Superinten-
dence of Buildings, and member of the
Académie Française, Perrault worked with
Colbert to create a cultural establishment
that would serve the absolute monarchy: a
system based on stipends and allowances, on
the founding of artistic and scientific institutions such as the Academy of Sciences and
the Académie Française in Rome, and the
renovation and construction of the Louvre
and Versailles.

An ardent defender of his times, fiercely
opposed to all those who, like Nicolas
Boileau, claimed that antiquity constituted an
unsurpassed model, he was, in a way, the
spokesman for women and the people at
court.

The polemics really got under way on Jan.
27, 1687. Louis XIV had just been operated
on for a fistula, and the Academy assembled
to express publicly its joy over the king's
recovery. Charles Perrault had a poem read
entitled "Le Siècle de Louis le Grand" (The
century of Louis the Great), in which he proclaimed the superiority of Louis XIV's epoch
over that of Augustus. Boileau's reply was
fierce, Racine's ironic, and La Fontaine, in his
Epître à Huet, professed his attachment to his
Greek and Roman masters.

Thus the Quarrel of the Ancients and
Moderns, which had begun in 1657 with
Desmarets de Saint-Sorlin, flared up again.
It enthralled the literary world not only in
France but in Italy, the Netherlands, and
England as well.

The publication in January 1697 of the
Histoires ou contes du temps passé, which were
intended to prove that the tales of contemporary times were more moral than those of
antiquity, did incontestably more for
Perrault's fame than the many works in
which he extolled the king. Returning to his
youthful pastime of writing verses with his
brothers, he reworked the tales that his
youngest son, Pierre Perrault d'Armancour,
sixteen years old, had transcribed during the
summer of 1694, based on stories told by old
ladies or wet-nurses. Hoping to obtain for his
son a position as secretary with Elisabeth
Charlotte d'Orléans, the niece of Louis XIV,
Perrault had the manuscript copied in a fine
hand and bound in red morocco stamped
with Mademoiselle's arms, and presented it
to her.

The album contains five prose tales: "La Belle au bois dormant" (Sleeping Beauty), "Le Petit Chaperon Rouge" (Little Red Riding Hood), "La Barbe Bleue" (Bluebeard), "Le Chat botté" (Puss 'n' Boots), and "Les Fées (The fairies). They were preceded by a dedicatory letter signed by his son but obviously written by Perrault. He added little illustrations he had drawn and carefully colored to each story, as well as a frontispiece corresponding to the subtitle: *Contes de ma mère l'Oye* (Mother Goose stories).

With a view to publication, he added three tales that Pierre had written down: "Cendrillon" (Cinderella), "Riquet à la Houppe," and "Le Petit Poucet" (Tom Thumb). His drawings were engraved on copper by Antoine Clouzier. The book was an immediate success. These stories taken straight from the mouths of nannies were followed by the publication of countless tales told by ladies in town or at court.

But the real triumph of Perrault's *Contes* dates from the 19th century. The stories became the great classic of children's books and mark the entry of the oral art of storytelling into written literature.

This small volume is extremely rare. Only four copies, one of which appears to be a second printing, are known to bibliographers. The copy belonging to the BNF is missing pages 105 and 106, these having been replaced by manuscript leaf.

Marie-Françoise Quignard

Marc Fumaroli, "Les enchantements de l'éloquence: *Les Fées* de Charles Perrault ou De la littérature," in *Le statut de la littérature: Mélanges offerts à Paul Bénichou* (Geneva, 1982), 153–86. Charles Perrault, *Contes,* ed. Marc Soriano (Paris, 1989).

127
Apotheosis of Claudius
Cabinet des Médailles, Babelon 265

Sardonyx cameo in three layers; 107 × 115 mm. Rome, A.D. 54. Attributed to Skylax the engraver. Square frame of enameled gold; 130 × 135 mm. Paris, 1685–1686. From the treasury of the monastery of Saint-Evre de Toul; purchased by Louis XIV in 1684.

This precious stone is one of the finest examples of cameo art, the art of carving hard stones in relief. It originated during the Hellenistic period and was very popular during the first two centuries A.D. This cameo shows the apotheosis of a Roman emperor taken, like Ganymede, to heaven by an eagle (shown frontally). The emperor, wearing Jupiter's aegis and the imperial cloak that falls to his ankles, is being crowned with a laurel wreath by a Winged Victory. In one hand he holds the *lituus,* the crooked rod that symbolizes the Pontifex Maximus (the religious title bestowed on emperors since the reign of Augustus). In the other hand he holds a cornucopia.

The apotheosis or deification of an emperor was a frequent subject of 1st-century art. The same iconography was used in monumental sculpture—as on Titus's arch of triumph, ca. 80–85—as well as on engraved gems, such as a cameo from the collection of the church of Saint-Nicolas du Port, now at the library of Nancy.

The cameo was initially thought during the Middle Ages to be a representation of

313

Saint John the Evangelist. When Louis XIV acquired it, the subject was identified as the apotheosis of Germanicus, prince of the imperial family, who died in Germania in the year 19. Several arguments, however, challenge this identification. The eagle and lituus are attributes reserved for emperors, as is the honor of apotheosis. Moreover, the vigorous lines and the contrast between the polished shiny sections and the unpolished sections make it possible to date the cameo to the era of Claudius (41–54) and to attribute it with probability to Skylax the engraver, who signed an intaglio amethyst portrait of Claudius with a similar profile, now in the Hermitage Museum. There is also an abundant iconography assimilating Claudius to Jupiter, identified by his wearing of Jupiter's aegis, such as the Vienna cameo depicting four figures also attributed to Skylax.

Moreover, the wrinkle across the emperor's forehead is absent from portraits of Germanicus, who died at the age of thirty-four, whereas it generally features in portraits of Claudius, who only became emperor at the age of fifty. Therefore, this would appear to be a portrait of Claudius, produced after his death in the year 54.

This cameo, acquired by Louis XIV in 1684 for his "Cabinet des Raretez," was set according to his orders in a gilt mount with blue, white, pink, and black enamel decoration, set off by diamonds, probably executed by the king's jeweler, Josias Belle, as early as 1685 or 1686. This is proof of the king's interest in his collection, which he kept in Versailles close to his apartments and visited every day.

Many of the most beautiful engraved gems in the current collection of the Cabinet des Médailles came from the Cabinet des Rois, the royal collection, which since the Middle Ages housed the coins, medals, gems, jewels, precious objects, and curios belonging to the kings of France. It became an administrative entity in 1560 on the orders of Charles IX. Considerable expansion took place under the impetus of Louis XIV. When he died, the collection was moved to the Bibliothèque Royale, where it continued to grow, notably through the confiscation of church property during the Revolution, and then by purchases, gifts, and bequests. Today, in addition to coins, medals, and antiques, the Cabinet des Médailles possesses approximately ten thousand engraved gemstones.

Mathilde Avisseau Broustet

E. Babelon, *Catalogue des camées de la Bibliothèque Nationale* (Paris, 1897), no. 265. G. Richter, *Engraved Gems of the Greeks, Etruscans, and Romans,* vol. 2 (London, 1971), no. 498. H. Jucker, *Jahrbuch des Bernischen Historischen Museums* 39–40 (1959–1960): 277ff., pl. 6, 1–2. W. R. Megow, *Kameen von Augustus bis Alexander Severus* (Berlin, 1987), no. A80, 199–200, pl. 27, no. 1.

128

FIRDAWSÎ TÛSÎ

Le Livre des Rois (The book of kings)

Département des Manuscrits, Division Orientale, Supplément persan 489, fol. 2v

Abû l-Qâsim Firdawsî Tûsî, *Shâhnâma*

Paper; 614 fols.; 265 × 380 mm. Binding decorated with arms of Napoléon I. Iran, 1543–1546. Purchased in Isfahan by Jean Otter for the Bibliothèque Royale ca. 1737–1739.

The original version of the *Shâhnâma,* the greatest Persian historical epic, was written about 995 by the poet Firdawsî Tûsî, who continued to add chapters to the work until about 1010. Depending upon the copy, the epic contains between 48,000 and 52,000 couplets and, using highly diverse sources, tells the history of Iran from its origins until the advent of Islam. This popular text was frequently illustrated with scenes of feasts or battles similar to those that once decorated the walls of Iranian palaces.

This unusual volume contains not one but two 16th-century copies of this epic. The first

copy is complete (fols. 1–551) and was produced between 950 and 953 of the Hegira (A.D. 1543–1546). Its sixty-eight paintings date from the 16th century, except for the image on folio 104, which was added during the 17th century at Isfahan. The name of the original owner has been erased from the opening folio. The second copy (fols. 552v–614), which is unfinished, dates from around 1520 and was written at Tabriz. Although five paintings were planned, only two were executed (fols. 558 and 566v). How the texts came to be bound together is not known.

The opening scene, on display here (fols. 2v–3) has no connection with the epic's text and depicts a scene of feasting in the countryside. The prince who appears on folio 2v has the effete characteristics typical of the period of Shâh Tahmâsb I, who ruled Iran from 1524 to 1576, and may be the ruler's son, Prince Bahrâm Mîrzâ, who died in 1549. Both men were famous patrons of the arts, and the manuscript may have been copied for a member of their entourage.

The miniature of Rûdâba entertaining Zâl (fol. 43) bears the tiny signature of the otherwise unknown artist, Rizâ'î, who is probably the artist of the opening image (fols. 2v–3) as well as a few others. Many of the small trees that dot the countryside in the scene of feasting have a broken branch, a motif already present in the *Shâhnâma* executed in Tabriz in 1520–1530 for Tahmâsb I. The broken branch is found again in the paintings on folios 59 and 70v. It is thought on the basis of these miniatures, all by the hand of Rizâ'î, that the artist worked at Tabriz in the shadow of the royal atelier. The remaining 16th-century miniatures appear to have been added several years later in central Iran.

A note on the flyleaf by Jean Otter, who was in Isfahan from 1737 to 1739 and purchased several Persian manuscripts for the Bibliothèque Royale, indicates that this manuscript comes "from the palace of the kings of Persia," pillaged in 1722 by the Afghans.

Francis Richard

I. Stchoukine, *Les peintures des manuscrits safavis de 1502 à 1587* (Paris, 1959), 86, no. 53. *Trésors d'Orient,* exhibition at the Bibliothèque Nationale (Paris, 1973), 91, no. 238.

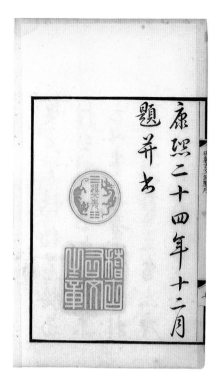

129
Yuzhi Guwen yuanjian
(Anthology of classical Chinese prose)

Département des Manuscrits, Division
Orientale, Chinois 3594, fols. 15v–16 and
imperial seal

*Woodblocks (19.3 × 14.2 cm), 9 columns per page, 20
characters per column; punctuation in red; notes in
the upper margin in blue, red, and yellow. 24 fascicles; original covers made of blue silk; labels made
of white silk with the calligraphed title. 8 bound
volumes (Chinois 3594–3601) (28.5 × 18 cm), calf
with Louis-Philippe's monogram. [China,] 1685.
Given to Louis XIV on Aug. 11, 1700; entered in the
registry of the Bibliothèque Royale on Oct. 7, 1700.*

According to an age-old Chinese tradition,
the emperors of the Qing dynasty (1644–1911),
of Manchurian origin, showed themselves to
be great patrons of the arts and literature.
Qing Shengzu in particular, usually referred
to in the West by his "reign title," Kangxi
(1662–1722), was a collector and connoisseur
of all forms of art. He enjoyed literature,
practiced calligraphy, and appreciated
Western painting and music, to which Jesuit
missionaries had introduced him.

In his concern to rally the educated class
(generally hostile to the Manchu dynasty)
around the monarchy, Kangxi initiated major
publishing projects: a translation into
Manchurian of the "classics" and basic texts

of Chinese literature, the writing of a history
of the Ming dynasty (1368–1644), and the compilation of dictionaries *(Kangxi Zidian, Peiwen
Yunfu)* and encyclopedias on calligraphy and
painting *(Peiwenchai Shuhuapu).* The *Anthology
of Classical Chinese Prose,* presented here, was
compiled on imperial orders under the direction of Xu Qianxue (1631–1695), a learned bibliophile who had been placed in charge of
writing the *Mingshi* (History of the Ming) several years earlier.

In sixty-four chapters, the anthology provides a selection of the most beautiful texts
written in prose between the 5th century b.c.
and the 12th century a.d., chosen by the
emperor and accompanied by notes in the
upper margin. Its major interest lies in its
provenance and in the way it was printed,
using a multicolor woodcut method.

Whereas in the West scribes were copying
texts by hand until Gutenberg invented a
means of printing with movable metal type in
the middle of the 15th century, by the 8th
century China had developed an original
process to duplicate images and texts known
as xylographic printing. The process first
involved cutting a block of wood to the
dimensions of a sheet of paper (paper having
been invented in China during the 1st century a.d. and widely used there as a medium
for writing since the 3d century). A thin sheet
of paper on which an artist had brushed was
then stuck, reverse side up, to the block. The
text or image could then be engraved into
the block; the engraved block would be laid
on a table and was inked, and then sheets of
paper were simply applied by hand, producing printed copies.

Practiced intensively by the 9th century,
woodblock printing was the preferred technique in China and the entire Far East right
up to the mid-19th century. Texts were usually
printed using black ink, like manuscripts, but
the use of several colors of ink during printing has been documented as early as the 14th
century.

During the final years of the Ming dynasty,
in the early 17th century, two families from
Wuxing in Zhejiang province, the Mins and
the Lings, rivaled one another in publishing
fine critical editions. The various commentaries, often placed in the upper margin, as

well as punctuation would be printed in red and blue. Each sheet of printed paper required as many engraved blocks as there were colors; and the sheet would have to be applied to every block in turn.

That is how the *Anthology of Classical Chinese Prose* was printed. The text is in black, with basic commentary in smaller characters in double columns; red was used for the punctuation and for the editors' comments printed in the upper margin. Commentaries by authors of preceding dynasties were printed in blue, and the emperor's comments appeared in a magnificent yellow.

This first print run, on superb white paper, was done at Wuyingdian, the imperial printing office that Kangxi had set up in 1680 within the very walls of the Forbidden City (Zijincheng), or at Shishuju in Yangzhou. The end of the preface, dated 1685, features the imperial seals in Chinese red ink. This copy was entered in the acquisitions registry of the Bibliothèque Royale on Oct. 7, 1700, by Nicolas Clément, after having been presented to Louis XIV on Aug. 11 at Versailles by Father Jean de Fontaney, a Jesuit. He had departed for China in 1685 with four other French Jesuits, "mathématiciens du Roi" (king's mathematicians), on Louis XIV's orders. Emperor Kangxi sent Fontaney back to the king of France with a mission and presents such as silk goods, tea, and books.

Monique Cohen

Trésors de Chine et Haute Asie (Paris, 1979), no. 39. *Europa und die Kaiser von China* (Berlin, 1985), no. 13/5. *Impressions de Chine* (Paris, 1992), no. 93.

130

JEAN-ANTOINE FRAISSE
Livre de dessins chinois
(Book of Chinese drawings)
Réserve des livres rares, Rés. V. 86, fol. 23

Paris: Lottin, 1735. Three pp. of texts and 54 plates, including 1 double, 1 triple, and 4 folding; folio. Plates engraved and drawn by J.-A. Fraisse. Contemporary red morocco gilt; sides decorated with the so-called dentelle du Louvre. *Confiscated with the Condé collections at Chantilly during the Revolution.*

After a frustrated political career, Louis-Henri de Bourbon-Condé, a well-informed collector and a man of taste, devoted himself to the embellishment of his castle at Chantilly and acquired a remarkable collection of objects from the Far East. The "Singeries," famous grotesque figures that were completed about 1735 for his rooms, bear witness to that even today. The vogue for fabrics, lacquer ware, and porcelains had continued to grow since the 16th century and the various companies of the Indies were unable to import enough to meet Western demand.

Condé–"Monsieur le Duc"–played a decisive role in the creation of manufactures intended to "imiter les ouvrages de la Chine" (imitate the works of China). The history of the porcelain factory set up in a house in Chantilly and placed under Cicaire Cirou's supervision is well known. The manufacture of Indian fabrics was established in the castle itself and about 1730 was entrusted to the direction of Jean-Antoine Fraisse from Grenoble, "peintre de son Altesse sérénissime" (painter to His Most Serene Highness). The *Livre de dessins chinois* that he published in 1735 under the duke's auspices is an ornamentist's catalogue intended to provide models for fabric and porcelain workshops. But it is no less a gorgeous book of pictures for use by amateurs, intended to celebrate the duke's remarkable Oriental collection. The album contains fifty-four plates, some of which are made up in long folding format, alternately depicting landscapes–genre scenes in which Chinese people fish and play with kites–and floral compositions. The plates differ from

317

those in the earlier "Orientalist" publications of Marot or Peter Schenk by their very thorough interpretation and respect for the simplicity of Oriental motifs. The Japanese orientation of the duke's collections is reflected in Fraisse's drawings and in the "kakiémon" motifs that would long characterize Chantilly porcelain.

The *Livre des dessins chinois* is very rare: a dozen copies are listed in Europe and only three are in watercolor. This one is especially valuable: it is in watercolor, has a binding decorated with the *dentelle* (lace) *du Louvre* (the copy belonging to the count of Egmont was described in 1743 as bound "avec le cordon du Louvre") lined in blue tabby. It was among the Condés' collections of objets d'art that were seized in 1793 during the Revolution and deposited in the Bibliothèque Nationale. The princes of Condé must therefore have kept it in the midst of the objects that had inspired it.

Isabelle de Conihout

Nicole Ballu, "Influence de l'Extrême-Orient sur le style de Chantilly au XVIIIème siècle," *Cahiers de la céramique* 1958: 100–117. Madeleine Jarry, *Chinoiseries: Le rayonnement du goût chinois sur les arts décoratifs des XVIIe et XVIIIe siècles* (Fribourg, 1981). Geneviève Le Duc, "Chantilly: Un certain regard vers l'Extrême-Orient, 1730–1750," illustrated lecture presented to the French Porcelain Society (London, 1993).

131

Condé Medal Cabinet

Cabinet des Médailles, Ancienne Collection
Condé no. 1

*Small wooden chest; tortoiseshell, brass, gilded
bronze. Length: 240 mm; height: 160 mm; depth: 200
mm. Workshop of André-Charles Boulle. Paris, end
of 17th century–first third of 18th century. Former
collection of the Princes of Condé, château of
Chantilly. Deposited in 1797.*

This wooden casket is inlaid with brass
arabesques on a tortoiseshell ground. A
chased, gilded bronze mascaron (decorative
head) adorns the lock and the sides. A handle, also in gilded bronze, is attached on top.
The interior is furnished with seven drawers
lined in blue velvet and separated into compartments by a framework of gilded bronze,
allowing for the storage of twelve coins or
medals; each point of intersection is decorated with a fleur-de-lis. The next-to-last drawer
has still more ornate decoration: a large
frame surmounted by a crown with fleurs-de-
lis and flanked by putti holding a scepter
covers two-thirds of the surface.

 This small medal cabinet was one of a
series of eight, only two of which are now in
the Cabinet des Médailles. They are mentioned in a 1715 inventory of furniture that
André-Charles Boulle (1642–1732), chief cabinetmaker of the king's household, left to his
four sons. These were probably pieces that
Boulle had crafted for Nicolas de Launay
(1647–1727), director of the currency, who by
virtue of his office had his lodgings, like
Boulle, in the galleries of the Louvre.
Although the great cabinetmaker apparently
began the construction of this small chest, it
was completed by one of his sons.

The craftsmanship exhibits the method
that bears the Boulle name. Probably invented at the end of the 16th century, the process
of *tarsia incastra,* later called the "Boulle
technique," consisted of superimposing
sheets of tortoise-shell and brass so that
ground and motif could be cut at the same
time. The two leaves were then separated and
the decorative part of each was set precisely
into the other, yielding highly refined inlay
work.

 Archival documents preserved at the
Bibliothèque nationale de France indicate
that this casket, which formed part of the collection of the princes of Condé in their
château of Chantilly, was confiscated along
with other objects in 1792 and deposited in
the Cabinet des Médailles in 1797. In fact,
shortly after the start of the French Revolution in 1789 the princes left the country, giving the signal for the emigration of nobles.
As early as 1793, the Convention's Committee
of Public Instruction demanded an inventory
of the collections in the château of Chantilly,
only a few months after the promulgation of
the laws calling for the confiscation of the
property of persons who had emigrated,
declaring their possessions to be "biens
nationaux" (national property) (February and
August 1792).

 Thus two small and precious pieces were
added to an already important collection of
furnishings in the Cabinet des Médailles. In
addition to the prestigious medal cabinets
built in 1741 for the Cabinet of Louis XV, the
Cabinet des Médailles also had the medal
cabinet of Louis d'Orléans (1703–1752), crafted by the cabinetmaker Cressent, and the
two medal cabinets owned by Joseph Pellerin
(one of Boulle inlay and lacquer, the other
made from Coromandel laquer screens), both
dating from about 1730.

Irène Aghion

319

H. Havard, *Les Boulle* (Paris, 1898). J.-P. Samoyault, *André-
Charles Boulle et sa famille* (Geneva, 1979), 15–16, 66, 81–82.
1789: Le patrimoine libéré, exhibition at the Bibliothèque
Nationale (Paris, 1989), 252–53, no. 186. *Collection Hubert de
Givenchy,* sales catalogue, Christie's, Monaco, Dec. 4, 1993, pp.
30–35, no. 10.

132

ABBÉ CLAUDE BERNOU

Amérique septentrionale... depuis l'embouchure de la rivière St Laurens jusqu'à l'isle de Cayenne avec les nouvelles découvertes de la rivière Mississipi ou Colbert (North America... from the mouth of the St. Lawrence River to Cayenne Island with the new discoveries of the Mississippi or Colbert River)

Département des Cartes et Plans, SH Pf. 122, div. 2, p. 0

Paper; watercolor manuscript; 1470 × 1630 mm. [Ca. 1681]. From the map collection of the Service Hydrographique de la Marine, deposited at the Bibliothèque Nationale in 1947.

This manuscript map, though incomplete, was prepared with great care. It was intended to make the minister of the navy (Jean-Baptiste Colbert, marquis de Seignelay, son of the great Colbert) aware of the voyage that Cavalier de La Salle was then undertaking—a voyage that culminated at the mouth of the Mississippi with a claim to possession of Louisiana in the name of Louis XIV on April 9, 1682. Along with the map, abbé Bernou sent Seignelay a memorandum that explained why the new territories explored by La Salle should be colonized (BNF Clairambault 1016, fols. 190–193), together with a report entitled *Relations des descouvertes et des voyages du sieur de La Salle* (1679–1681), edited by P. Margry.

Bernou, who blithely mingled the general good with his own private interest, was in contact with the coterie of the *Gazette* (the first weekly newspaper in France) and in particular with Eusèbe Renaudot, grandson of newspaper's founder (see cat. 91). Bernou hoped to be invested with a bishopric in the newly discovered territories. He pointed out to the navy minister how desirable it would be to beat the English to the territories just reached by La Salle—lands that could give France the monopoly of the fur trade.

In North America the map distinguishes three principal regions: *Terre du Labrador ou de Cortereal* (Labrador or Corterealland), *Canada ou Nouvelle France* (Canada or New

France), and, along the course of the Mississippi—which is drawn only as far as its confluence with the Ohio River—*Louisiane* (Louisiana). To the west, *Terres inconnues* (unknown land); to the south extended *Mexique ou Nouvelle Espagne* (Mexico or New Spain).

A comparison of Bernou's map with Franquelin's (see cat. 133) reveals that Franquelin drew New France much larger since he included Labrador and extended it down to the Gulf of Mexico. Bernou, on the other hand, furthered his own ambitions by separating Louisiana and New France. He also turned his attention to Mexico. In a memorandum of Jan. 8, 1692 (BNF Clairambault 1016, fols. 206–207), Bernou proposed the conquest of the northern part (New Biscay with its silver, gold, and lead mines) from the mouth of the Rio Bravo with the aid of buccaneers from Santo Domingo. This explains the significance on the map of the lovely arc made by the Antilles. In point of fact Louis XIV took more interest in the quickly exploitable mineral resources than in the Illinois territories so dear to La Salle—a fact Bernou fully appreciated.

The impatient abbé hastily dispatched his information about America to a Venetian monk named Coronelli, who from 1681 to 1683 was constructing in Paris a pair of enormous globes some four meters in diameter for Louis XIV's palace of Versailles. It was the ideal content for promoting global ambitions. The great Colbert, mindful of advances in cartography and concerned about French world trade, was certainly just as alert to the advantage of displaying Coronelli's works where they could be viewed by the king.

Monique Pelletier

M. Pelletier, "Les globes de Louis XIV," *Imago mundi* 34 (1982): 72–89. Pelletier, "From New France to Louisiana: Politics and Geography, in *The Sun King*, exhibition catalogue (New Orleans, 1984), 85–103. Pelletier, "L'Amérique septentrionale du globe de Louis XIV," in *Imago et mesura mundi* (Rome, 1985), 2:393–407.

133

JEAN-BAPTISTE FRANQUELIN

Carte de la Nouvelle France

(Map of New France)

Département des Cartes et Plans,
Rés. Ge DD 2987 (8536)

*Vellum; hand-drawn map highlighted with washes
and gold. [Between 1702 and 1711.] From the collection of the geographer J. B. Bourguignon d'Anville;
sold to Louis XVI on Feb. 18, 1782.*

This map of North America shows a much
enlarged New France whose predominant
role is highlighted by the view of Québec
delicately drawn in the cartouche. The map-
maker favored extending Canada down to the
Gulf of Mexico, in opposition to the views of
Lemoyne d'Iberville, who aspired to the gov-
ernorship of a distinct Mississippi region.

The map is dedicated to the grand
dauphin, son of Louis XIV, who died in 1711.
The indication of Fort Louis of Louisiana,
constructed in 1702, on the right bank of the
Mobile River makes it impossible to date it
before then.

The map closely resembles another
dated 1708 and dedicated to Count Jerôme
Phelypeaux de Pontchartrain, minister of
the navy, and preserved by the Service
Historique de la Marine. It bears the title
Carte générale de la Nouvelle France and was
signed by Jean-Baptiste Franquelin (b. 1651),
who noted that it was the fruit of twenty
years' work in the field. The two documents
are not altogether similar. There are differences in the graduations of longitude, in the
names of several Native American tribes, in
the representation of the mouth of the
Mississippi, and so forth. Nevertheless, both
maps provide an extremely interesting
overview of the division of the "Indian
nations." For the French, whose numbers
were insufficient, the backing of the "sav-
ages" was indispensable. They hoped that the
Indians (who it was said "naturally hated the
Spaniards") would become faithful allies. The
experience of New France, however, demonstrated that the balance of forces was highly
unstable. Besides, danger soon came from the

English colonists—a danger that Le Moyne d'Iberville tried immediately to stem. Franquelin's map may have figured in d'Iberville's analysis of the need to pacify the native tribes, but it is doubtful that the cartographer approved the other aspect of the policy promoted by the founder of Louisiana —the relocation of the inland population.

Franquelin had come to Canada in 1671 to trade, but Governor Frontenac persuaded him in 1674 to abandon commerce for cartography. Franquelin played a major role in this field, since it was thanks to him that maps of the French colonies in North America reached France with the same regularity as the reports of the governors and intendants. In 1683 Franquelin traveled to France with his own maps. He met Cavalier de La Salle, who persuaded him to draw a map of his recent expeditions. In 1687 he received the title of Hydrographer to the King at Québec. He took part in the war against England and constructed makeshift defenses to protect Québec. A new sojourn in Paris led to his employment by the military architect Vauban. He died in France sometime after 1712.

Monique Pelletier

G. Marcel, *Reproductions de cartes et de globes relatifs à la découverte de l'Amérique* (Paris, 1893) (reprod. of 1708 map as pl. 40). M. Giraud, *Histoire de la Louisiane française*, vol. 1, *1698–1715* (Paris, 1953). *Dictionnaire biographique du Canada,* vol. 2, *1701–1740* (Quebec, 1969), 236–39.

134

JUAN VICENTE DEL CAMPO
Carte du golfe du Mexique dédiée à l'amiral espagnol Morphi (Map of the Gulf of Mexico dedicated to the Spanish admiral Morphi)
Département des Cartes et Plans, SH Archives no. 27

Vellum; hand-drawn, illustrated map; 624 × 1011 mm. Havana, 1696. From the map collection of the Service Hydrographique de la Marine; deposited at the Bibliothèque Nationale in 1942.

This handsome 1696 Spanish portolan (early navigational) chart provided the French with valuable information about the then unfamiliar coasts of the Gulf of Mexico. A 1698 partial copy of the map (Département des Cartes et Plans, SH Pf. 141, div. 1, p. 3D) furnishes the following details about French acquisition of the map: "Copie d'une partie de la carte de l'Amérique pris [*sic*] aux Espagnoles par le vaisseau du Roy *le Bon* en 1697 aux isles de

323

l'Amérique" (Copy of part of a map of America taken from the Spanish by the royal ship *Le Bon* in 1697 in the islands of America); "Monsieur de Patoulet, capitaine de vaisseau, a l'original en parchemin" (Mr. de Patoulet, the ship's captain, has the original on parchment). Noted on the copy are details about Cavalier de La Salle's ill-fated attempt to find the mouth of the Mississippi by sea. Another copy (Département des Cartes et Plans, SH Pf. 141, div. 1, p. 2D), with more detailed toponomy, clearly refers to the original as the chart by "Jean Bisente, pilote," dated 1696. Capture of the portolan chart by the French occurred while Louis XIV was agreeing to the terms of the Treaty of Ryswick, under which France had to restore numerous territories in Europe to Spain. At the same time, France, under the watchful eyes of the English, was concerned about the future of the Mississippi basin.

This lovely portolan chart, drawn by the Spanish pilot Juan Vicente del Campo, enables us to resolve a question concerning a cartographic source. In 1700, Guillaume Delisle published the famous map *L'Amérique septentrionale dressée sur les observations de Mrs de l'Académie Royale des Sciences et quelques autres, et sur les mémoires les plus récens* (North America drawn from the observations of members of the Royal Academy of Sciences and others, and on the basis of the most recent accounts), which went through two editions. The second edition situated the mouth of the Mississippi somewhat farther east than the first. And a short time later, in 1703, Delisle published a *Carte du Mexique et de la Floride* with yet another drawing of the northwest coast of the Gulf of Mexico. Comparison with Vicente's portolan chart dispels all doubt: the correction was made possible by the capture of the Spanish map. In Delisle's papers, which are preserved in the Archives Nationales, the scholar indicates his textual and cartographic sources of information. His complex assemblage from various sources demonstrates the skill of desk-bound cartographers. For the *Carte du Mexique*, Delisle cites Herrera, J. de Laet, Thomas Gage, and a manuscript portolan chart about whose origin he is silent—it is probably the very one drawn up by our Vicente.

Guillaume Delisle contributed to the development of scientific cartography in France—a cartography that benefited from contributions by such 17th-century institutions as the Académie des Sciences and the Observatoire. The Spanish portolan chart illustrates how the new scientific cartographers made use of methods provided by many different sources. This included the calculation of positions by methods recommended by the Académie des Sciences, the comparison of documents in the growing royal collections, and the results of cartographic espionage and of expeditions tied to colonial expansion, as well as the critical examination of the documents passed on by predecessors.

Monique Pelletier

M. Giraud, *Histoire de la Louisiane francaise*, vol. 1, *1698–1715* (Paris, 1953). Bibliothèque Nationale, Département des Cartes et Plans, *Catalogue des cartes nautiques sur vélin* (Paris, 1963), 198. M. Pelletier, "Louis XIV et l'Amérique: Témoignages de la cartographie," *Bulletin du Comité Français de Cartographie* 115 (March 1988): 50–58.

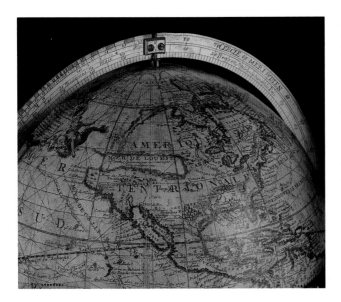

135

NICOLAS BION

Globe terrestre sur le quel les principaux points sont placez sur les dernières observations de Mrs de l'Académie royale des sciences... dédié au duc de Berry (Terrestrial globe on which are placed the most recent observations by members of the Royal Academy of Sciences... dedicated to the duke of Berry)

Département des Cartes et Plans, Ge A 402 (detail)

Engraved globe made of gores (strips of paper) mounted on a sphere; octagonal equatorial table; copper-engraved meridian; carved wooden legs. Sphere diameter: 250 mm. Paris, 1712. Purchased in 1943.

During the 17th century, France was flooded with Dutch-produced globes. At the end of the century, a Venetian named Vicenzo Coronelli took the lead with scale reductions of the large globes he had recently constructed for Louis XIV. His preeminence was challenged, however, by Claude Delisle and his son Guillaume, who were responsible for launching the 18th-century production of French globes. In 1697 they presented a hand-drawn terrestrial globe to Chancellor Boucherat. In 1700 they published a pair of engraved globes 32 centimeters in diameter, and at the same time a world map in two

hemispheres. The same year Jean-Baptiste Nolin published his own map of the world: "Ayant trouvé moyen d'avoir un globe manuscrit... qui était dans la bibliothèque d'une personne illustre, y a pris plusieurs choses singulières et en a fait une mappemonde" (Having managed to obtain a manuscript globe... which was in the library of a famous person, he copied several unique things from it and then made a world map; Claude Delisle in the *Journal des sçavans,* March 1700). Guillaume Delisle deplored above all the fact that Nolin had drawn the Western Sea in America, which thus far had figured exclusively on the manuscript globe. Referring to Nolin's plagiarism, he observed: "Il a représenté une mer à l'occident de la Louisiane, qu'il appelle mer de l'Ouest. Cette mer estoit une de mes découvertes, mais comme il n'est pas toujours à propos de publier ce que l'on sçait, ou que l'on croit sçavoir, je n'ai pas fait graver cette mer sur les ouvrages que j'ai rendus publics, ne voulant pas que les Etrangers profitassent de cette découverte quelle qu'elle pût estre avant que l'on eût reconnu dans ce Royaume si l'on en pourrait tirer quelque avantage" (He depicted a sea to the west of Louisiana, which he calls the Western Sea. This sea was one of my discoveries, but since it is not always appropriate to publish everything one knows or thinks one knows, I did not have this sea engraved in the works that I published. I did not want foreigners to take advantage of this discovery, whatever it might be, before it had been determined in this kingdom if some advantage might come from it). In 1708 Nolin was censured for plagiarism. The commission of experts, appointed in 1705, drew a distinction between the common geographical fund of knowledge (for example, data considered as solid that had been collected by the Académie des Sciences) and the discoveries that belonged to individual geographers (such as Delisle's claim to knowledge of the Western Sea).

In spite of Nolin's censure, Nicolas Bion (1652–1733) incorporated the famous Western Sea on two terrestrial globes without crediting Delisle. The first, 32 centimeters in diameter, was published between 1700 and 1709; the second, of 1712, is exhibited here. As for

325

California, Bion followed Delisle and Nolin for his first globe and represented it as a peninsula. But he returned to the tradition of drawing it as an island on the 1712 globe and on another smaller one that he probably produced afterward. Bion, who bore the title "king's engineer for mathematical instruments," had set up shop on the Quai de l'Horloge in Paris. His workshop at that time was reputed to be the best stocked of its kind. The fact that he did not consider himself a geographer perhaps spared him from the prosecution that befell Nolin.

The myth of the Western Sea arose from hypotheses that geographers formulated to connect the Atlantic with the Pacific. In France, official reports for the years 1717–1719 made use of it. It was revived in the middle of the 18th century by Guillaume de Delisle's brother, Joseph-Nicolas, and by his son-in-law Philippe Buache. Nevertheless, the latter failed to convince his colleagues of the Académie des Sciences.

Monique Pelletier

M. Daumas, *Les instruments scientifiques aux XVIIe et XVIIIe siècles* (Paris, 1953). N. Broc, "Une affaire de plagiat cartographique sous Louis XIV: Le procès Delisle-Nolin," *Revue d'histoire des sciences* 23 (1970): 141–53. M. Pelletier, "De l'objet de luxe au produit de consommation courante: L'évolution de l'édition des globes en France au XVIIIe et XIXe siècles," *Revue de la Bibliothèque Nationale* 21 (1986): 40–51. L. Lagarde, "Le passage du Nord-Ouest et la mer de l'Ouest, *Imago mundi* 41 (1989): 19–43. L. Lagarde, "L'information cartographique, la réalisation des cartes: Leur diffusion et utilisation au début du XVIIIe siècle," *Bulletin du Comité Français de Cartographie* 125 (September 1990): 26–31.

136

JACQUES CHRISTOPHE LEBLON
Portrait of Louis XV
Cabinet des Estampes, AA4 Rés.

Engraving; 610 × 448 mm (frame line). No type. Mezzotint; colors printed in register. 1739.

Jacques Christophe Leblon (1667–1741), a German miniaturist, painter, and engraver (also known as Jacob Christoph Leblon), began his research into color in Amsterdam, inspired by Newton's discoveries. But it was only after he moved to London that he learned the mezzotint technique and used it as the basis for his color engravings. As he explained around 1722 in a treatise titled *Coloritto*, he could print colors directly by using registration marks to print three plates one after another, inked with the primary colors red, yellow, and blue. The combination of these colors enabled him to attain secondary hues. After some initial success in England engraving reproductions of Dutch and Italian paintings, he went bankrupt and moved to Paris to try his luck around 1735. He managed to obtain a royal warrant from Louis XV, who, in 1739 granted Leblon exclusive rights for color engraving in France, on condition that he reveal his secret to two royal commissioners. The king also granted the artist a stipend (to revert to his daughter after his death) and lodging in the galleries of the Louvre, where the monarchy housed artists it wanted to reward.

After two trial prints (portraits of Cardinal de Fleury and the artist Van Dyck), Leblon executed his major work: a life-size bust portrait of his patron, Louis XV. As a model he chose a painting by his friend Blakey, an Irish painter living in Paris.

After Leblon died in 1741, one of his disciples, Jacques-Fabien Gautier-Dagoty, bought the royal warrant and unscrupulously tried to

claim credit for Leblon's discoveries, notably
the use of a fourth plate, inked in black, to
give greater range and texture to the colors.
Tardieu and Robert, two other followers,
tried to defend Leblon's reputation in 1756
by publishing a French version of *Coloritto*
under the title *L'Art d'imprimer les tableaux*
(The art of printing paintings).

Leblon's method, heavily based on the
English mezzotint technique little esteemed
in France, generally went unappreciated by
French connoisseurs; Gautier-Dagoty, and
later his sons, only managed to profit from
the method by engraving anatomical plates.

Corinne Le Bitouzé

Charles Maumene and Louis d'Harcourt, "Iconographie des
rois de France," *Archives de l'Art français* 16 (1929–1930):
481–83. Yves Sjöberg, *Inventaire du fonds français: Graveurs du
XVIIIème siècle* (Paris, 1974), 13:398. Otto M. Lililen, *Jacob
Christoph Le Blon, 1667–1741: Inventory of Three- or Four-Color
Printing* (Stuttgart, 1985).

137

LOUIS XV

*Cours des principaux fleuves et rivières
de l'Europe, composé et imprimé par
Louis XV, roy de France et de Navarre*
(Courses of the principal rivers and
streams of Europe, composed and
printed by Louis XV, king of France
and Navarre)
Réserve des livres rares, Rés. G. 2972,
front cover with the Pompadour arms and
frontispiece

*Paris: Imprimerie du Cabinet du Roi, 1718. [6] + 72
pp.; 4*^{*to*}*. Portrait of Louis XV engraved by C.
Audran in frontispiece. Red morocco with French
royal arms on covers; blue morocco doublures with
gilt dentelle border and the arms of Mme de
Pompadour, ca. 1750. Acquired in 1935.*

At the death of the Sun King on Sept. 1, 1715,
his successor was five and a half years old. A
precocious, handsome, and intelligent child,
he progressed rapidly under the authority of
the best teachers. Before he was seven years
old, it was said that "la géographie faisait ses
délices" (geography was his delight). His
teachers skillfully took advantage of their
royal pupil's likings and taught him mathematics and drawing by approaching them
through cartography. The traditional lessons
of Latin, ethics, and modern language
(Italian) were successfully combined with
practical activities and visits to scientific collections. In 1718 the Parisian printer
Collombat was asked to set up a little
printshop in the Tuileries where he could
teach the seven-year-old king the rudiments
of typography. At this Imprimerie du Cabinet
du Roi (King's Printshop), which operated
until 1730, Louis XV himself composed and
in part printed broadsheets of the divine
commandments, "precepts of wisdom," and
especially his own summary of Guillaume
Delisle's geography lessons, titled *Cours des
principaux fleuves et rivières de l'Europe*.

The use of a printshop as an "educational
toy" was not completely new. Already in 1648
the young Louis XIV on a visit to the
Imprimerie Royale (Royal Printing Office),
had enjoyed printing Commines's *Mémoires*.

327

138

JEAN-FRANÇOIS JANINET
La Toilette de Vénus (Toilet of Venus)
Cabinet des Estampes, Ef 105 Rés. fol., vol. 2

*Engraving; aquatint; etching and tools; colors
printed in register. 375 × 295 mm (frame line). 1784.
Signed under the frame line: "F. Boucher pinxit. F.
Janinet sculpsit 1783." In the lower margin, inscrip-
tion around a central cartouche:* "LA TOILETTE DE
VENUS/*Dédiée à madame La Comtesse de Coaslin/
Née Mailly." Lower right: "Par son très humble et
très obéissant serviteur Janinet." Lower left:*
"A PARIS, CHEZ CHEREAU, RUE DES MATHURINS,
PRES CELLE DE SORBONNE."

Both *La Toilette de Vénus* and its companion
piece, *Le Bain de Vénus* (Venus bathing), were
painted by François Boucher in 1751 for the
bathroom of the marquise de Pompadour's
Bellevue château. The marquise de
Pompadour (1721–1764), having become friend
and lover of Louis XV, soon fancied herself a
patroness of art and literature. Not only did
she do drawings and engravings herself, but
she had her many residences furnished and
decorated in the "financier" or "tax collector"
style that sought to prettify everything, a trait
still associated with the Pompadour name.

Boucher's painting of Venus at her toilet,
assisted by putti, was designed to be hung in
the marquise's private quarters and depicted
a subject close to her heart—in 1750 at
Versailles, she had played the leading role in
a little play titled *La Toilette de Vénus, ou Le
Matin* (The toilet of Venus, or Morning) which
itself was part of Laujon's ballet *La Journée
galante* (The flirtatious day). Contrary to what
was long believed, however, Boucher does
not seem to have endowed his Venus with
Pompadour's personal features.

This print of the painting was engraved by
Jean-François Janinet (1752–1814) in 1783 and
published the following year. The dedication
to Countess de Coaslin constitutes a knowing
wink to the public on the part of engraver or
publisher, since in her own day the countess
was one of Pompadour's rivals for the king's
attention.

Following Leblon's initial experiments,
research into color engraving continued. The
goal was to imitate a growing number of

Private presses multiplied in the 18th century
to give pleasure to the aristocracy. In Mme de
Pompadour's Versailles apartments Au Nord
were printed Quesnay's *Tableau économique*
and an edition of Corneille's *Rodogune* with
engravings by the marquise herself.

The marquise de Pompadour–née
Jeanne-Antoinette Poisson and famous for
her beauty and wit in Paris's upper bourgeois
circles–probably became the king's mistress
when entertainments were held to honor the
dauphin's marriage in 1745 (see cat. 139). Until
her death in 1764 she reigned over the king's
heart, thanks to her intelligence and artistic
talents. At an unknown date (though the
binding allows us to put it in the 1750s) Louis
XV gave her a copy of his childish "chef
d'oeuvre." Elegantly bound, the book
received the arms of the marquise, discreetly
gilded on the *contreplat,* with a title-page
manuscript note "ex dono authoris" (compli-
ments of the author). It testifies to the intelligence of a royal education and to the refinement of the ties that bound Louis XV to his
favorite.

Isabelle de Conihout

Henri Omont, "l'Imprimerie particulière du Cabinet du roi
au château des Tuileries sous Louis XV," *Bulletin de la Société
de l'Histoire de Paris* 1891: 33–45. Roderick Cave, *The Private
Press* (New York, 1983). Michel Antoine, *Louis XV* (Paris, 1989).

LA TOILETTE DE VENUS
Dédiée à Madame la Comtesse de Coaslin
(Née Mailly.

drawing and painting techniques. Janinet studied under Louis-Marin Bonnet (who perfected the engraving technique known as crayon manner and then developed the pastel manner) before going on to successfully invent and develop color aquatint engraving. He used an initial aquatint plate to print outlines, blacks, and grays, while three other plates, inked respectively in blue, yellow, and red, provided a range of color effects and gave an illusion of watercolor or gouache. Thanks to this method, Janinet became the prime interpreter of fashionable painters like Boucher and Fragonard.

Four different states of this engraving are known: a proof before all letters, one with signatures and date, a final state with all lettering (shown here), and one in which the putto doing Venus's hair has been eliminated.

Corinne Le Bitouzé

Henri Portalis, "La gravure en couleurs," *Gazette des Beaux-Arts* 1888: 441–57 and 1889: 29–41, 197–212. Michèle Hébert and Yves Sjöberg, *Inventaire du fonds français: Graveurs du XVIIIe siècle* (Paris, 1973), 12:23. *Graveurs français de la seconde moitié du XVIIIème siècle*, exhibition at the Louvre (Paris, 1985), 92. *François Boucher, 1703–1770*, exhibition at the Metropolitan Museum of Art (New York, 1986), 255–57.

329

VÛE PERSPECTIVE DE LA PLACE DE LOUIS LE GRAND,
avec la Représentation des Salles construites à l'occasion du Mariage de
MONSEIGNEUR LE DAUPHIN.

139
Fêtes publiques données par la Ville de Paris à l'occasion du mariage de Mgr le Dauphin les 23 et 26 février 1745
(Public festivities given by the city of Paris on the occasion of the marriage of monseigneur the Dauphin on February 23 and 26, 1745)
Réserve des livres rares, Rés. grand folio Lb³⁸. 508A

[Paris: François Blondel and Widow Chereau, 1751]. Title, frontispiece, 9 pages of engraved text, 8 single plates, and 10 double plates. Contemporary red morocco gilt. Acquired during the Second Empire.

The matrimonial and diplomatic arrangements between France and Spain had led to the decision to have a double wedding, Mme Première, the daughter of Louis XV, marrying the infante Don Philippe in 1739, with the dauphin, the king's only son, being promised to a Spanish infanta. The marriage of fifteen-year-old Maria Theresa of Spain to the dauphin was celebrated with extraordinary pomp in July 1745. The dauphine pleased her husband very much, and the rumor that she was pregnant spread after the victory at Fontenoy.

The princess died in July 1746 while giving birth to a daughter. Her funeral procession, orchestrated and decorated by the Slodtz brothers, was one of the great moments of the fading Rococo period. Two years later the dauphin, the sole male heir to the throne, was forced to overcome his grief and marry Marie-Josèphe of Saxony, who bore him eight children, the last three of whom were the last three legitimate kings of France.

The celebrations that had marked the wedding in 1745 were intended to prove that France had not been bled dry by the war. At Versailles itself, three famous prints by Cochin preserved the image of the rococo décor designed by the Slodtz brothers for the performance of *La Princesse de Navarre* (scripted by Voltaire, with music by Rameau), for the great ball, and especially for the masked ball, which may have begun the idyll between Mme de Pompadour and Louis XV, costumed as a yew tree. As was the case for Mme Première's wedding in 1739, and would be for the dauphin's second one in 1747, the city of Paris organized sumptuous festivities that this album commemorates. Six ball-rooms had been set up in various parts of the city and the designs for them revealed a most effervescent imagination: a profusion of gar-lands and floral motifs whose exuberance did not, however, mask a new taste for antique architectural features.

An advertisement in the *Mercure de France* reveals that the greater part of the designs were composed by the architect François Blondel, not by Cochin, to whom tradition attributes them, and that the two books depicting the celebrations given by the city for the dauphin's two subsequent marriages were put on sale at the same time, in November 1751.

The copy on display, in contemporary binding, is one of the rare deluxe copies and was made like the royal copy currently pre-served at the Versailles municipal library: two drawings for the frontispiece by Charles Eisen and the allegory of marriage by Charles Hutin, with delicate etchings retouched by pen and carefully colored for the various ballroom scenes, groaning side-boards, and triumphal arches.

Isabelle de Conihout

Henri Cohen, *Guide de l'amateur de livres à gravures du XVIIIème siècle* (Paris, 1912), 394 (with an erroneous attribution to Cochin). François Souchal, *Les Slodtz: Sculpteurs et décora-teurs du roi, 1685–1764* (Paris, 1967). Christian Michel, *Charles-Nicolas Cochin et le livre illustré au XVIIIème siècle* (Geneva, 1987). M. C. Moine, "Les fêtes du mariage de Madame Première à Versailles, les 26 janvier and 26 août 1739," *Bibliothèque de l'École des Chartes* 149 (1991): 107–29.

140
Louis XV
Cabinet des Médailles, Babelon 926

Three-layer sardonyx cameo; 74 × 60 mm. Versailles; signed by engraver Jacques Guay: GUAY F[ECIT] *1753. Gilt enamel setting from the period of Louis XV; 97 × 82 mm. Provenance: Cabinet du Roi.*

This portrait of King Louis XV, aged forty-three, was done by gem engraver Jacques Guay in 1753 and exhibited at the Salon of 1755. One of the few portraits of the king exe-cuted from nature, it is considered the mas-terpiece of engraving on stone of modern times, for the accuracy of the resemblance, the purity of the stone, and the high quality of the workmanship.

In a right profile, the king is shown with his head wreathed with laurels, dressed in a breastplate decorated with lion heads and a cloak fastened in the classical style on his right shoulder. The three horizontal layers of stone are skillfully used; the hair and gar-ments are engraved in the reddish upper layer and the face in the white middle layer, while the brown bottom layer highlights the composition. It reportedly took two years to engrave the cameo. The face and scalp were

331

engraved not with a lathe driven by a pedal-operated wheel but by hand, with a diamond point. Some parts were left dull while others were polished using a process invented by Guay.

Upon his return from a voyage to Italy, from which he had brought back classical-style intaglios, Jacques Guay (1711–1797), a student of François Boucher, was noticed by Louis XV's favorite, Mme de Pompadour, who became his patron. She moved him into Versailles and had him appointed the king's engraver. She herself began to do engravings on stone under his supervision and also reproduced Guay's works in a collection of prints. From 1745 until her death in 1764, she commissioned a series of cameo and intaglio gems from him, glorifying Louis XV by commemorating his military victories and the major events of his reign, as well as portraits and charming allegories of their love. Many of these works were set in jewels for Mme de Pompadour. Her death marked the end of Guay's career, despite several new commissions after the king's death, such as Louis XVI's and Marie-Antoinette's cameos.

Guay was described by Mariette in the *Traité des pierres gravées* and was considered by his contemporaries as "l'homme de génie de l'époque" (the genius of the era), putting him on a par with the most renowned gem engravers of antiquity, Pyrgoteles and Dioscorides. For us, he is still the best representative of modern glyptic.

Mathilde Avisseau Broustet

La Chau and Le Blond, *Description des pierres gravées du duc d'Orléans* (Paris, 1780), 2:197. J. Leturcq, *Notice sur Jacques Guay* (Paris, 1873), 44, 74, 197, 213, and pl. D, 1 (first print of Mme de Pompadour's collection). E. Babelon, *Catalogue des camées de la Bibliothèque Nationale* (Paris, 1897), 344–45, no. 926, pl. LXXV. *Louis XV: Un moment de perfection de l'Art français*, exhibition at the Hôtel de la Monnaie (Paris, 1974), 617ff. and 632–33, no. 940.

141
Patère de Rennes (Rennes patera)
Cabinet des Médailles, Chabouillet no. 2537

Dish made of solid 23-carat gold; hammered, chased, repoussé work. Diameter: 25 cm (medallion: 14 cm); height: 4 cm; weight: 1.315 kg. First half of the 3d century A.D. Found in Rennes in 1774 and deposited in the Cabinet des Médailles at the request of Louis XV.

This gold patera, a wide dish used as a cup for drinking or for libations, is decorated with a border of Roman imperial coins bearing representations of emperors from Hadrian to Geta (the most recent dates from the year 209). The sixteen *aurei* are set inside laurel wreaths for the emperors and acanthus wreaths for the empresses and young princes. In the center of the cup, a bas-relief illustrates a challenge between Bacchus and Hercules, symbolizing the triumph of wine over strength.

Bacchus, pictured among rocks, is surrounded by his retinue, notably Silenus, Pan playing panpipes, and a bacchant blowing into a double-flute. Crowned with ivy and vine branches, holding his thyrsus, Bacchus is seated on a throne with a panther at his feet. With a confident gesture, the god raises an empty rhyton (drinking horn). Hercules, seated near him and seemingly unsteady from the wine, is propped up against a rock on which he has deposited the slain lion and the club. He is holding his kantharus (a bowl-like cup) clumsily in the other hand. A bas-relief frieze ringing the central medallion evokes the Bacchic procession in which the god is half reclining in his chariot drawn by two panthers, preceded by a drunken Hercules. All of this imagery is surrounded by a chased decorative border of laurel leaves.

Found with this cup were about one hundred Roman gold coins dating from the time of Nero to Aurelian, one chain, and one gold fibula (or clasp). Buried six feet deep, the treasure was discovered in Rennes on March 26, 1774, while a chapterhouse in the city was being demolished. It was deposited by order of Louis XV in the Cabinet des Médailles et Antiques.

The exceptional nature of the patera presents a number of problems that have not yet been resolved: its place of production (Italy or Gaul), its homogeneity (the *emblema* was detached when it was discovered), and the reason for its burial (for hoarding or a votive offering). Nor has the archaeological context been determined. Today it is generally agreed that the cup was buried around 275 at the time of the first Frank raids in Gaul, only a few years after it was made. Although the jewelers of ancient Egypt used gold coins as decorative elements on finery as early as the Hellenistic period, goldsmiths in the Roman West did not use these components until the 3d century A.D.

Although the cup remains unique, quite a few pieces of jewelry incorporating coins have been found at archaeological sites, and some of them are in the Cabinet des Médailles. Coins were used as parts for pendants or clasps for necklaces, for rings, or for bracelets and fibulas. The treasure hoard discovered in 1809 in Naix-aux-Forges, in the Meuse region, also in the Cabinet des Médailles, includes not only seven necklaces made of gold, pearls, garnets, and glass beads but also a more valuable necklace with four set coins (aurei from the reigns of Hadrian, Septimus Severus, Caracalla, and Geta), two cameos, and five gold tubes that separate the medallions.

Irène Aghion

Lucien Decombe, *Notice sur la patère d'or découverte à Rennes en 1774* (Rennes, 1879). Cornelius C. Vermeule, "Numismatics in Antiquity: The Preservation and Display of Coins in Ancient Greece and Rome," *Revue Suisse de Numismatique* 54 (1975): 5–32. Claude Brenot and Catherine Metzger, "Trouvailles de bijoux monétaires dans l'Occident romain," *Cahiers Ernest Babelon* 4 (1992). *Vrai ou Faux? Copier, imiter, falsifier,* exhibition at the Bibliothèque Nationale (rev. ed., Paris, 1991) 56, no. 18. *Rome face aux Barbares,* exhibition at the abbaye de Daoulas (Daoulas, 1993), 144.

142

CHARLES-NICOLAS COCHIN THE YOUNGER

Pompe funèbre de Catherine Opalinska (Funeral ceremonies for Catherine Opalinska)

Cabinet des Estampes, Collection Hennin no. 8584

Etching and line engraving; 0.668 m × 0.455 m (frame line). 1747. Lower margin on both sides of a cartridge: "POMPE FUNEBRE DE CATHERINE OPALINSKA, REINE DE POLOGNE, GRANDE DUCHESSE DE LITHUANIE, DUCHESSE DE LOR-RAINE/ET DE BAR, EN L'EGLISE DE NOTRE DAME DE PARIS, LE XVIII.MAI M.DCC XXXXVII./*Cette Pompe ordonnée par M*ʳ*. Le Duc de Gesvres Pair de France Premier Gentilhomme de la Chambre du Roy,/A été conduitte par M*ʳ*. de Bonneval Intendant et Controlleur général de l'Argenterie Menus plaisirs et affaires de la Chambre de Sa* MAJESTÉ, *et exécutée par les s*ʳˢ·*Slodtz." Signed under the frame line:* "De Bonneval inv." *Drawn and engraved by C.-N. Cochin the Younger; completed with a burin by J. Ouvrier.*

333

A product of the Counter-Reformation, the custom of observing the death of the king or a member of the royal family (sometimes a foreign sovereign) by a special funeral display became widespread in France during the 17th century. During a commemorative ceremony marked by Italian baroque symbolism and a highly codified ritual, the deceased was glorified and underwent a veritable apotheosis. Like all court celebrations and ceremonies, funerals were arranged by the administrateur of the menus plaisirs (master of the revels), and various artists and craftsmen produced the sets and props designed by the dessinateur des menus plaisirs. These sets (featuring the deceased's cenotaph, hangings, and so on), made of plaster, cardboard, stucco, and cloth, were short-lived by definition, so that engravings were used to record them (an engraver was permanently employed by the Administration des Menus Plaisirs).

Catherine Opalinska, wife of the dethroned king of Poland, Stanislas Leszczinski, and mother of Marie Leszczinska, queen of France, died on March 19, 1747, in the duchy of Lorraine over which her husband had received nominal sovereignty after losing his kingdom. Louis XV declared six months of mourning in honor of his wife's mother and ordered a commemorative ceremony that took place at Notre-Dame de Paris on May 18, 1747.

The ceremony was organized by Sébastien-Antoine and Paul-Ambroise Slodtz, sculptors and decorators at the Menus Plaisirs. Under Louis XV and Louis XVI, they raised the art of funeral display to its apogee. The cenotaph produced for the occasion depicted the queen in person (custom normally dictated using an allegorical figure of death), giving up her earthly crown with one hand while receiving a crown of fame with the other. The designer of the queen's actual tomb in Bonsecours Basilica in Nancy used the same iconography and obviously drew inspiration from the cenotaph by the Slodtz brothers.

The engraving of the commemorative ceremony was produced by Charles-Nicolas Cochin the Younger (1715–1790), who, like his father, executed several engravings for the Menus Plaisirs. Cochin also did the preparatory sketch for the engraving, but he had to acquiesce to the whims of Monsieur de Bonneval, who was then the administrator of the menus plaisirs and, as Cochin explains in his *Mémoires inédits*, "avoit une petitesse de gloriole assés singulière: sur mes planches dont j'avois fait les desseins, il faisoit mettre *De Bonneval invenit*; on en rioit, personne n'en étoit la dupe, mais il étoit content" (was peculiarly petty in his vainglory: on plates that I myself had designed, I had to put *De Bonneval invenit*; everyone laughed about it, and no one was fooled, but he was happy).

Cochin received four thousand *livres tournois* "pour les desseins particuliers qu'il a faits et la planche qu'il a gravée" (for the special drawings he did and the plate he engraved). The plate is now in the Louvre's Chalcography Department. There are two known states of the engraving: before all letters and final proof (presented here).

Corinne Le Bitouzé

Charles-Nicolas Cochin, *Mémoires inédits... sur le Comte de Caylus, Bouchardon, les Slodtz publiés d'après le manuscrit autographe... par M. Charles Henry* (Paris, 1880). Marcel Roux, *Inventaire du fonds français: Graveurs du XVIIIème siècle* (Paris, 1946), 3:58–59. F. Souchal, *Les Slodtz: Sculpteurs et décorateurs du roi (1685–1764)* (Paris, 1967). Alain-Charles Grüber, *Les grandes fêtes et leurs décors à l'époque de Louis XVI* (Geneva and Paris, 1972). Christian Michel, *Charles-Nicolas Cochin et le livre illustré au XVIIIème siècle* (Geneva, 1987).

143

W O L F G A N G   A M A D E U S   M O Z A R T
Sonatas for the Harpsichord
Département de la Musique, Rés. 866

Sonates pour le clavecin qui peuvent se jouer
avec l'Accompagnement de Violon dédiées à
Madame Victoire de France Par J. G. Wolfgang
Mozart de Salzbourg Agé de Sept ans. Oeuvre
première. Gravé par Mme Vendôme Ci-devant
rue St. Jacques à présent rue St. Honoré Vis-à-
vis le Palais Royal. A Paris, aux adresses ordinaires. [1764] *(Sonatas for the harpsichord that
may be accompanied by the violin, dedicated to
Mme Victoire of France by J. G. Wolfgang Mozart
of Salzburg, age seven years. First work. Engraved
by Mme Vendome, formerly of rue St. Jacques, now
at rue St. Honoré opposite the Palais Royal. Paris,
at the usual addresses. [1764.] In-folio oblong; parts;
190 × 250 mm; 14 + 5 pp. Red morocco binding with
lace and the arms of Mme Victoire. Blue tabby covers. From Mme Victoire's library.*

The two sonatas for violin and piano (Köchel
nos. 6 and 7) in this edition, the first published in Paris by the very young Mozart, are
dedicated to Mme Victoire de France
(1733–1799), one of Louis XV's daughters.
Mme Victoire was a masterful harpsichord
player. One of her sisters, Mme Henriette,
played the bass viol; the other, Mme
Adélaïde, played the violin. In December
1763, during his first trip to Paris, the seven-
year-old Mozart (1756–1791) performed at
Versailles before Mesdames de France, who

made quite a fuss over the child prodigy. This
publication was announced in February 1764
by Leopold Mozart to one of his correspon-
dents from Salzburg: "Maintenant quatre
sonates de M. Wolfgang Mozart sont chez le
graveur. Imaginez-vous le bruit que feront
ces sonates dans le monde, lorsqu'on verra
sur la page de titre que c'est l'oeuvre d'un
enfant de 7 ans et que les incrédules seront
invités à en faire eux-mêmes la vérification. . . .
Vous entendrez en son temps combien ces
sonates sont bonnes; il y a un Andante d'un
goût tout particulier" (Four of Mr. Wolfgang
Mozart's sonatas are now at the engraver's.
Imagine the sensation these sonatas will
make in the world when people see on the
title page that the composer is a seven-year-
old child – and the nonbelievers will be invited to go and see for themselves. . . . You will
hear how good these sonatas are, and there
is an Andante with very special appeal) *(Correspondance,* 1:66–67; letter dated Feb. 1, 1764).
In his next letter, dated Feb. 22, Leopold
confirmed his thoughts: "Nous retournerons
à Versailles avant 15 jours pour présenter à
Madame Victoire, deuxième fille du roi, à qui
elle sera dédiée, *l'oeuvre 1er* des sonates
gravées du grand M. Wolfgang. *L'Oeuvre 2*
sera, je crois, dédiée à Madame la comtesse
de Tessé" (We shall be returning to Versailles
in less than a fortnight to perform for Mme
Victoire, the king's second daughter, to whom
the piece will be dedicated, the opus 1 of the

335

engraved sonatas by the great M. Wolfgang. I believe that opus 2 will be dedicated to the countess de Tessé). The newspaper *L'Avant-coureur* announced the publication of the work on March 5.

The dedication copy exhibited here quite naturally is bound with the arms of the dedicatee, although it does seem that an error was made in the choice of the color, because the scores in Mme Victoire's library are usually covered with olive-green leather as opposed to red morocco.

Mozart's opus 1, one of his first completed attempts at composition, shows the influence of Johann Schobert, a musician from Silesia living in Paris and the harpsichord player of the prince of Conti, who died tragically after being poisoned by mushrooms in 1767. While Mozart was in Paris, Schobert had already composed several collections of sonatas for the keyboard, sonatas for violin and harpsichord, and trio sonatas that were highly successful.

Catherine Massip

F. Lesure, *Mozart en France*, exhibition at the Bibliothèque Nationale (Paris, 1956), no. 39. Gertraut Haberkamp, *Die Erstdrucke der Werke von Wolfgang Amadeus Mozart* (Tutzing, 1986), 1:67–69 and 2:1–3. Facsimile ed. by François Lesure (Geneva, 1988). *1789: Le Patrimoine libéré*, exhibition at the Bibliothèque Nationale (Paris, 1989). W. A. Mozart, *Correspondance*, ed. Geneviève Geffray (Paris, 1986–1992). *Mozart à Paris*, exhibition at the Musée Carnavalet (Paris, 1991).

144

LOUIS DE ROUVROY,
DUKE OF SAINT-SIMON
Mémoires
Département des Manuscrits, NAF 23102,
p. 1,695

Paper; paginated 1,535–1,794 in 16 gatherings numbered 97–112; 370 × 240 mm. One of 11 portfolios bound in calf with the arms and monogram of the author; 420 × 300 mm. Autograph manuscript.

Upon Saint-Simon's death in 1755, his manuscript was confiscated on the king's order and deposited in December 1760 in the archives of the Ministry of Foreign Affairs. Duke Henri de Saint-Simon, a descendant of the memorialist, obtained restitution in 1828; it passed into the hands of the printer Lahure, then to the directors of Hachette, the publishing firm. In 1926 Hachette's board of directors gave it to the Bibliothèque Nationale to commemorate the firm's centenary.

Saint-Simon's account of Louis XIV's death presents some of the most representative figures from the last years of the Sun King's reign (p. 1,695: "Ainsi mourut un des plus grands rois de la terre entre les bras d'une indigne et ténébreuse épouse et de ses doubles bâtards..." [So it was that one of the greatest kings on this earth died in the arms of an unworthy and obscure wife and his double bastards...]). In addition to the inevitable servants, the scene depicts Mme de Maintenon, the dying king's legitimate spouse (unfortunately for her, the marriage occurred secretly), and Blouin, the *valet de chambre* and distinguished member of the clique headed by the *patronne* (Maintenon). Indeed, in that rarefied social atmosphere, the so-called valet was a great lord who held an enviable post at the center of a network of relations masterminded by Mme de Maintenon. The duke de Maine, natural son of the old monarch and Mme de Montespan, also figures for all sorts of reasons in the number of those close to Mme de Maintenon. Meanwhile, Father Tellier, also present, would join another faction—the one that had previously gathered around Fénelon and the duke of Burgundy, Louis XIV's grandson. Tellier's attachment did no harm to this Jesuit's high position at the Versailles court. As for Maréchal, the surgeon, he appears in the scene by virtue of his profession. This devoted practitioner wisely held aloof from the cliques, factions, coteries, and clans that were casting an eye on the soon-to-be-unoccupied seat of power, and he was hardly an evil influence in the political sphere.

In unexpected fashion, and independent of the factional maneuvers that were clearly in play here, Louis XIV's death opened up a period of substantial political thaw, symbolized by several illustrious names. First there was Cardinal de Noailles, who would reestablish satisfactory relations between the regent, Philippe d'Orléans, and the Jansenists, so influential in the Parisian clergy. Then there was abbé Dubois, who would soon direct foreign policy, followed by the Scottish financier John Law, judicious dispenser of paper inflation. The last member of the Regency's charmed foursome was the duke de Saint-Simon (1675–1755), an eccentric politician but a lucid political analyst. His initiative in

behalf of *polysynodie*, or governance by councils, represented a genuine attempt (despite certain utopian features) to provide for participation in the central government, even if only by the nobility. In sum, the dawning Regency would represent in every respect a systematic effort to open up and increase flexibility of government, which would mark France throughout the 18th century.

Emmanuel Le Roy Ladurie

Duc de Saint-Simon, *Mémoires (1691–1723)*, ed. Yves Coirault, 8 vols. (Paris, 1983–1988), esp. 5:600–601. John B. Wolf, *Louis XIV* (New York, 1968). E. Le Roy Ladurie, "Système de la cour (Versailles, vers 1709)," in *Le Territoire de l'historien*, vol. 2 (Paris, 1978), 275–99. François Bluche, *Louis XIV* (Paris, 1986). Le Roy Ladurie, *L'Ancien Régime: De Louis XIII à Louis XV (1610–1770)* (Paris, 1991).

337

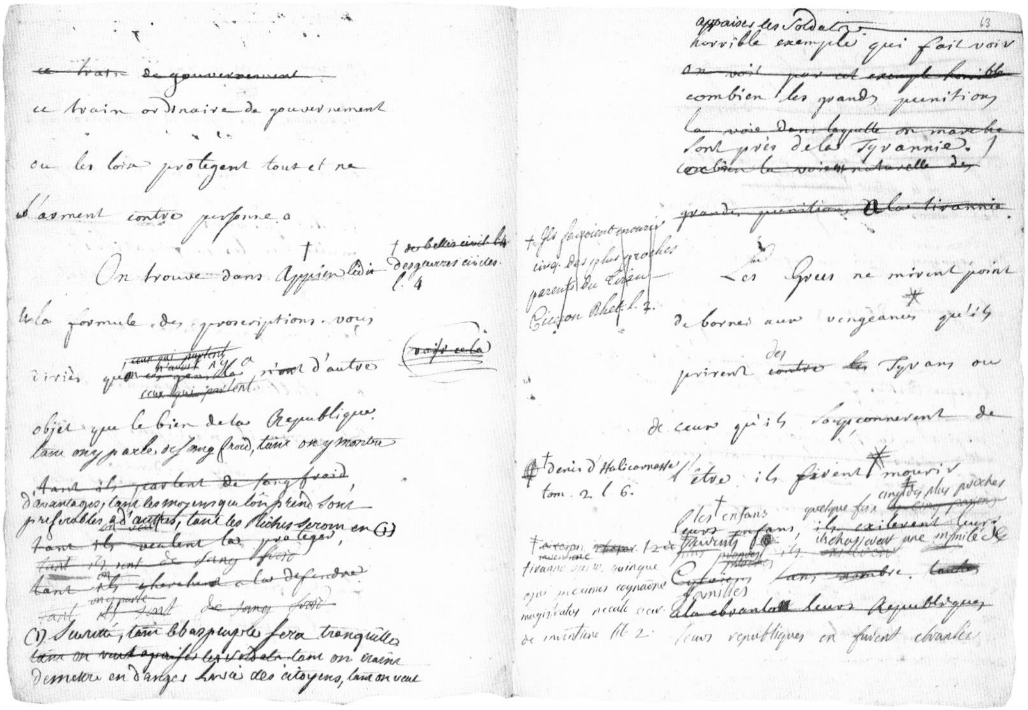

145

CHARLES-LOUIS DE
SECONDAT, BARON DE LA
BRÈDE ET DE MONTESQUIEU
De l'Esprit des lois
(On the spirit of laws), volume 3
Département des Manuscrits, NAF 12834,
fols. 62v–63

Paper; 244 fols.; 250 × 225 mm. Original manuscript comprised two handwritten states and secretary's copies. Purchased at the sale of the Montesquieu library (kept until then at the château de La Brède in Gironde), Paris, Hôtel Drouot, Feb. 23, 1939, no. 8.

Born in the Bordeaux region into a family of wealthy parliamentarians, Montesquieu (himself president of the Bordeaux Parlement) earned the reputation of having a brilliant mind in 1721 when he published the *Lettres persanes* (Persian letters), a stunning and instantly successful satire of Parisian society that has been imitated but never duplicated.

He left Parlement in 1726 and was elected to the Académie Française in 1728. He traveled throughout Europe from 1728 to 1731. To complete his masterwork, *De l'Esprit des lois*, would require fifteen more years of reading, research, compilation of all types of notes, and writing of various essays, including *Considérations sur les causes de la grandeur des Romains et de leur décadence* (Reflections on the causes of the grandeur and decadence of the Romans), in 1734, a meditation on the philosophy of history. Published in two volumes in Geneva in 1748, *De l'Esprit des lois* was the major turning point in the century of the Enlightenment. It was the harbinger of the new and critical grasp of knowledge embodied by the first volumes of Buffon's *Histoire naturelle* in 1749 and the *Encyclopédie* in 1751. Its complete title very clearly defined its purpose: *De l'Esprit des Loix, ou du rapport que les loix doivent avoir avec la Constitution de chaque Gouvernement, les Moeurs, le Climat, la Religion, le Commerce, etc., à quoi l'Auteur a ajouté des recherches nouvelles sur les Loix Romaines touchant les successions, sur les Loix françaises, et sur les Loix féodales* (On the spirit of laws, or the relationship that laws must have with the constitution of each government, with morals, climate, religion, trade, etc., to which the author has added new research on Roman laws on inheritance, French laws, and feudal laws).

The work is divided into thirty-one books subdivided into short chapters, with a clear and incisive style. Montesquieu substitutes a broader and more concrete conception for the purely political traditional classification of laws, based on a typology of political universes (despotic, monarchical, and republican). He associates the principles of governments and the constitutions of countries under consideration with physical, moral, economic, and geographical causes that are decisive for the formation and development of laws. One should emphasize the importance of Books XI and XII, from which emerges the concept of political liberty based on the separation of the three powers (legislative, executive, and judicial), for which

England seemed then to him to be the model. Also worth noting is the originality of Books XIV through XVIII containing his famous "theory of climates," which occasionally caused him to be accused of Spinozism.

Attacked as much as it was admired, the book was condemned by the church in 1751, but the depth of the analysis and the skill of the presentation, sprinkled with precise anecdotes, assured Montesquieu prodigious fame and considerable influence on the political thinking of the 18th and 19th centuries.

The last five books are in large part incomplete and are more historical in nature. The manuscript comprises handwritten passages and texts dictated to eight secretaries, whom Montesquieu had to utilize since he experienced periods of nearly total blindness. *De l'Esprit des lois* remains a unique testimonial to the working methods of one of the great writers of his century.

Annie Angremy

Original edition without the author's name: *De l'Esprit des loix...* (Geneva, [1748]). *Oeuvres complètes*, ed. A. Masson, vol. 3 (Paris, 1955). R. Shackelton, *Montesquieu: Une biographie critique* (Grenoble, 1977). S. Goyard Fabre, *La Philosophie du droit de Montesquieu* (Paris, 1973). P. Vernière, *Montesquieu et "L'Esprit des lois," ou La Raison impure* (Paris, 1977).

339

256   DE L'ESPRIT.

esprits ? que les hommes ne soient semblables à ces arbres de la même espece, dont le germe, indestructible & absolument le même, n'étant jamais semé exactement dans la même terre, ni précisément exposé aux mêmes vents, au même soleil, aux mêmes pluies, doit, en se développant, prendre nécessairement une infinité de formes différentes. Je pourrois donc conclure que l'inégalité d'esprit des hommes peut être indifféremment regardée comme l'effet de la nature ou de l'éducation. Mais, quelque vraie que fût cette conclusion, comme elle n'auroit rien que de vague, & qu'elle se réduiroit, pour ainsi dire, à un *peut-être*, je crois devoir considérer cette question sous un point de vue nouveau, la ramener à des principes plus certains & plus précis. Pour cet effet, il faut réduire la question à des points simples; remonter jusqu'à l'origine de nos idées, au développement de l'esprit; & se rappeler que l'homme ne fait que sentir, se ressouvenir, & observer les ressemblances & les différences, c'est-à-dire, les rapports qu'ont entr'eux les objets divers qui s'offrent à lui, ou que sa mémoire lui présente; qu'ainsi la nature ne pourroit donner aux hommes plus ou moins de disposition à l'esprit, qu'en douant les uns préférablement aux autres d'un peu plus de finesse de sens, d'étendue de mémoire, & de capacité d'attention.

*Le principe duquel
J'auteur déduire dans les chapitres suivants
l'égalité naturelle des esprits, et qu'il a tâché
d'établir au commencement de son ouvrage,
en que les jugements humains sont purement
passifs. Ce principe a été établi avec beaucoup de philosophie
et de profondeur dans l'Encyclopédie, article Evidence. J'ignore quel est
l'auteur de cet article; mais c'est certainement un très grand métaphysicien.
Je soupçonne l'Abbé de Condillac ou M. de Buffon. Quoiqu'il en soit,
j'ai tâché de le combattre et d'établir l'activité de nos
jugements, et dans les notes que j'ai écrites au commencement
de ce livre, et surtout dans la première partie de la profession
de foi du Vicaire savoyard. Si j'ai raison et que le principe de M.
Helvétius et de l'auteur susdit soit faux, les raisonnements des chapitres suivants
qui n'en sont que les conséquences tombent, et il n'est pas vrai que l'inégalité
des esprits soit l'effet de la seule éducation, quoiqu'elle y puisse influer
beaucoup.

CHAPITRE

DISCOURS III.   257

CHAPITRE II.
De la finesse des sens.

La plus ou moins grande perfection des organes des sens, dans laquelle se trouve nécessairement comprise celle de l'organisation intérieure, puisque je ne juge ici de la finesse des sens que par leurs effets, seroit-elle la cause de l'inégalité d'esprit des hommes?

Pour raisonner avec quelque justesse sur ce sujet, il faut examiner si le plus ou le moins de finesse des sens donne à l'esprit ou plus d'étendue, ou plus de cette justesse, qui, prise dans sa vraie signification, renferme toutes les qualités de l'esprit.

La perfection plus ou moins grande des organes des sens n'influe en rien sur la justesse de l'esprit, si les hommes, quelque impression qu'ils reçoivent des mêmes objets, doivent cependant toujours appercevoir les mêmes rapports entre ces objets. Or, pour prouver qu'ils les apperçoivent, je choisis le sens de la vue pour exemple, comme celui auquel nous devons le plus grand nombre de nos idées : Et je dis qu'à des yeux différents, si les mêmes objets paroissent plus ou moins grands ou petits, brillants ou obscurs; si la toise, par exemple, est aux yeux de tel homme plus petite, la neige moins blanche, & l'ébene moins noire qu'aux yeux de tel autre; ces deux hommes appercevront néanmoins toujours les mêmes rapports entre tous les objets : la toise, en conséquence, paroîtra toujours à leurs yeux plus grande que le pied; la neige, le plus blanc de tous

* Kk

146

CLAUDE-HADRIEN HELVÉTIUS
De l'Esprit (On the mind)
Réserve des livres rares, Rés. R. 895,
pp. 256–257

*Paris: Durand, 1768; [4] + XXII + 643 pp.; 4ᵗᵒ.
Copy owned by Jean-Jacques Rousseau, then by
Louis Dutens and Jean-Jacques Debure. Acquired
by the Bibliothèque Nationale in December 1853
after the sale of Debure's library.*

In 1758 Claude Hadrien Helvétius, former *fermier général* (tax collector), well-to-do bourgeois turned philosophe, anonymously published a book entitled *De l'esprit*. He thus participated in the Enlightenment, the philosophic movement which was developing in Europe and especially in France in the 18th century and which sought to base man's happiness on reason. Voltaire had published his *Dictionnaire philosophique* (Philosophical dictionary) in 1764; the great undertaking of the *Encyclopédie*, launched in 1750, would not be completed until 1772. In the Parisian salons Helvétius often met with Montesquieu, Buffon, Voltaire, Diderot, and d'Alembert.

Helvétius's book, condemned successively by the king, the Parlement, the Sorbonne, and the pope, created a great stir. Claiming inspiration from Locke, Helvétius declared that every idea comes down to sensation and that every human action is guided by sensations and needs. All men are born equal; their character is defined afterward by their education, their experience, and their social milieu. Philosophes of the day were divided in their reactions: Diderot emphasized the interest of certain analyses but challenged Helvétius's denial of individual uniqueness; Rousseau rejected the reduction of judgment to simple sensation.

The copy exhibited here belonged to Jean-Jacques Rousseau. Rousseau was considering a refutation of Helvétius's work and annotated the copy extensively, indicating in particular: "Le principe duquel l'auteur déduit . . . l'égalité naturelle des esprits, et qu'il a tâché d'établir au commencement de son ouvrage est que les jugements humains sont purement passifs. . . . J'ai tâché de le combattre et d'établir l'activité de nos jugements (The principle from which the author deduces . . . the natural equality of human intellect and which he attempted to establish at the beginning of his work is that human judgments are purely passive. . . . I have tried to combat it and to establish the active nature of our judgments; p. 256). Rousseau based his argument on the difference between "judging" and "sensing": "Appercevoir les objets, c'est sentir, appercevoir les rapports, c'est juger" (To perceive objects is to sense, to perceive relationships is to judge; p. 9). Nonetheless, he never published his refutation, refusing to join those who were then condemning Helvétius. On the other hand, in numerous passages of the *Profession de foi du vicaire savoyard* (Profession of faith of a Savoyard priest) he contested Helvétius's theses, sometimes violently.

Louis Dutens (1730–1812), an admirer of Rousseau, purchased the latter's library in London in 1766 and with it this copy of *De l'Esprit.* He pledged not to publish Rousseau's notes, however, as long as Rousseau was alive. Rousseau died in 1778. A volume titled *Lettres à M. Debure sur la réfutation du livre "De l'Esprit" par Jean-Jacques Rousseau* (Letters to M. Debure on the refutation of the book "De l'Esprit" by J.-J. Rousseau) was published in 1779. In it Dutens reproduced part of the notes, including his own comments on them. The notes did not appear in their entirety until 1911, when they were published by P. M. Masson in the *Revue d'histoire littéraire de la France.*

Nathalie Renier

Louis Dutens, *Lettres à M. Debure sur la réfutation du livre "De l'Esprit" par Jean-Jacques Rousseau* (London, 1779). P. M. Masson, "Rousseau contre Helvétius," *Revue d'histoire littéraire de la France* 18 (1911): 103–24. J. P. de Beaumarchais, Daniel Couty, and Alain Rey, *Dictionnaire des littératures de langue française,* vol. 2 (Paris, 1984), 1015–16.

147

DENIS DIDEROT

Le Rêve de d'Alembert
(D'Alembert's dream)
Département des Manuscrits, NAF 13727, fols. 9–9v

Paper; 32 fols.; 200 × 185 mm. Autograph manuscript, 1769. First draft of text. Bequest of the Singer-Polignac Foundation, 1952, along with all of Diderot's manuscripts purchased from the heirs of Baron Jacques Le Vavasseur, who were descendants of Diderot and his daughter, Mme de Vandeul.

Diderot the philosopher, Diderot the editor of the *Encyclopédie,* Diderot the playwright, Diderot the novelist, Diderot the art critic—all were facets of the man Voltaire called a universal "pantophile." This son of a knife maker from Langres forged every aspect of his protean oeuvre with equal felicity, though his contemporaries were aware of only a fraction of it. As early as 1759, following his imprisonment in the keep of Vincennes Castle in 1749 for his *Lettre sur les aveugles* (Letter on the blind), and the publication of the first volumes of the *Encyclopédie,* which earned him endless persecution and harassment from church, state, and even partners, Diderot took refuge in the secrecy of his attic and restricted most of his literary output for the few privileged readers of the *Correspondance littéraire,* the hand-written gazette that his friend Melchior Grimm parsimoniously dispatched to the grand courts and monarchs of northern Europe. Even during the Enlightenment, no man was a prophet in his own country.

In 1769 Diderot wrote the *Rêve de d'Alembert* trilogy. In a way it represented a response to questions concerning the origins of life and the organization of beings, raised at the end of the last philosophical text he had dared publish, back in 1754: *De l'interprétation de la Nature* (On the interpretation of

341

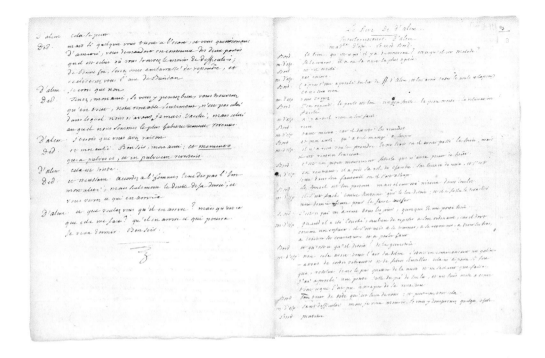

nature). The tone and spirit of the new work were wonderfully summarized in a letter to his closest confidante, Sophie Volland. "I've produced a dialogue between d'Alembert and myself. We chat merrily and even rather clearly, despite the dry and obscure topic. A second, much longer, dialogue follows, which serves to clarify the first one. This latter is entitled *Le Rêve de d'Alembert.* The speakers are d'Alembert, who is dreaming, his dear friend Mademoiselle d'Espinasse [sic], and Doctor Bordeu. . . . It is all greatly extravagant, being at the same time profoundly philosophical. There is a certain cleverness in having placed my ideas in the mouth of a dreaming man. Wisdom often has to be given an air of madness in order to gain acceptance. I prefer that people say, 'But that is not so outlandish as one might think,' rather than say myself, 'Listen now, here's some wisdom.'"

Just as in his *Neveu de Rameau* (Rameau's nephew) and *Jacques le Fataliste* (Jacques the fatalist), Diderot again found that the dialogue form best suited his dazzling storyteller's verve, this time developed around d'Alembert (with whom he was coediting the *Encyclopédie*), d'Alembert's lady friend (one of those influential Enlightenment women), and the scholarly Théophile de Bordeu. Diderot also attained the apogee of his materialist philosophy, ever more scientific and resolutely innovative, in a brilliant formulation of

transformism that predated Lamarck: "Life is a series of actions and reactions. Alive, I act and react as a mass. . . dead, I act and react as molecules. Being born, living, and passing away means changing form." In their complexity, mankind and the universe are the outcome of chemical and biological affinities between elements of heterogeneous matter.

The boldness of his ideas prevented Diderot from delivering his most accomplished philosophical work to the *Correspondance littéraire* prior to 1782. He nevertheless affirmed (as would his friend and first publisher, Naigeon, in 1798) that the original manuscript and copies had been destroyed at the request of Mlle de Lespinasse, who died in 1776. The text was only published in 1830 in the *Mémoires, correspondance et ouvrages inédits de Diderot* (Diderot's unpublished memoirs, correspondence, and works), based on St. Petersburg copies sent in 1785 to Catherine the Great, who had purchased the philosopher's entire library, over which he retained usufruct during his lifetime.

Annie Angremy

Mémoires, correspondance et ouvrages inédits de Diderot (Paris, 1830–1831). *Le Rêve de d'Alembert,* ed. J. Varloot (Paris, 1962). *Oeuvres complètes,* ed. J. Varloot, vol. 17 (Paris, 1987).

148
FRANÇOIS-MARIE AROUET, KNOWN AS VOLTAIRE
Oeuvres complètes (Complete works)
Réserve des livres rares, Rés. Z. 4450

*Kehl: From the press of the Société Littéraire
Typographique, 1785–1790*

*70 vols. (Rés. Z. 4450–4519); 108 engraved plates
after Moreau le Jeune's drawings; 8vo. Binding by
Bradel-Derôme in red morocco with the royal arms,
lined in blue watered silk, early 19th century. Gift of
Pierre-Augustin Caron de Beaumarchais to the
nation, July 2, 1791.*

This edition, referred to as "Kehl's edition,"
has been a symbol of the philosopher's oeuvre. François-Marie Arouet, alias Voltaire,
died in 1778, at the height of his glory.
Symbol of Enlightenment humanism, more
concerned with earthly happiness than with
eternal salvation, defender of human rights,
historian, author of plays and philosophical
tales, indefatigable correspondent, Voltaire
could escape censorship only by moving, in
1759, to Ferney near the Swiss border. For
nineteen years, the "patriarch of Ferney"
received at his château there the elite of
Europe, all eager to meet the "great man."
Back in Paris shortly before his death, he was
triumphantly received into the Académie and
at the Comédie Française, where his bust was
crowned on stage during a performance of
Irène. He was preparing a new edition of his
works for Panckoucke, the publisher, who, in
1779, sold the rights and manuscripts to
Pierre-Augustin Caron de Beaumarchais,
journalist and man of letters, author of *The
Marriage of Figaro* (cat. 154).

Beaumarchais took charge of gathering as
many new texts as possible, by approaching
the philosopher's numerous friends, thus
succeeding in assembling some 4,700 letters.
In order to publish this edition he became a
stationer, printer, and editor, purchasing the
typographical equipment of the famous
British printer John Baskerville from his
widow. The elegance of the Baskerville typefaces was admired throughout Europe. In
order to escape the censors, Beaumarchais
set up his printing firm at Kehl in Germany.

343

Between 1785 and 1790, seventy-four volumes were published at great expense, leaving Beaumarchais on the verge of financial ruin, despite his numerous appeals for subscriptions.

The edition displayed here, printed on vellum with wide margins, was presented by Beaumarchais to the royal library. In an accompanying letter addressed to the royal librarian, the abbé des Aulnays, he states: "Cette collection des fruits d'un immortel génie aura sa place, à la translation de Voltaire, devant les gens de lettres, ses disciples et ses enfants" (When Voltaire's remains are translated, this collection of the fruit of an immortal genius will be placed before all the literati, disciples, and heirs). And, indeed, when Voltaire's ashes were moved to the Panthéon on July 11, 1791, seventy volumes of unbound sheets, enclosed in a chest in the shape of a bookcase, featured prominently in the triumphal procession. The red morocco bindings were done by Bradel, the nephew and successor of the great Derôme, after the *Oeuvres complètes* entered the Bibliothèque Nationale.

Nathalie Renier

Georges Bengesco, *Voltaire: Bibliographie de ses oeuvres*, vol. 4 (Paris, 1890), 105–46. John Dreyfus, "The Baskerville Punches, 1750–1950," *The Library*, 5th ser., 5 (1950): 26–48. *Voltaire: Un homme, un siècle*, exhibition at the Bibliothèque Nationale (Paris, 1979), no. 684. *1789: Le Patrimoine libéré*, exhibition at the Bibliothèque Nationale (Paris, 1989), no. 76.

149

CÉSAR FRANÇOIS CASSINI DE THURY

Triangulation de la Seine, feuille de Paris (Triangulation of the Seine, Paris sheet)

Département des Cartes et Plans, Bibliothèque de la Société de Géographie, SG B 107 (6)

Paper; manuscript colored by hand; 630 × 940 mm. [1747.] From the bequest of the Société de Géographie, deposited in the Bibliothèque Nationale de France.

Prompted by Colbert, who wanted accurate maps to better govern the kingdom, the mapping of France was one of the first new topics debated by the Académie des Sciences (founded in 1666). After initial trials made near Paris under the academy's aegis, in 1681 abbé Jean Picard suggested producing a general framework, meaning a network of large triangles covering France. The triangles were to be established by connecting landmarks (bell towers, windmills, towers, aqueducts) from which long sightings could be made thanks to new telescopic lenses. Picard's purpose was to provide cartographers with key reference points on which local surveys could be based. Colbert was in favor of the project. After Picard died in late 1682, the work was entrusted to a famous Italian astronomer, Jean-Dominique Cassini, who ran the Paris Observatory at the time. After several interruptions, the measurement of the meridian of the observatory, which followed the route from Dunkirk to Collioure, was completed in 1718. Jacques Cassini, Jean-Dominique's son, used it to show that the earth was prolate.

Measurement of France only resumed in 1733 "pour le bien de l'Etat et l'utilité du public" (for the good of the state and the public utility). This time, the driving force was the Administration des Ponts et Chaussées (Office of Bridges and Roads), which intended to redraw and improve the French road system. The triangle network was completed in 1744 and gave rise to the publication of the first map. In 1746–1747, to

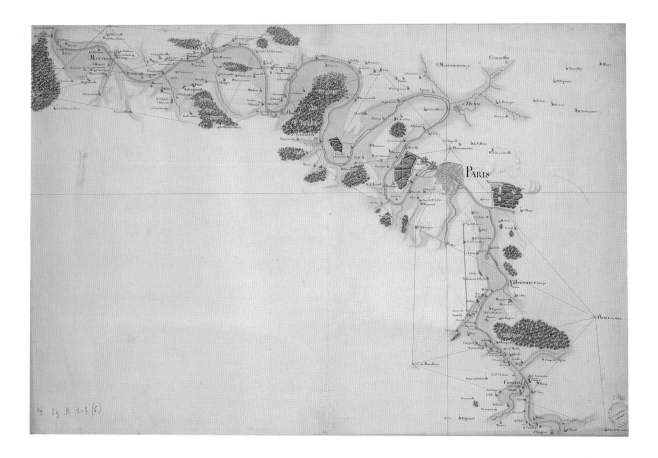

accompany the publication of all the measurements, César-François Cassini de Thury, son of Jacques and grandson of Jean-Dominique, produced a second map of triangles on which he noted that the river system was inaccurately represented on even the best maps of France. The triangulation operations did not take the rivers of the kingdom into account, save for the Loire.

Therefore, when Louis XV made the decision in 1747 to have Cassini de Thury prepare detailed maps of the entire kingdom, Cassini began by supplementing the series of triangles along the Seine and its tributaries. This preceded the publication of the map of France, which began in 1756 and was not entirely completed when, in 1793, the revolutionary government confiscated Cassini's work and transferred it from the Paris Observatory to the War Ministry archives.

Monique Pelletier

C.-F. Cassini de Thury, "Sur la description géométrique de la France," *Mémoires de l'Académie Royale des Sciences* 1745: 553–60. J. Konvitz, "Redating and Rethinking the Cassini Geodetic Surveys of France, 1730–1750," *Cartographica* 19, no. 1 (1974): 1–15. M. Pelletier, *La carte de Cassini* (Paris, 1990).

345

Vue du Port de Dieppe

150

View of the Port of Dieppe

Engraving by Charles-Nicolas Cochin the
Younger (1715–1790) and Jacques-Philippe
Le Bas (1707–1783)
Cabinet des Estampes, Va 426, format 4

*Etching and line-engraving; 0.478 × 0.738 m (frame
line). 1778. Under the frame line: "J. Vernet pin
1765"/"P. Martini scul., aqua forti 1775." In the
lower margin: "Vue du Port de Dieppe/Gravé
d'après le Tableau Original appartenant au Roi, et
faisant partie de la Collection des Ports de France
ordonnée par Mr. le Marquis de Marigny/
Conseiller d'Etat ordinaire d'Epée,/Commandeur
des Ordres du Roi, Lieutenant Général de
l'Orléanois et Beauce, Directeur et Ordonnateur
des Bâtiments/du Roi, Jardins, Arts, Académies, et
Manufactures Royales./Peint par J. Vernet de
l'Académie Royale de Peinture et Sculpture/C.-N.
Cochin filius et J.-P. Le Bas socii Sculpserunt 1778.
A.P.D.R."*

While in Italy to complete his education
before becoming director of the Administration Royale des Beaux-Arts, the marquis
de Marigny, youngest brother of the marquise
de Pompadour, met Joseph Vernet, a painter
of seascapes who had been living in Rome
for several years. Marigny returned from Italy
with the firm resolve to redirect French

tastes to a more classical tradition. In 1751 he became director of the king's buildings and commissioned a series of paintings representing various French ports from Vernet, who had returned to France in 1752.

Marigny's orders were very specific: he wanted the paintings to be not only of seascapes but also of genre scenes at the seashore. And so Vernet had to visit every port he was asked to paint and make a sketch and note the features at the site. For nearly ten years, from 1753 to 1762, the painter had some short and long stays in several towns on the Mediterranean and then on the Atlantic. His long voyage was interrupted in 1762 owing to the financial difficulties experienced by the Royal Treasury. By that time, Vernet had painted fourteen of the twenty-four commissioned paintings. The ports of the English Channel were never executed, except for Dieppe, which was painted in 1765.

As early as 1758 Marigny decided to have the paintings engraved and chose Le Bas and Cochin. Cochin had traveled to Italy with Marigny and was his friend and adviser. A subscription was issued and, between 1760 and 1778, the two engravers published the fifteen plates of the series one after another.

The port of Dieppe was the final painting in the series. Vernet was tired and had lost some of the enthusiasm that had buoyed him for ten years, so the Dieppe canvas shows little inspiration. The engraving was done in 1778 and, as was the case for the other plates, Cochin executed the etched figures, while Le Bas and his atelier handled the rest. Le Bas worked with many students (such as Pierre-Antoine Martini, who is credited in the caption) who prepared the etched plates for him, to which he added the finishing touches.

In his articles on art, Diderot was very severe with this series of engravings that he deemed of no interest.

Cochin and Le Bas completed the series with a view of Le Havre and two views of Rouen, engraved after Cochin's drawings.

Corinne Le Bitouzé

Florence Ingersoll-Smouse, *Joseph Vernet: Peintre de marine, 1714–1789*, 2 vols. (Paris, 1926). Marcel Roux, *Inventaire du fonds français: Graveurs du XVIIIeme siècle* (Paris, 1946), 3:96. Pierre Arlaud, *Catalogue raisonné des estampes gravées d'après Joseph Vernet* (Avignon, 1976).

151

CHARLES-CLÉMENT BERVIC
Louis XVI

Cabinet des Estampes, AA5 Rés.

Line-engraving; 0.690 × 0.520 m (frame line). 1790. In the lower margin: "LOUIS SEIZE / ROI DES FRANÇAIS, RESTAURATEUR DE LA LIBERTE. / PRESENTE AU ROI ET A L'ASSEMBLEE NATIONALE. *Par l'Auteur." Signed under the frame line:* "Peint par Callet, Peintre du Roi / Se vend à Paris, chez Bervic, aux Galleries du Louvre / Gravé en 1790, par Bervic, Graveur du Roi."

Depicting the monarch in his coronation robes was one of the traditions of the French monarchy. The king is shown in a full-length portrait, with the attributes of his charge: ermine coat, scepter, hand of justice, crown, and so on. These official portraits have followed a somewhat stereotyped image, since the model was established once and for all beginning with Louis XIV. The king wanted the painting to magnify his majesty and hence placed great importance on making sure that the manifestations of his power

347

were accurately represented. Thus he ordered the prior of Saint-Denis, who was in charge of the coronation regalia, to lend them to the painter. There were often several copies of such portraits that the king would send to foreign courts, present to his ambassadors, or give to people he wanted to honor.

This portrait was officially commissioned by the Direction des Bâtiments du Roi (Office of the Kings' Buildings), which under the monarch's direct authority was responsible for management of the royal manufactories and oversight of the Royal Academy of Painting and Sculpture, as well as relations with artists. The director general of the Bâtiments du Roi distributed favors, assistance, posts, pensions, and housing in the Louvre galleries, thereby exercising much influence over trends in the arts.

The count d'Angiviller, as the successor to the marquis de Marigny (the marquise de Pompadour's brother), was the director general under Louis XVI from 1774 to 1791. He deplored the triumph of insipid art and attempted to create a renaissance of "le grand genre," focusing on historical paintings and portraits of great Frenchmen. His choice of the engravers Bervic and Müller in 1785 to reproduce two of Louis XVI's coronation portraits (one by Joseph-Sifred Duplessis and the other by Antoine Callet) bears witness to this. Both engravers practiced line-engraving, a technique quite different from "free handling" permitted by etching, which had been preferred during the first two-thirds of the century. This trend toward a more severe manner followed public taste, which was rediscovering classical antiquity at that time.

Bervic (1756–1823)—whose his real name was Charles-Clément Balvay—was typical of the artists esteemed by Angiviller. In 1784 he was housed in the Louvre by the king and was chosen in 1785 to engrave Louis XVI's portrait after Callet. He rejected the official commissioning system, preferring to launch a subscription on his own behalf and thereby profit directly from the sale of his work.

The plate was only completed in 1790 and was immediately praised by connoisseurs. But, with the advent of the Revolution, the plate soon became a burden to its creator.

During the Terror, the remaining proofs were destroyed. As a precaution or as a token gesture to the new regime, Bervic himself broke the plate in half. Once the Bourbons returned to power, he resoldered the copper plate and touched up the engraving to make new proofs from it. Prints exist in six known states: three before the plate was broken and three after it was repaired.

Corrine Le Bitouzé

Charles Maumène and Louis d'Harcourt, "Iconographie des rois de France," *Archives de l'Art français* 16 (1929–1930): 481–83. Marcel Roux, *Inventaire du fonds français: Graveurs du XVIIIème siècle* (Paris, 1933), 2:471–72. Sean T. Tailor, "Le portrait du sacre gravé de Drevet à David," *Les Nouvelles de l'Estampe* 1986: 6–16.

152

JEAN-FRANÇOIS JANINET
Marie-Antoinette
Cabinet des Estampes, Ef 105 Rés. fol., vol. 1

Engraving; aquatint and tools, colors printed in register; 255 × 205 mm. 1777. Signed under the frame line: "Gravé par Janinet en 1777." In the lower margin: "Marie-Antoinette d'Autriche/Reine de France et de Navarre/Née à Vienne le 2.9^{bre} 1755/Mariée à Versailles le 16 de may 1770."

Janinet's engraving uses as a model a full-length portrait of Queen Marie-Antoinette by Jean-Baptiste-André Gautier-Dagoty. This portrait, painted in 1775, was presented to the royal family by the painter in July of the same year in the Hall of Mirrors at the château of Versailles. The queen gave her permission to exhibit it temporarily and then gave it to Prince von Starhemberg in 1777. The painting is now at the château of Versailles (MV 8061, no. 1851 of the *Catalogue des peintures du Musée du château*).

As early as 1775, Fabien Gautier-Dagoty, brother of Jean-Baptiste-André and son of Jacques-Fabien Gautier-Dagoty, decided to undertake an engraved reproduction of the painting. The Gautier-Dagoty family had been specializing in color engraving ever since Jacques-Fabien studied with Leblon and learned the process Leblon had developed. This process, based on the mezzotint technique, used four or more plates—one for each color—printed one after another "in reg-

Marie Antoinette d'Autriche
Reine de France et de Navarre,
Née à Vienne le 2. 9bre 1755.
Mariée à Versailles le 16. de May 1770.

ister," that is, carefully aligned (see cat. 136). Leblon's method was not highly valued by connoisseurs, who preferred those developed by Bonnet or Janinet. Fabien Gautier-Dagoty did not reproduce the entire painting but restricted himself to a bust portrait. He presented his engraving to the queen in November 1775. Two years later, Jean-François Janinet (1752–1814) wanted to demonstrate his skill and began to engrave the same painting—also as a bust. He used the process he had developed himself, based on the aquatint technique rather than mezzotint (see cat. 138).

Corrine Le Bitouzé

Ronarl S. Gower, *Iconographie de la reine Marie-Antoinette* (Paris, 1883). Michèle Hébert and Yves Sjöberg, *Inventaire du fonds français: Graveurs du XVIIIème siècle* (Paris, 1973), 12:29. Claire Constant, *Musée national du château de Versailles: Catalogue des peintures* (Paris, 1980). *Graveurs français de la seconde moitié du XVIIIeme siècle*, exhibition at the Louvre (Paris, 1985), 92.

153

PIERRE-AMBROISE-FRANÇOIS
CHODERLOS DE LACLOS
Les Liaisons dangereuses
(Dangerous liaisons)
Département des Manuscrits, Fr. 12845, fols. 35–127; fol. 104v

Paper; 93 fols.; 255 × 200 mm. Quarter-binding in ivory-grained leather. Autograph manuscript; intermediate draft. Ca. 1778–1781. Gift of Mme de Laclos, the author's daughter-in-law, 1849.

"J'ai vu les moeurs de mon temps et j'ai publié ces lettres" (I witnessed the morals of the day and I've published these letters). By choosing a sentence from the preface to Rousseau's *Nouvelle Héloïse* as the epigraph to his own *Liaisons dangereuses,* Laclos honored the popular 18th-century tradition of the epistolary novel. Yet how he revitalized the genre! And with what perversity! In the relentless dramatic construction of the novel, letters shorn of all irrelevant information become the decisive element in a libertine campaign that Laclos—a peaceable artillery officer in real life—conducted with the virtuosity of a great military leader.

Baudelaire, a great exegete of *Les liaisons dangereuses,* described it as a "devastating critique of society, but presented with playful decorum." The double-dealing of the novel's protagonists, Valmont and the marquise de Merteuil—"methodical scoundrels" more than libertines, the ultimate products of an overly policed Ancien Régime—springs an infernal trap into which they themselves fall. And

349

even Valmont, a skillful tactician and carefree Don Juan until his encounter with Mme de Tourvel, is perhaps no more than a puppet in the hands of she who really pulls the strings, the marquise de Merteuil. The only outlet for the diabolical pair is passion, which takes the form of vengeance for Merteuil, while Valmont vainly attempts to deny that very passion ("One becomes bored with everything, angel, it's a law of Nature"). Their stooges are easy prey, dupes to the respectability that Laclos claimed he was defending. Then there is the highly moving Mme de Tourvel, a worthy heir to the princess de Clèves, who dies of a broken heart in the purest tradition of Rousseau.

The novel, originally titled on the manuscript *Le Danger des liaisons* (The danger of liaisons), draws its morality from its tragic end. Many other writers throughout the 18th century, such as Claude Crébillon, Pinot Duclos, Nerciat, and Fougeret de Montbron, had published straightforwardly licentious, indeed erotic novels. *Les Liaisons dangereuses* was enormously successful right from its first publication in 1782, a year in which no fewer than sixteen other editions saw the light. Obviously, success derived from its scandalousness, yet the novel was also recognized as a pure masterpiece that sprang from the imagination of a modest officer bored with bleak barracks life. Laclos wanted "to write a book that left the trodden path, that would

create a bang, would still resound on earth long after [I'm] gone." Mission accomplished.

Laclos's tense handwriting, seen on this manuscript bequeathed by his daughter-in-law, seems to reflect the dramatic intensity of the tale. However, this is a copy of a first draft—no longer extant—and was executed in two phases, as indicated by the use of two different colors of paper. White paper was used for letters I–LXXIX, blue for the subsequent ones (written in an even tighter hand) and for the author's note and preface. The dates on certain letters cover a four-year period, from 1778 to 1781, that putatively date the composition of the novel, although in fact it was drafted in six months. The only remnant of the original draft is an unfinished love letter from Mme de Tourvel to Valmont, which Laclos did not include in the final version.

Annie Angremy

Les Liaisons dangereuses, [or] *Lettres recueillies dans une Société et publiées pour l'instruction de quelques autres...* (Amsterdam and Paris, 1782). Charles Baudelaire, "Notes sur *Les Liaisons dangereuses,*" in Baudelaire, *Oeuvres complètes,* vol. 2, ed. C. Pichois (Paris, 1976), 66–75. L. Versini, *Laclos et la tradition: Essai sur les sources et la technique des "Liaisons dangereuses"* (Paris, 1968). Laclos, *Oeuvres complètes,* ed. L. Versini (Paris, 1979). R. Pomeau, *Laclos* (Paris, 1975). M. Delon, *Les Liaisons dangereuses* (Paris, 1986).

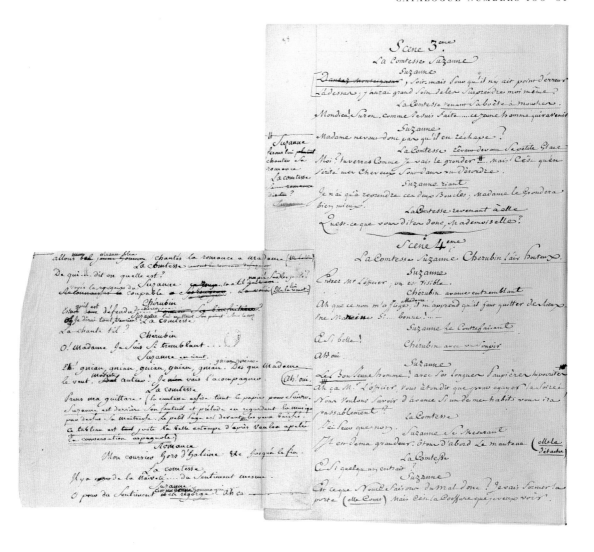

154

PIERRE-AUGUSTIN CARON
DE BEAUMARCHAIS
*La Folle journée, ou Le Mariage de
Figaro* (The crazy day, or The mar-
riage of Figaro)
Département des Manuscrits, Fr. 12544,
fols. 38–38*bis*

*Paper; 175 fols.; 310 × 210 mm. Copy with auto-
graph additions and corrections. Purchased from
the heirs of a certain Delaporte (probably the secre-
tary-prompter at the Comédie Française from 1765
to 1795), 1833.*

The future creator (and worthy equal) of
Figaro started out as Caron the Younger,
clockmaker to the king, a position which
served as a springboard for a checkered
career full of imbroglios and plot twists.
Beaumarchais was, in turn, music teacher to
"Mesdames" (Louis XV's sisters), occasional

351

judge, relentless businessman, secret agent, enthusiastic advocate of the American Revolution, and, of course, a towering theatrical figure. This "playwright-for-the-fun-of-it" provided striking proof that love of literature is compatible with a flair for business.

Le Mariage de Figaro, a merry comedy in a style inherited from the commedia dell'arte, has an ultimately conventional plot (hinging on a lord's prerogatives over a vassal's bride, which had been lampooned for centuries and was a symbol of the most contemptible privileges of the Ancien Régime). Nevertheless, it carried an ambivalent message that people interpreted to suit their own views. It could be seen either as a lightly satirical depiction of a fin-de-siècle society with its touching love stories (focusing on Figaro and Suzanne, or on the chaste Countess Almaviva, who is nevertheless flustered by the attentions of the little page Chérubin, Beaumarchais's most wonderful character after Figaro), or as a vibrant plea for the new ideas that would rock France just a few years later. *Le Mariage de Figaro* transcends its own theatrical genre through trenchant rejoinders, always on target ("You put yourself to the trouble of being born—nothing else"), and long monologues by Marcelline and Figaro under the old chestnut tree (commentaries that underpin the play without disrupting its fast-paced rhythm).

Louis XVI was right when he commented, after hearing Figaro's monologue read aloud, that "the Bastille would have to be demolished if this play were to be performed without creating a dangerous inconsistency." Censured six times, delayed for nearly two and half years, *Le Mariage de Figaro* was an unprecedented hit from its first performance at the Comédie Française on April 27, 1784. An oblivious nobility raced to applaud the prophetic lines of Figaro, who became the spokesman for freedom-loving men in 1792,

when they transformed the play's closing line—"Tout finit par des chansons" (Everything ends with a song)—into "Tout finit par des canons" (Everything ends with a gun).

The copy of the play exhibited here, heavily corrected by Beaumarchais, must have been used during the private readings that he gave in salons during the three years that censorship prohibited official performances. It is preceded by two drafts of an "Introduction to the Reading," a harangue in which Beaumarchais compared the reticence of sought-after writers to the coquetry of young ladies who resist advances for fear of disappointing. This indicates that the text predates the performance. Initially set in France, the action had already been shifted to Spain in order to blunt the social criticism, but there remain many bold passages as well as many developments that weaken the overall dramatic balance of the play.

Annie Angremy

La Folle journée, ou Le Mariage de Figaro ([Paris], 1785); ed. J. H. Ratermanis in *Studies on Voltaire and the Eighteenth Century*, vol. 63 (Geneva, 1968). Beaumarchais, *Oeuvres*, ed. P. Larthomas (Paris, 1988). J. Scherer, *La Dramaturgie de Beaumarchais*, 3d ed. (Paris, 1980).

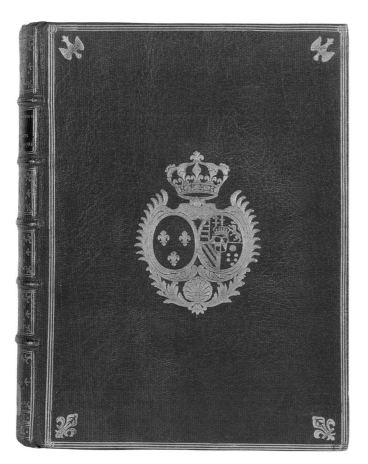

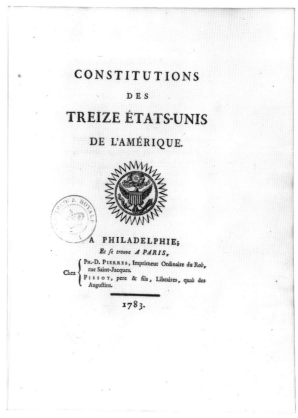

155

Constitution des treize Etats-Unis de l'Amérique (Constitution of the thirteen United States of America)
Réserve des livres rares, Rés. 4to Pb. 746, title page

Paris: Ph.-D. Pierres, Pissot, father and son, 1783. (8) + 540 pp.; 4to; 260 × 200 mm. 18th-century binding, red morocco gilt, with the arms of Marie-Antoinette, queen of France. Provenance: Collections of Queen Marie-Antoinette; deposited in the Bibliothèque Nationale in 1792.

Several weeks before the Treaty of Versailles was signed on Sept. 3, 1783, a French-language edition of the *Constitution des treize Etats-Unis de l'Amérique* was printed at the behest of Benjamin Franklin, who considered the document useful in supporting the recognition of the new country by European courts.

An English-language edition had been printed in Philadelphia in 1781. For the translation into French, Franklin turned to Duke Louis-Alexandre de La Rouchefoucauld d'Enville, a friend of the American cause who had fought at LaFayette's side. The texts were circulated somewhat unofficially in Europe. A semiclandestine periodical, *Les Affaires de l'Angleterre et de l'Amérique,* featured a column by a London banker that brought these documents to the attention of Europeans.

Fortunately, this official edition arrived at the right time. Franklin supervised the content and many notes accompanied the documents, hence the "Note d'un Américain" (Note by an American) included in the Massachusetts Constitution. He was also most certainly interested in the form, and he probably provided the model for the seal of the United States, depicted for the first time, which appears in the title. Nor was he a stranger to vellum paper used for several select copies. Philippe-Denis Pierres, the king's printer in ordinary, who respected Franklin and with whom Franklin had occupational interests in common, was asked to print the document. One hundred copies were made in quarto, printed on Annonay paper and bound for members of European

353

courts. Five hundred unbound copies were produced in octavo format, and a few copies were printed on vellum paper manufactured by M. Réveillon's plant.

The project began on March 24, 1783, with a letter from Franklin to Louis XVI's minister of foreign affairs, Count Gravier de Vergennes, and was completed four months later. Permission was granted on April 5, and on July 24, 1783, Franklin sent one copy to Vergennes and to each member of the royal family.

This copy, on Annonay paper, was produced for Queen Marie-Antoinette and bound with her arms: two adjacent shields with the arms of France and Austria surmounted by the large royal crown (the corners and spine are decorated with the fleur-de-lis and the Austrian eagle). We know its exact location in the queen's library at Versailles (bookcase H, shelf 4) and then at the château des Tuileries (bookcase B, shelf 2), before it was deposited at the Bibliothèque Nationale in 1792.

Catherine Allix

L. S. Livingston, *Franklin and His Press at Passy...* (New York, 1914). G. Chinard, "Notes on the French Translations of the 'Forms of Government or Constitutions of the Several United States' 1778 and 1783," in *American Philosophical Society Year Book* 1943: 88–106. B. Watts, *Philippe-Denis Pierres, First Printer Ordinary of Louis XVI* (Charlotte, N.C., 1966).

156
Preparatory Map for the Lapérouse Expedition

Département des Cartes et Plans, SH Pf. 174, p. 1 (2)

Paper; 3 hand-drawn sheets in watercolor backed in blue silk; 625 × 1,625 mm, 595 × 1,820 mm, and 625 × 1,820 mm. [1785–1793]. Copy owned by Louis XVI, acquired by the Bibliothèque Nationale in 1947 through deposit of the map collection of the Service Hydrographique de la Marine.

In 1785 conditions in France favored the launching of an important exploratory expedition to the Pacific. The end of the war in America (1778–1783) left idle a powerful and victorious royal fleet, led by men increasingly well trained in the methods of scientific navigation ever since the founding of the Académie de la Marine in 1752. The perfection of reliable marine chronometers in the 1760s in France and England (Harrison, Le Roy, and Berthoud timepieces) satisfactorily solved the thorny problem of how to determine longitude at sea. It thereby became possible in the final third of the century to dispel the last important geographical enigmas, especially those about the "Southern Sea" (the Southern Pacific, where earlier reliance on navigation by dead reckoning had prevented positive identification of islands). Besides, maritime affairs had never aroused such popular interest in France as in the 1770s and 1780s, after the stir caused by Bougainville's voyage and the writings of Bernardin de Saint-Pierre.

The expedition undertaken by Lapérouse— an expedition known for its tragic end (the two frigates wrecked in 1788 after a stopover in Australia)—differed from previous French voyages of discovery by Surville (1769–1770), Marion-Dufresne (1772), and even Bougainville (1766–1769) in one innovative respect: government involvement. The monarchy desired, meticulously planned, and entirely financed the expedition without leaving the slightest place to private initiative. Louis XVI, who was receptive to scientific advance and notably educated in geographic matters by Philippe Buache, the best master geographer of the age, fully appreciated the benefit

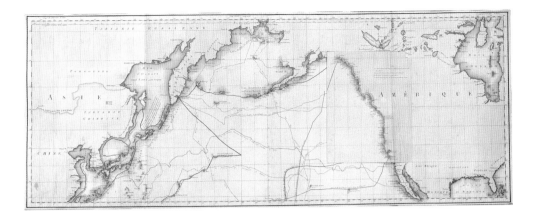

of a voyage of exploration that would complete Cook's discoveries in the Pacific in two specific areas: the coasts of North America (the question of a Northwest Passage still being unresolved) and the regions located between kabuki and Japan (which the English had neglected).

Scientific curiosity was not the sole motive; concerns of a political, colonial, and commercial nature were also intermingled in the plan of discovery. Although the Treaty of Versailles (1783) had restored France to a prestige in Europe which had been seriously shaken after the French and Indian Wars, it offered no compensation for the colonial losses previously imposed by the English in the 1763 Treaty of Paris (Canada, Louisiana, and India). Cook's voyages, while they definitively dispelled the myth of a Southern Continent, also increased the English lead in the exploration of new lands and potential trading posts. The extensive geographical and scientific objectives of the French undertaking—astronomers, naturalists, and "gardeners" were brought along—were accompanied by less disinterested goals: monitoring the activities of European countries (especially Britain) in the distant seas, and seeking new French commercial outlets in the Far East—for example, shipping North American furs to China and Japan.

Claret de Fleurieu, as the director of ports and arsenals and as assistant inspector for the registry of naval maps, was the principal promoter and organizer of the expedition. He entrusted Buache de La Neuville, hydrographer and chief geographer of the king, with the task of drawing up charts for the voyage, among which is to be found this great map of the Pacific Ocean. Showing the projected itinerary for the voyage as well as tracings of the principal European voyages hitherto undertaken, "afin de rapprocher les découvertes récentes de celles qui ont été faites dans les siècles précédens, et de prouver, dans quelques cas, leur identité" (in order to compare recent discoveries with those that had been made in previous centuries and to demonstrate that in some cases they were the same), this map was a veritable catalogue of the remaining geographical uncertainties. It showed all the coasts known in 1785 and indicated unexplored areas with dotted lines. In Oceania gaps appeared for certain sections of the coasts of New Holland, New Caledonia, and the Terre des Arsacides (Solomon Archipelago), as well as for the uncertain junction of Louisiade and New Guinea. In Asia, Europeans knew little about the Kurile Islands or the coasts of Japan, Korea, and Tartary. In North America a large part of the coast between Mount St. Elias and Monterey was yet to be explored.

Of the five copies that were made of the map, two were handed over to the captains of the two frigates in the expedition, Lapérouse and Fleuriot de Langle, and the other three were given to Marshal de Castries (secretary of state for the navy), to Claret de Fleurieu, and to Louis XVI. It is the copy "provenant du cabinet du ci-devant roi" (from the cabinet of the former king; manuscript note on the verso) that is exhibited here. It is also the most complete copy—for two reasons. Louis XVI, on the basis of reports he had received, ordered that the route actually taken (as far as China) be drawn in red ink alongside that of the anticipated itinerary, which had been

355

drawn in a thick black, crinkly line. The
results of the exploration of the northern
coasts of America, on the other hand, were
noted on a loose leaf that could be superimposed there to illustrate the discoveries of
Cook, of the Spaniards, and of Lapérouse,
respectively–the principal goal of the
expedition.

Catherine Hofmann

L. M. A. Destouff, baron de Milet-Mureau, *Voyage de La
Pérouse autour du monde, publié conformément au décret du 22
avril 1791* (Paris, 1797). Numa Broc, *La Géographie des
philosophes: Géographes et voyageurs français au XVIIIe siècle*
(Paris, 1975). E. Archier, "Introduction aux sources car-
tographiques de l'histoire du Pacifique, conservées à la
Bibliothèque Nationale, Département des Cartes et Plans," in
L'Importance de l'exploration maritime au siècle des lumières
(Paris, 1978). *A la découverte de la Terre: Dix siècles de cartogra-
phie,* exhibition at the Bibliothèque Nationale (Paris, 1979). C.
Gaziello, *L'Expédition de Lapérouse, 1785-1788: Réplique
française aux voyages de Cook* (Paris, 1984).

157

Le serment du Jeu de Paume (The Jeu de Paume oath)

Cabinet des Estampes, Ef 236f, vol. 1,
format 6

*Aquatint retouched with outils by Jean-Pierre-
Marie Jazet (1788–1871) based on a drawing by
Jacques-Louis David (1748–1825). "A Bruxelles, chez
Michel Stapleaux éditeur, Marché aux Herbes." Ca.
1825. 65 × 99.8 mm.*

The Estates General had been convoked on
May 1, 1789. The opening session took place
in the great hall of the Menus Plaisirs in
Versailles on May 5 and 17, where the assembled deputies solemnly declared themselves
to be an Assemblée Nationale. A little later,
the king announced that a royal session
would be held on June 22 and that as a result
deliberations would be suspended to allow
for decoration of the hall. The deputies then
found another place to meet in a nearby
building used for playing *jeu de paume*, the
precursor to modern tennis.

The Jeu de Paume hall, built at the end of
the 17th century, consisted of a rectangle 29
by 10 meters, with a covered gallery that ran
along three sides pierced by seven large windows and framed by columns supporting the
structural framework. It naturally lacked any
furniture appropriate to the needs of an
assembly.

The deputies swore to meet anywhere circumstances might require until a constitution for the kingdom could be solidly established. The artist David was probably not in
Versailles, since he was quite busy finishing
his *Brutus,* but he was charged with the
responsibility of painting a large canvas of
the event at state expense. He finished a large
drawing of it in May 1791 and exhibited it at
the Salon the following September. He urged
the deputies to come to his studio so that he
could do their portraits. The painter worked
on his great project until his election to the
Convention in 1792. But political developments rapidly made the depiction of certain
persons in the painting an embarrassment,
and it remained in a preliminary state. The
immense canvas (nearly 7 by 10 meters) was
abandoned and rolled up. It is kept now in

SERMENT DU JEU DE PAUME.

the National Museum at the château of Versailles.

During David's exile in Brussels (Louis XVIII banished him as a regicide), the painter was occupied in getting his works engraved. In October 1820 he commissioned a certain Daniel Isoard de Martouzet to have the *Serment du Jeu de Paume* engraved. Martouzet engaged Jazet to make the engraving and Stapleaux to publish it. Four different versions of it were completed; this is the largest.

In the center, standing on a makeshift table – a door placed on two barrels – Bailly, the mayor of Paris, can be identified. In front of him are three people: the Carthusian monk Dom Gerle, who was one of the first members of the clergy to join the Third Estate; abbé Grégoire; and pastor Rabaut Saint-Etienne. Seated on the left of this group, taking notes, are Barère de Vieuzac and, at Bailly's feet, the somber-eyed Sieyès. Gérard folds his hands while Mirabeau, holding his hat, raises his right hand. Robespierre

brings his hands to his chest in a gesture of exaltation, but below on the right, lying prostrate, Martin d'Auch shows his disapproval. On the left is Maupetit de la Mayenne, who though ill had had himself carried in to be present at the session. The engraving popularized what ought to have been the greatest artistic masterpiece of the French Revolution and would have constituted a magisterial counterpart to David's *Coronation of Napoléon*.

Laure Beaumont-Maillet

Philippe Bordes, "*Le Serment du Jeu de Paume* de Jacques-Louis David," in *Notes et documents des musées de France* 8 (1983).

357

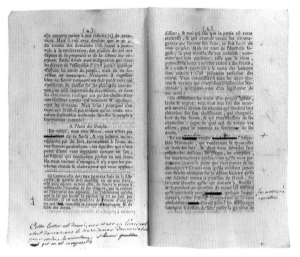

158

L'Ami du peuple (The people's friend),
copy annotated by Jean-Paul Marat

Réserve des livres rares, Rés. p. Z. 2681, p. 4

*Paris, 1789–1794. 12 vols. in 8ᵛᵒ. Green half-roan
binding. Purchased at auction, Sotheby's, London,
Nov. 20, 1990.*

In September 1789, Jean-Paul Marat
(1743–1793) founded a newspaper, *Le Publiciste
parisien* (The Parisian publicist), whose title
quickly changed to *L'Ami du peuple*. For nearly four years, until his assassination by Charlotte Corday on July 13, 1793, Marat almost
singlehandedly published 685 issues of the
Ami du peuple, as well as 242 issues of the
Journal de la République française that succeeded it, beginning in September 1792. His
permanent opposition to the government
(the king and Necker in 1789, the Girondins
in 1792), and his chosen mission to thwart the
counterrevolution then under way—by urging
the people to be vigilant and if necessary violent—forced him to lead the hectic life of an
outlaw. Lack of money caused an interruption in the publication of the *Ami du peuple*
from December 1791 to April 1792, but Marat
took advantage of the time to devote himself
to reflection about his action and his thought.

In 1990 the BNF acquired twelve volumes
with annotations in Marat's hand. The collection is composed for the most part of the
Ami du peuple but also contains pamphlets
and issues of other broadsheets on which he
collaborated, such as the *Orateur du peuple*
(People's orator). The volumes displayed here
(which were in part compiled and bound
after Marat's death) come from his sister
Albertine. They were acquired in 1859 by one
of the principal collectors of the period, Félix
Solar. Auctioned off two years later for the
substantial sum of 1,500 francs, this copy of
L'Ami du peuple went next to Prince Jérôme
Napoléon; it then found its way into
Nadaillac's library of revolutionary material,
and finally in 1885 it was acquired by a great
English amateur, the earl of Rosebery, whose
descendants kept it until recently in a castle
in Scotland.

Volumes 3 to 5 of this copy are the most
abundantly annotated and are valuable for
the information supplied on the complex
bibliography of *L'Ami du peuple*. They make it
possible to distinguish authentic issues from
their numerous forgeries, provide issues in
proof state, contain Marat's notes about the
printers and about the authorship of letters
published in the newspaper, and contain
Marat's manuscript corrections and additions
and retrospective comments on his impact:
"décret que j'ai fait passer," "mon histoire"
("decree which I had passed," "my story").
The BNF, which also houses the manuscript
from the La Bédoyère collection containing a
dozen issues rewritten by Marat at the end of
November 1789, thus remains the principal
center for research on "l'ami du peuple" (the
"People's Friend") and his newspaper.

Isabelle de Conihout

Eugène Hatin, *Bibliographie historique et critique de la presse
française* (Paris, 1886), 101ff. Maurice Tourneux, *Bibliographie
de l'histoire de Paris pendant la Révolution* (Paris, 1894), nos.
10320 and 10829. Louis R. Gottschalk, *Jean-Paul Marat: A
Study in Radicalism* (Chicago, 1967). Charlotte Goëtz and
Jacques De Cock, *Marat corrigé par lui-même* (Brussels, 1990).
The Press in the French Revolution (Oxford, 1991).

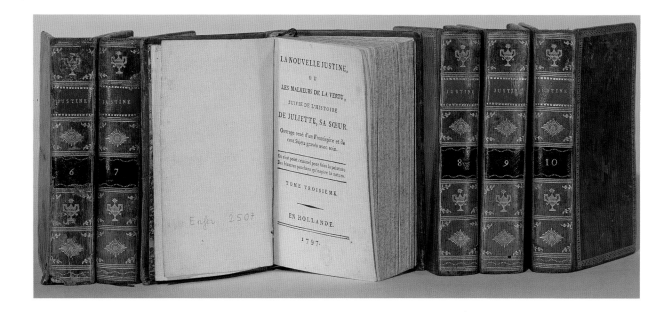

159

DONATIEN-ALPHONSE-
FRANÇOIS, MARQUIS DE SADE
*La Nouvelle Justine, ou Les Malheurs
de la vertu, suivie de L'Histoire de
Juliette, sa soeur*
(The new Justine, or The misfortunes
of virtue, followed by The history of
Juliette, her sister). Ouvrage orné
d'un frontispice et de cent sujets
gravés avec soin (Work decorated
with a frontispiece and one hundred
scenes carefully engraved).
Réserve des livres rares, Rés. Enfer 2507

*In Holland [recte Paris: Nicolas Massé], 1797 [recte
1799 and 1801]. 10 vols. in-18mo. First edition.
Contemporary binding, tree-marbled calf, with gilt
Greek key border. Acquired in 1985.*

Sixteen years of confinement in different
prisons, followed by eleven years in the
Charenton insane asylum–such is the real
scandal of the marquis de Sade's life
(1740–1814) as viewed by admirers of the man
whom Apollinaire judged "cet esprit le plus
libre qui ait encore existé" (the freest spirit
who has ever existed). For his contemporaries, the three sex cases that landed Sade in
the Bastille were simply revealing glimpses of
a debauched life that aroused their worst
suspicions. Later on, what they knew and
what they imagined about his work only
strengthened their condemnation: Sade, that
infernal genius, that "monstre auteur" (mon-

strous author), in the words of Restif de La
Bretonne, deserved nothing more than to
disappear from society–and with him his
infamous books that another of his enemies
said might have been produced by a bunch
of raving executioners during a filthy orgy.

Such judgments hardly referred to *La
Philosophie dans le boudoir* (Philosophy in the
boudoir, 1795), which at that time had but few
readers, or to *Les Cent vingt journées de Sodome*
(The 120 days of Sodom), which was to
remain in manuscript form until 1904. They
were aimed still less at the plays–some of
which were performed–or at the epistolary
novel (*Aline et Valcour*, 1795) or at the tragic
short stories (*Les Crimes de l'amour*, 1800)
which their author had no qualms in signing
and which placed him among the initiators
of the Gothic novel.

A single title epitomized the scandal:
Justine (1791), a book that Sade published
anonymously and whose paternity he fero-
ciously denied. Restif, his first accuser and
the hypocritical author of *Anti-Justine* (1798),
had begun to attribute to Sade this "execrable novel" (printed in two volumes with
engravings), while at the same time he took
advantage of the great success of "the divine
marquis" and his book, reprinted many times
and sold openly at the Palais Royal.

After *La Philosophie dans le boudoir*,
exploiting the loose morality that reached its
peak during the Directory (1795–1799), Sade
devoted himself to the ultra-secret writing of
works that amounted to some ten known

titles, only two of which could be printed: *La Nouvelle Justine* (1799), a still more scandalous expansion on the first version, and *L'Histoire de Juliette* (1801). The two texts formed a series of more that 3,600 pages, in ten volumes, illustrated by 101 engravings. Such a publication, "the most important clandestine publication of a pornographic book ever seen in the world" (J.-J. Pauvert), involved the collaboration of too many intermediaries for Fouché's police not to find a weak point in the network of accomplices. In August 1800 a new edition of *La Nouvelle Justine* was seized at the book sewer's. In the last days of February 1801 the prefect Dubois was informed that publication of *Juliette* was imminent. On March 6 Sade was arrested at his publisher's; all of his manuscripts were confiscated and a large part of the printed material was seized by the police, whom Massé had guided to the hiding places in exchange for his freedom. Sade was never to recover his own. Led away to Sainte Pélagie prison, then to Bicêtre, he was institutionalized on April 27, 1803, at the asylum of Charenton, where he died eleven years later.

Indomitable monument of literary obscenity, constantly reprinted in spite of grave risk of punishment, *La nouvelle Justine. . . suivie de L'histoire de Juliette* is inordinately rare in first edition.

Antoine Coron

Guillaume Apollinaire, introduction to *L'Oeuvre du marquis de Sade* (Paris, 1909). Maurice Blanchot, *Lautréamont et Sade* (Paris, 1949). Pierre Klosowski, *Sade, mon prochain* (Paris, 1967). Jean-Jacques Pauvert, *Sade vivant*, 3 vols. (Paris, 1986–1990). Pascal Ract-Madoux, "L'édition originale de la 'Nouvelle Justine' et 'Juliette,'" *Bulletin du Bibliophile* 1 (1992): 139–58.

160

Thèbes, Medynet-Abou: Vue intérieure du péristyle du palais (Thebes, Médinet-Abou: Interior view of the peristyle of the palace)

Cabinet des Estampes, Ub 181c

Drawn by Charles-Louis Balzac (1752–1820) for vol. 2 of the Antiquités *of the* Description de l'Egypte *(1809–1824). Pen and ink with gray wash; 37.2 × 56 cm.*

Charles-Louis Balzac, an architect, drew the interior of the peristyle of one of the funeral temples of Médinet-Abou, located on the left bank of the Nile and part of the large series of the funeral temples of Thebes. On the right, two French scholars are visiting and commenting on the peristyle's sculpted reliefs, while the exhausted draftsman rests near his drawing portfolio, and the scholars' local guides, whose clothing is better suited to the heat of the country, are talking while seated on the ground.

This watercolor illustrates the monumental *Description de l'Egypte*, published between 1809 and 1824. It consists of nine books of texts with descriptions, commentary, and accounts, and ten volumes containing 841 engraved plates comprising more than 3,000 other illustrations printed on large paper, making it the largest printed work of this type ever undertaken. The *Antiquités* contains four volumes of text plus five volumes of 426 plates; *L'Etat moderne* contains three volumes of text plus two volumes of 171 plates; *L'Histoire naturelle* contains two volumes of text plus three volumes of 244 plates. The *Atlas géographique,* the *Préface,* and the *Explications des planches* complete the work.

To store this encyclopedia, a special piece of furniture with mahogany veneer, horizontal shelves, and vertical compartments was offered to subscribers. The upper part of the piece opened to make a desk.

How did the *Description de l'Egypte* originate? In 1798, the government of the Directory dreamed of sending the turbulent and ambitious general Napoléon Bonaparte, brilliant victor of a recent military campaign in Italy, far from the political arena. The

expedition to Egypt was decided in an attempt to cause harm to England, at war with France, by occupying Egypt in order to cut off the India trade route to the commercially powerful British Isles.

In May 1798, Napoléon took to the sea with 34,000 sailors and soldiers and more than 500 scholars, technicians, and artists who were to help develop the country. At the same time, a complete map of Egypt was to be drawn. For this purpose, a large library was taken along, including instruments used for astronomy, physics, and topography. Workers from the Vatican Press were even hired who were capable of writing in Arabic, Greek, and Syriac.

While military victories were followed by defeats in a continuing cycle, cultural and technical missions crisscrossed the country, often under hazardous and extremely uncomfortable conditions. The comprehensive research into ancient monuments was to be the main task of the scholars of the Eastern Army, under the dynamic leadership of Dominique-Vivant Denon, whose "antiquarian" mentality and cultivation would be decisive factors in the completion of this extravagant undertaking in publishing. With their thousands of notes, sketches, and watercolors, the scholars returned to France early in 1802 and began preparing this admirable encyclopedia. In February 1802, a committee of eight was appointed to coordinate the project. The texts had to be filed and inventory had to be taken. Owing to the large number of authors, the texts had to be written and checked to transform the work into a bona fide synthesis.

Besides the intellectual problems to be solved, new solutions had to be found for new technical problems, such as obtaining vast quantities of large sheets of paper (over two million sheets were to be delivered) and executing copper engravings of very large dimensions. Two hundred engravers came together to transpose the scholars' surveys onto copper plates. To economize their effort and improve their performance, Conté, an engineer, invented a machine that executed immense skies, uniform masses of monuments, and the backgrounds of bas-reliefs. Many plates were colored mechanically and touched up subsequently with watercolor. The undertaking would never have been completed without Conté's machine, which printed 820,000 sheets, 60,000 of which were in color. The *Description de l'Egypte* took twenty years to be published and one thousand copies were made.

Françoise Jestaz

Monuments of Egypt: The Napoleonic Edition, ed. Charles Coulston Gillipsie and Michel Dewachter (Princeton, 1987).
Mémoires de l'Egypte: Hommage de l'Europe à Champollion, exhibition in Strasbourg, Paris, and Berlin (Strasbourg, 1990).

161

Constitution républicaine des colonies
française [sic] de Saint-Domaingue...
envoyé [sic] au premier consul de France
par le citoyen Toussaint-Louverture...
(Republican constitution of the
French colonies of Santo Domingo...
sent to the first consul of France by
the citizen Toussaint-Louverture...)
Réserve des livres rares, 8º, Lk¹². 554,
title page
[Paris]: Widow Leroux, [1801]. 8 pp.; 8ᵛº.

This constitution, the first for a black state,
was drawn up by "une assemblée centrale" (a
central assembly) of the population of Santo
Domingo—an assembly which had been
called by Toussaint-Louverture. The constitution was formally proclaimed on July 8, 1801.
It instituted a certain de facto autonomy for
the colony whose sole tie with France was
nothing more than the personal bond
between the governor of Santo Domingo and
the head of the French government. It
affirmed that "chaque homme, de quelque
couleur qu'il puisse être, est éligible à toute
[sic] les places. Il n'y a parmi eux d'autre distinction que celui [sic] des talens et des vertus" (every man of whatever color is eligible
for all offices. The only distinctions among
them are those of talents and virtues").

Since the 17th century France had occupied the western part of Santo Domingo
island. The island's economy was based on
agricultural plantations worked by slaves.
Beginning in 1789 and encouraged by the
French Revolution, social agitation increased:
free people of color demanded the same
rights as whites and the black slaves wanted
their freedom. Numerous insurrections followed one another starting in 1791. It was in
this context that Toussaint-Louverture, former slave, self-taught and freed in 1776, a
militant for black freedom, saw his power
grow. The abolition of slavery decreed by the
Convention in 1794 rallied him to the French
cause against the Spaniards who held the
other part of the island. From that point on,
his political influence constantly grew firmer.
In 1797 he was named commander in chief of
the colony of Santo Domingo.

Since the French Revolution, the status of the colonies had remained uncertain. The Consular Constitution of Dec. 13, 1799, foresaw special laws to determine their governance. Based on this provision, Toussaint-Louverture decided to convene an elected assembly to draft a local constitution. The constitution instituted a military dictatorship that named Toussaint-Louverture governor for life and gave him the right to choose his successor. It sought to reestablish for black profit the plantation regime and bound each agricultural worker to his land with the goal of restoring agricultural prosperity to the island. It created a de facto autonomy for the colony, inasmuch as every law concerning it needed to be proposed by the governor and promulgated by the central assembly.

After its proclamation, the constitution was forwarded for approval to Napoléon Bonaparte, who was himself preparing an administrative reorganization for Santo Domingo. Napoléon could not accept such a manifestation of autonomy and dispatched General Leclerc with an expeditionary corps to reestablish French authority over the colony. Toussaint-Louverture yielded in May and was deported to France, where he died in the Fortress de Joux in 1803, a year before the proclamation of Haitian independence.

The copy of the constitution exhibited here is the only one known.

Nathalie Renier

Jean Tulard, ed., *Dictionnaire Napoléon* (1987). Pierre Pluchon, *Toussaint Louverture: De l'esclavage au pouvoir* (Paris, 1989).

363

IV

Revolution, Empire, and the Independence
of Culture

RÉSISTANCE

BULLETIN OFFICIEL DU COMITE NATIONAL DE SALUT PUBLIC

n.1   15 décembre 1940

Résister! C'est le cri qui sort de votre coeur à tous,dans la détresse où vous a laissés le désastre de la Patrie.C'est le cri de vous
tous qui ne vous résignez pas,de vous tous qui voulez faire votre devoir.

Mais vous vous sentez isolés et désarmés,et dans le chaos des idées,
des opinions et des systèmes,vous cherchez où est votre devoir.Résister,
c'est déjà garder son coeur et son cerveau.Mais c'est surtout agir,faire
quelque chose qui se traduise en faits positifs,en actes raisonnés et
utiles.Beaucoup ont essayé,et souvent se sont découragés en se voyant im-
puissants.D'autres se sont groupés.Mais souvent leurs groupes se sont
trouvés à leur tour isolés et impuissants.

Patiemment,difficilement,nous les avons cherchés et réunis.Ils sont
déjà nombreux (plus d'une armée pour Paris seulement),les hommes ardents
et résolus qui ont compris que l'organisation de leur effort était néces-
saire,et qu'il leur fallait une méthode,une discipline,des chefs.

La méthode? Vous grouper dans vos foyers avec ceux que vous connais-
sez.Ceux que vous désignerez seront vos chefs.Vos chefs trouveront des
hommes éprouvés qui orienteront leurs activités,et qui nous en rendront
compte par différents échelons.Notre Comité,pour coordonner vos efforts
avec ceux de la France non occupée et ceux qui combattent avec nos Alliés,
commandera.Votre tâche immédiate est de vous organiser pour que vous
puissiez,au jour où vous en recevrez l'ordre,reprendre le combat.Enrôlez
avec discernement les hommes résolus,et encadrez les des meilleurs.Ré-
confortez et décidez ceux qui doutent ou qui n'osent plus espérer.Recher-
chez et surveillez ceux qui ont renié la Patrie et qui la trahissent.
Chaque jour réunissez et transmettez les informations et les observations
utiles pour vos chefs.Pratiquez une discipline inflexible,une prudence
constante,une discrétion absolue.Méfiez-vous des inconséquents,des ba-
vards,des traîtres.Ne vous vantez jamais,ne vous confiez pas.Efforcez
vous de faire face à vos besoins propres.Nous vous donnerons plus tard
des moyens d'action que nous travaillons à rassembler.

En acceptant d'être vos chefs,nous avons fait le serment de tout sa -
crifier à cette mission,avec dureté,impitoyablement.

Inconnus les uns des autres hier,et dont aucun n'a jamais participé
aux querelles des partis d'autrefois aux Assemblées ni aux Gouvernements,
indépendants,Français seulement,choisis pour l'action que nous promettons
nous n'avons qu'une ambition,qu'une passion,qu'une volonté:faire renaître
une France pure et libre.

                         LE COMITE NATIONAL DE SALUT PUBLIC.

7 From the French Revolution to the Present

Peter Gay

Printing has been dangerous since its invention, in France no less than elsewhere. It has been dangerous—or thought dangerous—to the holders of power and therefore to writers even more. It was an old story. One thinks of the pamphlet wars enlivening the decades of the French Wars of Religion, or of Pascal's polemics against the Jesuits a century later. Yet it was the French Revolution that gave the printed word its most visible role. To be sure, the virulent controversies that marked France from 1789 on had been thoroughly prepared during the age of the Enlightenment. Voltaire, Rousseau, and their fellows were men of words—printed words; so was Diderot, who wished, he announced, to change the general way of thinking with his *Encyclopédie*. But that change, whatever conservative nineteenth-century historians like Hippolyte Taine might say, did not prove easy. Religious orthodoxy, tenacious habits of conformity and obedience, self-interested loyalties to constituted authorities, and more or less alert royal censors made printed challenges a risky, often an unprofitable, business.

One legacy left by these writers, which has lasted to present-day France, was the prestige of what the nineteenth century would come to call intellectuals. To the astonishment of foreign observers—many of them no doubt committed philistines, but others sober realists—the French have long given excessive credit, and lent unwarranted authority, to people of ideas, even bad ideas. Certainly the French Revolution was an event in culture as much as in power, and in their intertwining; it was both consequence and cause of an avalanche of treatises, pamphlets, broadsides, and editorials. Historians have observed that the leading revolutionaries were aspiring or published authors who used the stage these excited times provided to add their bit. Willing, efficient printers were agents of popular politics. "Where does so much agitation come from?" asked the Parisian magistrate Pierre Gerbier in June 1789, and answered his own question: "From a crowd of minor clerks and lawyers, from unknown writers, starving scribblers, who go about rabble-rousing in clubs and cafés. These are the hotheads who have forged the weapons with which the masses are armed today."[1] This was a time when the distinction between words and acts, never very firm, seemed to disappear altogether. To write a pamphlet, even to read one, was a political commitment, lining up the author, or the reader, with Jacobins, Girondins, royalists. Few documents of the age drew as wide a circle of impact as the notorious Brunswick manifesto of July 1792, which threatened to level Paris to the ground if a hair on the heads of the royal family was harmed.

The French Revolution was, then, significantly, an experiment in the popular invasion of politics. In the Old Regime, political culture had been a strictly circumscribed affair, confined to reading circles, provincial academies, and internecine struggles near the throne. But the *cahiers* of grievances of early 1789 mobilized a public becoming aware for the first time not so much of its power as of its very existence as a public, as a potential judge of what was in its best interests. And the proliferation of publications during the Revolution itself, like the replacement of aristocrats in authority in Paris and in the provinces by men of the law and gradually of lesser folk, gave the new, still untried French political public an unprecedented platform for action. Papers propagating a strong line, like Marat's *L'Ami du peuple* (cat. 158), appeared in great numbers. This democratization of printing—everyone his own political philosopher—was anything but straightforward. There continued to be a tension between authorities repressing printed opinion, whether uttered in words or caricatures, and a growing political elite presuming to speak—and at times actually speaking—for a general public of readers. The Revolution was the first battleground. There would be more.

The First Modern Caesar

When Napoléon Bonaparte wrested power from the Directory on 18 brumaire of the year VIII (Nov. 9, 1799), he found strong public support. After a decade of turmoil—constitution making, regicide, civil conflict, de-Christianization, European war, terror and counterterror, and, during the five years of the Directory, drift and corruption—the country yearned for stability. Perhaps that remarkable, domineering Corsican general could supply it without jeopardizing the Revolution's gains. Looking back from 1818, the liberal politician and philosopher Charles de Rémusat remembered that Napoléon Bonaparte "appeared like a savior."[2] Tightening his grip, the general met little opposition and easily crushed whatever antagonists he found or imagined. They were coopted, bribed, or shot. Having taken power, Napoléon meant to keep it.

But control resting on guns, gold, and concessions to Roman Catholic sensibilities was not enough to secure the legitimacy Napoléon craved. Lacking the mantle of an old dynasty or a living tradition, he resorted to a resource he privately despised: the French people. The first of the modern Caesars, he coupled absolute rule with populist admixtures. This apparently self-contradictory political principle, first adumbrated by Julius Caesar some eighteen centuries earlier, included the plebiscite: Napoléon had each of his steps up the ladder of power sanctioned by popular approval.[3] These charades were exercises in managing consent. In 1800, the official figures had 3,011,007 sanctioning Napoléon's rule as First Consul, with only 1,562 objecting. In 1802, 3,600,000 were reported as voting in favor of his consulship for life, with a mere handful, 8,374, voting against it. And in 1804, 3,572,329 were listed as having supported his bid for the imperial purple, while only 2,569 opposed it. These were, of course, literally incredible numbers, compiled by means of open voting, propaganda, intimidation, and plain fraud. But they were also a wry tribute to that modern phenomenon, the emerging political culture which demanded at least lip service. Appearances had always mattered—the "Sun King" had cultivated the prestige of distance from the common herd—but now they were taking new forms: ordinary people's ideas about themselves and their right to power. The sumptuous coronation ceremony Napoléon arranged for himself in December 1804 was part of his legitimation by show. He had it staged at Notre-Dame, with scores of dignitaries including Pope Pius VII in attendance. Visibility was the road to respectability.

The new Emperor Napoléon I had recognized the benefits of image making ever since the mid-1790s, when he had been General Bonaparte. In his Italian campaigns, he had used bulletins or carefully orchestrated interviews to show himself the hardworking, self-sacrificing, brilliant public servant. During his years as consul and emperor, he continued to manipulate the printed word, silencing critics and rewarding adulators. Napoléon's severity with Madame de Staël—she and her allies called it persecution—is a case in point.

Germaine de Staël was a formidable antagonist, rich, well connected, intelligent, learned, passionate, and a political liberal with romantic inclinations. In 1800, not long after 18 Brumaire, she published *De la Littérature*, a sociological treatise drawing on the French Enlightenment from Montesquieu to Condorcet. She would have been at home in this exhibition; her book relates high culture to political power and argues that the first draws strength from the second. Napoléon glanced at it, distrusted its independent-minded author, and inspired a press campaign to discredit her. Soon he went further. Her salon, attended by liberal intellectuals like her lover, Benjamin Constant, annoyed and obscurely frightened him. By 1802 he banished her from Paris; three years later, now emperor, he renewed the ban.

De Staël's *De l'Allemagne* of 1810 turned these skirmishes into outright war. While the censors found little that was objectionable, the emperor ordered the book destroyed—only five copies of the first edition, including proofs belonging to Joseph Marie Portalis, the empire's chief censor, have survived (cat. 166). Published in England, it reached France only after Napoléon's ouster. *De l'Allemagne* offers partisan praise of Germany, the country of romanticism, and a plea for freedom of thought and the pen. In Madame de Staël's mind, the two were related: only a free country can absorb valuable imported ideas. This was not the kind of political culture Napoléon found tolerable. Freedom of expression had to wait until his final exile to Saint Helena.

From Uncle to Nephew

The thirty-three years between Waterloo and the revolution of 1848 were more than a parenthesis between Napoléon I and Napoléon III, though they have been portrayed that way. It was a time when France's political culture tested the possibilities of loosening the grip of repression that the emperor had imposed on the country. The efforts proved fitful.

369

The Restoration, which came to an inglorious end in 1830, was born twice: in 1814, after Napoléon's debacle in Russia (see cat. 165) and on German battlefields, and in 1815, after his astonishing brief return to power following his escape from Elba.

Louis XVIII, younger brother of the martyred Louis XVI, undertook to govern with a charter that promised to give breathing room to dissenting opinion. Article 8 of the charter explicitly stated: "The French have the right to publish and to have their opinions printed as long as they conform to the laws that must curb the abuses of that liberty."[4] The formulation allowed contradictory interpretations: it might, in the government's view, permit prepublication censorship or, as liberals contended, apply only to matter already printed. The revised constitution of 1815 removed some but not all of these ambiguities.

Significantly, the constraints the government exercised over opinion concentrated on brief pamphlets and, above all, on that modern invention, the daily newspaper. Times were changing, and repression was changing with it. France during the Restoration could hardly boast of a developed political culture: "The application of ideas of equity, moderation, even of humanity to politics," wrote Rémusat, "was still, so to speak, in its infancy."[5] Paris boasted a mere seven political newspapers, and their circulation amounted to a few thousand copies; the provincial dailies were thin on the ground. And France had a parliament, but not a parliamentary regime: the king appointed his "servants," and they were responsible to him. Moreover, the active political public was tiny: some 72,000 enjoyed the suffrage, and only about 16,000 among them were eligible for a seat in the Chambre des Députés—1.5 percent of adult males. Party politics, that essential ingredient in any real political education, and the idea of a legal—and loyal—opposition, were still (to borrow from Rémusat) in their infancy. Yet this relative relaxation was congenial to the development and expression of political thought. The historian and politician François Guizot insisted on the need for a political opposition. Benjamin Constant, the most original mind among the liberals, argued for widening the suffrage to include all property owners and for maintaining a free press as a source not of public unrest but of public tranquility. Interestingly enough, when the Restoration collapsed, one prominent cause was the government's attack on the press.

In 1824 the count of Artois, the younger brother of Louis XVIII, more pious and more reactionary than his predecessor, mounted the throne as Charles X. His policies, a signal defeat for the liberals, supported a resurgent clericalism. But, far from disarming the opposition, the regime only strengthened it, especially among the romantics. Romanticism had come to France, wedded to neoclassical ideals in drama, architecture, and painting, later than elsewhere. The romances of Chateaubriand, German doctrines mediated through Madame de Staël's *De l'Allemagne*, set the stage. But when Charles X acceded, critics could still belittle the romantics as a mere nuisance, as self-important young malcontents.

Nevertheless, the romantics were making themselves heard. While in a bitter mood, Alfred de Vigny and Alfred de Musset, even at times Benjamin Constant, caressed the *mal de siècle*, a mixture of melancholy and aimlessness. Most of them took political positions at odds with the government. Stendhal was an unreconstructed Bonapartist; Victor Hugo, whose youthful verse was gaining him fervent admirers, began as a loyal monarchist rewarded by Charles X with the Légion d'Honneur but moved rapidly to the left. With his allies on the brilliant literary-political daily *Le Globe*, founded in 1824, he increasingly committed himself to the opposition. "Liberty in the arts," he proclaimed in the preface to *Hernani*, "liberty in society: that is the double aim toward which all consistent and logical spirits must tend in step."[6] By the time he wrote *Hernani*, a drama that called forth riots in the theater, Hugo was a forceful liberal in politics, religion, and the drama.

The year was 1830. The Bourbons were being chased from the throne they had occupied, with an interruption of a revolutionary and imperial quarter-century, for more than three centuries. The elections of June and July 1830, defying the habitual official efforts to secure a complaisant Chambre des Députés, produced an overwhelming majority for the opposition. The government responded by enacting the notorious Four Ordinances, which among other things dissolved the new legislature, reduced the already narrow franchise, and circumscribed the freedom of the press, placing pamphlets under renewed censorship and, more ominous, requiring that newspapers obtain royal permission to publish. The popular reaction was electric: political education had generated enough self-confidence to encourage journalists to strike back. Braving the ordinance, opposition newspapers kept printing and on July 26 issued a revolutionary declaration: "Today the government has lost the quality of legality that commands obedience." Four days later, after three days of street fighting known as *les trois glorieuses* (July 27, 28, and 29, 1830), Charles was in exile.

The Orléanist regime of Louis Philippe that governed France for the next eighteen years has been denounced, by the English historian Alfred Cobban, as "so lacking in principle that it could only be known by the name of the month of its founding, as the July Monarchy."[7] But at the outset, the king made efforts to avoid the mistakes of his predecessors by tempering order with liberty. The constitution of 1830 assiduously cultivated public opinion. Louis Philippe was styled king of the French and the Bourbon fleur-de-lis was exchanged for the tricolor. In matters of religion, for so long the flash point in France, the charter provided that Roman Catholicism was no longer the official religion of the state but merely that of the majority of the French people. Above all, censorship of books and newspapers was abolished. French power seemed secure and generous enough to permit a legitimate opposition.

These hopes were soon disappointed. The men of 1830, the opposition journalists and academics who had brought down a regime, were coopted into the new one, and this paralyzed their will to criticism. Their defection made the remaining opposition all the noisier. Legitimists agitated for a return of the Bourbons; republicans wanted an end to monarchy. These dissenters appeared to endanger the stability that the Orléanist regime had promised and was determined to maintain. In April 1834 a weavers' strike in Lyon, supported in other cities, was put down with considerable loss of life. And in July 1835 a bomb aimed at Louis Philippe killed a number of bystanders and several National Guardsmen. Although the king himself escaped unscathed, these events strengthened the government's resolve to clamp down on words capable of causing so much mischief.

371

Even without formal censorship, the authorities had prosecuted writers deemed to have insulted the king's majesty or the government's probity. In 1835, with menace in the air, Louis Philippe's ministers sharpened the laws of libel, made convictions easier to obtain, increased penalties, and criminalized any ridicule of—or even allusion to—the king in a political context. The enactments had their critics. Were the king and his ministers using a detestable assassination attempt to stifle the liberty they had sworn to uphold? Yet many deputies voted for the bills, however reluctantly, because they were persuaded, in the words of Irene Collins, "that newspapers had contributed toward the state of mind in which a fanatic had made a hideous attempt on the king's life."[8]

A look at Daumier's lithographs shows that protest did not disappear; it merely grew subtler, more indirect. Daumier put his impressive gifts in the service of the radical opposition. In association with Charles Philipon, an editor of genius and a principled republican, he developed scathing critiques of the government and its head. Philipon had launched a weekly, *La Caricature,* in November 1830, and two years later the daily *Le Charivari.* Both were steadily beset by confiscations and prosecutions, fines and jail sentences. In late 1832 Daumier spent some months in prison for a highly disrespectful, scatological lithograph about Louis Philippe showing the king shitting out decorations and patents of nobility. Inspired by Philipon, he caricatured the king's slightly bulbous head by depicting him as a pear (cat. 170). In other prints, Daumier assailed government repression with grim wit. With the legislation of 1835, *La Caricature* disappeared and *Le Charivari* became more circumspect. Instead of caricaturing the king, Daumier adapted a raffish stage character, Robert Macaire, to stand for all the ills of the country. Macaire was swindler, thief, fraudulent bankrupt, cynic, liar—the very embodiment, Daumier hinted, of the July Monarchy. But Daumier was not vindictive: after the February revolution of 1848, a dénouement to which he had contributed his bit, he refused to lampoon the fallen monarch. But Daumier would soon have another ruler to think about.

For all its brave beginnings, the Second Republic looks in retrospect like a showcase for the nephew of Napoléon I, the later Napoléon III (see cat. 175). From December 1848, Louis-Napoléon Bonaparte was president of a republic he plotted from the outset to destroy. And its last year was a dictatorship under his aegis. He was much like his uncle and tried to be even more so, shrewdly invoking, and exploiting, the immortal name he bore. Like Napoléon I, he was a devotee of Julius Caesar and had a superb flair for publicity. In 1839 he published a deft polemic, *Idées napoléoniennes,* arguing that France needed an injection of the emperor's ideas and hinting not very subtly that he was the man for the job. On trial in 1840 for a pathetic attempt to overthrow the government, he used his time in the dock to make unapologetic speeches that spread his name to an even wider public. Comfortably detained in a fortress, he kept on writing and plotting.

Ironically, it had been the February revolution and its democratic innovation, universal male suffrage, that gave Louis-Napoléon his chance. His triumph in the electoral campaign for president had been stunning—many had voted for him under the illusion that he was his uncle—and he spent much time traveling across the country orating on every occasion, enforcing the point that he was the indispens-

able man of the hour. Buoyed up by popular nostalgia for the days of French greatness, he skillfully elevated himself as he deified his uncle. Everything was
Bonapartist magic: he was crowned Emperor Napoléon III on December 2, 1852,
exactly a year after launching his successful coup d'état and forty-eight years after
Consul Napoléon had made himself Emperor Napoléon.

Louis-Napoléon's message, given out as president and emperor alike, was a lesson
he had absorbed from his uncle and applied even more consistently: that his authority rested entirely on the French people. They had chosen him and they could dis-
miss him. The master was masquerading as a slave. But as a modern Caesar, he took
care not to give the people its opportunity. He had inconvenient booksellers, printers, journalists, and editors fined and jailed. Newspapers and publishing houses
were shut down when it suited him. Broadsheets, songs, and almanacs, to say nothing of political pamphlets, that deviated from his line were suppressed. Political
meetings were supervised, independent politicians harassed, suspicious foreigners
deported. He repeatedly appealed to the people—the time-honored technique of the
plebiscite suited him, since he could manipulate it through bribery, intimidation,
and fictitious majorities. True, Napoléon III was genuinely popular: "There has been
terror," wrote George Sand to Mazzini after the French electorate had approved his
coup by a stunning majority of 7.5 million to 600,000 votes, "but the people would
have voted as it had without this."[9] Like other countries, France showed itself far
from immune to the blandishments of demagogues.

Curiously, the most conspicuous cases pitting culture against power during the
empire, fought out in 1857, were not directly about politics but about morality in literature. Gustave Flaubert was accused of obscenity in *Madame Bovary* and Charles
Baudelaire of obscenity and blasphemy in *Les Fleurs du mal* (see cat. 183). Both rallied support among poets, novelists, and critics, but a number of them, in government employ or fearful of retaliation, preferred prudence—not without reason.
Flaubert was acquitted; Baudelaire exonerated of blasphemy but fined three hundred francs and compelled to omit six poems from his collection which allegedly
offended public morality. There was, it seems, more than one way of arousing the
wrath of power holders.

The ordeals of these two ornaments to imperial culture (though then hardly recognized as such) suggest the prominence of a theme other than censorship in the
contest between culture and power: the alienation from respectable society of what
was coming to be called the avant-garde. That contest had not begun in France—
one may date its start with the self-isolated, bourgeois-hating protagonist of
Goethe's *Werther*. The rebellious sentiments of an E. T. A. Hoffmann or Heinrich
Heine—both well known in France—were echoed by French aesthetes like Théophile
Gautier, to say nothing of Flaubert and Baudelaire. By mid-century, venturesome
French writers, critics, painters, and composers were distancing themselves from the
bien-pensants, from good bourgeois who, the charge went, loved money and hated
art—or, if they loved art, loved only the unadventurous, falsely heroic, at times sala-
cious art favored by the official academies. This disgust with bourgeois taste could
rise to neurotic intensity: witness Flaubert's letters, which harp on the need to extir-
pate the bourgeois, a class, he said, that made him want to vomit. But, justified or

373

self-serving, the split between the avant-garde and the bourgeoisie grew into a serious issue for French culture from the 1850s onward.

Napoléon III was not indifferent to art: his tastes ran to slick, creamy nudes like Alexandre Cabanel's Venus rising from the foam. And in 1863, he struck a blow for unconventional painters—and for his own popularity—by adroitly ordering a Salon des Refusés to compete with the Academy's salon of that year. Many of the pictures the judges had rejected, now given their chance for display, were miserable daubs, but some of them, like Edouard Manet's *Déjeuner sur l'herbe*, were masterpieces. The incident once again demonstrates the complicated relation of power to culture.

Yet, not surprisingly, what mattered more to the emperor and his ministers than high culture were the rebuilding of Paris and international prestige. In search of the latter the aging emperor, still popular, made an irreparable mistake: falling into the trap Bismarck had set, he declared war on Prussia. The result: defeat at Sedan in September 1870, abdication of the emperor, and the imposition of a humiliating, extortionate peace in early 1871. Power had broken down. Was it, Frenchmen disconsolately asked themselves, the fault of culture?

The Third Republic: Trials, Consolidation, Affaires

The Third Republic provided no quick answers. Agonized self-examination called for educational policies which would enable the French to compete with those noted schoolmasters, the Prussians, and for recreational programs which would make them fit to take revenge on the Germans. But the regime hastily assembled after Napoléon's abdication in September 1870 had more immediate tasks: paying off the gigantic indemnity the victorious Prussians had imposed, restoring order in the country, and establishing a new constitutional structure. The first task it accomplished with impressive rapidity: by September 1873, the Germans had got their two billion francs and withdrawn their occupying troops from France. The second it accomplished with vindictive ruthlessness after defeating the republican Paris Communards in late May 1871, executing thousands and exiling thousands more to the penal colonies. The last and probably the most difficult task was accomplished in a curiously backhanded way: the Third Republic was built on fundamental laws hammered out across some six years, laws it never got around to incorporating into a formal constitution.

The first elections after the end of empire, held in February 1871, gave royalists an impressive majority in the Assemblée. The country looked like a republic without republicans. But, fortunately for them, royalists could not agree on a candidate for restoration: the legitimists wanted the Bourbon count of Chambord, the Orléanists the count of Paris. And, as the country recovered economically and republican politicians showed themselves responsible citizens, the monarchist majority in the Assemblée melted away. By 1877, after a series of skirmishes, the republic was firmly in the saddle.

Firmly, but not without formidable antagonists. A century before, Rousseau had asserted that everything is fundamentally linked to politics, and culture in the Third Republic confirmed that saying. In some eighty years, the country had undergone one upheaval after another—in 1789 and 1792, in 1799 and 1804, in 1814–1815, in 1830,

1848, 1851–1852, and 1870. It had been governed by two dynasties, two emperors, and it was now experimenting with a third republic. Yet none of these drastic reversals had succeeded in quieting the regional, economic, and religious strife that had long polarized Frenchmen. Power was necessarily the central issue. This was most visible, no doubt, in the religious sphere: the state had everything to say about who taught the children, whether priests and nuns or laymen; everything to say about what went into the textbooks, whether Christian pieties or secular patriotism. And, although the Third Republic, once stabilized, flourished in the arts, in literature, and in the sciences–Louis Pasteur had made major scientific discoveries during the empire and became a cherished household name in the early years of the republic– the tensions around authority, faith, and social programs tore at the country's tranquility.

Not surprisingly, tensions did not spare the arts. Academic painters continued to enjoy highly placed patronage and high prices. But toward the end of empire, and especially in the 1870s, a band of disaffected artists was turning to a lighter palette, quick brush strokes, and brilliant optical effects. They went outdoors for their subjects and, some of them close friends, together chose favorite spots in Paris and the countryside, outdoing the Barbizon landscape artists in their daring colors and evocation of ephemeral impressions. Indeed, in 1872 the movement was baptized, at first derisively and then appreciatively, "Impressionism" after a canvas by Claude Monet, *Impression: Sunrise*. Monet, Auguste Renoir, Camille Pissarro (the eldest in the group), Alfred Sisley, and Paul Cézanne (who later took his own way into post-impressionism) were the leading spirits, joined by gifted colleagues like Berthe Morisot, Mary Cassatt, Gustave Caillebotte, and (rather reluctantly) the great draftsman Edgar Degas. In 1874, after the official salon of the previous year had shown itself more starchy about unconventional work than ever, the rebels launched an exhibition of their own, a signal that government-approved culture had lost its hold over many creative artists. Down to 1886, the Impressionists staged seven Salons des Indépendants, and although the first salon was hooted down by the critics, a dozen years later it was plain that these innovators were changing the history of art–forever. Only Manet, in his own vision as subversive as the Impressionists, continued to try his luck with the academic painters, although he too, in the mid-seventies, did some fine impressionist work.

In contrast with such unbloody combats, an ominous episode, only in retrospect more comical than tragic, gave loyal supporters of the Third Republic reason for worry: the rise and fall of Gen. Georges Boulanger. A military man who looked good on a horse, thought to be a sound republican, he was appointed minister of war in January 1886. With a gift for self-promotion rivaling that of Louis-Napoléon, he made himself into a national icon by instituting reforms in the army and giving popular anti-German speeches. Worried by the monster it had created, the government stripped Boulanger of his post in May 1887, but by then he was a name to conjure with. With scandals discrediting high officials and the governing coalitions unstable, the right wing, in search of a deliverer to restore credibility to France–that is, the monarchy or perhaps a personal dictatorship–adopted him as a favorite. In 1887 Boulanger contested by-elections across the country, easily winning them all.

375

When in January 1889 he won a by-election in Paris with 60 percent of the vote against a strong republican opponent, the call for a coup d'état became clamorous. But the republic was fortunate: whether too confident that he would be voted into power, or too timid to mobilize his impetuous supporters, Boulanger did nothing. Fearing an indictment, he fled the country and committed suicide in Brussels at the grave of his mistress.

A second shock dating from the 1890s divided France even more decisively; it pitted culture against power and split each internally more painfully than any conflict in living memory. What is significant about the *affaire Dreyfus*—too familiar to require detailed retelling—is that an apparently routine conviction of an officer for treason mushroomed into a threat to the republic. The artillery captain Alfred Dreyfus, an Alsatian Jew working in the Ministry of War, was wrongfully accused, and convicted in a secret court-martial, of selling secret documents to the Germans. The army, eager not to offend noisy anti-Semitic publicists, stooped to forged documents to railroad Dreyfus to the deadly prison on Devil's Island. But sympathizers leaked the truth in the newspapers, at dinner parties, in the legislature. "Families were split," writes Gordon Wright, "there were frequent clashes in the streets, and duels were fought daily."[10] The debate haunts the middle volumes of Marcel Proust's *A la Recherche du temps perdu* (cat. 197), the most remarkable novel the Third Republic produced, and much other fiction of the time.

Conservatives anxious to save the army's reputation, anti-Semites convinced that no Jew could be a loyal Frenchman, clericals seeing attempts to rehabilitate Dreyfus as typical for a regime lost to higher feelings—all closed their eyes to persuasive evidence of Dreyfus's innocence. The army's cover-up grew more desperate; forgery was piled on forgery. But liberal and left-wing politicians, emphatically seconded by a substantial number of French intellectuals, declared themselves committed Dreyfusards. Most militant among these was Emile Zola: in January 1898 he published an eloquent open letter to the President of the Republic in Georges Clemenceau's newspaper *L'Aurore*, charging the government with a vicious cover-up. This was the celebrated "J'accuse. . . !" the manuscript of which is one of the treasures in this exhibition (cat. 193). The dénouement, though delayed by more lies, was inevitable; all too slowly, Dreyfus's innocence was admitted and he was ceremoniously reinstated in all honor in 1906.

Having threatened to weaken the republic, the Dreyfus Affair in the end strengthened it. While reactionary and Catholic writers continued to trumpet anti-Dreyfusard slogans, and while chauvinist nationalists gained strength after the turn of the century, anticlericals and left-leaning politicians took advantage of the shame that the forces of reaction, including the army, had brought on themselves. Until the outbreak of the First World War, they remained in control of legislation. The separation of church and state, moves toward a permanent income tax, and increasing acceptance of trade unions and socialist ideas all followed—and in some measure profited from—the affair. Yet it would have been too much to expect that the notorious splits—economic, social and religious—that had produced the proverbial Two Frances, one clerical, the other anticlerical, would be eradicated. But the republic now seemed secure. Then came August 1914, when the war made everyone, including

Marxist socialists on the left and nostalgic Catholics on the right, into anti-German patriots.

From World War to World War

Many in France and elsewhere expected war, but none predicted that it would last four years and murder the flower of the youth among all contending nations. Before the World War was over, some five million Frenchmen had been killed or wounded and the economy devastated. The prewar world seemed increasingly unified by international trade and European diplomacy that was, on the whole, adroit. But there were also temptations to conflict: chauvinists (including the French variety) beating the drum, the naval race between Britain and Germany, clashes between imperial powers in Africa and elsewhere, the crumbling of the old Turkish empire on southeastern European soil. But potentiality became actuality as the Germans pushed their Austrian allies toward a bellicose stance in the Balkans and as they invaded neutral Belgium on August 3, 1914, to march toward Paris. President Raymond Poincaré proclaimed a *union sacrée* among all Frenchmen, as chiefs of state elsewhere rallied their citizens. For a time, it was a war of patriots against patriots, including socialists who had earnestly preached that workers belong to no country and that war can only enrich bankers and industrialists.

Inevitably, as the war dragged on and casualties mounted to horrifying totals, this unity—which writers and artists, setting aside their customary squabbles, actively fostered—began to fray. Offenses expensive in manpower and meager in results, the obstinate and essentially meaningless defense of Verdun, the absence of any signs of victory, revived old quarrels. In November 1917 the aged Clemenceau, known for his intransigence, was appointed premier and showed himself ruthless against even reputable opposition: war was no time for free speech, and criticism could be distorted into treason. Power triumphed, as so often before, over culture.

These conflicts were only exacerbated by the peace making. Clemenceau, who led the French delegation at Versailles, was attacked from all sides. Some thought his demands too harsh for a new Germany attempting to make itself into a democratic republic; others thought him too soft on a vengeful enemy only awaiting a chance to remilitarize. Nor did social and intellectual conflicts vanish during the twenty years before France went to war again. Communists, Socialists, radicals, moderates, conservatives, royalists, with a sprinkling of partisans of fascism thrown in, competed for public attention. And in the 1930s, with the Great Depression gripping the country, Hitler just across the border to the east, the Spanish republic in mortal danger to the south, and ugly scandals soiling the reputations of leading politicians, the energetic took to the streets. The unbuttoned partisan malice in the daily press did not abate. Looking back after the war, Raymond Aron, the political sociologist and astute observer of the public scene, said of the thirties, "In essence, France no longer existed. It existed only in the hatred of the French for one another."[11]

But high culture blossomed in France just the same—most impressively, of course, in Paris. Janet Flanner, who from 1925 (under the *nom de guerre* Genêt) wrote for the *New Yorker* a fortnightly column as acerbic as it was affectionate, called the city "the capital of hedonism of all Europe." Paris, she recalled decades later, "was still a beautiful, alluring, satisfying city. It was a city of charm and enticement, to foreigners and even the French themselves."[12] The way that foreigners, notably Americans–composers, writers, painters, would-be geniuses–flocked to Paris was a tribute to its vitality, its intellectual and erotic freedom. Gertrude Stein and her loyal Alice B. Toklas were only the best known among these Parisophiles. James Joyce's *Ulysses* was published in Paris in 1922, and Marcel Proust, fighting a brave rear-guard action against deteriorating health to rewrite and rewrite the galleys of his river of a novel, died there in the same year. It was in Paris that Josephine Baker made a sensation dancing in the nude, and in Paris that Picasso and Braque, though their breakthrough to cubism had predated the war, continued to experiment with the medium. The Symbolist poet and brilliant essayist Paul Valéry lived there (cat. 200), and the plays of Jean Giraudoux were first performed there. It was to Paris, too, that such great historians as the medievalist Marc Bloch and the Reformation specialist Lucien Febvre came to advocate and practice a new social history, a history that made its mark, to its benefit, on the profession across Europe and the United States. French ideas (not always happily) have always been a favorite export.

In 1936 France even saw an intellectual, Léon Blum, appointed prime minister. His premiership, which lasted only a year–as in earlier decades, cabinets came and went with distressing frequency–was a novelty: Dreyfusards had held this post before, but never a Socialist or a Jew. He attempted to govern with a broadly based Popular Front, to introduce long-needed economic reforms, and to develop a foreign policy adequate to the pressures from the dictators. It was hardly Blum's fault–though his hopes for working-class solidarity were illusory–that he failed at every point. The republic was too deeply polarized on domestic and diplomatic issues alike. When Hitler marched into Poland on September 1, 1939, France was not prepared, emotionally or militarily, to face him.

De Gaulle: Substance and Shadow

The next five years are among the most painful in a history which, though rich in glory and intelligence, was not unacquainted with disaster, folly, and cowardice. The "phony war" that succeeded Hitler's conquest of Poland gave the French government nearly a year's respite, but once the Germans invaded the Low Countries on May 10, 1940, France's doom was only a matter of weeks. On June 14 the Nazi armies entered Paris, and within days hastily negotiated armistices with Germany and Italy had taken France out of the war. Writing in 1940, Marc Bloch, soldier, patriot, unsurpassed observer, and Resistance fighter, was as severe as he was just, blaming his country's unexampled defeat on "the utter incompetence of the High Command,"[13] the passivity of France's elite, and the unwillingness of the bourgeoisie to educate the working classes in the pressing issues of the day.

The new regime installed at Vichy had little room for maneuver, and even less after the Germans took over the unoccupied south of France in November 1942. By then French republicanism seemed only a memory. The aged Marshal Pétain, and those speaking in his name, discarded the time-honored slogan of *Liberté, Egalité, Fraternité* (liberty, equality, fraternity) and substituted *Famille, Travail, Patrie* (family, work, country)–innocuous-sounding ideals, but in historical context a betrayal of the principles carried down from the French Revolution and a strong hint at an organic society uncomfortably close to the German model. Under the Nazi heel, the old Two Frances continued at war with one another, often literally so. At one extreme were the men and women of the Resistance, many of them slaughtered for their commitment to the France they loved (see cat. 203). Bloch, fifty when he volunteered, was only one Resistance fighter, and one of the bravest, to be tortured and shot. On the right were the collaborators, some opportunistic and others ideological, the latter welcoming Nazi doctrine and practice as a refreshing change from bickering parliaments, corrupt politicians, and the secular cosmopolitanism that, they thought, had poisoned the bloodstream of France. There were Frenchmen who happily turned over Jews, children and adults alike, to the Nazis making ready to ship them east for extermination–some even who anticipated their conquerors.

In the turmoil of France's collapse, though, one voice came to embody the hope that France would rise again, shake off the victorious barbarians, and restore to the country its lost dignity. That voice, of course, belonged to Gen. Charles de Gaulle. An officer whose modern ideas of warfare had been shunted aside by his superiors in the 1930s, he reached London on June 17, 1940, and immediately launched his broadcasts on the BBC. France, he insisted, had lost a battle but not the war. "Believe me, for I know what I am talking about and I tell you that nothing is lost for France," he said in his first address on June 18. "The same means that beat us may one day bring victory. For France is not alone. She is not alone! She is not alone!"[14] But for much of the time it was de Gaulle who seemed to be alone. At first, his message reached few French ears and found only limited responses among those it did reach. And the Allies, especially the Americans, harbored a deep distrust of this self-righteous rhetorician who might be a new Boulanger, if not a new Napoléon III.

Yet, as the war went on, it became clear, especially to the British, that de Gaulle was the man to rally, and eventually lead, his compatriots. After June 6, 1944, when the Allies made good on their promise of a second front in the west, de Gaulle's men took over the liberated territories. On August 26, after local citizens and troops had bravely defeated the German occupying forces, the general entered Paris. Sweeping aside attempts to proclaim a new republic, de Gaulle, unbending and imperious, proclaimed that the republic had never ceased to exist. Vichy had been but an illegitimate, appalling interlude.

Still, the unlamented Third Republic soon received an official burial, to be succeeded by the Fourth, in effect almost a carbon copy of the Third. It did little to still the partisan altercations that had so often paralyzed its predecessor. De Gaulle did not tolerate it long. In January 1946 he resigned as head of state, continued to advocate a strong presidential regime, and began thinking about his memoirs (cat. 204). His views, and his supporters, retained considerable prestige, and he was swept back into power in June 1958 after a rebellion of colonials in Algeria (led by French officers to thwart freeing that colony) produced a crisis at home. De Gaulle was the answer. He returned, and a Fifth Republic, a far more resilient structure, emerged with de Gaulle as its president.

One opponent de Gaulle had to deal with from start to finish of his political career was the French Communists. He was not unwilling to make strategic deals with the Soviet Union, but he had always seen the possibility of the Communist party, that willing tool of Moscow, taking power as a threat to be checked before it could gather steam. Yet the party secured, and long kept, a measure of influence in part because fellow-traveling intellectuals sustained its dubious ideology and even more dubious political course. This should surprise no one. In France, culture and power, as we have seen, were not only formidable antagonists but equally formidable allies. After the turn of the century down to its collapse with the Nazi victory, the reactionary Action Française had been influential among journalists and politicians out of all proportion to its numbers and in defiance of its contribution to political rationality.[15] And its left-wing competitor and deadly rival, communist ideology, exercised similar charms.

One reason, traceable to the emergence of the avant-garde in the days of Flaubert and Baudelaire, was the contempt of eloquent writers, artists, and philosophers for the bourgeoisie. They, and their twentieth-century heirs, made feverish attempts to flee the middle. Anything seemed better to them than the reign of mediocrity and vulgarity–even Hitler, some said in the 1930s and after; even Stalin, more of them said in those years. Just as some gullible visitors to Nazi Germany came back full of praise, so did more visitors to the Soviet Union. The political instability of the Third Republic, which masked the underlying equilibrium of the administration and (except during the Great Depression) of the economy, seemed an added reason for an infatuation with ideological solutions. The affection that generations of French had felt for Caesars, for men of personal charisma and simple solutions, and their secret–often not so secret–infatuation with the romance of violence, only gave this dangerous current of thought all the greater appeal. Hence apologias for Stalin's show trials and labor camps became a recurrent theme of postwar French intellectual life among writers and artists who preferred blindness in the face of overwhelming evidence to humble admissions of error. Jean-Paul Sartre was only the best known of these apologists, though it is important to remember that he did not speak for a majority of intellectuals. There were good Christians among them, solid republicans, humanists horrified by the notion that Lenin's prescription for political conduct–one must break eggs in order to make an omelet–should govern rational French men and women.

The much maligned Fourth Republic over whose demise de Gaulle presided had not been inactive. It had disentangled France from some of its untenable colonies in Southeast Asia and northern Africa, taken the first steps toward European economic integration, passed some much needed social legislation. But shifting voters' favor continued to underscore the difficulty of governing a nation of individualists with strongly held and clashing opinions, a difficulty that even de Gaulle's Fifth Republic could not quite overcome. Before his death in 1970, he had to endure continuing unrest in Algeria, a measurable decline in popularity, and, in May and June 1968, the *Événements* at the universities, when students took over streets in Paris and were joined by workers who started a massive strike. Still, when he died, even his detractors had to admit that he was what Hegel would have called a world-historical personality. "In his youth," Gordon Wright has written, "de Gaulle had arrived at the belief that destiny had chosen him to lead France in a time of crisis. Destiny—or chance—had done its work: de Gaulle had indeed led his country, and had left an enduring mark on its history."[16] The quarter-century since his death has shown that there is life after de Gaulle, in some respects rather different from what came before. But French independence in international affairs—critics would call it intransigence—and resurgent French pride show that the shadow of de Gaulle still lingers. Even someone not committed to Gaullism can admit that a country could choose a less creditable hero than this.

1 Quoted in Robert Darnton, *The Literary Underground of the Old Regime* (Cambridge, Mass., 1982), 1.

2 Rémusat, "La Révolution française," in *Critiques et études littéraires; ou Passé et présent* (1847; rev. ed., 1859), 102.

3 For a study of 19th-century Caesarism, see Peter Gay, *The Bourgeois Experience: Victoria to Freud,* vol. 3, *The Cultivation of Hatred* (New York, 1993), 235–65.

4 See Irene Collins, *The Government and the Newspaper Press in France, 1814–1881* (London, 1959), 1.

5 Rémusat, *Mémoires de ma vie,* ed. Charles H. Pouthas, 5 vols. (Paris, 1958–1967), vol. 1, *Enfance et jeunesse: La restauration libérale (1797–1820),* 278.

6 Hugo, preface to *Hernani,* signed March 9, 1830; in *Oeuvres complètes,* 15 vols. (1985–); *Théâtre,* vol. 1, ed. Anne Ubersfeld (1985), 539–40.

7 Alfred Cobban, *A History of Modern France,* vol. 2, *From the First Empire to the Second Empire, 1799–1871* (1961; 2d ed., New York, 1965), 131.

8 Collins, *Government,* 83.

9 Sand to Giuseppe Mazzini, May 23, 1852. Quoted in Roger Price, *The French Second Republic: A Social History* (London, 1972), 215.

10 Gordon Wright, *France in Modern Times: From the Enlightenment to the Present* (1974; 4th ed., New York, 1987), 250.

11 Quoted in Tony Judt, *Past Imperfect: French Intellectuals, 1944–1956* (Berkeley, 1992), 15.

12 Janet Flanner (Genêt), *Paris Was Yesterday, 1925–1939,* ed. Irving Drutman (New York, 1972), xx–xxi.

13 Bloch, *Strange Defeat: A Statement of Evidence Written in 1940,* trans. Gerard Hopkins (London and New York, 1949), 25.

14 Jean Lacouture, *De Gaulle: The Rebel, 1890–1944,* (1984; trans. Patrick O'Brian, London, 1990), 224-25.

15 See the comments in Judt, *Past Imperfect,* 297–98.

16 Wright, *France in Modern Times,* 429.

nᵒ 18 · a ·

8 National Collections and Private Donors

Florence Callu

During the Napoleonic era, French cultural life was largely a continuation of what it had been in the eighteenth century and would continue to be until the Restoration. The confiscations of the property of clergy and *émigrés* during the Revolution enriched the Bibliothèque Nationale's collections with a considerable number of volumes and documents of various origins in every area of knowledge.

Napoléon I's appetite for books and libraries is well known. The Bibliothèque Impériale was among his greatest concerns, as illustrated by the following note written in 1807: "We must be involved with the Bibliothèque Impériale, first to organize it. . . . The library must have able administrators: one administrator with the appropriate number of men under him." His intentions never came to fruition, however, nor did the move from the Bibliothèque to the Louvre that was so dear to the heart of the emperor. Nevertheless, in 1810 Napoléon permanently reinstated the *dépôt légal* (legal deposit), which had been eliminated early in the Revolution and made optional in 1793. The extraordinary seizures conducted during his victorious campaigns in Europe enriched the national collections, but most of the material was returned after the Congress of Vienna in 1815.

Even as the Napoleonic conquests went on, the traditional policy of the Bibliothèque Royale continued as it had been pursued under the Ancien Régime. The library acquired in many disciplines, accepting donations and purchasing old documents and collections of bibliophiles or scholarly papers. In 1801 the archives of the former Chambre Syndicale de la Librairie et Imprimerie de Paris of the seventeenth and eighteenth centuries were deposited, replete with hundreds of documents of extraordinary interest for the history of books. In 1804 the "Chansonnier de Maurepas" was purchased, comprising forty-one collections of songs and epigrams from the fourteenth to the eighteenth centuries, followed in 1806 by a Terence copied in the eleventh century. Curiously, the manuscript of Rousseau's *Nouvelle Héloïse,* offered for the price of twelve thousand francs, was rejected in

383

1805, even though the philosopher's widow had given some of his manuscripts to the Convention in 1794.

Under the Restoration, special funding was provided to the Bibliothèque Nationale as needed to purchase individual manuscripts: a Horace from the tenth century, the *Pontifical d'Egbert* from the eleventh century, series such as the charters of the abbey of Cluny, some of which had been sequestered under the Revolution, and even some incunabula on vellum, including the famous *Psautier de Mayence*, printed in 1457.

The July Monarchy maintained the same policy by receiving prestigious manuscripts–*Diurnal* by René de Lorraine, Gaston Phébus's *Livre de la chasse*–and by purchasing large collections such as those of Joursanvault (historical), Joly de Fleury (administrative), and de Soleinne (theatrical and literary). The collections of medals and manuscripts profited from scientific discoveries. A law of April 24, 1833, ordered the purchase of Champollion's papers, an indispensable monument for the Egyptology studies that were so fashionable at the time. On the whole, however, the first half of the nineteenth century was a precarious period for the library's management, confronted with a sudden influx of collections that there was no longer room to store. As a result of these poor conditions, it became very difficult to put the collections in order and to make them available to the public. The government's failure to act effectively exacerbated the problem.

As these periods of political instability drew to a close, the government regained control of the situation and played a decisive role in the reorganization of the library under Napoléon III. In 1857 the emperor gave the author Prosper Mérimée, who was then the inspector general of historical monuments, the task of chairing a commission that eventually took the necessary action. Moving the library to a different site was not an option, so in 1858 the commission decided to rearrange the original buildings to improve and expand existing space. The architect Henri Labrouste was commissioned for the project. In 1868 he completed the celebrated reading room for printed materials with nine cupolas and related storage areas.

The role played by Jules Taschereau within the Bibliothèque Nationale should be noted. As administrateur général from 1858 to 1874, his main task was to enact reforms and to make the newly designed grand library functional for its users. He also enriched the library with the collection of Eugène Burnouf, the Orientalist, and those of Payen (Montaigne) and de la Bédoyère (the French Revolution). The numbers of engravings and medals grew substantially, while the collection of maps and plans swelled under the impetus of the conservator Edme-François Jomard. It was under Taschereau that the first volumes of the *Catalogue général des manuscrits français* were published.

During the Third Republic, the Bibliothèque Nationale's influence was extended thanks to Léopold Delisle, administrateur général from 1874 to 1905. Acquisitions were stepped up in every department. Delisle added an impressive number of printed books to the collection, as well as new types of images made possible by technological advances, such as lithographs and photographs. (These are now housed in the Cabinet des Estampes.) Delisle was particularly fond of manuscripts, having served as curator of that collection for a long time. He purchased the Bible of Philip the Fair, many charters and diplomas, the Visigoth manuscripts from the Silos Abbey in Spain, and diplomatic and political correspondence.

In 1885 Victor Hugo bequeathed his manuscripts to the Bibliothèque Nationale, which he saw as the future "Library of the United States of Europe." Beginning with Rousseau and Diderot, writers had begun to retain their manuscripts instead of destroying them or giving them away. At the confluence of the philosophical doctrines of the eighteenth century and the romanticism that was blowing across Europe, Madame de Staël carefully preserved her manuscripts of *Delphine* and *Corinne, ou l'Italie* and even succeeded in saving fragments of *De l'Allemagne*, despite Napoléon's efforts to eliminate every trace of it.

For romantics, manuscripts in all forms—notes, drafts, and final versions that preceded the original edition—became an integral part of their intellectual universe. Collections of authors' papers tweaked the interest of bibliophiles beginning in the second half of the nineteenth century. It was then that the first private collections were established in France and abroad; the model is still the collection of Vicomte Spoelberche de Lovenjoul. It does not appear, however, that public institutions immediately shared this fascination. Hugo's bequest mobilized interest in literary manuscripts, and beginning in 1890 donations and bequests of papers by contemporary authors streamed into the Bibliothèque Nationale: Edgar Quinet, Ernest Renan, Adolphe Thiers, Edmond and Jules de Goncourt, Emile Zola, Anatole France, and Gustave Flaubert, to mention only the most renowned. Although the library welcomed these documents, no active manuscript acquisition policy was developed, and the library continued to place greater emphasis on adding to its existing collections than on acquiring new ones.

Not until Julien Cain's arrival as head of the institution in 1930 did the preservation of contemporary literary works gradually come to be seen as an equally important mission. The increasing scarcity of old manuscripts on the market was a major influence on this new outlook. The purchase of *Empédocle d'Agrigente et l'âge de la haine* in 1945 was quite an event, even if it was not one of Romain Rolland's major works. (Rolland's widow donated all of his manuscripts to the Bibliothèque Nationale forty years later.) Cain's determination to acquire modern works was further attested by the purchase of letters and poems by Max Jacob in 1950, followed shortly by works about surrealists. The new policy was firmly established in 1962 when Marcel Proust's manuscripts were confiscated by Customs, leading to a degree of interest by readers that has never diminished over the last thirty years.

Cain's policy survived his departure in 1964, and the library purchased works by such giants of French literature as Paul Valéry, Victor Ségalen, Jean Giraudoux, Paul Claudel, Colette, Albert Camus, and Jean-Paul Sartre. At the same time, prestigious donations and bequests continued: Apollinaire, Maurice Barrès, Roger Martin du Gard, Jules Romains, Georges Duhamel, General de Gaulle, Georges Bernanos, Georges Bataille, Raymond Roussel, Antonin Artaud, and the rich trove of about forty thousand letters received by Michel Butor. The French government created another means of enhancing the collections with the Law of December 31, 1968, which gave heirs the option of paying their inheritance taxes by donating art or similar objects to a public institution. Used extensively by museums, this procedure made it possible for the library to obtain the manuscripts of Roger Martin du Gard (1977), Marcel Proust (1984), and Simone de Beauvoir (1989).

Even as manuscripts become increasingly scarce with the growing use of word processors by some writers, depriving us of precious handwritten drafts, the library continues to acquire medieval manuscripts of exceptional quality. Among them are the *Missel d'Aix,* decorated with five full-page paintings by Enguerrand Quarton; the *Heures à l'usage d'Angers,* colored by the Master of Jouvenel des Ursins and enhanced with scenes drawn by Jean Fouquet; the *Heures de Jean de Châteauneuf,* entirely illustrated by Georges Trubert, Réne de Lorraine's painter; and the admirable *Guirlande de Julie.* None of these acquisitions would have been possible without substantial contributions from the Ministry of Culture's Fonds du Patrimoine (Patrimony Fund). The purchase in 1988 of an Arab astrology treatise, translated from the Latin into French at the request of the future king Charles V, founder of the royal "librairie," is a symbol of continuity. The return to the shelves of the Bibliothèque nationale de France of the sixty-fifth volume from Charles's library—recovered from the thousand or so collected by the sovereign and scattered in 1422—further attests to the eternal alliance between power and culture.

PARIS. — Nouvelle Salle de lecture de la Bibliothèque impériale.

387

ATLANTIC OCEAN

NORTH SEA

IRELAND

UNITED
KINGDOM OF
GREAT BRITAIN
AND IRELAND

London

English Channel

DENMARK

Copenhagen

Lübeck

Hamburg

Danzig

Friedland
1807
Eylau

Berlin

Warsaw
GRAND DUCHY
OF WARSAW

Cherbourg

Brest

KINGDOM OF HOLLAND
1806–1810

OLDENBURG
1810

BELGIUM
1797

CONFEDERATION

OF THE

RHINE

Leipzig
Dresden

Pillnitz

Prague

Paris

Fontainebleau

Nantes

MULHOUSE
1798

MONTBELIARD
1798

Neuchâtel
1805

1806

Bern

Munich

Austerlitz
1805

Wagram
1809

Vienna

FRENCH

EMPIRE

Geneva
1798

SWISS
CONFEDERATION
1803

CARINTHIA
1809

AUSTRIAN EMPIRE

Bordeaux

Lyon

SAVOIE
1792

Milan

KINGDOM OF

ILLYRIAN PROVINCES

Turin

Campoformido

ISTRIA
1805

Bayonne

Toulouse

COMTAT
1791

NICE
1793

Genoa

ITALY
1808

Belgrade

Nice

Toulon

Saragossa

Barcelona

Corsica

ETRURIA
1800–1807

Rome

Madrid

KINGDOM OF SPAIN

KINGDOM
OF
SARDINIA

Naples

KINGDOM OF
NAPLES
1806

Seville

Trafalgar
1805

MEDITERRANEAN SEA

THE NAPOLEONIC EMPIRE

French territory in 1789

French annexations between 1791 and 1804

French annexations between 1804 and 1812

Border of Cisalpine Republic

Vassal states of the empire

Confederation of the Rhine, 1806–1813 and

Grand Duchy of Warsaw, 1807–1815

Catalogue Numbers 162–207

162
Code Napoléon (Napoleonic code), copy printed on vellum

Réserve des livres rares, Rés. Vélins 994,
binding

*Paris: Imprimerie Impériale, 1807. 610 pp.; folio.
Contemporary embroidered velvet binding with
Napoléon's arms. Napoléon's own copy, "Cabinet
de l'Empereur" at the Tuileries; Bibliothèque Royale
at the Louvre after 1815; Musée des Souverains in
1852; transferred to the Bibliothèque Nationale in
1871.*

The French Revolution swept away the judicial structure, inherited from the Middle
Ages, that had remained virtually intact until
1789. Immediately after the coup d'état of 18
brumaire (November 1799), Napoléon took up
the project of French legal unification that
the revolutionary assemblies had failed to
complete. Drafted in less than four months
by a four-member commission whose work
Napoléon, as first consul, carefully scrutinized, then submitted for discussion and
revision, thirty-six legal texts were combined
and promulgated under the title *Code civil des
Français* on 30 ventôse, year XII (March 21,
1804). Reconciling Roman law and customary
law, the *Code civil* ratified the accomplishments of the French Revolution: equality and
individual and religious liberty. But in
affirming the principles of authority and
property, it also recognized the preeminence
of *notables* (propertied establishment). The
new code, which was more a monument to
Napoléon than to the Revolution, served as a
model for numerous foreign countries.

The rapid march, however, toward the
imperial monarchy and the creation of an

imperial nobility required modification of
the system of inheritance established in 1804.
A modified version of the *Code civil* was
therefore promulgated on Sept. 13, 1807, as
the *Code Napoléon*. The task of printing it was
entrusted to the Imperial Printing Office,
heir to the Royal Printing Office which had
been founded in 1640 to publish official acts
and which had enjoyed an excellent reputation for the quality of its work. From 1803 to
1815 the printing office was directed by the
Orientalist Jean-Joseph Marcel (who in 1807
drafted the table of contents for the *Code
Napoléon*). The press had already printed the
first edition of the *Code civil* in 1804, of which
three copies were specially printed on vellum, intended respectively for Napoléon, for
Cambacérès (1753–1824, second consul then
archchancellor of the empire), and for
Lebrun (1739–1824, third consul then
archtreasurer of the empire). When the second official edition of the code henceforth
called the *Code Napoléon* was printed, the
emperor, as sole master of France, received
the unique copy printed on vellum.

The *Code*, representative of the luxury displayed at the imperial court, is bound in dark
purple velvet embroidered in gold, silver, and
silk with the emperor's arms. An emblematic
motif is placed at the four corners of the
boards: the *Code Napoléon*, surmounted by
the imperial crown, and upheld by a sword,
is accompanied by a scale balanced by a
hand of justice and Charlemagne's scepter.

This volume, embodying the identification
that imperial propaganda established
between Napoléon and the code bearing his
name, was shown in the emperor's hand in
official portraits. The volume was deposited
in the Musée des Souverains at the beginning of the Second Empire, and thereby
escaped destruction when the Commune
destroyed the library of the Louvre in 1871.

Isabelle de Conihout

J. Van Praët, *Catalogue des livres imprimés sur vélin...*, vol. 3
(Paris, 1824), no. 58ter. A. Guillois, *Napoléon: L'homme, le politique...*, vol. 2 (Paris, 1889), 548. H. Beraldi, *La reliure du
XIXème siècle* (Paris, 1895), 12. R. Savatier, *L'Art de faire les lois:
Napoléon et le Code civil* (Paris, 1927). J. Imbert, *Histoire du droit
privé* (Paris, 1985), 80–96. Pierre Nora, ed., *Les Lieux de
mémoire* (Paris, 1989), vol. 2, s.v. "Code civil."

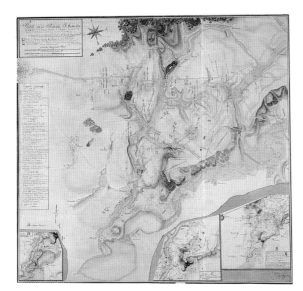

163

CALMET-BEAUVOISIN
Plan de la bataille d'Austerlitz
(Map of the battle of Austerlitz)
Département des Cartes et Plans,
Rés. Ge AA 585

*Paper; one hand-drawn sheet in color; 860 × 950
mm. [After 1805.] Purchased Dec. 1, 1863.*

Wars in the period of the French Revolution
and Empire conferred great importance on
maps because military operations required
exact topographic information. Map making
was especially intense between 1804 and 1811
and concentrated particularly on the regions
located beyond French frontiers where the
warfare constantly occurred. Although topographic maps made up the bulk of the production, geographers and military engineers
also created "war maps" to display military
operations. Some of the latter related directly
to military plans and consisted of maps
showing the advance of armies, along with
reconnaissance sketches; others were intended as a historical record of the fighting (battles and sieges) with a twofold objective: to
furnish the government with propaganda by
establishing "memorials of great actions" and
to provide a body of materials needed for the
tactical and strategic education of officers.

The battle maps of Austerlitz provide a
perfect example of this dual purpose.

Calmet-Beauvoisin, a captain in the corps of
engineers, drew a fine one with great care
shortly after the battle. The victory of
Napoléon I over the Austro-Russian armies
led to the break up of the Third Coalition
consisting of England, Austria, and Russia.
The battle therefore assumed great symbolic
significance for the Napoleonic regime, since
it took place on Dec. 2, 1805, the first anniversary of the emperor's coronation. Furthermore, the operations had been conducted
brilliantly. Occupying Ulm and Vienna, the
Grande Armée was perilously exposed, far
from its bases; with the threat of Prussian
entry in the war increasing, Napoléon needed an overwhelming victory over the Austro-
Russian armies entrenched at Olmütz. The
"battle of the three emperors" occurred
between Brunn and Austerlitz over a terrain
which Napoléon had reconnoitered and chosen. Having deployed his 74,000 men behind
the Goldbach, facing the plateau of Pratzen
which the enemy occupied with some 86,000
men, the emperor enticed the Austro-
Russian forces into his trap. Leaving a
reduced force to his right, he lured them
into flanking the Grande Armée from the
south to bar his route to Vienna; but by so
doing, they gravely exposed their center on
the plateau. Napoléon used his advantage to
strike at Pratzen and cut the opposing army
in two. His victory was complete and led to
the signature of the Treaty of Pressburg.

Nothing was spared to exploit this
resounding success. Starting in 1806 work
began on a relief map as well as on a smaller
engraved version of the battle plan destined
for wide distribution. Designed for military
instruction, the war maps were also intended
to represent accurately and precisely the various stages of the military action. Production
corresponded, in fact, with the first attempts
to represent the action and therefore the
chronological factor in the maps' dual

391

dimensions. For this purpose the engineers used several graphic techniques of which Calmet-Beauvoisin's map provides some samples: dotted lines and arrows of different colors to indicate various troop movements, the use of lettering (explained in the captions) to identify the successive positions of the same army corps, and reliance on insets to depict certain critical episodes of the battle (notably inset C: the capture of the village of Pratzen). Military cartography was also characterized by the attention given to all those factors about which knowledge is indispensable for successful military operations; rivers, streams and ponds, roads, irregularities of terrain (cross-hatching, tints), vegetation (woods, vineyards, marshes), and inhabited areas. The Napoleonic period was marked by increased simplification and uniformity in graphic modes of expression. The Topography Commission, formed in 1802 by the War Registry, laid down a number of rules for that purpose, thus preparing the way for the ordinance survey maps—the great invention of the 19th century.

Catherine Hofmann

Berthaut (Colonel), *Les Ingénieurs géographes militaires, 1624–1831: Etude historique,* 2 vols. (Paris, 1902). *A la découverte de la Terre: Dix siècles de cartographie,* exhibition at the Bibliothèque Nationale (Paris, 1979). H. Ozanne, "Etude d'une carte inédite sur les préliminaires de la bataille d'Austerlitz," in *Imago et mensura mundi: Atti del IX congresso internazionale di storia della cartografia* (Florence, 1981), 99–106. *Mémoire de l'armée, 1688–1988: Tricentenaire de la création du "Dépot de la Guerre,"* exhibition organized by the Historic Service of the Army (Paris, 1988).

164
Vue de l'arc-de-triomphe du Carrousel (View of the Carrousel Arch of Triumph)
Cabinet des Estampes, Ve 53c Rés., nos. 28–29

1 View of the east facade, seen from the Louvre; watercolor; 28.8 × 24.8 cm; lower left: Percier.

2 View of the south side; watercolor; 31 × 23.2 cm.

Built on a rectangular base 19.5 meters long by 6.54 meters wide, and rising 14.5 meters high, this triumphal arch was planned as the main entrance to the courtyard of the Tuileries Palace, and at the same served to commemorate the 1805 victory of Austerlitz (see cat. 163). It was the work of architects Charles Percier and Pierre Fontaine, in imitation of an arch erected by Emperor Septimius Severus in Rome.

The monument features three semicircular arches perpendicular to a transversal axis, with vault decoration of caissons and mezzo-relievo figures. The pedestals of the arches bear eight Corinthian columns of pink marble from the Languedoc region, which support an entablature adorned with six bas-reliefs. Above the entablature is a frieze with trophies and inscriptions glorifying Napoléon and his Grande Armée, victors over the Third Coalition. The top is occupied by a quadriga (four-horse chariot) originally featuring the four gilded bronze horses that Napoléon carried off from Saint Mark's Basilica in Venice as war booty during his Italian campaign of 1797–1798. The horses are

harnessed to a chariot in which stands Napoléon, flanked by statues of Peace and Victory.

A decree dated Feb. 26, 1806, announced the construction of the arch. "Title III, art. 8: A triumphal arch shall be erected to the glory of our armies at the grand entrance of our Tuileries Palace, on the parade ground. Art. 9: This triumphal arch will be erected prior to November 1; the works of art . . . shall be completed and set in place prior to January 1, 1809."

The architect was Pierre Fontaine, assisted by Charles Percier. Baron Denon, director of the Napoléon Museum (the future Louvre), was placed in charge of the artwork. A painter named Meynier was responsible for designing the six bas-reliefs and eight statues.

The first stone was laid on July 7, 1806, and the horses from Saint Mark's were hoisted to the top of arch in April 1808. The sculptor François Lemot produced the models for the statue of Napoléon and those of Peace and Victory.

The six bas-reliefs evoke the high points of the war against the Third Coalition, notably the *Capitulation before Ulm* (Oct. 27, 1805) and the *Victory of Austerlitz* (Dec. 2,

1805) on the east facade, and the *Peace of Pressburg* (Dec. 26, 1805) on the south side. The entablatures of the eight columns were topped by statues of soldiers of the Grande Armée, representing four cavalrymen and four infantrymen.

After Napoléon's abdication in 1815 and his imprisonment on Saint Helena, the Austrians reclaimed the horses from Saint Mark's. The marble bas-reliefs and the statue of the emperor were removed and replaced by plaster bas-reliefs evoking the Spanish victories of the duke of Angoulême (son of the restored king Charles X). In 1828 four new horses and a chariot were commissioned from the sculptor François Bosio, who also sculpted the figure of Restoration that drove the chariot.

Then, in March 1830, the Napoleonic bas-reliefs were replaced. Ultimately, only the main body of the monument erected by Napoléon remained, for the entire upper decoration henceforth glorified the legitimists, resulting in an intellectually disconcerting ensemble.

Françoise Jestaz

Charles Galbrun and H. Cornus, "L'Arc de triomphe du Carrousel," *L'Artiste* 1898: 250–72. Louis Hautecoeur, *Histoire de l'architecture classique en France*, vol. 5, *Révolution et Empire* (Paris, 1953). Marie-Louise Biver, *Pierre Fontaine: Premier architecte de l'empereur* (Paris, 1964). Geneviève Bresc and Anne Pingeot, *Sculptures des jardins du Louvre, du Carrousel et des Tuileries*, 2 vols. (Paris, 1986). *Clodion*, exhibition at the Louvre (Paris, 1992).

165

THÉODORE GÉRICAULT
Le Retour de Russie
(The return from Russia)
Cabinet des Estampes, Dc 141b Rés., vol. 1

*Watercolor over pencil on Bristol board and litho-
graph signed in the lower right-hand corner; 32.2 ×
23.7 cm and 50 × 39 cm. [Ca. 1818.]*

This work is at the heart of a series of studies on the misfortunes of war and the retreat
from Russia which was to result in the
famous lithograph entitled *Retour de Russie*,
executed around 1818. As Kate Spencer has
remarked, the two-tone lithograph "was
clearly exploring the painterly possibilities of
multi-stone lithography. . . as a special kind
of painting." Therefore, it comes as no surprise that the artist took up his subject again,
in this case in the form of a highly accomplished watercolor in which brown tones
dominate, as if to provide an absolute point
of reference for effects of color he tried to
obtain from lithographs. The subject is handled on the same scale and in the same orientation, which suggests an initial transfer of
the lithograph before adding the watercolor;
however, the lower portion of the scene has
been cut off, eliminating the field of snow,
the dog at the soldier's feet, and the horse's
hoofs.

Other drawings preceded or derived from
this most famous of lithographs by Géricault

(1791–1824). Two are ink drawings (in Rouen
at the Musée des Beaux-Arts, Chéramy
Collection; and in Paris, Ecole des Beaux-
Arts, M. A. Valton Collection), and one is in
gouache (private collection, exhibited at
Bernheim in 1957). Several preparatory studies are found in the sketchbook now at the
Art Institute of Chicago. The description
Nicolas Clément gives of this scene in the
catalogue of Géricault's lithography perfectly
summarizes the mood of heroic nostalgia in
which the artist conceived this plate, so similar to the *Cuirassier blessé* (Wounded cavalry-
man) of the same year: "In terms of lofty
ideas and sentiments, of poetic and dramatic
conception, this is perhaps Géricault's most
complete and most powerful work. It draws
on the same inspiration as the *Cuirassier
blessé*, but the execution is more skillful and
the inspiration is more grandiose and even
more heartbreaking. In the middle of the icy
plain comes a one-armed grenadier leading
by the bridle the exhausted horse of a blind
cuirassier whose left arm in in a sling. A dog
half-dead from fatigue is following them.
Farther to the right, there is an infantry soldier carrying his fellow soldier on his back.
These figures summarize in the most dramatic manner this horrible disaster. The expres-
sions on the faces are admirable and heart-
rending. One seems filled with resignation,
the other with deep pain and despair. The
Retour de Russie is one of those works of candid and powerful inspiration, and although
the figures appear to be a bit short, they are
of an admirable execution which captures
the eye and the imagination."

François Fossier

K. H. Spencer, *The Graphic Art of Géricault,* exhibition at the
Yale University Art Gallery (New Haven, 1969), 21. L. Eitner,
Géricault: An Album of Drawings in the Art Institute of Chicago
(Chicago, 1960), fol. 7. Not quoted in the catalogue of the
exhibit at the Grand Palais in 1991, *Géricault,* no. 63.

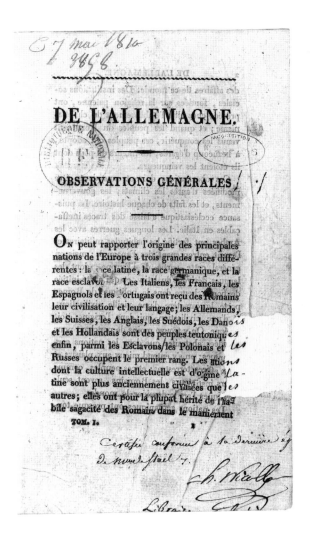

166

De l'Allemagne (On Germany)

Réserve des livres rares, Res. p. M. 149,
p. 1

*Paris: Nicolle, 1810; 3 vols.; 8ᵛᵒ. Contemporary
half-roan binding, with Portalis's monogram P on
the spine. Proof copy formerly belonging to Baron
Portalis, the director of the Librairie during the
First Empire. Acquired in 1926.*

Too attached to liberty not to make herself
non grata to the various postrevolutionary
governments, Anne Louise Germaine Necker,
Mme de Staël, the daughter of Louis XVI's
former minister of finances, owes her discovery of Germany to the exile to which she was
sentenced. Back in her Swiss château in
Coppet, she wrote *De l'Allemagne.*
"J'attachais un grand prix à ce livre, que je
croyais propre à faire connaître des idées
nouvelles à la France" (I set great store by
this book, which I considered an appropriate
means for introducing new ideas into
France).

In February 1810, she signed a contract
with Nicolle, a Parisian editor. He underesti-
mated the difficulties that Napoléon's hostility to Mme de Staël would cause and started
printing in conformity with the new demands
imposed on publishers by the reestablishment of censorship, regularly sending proofs
for examination to the Direction de la
Librairie, a body recently formed to keep the
written word under surveillance. But
Napoléon, whom Mme de Staël had mightily
annoyed, ordered his minister of police to
short-circuit the Direction de la Librairie
and have all copies of the book confiscated
directly from the printer, Mame. The manuscripts and the few proof copies available
were eagerly sought, although no manuscripts were found. Mme de Staël was refused
permission to travel to America and was
soon back in exile at Coppet. The emperor
complained that this book, one of the first
manifestos of romanticism and containing
vital insights into poetic mysticism, discussed
the customs and literature of the Germans
without devoting so much as a single line to
the glorious military exploits of the French
in Germany.

Four copies of proofs escaped destruction. This one was presented by Nicolle to
the Direction de la Librairie for scrutiny by
the censor and preserved by Portalis, the
director of the Librairie.

Having succeeded in getting to England
after a perilous trip across Russia, Mme de
Staël published a new edition in 1813, thus
opening, in the words of Goethe, "the first
breach in the wall of antiquated prejudices
which has been erected between France
and us."

Isabelle de Conihout

Simone Balayé, "Madame de Staël et le gouvernement impér-
ial en 1810: Le dossier de la suppression de 'De
l'Allemagne,'" *Cahiers staëliens* 19 (1974). Simone Balayé, *Mme
de Staël: Lumières et liberté* (Paris, 1979). Bernard Vouillot, "La
Révolution et l'Empire: Une nouvelle réglementation," in
Histoire de l'édition française, vol. 2 (Paris, 1984), 526–35.

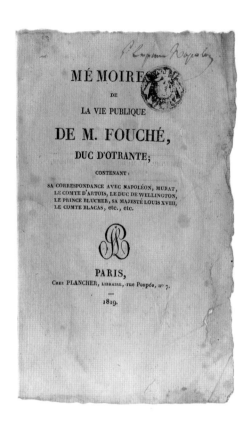

167

*Mémoires de la vie publique de
M. Fouché, duc d'Otrante*
(Memoirs of the public life of
M. Fouché, duke of Otrante)
Réserve des livres rares, Rés., 8º, La³³. 57,
title page, ex-libris

*Paris: Plancher, 1819. 158 pp.; 8ᵛᵒ. Stitched, blue
paper. From the library of Napoléon I on Saint
Helena. Acquired by the Bibliothèque Nationale at
public sale at the Hôtel Drouot, Nov. 13, 1956.*

Between 1817 and 1830 many books of
mémoires–true or false–were published
regarding the period of the French
Revolution and Empire, fascinating because
of the upheavals it brought. The *Mémoires*
exhibited here are a sort of defensive plea in
behalf of Joseph Fouché, then in exile in
Trieste.

Fouché was at first a teacher with the
Oratorians at Arras, where he met
Maximilien Robespierre before embarking
on a political career. Elected a deputy at the
Convention in 1792, he voted for the king's
death. After having been selected for a mission to the Nièvre, then to Lyon, he experienced a period of disgrace. Minister of police
for the Directory in 1799, he favored
Napoléon's coup d'état. His relations with
Napoléon were ambiguous: the emperor distrusted this minister who compiled files on
everyone and everything and who had the
know-how to organize a fearsome intelligence network. However, Fouché kept his
ministry post until 1810, at which time he was
dismissed for having conducted secret negotiations with England without Napoléon's
knowledge. He resumed his post again during the Hundred Days but negotiated at the
same time with Wellington, who persuaded
Louis XVIII to appoint Fouché his minister
and secretary in 1815. However, he was exiled
as a regicide in 1816 and died in Trieste
in 1820.

The *Mémoires de la vie publique de M.
Fouché, duc d'Otrante* differ from the
Mémoires de Joseph Fouché that were written
in part by Alphonse de Beauchamps and
published in 1824. The text exhibited here, of
unknown authorship, endeavored to put
Fouché's intrigues during the Empire in a
favorable light: how he had sought to protect
France and how he had tried to reason with
the emperor.

This copy bears Napoléon's signature and
the stamp of the library on Saint Helena,
which contained about 3,500 volumes at
Napoléon's death. Napoléon read voracious-
ly–he had even had a portable library constructed that accompanied him on all his
military campaigns–and he did not hesitate
to annotate his books. The *Mémoires de la vie
publique de M. Fouché, duc d'Otrante*, which
passes judgment on his reign, naturally provoked reactions, and the copy contains
numerous notes written in lead pencil: the
text is punctuated by exclamations–"quelle
plaisanterie," "mensonge" (what a joke, lie)
expressing his intense indignation.

Nathalie Renier

Louis Madelin, *Fouché* (Paris, 1901). Stephan Zweig, *Joseph
Fouché: The Portrait of a Politician,* trans. Paul Eden and Paul
Cedar (New York, 1930). Jean Tulard, ed., *Dictionnaire
Napoléon* (Paris, 1989), 214–15 and 746–51.

168

LONGUS

Daphnis et Chloé (in Greek)

Réserve des livres rares, Rés. Vélins 835, p. 20

Paris: Pierre Didot the Elder, 1802; 103 pp.; folio. Original drawings by Pierre-Paul Prud'hon and François Gérard, with nine engravings. English straight-grained morocco gilt by Charles Lewis, ca. 1823. Acquired in 1956.

Daphnis et Chloé, a novel written in the 3d century B.C. by the Greek writer Longus, owes to its rustic atmosphere and the delicacy of its psychological analysis a popularity such that we may call it an "unknown bestseller." The amorous intrigue that takes shape between two children found by shepherds has been often illustrated, most famously by Crispin de Pas in 1626, in the famous Regent's edition, with figures drawn by the great libertine prince in the early 18th century, and by Bonnard, Maillol, and Chagall in the 20th century.

In 1800 Pierre Didot the Elder issued a milestone edition of this classic. He was the scion of a dynasty of printers that revolutionized the aesthetic of the book in France by breaking with the rococo, introducing the new typefaces that still bear his name, and contributing to the introduction of new techniques, vellum paper, and stereotype. One of the family's finest claims to fame is the production of what may be considered the first artist's books: the illustration of the great classical texts sought by revolutionary France was entrusted to the foremost painters, heralds of the neoclassical style perfectly in harmony with the Didots' austere and elegant typography. Several rare copies on vellum were printed of these "classiques du Louvre"—so called because Pierre Didot had acquired permission to set up his printing press in the former royal palace—La Fontaine, Virgil, Horace, and Racine, illustrated by Fragonard, David, Gérard, Girodet, Prud'hon, or Percier, Napoléon's architect and decorator. The most precious of these copies was the one that included the original drawings.

As early as 1793 Didot had asked Prud'hon to illustrate *Daphnis et Chloé.* Exhibited at the Salon of 1796, Prud'hon's three remarkable drawings had to be supplemented (because he was so slow) by another six commissioned from another prominent artist, Gérard. The novel appeared first in French, in 1800, and then in Greek, in 1802. Five years later a copy was printed on vellum especially for the maréchal d'empire Junot, a bibliophile. This copy contained, in addition to the artists' proofs for the engravings, the original drawings done by Gérard and Prud'hon. Sold in England by Junot's widow after he had killed himself in a fit of madness, it was subsequently acquired by Watson Taylor, who had it bound by Lewis. This copy had been part of several important private collections before being reunited with the vellum collection of the BN in 1956.

Isabelle de Conihout

Jean Guiffrey, "L'oeuvre de Pierre-Paul Prud'hon," *Archives de l'Art français,* n.s. 13 (1924). Carol Margot Osborne, *Pierre Didot the Elder and French Book Illustration* (New York and London, 1985). Giles Barber, *Daphnis and Chloe: The Markets and Metamorphoses of an Unknown Best-Seller* (London, 1988). François Fossier, *Da David à Bonnard: Disegni francesi del XIX secolo dalla Biblioteca Nazionale di Parigi,* exhibition in Florence (Milan, 1990), no. 4.

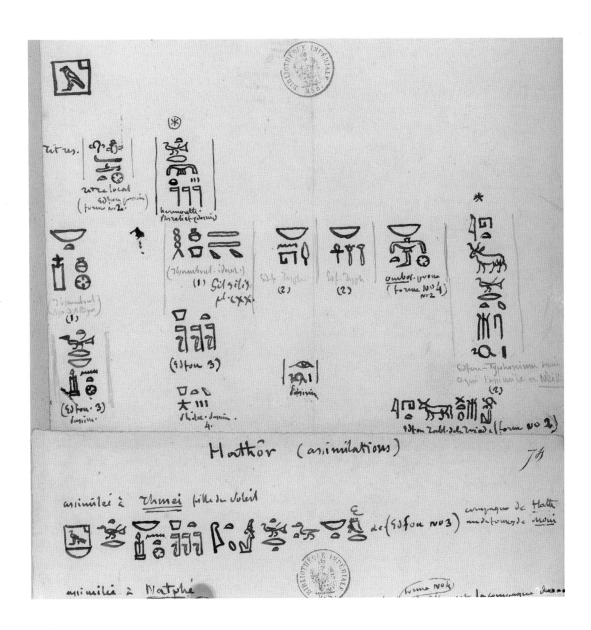

169

JEAN-FRANÇOIS CHAMPOLLION

Panthéon égyptien

Département des Manuscrits, NAF 20323,
fol. 88 (detail)

Paper; 314 fols.; 405 × 260 mm. Autograph manuscript. Paris, ca. 1815–1825. Entered the Bibliothèque Royale in 1833, with all of Champollion's papers, after a nearly unanimous vote of the two houses of Parlement.

Among the sixty-eight volumes containing Champollion's papers, including letters, travel diaries, and manuscripts of his works, five are entitled *Panthéon égyptien*. They represent the preparatory efforts for a work which its author hoped would be vast but which he published prematurely in 1825, prodded by the many people who were eager to see it in print.

This undertaking went hand in hand with the deciphering of hieroglyphics. Until then, information about the Egyptian religion could be obtained only from classical Greek and Latin authors. Yet Champollion was convinced that the hieroglyphics engraved and drawn around divine images on Egyptian monuments or papyri spoke of gods, describing their attributes and telling their story. Therefore, he thought he would obtain considerable information from them. And the more he read these documents, the more he discovered the richness, variety, and interest of the "panthéon égyptien."

After several genealogical sketches of gods, vol. 1 presents the beginning of an alphabetical catalogue. For each god there are the testimony of the classical authors, philological discussions, and excerpts from hieroglyphic texts taken from the works of early Egyptology or done by Champollion himself during time spent at the Museum of Turin. Some of the accompanying drawings are in pencil and others in pen intended for coloring, while still others are perfectly finished and ready for publication. Overall, this is an exceptional document, in terms of both quantity and accuracy of presentation and painstaking attention to detail.

Folio 88 reproduces the upper register of a stele of adoration from the Museum of Turin. It contains the principal symbols of one of the most widely known goddesses in Egypt, Hathor. On four columns of hieroglyphics there is the motto of the goddess: "Hathor, lady of the offerings, eye of the sun residing in its disk, mistress of the heavens, spirit of all the gods." To the right, a frontal view of a head on a pedestal, with cow's ears (a typical representation of the goddess), symbolizes fertility, as does the red *modius* above it. "Hathor" means "Horus's worldly residence," hence the building that dominates everything. In the middle, on another pedestal, a profile of a human head, crowned with a vulture (maternal fertility) on top of which is the *modius*, a sign of abundance. The side of the headdress is masked by the detailed illustration of a neck clasp on which figure the titles attributed to the goddess: Hathor thus also presides over feminine beauty.

Anne Boud'hors

Jean-François Champollion, *Panthéon égyptien* (collection of mythological characters from ancient Egypt, according to the monuments, with an explanation by M. J.-F. Champollion the Younger and the figures according to the drawings of M. L.-J.-J. Dubois) (Paris, 1823–1825; fifteen deliveries in 4to; repr. Paris, 1986). Hermine Hartleben, *Champollion: sa vie, son oeuvre*, trans. D. Meunie (Paris, 1983). Wolfgang Helck and Eberhardt Otto, *Kleines Wörterbuch der Ägyptologie* (Wiesbaden, 1987). Jean Lacouture, *Champollion: une vie de lumières* (Paris, 1988). Michel Dewachter, "Champollion au bout de son rêve," in *Mémoires d'Egypte*, exhibition in Strasbourg, Paris, and Berlin (Strasbourg, 1990), 173–99.

170

CHARLES PHILIPON

La Métamorphose du roi Louis-Philippe en poire (The metamorphosis of King Louis-Philippe into a pear)

Cabinet des Estampes, B 16, Rés. Philipon

Pen-and-bister-ink drawing; four sketches on one leaf: 247 × 217 mm. First head: 82 × 68 mm; second head: 86 × 74 mm; third pear-shaped head: 83 × 69 mm; fourth sketch (the pear): 95 × 81 mm (including the lines lightly drawn in pencil). Paris, November 1831. Signed "Philippon" [sic] in black or sepia ink, by a different hand in the lower left. On the reverse, a handwritten inscription in pencil: "Coursaget No. 2." Preliminary drawing for the autolithograph published in La Caricature *of Nov. 24, 1831. Gift of Pierre Coursaget to the Bibliothèque Nationale in 1992.*

Although W. Hofmann has discovered an earlier example of a pear-shaped caricature of Alexandre du Sommerard by J.-B. Isabey in 1827 (Réserve des Estampes), this in no way devalues the novelty of Philipon's "invention." After the Revolution of 1830, Charles Philipon (1800–1862) published *La Caricature* from 1830 to 1834, with lithographs by Daumier, Monnier, Traviès, and many others. He also founded *Le Charivari* (1832–1842) and created the character of Robert Macaire. Louis-Philippe, the "Citizen King," assumed a bourgeois lifestyle and strolled through Paris on foot with his gray hat and large umbrella. He was the target of republican caricaturists until censorship was reinstated with the laws of September 1835. The government filed proceedings against Philipon on several occasions from 1830 to 1835.

Philipon was hauled before the courts on Nov. 14, 1831, for having published an antiroyal caricature several months earlier. Entitled *Le Replâtrage*, it shows a mason plastering over the slogans of the "Three Glorious Days" of unrest that deposed Charles X and

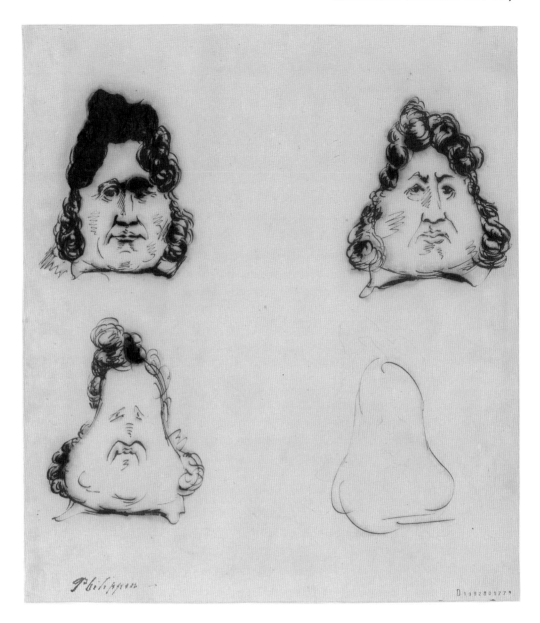

brought Louis-Philippe to the throne. "Il argua du fait que le maçon ressemblait au Roi, mais n'était pas le Roi. Pour appuyer sa démonstration, il dessina quatre croquis sur une feuille" (He argued that the mason may have resembled the king but was not the king. To support his case, he drew four sketches on a piece of paper) (Laure Beaumont-Maillet, 1993). Beginning with an accurate portrait, he gradually changed the monarch's face until he obtained the shape of a pear.

Philipon was sentenced to six months in prison and was ordered to pay a fine of two thousand francs. In all probability, this drawing is the first (incomplete) sketch, executed during the hearing while the judges were looking on. Philipon reproduced it as an almost identical autolithograph, finishing the fourth motif and explaining his defense in a handwritten commentary. The whole thing was published in the issue of *La Caricature* dated Nov. 24, 1831. The government immediately seized the publication! Another variant, *Les Poires*, was engraved on wood with a text printed in *Le Charivari* of Jan. 17, 1834.

The caricaturist extended the graphic tradition of Lebrun's heads of expression (the morphology of an animal transmuted into a human) and Lavater's physiognomonic theory. He based his innocence on the visual evidence of resemblance and then used the sequence of sketches to plead his case. This prototype of a pear, as a perfect symbol of the corpulent and soft king, met with immediate and smashing success.

The Département des Estampes has many lithographs by Daumier, Grandville, and

401

other press caricaturists in the portrait collection and the De Vinck Collection. In 1833–1834, at Philipon's initiative, Daumier replaced grease pencil with ink lithography, which matched the linear subtlety of woodcuts that appeared in the publication ("La poire royale," in *Le Charivari* of Sept. 7, 1834). The most striking images include *La Poire et ses pépins* (The pear and its seeds–i.e., the king's ministers) and the *expiapoire* ("ex*pear*atory" [expiatory]) monument at the Place de la Concorde. In a charming scene from *Les Misérables*, Victor Hugo took inspiration from two lithographs by Bouquet and Traviès in 1833, where two children were caught doing graffiti drawings of the king's head on a wall: "One summer evening, Louis-Philippe, returning home on foot, saw a child, a tiny one, only so big, who was struggling and stretching to make a charcoal drawing of a gigantic pear on the pillars of the Neuilly gate. The king, with the bonhomie reminiscent of King Henri IV, helped the child, completed the pear, and gave the child a Louis as he said: 'The pear is on the coin as well.'"

This historic drawing, the most famous of French caricatures, has just been acquired by the Bibliothèque nationale de France (Département des Estampes et de la Photographie), a generous gift of Pierre Coursaget in accordance with the wishes expressed by his father, the collector René Coursaget.

Claude Bouret

Werner Hofmann, *La Caricature de Vinci à Picasso* (Vienna, 1958; French trans. Paris, 1958), 32–35. Nicole Villa, *Collection De Vinck: Inventaire analytique*, vol. 6, *La Révolution de 1830 et la Monarchie de Juillet* (Paris, 1979), chap. 12, nos. 12, 249–370. James Bash Cuno, "Charles Philipon and 'La Poire': Politics and Pornography in Emblematic Satire, 1830–35," in *Proceedings of the Consortium on Revolutionary Europe* (Athens, 1984), 147–56. Ségolène Le Men. "Calligraphie, calligramme, caricature," in *Langages* 75 (September 1984): 83–101. Cuno, *Charles Philipon and La Maison Aubert: The Business, Politics, and Public of Caricature in Paris, 1820–1840* (Cambridge, 1985; repr. Ann Arbor, 1987), 193–258. Robert Justin Goldstein, *Censorship of Political Caricature in Nineteenth-Century France* (Kent, Ohio, 1989), 120–54.

171

FRANÇOIS-RENÉ DE CHATEAUBRIAND

[*Amour et Vieillesse* (Love and old age)]

Département des Manuscrits, Fr. 12454, fols. 25–38; fol. 34

Paper; 14 fols.; 210 × 170 mm. Bound with other papers of Chateaubriand, notably an autograph letter from Benjamin Constant to Mme Récamier (fol. 22). Half-binding. Autograph manuscript with corrections, [1829–1835]. Given to the Bibliothèque Nationale by Edouard Bricon, May 16, 1852.

The special affinity that unites political life and literature in France sometimes leads to contradictory if not comical situations. So what were the literary options of a convinced legitimist (or "royalist") in the early 19th century? If he wanted to be fashionable, he was supposed to write like a romantic, that is, sometimes showing a freedom of tone and morals incompatible with the moralizing Catholicism of his political opinions. Proust had not yet arrived on the scene with his distinction between a writer's social self and his literary self, thereby justifying certain hypocrisies. There remained, then, three solutions for our politically conscious writer: to present himself as a liberal legitimist (if such an association of terms is possible), lauding the principle of freedom of the press and claiming it for himself; to argue for a radical distinction between public life and private life and thus pretend that amorous adventure by no means signified political adventurism; or finally, an extreme solution, to arrange to have his most embarrassing works published only after his death.

Chateaubriand resorted, more or less, to the first two solutions. But it is to the last that we owe the *Mémoires d'Outre-tombe* (Memoirs from beyond the grave), a sort of time-bomb that he adjusted meticulously during the whole last part of his life but whose explosive power was such that excessive scruples made whole sections of it disappear even before publication. Not until the middle of this century was it possible to reconstitute the work in its entirety. The manuscript on exhibit here bears witness to this troubled story.

The manuscript belonged to a group of miscellaneous papers which were sold by Chateaubriand's rather unprincipled secretary to a certain Edouard Bricon, poet by trade and admirer of the great man. Seven years later, perhaps overcome by remorse, this same Bricon donated the treasure to the BN, and to authenticate its origin, without any pretense at shame, he attached to it the contract he made with the dishonest secretary. Nearly a half-century would pass before anything more was heard about the text. To be sure, on April 21, 1862, Sainte-Beuve had indeed cited an unpublished fragment from Chateaubriand in an article in *Le Constitutionnel*, saying that the wind had blown it to him through a "fenêtre entr'ouverte" (half-open window). But no one seems to have accorded any importance to this long citation. It was only in 1899 that the section in question was identified as belonging to the papers donated by Bricon. And from that time forward studies and commentaries have not ceased to accumulate about this mysterious passage.

For these few pages, no doubt written in the early 1830s – we do not know whether or not they belong to a primitive version of the *Mémoires d'Outre-tombe* – are unprecedented in the writer's work. In the first place, the narrator addresses himself to an unknown woman. Interpreters have worn themselves out trying to guess her identity in a sort of romantic litany: some have called her "L'Occitanienne" (the southerner), others Mme de C., Mme de Vichet, Mme de Villeneuve. . . . The list drawn up for the occasion resembles less a university work than it does the *mille e tre* from *Don Giovanni* and pays more tribute to Chateaubriand's talents as a seducer than to his commentators' intellectual virtues. No matter. Besides, that is not the crux of the question, and perhaps the factual commentaries unconsciously only seek to mask what gives this text such impact.

The usual title of the fragment, even if it is not the author's, indicates its originality: *Amour et Vieillesse*. Chateaubriand – or the narrator who represents him – has more than sixty years behind him. He is no longer the dashing young man who appeared in *René* but already an old man by the standards of his period. He can love; he still wants to. But does he still have the right? For to love is not all; he must still be loved. And then imagine, hour after hour, his mistress dying "de volupté dans les bras d'un autre" (of sensual delight in the arms of another). And then mentally devise the crimes that could assuage his torment. And thereby enrich French literature with one of the most perfect renderings anywhere of a lover's jeal-

403

ousy, before Proust's characterization of
Swann. . . .

It is indeed an intense text, an impassioned text, so unseemly that Sainte-Beuve thought it his duty to censor the largest part of the work, which, in his view, was worthy only of the *Song of Songs*. Perhaps he was not entirely wrong: in love, as in politics or literature, the most difficult thing for a great man is not to die but to grow old. For heroes grow old too. Finally, if the text had not been stolen at the outset by an unscrupulous copyist, would we ever have been privy to such an exercise in sincerity?

William Marx

Charles Sainte-Beuve, "*Le Poème des champs* de Calemard de Lafayette," in *Le Constitutionnel*, April 21–22, 1862; repr. in *Nouveaux Lundis* 2 (Paris, 1864): 257–60. François René de Chateaubriand, *Amour et Vieillesse*, facsimile, ed. Victor Giraud (Paris, 1922). Jean Pommier, "Le véritable texte d'*Amour et Vieillesse*," in *La Table ronde*, January 1946. Chateaubriand, *Mémoires d'outre-tombe*, ed. Maurice Levaillant (Paris, 1964). George D. Painter, *Chateaubriand: A Biography* (London, 1977). Charles A. Porter, *Chateaubriand: Composition, Imagination, and Poetry* (Saratoga, Calif., 1978).

172

LOUIS DE ROUVROY,
DUKE OF SAINT-SIMON
*Mémoires complets et authentiques. . .
sur le siècle de Louis XIV et la Régence*
(Complete and authentic memoirs. . .
on the century of Louis XIV and the
Regency), annotated by Stendhal
Réserve des livres rares, Rés., 8° Lb^{37} 216a
(1–21), vol. 1, pp. 392–393

*Paris: Sautelet, 1829–1830; 21 vols. in-8vo.
Contemporary half-roan binding. Former collection
of Emmanuel Modigliani-Edouard Kann (sale
1930), then of Mme Cotreanu. Purchased in April
1989 at the Colonel Sickles sale.*

In 1830 Stendhal finally acquired literary celebrity in Paris with the November publication of *Le Rouge et le noir* (The red and the black). Approaching age fifty, he was prompted by financial difficulties and by concern over his retirement to request a post as consul. After some troubles resulting from his liberal reputation, Stendhal wound up in April 1831 as consul at Cività-Vecchia, a depressing little port that belonged to the Papal States. To forget his boredom, he devoured Saint-Simon's *Mémoires*, which had just been published in an authentic edition based on the original manuscript. It was not Stendhal's first reading of the memorialist, as he recalled in *La Vie de Henry Brulard* (The life of Henry Brulard): "Mon seul plaisir en lecture était Shakespeare et les *Mémoires* de Saint-Simon, alors en sept volumes que j'achetai plus tard en douze, passion qui a duré comme celle des épinards au physique et qui est aussi forte pour le moins à cinquante-trois qu'à treize ans" (The only books I enjoyed reading were Shakespeare and the *Mémoires* of Saint-Simon in seven volumes, which later I purchased in twelve volumes, a passion which has lasted like a craving for

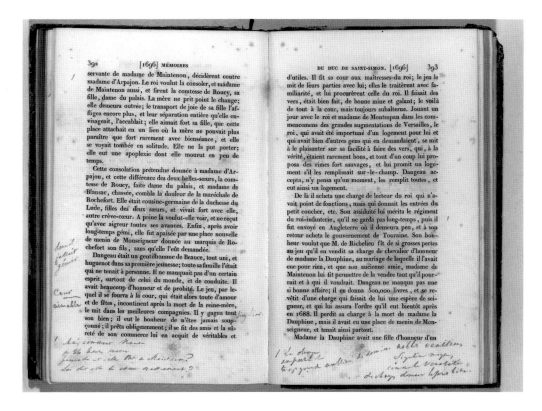

spinach and which is at least as strong at 53 as at 13). His advice to his sister Pauline testified to this longtime passion as early as 1804–1805: "Lis et relis sans cesse Saint-Simon" (Read and reread Saint-Simon constantly), as did notes and allusions all through his work.

Two copies of the *Mémoires* with annotations by Stendhal have come down to us: the Treuttel edition of 1791, which he read and reread from 1808 to 1818 and which is now in the Bibliothèque Municipale of Grenoble, and the copy which the BN acquired of the 1829–1830 edition in twenty-one volumes, of major importance because of its annotations.

More than a thousand annotated pages indicate the depth of Stendhal's three successive readings from 1833 to 1841 of his favorite historian during his last Italian exile. The notes relate to persons described, their character, and to court intrigues and morals. Stendhal's fascination with the memorialist became ever deeper. True, he reproached Saint-Simon for narrowmindedness and "ducomanie" (obsession with the aristocracy), but he constantly pays tribute to Saint-Simon's style and to his literary and narrative excellence. Stendhal also made autobiographical notes on the climate, on his trips,

and about his health. These marginalia replaced the diary that the author of the *Journal d'égotisme* (Diary of egotism) abandoned.

Saint-Simon's influence on Stendhal was unquestionable. It is revealed in his taste for ordinary events and the study of individuals (it is by reading memorialists, including the greatest, Saint-Simon, that "on tire le jus de la connaissance de l'homme" [one obtains a pithy knowledge of humanity]), as well as in Stendhal's characters and the political milieus portrayed in the great novels of the 1830s.

Isabelle de Conihout

Ferdinand Boyer, *Les lectures de Stendhal* (Paris, 1925). François Michel, *Fichier stendhalien* (Paris, 1964), 3:342–43. Théo Gieling, "Stendhal, lecteur de Saint-Simon," *Stendhal Club* 1964–1966: nos. 24–26. Stendhal, *Oeuvres complètes,* vol. 35, *Journal littéraire,* vol. 3 (Paris, 1970), 269–86. Stendhal, *Oeuvres intimes* (Paris, 1982). Michel Crouzet, *Stendhal ou Monsieur Moi-même* (Paris, 1990).

173

HECTOR BERLIOZ

Symphonie funèbre et triomphale composée pour l'inauguration de la Colonne de la Bastille et la translation des restes des combattants de Juillet. A son altesse Royale Monseigneur le duc d'Orléans (Funeral and triumphal symphony composed for the inauguration of the column of the Bastille and the transfer of the remains of the July combatants.

To his royal highness, monseigneur the duke of Orléans)

Département de la Musique, MS 1164, title page and Berlioz's signature

Score; 108 pp.; 33.5 × 26 cm. Manuscript partly autograph, 1842.

In 1840 "le gouvernement français voulut célébrer par de pompeuses cérémonies le dixième anniversaire de la Révolution de 1830 et la translation des victimes plus ou moins héroïques des trois journées, dans le monument qui venait de leur être élevé sur la Place de la Bastille" (the French government wanted to celebrate the tenth anniversary of the Revolution of 1830 with solemn ceremonies and with the transfer of the victims, more or less heroic, of the Three Days to the monument which had just been erected for them on the Place de la Bastille). So it was that Hector Berlioz (1803–1869) explained the circumstances which, after the Requiem, accounted for his second official commission from the July Monarchy. Berlioz had not taken part in the popular movement, since at the time of the insurrection (July 27–29, 1830), he was participating for the fifth time in the Prix de Rome competition.

He conceived his work in three parts. The first should "rappeler les combats des trois journées fameuses au milieu des accents de deuil d'une marche à la fois terrible et désolée qu'on exécuterait pendant le trajet du cortège" (recall the combats of the three famous days in the midst of the mournful accents of a march, at once terrible and full of grief, to be played during the passing of the procession). The second—in which an imposing trombone replays a theme from his unfinished opera, *Les Francs-Juges*—should "faire entendre une sorte d'oraison funèbre ou d'adieu adressée aux morts illustres au moment de la descente des corps dans le tombeau monumental" (should project the impression of a funeral sermon or farewell addressed to the illustrious dead at the moment when their bodies were being lowered into the monumental tomb). The third should "chanter un hymne de gloire, l'apothéose, quand, la pierre funèbre scellée, le peuple n'aurait plus devant les yeux que la haute colonne surmontée de la liberté aux ailes étendues" (sing a hymn of glory, the apotheosis, when, with the funeral stone sealed into place, the people would have before their eyes only the tall column surmounted by liberty with wings extended).

The composition, lacking string instruments because the musicians had to march, is related to the great musical compositions for open-air ceremonies that were all the rage during the Revolution. Berlioz himself conducted the work on July 28, 1840. "Notre scène était Paris, ses quais, ses boulevards" (Our stage was Paris, its quays, its boulevards), he wrote lyrically. Between Saint-Germain l'Auxerrois, the Place de la Concorde, the Madeleine, and the Bastille through the great boulevards, the *Marche funèbre* was played at least six times. As a matter of fact, Parisians heard very little despite the 210 musicians. Prudently, however, Berlioz had taken care to invite musicians and critics to the July 26 rehearsal in the Salle Vivienne. The work was played there

again on Aug. 7 and 14. Wagner enthusiastically attended one of the concerts. "Tout cela est neuf, beau, grand" (All of it is new, beautiful, great), Henri Blanchard would exclaim.

When he was requested some time later to write a march for the return of the Emperor Napoléon's ashes, Berlioz for lack of time refused and wrote to his father that he was very annoyed to have composed a short while before a "marche triomphale pour nos petit Héros de Juillet" (triumphal march for our minor Heroes of July) when it "eût presque convenu pour le grand Héros." (might almost have been suitable for the great Hero).

The original manuscript of the *Symphonie funèbre et triomphale* is lost: no doubt destroyed after the careful working through of the 1842 copy, exhibited here, in which the composer revised the orchestration and the third movement. Only the six first pages as well as the corrections and certain instrumental parts are in Berlioz's hand; the rest was done by his copyist Rocquemont. The text was written afterwards by Anthony Deschamps. The *Symphonie* was dedicated to the king's eldest son, who died accidentally that same year.

Owing to its somewhat special nature, this work is hardly ever played today. Richard Franko Goldman gave it an open-air performance in Central Park, New York, in 1947.

Pierre Vidal

Hector Berlioz, *Correspondance générale,* ed. Pierre Citron, vol. 2, *1832–1842* (Paris, 1975). *The Memoirs of Hector Berlioz... 1803–1865,* trans. David Cairns (London, 1969). *Revue et Gazette musicale de Paris* 1840, no. 47. Berlioz, *Grande Symphonie Funèbre et Triomphale,* ed. Hugh Macdonald (London, Cassel, and Basel, 1967). Jacques Barzun, *Berlioz and the Romantic Century,* 3d ed. (New York, 1969), 1:350–65.

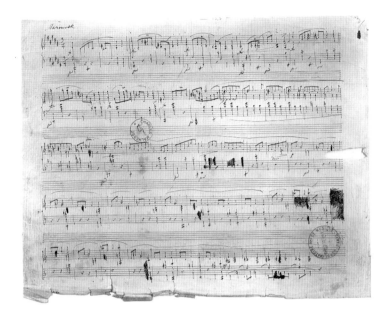

174

FRÉDÉRIC CHOPIN

Mazurka en si majeur, op. 63, no. 1

(Mazurka in B major, op. 63, no. 1)

Département de la Musique, MS 112

Original title: "Mazourek." Autograph manuscript; 2 fols.; 220 × 284 mm. Signed and dated: Nohant 1846 F Chopin. Stamp of Charles Malherbe. Written during Chopin's last stay at the château of Nohant in Berry before the break-up of his long love affair with the writer George Sand.

Chopin wrote nearly fifty mazurkas, whose thematic roots express the profound ties which, despite his exile, bound him to his native Poland. The last two compositions to occupy him before his premature and painful death in 1849 were two mazurkas (op. 67, no. 2 and op. 68, no. 4): "Je dois tirer des mazurkas de ce coeur lacéré" (I must draw some mazurkas from this broken heart), he would write to one of his friends.

This dance in triple time with a strongly accented second beat originated in the plains of Mazovia, a region in Poland. It was often based on folk tunes, which Chopin's harmonic genius transformed into an excuse for innovation and experimentation. In the op.

63, no. 1 mazurka he chose to write the central section in A major, one tone below the tonic B and not in a customary relative key, thereby creating a feeling of harmonic destabilization; hence the melody, woven around itself and often sustained by fifths, suggests the association between fife and tambourine present in other mazurkas.

Liszt spoke of these pieces as "tableaux de chevalet" (easel paintings) while Schumann called the mazurka "une petite forme d'art" (a little art form). This indicates the mazurka's importance in the history of 19th-century piano music, in spite of its brevity and unspectacular pianistic technique, as compared with the polonaise and other forms Chopin used.

Chopin's mazurkas were to inspire a plentiful production of salon pieces that Parisian music publishers sold in the second half of the 19th century. However, none of the imitators approached either the grace, the studied simplicity, or the originality of these little jewels.

This autograph manuscript reveals the care with which Chopin set down markings for shading, phrasing, and tempo, as well as use of the pedal.

Previously regarded as a symbol of the romantic artist—a salon hero torn between unhappy loves and nostalgia for a lost homeland—Chopin has acquired quite another dimension, thanks to modern historical research. This independent artist who earned his living as a virtuoso, from the lessons he gave, and from the publication of his compositions, profoundly changed not only piano music but also musical language in its most fundamental elements of form and aesthetics, opening the way to the 20th century.

Catherine Massip

Camille Bourniquel, *Chopin* (Paris, 1957). Krystyna Kobylanska, *Manuscripts of Chopin's Works: Catalogue* (Krakow, 1977), no. 836.

175

GUSTAVE LE GRAY

*Portrait of Prince-President Louis-
Napoléon Bonaparte*

Cabinet des Estampes, Eo 13 fol., vol. 1

*Salt print from a paper negative; 203 × 144 mm;
signed (stamp). Paris, 1851–1852.*

Gustave Le Gray (1820–1882), a photographer
of superior talent, did not excel in portraiture, but in this instance he put his name to
a beautiful portrait. The circumstances under
which it was produced are unknown. However, in 1856, shortly after the crown prince
Eugène was born, Le Gray took a series of
portraits of Empress Eugénie, beautiful and
majestic on her prie-dieu surrounded by the
floods of lace from her dress. In 1857, the
military camp at Châlons again afforded him
the opportunity of giving a masterful demonstration of his talents. This bit of reporting
on the occasion of the emperor's visit–if not
done at the emperor's request, then at least
with his approval–was proof that the earlier
portrait of the prince-president was appreciated by him. It is true that it was better than
most of the photographs of Louis-Napoléon,

who posed obligingly for the lens. This portrait might even be preferred to the fine
painting by Hippolyte Flandrin, for photographic realism converges here with psychological verity. Moreover, the calotype's slightly
misty technique is nicely matched to the
rather foggy personality of the future sovereign with that strange gaze which struck
everyone who came near him.

This portrait was the first of a series of
photographic portraits of French statesmen,
although it did not immediately become the
model for them, doubtless owing to the still
uncertain political status of the pretender in
1852 when the photo was taken.

Louis-Napoléon is seated rather than
standing, probably the better to convey his
unproclaimed right to the throne, hinted at
by the Empire-style armchair. The composition tends to the hieratic–appropriate for a
sovereign haloed in the radiance of the
Napoleonic legend–but the disturbed
frontality (the somewhat casual oblique angle
of the legs) also reminds us that the prince,
"glissé dans l'habit du premier consul" (having slipped into the attire of the first consul),
is for the time being a president elected for
ten years. Everything in this print points to
the reestablishment of the empire by this
man who had perhaps not yet really made up
his mind.

Bernard Marbot and Sylvie Aubenas

*Regards sur la photographie en France au XIXe siècle: 180 chefs-
d'oeuvre de la Bibliothèque Nationale*, exhibition catalogue
(Paris, 1980), nos. 79–84. *Le corps et son image*, exhibition catalogue (Paris, 1986), 133. Eugenia Parry Janis, *The Photography
of Gustave Le Gray* (Chicago, 1987), 91 and 101.

176

HONORÉ DAUMIER

Grand défilé de l'armée qui vient d'être levée pour entreprendre la fameuse expédition de Rome à l'intérieur (Grand procession of the army that has just been raised to undertake the great expedition to Rome in the interior; Paris, 1850)

Cabinet des Estampes, B 16b Rés.

Shows the representatives of the majority in the legislative body. Charcoal, blender, black chalk, highlights with pen and brown ink; 318 × 494 mm; unsigned. Maison 823. Preliminary study for the lithograph Grand défilé de l'armée... , *published in* Le charivari, *July 6, 1850. Acquisition 67833 in 1977.*

The Revolution of 1848 in France provoked chain reactions all across Europe and, when it spread into Italy, unleashed the war of national unity. The French government decided to send an expeditionary army to Rome during the summer of 1849. This foreign policy initiative divided the Assemblée and created conflict between the majority of moderate Republicans who were favorable to intervention and the minority of the "Montagne," led by Ledru-Rollin. In 1848 and 1849, Louis-Napoléon relied on the partisans of order, a political coalition of Orléanists, legitimists, and Catholics. Thus, under the influence of Thiers, laws were enacted aiming at strengthening moral foundations and at reestablishing social peace (for example, the Falloux Law of March 1850). Universal suffrage was modified by effective restrictions (Electoral Law of May 31, 1850). In July 1850, the imposition of an obligatory bond and stamp delivered a severe blow to freedom of the press. That explains why Daumier made ironic allusion to the Rome expedition of the preceding year and doubly ridiculed the docile and easily manipulated attitude of the defenders of the moral order who had not changed ("Rome à l'intérieur" means Paris).

From this moment on there was open rivalry between the majority of the Assemblée, which tended toward the overturn of the Republic in favor of a restoration of the monarchy, and Louis-Napoléon, who wanted to strengthen his power by drawing closer to the people and by disapproving the Assemblée's reactionary measures. In Daumier's drawing and in his lithograph, the marquis de La Rochejacquelin, leader of the legitimists, is depicted at the head of a grotesque group. Thiers is there, a tiny silhouette, followed by representatives of the press (*Le Constitutionnel* and *L'Assemblée nationale*); farther behind, Baroche, attorney general of the Republic, then Léon Faucher, minister of the interior. Véron, present in the drawing, would be replaced in the lithograph. Montalembert, Falloux, and the lawyer Berryer are identifiable in the second group.

Daumier (1808–1879) drew directly on stone and so his paper sketches, which were preliminary to the lithograph, are extremely rare. Another instance which is just as exceptional can be cited, the "Grrrrand Déménagement du Constitutionnel," a study for the 1846 lithograph. Here the composition and the dimensions are very close to the lithograph (Delteil 1979: 261 × 448 mm), but numerous details differ in the execution, which seems to exclude the hypothesis that the drawing was transferred directly to the limestone. The power and spontaneous quality of the style and the movement of the processional body are more dynamic in the drawing. In the lithograph Daumier strove harder to individualize the facial resemblances. Technical examination reveals a composition in three stages: a tracing in charcoal, a reprise in black chalk, and some parts made more distinct with pen. As Arsène Alexandre tells us, the artist often sketched his subject in charcoal right onto the stone before fixing the final lines with a grease pencil.

This work, long known, appeared in the 1923 exhibition *Daumier et Gavarni* in the Maison de Victor Hugo. It was acquired for the Viau collection at the June 1, 1932, Hôtel Drouot sale in Paris. Maurice Loncle purchased it at the Dec. 8, 1966, sale at Drouot. Finally, the Bibliothèque Nationale exercised its right of preemption at the Loncle sale on Nov. 22, 1977, also at Drouot.

Claude Bouret

Jean Adhémar, *Honoré Daumier* (Paris, 1954). Karl Eric Maison, *Honoré Daumier: Catalogue Raisonné of the Paintings, Watercolours, and Drawings* (London, 1968), vol. 2, no. 823. *Nouvelles de l'estampe* 46–47 (July–October 1979), special issue on Daumier, reprod. p. 25. Roger Passeron, *Daumier témoin de son temps* (Paris and Fribourg, 1979). Bruce Laughton, "Some Daumier Drawings for Lithographs," *Master Drawings* 22, no. 1 (Spring 1984). François Fossier, *Da David à Bonnard: Disegni francesi del XIX secolo dalla Biblioteca Nazionale di Parigi,* exhibition in Florence (Milan, 1990), no. 46, pp. 112–13.

411

177

EDOUARD-DENIS BALDUS

La Bibliothèque impériale du Louvre
(The Imperial Library at the Louvre)

Cabinet des Estampes, Eo 7a grand folio,
vol. 2

Albumen print from wet collodion on glass nega-
tive; 442 × 344 mm; signed. Paris, ca. 1855.

178
CHARLES MARVILLE
L'Hôtel de Ville de Paris
(Paris City Hall)
Cabinet des Estampes, Eo 8 grand folio,
vol. 3

Albumen print from wet collodion on glass negative; 485 × 390 mm; signed. Paris, ca. 1860.

Edouard-Denis Baldus (1813–1882) and Charles Marville (1816–after 1879) both studied painting, both were dissatisfied, and both turned to photography early in the Second Empire. Official commissions were forthcoming and they specialized in photographing architecture and monuments.

In 1851 the Historical Monuments Commission asked Baldus to photograph the threatened architectural treasures of Burgundy, Dauphiné, and Provence. From 1854 to 1856, at the request of the Ministry of the Interior, he reported on the construction of Lefuel's new Louvre, reproducing in particular the sculptures and decorative motifs. In this overview of the library's facade, looking out onto the rue de Rivoli, the full sun that splashed the stones was skillfully used to highlight the rich ornamentation. The three doors still obstructed with scaffolding, in

contrast to the stunning whiteness of the facade punctuated with the imperial *N*, attest to the fact that this was a testimonial to the construction of the palace. Is it because it was a working document that the artist tolerated a prosaic horse cart in the foreground? Did he use it to indicate scale, as was frequently done, or did he take advantage of the opportunity to temper the excessive rigidity of the rest of the picture using this living component?

The same sensitivity is found in the photo of the Paris Hôtel de Ville (City Hall) by Marville. After numerous voyages throughout France and Europe from 1851 to 1858 on behalf of Blanquart-Evrard, a printer-publisher who distributed about one hundred of his photos, Marville still never stopped taking photos of Paris. For the city, beginning in 1858, he took pictures of the old streets destined to disappear during the urban renewal directed by Haussmann. He left behind several pictures of City Hall, expanded between 1837 and 1871, burned during the Commune, and then rebuilt from 1874 to 1882. In this view of the oldest, central part of the facade, the richly sculpted Renaissance décor seems carved out by the light projected by the anachronistic street lamps onto the stones, while several pedestrians and an open carriage, as in Baldus's work, give the building a human scale. The plethora of details is tempered by the implacable symmetry of the whole, reflected in the framing and the central axis established by the little belfry, the clock, and the equestrian statue.

These two commissioned photographs of the places where imperial power was exercised do not appear cold or servile; rather, they demonstrate the sensitive virtuosity that masters such as Baldus and Marville had succeeded in attaining.

Sylvie Aubenas

413

Charles Marville: Photographe de Paris de 1851 à 1879, exhibition catalogue (Paris, 1980). *La Mission héliographique: Photographies de 1851*, exhibition catalogue (Paris, 1980), 33–51. Isabelle Jammes, *Blanquart-Evrard et les origines de l'édition photographique française* (Geneva and Paris, 1981). *La photographie comme modèle: Aperçu du fonds de photographies anciennes de l'Ecole des Beaux-Arts*, exhibition catalogue (Paris, 1982), 45–71 and 96–102. Françoise Heilbrun and Philippe Néagu, "Baldus: Paysages, architectures," *Photographies*, test issue (Winter 1982–1983): 60–83.

¹79

RODOLPHE BRESDIN

Abd el-Kader secourant un chrétien, or
Le Bon Samaritain

(Abd el-Kader caring for a Christian,
[or] The Good Samaritan)

Cabinet des Estampes, Ef 362 fol. Rés., vol. 1

*Pen-and-wash drawing in India ink on Bristol
board; 418 × 255 mm. Toulouse, 1860. Signed and
dated "Rodolphe Bresdin/1860." Monogram RB on
the camel's leg. Embossed stamp in the lower right:
"Reichmann marchand de dessin, 15 rue Saint-
Benoît à Paris." Van Gelder, 1:73. Preparatory study
for the lithograph* The Good Samaritan *(Van
Gelder, no. 100). Purchased from Paul Prouté on
Dec. 31, 1947.*

As surprising as it may seem, this magnificent drawing by a reclusive engraver is a
significant testimonial of French foreign policy and cultural patronage under the Second
Empire. Bresdin (1822–1885) exhibited six
compositions at the Salon of 1861, including
the following two: "413. Abd el-Kader secourant un chrétien (lithograph)./414. Same
subject (drawing done in 1859 and dated
1860)."

The subject must be understood in the
context of French colonial politics, notably
the conquest of Algeria beginning in 1830. It
should also be related to the evolution of the
popular image of Emir Abd el-Kader from
1836 onward. Before 1847, the Arab chief was
perceived as the fiercest adversary of the

French. In 1847 he was taken prisoner and was suddenly portrayed as a noble patriot. His legendary figure was depicted by the likes of Gustave Doré, Horace Vernet, and Jean-Baptiste Carpeaux. The myth took on a new dimension when the future Napoléon III freed Abd el-Kader from the château d'Amboise and officially met with him in Saint-Cloud in October 1852. From that moment on, Abd el-Kader became a friend of France. His fate as a valiant loser was even compared to that of Napoléon I. In the late 1850s the emperor allowed him to retire to Syria. In June 1860, when the Druses invaded Syria and massacred the Maronites of Damascus, the former emir managed to repel the fanatics and, from July 9 to 16, saved eleven thousand Christians. Numerous engravings recount this act of bravery, such as the image d'Epinal entitled *Abd el-Kader arrive au secours des chrétiens* (comes to the aid of the Christians).

Bresdin undoubtedly chose his title at that time. It is perhaps worth mentioning the role played by Princess Mathilde, Napoléon III's cousin. She received authors such as Taine, Renan, Gautier, Flaubert, Saint-Beuve, and the Goncourt brothers in her salon, not to mention artists such as Gavarni, Hébert, Meissonier, and Eugène Giraud. Her sobriquet was "Notre Dame des Arts" (Our Lady of the Arts) and she relied on Nieuwerkerke, the powerful director of the Administration des Beaux-Arts, to support artists. During the early years of the Second Empire, Abd el-Kader was a frequent guest at her private residence, impressing Parisian society by his superb clothing and his Muslim seriousness. It should be added that, on the recommendation of Champfleury (author of a book about Bresdin entitled *Chien-Caillou*) in the summer of 1860, Princess Mathilde paid a handsome sum to the engraver to encourage him. The needy artist then decided to thank his benefactor by giving her his largest print,

which had been an instant hit and his best-selling work.

Van Gelder has described the genesis of the lithograph, the product of this drawing and many other painstaking studies of camels (Washington, National Gallery of Art) and lush vegetation (The Hague, Gemeentemuseum). This beautiful drawing, a success in its own right, is sufficient to show Bresdin's incomparable mastery of graphics. Even more than the lithograph, it reveals a taste for Oriental motifs fostered by Napoléon III's foreign policy. But for Bresdin this merely served as the point of departure for a multifarious transformation of the landscape. He elaborated teeming foliage, enlarged the format, and packed the composition with other animals and strange details. This metamorphosis enlightens us as to the engraver's paradoxical genius; at the very moment he sought and attained public recognition by way of a political subject, the artist tended to project his inner universe through a sort of concentric proliferation that was not only expansive and pantheistic in nature but also instinctively served as protective clothing for his innermost being.

The Département des Estampes has many drawings by Bresdin. François Fossier has listed seventeen that were certainly his and ten more that are attributed to him (*De David à Bonnard*, 1990). Of this total group, which includes major works, twenty-four were purchased from Paul Prouté on Dec. 31, 1947.

Claude Bouret

415

Rodolphe Bresdin, *Le bon Samaritain,* 1st ed. (1861) (proof from the E. Chausson sale, acq. 9188), Van Gelder, no. 100. Jacques de La Faye, *La Princesse Mathilde (1820–1904)* (Paris, 1928). D. Bernasconi, "Mythologie d'Abd el-Kader dans l'iconographie française au XIXe siècle," *Gazette des Beaux-Arts,* January 1971: 51–60. Dirk Van Gelder, *Rodolphe Bresdin,* 2 vols. (The Hague and Paris, 1976). *L'Art en France sous le Second Empire,* exhibition at the Grand Palais (Paris, 1979). François Fossier, "Rodolphe Bresdin: Un graveur solitaire," *Dossiers du Musée d'Orsay* 40 (1990). Bruno Etienne, *Abdelkader: Isthme des isthmes (Barzakh al-barazikh)* (Paris, 1994).

180

VICTOR HUGO

Les Misérables

Département des Manuscrits, NAF 13483,
fol. 9 (above); NAF 13379, fol. 688 (opposite)

*Paper; 2 vols. (NAF 13379–13380); 945 and 828 fols.;
290 × 240 mm. Bindings in full white parchment,
title and author's name in red letters; bindings
restored in the style of those which Hugo had made
on Guernsey by his binder, Turner, May 4–7, 1869.
Autograph manuscript. Bequest of Victor Hugo to
the Bibliothèque Nationale; in the estate inventory
drawn up by the notary, Maître Gâtine, the manuscript bears the call number 84.*

When *Les Misérables* was published, thirty
years had elapsed since Victor Hugo had
imagined the project. Begun in November
1845, the writing of *Les Misères* (Misfortunes)
was interrupted in 1848 when the revolution
broke out, and then again by the political
activity in which Hugo was engaged. It was
on Guernsey in 1860 that the poet revised
the first four parts written before the exile,
recording in little notebooks the additions
and modifications to be applied to the novel.
Then he launched into the writing of a fifth
part, specifying in his manuscript: "Ici le pair
de France s'est interrompu et le proscrit a
continué 30 déc. 1860" (Here the peer of
France broke off and the exile continued
Dec. 30, 1860). Finally, on July 1, 1861, the

author could write to Hetzel: "*Les Misérables*
sont finis, mais ne sont pas terminés" (*Les
Misérables* is concluded but not finished).

As early as 1848 the framework of the
novel was defined. It would be "l'histoire
d'un saint/l'histoire d'un homme/l'histoire
d'une femme/l'histoire d'une poupée" (the
story of a saint, the story of a man, the story
of a woman, the story of a doll). The central
character of the novel is Jean Valjean, former
convict, who owes his salvation to Monseigneur Myriel, bishop of Digne. With Fantine,
Hugo addressed the issue of the redemption
of prostitutes, victims of society. It was a
recurrent theme in Hugo's work from *Marion
Delorme* to *Chants du crépuscule*: "Oh! n'insul-
tez jamais une femme qui tombe!" (Never
insult a fallen woman!). The character of
Cosette brings charm and freshness. (In an
album used in 1864–1865, Hugo sketched a
portrait of a little girl, perhaps an evocation
of Cosette as a child: BNF NAF 13345, fol. 50).
Revolving around them are also the figures
of Gavroche, the Paris street urchin, full of
cocky humor (whose portrait Hugo traced in
a notebook used in 1869: BNF NAF 13483, fol.
9), Javert the implacable police inspector,
Thénardier, and especially the impassioned
Marius, whose attributes are indeed those
of the author. Hence Marius, like Hugo, was
successively royalist, Bonapartist, and
republican.

Long expository passages were inserted in
the text, on the convent of Picpus, on slang,
on the sewers of Paris, or on the battle of
Waterloo (where, in his concern for historical
truth, Hugo completed the novel in 1861).
Through this apparent diversity Hugo pursued a unique plan announced in the preface: "Tant qu'il existera, par le fait des lois et
des moeurs, une damnation sociale créant
artificiellement, en pleine civilisation, des
enfers, . . . tant que les trois problèmes du
siècle, la dégradation de l'homme par le pro-
létariat, la déchéance de la femme par la
faim, l'atrophie de l'enfant par la nuit, ne
seront pas résolus. . . des livres de la nature
de celui-ci pourront ne pas être inutiles" (As
long as social condemnation exists because
of laws or customs which artificially create

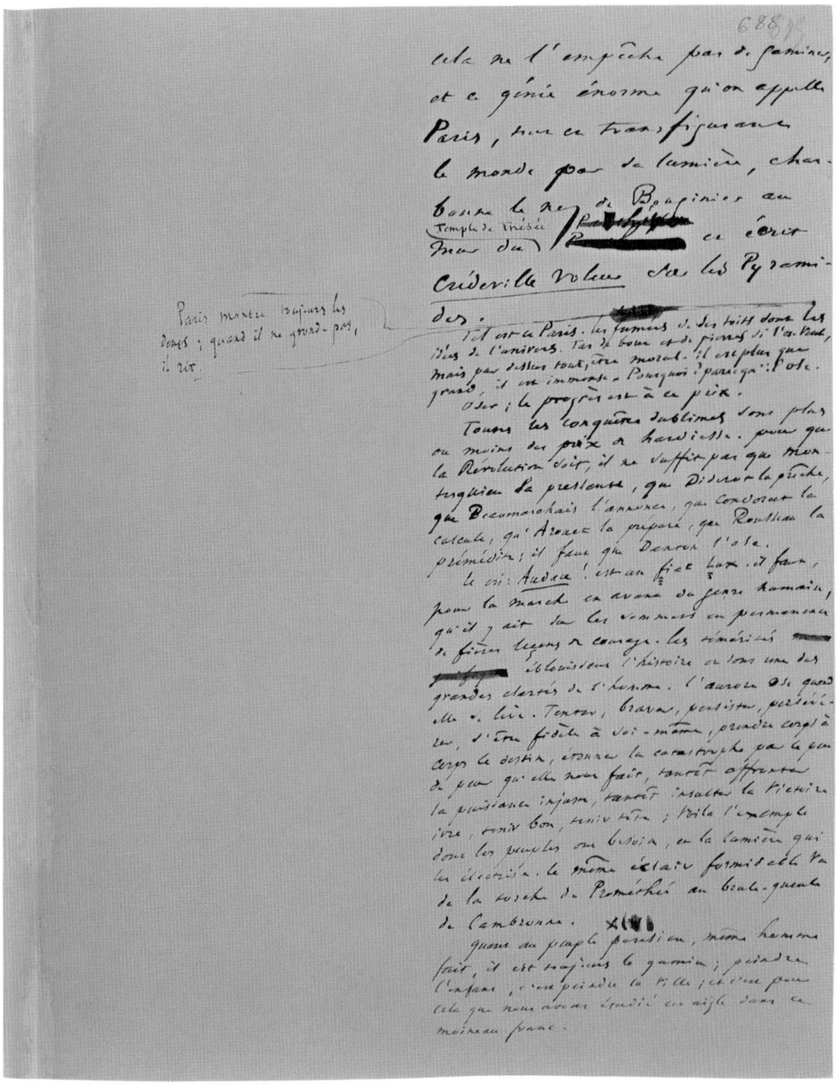

hells in civilization's midst, . . . as long as the three problems of the century have not been resolved—the degradation of man by poverty, the ruin of woman by hunger, the wasting of the child by night, . . . books like this will be needed). Indeed, few works have been so closely linked to political life as *Les Misérables* in the circumstances and places of its writing and in its general plan.

From the moment of its simultaneous publication in Paris and Brussels in the spring of 1862, the novel met with great success. It went through numerous new editions; was adapted for the stage by Charles Hugo, the poet's son, and Paul Meurice; was subjected to parodies (another kind of homage);and was filmed as early as 1909 by Stuart Blakton and by K. W. Linn F. Wolf in 1913. Finally, the publication of *Les Misérables* was to have consequences as much on the social front—working conditions for women

and children became the order of the day— as on the penal front: a revision of the penal code would be voted on May 13, 1863.

As for the manuscript, it was bequeathed to the Bibliothèque Nationale with the ensemble of Hugo's works, according to the author's wishes. In the history of literary collections, Hugo's testament is a milestone: "Je donne tous mes manuscrits, et tout ce qui sera trouvé écrit ou dessiné par moi, à la Bibliothèque Nationale de Paris, qui sera un jour la Bibliothèque des Etats-Unis d'Europe" (I give all my manuscripts and all that I may have written or drawn to the Bibliothèque Nationale of Paris, which will some day be the Library of the United States of Europe).

Marie-Laure Prévost

Victor Hugo, *Les Misérables* (Brussels and Paris, 1862), 10 vols. René Journet and Guy Robert, "Le manuscrit des 'Misérables,'" *Annales de l'Université de Besançon* (Paris, 1963).

417

Hugo's caricatural inspiration tended to fade with his departure into exile but revived in his last years on Guernsey about 1866–1869. Then a series of "figurines" took shape under the writer's pen. Some of them he brought together in an album entitled *Théâtre de la Gaîté*. But, as Jean Massin has noted, by way of gaiety these drawings propose a spirit of cutting satire aimed at the army, the clergy, the judiciary, indeed the government, as seen in this caricature of Napoléon III. This portrait-indictment with its ambiguous caption harks back to Hugo's literary works from the beginning of his exile, *Histoire d'un crime, Napoléon le Petit*, and *Châtiments*, all written after the coup d'état of Dec. 2, 1851.

Marie-Laure Prévost

Victor Hugo, *Théâtre de la gaîté* (selected drawings from album BNF NA Fr. 13352), ed. René Journet and Guy Robert (Paris, 1961).

181

VICTOR HUGO

Dessin portant la légende: "admire Napoléon III" (Drawing bearing the caption: "admire Napoléon III")

Département des Manuscrits, NAF 13352, fol. 26v

Pen and brown ink on paper; 1 fol., 230 × 147 mm. Bequest of Victor Hugo.

In his preface to the album of Victor Hugo's drawings engraved by Paul Chenay (1863), Théophile Gautier declared, "S'il n'était pas poète, Victor Hugo serait un peintre de premier ordre" (If he weren't a poet, Victor Hugo would be a first-rate painter). Associated with numerous artists like the painter Alaux, David d'Angers, the Deverias, Louis Boulanger, and Célestin Nanteuil, as early as 1819 Hugo was also writing the art column in the *Conservateur littéraire*, the review he founded with his brothers.

His graphic work developed more slowly than his literary work, beginning about 1830–1835, as souvenir sketches of his travel, or with modest caricatures that the writer called "choses à la plume" (things in ink). This first series of caricatures–as Judith Petit has emphasized–should be related to his notorious preface to his 1827 play *Cromwell*: "le beau n'a qu'un type; le laid en a mille" (beauty has but one face; ugliness has a thousand).

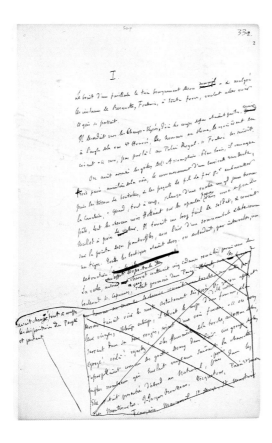

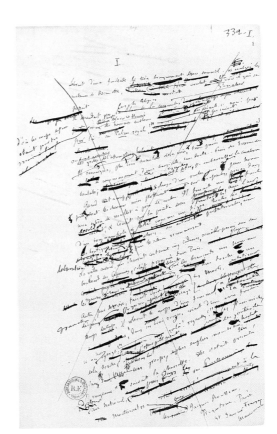

182

GUSTAVE FLAUBERT

L'Education sentimentale
(Sentimental education)

Département des Manuscrits, NAF 17607,
fols. 1 and 2

*Paper; 12 vols. (NAF 17599–17611), 360 × 280 mm,
and 1 vol., 450 × 360 mm (scenarios). Half-binding
in shagreen, with violet corners. Second version of
1864–1869. First manuscript. Inheritance of Mme
Franklin-Grout-Flaubert, Hôtel Drouot, Nov.
18–19, 1931, no. 183. Collection Sacha Guitry.
Purchased at the Drouot sale, Nov. 15, 1977, nos.
31–32.*

While completing *Salammbô,* Gustave
Flaubert began planning a pantomime, the
Château des coeurs, and considered writing
either "un immense roman" ou "deux ou
trois petits romans... tout simples" (an
immense novel or two or three little
novels... very straightforward).

Apparently, *L'Education sentimentale* was
already one of those projects over which the
writer was hesitating. In a letter of April 7,
1863, he declared that he was working on
L'Education sentimentale. Reusing the title of a
youthful novel he had written about
1843–1845, he set to work on a new one. He

began drafting it in 1864 and finished it "le 16
mai [1869] à 5 heures moins quatre minutes"
(May 16, [1869], at four minutes before five
o'clock) (letter from Flaubert to his niece).

For five years Flaubert accumulated background material, taking notes on his reading,
collecting evidence, delving as well into his
personal recollections of events in February
1848 to which he had been witness together
with Maxime Du Camp and Louis Bouilhet.
Scenarios and rough drafts followed one
after the other. In the process the novelist
covered rectos and versos of the approximately 2,500 sheets that now constitute the
"old manuscript" of *L'Education sentimentale.*
In his concern for perfection, Flaubert constantly revised his text and in the same passage might offer some ten successive versions. Besides which, the text was also put to
a test the writer called the *gueuloir,* or "brawl
room." "Il écoutait le rythme de sa prose,
s'arrêtait pour saisir une sonorité fuyante,
combinait les sons, éloignait les assonances,
disposait les virgules avec conscience,
comme les haltes d'un long chemin" (He listened to the rhythm of his prose, stopped to
seize a fleeting resonance, combined sounds,
spaced assonances, conscientiously arranged

419

183

CHARLES BAUDELAIRE

L'Avertisseur (The cautioner)

Département des Manuscrits, NAF 19799, fol. 3

Paper; 1 sheet; 298 × 194 mm; bound with other poems by Baudelaire. Signed autograph manuscript. 1861.

commas like rest stops on a long road) (Maupassant).

The initial project to construct a novel "ayant pour acteurs le mari, la femme, l'amant tous s'aimant, tous lâches" (having for characters a husband, a wife, and a lover, all loving one another, all cowards) continued to evolve. Flaubert set out to "montrer que le sentimentalisme suit la Politique et en reproduit les phases" (show that sentimentalism follows politics and goes through the same phases); he strove "d'écrire l'histoire morale de [s]a génération" (to write the moral history of his generation).

As an account that drew upon the writer's own autobiography–notably, the recollection of his passion for Elisa Schlésinger, whom he had met at Trouville–*L'Education sentimentale* is also a historical novel that paints a picture of Paris from 1840 to 1851, which must have disconcerted its first readers. It was a disillusioned and flowing account which Théodore de Banville termed "mystérieux comme la vie même" (mysterious like life itself).

Marie-Laure Prévost

Madeleine Cottin, "Flaubert: Le vieux manuscrit de 'L'Education sentimentale,'" *Bulletin de la Bibliothèque Nationale*, December 1976: 99–108. *L'Education sentimentale*, ed. P. M. Wetherill (Paris, 1984). *L'Education sentimentale*, pictures and documents, ed. P. M. Wetherill (Paris, 1985). D. A. Williams, "L'Education sentimentale: Le classement des scénarios," *Etudes normandes* 1988: 47–52.

In 1861 a new edition of *Les Fleurs du mal* (The flowers of evil) was published, minus the parts banned in 1857 for offending public morality. But other poems came to light, such as "L'Avertisseur" (The cautioner), published in the *Revue européene* in September 1861. "L'Avertisseur" was included, along with eleven other poems, in the third and final edition of *Les Fleurs du mal*, dated 1868.

The poem is similar to a sonnet in form (although the two tercets precede the second quatrain) and emphatically sums up the inner contradictions that made Baudelaire (1821–1867) a tortured being who bore a painful secret. He was obsessed by feelings of guilt and moral failure, and his soul was the site of a harsh mental struggle against what he called his "dark enemy." Rather than a tendency to evil, this obsession should be understood as his awareness of the mutual existence within himself of two contradictory feelings, "horror of life and the ecstasy of life." They prompted him to write in a letter dated February or March 1861 that "something terrible is telling me 'never' while something else is telling me to 'try.'" "L'Avertisseur," which conveys this awareness, is probably contemporary with the letter.

This existential dread and the conflict of self against self were certainly carried to an expressive pitch by Baudelaire's genius, yet they also bear the mark of a general transition from one form of civilization to another, the one Baudelaire himself identified with "modernity." The "self" of consciousness occupied the vacuum left by the collapse of the grand traditional frames of reference (nature having been judged bleak and boring, while God no longer served as guarantor of all things). The flashes of insight afforded by a suddenly liberated consciousness often become excesses of self-centeredness that

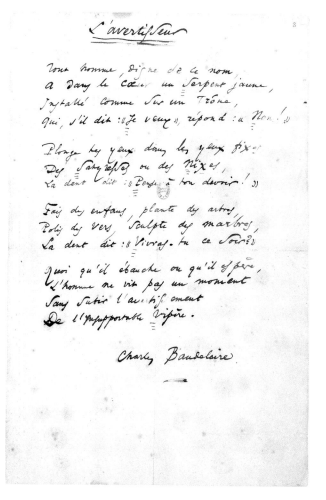

themselves engender ennui and a "what's the point?" attitude. ("Reader, you know this dainty monster too," he asserted in the prologue to *Les Fleurs du mal* [trans. James McGowen]). Such feelings can be followed by bitterness accompanied, at its most extreme, by rebellion and total rejection. Baudelaire referred to this dethroning of the Absolute as the "Irremediable" or the "Irreparable" ("The Irreparable with cursed tooth gnaws souls," *L'Irréparable*).

Baudelaire's satanism is merely the transposition of the malaise gnawing at a dandy exasperated by a society that hypocritically upheld an intransigent morality while prosecuting him in a scandalous, idiotic way.

Florence de Lussy

Guy Sagnes, *L'Ennui dans la littérature française de Flaubert à Laforgue (1848–1884)* (Paris, 1969). Benjamin Fondane, *Baudelaire et l'expérience du gouffre* (Paris, 1972). Marcel A. Ruff, *L'Esprit du mal et l'esthétique baudelairienne* (Geneva and Paris, 1972). Claude Pichois and Jean Ziegler, *Baudelaire* (Paris, 1987). *Les plus beaux manuscrits des poètes français* (Paris, 1991), 218–21. Yves Bonnefoy, "Baudelaire contre Rubens," in *Le Nuage rouge* (Paris, 1992). *The Flowers of Evil*, trans. James McGowen (Oxford, 1993).

184

ISIDORE DUCASSE

Poésies I et II (Poems I and II)
Réserve des livres rares, Rés. p. Ye. 870,
title page

Paris: Journaux politiques et littéraires (Librairie Gabrie), [April and June] 1870. 15 + [1] and 16 pp; two fascicles in one 8⁰ volume (22.2 cm). First edition. Citron morocco binding, ca. 1950. Copyright registration copies (Seine, 1870, nos. 2327 and 4074).

"*Les Chants de Maldoror* [The lay of Maldoror] and *Poésies* shine with incomparable radiance; they express a total revelation that seems to surpass human possibilities. . . . His magic law already contains the formulation, in advance, of all the boldest thoughts and undertakings of centuries to come." These two sentences from André Breton's preface to the 1938 edition of the complete works of Isidore Ducasse, count of Lautréamont, demonstrate the extent to which the poet—almost totally overlooked by literary criticism until then—assumed capital importance in the eyes of the surrealists. Even André Gide, who had relished reading the sixth song of *Maldoror* "to the point of delirium" as early as 1905, later praised Breton's group "for having recognized and proclaimed the ultra-literary importance of marvelous Lautréamont."

Although Philippe Soupault, in his excessive cult of admiration, forbade literary criticism from even approaching "M. le Comte," critics have made appreciable progress in unearthing biographical information about Ducasse. Almost nothing was known of him at the turn of the century. Today his life no longer needs to be fleshed out with myths. Yet his death in a besieged Paris on the eve of the Commune has fixed his literary oeuvre into two uneven and contrasting books, the keys to which are perhaps permanently lost.

Exegetes have nevertheless been unsparing in their efforts to decipher this complex literary mystery, concentrating especially on elucidating the significance of the *Chants de Maldoror* (1869), the powerful torrent of poetry that Valéry Larbaud called "the supreme expression of flamboyant romanticism." The

421

two fascicles of *Poésies*, meanwhile, took exactly the opposite tack, being a series of unexpectedly conformist aphorisms conceived as the preface to a future book that the poet's death five months later consigned to oblivion. The difficulty of relating the intention of *Poésies* to the verbal profusion of *Maldoror*, along with the impossibility of analyzing *Maldoror* while ignoring the later recantation of *Poésies* (the only text for which Ducasse took responsibility), have contributed greatly to the perplexity of critics, who generally find it easier to identify the multiple plagiarisms than actually to explain this strange treatise of antiliterature.

Finally, it should be noted that *Poésies*, that permanent obstacle to a relatively coherent interpretation of Lautréamont's oeuvre, almost vanished without a trace. All that survived of the first edition, which Lautréamont probably sent to the twelve people to whom *Poésies I* is dedicated, is the first fascicle addressed to Henri Mue, Ducasse's former schoolmate from Tarbes. This means that only a single complete set of *Poésies* exists, the one legally deposited for copyright registration, which André Breton copied in 1919 in order to publish the text in *Littérature*. The protection offered by the Bibliothèque Nationale was far more reliable than the disdainful neglect shown by the poet's ungrateful friends.

Antoine Coron

Isidore Ducasse, count of Lautréamont, *Oeuvres complètes*, facsimiles of the original editions (Paris, 1970). Michel Philip, *Lectures de Lautréamont* (Paris, 1971). François Caradec, *Isidore Ducasse, comte de Lautréamont*, enlarged ed. (Paris, 1975). Jacques Lefrère, *Le Visage de Lautréamont* (Paris, 1977). Maurice Blanchot, Julien Gracq, and J.-M. G. Le Clézio, *Sur Lautréamont* (Brussels, 1987). Lautréamont, *Les Chants de Maldoror*, and Isidore Ducasse, *Poésies*, ed. Jean-Pierre Goldenstein (Paris, 1992).

185

GEORGES BIZET

Carmen. Livret de Henri Meilhac et Ludovic Halévy d'après Prosper Mérimée. . . .

Département de la Musique, MS 436[/9], fols. 177v–178r

Opera in 4 acts; score; 4 vols.; 36 × 29 cm. Autograph manuscript, ca. 1875.

More than a century after its première, Bizet's opera gloriously pursues its path of shadow and light, fame and ambiguity. Sung in every language (sometimes even in several at the same time), it has been adapted to all kinds of staging (from the plainest to the most "Hollywood," from the most classic to the most "committed"), arranged for cinema, song, and musical comedy, and acclaimed by feminists who see in it a modern myth and a key persona, while others mock the protagonist's "bitchy" character as simplistic and shallow.

The opera was itself the adaptation of a story published in 1847 by Prosper Mérimée. Spare, concise, without grandiloquence, Mérimée's story presented with almost ethnographic naturalism a sharply etched narrative centered around an intuitive, primitive, almost organic character.

The librettists who were assigned the task of adapting the work to the rules or traditions of the lyric stage were long-time professionals whose specialty was operetta rather than opera. It is amusing to note that ten years before tackling *Carmen*, Henri Meilhac and Ludovic Halévy had written the libretto for an Offenbach "espagnolade" (situated in Peru), likewise adapted from a (more pleasant) novel by Mérimée. Thus *La Périchole* and *Carmen* have the same three literary fathers.

The working out of the libretto for *Carmen* does not seem to have posed any problem. Mérimée had died in 1870 and his heirs gave up their rights unconditionally. In Bizet's correspondence there are letters proving that he involved himself in the elaboration of the text—his wife was even Ludovic Halévy's first cousin. Whatever the case, the

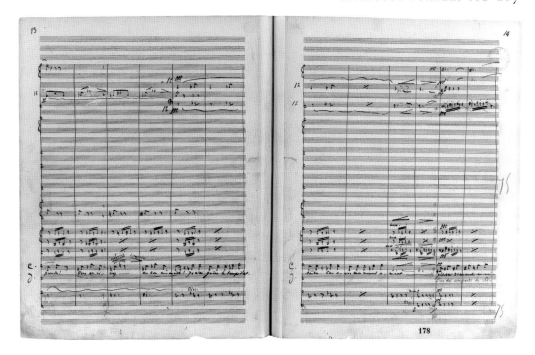

178

librettists rendered it markedly insipid compared with the original novel by creating, among others, two important characters, the pure and blond Michaela, the antithesis of Carmen, and, just as conventional, Escamillo, the "toreador"—a neologism that has since become part of the French language.

The two essential characters were travestied by the theatrical adaptation. Mérimée's Don José was a somber figure, a murderer many times over, conscious of his degeneration and hardly recognizable in the naive hero of the opera. Carmen herself employs a shopgirl's vocabulary ("Et c'est bien en vain qu'on l'appelle/S'il lui convient de refuser" [And it is indeed in vain to call him if it suits him to refuse]) and ideas ("Je suis amoureuse" [I'm in love], "là-bas, là-bas dans la montagne/Là-bas, là-bas si tu m'aimais. . ." [over there, over there in the mountains, over there, over there if you loved me. . .]). Nonetheless, some things touched by the novel's *souffle,* or inspiration, do remain, if only the important borrowings of original spoken dialogue from the text and the implacable dramatic progression that renders the opera ever more somber from act to act.

The stormy, indeed shocked reception with which the public and the critics greeted the work at the time of its première at the Opéra-Comique on March 3, 1875, indicates that even when smothered with the "sauce" of comic opera, *Carmen* was nevertheless a powerful new work of a disturbing kind—all the more so because Bizet's music, rapid without bombast, with contrast, now sober, now glittering, transcended the conventionality of the libretto. Despite the uproar, a slightly altered version of the work held the stage and soon became popular with the general public and with intellectuals. Bizet's death on June 3, 1875, heightened the disturbing aura around the work. The Vienna Opera called for it the same year and transformed it for the occasion into grand opera with the aid of Ernest Guiraud, who substituted recitatives for the spoken dialogue characteristic of comic opera. This version ran throughout the world for nearly a century. Only recently has the original spoken text made a comeback.

Despite that, the quarrels over the return to an authentic *Carmen* are far from over. Musicologists in every country argue sharply about the work's different sources. These include the manuscript copy (from the library-museum of the Paris Opéra), which the orchestra director used for the première; the Choudens piano-vocal edition of 1875, which contains some cuts approved by Bizet; the present autograph manuscript, which incorporates some cuts and autograph changes; and the recitatives of Guiraud and the cuts and additions made after Bizet's death. Fritz Oeser's edition, far from serenely establishing the longed-for synthesis, has

423

unleashed the musicologists' quarrels anew with even greater intensity.

The two pages on exhibit (fols. 177v and 178r) are taken from Bizet's original manuscript (offered by his widow to the library of the Paris Conservatoire), which was altered by a series of changes and additions, as noted above. The *seguidilla* from the end of the first act looks to be completely from Bizet's hand. The scene is interesting in terms of role characterizations (seduction scene) and action (José succumbs to the provocation). Bizet's original music seems very Spanish. Carmen beguiles José while gliding through a significant portamento, "Vous arrivez" (You're coming), while a flute that is at once mocking and erotic repeats or anticipates what the voice is singing. Bizet's corrections in blue pencil eliminate a theme for the second flute and transform the quite naturalistic text of "J'irai dimanche en voiture" (I'll take a coach on Sunday) into "près des remparts de Séville" (near the ramparts of Seville), which "sounds" more like comic opera.

Pierre Vidal

Fritz Oeser, *Carmen... Kritische Neuausgabe...* (Cassel, 1964). *Carmen*, in *L'Avant-scène opéra* 26 (March–April 1980; rev. March 1993). Bizet, *Carmen* (London and New York, 1982). Susan McClary, *Georges Bizet: Carmen* (Cambridge, 1992).

186
Premier projet pour la peinture de la coupole de la salle de spectacle de l'Opéra Garnier (Initial plan for painting the inner dome of the Garnier Opera House)
Bibliothèque du Musée de l'Opéra, Mus. 642

Painted by Eugène Lenepveu (1819–1898). Oil on canvas in a carved circular frame representing the inner dome and the central boss from which the chandelier was to hang. Diameter: 0.85 m. Signed and dated on the exterior side: "Lenepveu 1867." Donated by Mme C. de Nieville in 1926.

The ceiling depicts the hours of the day and night in a vast composition that included Olympian gods, the Graces, cupids, and many mythological figures. The sketch exhibited here was simplified when the full-scale execution was done. Paint was applied directly to the flat dome of copper that covered the theater. Of special note are the magnificent sculpted frame and the central grill, representing the sun's rays, which opened directly to the outside to provide ventilation for fumes from the gas chandelier.

Lenepveu's ceiling is still in place beneath the ceiling of Marc Chagall, which now covers it.

Martine Kahane

187

Coupe longitudinale du Grand Foyer de l'Opéra (Longitudinal section of the Grand Foyer of the Paris Opera House)

Bibliothèque du Musée de l'Opéra, Plan Garnier 014

From the side of the fore-foyer. Pencil, India ink, wash, and gouache; 80.5 × 146 cm. Studio of Charles Garnier.

Construction of the Paris Opéra by the architect Charles Garnier (1825–1898) lasted from 1860 until 1875 and encompassed many changes. These initial plans for the decoration of the Grand Foyer were profoundly modified after the fall of the Second Empire in 1870. The eagles, emblems of the imperial regime, were replaced by large female figures and child musicians. Any decorative elements that might evoke the Second Empire were eliminated. Garnier replaced them with figures devoid of political connotation, Sèvres vases, and so on.

188

EDGAR DEGAS

Danseuses s'exerçant au Foyer de l'Opéra (Ballet dancers practicing in the Opéra's practice room)

Bibliothèque du Musée de l'Opéra, Mus. 1751

Pastel signed at bottom left; 685 × 590 mm.
Acquired in 1992 with the support of the Association pour le Rayonnement de l'Opéra de Paris.

Until very recently the museum of the Paris Opéra owned no work by Edgar Degas (1834–1917). Indeed, this one is the first to enter its collection. Acquired when the art dealer Durand-Ruel, Degas's friend and patron, sold the artist's studio, it had previously remained in his collection.

It shows four female ballet dancers stretching in the ballet practice room of the Opéra. Degas's lines are heavily marked, and highlights in dark tones of pastel give them unusual power.

This large pastel by Degas is undated. It apparently belongs to the last period of the artist's life, a period which, strangely enough, is poorly represented in French museum collections.

Martine Kahane

189
Three-dimensional Model for Verdi's Aïda
Bibliothèque du Musée de l'Opéra,
Maquette 130

Opera in 4 acts and 7 scenes by Antonio Ghislanzoni, after Auguste Mariette Bey; music by Giuseppe Verdi

Act I, scene 1. Cardboard cut out and painted; 83 × 66 × 66 cm. By Antoine Lavastre and Eugène Carpezat.

The première of Verdi's *Aïda* took place at the Paris Opéra on March 22, 1880, in a French-language version by Camille Du Locle and Charles Nuitter, directed by Régnier and Adolphe Mayer, with costumes by Eugène Lacoste. This production benefited from the enlightened advice of Auguste Mariette Bey, the famous Egyptologist. The scenery and costumes were designed with the greatest archeological precision.

Exhibited here is the model for act I, scene 1. It represents a hall in the king's palace. On the left is a gallery, in the middle a large entranceway leading to the subterranean hall of judgment. On the right is a gallery leading to the prison of Radamès.

Martine Kahane

190
Portrait du comte Savorgnan de Brazza (Portrait of Count Savorgnan de Brazza)
Département des Cartes et Plans,
Bibliothèque de la Société de Géographie,
Portrait 10154

Print enlarged using silver salts, 57.6 × 42 cm; glued onto cardboard for mounting with gilded beveled edges, 67 × 47 cm. Printed at the bottom of the board in gilded letters: "grand prix 1889, Nadar, Paris." Handwritten on the label: "Comte Savorgnan de Brazza, 1886." From the deposit of the Société de Géographie at the Bibliothèque Nationale.

"Il faut aller là . . . à la recherche des lacs ou du fleuve par où doit s'écouler la grande masse d'eau qui tombe sous l'équateur" (One must go there looking for the lakes or river through which the great mass of water that descends below the Equator must flow). It took Pierre Savorgnan de Brazza twenty years to fulfill the project set out in these few lapidary words. It was the minister of the navy, to whom Savorgnan de Brazza also owed his admission to the Naval School as an alien (he was born in Rome in 1852), who gave him his first mission (1875–1878) to explore the Ogooué River in West Africa. During his second mission (1879–1882), having founded Franceville on the Upper Ogooué, he traveled to the Congo along the Léfini, another tributary of the great river. That is where he met Makoko, king of the Batekes, before setting up the first post at the site of the future Brazzaville. During his third voyage from 1883 to 1885, he began a new series of explorations even higher toward the

427

Sangha and Ubangi Rivers, which he continued during his fourth voyage beginning in 1886, while setting up the French settlement in the Congo.

Savorgnan de Brazza (1852–1905) had an exceptional career. One seldom finds such a young man entrusted with such an important official mission and such substantial financial resources. He was twenty-three years old in 1875 and had not yet proven himself. He received funding and authority from the French government in 1883 with the title of government commissioner. He was appointed commissioner general in 1886. In the meantime, by a treaty signed with King Makoko in 1882, he had given France—which had not asked for that much—the entire right bank of the Congo River from the Ubangi, a region he had taken from his great rival, Stanley, an explorer serving the Belgian king, with whom Brazza had refused to cooperate. A member of the Société de Géographie, which, at the conclusion of his first voyage, had awarded him its grand gold medal in 1879 (he was inducted into the Légion d'Honneur the same year), he peacefully opened the road to exploring central Africa. He quickly earned fame while upholding the legendary image of the humanistic explorer that he would keep for his entire life, albeit a life shortened by disease. He dedicated his life to travels and died in Dakar in 1905, upon returning for the last time from his beloved Congo. He was an administrator and had high official duties, such as advisor to the government for colonial issues. He remained an explorer throughout his life, even when he posed in Paul Nadar's studio in 1886, in his "native" costume as others before him had done, for the long unpublished photograph that now immortalizes him.

France Duclos

Pierre Savorgnan de Brazza, *Conférences et lettres sur les trois explorations dans l'Ouest africain de 1875 à 1886* (Paris, 1887). Général de Chambrun, *Brazza* (Paris, 1930). Catherine Coquery-Vidrovitch, *Brazza et la prise de possession du Congo: La mission de l'Ouest africain...* (Paris, 1969). Henri Brunschwig, *Brazza explorateur* (Paris, 1966–1972). Paul Nadar, *Photographs*, vol. 1 (Paris, 1979). Numa Broc, *Dictionnaire illustré des explorateurs et grands voyageurs français du XIXe siècle*, vol. 1, *L'Afrique* (Paris, 1988).

191

PAUL CLAUDEL
Tête d'or

Département des Manuscrits, Collection Paul Claudel, pp. 116–17

Paper; 1–171 (Claudel's pagination); 260 × 230 mm. Plain royal blue morocco binding (by C. Septier), lined with mauve morocco; endpapers of purple silk brocade. Second version, 1894. Autograph manuscript used for printing. On fol. 1, headed "Commission Internationale du Slesvig," the autograph title appears: "Tête d'Or. Ms. de la 2e version. Boston, 1894, P. Claudel." Library of Paul Voûte, no. 587, ex libris "P.V." Collection of the marquis Emmanuel du Bourg de Bozas. Ex libris "Du Bourg de Bozas Chaix d'Est Ange" with the family arms. Purchased at Drouot sale, June 27–28, 1990, lot 301.

The theater definitely seems to have been Paul Claudel's first mode of poetic expression. When he composed *Tête d'or* in 1889, he had just turned twenty. With it, he successfully translated his fierce inner turmoil into an original style, exorcising the fantasies that had been haunting him. The play was sparked, moreover, by a special situation: the poet later defined *Tête d'or* as "l'oeuvre de l'époque tragique de ma vie" (the work of the tragic period of my life). The year 1886 had been a crucial one for Claudel, since it was marked by his passionate encounter with Rimbaud's *Illuminations* and *Une saison en*

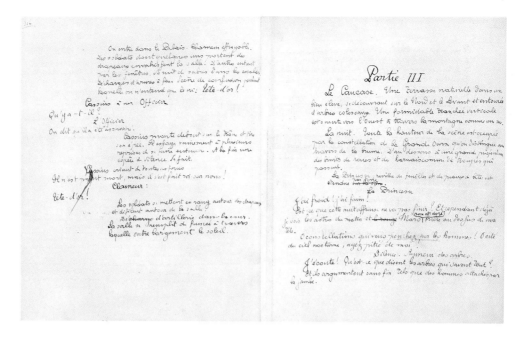

enfer, followed by his conversion to Roman Catholicism on Christmas Day in Notre-Dame in Paris. But he only managed to achieve some degree of peace in 1890, when he fully acknowledged his conversion by resuming religious practices.

Claudel's personal anguish was intensified by the climate of the 1880s in France, when the younger generation was prey to a profound alienation born of Baudelaire's pessimism, nurtured by the scientism of Taine and Renan, and made still worse by the bleak political outlook. With all the violence of youthful despair, *Tête d'or* embodies the mythical pursuit of a heroic ideal at grips with a decadent world. The unquenchable thirst for conquest, symbol of immoderation, ultimately destroys the hero, all haloed in gold like a child of the sun. It should be noted that Claudel's personal culture during these salad days was deeply imbued with his readings of Shakespeare and Greek tragedies. *Tête d'or*, a play in three acts, shows in varying degrees the effects of this compound inspiration, at least thematically. At the stylistic level, Aeschylean metrics and images from classical mythology have left traces on his staccato verses with their dazzling lyricism, foreshadowing all his subsequent poetic work. When it was published in 1890 by the Librairie de l'Art Indépendant in a printing of one hundred copies, *Tête d'or* did not bear its author's name. Only a limited, but enthusiastic, public took note.

After Claudel was appointed head of the French consulate in Boston in 1893, he found a certain degree of serenity and gained theatrical experience by writing two more plays: *La Ville* and *L'Échange*. Naturally inclined to revise his texts, he began by making notes in the margins of his edition of *Tête d'or* before rewriting those passages whose stylistic audacity now seemed excessive. He also increased the number of stage directions; part 3 is set geographically in the Caucasus, a reference to Aeschylus's *Prometheus Bound*, and is dominated by the "constellation Ursa Major."

Completed in July 1894, the second version, on exhibit here (pp. 116–17, the beginning of part 3), was published by Mercure de France in 1901 at the head of a small anthology of Claudel's plays called *L'arbre*. In accordance with the author's expressed wishes, it was never performed in his lifetime. Jean-Louis Barrault gave the première of *Tête d'or* for the grand opening of the Odéon/Théâtre de France in 1959 (see cat. 192).

Florence Callu

"*Tête d'Or*" *et les débuts littéraires* (Paris, 1959). J. Madaule, *Le Drame de Paul Claudel* (Paris, 1964). C. Sarrazin, *La Signification spirituelle de "Tête d'Or,"* Annales de la Faculté des Lettres d'Aix-en-Provence (1966). M. Lioure, "*Tête d'Or*" *de Paul Claudel*, with an introduction and notes, Annales littéraires de l'Université de Besançon (Paris, 1984).

Illustration courtesy of the Société Paul Claudel

429

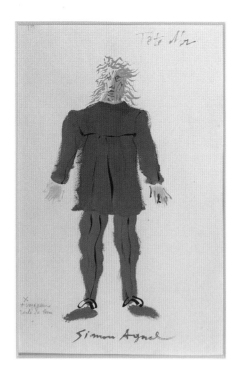

192

ANDRÉ MASSON

Set and Costume Designs for Paul Claudel's Tête d'or, *directed by Jean-Louis Barrault, Odéon/Théâtre de France, 1959*

Département des Arts du Spectacle, Maquettes 989, 91–120, 985

Simon Agnel. *Gouache; 50 × 32 cm. Unsigned.* Set for Act III. *Pencil and India ink; 42 × 55 cm. Signed (embossed stamp), lower right.* Banner for Act III. *Pencil, India ink, and gouache; 65 × 47.5 cm. Unsigned.*

Jean-Louis Barrault, whose friendship with Paul Claudel began in 1936, harbored a dream of producing *Tête d'or* for twenty years. In 1959, André Malraux, minister of culture, gave him the opportunity to produce the play for the grand opening of the Théâtre de France (previously known as the Théâtre de l'Odéon), the administration of which had just recently been entrusted to him (by the Decree of Oct. 3, 1959). The appointment of Barrault to head up the Odéon, and at the same time selecting a play combining scope with boldness, was in keeping with the new minister's cultural agenda.

The opening of the Théâtre de France on Oct. 29, 1959, skillfully orchestrated by Malraux himself for the first official evening at the theater of the new president of the Fifth Republic, brought together a select audience around General de Gaulle: fifteen ministers, several generals, the most senior government officials, ten members of the Académie Française, ambassadors, and distinguished representatives from the world of the arts, letters, industry, and high society.

To commemorate the event, the seating plan for the theater was published the following day in the daily press. Names listed included Michel Debré, Georges Pompidou, Valéry Giscard d'Estaing, Francis Poulenc, René Clair, Louis Aragon, Yves Saint-Laurent, Pierre Cardin, Jeanne Moreau, and Charles Aznavour. The event was a political and artistic success, a première that left reporters with a lasting impression of "a most imposing display of the world of officialdom and pompous splendor," although it may have seemed quite daring to confront all these well-placed people with a play about people who could find no place at all in this world.

On stage, Alain Cuny played the role of Simon Agnel/Tête d'or, Laurent Terzieff played Cébès, Barrault was the King and Catherine Sellers the Princess. Sets and costumes were designed by André Masson, and the play was set to the music of Arthur Honegger. Masson (1896–1987), a surrealist painter, had met Malraux in 1921 and Barrault in 1936. While shooting a film, Masson gave Barrault the idea for his first production, *Numance* by Cervantes (first performed at the Théâtre Antoine in 1937), with sets and costumes by Masson himself.

A deeply creative artistic collaboration between two friends was the result. During the war, André Masson went to the United States. When he arrived in New York on May 29, 1940, U.S. Customs confiscated a series of drawings he was bringing into the country on the grounds that they were obscene. Archibald MacLeish, the Librarian of Congress, had been an admirer of Masson since his purchase in 1927 of *La Tour des cartes*, a drawing now in the Museum of Modern Art, and managed to get the drawings returned to their owner. (Masson and his family lived in the countryside near New Preston, Connecticut. Trees were a major theme in his work. He often spoke of

Connecticut's "tortured trees.") In 1946, when the Renaud-Barrault Company was formed at the Théâtre Marigny, Barrault asked Masson, just back from the United States, to design the sets and costumes for *Hamlet*. To inaugurate the third major phase of his theatrical career in 1959, Barrault once again thought of Masson, knowing that the artist would put "sa puissance particulière en ce qui concerne la forme et la couleur au service de l'art théâtral" (his particular control of form and color in the service of the theater), no matter whether it was a matter of "la couleur psychique d'un personage" (the psychic coloring of a character), of the "mouvement dramatique d'une action dans son évolution scénique" (dramatic movement as the play's

action evolves), or of "la recherche d'une symbole profond, totémique" (finding a profound, totemic symbol).

The designs, two of which are reproduced here, bear out Barrault's judgment:
(1) The profound solitude of Simon Agnel with his flamboyant hair, wearing a modest peasant blouse and armed with the spade of the part-time gravedigger, is evident in the destitute image of this Nietzschean hero (second version, part I: scene between Simon and Cébès).
(2) The "totem" is the "arbre emblématique du dernier acte" (emblematic tree in the final act), "l'arbre du champ de bataille" (the tree on the battlefield), which the painter admit-

ted had given him "beaucoup de soucis" (a great deal of trouble). Masson at first conceived this grandiose and imposing black tree more naturalistically, but after discussing the matter with Barrault, he made the model clearly "symbolist," in keeping with the period when *Tête d'or* was written, and in accordance with the transcendental value of trees in Claudel's poetry. This is the tree to which the Deserter nails the Princess by her hands, with the débris of the battlefield lying all around (part III): human and animal remains, "un côté de boeuf, un crâne d'homme, des ronces" (cattle ribs, a human skull, brambles), stylized débris, somewhat reminiscent of *Numance*, and the skull on the horns of a bull, which became the emblem of the Renaud-Barrault Company.
(3) A dozen banners, "rêves peints" (painted dreams), "d'étranges légendes" (strange legends), "des dragons, des panthères qui mangent les dieux" (dragons and god-eating panthers), tower above the battlefield.

Claudel's poetic and philosophical elan was quite naturally echoed by Masson's "dépouillé" (bare) and "efficace" (efficient) work. Elsa Triolet noted in *Lettres françaises* (Oct. 29, 1959) the extent to which set design and costume help reveal the meaning conveyed by the play. Claudel (1868–1955) was no longer there to let his opinion be known. In a letter to Louise Lara dated May 6, 1920, he had enthusiastically mentioned Gordon Craig as a possible set designer for *Tête d'or*. (During Claudel's lifetime, this play was performed by the Art et Action Experimental Theater by the Autant-Laras in the famous "Yellow Attic" on rue Lepic with a neutral set; it had four performances in 1924 and three in 1927). Masson would surely have met with Claudel's approval.

Cécile Giteau　431

Collection of press articles compiled at the Département des Arts du Spectacle relating to the production of *Tête d'or* at the Théâtre de France (R. supp. 6272/1). Ghislain Uhry, *André Masson et le théâtre*, exhibition at the Maison Internationale du Théâtre Renaud-Barrault (Paris, 1983). I am grateful to Mr. Uhry for information about André Masson's time in the United States.

Illustration courtesy of the Comité André Masson

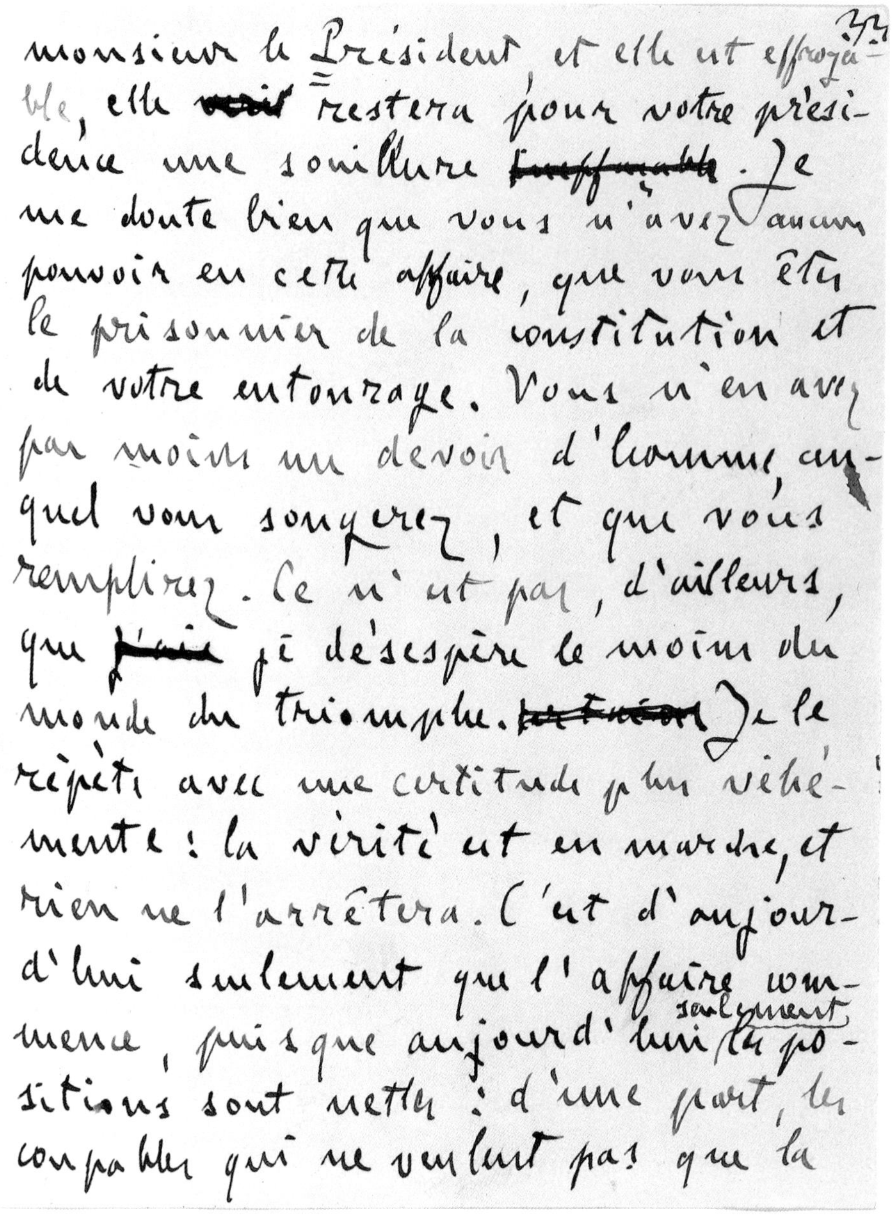

33

monsieur le Président, et elle est effroya-
ble, elle ~~sera~~ restera pour votre prési-
dence une souillure ~~ineffaçable~~. Je
me doute bien que vous n'avez aucun
pouvoir en cette affaire, que vous êtes
le prisonnier de la constitution et
de votre entourage. Vous n'en avez
pas moins un devoir d'homme, auquel vous songerez, et que vous
remplirez. Ce n'est pas, d'ailleurs,
que ~~j'aie~~ je désespère le moins du
monde du triomphe. ~~et rien~~ Je le
répète avec une certitude plus véhé-
mente : la vérité est en marche, et
rien ne l'arrêtera. C'est d'aujour-
d'hui seulement que l'affaire commence, puisque aujourd'hui seulement les positions sont nettes : d'une part, les
coupables qui ne veulent pas que la

193

EMILE ZOLA

J'accuse. . . ! (I accuse. . . !)

Département des Manuscrits, NAF 19951, fol. 33

Paper; 39 pp.; 200 × 150 mm, with envelope bearing the autograph note "Manuscrit de ma 'Lettre à M. F. Faure.'" Red morocco binding with slipcase. Autograph manuscript. Jan. 11–13, 1898. Purchased from the Zola family in 1991.

On Dec. 22, 1894, the Ministry of War unjustly sentenced Capt. Alfred Dreyfus to exile and internment for life. He had been falsely accused of having passed secret documents to Germany. After an odious ritual in which he was publicly drummed out of the army, Dreyfus was sent to Devil's Island, off French Guiana, where he was subjected to extremely harsh detention.

Three years after these deplorable events, another officer suspected of being the real spy, M. C. Esterhazy, was placed on trial. Public opinion, hoodwinked by those who had mounted the whole complicated affair, still generally considered Dreyfus to be a traitor guilty of the most heinous of crimes. The captain's defenders, however, who had struggled tenaciously behind the scenes to have the verdict overturned, saw a glimpse of hope in Esterhazy's indictment. General Gonse, head of the army intelligence unit, was convinced of Esterhazy's guilt, while nei-

Veuillez agréer, monsieur le Pré-sident, l'assurance de mon profond respect.

Emile Zola

ther General Boisdeffre nor General Billot (chief of general staff and minister of war, respectively) disputed that the incriminating "memo" was in Esterhazy's handwriting; yet despite such evidence, Esterhazy was unanimously acquitted and left the courtroom in triumph on Jan. 10, 1898.

Though ill-prepared for political confrontation, Emila Zola was a famous writer who had joined the struggle to clear Dreyfus's name the previous summer. He now decided to strike a major blow by throwing all caution to the winds in an effort to pull public opinion out of its grim lethargy. Burning his bridges, Zola wrote a third open letter on the issue, this time addressed directly to Félix Faure, president of France. Zola's case was full of errors and omissions, and almost every paragraph was open to attack due to the violence of his libelous accusations. The courageous writer was courting a lawsuit, but that was precisely what Zola wanted—a trial before a civilian court, in full public view, which would oblige the authorities to reopen the Dreyfus files and place the general staff on the defensive.

A fuss had to be made, and Zola's letter kicked up a huge one. Written in two days and two nights, his scathing attack was print-

ed on the front page of *L'Aurore* on Jan. 13, 1898, thanks to Georges Clemenceau who was influential on the newspaper. It was Clemenceau who came up with the title "J'accuse. . . !" which, printed in large bold capitals, aroused extraordinary passions. Over 200,000 copies of the newspaper were sold, finally launching the first trend of public opinion favorable to Dreyfus.

Zola hit hard, publicly accusing five generals, two war ministers, and a chief of general staff. The government filed suit against him on Jan. 18 and the trial began on Feb. 7 in the Court of Assises. But, as the brave writer himself predicted, "the truth is emerging and nothing can stop it. Today is just the beginning of the affair" (fol. 33).

Florence de Lussy

Emile Zola, *L'Affaire Dreyfus: La Vérité en marche*, chronology and preface by Colette Becker (Paris, 1969). Marcel Thomas, *L'Affaire sans Dreyfus*, 2d ed., 2 vols. (Geneva, 1978–1979). *Le Procès Zola (7–23 février 1898)*, extracts from the report of the debates, selected and edited by Marcel Thomas (Geneva, 1980). Emile Zola, *L'Affaire Dreyfus: La Vérité en marche*, edited by Jean-Denis Bredin (Paris, 1992).

433

194

GEORGES CLEMENCEAU

Au pied du Sinaï (At the foot of Sinaï).
Illustrations by Henri de Toulouse-
Lautrec

Réserve des livres rares, Rés. Z. Audéoud
223, opposite p. 59

*Paris: Henry Floury, April 20, 1898. [8] + 107 + [5]
pp. and [45] ll. of plates; 4ᵗᵒ (30.2 cm). First edition.
No. 1 of 28 copies on old Japan paper, with a tripli-
cate set (in different colors and on different kinds of
paper) of the 10 lithographs, of which the third set
is signed by the painter, plus 4 lithographs not used.
Binding signed by Marius-Michel: brown morocco,
the front cover inlaid with letters of beige and dark
green morocco, ca. 1900. Bequest of Maurice
Audéoud, accepted by the Bibliothèque Nationale
on Feb. 17, 1909.*

Of all the books illustrated by Henri de
Toulouse-Lautrec, *Au pied du Sinaï* is probably the least known. No study seems to have
been made of it, and exhibitions of the
painter's graphic works often overlook this
book. It is indeed small in format. Its ten
lithographs are not decorative. They are
monochromatic, as are most of the plates
drawn by Toulouse-Lautrec from 1897 on.
The artist's last book, *Histoires naturelles*
(1899), however, equally modest in size and
limited in color, has been far more popular.
The point is that *Au pied du Sinaï* is a book
unlike the others.

When it was published, France was
embroiled in the Dreyfus affair, so called
after the Jewish captain of that name falsely
accused of spying for Germany yet convicted
and deported to Devil's Island. "J'accuse...
!," Emile Zola's indictment of military justice,
was published in *L'Aurore* on Jan. 13, 1898
(cat. 193). During the proceedings filed in
February against the novelist and the publisher of the journal, Clemenceau, who was
not an attorney, publicly defended them
both. From November 1897 until November
1901, there were no fewer than 660 articles in
the press written by the future statesman, all
obviously pro-Dreyfus, with the intent of
having the verdict overturned.

When Gustave Geffroy put Clemenceau
in touch with Toulouse-Lautrec, the writer
had not yet taken his passionately pro-
Dreyfus stand. The first two "Jewish stories"
to which the project seems to have been initially limited in May 1897 presented a
sufficient number of preconceptions so that,
in a letter to his mother, Toulouse-Lautrec
told her of a book in preparation that was
"contre les Juifs" (anti-Jewish). Subsequently,
when he was completing the work, the illustrator corrected himself: "sur les Juifs" (about
Jews). In the meantime, Clemenceau had
begun his struggle on Dreyfus's behalf and
added four new stories to the volume, one of
which was about the faith of the Orthodox
Jews of Carlsbad, another about the Krakow
ghetto, and a third on the poverty of the Jews
in Busk, "village désolé de l'extrême Galicie"
(a desolate village deep in Galicia). These
candid accounts, collected during summer
trips to Central Europe, counterbalanced
more fanciful portraits of Baron Moses and
Mayer the friendly crook.

Denouncing the methodical extermina-
tions already proposed by some against a
people who, "sorti vivant du moyen âge, ne
peut être supprimé" (having survived the
Middle Ages, can no longer be suppressed),
Clemenceau, as a man of the left, believed
that raising the "Jewish question" meant
making a travesty of what could only be

understood as a part of a larger "social question." Clemenceau's ultimate appeal to all oppressed people–"chrétiens de Paris ou juifs de Busk" (Christians of Paris or Jews of Busk)–must have moved Toulouse-Lautrec: to illustrate Clemenceau's text as closely as possible, he also delved into some first-hand reporting in la Tournelle, the Jewish quarter–walking its streets, studying its inhabitants. The picture he painted, an echo of his own wretchedness, makes this "livre de peintre" one of the most moving and least conventional of all.

The copy exhibited here is probably the most precious. Its binding, strictly contemporary and soberly Art Nouveau, is one of the boldest of all those produced by Marius-Michel.

Antoine Coron

Wolfgang Wittrock, *Toulouse-Lautrec: Catalogue complet des estampes* (Paris, 1985), nos. 187–201. Götz Adriani, *Toulouse-Lautrec: Das gesamte graphische Werk, Sammlung Gerstenberg* (Cologne, 1986), nos. 213–27. Jean-Baptiste Duroselle, *Clemenceau* (Paris, 1988). Toulouse-Lautrec, *Correspondance* (Paris, 1992).

195

CLAUDE DEBUSSY
Pelléas et Mélisande
Département de la Musique, MS 963, p. 15

Lyric drama by Maurice Maeterlinck in 5 acts and 12 scenes

Orchestra score for act III; 410 × 330 mm. Autograph manuscript used for the printed score.

The conception and composition of *Pelléas et Mélisande*, the only opera Debussy completed and one of the major works of the 20th century, well illustrates the latent conflicts between dominant cultural authorities and an artist aware of the revolutionary character of his work.

Maurice Maeterlinck's play was performed in Paris on May 13, 1893. The same year Debussy asked the playwright, through Henri de Régnier, for authorization to set *Pelléas et Mélisande* to music. From September–October 1893 to August 1895, Debussy worked almost continually to develop the work, as a complex and scattered series of manuscript sources reveal. Only two major projects interrupted its progress: the prelude *A l'après-midi d'un faune* and the unfinished opera *Cendrelune*. After the première of *Pelléas*, Debussy explained his approach: "Depuis longtemps je cherchais à faire de la musique pour le théâtre, mais la forme dans laquelle je voulais la faire était si peu habituelle qu'après divers essais j'y avais presque renoncé. . . . Je voulais à la musique une liberté qu'elle contient peut-être plus que n'importe quel art, n'étant pas bornée à une reproduction plus ou moins exacte de la nature, mais aux correspondances mystérieuses de la nature et de l'imagination" (I tried for a long time to compose music for the theater, but the form in which I wanted to do it was so unusual that after a number of tries I almost gave up. . . . I wanted the music to have a freedom that perhaps music embodies more than any other art, since it is not restricted to a more or less exact reproduction of nature, but to the mysterious correspondences of nature and imagination). From 1895 to 1901 Debussy made every effort to find a theater in London, Brussels, or

435

Paris that would agree to stage an operatic work that deliberately eschewed the reigning styles, whether influenced by Wagner or verismo.

Albert Carré's arrival as the head of the Opéra-Comique in 1898, and the constant support of the composer and orchestra conductor André Messager, allowed Debussy to overcome the last obstacles, among them the death in 1900 of the publisher Hartmann and a squabble over the role of Mélisande between Georgette Leblanc, wife of Maeterlinck, and Mary Garden, who eventually created the role. The dress rehearsal of *Pelléas* at the Opéra-Comique on April 28, 1902, took place in an atmosphere of agitation and intrigue but did not prevent the work from achieving success in the following months.

The orchestra score exhibited here was used in the first performances of the opera, conducted by Messager ("Vous avez su éveiller la vie sonore de *Pelléas* avec une délicatesse tendre" [You were able to awaken the resonant life of *Pelléas* with a gentle refinement], Debussy would write him). Henri Busser conducted later performances. This score would also be used to engrave the plates of the first edition of the orchestra score published in 1904. It contains some annotations by Messager and Busser and some revisions of orchestration. Some anomalies in the pagination are to be noted; they correspond to changes introduced in the interludes, which were judged too short at the time of the rehearsals.

Catherine Massip

Jean Barraqué, *Debussy* (Paris, 1962). François Lesure, *Catalogue de l'oeuvre de Claude Debussy* (Geneva, 1977), no. 88. Claude Debussy, *Lettres, 1884–1918*, ed. François Lesure (Paris, 1980). David Grayson, *The Genesis of Debussy's "Pelléas et Mélisande"* (Ann Arbor, 1983).

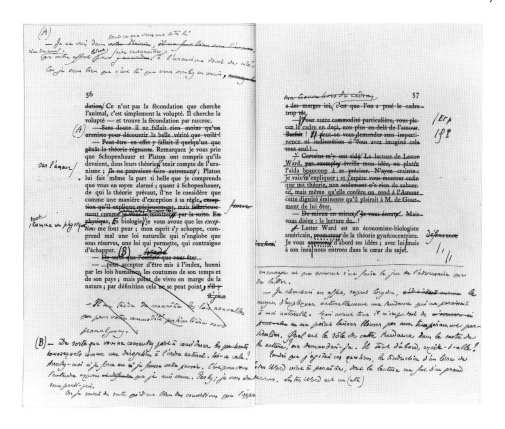

196

[ANDRÉ GIDE]

C.R.D.N.

Réserve des livres rares, Rés. p. Y². 2566,
pp. 56–57

*Proof copy, corrected and expanded. [Bruges: The
St. Catherine Press, Ltd,] May 22, 1911. 124 + [1] pp.
and [2] ll. added; 8ᵛᵒ (18.7 cm). Binding signed by
Huser: blue morocco, doublures and endleaves of
gray morocco. André Gide's copy (his sale, April
27–28, 1925). Acquired March 22, 1966, at the Palais
Galliéra (auction of René Gaston-Dreyfus's
library).*

Although homosexuality had been tolerated
since the French Revolution—provided it was
practiced by adults—a century later most
French people deemed it a subject for scandal or ridicule. Then the topic began to surface in literature: Lautréamont, Verlaine,
Rimbaud, Gide, Proust (see cat. 197), and
Cocteau—to mention only the most famous
authors—introduced it in their writings. But,
except in some editions circulating clandestinely, homosexual desire was veiled in ambiguity and usually presented in transposed
form.

The obligation to compromise with society's prejudices and to conceal his desires

was something André Gide lived with not only in his work (*L'Immoraliste* in 1902) but in his personal life. In 1895, some months after Oscar Wilde opened Gide's eyes to his own real tendencies, Gide married his cousin, with whom he lived for twenty-three years. In the course of time, he found bourgeois constraints and the shackles of family ties increasingly burdensome. The painful memory of Wilde's trial, revived in 1909 by that of Pierre Renard, which ended in another miscarriage of justice where the victim was homosexual, prompted him to start work again on a treatise in the form of a dialogue that he had probably outlined in rough form the previous summer.

"Je ne veux pas apitoyer avec ce livre," Gide wrote in 1910, "je veux GÊNER" (I do not want to arouse pity with this book, I want to DISTURB). *Corydon*, which was presented as a new theory about love, is the first work to propose a defense for homosexuality based on scientific readings (Bohn, J.-H. Fabre, Edmond Perrier, Lester Ward, and others) in order to demonstrate that *uranisme* (Gide's term for pederasty) not only conformed with nature but was beneficial for both social harmony and social morality.

At the end of summer 1910, after having entirely reworked his treatise, Gide read it to several friends, including his brother-in-law Marcel Drouin, who convinced him to abandon such a "subversive" project. *Corydon* then consisted of only two complete dialogues and the first part of a third. Gide had them printed the following year by Edouard Verbeke in Bruges, where he went specifically to supervise the work. According to a note from the printer, the press run for *C.R.D.N.* (its code title) was twenty-two copies on Holland laid paper. In his 1920 preface Gide mentioned only twelve. The volume on exhibit here is in addition to one or the other of those figures. Printed on thin wove paper and styled as a "proof copy" in the auction catalogue of his library, which Gide drew up before setting off on a trip to the Congo, it is replete with corrections and additions. It served to prepare the second edition of four dialogues that Gide finished just as he was breaking up with his wife. It was not printed, however, until two years later, in 1920. Even though Jacques Doucet paid half the cost, it was once again a private edition carrying no mention of the author's name and printed in only twenty-one copies. Not until 1924 did the first "public" edition of the text appear, immediately precipitating a scandal despite a total lack of publicity by Gallimard, the publisher. These days, it is feminists who are likely to be shocked on reading it—so singular was the author's attitude toward women.

Gide, who judged *Corydon* "the most *serviceable*" of his writings, gradually became critical of its form—not for its style, which some of his friends criticized, but because he viewed his use of dialogue as a literary dodge to avoid a sharper attack on the problem. By 1946, even to the aging writer who aspired to the Académie Française, the book seemed too timid. Time—and *Corydon*, to which Gide still paid tribute—had no doubt had their effect on attitudes.

Antoine Coron

Arnold Naville, *Bibliographie des écrits de André Gide* (Paris, 1949). André Gide, *Journal, 1889–1949* (Paris, 1951–1954). Bibliothèque Nationale, catalogue for André Gide exhibition (Paris, 1970). François Chapon, "Note sur l'édition du second Corydon," in *Bulletin du bibliophile* 1 (1971): 1–9. Auguste Anglès, *André Gide et le premier groupe de La nouvelle revue française*, 3 vols. (Paris, 1978–1986). André Gide and Jean Schlumberger, *Correspondance, 1901–1950* (Paris, 1993).

Illustration courtesy of Mme Catherine Gide.

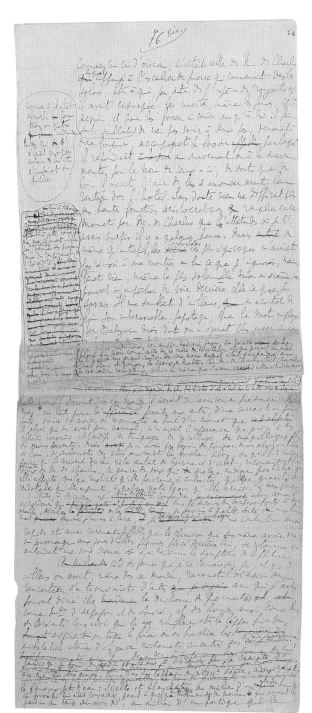

197

MARCEL PROUST

A la Recherche du temps perdu:
Sodome et Gomorrhe
(Remembrance of things past:
Cities of the plain)

Département des Manuscrits, NAF 16709,
fol. 14

Paper; 86 fols.; 330 × 240 mm. Quarter-binding in
red morocco. School notebook with cover of gray
cloth, labeled in Proust's handwriting, "Sodome et
Gomorrhe (I) (Deuxième cahier)." Final autograph
revision, 1915–1916. Purchased by the Bibliothèque
Nationale in 1962 along with the entire Proust col-
lection held by Suzy Mante-Proust, the author's
niece and sole heiress.

It was not by chance that Marcel Proust's
choice of epigraph for *Sodome et Gomorrhe*
was a famous line from one of the poems in
Alfred de Vigny's *Destinées:* "Woman will
have Gomorrah, Man will have Sodom." The
French title of this volume of *A la Recherche*
du temps perdu immediately indicates the
theme to be developed – homosexuality within the society that Proust, like some chronicler, took so much delight in describing.

The text is the culmination of a long-
matured plan. The theme of homosexuality
was already present in early drafts predating
1909, when Proust was writing the essay on
Sainte-Beuve that over the years would give
birth to *A la Recherche.* It was in August 1909,
while seeking a publisher, that Proust wrote
a letter to Alfred Vallette, editor of the
Mercure de France, in which he sketched a
portrait of the character that would become
Baron de Charlus: "*Contre Sainte-Beuve,*
Souvenir d'une matinée is a veritable novel, a
novel which is extremely indecent in certain
parts. One of the main characters is homosexual."

During the successive drafts that led to
the completed version of the first novel in
1912, Charlus (long called the marquis de
Guercy), showed his true colors. But nothing
yet was obvious in the part of the text published as *Du côté de chez Swann* (Swann's way)
in 1913. World War I brought publication of
the whole work to a brutal halt, even though

a second volume, *Le Côté des Guermantes* (The Guermantes way) was already in proof stage in June 1914. Proust would later seriously rework the version of the story presented in this volume, giving it a dimension he had not initially foreseen.

Sodome et Gomorrhe fills the first seven of the twenty notebooks he used for the revised copies of the latter parts of the novel. The rest contained *La Prisonnière* (The captive), *Albertine disparue* (The sweet cheat gone), and *Le Temps retrouvé* (The past recaptured). A close examination of *Sodome et Gomorrhe* reveals that the novel's unity is admirably constructed, within the Proustian universe, around a binary structure based on the two main characters, Charlus and Albertine, whose true tendencies are revealed by the two dramatic incidents that open and close the volume.

The virile act put on by Charlus could still deceive readers in the volumes published in 1918 and 1920, *A l'ombre des jeunes filles en fleurs* (Within a budding grove) and *Le Côté des Guermantes*. His homosexual personality only became fully evident in the opening pages of *Sodome et Gomorrhe*. Unlike Charlus, the character of Albertine was a relatively recent invention, since she did not figure in the novel prior to 1914. The narrator foreshadows her ambiguous nature during the second stay at Baalbec, but it is only after having learned of her former relationships with Mlle Vinteuil and a girlfriend that he decides to marry her in a fit of jealousy at the end of *Sodome et Gomorrhe*. This unexpected twist allowed Proust the freedom to develop "Albertine's story" (*La Prisonnière* and *Albertine disparue*) before capping his masterpiece with *Le temps retrouvé*.

The notebook displayed here corresponds to the beginning of *Sodome et Gomorrhe II*, which opens (fol. 14) with a glittering high-society party given by Princess de Guermantes, at which Baron de Charlus sparkles.

Florence Callu

Marcel Proust, *A la Recherche du temps perdu*, vol. 5, *Sodome et Gomorrhe* (Paris, 1922). *A la Recherche du temps perdu*, vol. 3, *Sodome et Gomorrhe*, critical edition by Antoine Compagnon (Paris, 1988). M. Bardèche, *Marcel Proust, romancier* (Paris, 1971). A. Winton, *Proust's Additions: The Making of "A la Recherche du temps perdu"* (Cambridge, 1977).

198

BLAISE CENDRARS

La Prose du Transsibérien et de la Petite Jehanne de France (Prose of the Transsiberian and of the Little Jehanne de France). "Couleurs simultanées de Mme Delaunay-Terk" (Simultaneist illustration by Sonia Delaunay-Terk).

Réserve des livres rares, Rés. p. Ye. 2730

Paris: Editions des Hommes Nouveaux, [November] 1913. Four sheets forming a foldout of 197.5 × 35.5 cm (17.8 × 10 cm folded). First edition. In its original black kid wrapper (19.2 × 22.4 cm), painted and stenciled in oil colors by Sonia Delaunay. Number 16 of an announced run of 28 copies on Japan paper, signed by author and artist. This copy belonged to Guillaume Apollinaire. Donated to the Bibliothèque Nationale by Bernard Poissonnier, 1989.

Blaise Cendrars was unknown prior to *La Prose du Transsibérien*. The publication of *Pâques* (Easter) in November 1912 had certainly impressed Guillaume Apollinaire, but the impact made by the rare little booklet did not extend beyond the circle of Apollinaire's friends, which included Robert Delaunay and his wife, Sonia Delaunay-Terk. Moreover, it was in Apollinaire's new apartment at 202 boulevard Saint-Germain that Sonia first met Cendrars, who swiftly became a regular at the Delaunays' own place on the rue des Grands-Augustins.

Early in 1913, a first draft of *La Prose* was submitted to Sonia Delaunay, who was to provide the illustration. The theme of the poem—an imaginary voyage from Moscow to

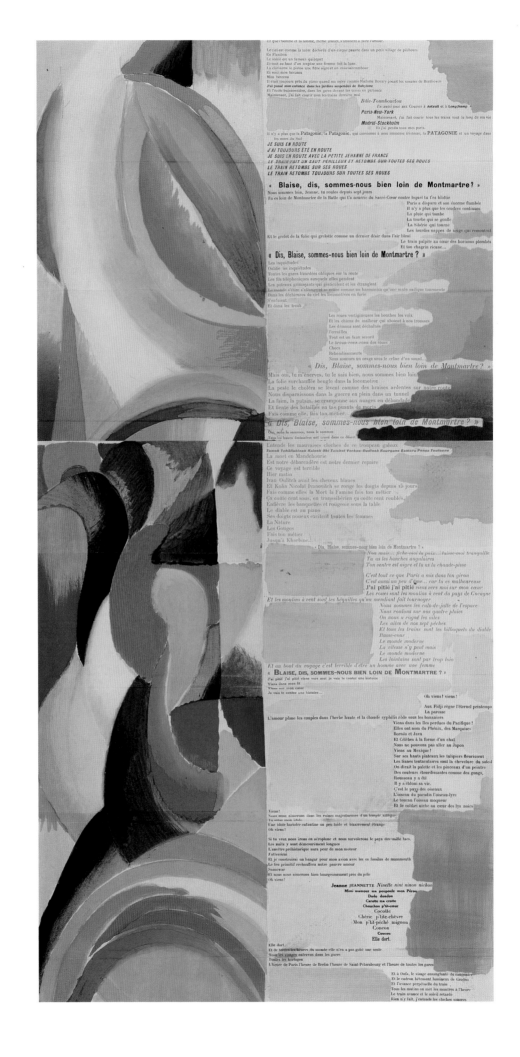

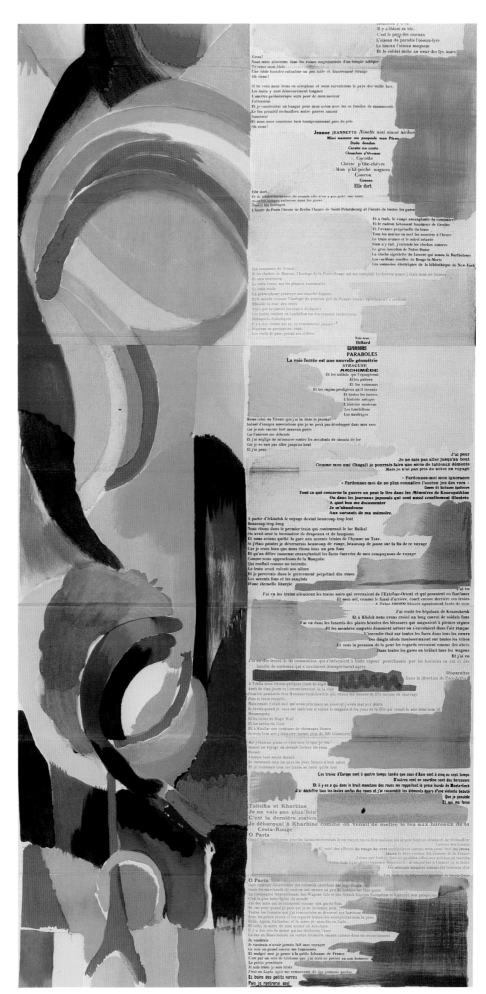

Harbin (Manchuria)—was certain to spark her enthusiasm. As soon as the text was completed, apparently in April or May, Delaunay and Cendrars decided to publish the work in the form of a long foldout permitting "synchronous presentation" that directly linked colored typeface to the painter's abstract illustrations. Although little is known about the details and chronology of the preparatory stages, the publication date of November 1913 has been reliably determined.

As early as October, a controversy had arisen between the creators of the "first simultaneist book" (who were convinced, in Delaunay's words, that they had "established the starting point for a new vision of the world which would shatter old conceptions in the realms of visual arts and poetry") and H. M. Barzun, who claimed to be the sole inventor of "simultaneism." The heated dispute might have been resolved swiftly but dragged on for eight months, until Apollinaire finally took a stand. For although he had momentarily distanced himself from Cendrars and saw less of the Delaunays (his copy bears no dedication from author or illustrator), the article he published in the *Soirées de Paris* on June 15, 1914, put Barzun in his place and described *La Prose* as the "first attempt at written simultaneity in which contrasts of color accustom the eye to read the whole poem in a single glance, the way an orchestra conductor reads the superimposed notes of score, the way one grasps all at once the visual and typographic elements of a poster." Although somewhat stinting in its praise, this defense was the only favorable review of *La Prose* at the time of its publication.

The format, inventive typography, and beautiful composition painted by Sonia Delaunay (not to mention Cendrars's poem) probably merited more than Apollinaire's few lines. But at least his comments put an end to the dispute. The book was not, however, a publishing success. In a cautious move, since the stenciled painting was relatively expensive to reproduce, the Crété firm actually produced only some sixty copies, the rest of the print run being planned for later. But subscribers were so few and war came so quickly that the print run was never completed. By the time *La Prose* was recognized as a key event in the history of illustrated books and modern painting, it was much too late. Apollinaire's copy, exhibited here, is one of the very few on Japan paper, complete with its original wrapper of painted black kid.

Antoine Coron

Michel Hoog, *Robert et Sonia Delaunay* (Paris, 1967). *L'année 1913*, ed. L. Brion-Guerry (Paris, 1971). *Sonia et Robert Delaunay*, exhibition at the Bibliothèque Nationale (Paris, 1977). Antoine Sidoti, *Genèse et dossier d'une polémique: La prose du Transsibérien et de la Petite Jehanne de France* (Paris, 1987). Blaise Cendrars, *La prose du Transsibérien et de la Petite Jehanne de France* (Paris: Editions des Hommes Nouveaux, [November] 1913). Copyright © ADAGP, Paris, 1995.

445

199

GUILLAUME APOLLINAIRE

Le Poète assassiné

(The assassinated poet)

Réserve des livres rares, Rés. p. Y². 2342

Paris: L'Edition (Bibliothèque des Curieux), [October] 1916. [2] + 316 + [2] pp. and 17 letters or cards; 8⁰ (18.5 cm). First edition. Red morocco binding signed by Huser. René Gaffé's copy, mounted at the front of which are 17 autograph letters from the Apollinaires to André Breton, 15 being from Guillaume and 2 from Jacqueline, his wife. Purchased at Drouot sale, Feb. 5, 1957.

With the exception of a few limited editions (whether illustrated by painters or not), Guillaume Apollinaire's oeuvre prior to *Le Poète assassiné* comprised only two books accessible to a general public–a 1910 prose volume, *L'Hérésiarque et Cie* (Heresiarch and Co.) and *Alcools* (Alcohols), a 1913 anthology of poems in a highly modern idiom that brought a breath of fresh air and whimsy to French lyrical poetry, suffering as it was from the anemic atmosphere of symbolism. Pierre Reverdy asserted with conviction in 1917 that Apollinaire, more than anyone else, had forged new paths and opened new horizons. For André Breton, who took the term *surrealism* from Apollinaire, the prose of the writer he called "the last poet" in 1922 was at least as worthy of interest as the poetry in *Alcools* and *Calligrammes*.

Breton wrote to a friend, René Hilsum, as early as November 1916 to recommend *Le Poète assassiné* as "marvelous for its color and modern meaning." Ever since his first meeting with Apollinaire on May 10, 1916 (the day after Apollinaire underwent an operation for war wounds), Breton had eagerly awaited publication of the volume (which, except for the last story, had been compiled by July 1914 and had been held up only by events). Scarcely had Breton finished reading it on Nov. 6 than he told Apollinaire how "enchanting" he found it. Later, in October 1918, Breton devoted his first piece of criticism to Apollinaire, in which he described *Le Poète assassiné* as a defense and illustration of "surprise" as the driving force of modernism. Charmed by the book's whimsy, mingling of genres, and temporal complexity, Breton was especially interested in the autobiographical elements scattered throughout the tales, in which he also noted "vast glimmerings" of eroticism.

Indeed, Apollinaire enjoyed a strong power of attraction over young writers. Those who would form the first surrealist group had gathered around him, even met one another through him. They were captivated by everything about him. Breton was already insisting that "many years hence, those of us who will have lived long enough to be solicited for our recollections, will speak of Guillaume Apollinaire. Just having known him will be considered a rare boon." Their memory of the "enchanter" was so vivid that it mitigated whatever disaffection they may have felt for an overly sentimental and chauvinistic poet. Thirty-four years after Apollinaire's death, Breton was still insisting that "he was a very great figure, at any rate such as I have never seen since. . . . Lyricism in person. He drew Orpheus's procession along in his footsteps."

The copy displayed here, designed to bear witness to a treasured relationship, contains fifteen of the twenty-two letters and cards Breton received from Apollinaire between December 1915 and October 1918. Breton assembled them for René Gaffé, the surrealists' Belgian patron, to whom Breton also sold the manuscript of *Le Poète assassiné*, which the BN purchased on April 10, 1987.

Antoine Coron

André Breton, "Guillaume Apollinaire," in *Les Pas perdus* (Paris, 1924). Breton, *Entretiens (1913–1952)* (Paris, 1952). Breton, "Ombre non pas serpent, mais d'arbre, en fleurs," in *Le Flâneur des deux rives* 1 (March 1954). "Lettres de Guillaume Apollinaire à André Breton," ed. Marguerite Bonnet, in *Apollinaire et les Surréalistes*, special issue of *Revue des lettres modernes* 104–07 (1964): 13–37. Bonnet, *Aux sources du surréalisme: Place d'Apollinaire*, ibid., 38–74. Apollinaire, *Oeuvres en prose*, ed. Michel Décaudin (Paris, 1977).

Illustration courtesy of M. Gilbert Boudar

2

CABINET DU MINISTRE

Bref, M. Paul Valéry qui ne nourrit aucune prévention contre un auteur comme André Lebey, charmant mais le plus ennuyeux du monde, ne persistera pas dans son dédain pour votre poème.

Du moins, reconnaîtra-t-il votre bonne foi et même votre droit à en manger quand il s'agit de choses de l'esprit. Il est bien singulier que l'on ne veuille plus admettre la légitimité

447

200

PAUL VALÉRY

La Crise de l'esprit

(The spiritual crisis)

Département des Manuscrits, NAF 19061,
fol. 19

Paper; 9 fols. and 6 fols.; 230 × 180 mm and 270 × 210 mm. Bound manuscripts with notes and the preliminary rough drafts and the document of Note ou L'Européen, *to form vol. 1 of "Regards sur le monde actuel" (Observations on the world today) (370 × 310 mm). Quarter-binding in blue-green grained leather. Two autograph manuscripts, March–April 1919. The 740 volumes forming the Valéry Collection of the Bibliothèque Nationale were acquired in 1972 by purchase and donation.*

John Middleton Murry, who reviewed French literature for the *Times Literary Supplement*, took over the famous London publication, *The Athenaeum*, in 1919. He immediately sought the assistance of Paul Valéry: "I have suddenly been appointed editor of *The Athenaeum*. . . . Would you be prepared to write, at least once a month, a letter about 2,000 words [sic] describing events of literary and artistic importance in France? . . . You have complete liberty."

Tearing himself away from his "entraînement spécial" (special vocation) of writing poetry (he was a "full-time" poet from 1913 to 1923), Valéry wrote two "letters" which were published in April and May under the title of "The Spiritual Crisis." A few months later, both pieces appeared in *La Nouvelle Revue Française* under their permanent title, "La Crise de l'Esprit."

Valéry did not exactly meet Middleton Murry's expectations–he exceeded them. He took a very broad approach and decided to talk about France in general as a nation and as the guiding light of the European spirit. He also decided to use as a basis the now famous saying regarding the death of civilizations, which was especially meaningful at a time when people were recovering from the carnage of the war that had just ended: "Nous autres, civilisations, nous savons maintenant que nous sommes mortelles" (We, as civilizations, are now aware of our mortal condition; fol. 19).

It was not the first time that Valéry had taken up this sort of political essay ahead of his time. In 1897 he contributed an article to the *New Review* entitled "La conquête allemande" (The German conquest), later published in a booklet entitled *Une conquête méthodique* (A methodical conquest), which had a strong impact in literary and even political circles, though not on the public at large.

The ideas included in these two letters on the spiritual crisis were taken up again and expanded in a lecture he gave in Zurich in 1922—the first in his full career. This highly farsighted speech on Europe can still provide food for thought. Not only did Valéry refer to "l'Esprit européen" (the European spirit, rather than Europe as a federation of nations), "dont l'Amérique est une création formidable" (of which America is a wonderful product), but he also exposed the source of the many conflicts we have known throughout the 20th century. He spoke not only of the now classic conflict between science and religion but also of the conflict between science and art, of the brutality of society contrasted with the fragility of culture, of "democratism" as the enemy of "forms," and of mass education as a hindrance to the blossoming of individual minds destined for greatness.

Henceforth, domination is no longer achieved by means of military power. The stronger nations dominate the weaker ones by creating needs and values which are not always based on lofty ideals and a sound conception of civilization—indeed, far from it.

Florence de Lussy

Jean Mistler, "La Coopération intellectuelle," lecture, Feb. 11, 1931, Paris, Nouvelle Ecole de la Paix. Pierre Roulin, *Paul Valéry, témoin et juge du monde moderne* (Neuchâtel, 1964). François Valéry, in Paul Valéry, *Principes d'anarchie pure et appliquée* (Paris, 1984).

Illustration courtesy of Mme Rouart-Valéry

201

DARIUS MILHAUD

Christophe Colomb
(Christopher Columbus)

Département de la Musique, MS 15372 (1), pp. 398–99

Opera in 27 scenes to a libretto by Paul Claudel

Score; 2 vols.; 40 × 29 cm. Autograph manuscript, 1929.

The birth of *Christophe Colomb* was long and complicated. It would seem that the original idea came to the Catalan painter and set designer Jose Maria Sert, who was thinking of Claudel. This idea engendered two projects whose chronology is not quite clear: a ballet for Spain with music by Falla and a great theatrical or cinematographic construction created by the Austrian producer Max Reinhardt for America, along the lines of the success enjoyed by his production of the *Miracle* by Karl Vollmoeller and Engelbert Humperdinck.

Claudel, whom Reinhardt had approached about the matter in early summer 1927, was more than slightly reticent. "On parlait de Richard Strauss pour la musique, ce qui ne me convient pas du tout" (They were talking about Richard Strauss for the music, which doesn't suit me at all), he wrote to Darius Milhaud (1892–1974). "On m'a suggéré comme sujet l'histoire de Christophe Colomb ce qui ne m'a nullement enthousiasmé" (They suggested the story of Christopher Columbus, which utterly failed to inspire me). But, while he was talking "sans beaucoup de conviction" (without much conviction) to Reinhardt, he got an idea that set him off to such an extent that he wrote "dans l'enthousiasme non pas le scénario. . . mais la pièce toute entière" (not just the scenario. . . but the whole play in my enthusiasm.)

Claudel could conceive only of Milhaud as the one to put this play to music. He was very close to Milhaud, because of their fifteen-year collaboration on a large number of diverse works (songs, incidental music, opera, ballet) and because of their professional ties in the diplomatic corps (Milhaud

449

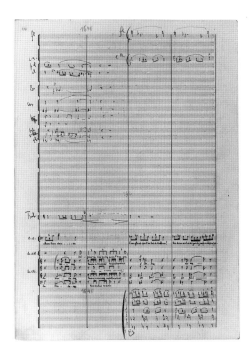

had been Claudel's secretary when he was ambassador to Brazil in 1918).

In the end, Reinhardt abandoned the project, and it was at the Staatsoper unter den Linden in Berlin that the work had its première on May 5, 1930, under the direction of Erich Kleiber. *Christophe Colomb*, which was called an "opera," is also part spoken theater, part oratorio, and part movie. The libretto contains a reading of Christopher Columbus's book read by an "expositor" (a spoken part) who addresses a chorus that comments on and examines both the conscience of the public and the people in Columbus's life. Columbus is himself divided in two at times, so as to be able to look at himself and ask himself questions as well.

There are also two filmed parts projected on a movie screen where "se peignent avec des degrés divers d'insistance et de précision toutes sortes d'images nettes ou confuses indiquant leur plus ou moins de présence dans le passé, dans le présent, dans le possible et dans le rêve" (with varying degrees of emphasis and sharpness all sorts of precise or diffuse images are cast indicating their being more or less in the past, the present, the potential, or a dream).

These few elements give us a glimpse of the technical complexity involved in producing the work, which required in addition to an orchestra a large chorus, nine soloists, and thirty-seven smaller sung parts. Berlin mounted a very good production but subsequently the work was "staged" as an oratorio, thus eliminating the technical and financial difficulties of having it produced.

Moreover, the oratorio form is quite in keeping with Claudel's message: Christopher Columbus, as indicated by his name, is the *Christ-bearer*, the dove (*Colombe*) of the Holy Ghost and the dove of Noah's Ark, which after many tribulations on the water finally lands on a place marked with the seal of God.

The twenty-seven scenes of *Christophe Colomb* really do not offer any kind of dramatic progress. They constitute separate but juxtaposed worlds which spectators have to bring together in their own minds. In any event, in spite of the intent to make comments on the life of Columbus from the beginning to the end of the work, the two parts of it are quite different. In the first part, the almost obligatory traditional episodes in the life of Columbus predominate: *Christophe Colomb et ses créanciers* (Christopher Columbus and his creditors), *Christophe Colomb fait le siège du roi* (Columbus besieges the throne), *Le Recrutement pour les caravelles* (Recruiting for the caravels), *Christoph Colomb et les marins* (Christopher Columbus and the sailors). This part is more dramatic and gives the music the opportunity for brilliant orchestral preludes, comic or dramatic scenes, lyrical developments, spirited choruses, and, in short, contrast. The second part, reflective, mystical, allegorical, is almost an unrelieved meditation on Columbus, as is shown by the titles of the scenes: *Controverse* (Controversy), *La Conscience de Christophe Colomb* (The conscience of Christopher Columbus), *Au Paradis de l'Idée* (In the heaven of ideas).

Doubtless more profound than the first part from a literary standpoint, the second gives the musician fewer characters, fewer contrasts or dramatic effects, frequently showing the meditations of Columbus alone, handled through a sort of recitative rather than through long lyrical and melodic pages (except for Queen Isabella's aria).

Milhaud was not completely satisfied with this part, which ends the play. In 1955 his wife Madeleine got the idea of reversing the two parts, which may be acceptable from the standpoint of the text and which is really more satisfying from the musical standpoint.

In this new version, the two pages exhibited here (pp. 398–99) are near the end of the work: the sailors despair of ever sighting land in a four-part chorus over which the spoken voice of the delegate and Columbus's singing voice intervene, conjuring up, highly inappropriately, the seventy fountains of Grenada, none of which tastes like any other. These sung parts were done by a copyist, unlike the orchestral part, which Milhaud himself wrote. There, wood and brass instruments translate the haunting omnipresence of water, and they become more and more prominent until the outburst at the end: "Terre!" (Land!).

Pierre Vidal

Paul Claudel, *Christophe Colomb* (Vienna and Leipzig, 1929). *Cahiers Paul Claudel*, vol. 3, *Correspondance Paul Claudel–Darius Milhaud* (Paris, 1961), 78–165. Jeremy Drake, *The Operas of Darius Milhaud* (New York, 1989), 242–62.

Illustration courtesy of Mme Madeleine Milhaud

202

ANDRÉ MALRAUX
La Condition humaine (Man's fate)
Réserve des livres rares, Rés. p. Y². 2923, fol. 3

Paris: Editions de la Nouvelle Revue Française, May 5, 1933. [2] + 404 + [6] pp.; a press clipping and 13 ll. mounted at the front; 4ᵗᵒ foolscap (21.5 cm). First edition. No. 1 of 39 copies reimposed on laid all-rag paper Lafuma-Navarre, this copy is preceded by an episode not retained from the fifth part, an excerpt from the weekly Marianne *(Dec. 13, 1933), and autograph fragments in first state of two episodes from the fourth and second parts. Binding signed by Huser: red morocco, doublures, and endleaves in red morocco. From René Gaffé's library (sale, April 26–27, 1956, no. 167). Acquired at one of the sales of the library of Col. Daniel Sickles (June 13–15, 1983, no. 339).*

Anticolonialist activist in Saigon in 1925, communist fellow traveler in the 1930s, leader of the republican squadron "España" in 1936, "Colonel Berger" in the Resistance, head of the Alsace-Lorraine brigade in 1944–1945, and then government minister under General de Gaulle for a dozen years, André Malraux was clearly "engagé" (committed) on every issue that arose in his time–an era rich in ideological conflicts. In Malraux's work, the heroism of the combatant and the activism of the militant were cleverly exalted by the writer yet monitored by the exceptional lucidity of his intelligence and culture.

La Condition humaine, his third "Asiatic" novel, continued the series begun by *Les Conquérants* (The conquerors, 1928) and *La Voie royale* (The royal way, 1930). It is without doubt his masterpiece. Through this account of the communist insurrection in Shanghai led by Chou En-lai in March 1927, which was crushed on April 12 by Chiang Kai-shek, Malraux first revealed to Western readers the conditions and the stakes of the political and military upheavals that would shake China

451

continued to rework the text right into the proof stage, in April 1933, which accounts for the numerous differences between the first edition and the sole complete manuscript, bequeathed to the Bibliothèque Nationale by General de Gaulle (NAF 16587). Since the volume exhibited here and the manuscript both belonged as early as 1933 to the Brussels collector René Gaffé, one may suppose that the two autograph fragments mounted at the front of the exhibition copy were detached from the body of the manuscript texts, where they fit poorly, when those texts were being bound. These two "chapters" (which apparently remain unstudied) actually supply two episodes of the novel in a textual state that antedates the manuscript. Their main features—as in the manuscript there are different drafts pasted in strips—reappear in the printed version, scattered among four different episodes.

Antoine Coron

Jean Lacouture, *André Malraux: Une vie dans le siècle* (Paris, 1973). Christiane Moatti, *La Condition humaine: Poétique du roman, d'après l'étude du manuscrit* (Paris, 1983). Curtis Cate, *André Malraux* (Paris, 1994).

Illustration courtesy of Mme Florence Malraux

for twenty years. For him this book was especially an expression of "le drame de la conscience" (the drama of conscience) that occupied his thought in an almost obsessive way (letter to E. Jaloux, Jan. 7, 1934). Paul Nizan would soon specify the meaning of a work in which action serves as a shelter from existential angst, heroism as a refuge, and revolution as the supreme tragic theater. Such a conception of existence so evidently bears the stamp of his age that it now hardly seems "modélisable" (useful as model), to use current French jargon. Nonetheless, *La Condition humaine* remains a 20th-century "classic." Cut like a film, constantly demanding the reader's attention, dense and allusive like a poem, the novel employed a kind of writing which was so new that at first it surprised even experienced readers like André Gide. However, it was through it that Malraux reached his greatest public.

He began to draft the novel in September 1931, when a trip to China allowed him to discover Canton (where he had set the action of *Les Conquérants*) and Shanghai, and he

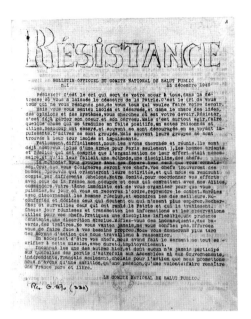

203

Résistance: Bulletin officiel du Comité national de Salut public (Resistance: Official bulletin of the National Committee for Public Safety)
Réserve des livres rares, Rés. G. 1470 (334), title page

No. 1, Dec. 15, 1940. [6] pp.; 26.7 cm. Given to the Bibliothèque Nationale shortly after the Liberation.

"Résister! C'est le cri qui sort de votre coeur à tous, dans la détresse où vous a laissés le désastre de la Patrie..." (Resist! That's the shout that goes out from everyone's heart in the anguish of our country's disaster...). On Dec. 15, 1940, the editorial in the first issue of *Résistance* began with the word the Camisardes, imprisoned in Aigues-Mortes two centuries earlier, had scratched on the wall of the Constance Tower. *Résister!* was the title that protestant Yvonne Oddon would have liked to give the clandestine newspaper. Jean Cassou had suggested *Libération*, but it was judged premature. Boris Vildé imposed *Résistance*, a word that crystallized his vision of a concerted enterprise that would draw together all clandestine activities against the German occupying forces.

The editorial of the first issue called, moreover, for a regrouping of patriots into small disciplined units under the direction of a National Committee for Public Safety, with *Résistance* as its official bulletin. These terms, which were selected with an eye toward Robespierre and the *Patrie* in peril, sanctioned the collaboration of a number of groups without party affiliation, composed primarily of intellectuals whose anti-German activities (tracts, intelligence, networks to London) had begun as early as August 1940. Included among them were lawyers and jurists grouped around Albert Jubineau and Léon-Maurice Nordmann, the circle of the "Français libres de France" (Free French of France) of Claude Aveline and Jean Cassou, agents of the Intelligence Service (Georges Ithier and Pierre Walter), and the active Musée de l'Homme network, whose three leading figures were the anthropologist Anatole Lewitsky, the librarian Yvonne Oddon, and the ethnologist Boris Vildé.

Vildé, born in St. Petersburg in 1908, a specialist in Arctic societies, had assumed a leading role explained by his calm audacity and exceptional intellectual and moral qualities. Gide had taken him under his wing upon his arrival in Paris in 1932. Four years later he became a naturalized French citizen, having in the meantime married the historian Ferdinand Lot's eldest daughter.

Although essentially Parisian, the Musée de l'Homme network had likeminded per-

453

sons available to it in the provinces, notably in Brittany, and had a branch in Béthune in the north. Its much desired national growth was, however, quickly stifled. The group sadly lacked resources, as is evident from the modest appearance of the five issues of *Résistance* (December 1940–March 25, 1941), mimeographed on an old machine that came from the basements of the Musée de l'Homme and was carried into a vacant apartment, later to be set up in Jean Paulhan's own room. The Nazi police were especially to be feared, aided as they were, unfortunately, by the *résistants'* inexperience and the treachery of one of their members. Beginning in January 1941 arrests quickly followed one after the other and the committee was broken up. A year later its principal members, excepting Jean Cassou and his friends, who had crossed into the Southern Zone of France, were tried before a military tribunal. On Feb. 23, 1942, seven of the condemned – Vildé, Lewitsky, Walter, Ithier, Nordmann, Jules Andrieu, and René Sénéchal – were shot at Mont-Valérien, a fortress outside Paris.

In this brief adventure the Resistance had found a name. It had acquired one of its future leaders, Pierre Brossolette, sole editor of the fifth and last issue of *Résistance*. The reception given to Vercors's *Silence de la mer*, which circulated clandestinely immediately after the executions, would very likely have been less favorable had public opinion not been touched by the death of Vildé and his companions, innocent themselves of having caused any German deaths.

Antoine Coron

Agnès Humbert, *Notre guerre* (Paris, 1946). Germaine Tillion, "Première Résistance en zone occupée," *Revue d'histoire de la Deuxième Guerre mondiale* 30 (April 1958): 5–22. Henri Noguères, *Histoire de la Résistance en France*, 2 vols. (Paris, 1967 and 1969). Simone Martin-Chauffier, *A bientôt quand même* (Paris, 1976). Martin Blumenson, *The Vildé Affair: Beginnings of the French Resistance* (Boston, 1977). Boris Vildé, *Journal et Lettres de prison: 1941–1942*, ed. François Bédarida, *Cahiers de l'IHTP* 7 (February 1988).

204

CHARLES DE GAULLE
Mémoires de guerre: L'Unité (War memoirs: Unity)

Département des Manuscrits, Fonds de Gaulle, *L'Unité*, second draft, vol. 2, fol. 194

Paper; 384 fols.; 280 × 240 mm. Handwritten manuscript. Second draft [1955]. Donated to the Bibliothèque Nationale in 1960.

When he wrote his *Mémoires de guerre*, which he began to plan as soon as he resigned as president of the provisional government in January 1946, Charles de Gaulle did not intend to write a history book – "nul ne peut être à la fois juge et partie" (no one can be both a participant and judge) – but rather the story of a decision: the decision, during the disaster of June 1940, to assume the mantle of French sovereignty until the final victory. "Enorme travail" (enormous task) in terms of documentation but also in terms of writing for a memorialist, who wanted to elaborate an entire "oeuvre" (work) and who, in a passage from *Salut* (Salvation), complained about not being handy with a pen.

The first two volumes, *L'Appel* (The call) and *L'Unité* (Unity), were published in 1954 and 1956. When de Gaulle published the third, *Le Salut*, in 1959, he had been president of France for several months. *Mémoires de guerre* met with immediate success and has been translated into twenty-three languages.

French sovereignty is certainly the key word in *Mémoires*. It also explains the difficult relations between the president of the United States and the leader of Free France, who wanted France to participate fully in solving international problems. The two men had already met at the Anfa conference in January 1943, but when General de Gaulle traveled to the United States in July 1944, the situation had changed. De Gaulle

going to weaken the very cause he meant to serve–that of civilization?). And de Gaulle concluded that "dans les affaires entre Etats, la logique et le sentiment ne pèsent pas lourd en comparaison des réalités de la puissance" (in foreign affairs, logic and sentiment do not weight heavily in comparison with the realities of power; fol. 196).

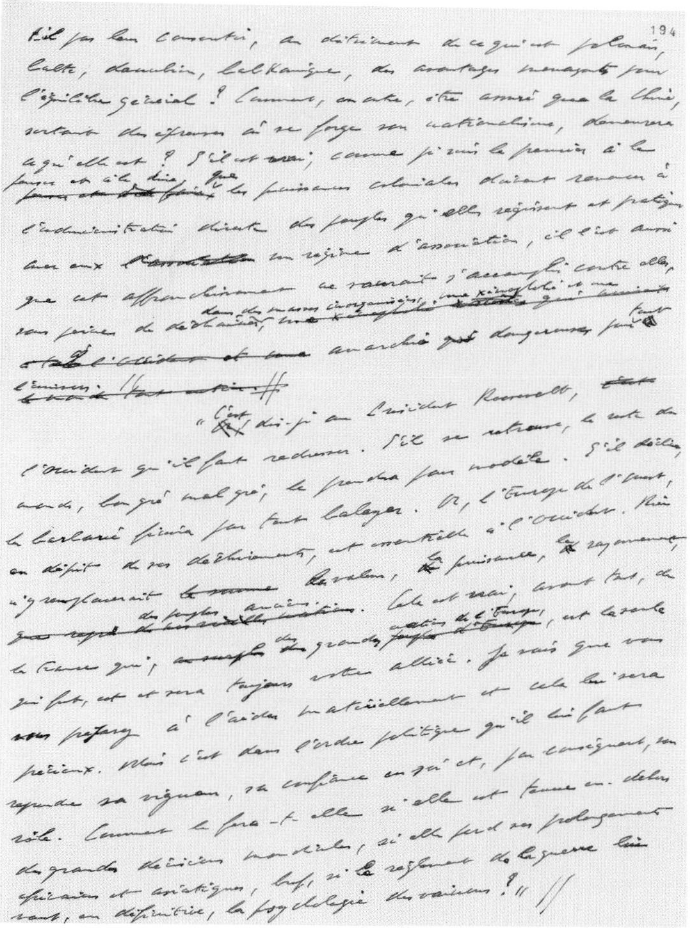

All the manuscripts for *Mémoires de guerre* (first draft manuscript, second draft manuscript, typescript, and corrected proofs) were donated by de Gaulle to the BN in 1960, with a 50-year restriction on access. Special permission was granted by Adm. Philippe de Gaulle to display them here.

Michèle Le Pavec

Charles de Gaulle, *Mémoires de guerre*, 3 vols. (Paris, 1954–1959). Jean Lacouture, *De Gaulle*, 3 vols. (Paris, 1984–1986); vols. 1 and 2 trans. Collins Harvill (London, 1990 and 1991). *Charles de Gaulle: La conquête de l'histoire*, exhibition at the Bibliothèque Nationale (Paris, 1990). *War Memoirs of General de Gaulle: The Call of Honour, 1940–1942*, 2 vols. (New York, 1955). *Unity, 1942–1944* (New York, 1959). *Salvation, 1944–1946* (New York, 1960). Charles Williams, *The Last Great French Man* (London, 1993).

had become president of the provisional government of the French Republic and Allied troops had just landed in Normandy.

Written twelve years after that meeting, these pages from *L'Unité* still convey the vividness of de Gaulle's impressions. The portrait he paints of Roosevelt's "personnalité étincelante" (glittering personality) is still famous: "J'écoute Roosevelt me décrire ses projets. Comme cela est humain, l'idéalisme y habille la volonté de puissance [. . .] C'est par touches légères qu'il dessine, si bien qu'il est difficile de contredire catégoriquement cet artiste, ce séducteur" (I listened to Roosevelt describe his plans to me. As was only human, his will to power cloaked itself in idealism [. . .] It was by light touches that he sketched in his notions and so skillfully that it was difficult to contradict this artist, this seducer in any categorical way; fol. 193). But the American president's grandiose design did not cause his French counterpart to be concerned: "En tenant l'Europe de l'Ouest pour secondaire, ne va-t-il pas affaiblir la cause qu'il prétend servir: celle de la civilisation?" (By considering Western Europe as a secondary matter, was he not

455

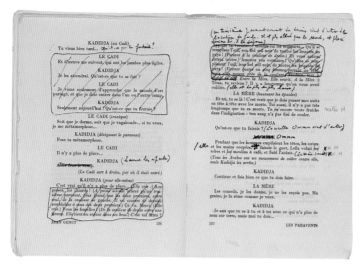

205

JEAN GENET

Les Paravents (Screens)

Réserve des livres rares, Rés. g. Yf. 102,
pp. 136–37

*Dossier (1961–1967) in view of the definitive edition.
Comprises: first edition (Décines: Marc Barbezat,
Feb. 3, 1961). 259 + [3] pp., 8vo, corrected by Jean
Genet, plus 113 ll. in different formats, 19 of which
are handwritten by Genet, the others for the most
part typed by Paule Thévenin, 15 of which have
Genet's annotations. Acquired in 1992 from the
library of Paule Thévenin.*

By the time Sartre published *Saint Genet,
comédien et martyr*, Jean Genet had already
ceased producing novels–written entirely
from 1942 to 1947–and in his new career as
dramatist had produced only two plays, *Les
Bonnes* and *Haute Surveillance*. After a rather
long unproductive period, he wrote, from
1955 to 1957, his two best essays on art
(*L'Atelier de Giacometti* and *Le Funambule*) and
his three longest theatrical works: *Le Balcon,
Les Nègres*, and *Les Paravents*. To his agent,
Bernard Frechtman, he wrote à propos of *Les
Paravents*: "Je crois que ce sera ma première
vraie pièce" (I think that it will be my first
real play), and added, "Il s'agit enfin, pour
moi, d'une véritable tragédie" (For me it is,
finally, truly a tragedy.)

Although the action of *Les Paravents* was
not precisely localized, the setting could only
be Algeria, where the French army was
engaged at that time.

This work, the last published during
Genet's lifetime, is one of the most abundant

in 20th-century theater. Played without interruption, the drama runs five hours, with
ninety-six roles. Before its performance in
Paris at the Odéon Theater on April 16, 1966,
the text had more than ten years of history
behind it. Already started in February 1956, a
first draft entitled *Saïd* was completed in
March 1958. Genet almost immediately
picked it up again to have a second version
typeset by Gallimard in June 1959, entitled
Les Mères, then *Ça bouge encore. . .*, before
finally giving the play to the publisher
Barbezat–with whom he had signed a contract in June 1956, under the original title.
Hardly was the book published than Genet
began reworking the text while at the same
time returning to *Le Balcon* and *Les Nègres*.

The wounds from the war in Algeria had
hardly closed when the play was programed
at the Odéon, then directed by Jean-Louis
Barrault. Produced by Roger Blin with
scenery by André Acquart, it achieved a turbulent success. Right-wing extremists
demonstrated in front of the theater, while
those nostalgic for a French Algeria regularly
interrupted the play with violent incidents
during the famous "farting scene."

Genet participated more in the prepara-
tions for this production than he had done
for any of his other plays. Often on hand at
the extremely long rehearsals, he intervened
with messages to the actors, letters to the
director, and innumerable recommendations
passed on through the intermediary of Paule
Thévenin, one of his closest friends. The text
was markedly altered, as Blin's copy bears
witness. When at the end of 1966 the publishing house Gallimard envisaged including
Les Paravents in the fourth volume of the
Oeuvres complètes, Genet insisted that these
stage alterations be taken into account. A
volume from the first edition was sent to him
in which the some 350 corrections from
Blin's copy had been entered. In early 1967

Genet added nearly 600 other alterations, notably in the twelfth, fourteenth, and fifteenth scenes, fusing the last two and from then on placing the intermission immediately after. He also included in the text at that time the "commentaries" published at the end of most of the scenes.

When Thévenin finished the final version of this new edition, opposition from Barbezat prevented its publication and volume 4 was published in 1968 without the play. Since Genet resisted any reprinting of it by his first publisher, ten years had to pass before the dossier exhibited here could be used in what would be the definitive edition of *Les Paravents* (1976).

Antoine Coron

Jean Genet, *Lettres à Roger Blin* (Paris, 1966). Jean Genet, *Les paravents* (Décines, 1976). Paule Thévenin, "L'Aventure des Paravents," in *La Bataille des Paravents*, ed. Lynda Bellity Peskine and Albert Dichy (Paris, 1991), 5–11. Edmund White, *Jean Genet* (Paris, 1993).

206

JEAN-PAUL SARTRE

La Nausée (Nausea)

Département des Manuscrits, NAF 17900, fol. 109

Paper; 514 + 9 fols., paginated 5²–5¹⁰; 230 × 180 mm. Binding signed by Monique Mathieu. Full black calf with two seams of brown hemp thread on both boards. Endleaves of dark gray-green suede.

Title on spine embossed in dark green leather. Autograph manuscript, 1931–1936. Purchased by the Bibliothèque Nationale in 1979 and nine leaves purchased in 1984.

Intellectual mentor to several generations in the 20th century, much as was Voltaire in the 18th, and representative of the French intelligentsia throughout the world, Jean-Paul Sartre made a sensational writing debut in 1938 with the publication of *La Nausée*. Until his death—or rather, until the 1970s, when he lost his eyesight—he continued to publish novels, plays, essays, philosophical treatises, and even political texts, works all stamped with his own philosophy of existence, attesting to one of the most powerful and original minds of our era.

Half novel, half philosophical tract, *La Nausée* was published by Gallimard and nearly won the prestigious Prix Goncourt for its author. Written between 1931 and 1936 and revised several times, as shown by the different inks and handwriting that filled four spiral notebooks and school graph paper, *La Nausée* looked at first like a "factum sur la contingence" (attack on [the idea of] contingency).

Thanks to the *Mémoires* of Simone de Beauvoir, to whom, under the name "Castor," *La Nausée* was dedicated, we can easily follow the inception of this text. This privileged witness reports, in fact, that the "attack" on which Sartre had been working when he began his career as a philosophy professor in Le Havre was resumed and fleshed out in Berlin in 1934. And then, at the advice of de Beauvoir, he added a novelistic dimension to this "longue et abstraite méditation sur la contingence" (long and abstract meditation on contingency). He then sent the novel to

457

Gaston Gallimard, who accepted it in the end in 1937, but on several conditions: Sartre was to delete some overlong passages, censor the text, and agree not to use the title *Melancholia*, which he had chosen "à cause de la gravure de Dürer qu'il aimait" (because of Dürer's engraving, which he liked).

The sole manuscript of the text includes these forty-five deleted passages–reproduced in the 1981 Pléiade edition–as well as the original title, which Gallimard replaced with *La Nausée*.

Given by Sartre to one of his students, the manuscript changed hands several times and was very quickly relieved of the first nine leaves. The Bibliothèque Nationale was fortunate enough to be able to purchase the missing leaves and even reinsert them into the manuscript, which it bought in 1979 and entrusted for rebinding to Monique Mathieu, a great contemporary binder.

With over two million copies sold since its publication and translated into over twenty languages, *La Nausée,* which Sartre never disavowed, occupies a special place in the author's work and in contemporary French literature. Outside France, this benchmark work is and will always be a major work in the history of 20th century, not only as literature, but philosophically and culturally as well–a universal work.

Mauricette Berne

Jean-Paul Sartre, *La Nausée* (Paris, 1938). Sartre, *Oeuvres romanesques,* ed. Michel Contat and Michel Rubalka (Paris, 1981). *The Writings of Jean-Paul Sartre,* vol. 1, *A Bibliographical Life,* trans. Richard C. McCleary (Evanston, Ill., 1985).

Illustration courtesy of Mme Elkaïm-Sartre

207

LÉOPOLD SÉDAR SENGHOR

Elégie pour Martin Luther King
(Elegy for Martin Luther King)
Département des Manuscrits, NAF 17885,
fol. 3

Paper; 4 fols., 305 × 250 mm. Autograph manuscript. Stanza V, third version [1976]. Donated to the Bibliothèque Nationale in 1979 as a token of thanks for the exhibit entitled Léopold Sédar Senghor, écrivain et poète.

On April 4, 1968, as Senegal was celebrating the eighth anniversary of its independence from France, Martin Luther King, Jr., was assassinated in Memphis when a bullet struck his throat, silencing the voice that had called on the black community in America to engage in nonviolent combat against racial segregation.

There are too many affinities between the pastor from Atlanta and the African statesman for Senghor not to have felt that this death was another sacrifice that black people were being asked to make. Men of culture, both nurtured their pride of being black with the works of the authors of the Harlem Renaissance. Men of faith, they were able to overcome their hatred for the white slave-owners, colonizers, and segregationists and issued an appeal for reconciliation. Men of action, they took on the mission of leading their people to the Promised Land of freedom and to fight for the dignity of black people. It is impossible not to compare the verse from Senghors's *Chants d'ombre* (1945): "j'ai rêvé d'un monde de soleil dans la fraternité de mes frères aux yeux bleus" (I have dreamed of a world of sunshine and fraternity with my blue-eyed brothers) with the speech King made at the march on Washington in 1963: "I have a dream that one day, on the red hills of Georgia, sons of former slaves and the sons of former slave-owners will be able to sit together at the table of brotherhood."

After a long period of gestation, "Elégie pour Martin Luther King" was written in 1976 and published in both editions of *Elégies majeures* in 1979 and 1984. Longer than the elegies published in 1961 in *Nocturnes*, these are also more exclusively about mourning those dear to him: his friend, Georges Pompidou, and his son, Philippe-Maguilen Senghor.

But the symbol that King represents singularly broadens the scope of this elegy, dedicated to the long suffering of Africa, and whose bitter and painful accents remind us of the poems of *Hosties noires*, which Senghor wrote during World War II. Just as *Hosties noires* concluded with a "Prière de paix," "Elégie pour Martin Luther King" concludes in stanza V with the vision of a heaven of peace where white and black voices blend in the symphony of brotherhood King dreamed about. Amid the symbolic figures of those who, from Benjamin Franklin to John F. Kennedy (fol. 3), struggled for the freedom and rights of black people, Martin Luther King thus takes his place in eternity.

Michèle Le Pavec

459

Léopold Sédar Senghor, "Elégie pour Martin Luther King," in *Elégies majeures* (Paris, 1979). Senghor, *The Collected Poetry*, trans. Melvin Dixon (Charlottesville, Va., 1991). Sylvia Washington Ba, *The Concept of Negritude in the Poetry of L. S. Senghor* (Princeton, 1973). J. L. Hymans, *L. S. Senghor: An Intellectual Biography* (Edinburgh, 1971).

Contributors

Elizabeth A. R. Brown, *Professor of History Emerita, Brooklyn College,*
City University of New York

Florence Callu, *Conservateur général, Directeur du Département des Manuscrits,*
Bibliothèque nationale de France

John J. Contreni, *Professor of History, Purdue University*

Antoine Coron, *Conservateur général, Directeur de la Réserve des livres rares,*
Bibliothèque nationale de France

Peter Gay, *Sterling Professor of History, Yale University*

Prosser Gifford, *Director of Scholarly Programs, Library of Congress*

Emmanuel Le Roy Ladurie, *Professeur au Collège de France*

Orest Ranum, *Professor of History, The Johns Hopkins University*

Marie-Hélène Tesnière, *Conservateur au Département des Manuscrits (Section*
Occidentale), Bibliothèque nationale de France

Catalogue Entries

Irène Aghion, *Conservateur en chef au Cabinet des Médailles*

Catherine Allix, *Bibliothécaire à la Réserve des livres rares*

Michel Amandry, *Directeur du Cabinet des Médailles*

Annie Angremy, *Conservateur général au Département des Manuscrits*
(Section Occidentale)

Sylvie Aubenas, *Conservateur au Département des Estampes et de la Photographie*

Mathilde Avisseau-Broustet, *Conservateur au Cabinet des Médailles*

François Avril, *Conservateur général au Département des Manuscrits (Section Occidentale)*

Ursula Baurmeister, *Bibliothécaire spécialiste à la Réserve des livres rares*

Laure Beaumont-Maillet, *Directeur du Département des Estampes et de la Photographie*

Mauricette Berne, *Conservateur en chef au Département des Manuscrits*
(Section Occidentale)

461

Annie Berthier, *Conservateur en chef au Département des Manuscrits (Section Orientale)*

Anne Boud'hors, *Chercheur à l'Institut de Recherche et d'Histoire des Textes*

Claude Bouret, *Conservateur en chef au Département des Estampes et de la Photographie*

Annie Charon, *Professeur de Bibliographie et Histoire du Livre à l'Ecole Nationale des Chartes*

Monique Cohen, *Conservateur général, Directeur de la Section Orientale du Département des Manuscrits*

Isabelle de Conihout, *Conservateur à la Réserve des livres rares*

Michel Dhénin, *Conservateur en chef au Cabinet des Médailles*

France Duclos, *Conservateur en chef, chargée des collections de la Société de Géographie*

François Fossier, *Professeur d'Histoire de l'Art à l'Université Louis Lumière–Lyon II*

Michel Garel, *Conservateur en chef au Département des Manuscrits (Section Orientale)*

Marie-Odile Germain, *Conservateur en chef au Département des Manuscrits (Section Occidentale)*

Cécile Gîteau, *Directeur du Département des Arts du Spectacle*

Marie-Thérèse Gousset, *Ingénieur de Recherche au Département des Manuscrits*

Marianne Grivel, *Maître de Conférences à l'Université Rennes II–Haute-Bretagne*

Geneviève Guilleminot-Chrétien, *Conservateur en chef à la Réserve des livres rares*

Denise Hillard, *Conservateur en chef à la Réserve des Livres rares*

Catherine Hofmann, *Conservateur au Département des Cartes et Plans*

Françoise Jestaz, *Conservateur général au Département des Estampes et de la Photographie*

Martine Kahane, *Directeur du Service Culturel de l'Opéra National de Paris*

Corinne Le Bitouzé, *Conservateur au Département des Estampes et de la Photographie*

Michèle Le Pavec, *Conservateur en chef au Département des Manuscrits (Section Occidentale)*

Florence de Lussy, *Conservateur en chef au Département des Manuscrits (Section Occidentale)*

Bernard Marbot, *Conservateur en chef au Département des Estampes et de la Photographie*

William Marx, *Chargé de Recherches à l'Université de Paris–Sorbonne et à la Bibliothèque nationale de France*

Catherine Massip, *Directeur du Département de la Musique*

Jacqueline Melet-Sanson, *Directeur de l'Imprimé et l'Audiovisuel de la Bibliothèque nationale de France*

Danielle Muzerelle, *Conservateur en chef à la Bibliothèque de l'Arsenal*

Myra D. Orth, *The Getty Center for the History of Art and the Humanities (Collection Development)*

Monique Pelletier, *Directeur du Département des Cartes et Plans*

Marie-Laure Prévost, *Conservateur en chef au Département des Manuscrits (Section Occidentale)*

Marie-Françoise Quignard, *Conservateur à la Réserve des Livres rares*

Natalie Renier, *Conservateur à la Réserve des Livres rares*

Nicole Reynaud, *Directeur de Recherche honoraire au Centre National de la Recherche Scientifique*

Francis Richard, *Conservateur en chef au Département des Manuscrits (Section Orientale)*

Michèle Sacquin, *Conservateur en chef au Département des Manuscrits (Section Occidentale)*

✝Yvette Sauvan, *Bibliothécaire spécialiste au Département des Manuscrits (Section Orientale)*

Sylvie de Turckheim-Pey, *Conservateur au Cabinet des Médailles*

Laurence Varret, *Conservateur au Département des Livres Imprimés (Périodiques)*

Pierre Vidal, *Directeur de la Bibliothèque de l'Opéra*

✝Deceased

Index

475

477

Illustration Captions

Frontispiece
Bibliothèque nationale de France (Richelieu and Tolbiac)

p. 2
Flavius Josephus presenting his book, protected from contact with his hands by cloths, to the emperors Vespasian and Titus. From Flavius Josephus, *De bello judaico*, abbey of Moissac, ca. 1100. *Cat. 11, fol. 3*

p. 17
The decoration of this illuminated initial calls to mind the capitals of the abbey of Moissac where the book was made. From Flavius Josephus, *De bello judaico. Cat. 11, fol. 7*

p. 18
The wise king Charles V, who transferred the Royal Library to the Falconry Tower of the Louvre, consults a manuscript at his bookwheel. From John of Salisbury, *Policraticus*, translated by Denis Foulechat, Paris, ca. 1372. *Cat. 25, fol. 2*

p. 33
An illustration from a book that was among those that Charles V assembled in a tower of the Louvre shows Saint Louis worshipping the crucified Christ. From Guillaume de Saint-Pathus, *Vie et miracles de Saint Louis*, Paris, ca. 1330–1340. *Cat. 23, p. 63*

p. 130
The Master of the Getty Epistles pictures Henry II healing scrofula with the royal touch after his coronation at Reims. From the Hours of Henry II, 1547–1550. *Cat. 80, fol. 107v*

p. 149 (top)
The reverse of the sixteenth-century gold coin pictured on page 126 shows a cross and fleurs-de-lis. Charles VII, *royal d'or*, Lyon, 1429–1431. *Cat. 54, no. 9, reverse*
(bottom)
The sun is engraved on the obverse of a gold *écu* of Brittany. Charles VIII, *écu d'or de Bretagne*, Rennes, 1491–1498. *Cat. 54, no. 10, obverse*

p. 150
A detail of Androuët de Cerceau's engraving of the château of Blois *(top)* shows the facade of the library; in another engraving he pictures the château of Fontainebleau (BnF, Cabinet des Estampes, Ed. 2a fol.).

p. 167
One of the twenty-nine flowers in *La Guirlande de Julie*, Paris, 1641. *Cat. 93, fol. 46*

p. 248
Two medals from Louis XIV's *Histoire métallique*, a series of historical medallions publicizing the king's achievements and using his emblems and mottos. A raidant sun illustrates the king's motto *(top)*. Cabinet des Médailles, série royale 2830, 1674. (*Cat. 114, no. 10, reverse, silver.*) The portrait below shows Louis XIV wearing a breastplate decorated by a sun. Cabinet des Médailles, série royale 3080, 1665. *Cat. 114, no. 11, obverse, gold*

p. 270
Place Louis le Grand was lavishly decorated for the wedding of the dauphin and Maria Theresa of Spain in July 1745. *Fêtes publiques donées par*

la Ville de Paris à l'occasion du mariage de Mgr le Dauphin les 23 et 26 février 1745, Paris, 1751. *Cat. 139*

p. 275
A Persian prince enjoys a feast in the countryside. Opening scene from Firdawsî Tûsî, *Le Livre des Rois,* 1543–1546. *Cat. 128, fols 2v–3*

p. 367
Résistance: Bulletin officiel du Comité National de Salut Public, no. 1, Dec. 15, 1940. *Cat. 203, title page*

p. 382
Champollion's studies of the Egyptian gods and the hieroglyphics that described them were preserved in five published volumes; the autograph manuscript entered the Bibliothèque Royale in 1833. Jean-François Champollion, *Panthéon égyptien,* Paris, ca. 1815–1825. *Cat. 169, fol. 73*

p. 387
The Salle Labrouste, the multidomed reading room on the rue de Richelieu.